International Economics

EIGHTH EDITION

Robert J. Carbaugh

Professor of Economics

Central Washington University

SOUTH-WESTERN

THOMSON LEARNING

Australia · Canada · Mexico · Singapore · Spain · United Kingdom · United States

International Economics, 8e
by Robert J. Carbaugh

VICE PRESIDENT/PUBLISHER: Jack W. Calhoun
ACQUISITIONS EDITOR: Michael Worls
SENIOR MARKETING MANAGER: Lisa L. Lysne
DEVELOPMENTAL EDITOR: Andrew J. McGuire
PRODUCTION EDITOR: Elizabeth A. Shipp
MEDIA TECHNOLOGY EDITOR: Vicky True
MEDIA DEVELOPMENTAL EDITOR: Peggy Buskey
MEDIA PRODUCTION EDITOR: John Barans
MANUFACTURING COORDINATOR: Charlene Taylor
INTERNAL DESIGN: Jennifer Lambert/Jen2 Design
COVER DESIGN: Jennifer Lambert/Jen2 Design
COVER IMAGES: © PhotoDisc, Inc.
PRODUCTION HOUSE: Rebecca Gray Design
PRINTER: R.R. Donnelley & Sons Company—Crawfordsville Manufacturing Division

Printed in the United States of America
1 2 3 4 5 04 03 02 01

For more information contact South-Western, 5101 Madison Road, Cincinnati, Ohio, 45227 or find us on the Internet at http://www.swcollege.com

For permission to use material from this text or product, contact us by
• telephone: 1-800-730-2214
• fax: 1-800-730-2215
• web: http://www.thomsonrights.com

Library of Congress Cataloging-in-Publication Data
Carbaugh, Robert J.
      International economics / Robert J. Carbaugh.-8th ed.
          p. cm.
      Includes bibliographical references and index.
      ISBN 0-324-05589-7 (alk. paper)
        1. International economic relations. I. Title.
HF1359 .C37 2001
337—dc21   00-049248

PREFACE

My belief is that the best way to motivate students to learn a subject is to demonstrate how it is used in practice. The first seven editions of *International Economics* reflected this belief and were written to provide a serious presentation of international economic theory with an emphasis on current applications. Adopters of these editions strongly supported the integration of economic theory with current events.

This edition has been revised with an eye toward improving this presentation and updating the applications as well as toward including the latest theoretical developments. Like its predecessors, this edition is intended for use in a one-quarter or one-semester course for students who have more background than principles of economics. This book's strengths are its clarity and organization and its applications, which demonstrate the usefulness of theory to students. The revised and updated material in this edition emphasizes current applications of economic theory and incorporates recent theoretical and policy developments in international trade and finance. New or substantially revised topics in the eighth edition include:

- Common fallacies of international trade—Ch. 1
- Has globalization gone too far?—Ch. 1
- What the U.S. lost and gained from Asia's economic downturn—Ch. 1
- Even the Boeing 777 isn't all American; neither is the Airbus A330 all European—Ch. 1
- The anxiety behind globalization and trade—Ch. 2
- Boeing, Airbus, and industrial policy—Ch. 4

- Nike and Reebok respond to sweatshop critics, but wages remain at poverty level—Ch. 4
- Steelmakers complain about regulatory burdens—Ch. 4
- Lamb tariffs fleece U.S. consumers—Ch. 5
- U.S. puts squeeze on Chinese apple juice—Ch. 6
- Does the WTO reduce national sovereignty?—Ch. 7
- WTO rulings outrage environmentalists—Ch. 7
- Conflicting agendas at the WTO's Seattle Round—Ch. 7
- Fair trade movements helps poor coffee farmers—Ch. 8
- China and permanent normal trade relations—Ch. 8
- China and the WTO: unions are wrong—Ch. 8
- OPEC's price band: moderating fluctuations in oil prices—Ch. 8
- Did Britain gain from entering the European Union? Trade creation and trade diversion—Ch. 9
- Economic costs and benefits of a common currency: the European monetary union—Ch. 9
- Europe can't handle the euro—Ch. 9
- Is a current account deficit a problem?—Ch. 11
- Can the U.S. continue to run current account deficits year after year?—Ch. 11
- Do current account deficits cost Americans jobs?—Ch. 11
- Weak euro is a bonanza for American tourists—Ch. 12
- Does foreign-currency hedging always pay off?—Ch. 12
- Traders run currency markets—Ch. 12

- Inflation differentials and the exchange rate—Ch. 13
- Financial assets as determinants of exchange rates—Ch. 13
- The dollar and U.S. manufacturing—Ch. 15
- Inflation works against the gains of depreciation—Ch. 15
- Stabilizing currencies of developing countries: currency boards versus dollarization—Ch. 16
- The Asian financial crisis of 1997 and 1998—Ch. 18
- Mexico: elections and currency crises—Ch. 18

Although instructors generally agree on the basic content of the international economics course, opinions vary widely about what arrangement of material is appropriate. This book is structured to provide considerable organizational flexibility. The topic of international trade relations is presented before international monetary relations, but the order can be reversed by instructors who choose to start with monetary theory. Instructors can begin with Chapters 11–18 and conclude with Chapters 2–10. Those who do not wish to cover all the material in the book can omit Chapters 7–10 and Chapters 16–18 without loss of continuity.

In this age of computing, no text package would be complete without Web-based resources. An international economics Web site is offered with the eighth edition. This site, http://carbaugh. swcollege.com contains many useful pedagogical enrichment features including NetLink Exercises, which draw upon the expanded NetLinks feature at the end of each chapter. While the NetLinks direct the student to an appropriate international economics Web site to gather data and other relevant information, the NetLink Exercises allow students to access these Web sites to answer pertinent and practical questions that relate to international economics. As an added enrichment feature, a Virtual Scavenger Hunt engages and encourages students to search for international economics answers at various Internet Web sites.

This edition also includes Microsoft® PowerPoint slides created by Steve Norton of Okno Consulting Group, Ann Arbor, Michigan. These slides can be easily downloaded from the Carbaugh Web site.

The slides offer professors flexibility in enhancing classroom lectures. Slides may be edited to meet individual needs. They also serve as a study tool for students.

In addition, students and instructors alike can address questions and provide commentary directly to the author with the Talk to the Author feature. Return often to http://carbaugh.swcollege.com to access the most current economic policy debates, written by John Kane from SUNY Oswego, as well as *EconNews Online*, a news summary service of important news-breaking reports. For other high-tech study tools, visit the South-Western Economics Resource Center at http://economics.swcollege.com.

To assist instructors in the teaching of international economics, I have written an *Instructor's Manual/Test Bank* (0-324-10691-2), which accompanies the eighth edition. It contains: (1) brief answers to end-of-chapter study questions; (2) multiple-choice questions for each chapter; and (3) suggestions for further readings.

To accompany the eighth edition of the international economics text, Professor Jim Hanson of Willamette University has prepared a *Study Guide* (0-324-05590-0) for students. This guide reinforces key concepts by providing a review of the text's main topics and offering practice problems, true-false and multiple-choice questions, and short-answer questions.

Besides serving the educational needs of resident college students, the eighth edition of *International Economics* addresses the needs of distant-learning students; it is the recommended text for the telecourse, *Inside the Global Economy*, provided by the Annenberg/CPB Project. *Inside the Global Economy* includes 13 one-hour television programs that present an in-depth examination of the basic principles of international economics. Each program features two documentary case studies that illustrate the connection between economic theory and global trade, business, and finance in concrete, highly visual terms. The 26 case studies were produced in more than 20 countries. Besides the case studies, each program provides an introduction and analysis of the economic principles by the project's director of content, Dr. Nariman Behravesh. A distinguished group of international economists from Australia, Sweden, Venezuela, and the United States wraps up each program with an illuminating round-table discussion of a major economic issue. To purchase the series or request a VHS preview cassette, phone 1-800-LEARNER or write Annenberg/CPB Collection, P.O. Box 2345, South Burlington, VT 05407-2345. To accompany *Inside the Global Economy*, I have also prepared a reader, *Inside the Global Economy: A Case Study Reader and Review Guide.*

I am pleased to acknowledge those who aided me in preparing this textbook. Helpful suggestions and often detailed reviews were provided by:

- Burton Abrams, University of Delaware
- Richard Adkisson, New Mexico State University
- Richard Anderson, Texas A & M
- Richard Ault, Auburn University
- Robert Blecker, Stanford University
- John Charalambakis, Asbury College
- Charles Chittle, Bowling Green University
- Elanor Craig, University of Delaware
- Gopal Dorai, William Paterson College
- Veda Doss, Wingate University
- Daniel Falkowski, Canisius College
- Patrice Franko, Colby College
- Norman Gharrity, Ohio Wesleyan University
- Jim Hanson, Willamette University
- Pershing Hill, University of Alaska-Anchorage
- Mohamad Khalil, Fairmont State College
- Robin Klay, Hope College
- William Kleiner, Western Illinois University
- Peter Karl Kresl, Bucknell University
- Edhut Lehrer, Northwestern University
- Jim Levinsohn, University of Michigan
- Mike Marks, Georgia College School of Business
- Al Maury, Texas A&I University
- Jose Mendez, Arizona State University
- Mary Norris, Southern Illinois University
- John Olienyk, Colorado State University
- Gary Pickersgill, California State University, Fullerton
- Chuck Rambeck, St. John's University
- Nindy Sandhu, California State University, Fullerton
- Anthony Scaperlanda, Northern Illinois University
- Ben Slay, Middlebury College (now at PlanEcon)
- Robert Stern, University of Michigan
- Darwin Wassink, University of Wisconsin—Eau Claire
- Peter Wilamoski, Seattle University
- Harold Williams, Kent State University

I would like to thank Wahhab Khandker, of the University of Wisconsin—La Crosse, for creating the NetLinks for this edition. I would also like to thank my colleagues at Central Washington University—Don Cocheba, Tim Dittmer, Ron Elkins, Wolfgang Franz, Koushik Ghosh, Richard Mack, Peter Saunders—for their advice and help while I was preparing the manuscript. I am also indebted to Jami Mays, who assisted in the manuscript's preparation.

It has been a pleasure to work with my editor, Andy McGuire, who provided many valuable suggestions and assistance in seeing this edition to its completion. A special thanks is given to Libby Shipp, who orchestrated the production of this book in conjunction with Rebecca Gray, project manager at Rebecca Gray Design. I also appreciate the fine job that Rebecca Roby did in the copyediting of the manuscript. Moreover, Lisa Lysne did a wonderful job in advertising and marketing the eighth edition. Finally, I am grateful to my students who commented on the revisions included in this new edition.

I would appreciate any comments, corrections, or suggestions that faculty or students wish to make so I can continue to improve this text in the years ahead. Please contact me! Thank you for permitting this text to evolve to the eighth edition.

Bob Carbaugh
Department of Economics
Central Washington University
Ellensburg, Washington 98926
Phone: (509) 963-3443
Fax: (509) 963-1992
Email: Carbaugh@CWU.Edu

CONTENTS IN BRIEF

PART TWO
International Monetary Relations 339

CONTENTS

CHAPTER *3*

International Equilibrium 59

CHAPTER *4*

Trade Model Extensions and Applications 75

CHAPTER 5

Tariffs   113

CHAPTER 6

Nontariff Trade Barriers   151

CHAPTER 7

Trade Regulations and Industrial Policies 187

CHAPTER 8

Trade Policies for the Developing Nations 231

CHAPTER **9**

Regional Trading Arrangements   **267**

C H A P T E R **10**

International Factor Movements and Multinational Enterprises   305

PART TWO
International Monetary Relations 339

C H A P T E R **11**

The Balance of Payments   341

C H A P T E R 12

Foreign Exchange   361

C H A P T E R 13

Exchange-Rate Determination   395

CHAPTER **14**

Balance-of-Payments Adjustments Under Fixed Exchange Rates   431

CHAPTER **15**

Exchange-Rate Adjustments and the Balance of Payments   447

CHAPTER **16**

Exchange-Rate Systems   469

CHAPTER **17**

Macroeconomic Policy in an Open Economy   497

CHAPTER **18**

International Banking: Reserves, Debt, and Risk   513

introduction

chapter 1

The International Economy

In today's world, no nation exists in economic isolation. All aspects of a nation's economy—its industries, service sectors, levels of income and employment, living standard—are linked to the economies of its trading partners. This linkage takes the form of international movements of goods and services, labor, business enterprise, investment funds, and technology. Indeed, national economic policies cannot be formulated without evaluating their probable impacts on the economies of other countries.

The high degree of **economic interdependence** among today's economies reflects the historical evolution of the world's economic and political order. At the end of World War II, the United States was economically and politically the most powerful nation in the world, a situation expressed in the saying, "When the United States sneezes, the economies of other nations catch a cold." But with the passage of time, the U.S. economy became increasingly integrated into the economic activities of foreign countries. The formation in the 1950s of the European Community (now known as the European Union), the rising importance of multinational corporations in the 1960s, and the 1970s market power in world oil markets enjoyed by the Organization of Petroleum Exporting Countries (OPEC) all resulted in the evolution of the world community into a complicated system based on a growing interdependence among nations.

In recent years, the character of global economic interdependence has become much more sophisticated. Rather than emphasizing only the economic issues of the industrial countries, world

KEY CONCEPTS AND TERMS

- *Economic interdependence*
- *Law of comparative advantage*

WHAT THE UNITED STATES LOST AND GAINED FROM ASIA'S ECONOMIC DOWNTURN

In this chapter, we learned about the linkages between economies. Indeed, economic adversities in one part of the world can have significant effects on other parts of the world. Consider the Asian economic crisis of 1997–1999.

From the 1960s to the mid-1990s, Asian economies realized remarkable rates of economic growth and rising standards of living. Their annual growth rates in real per capita incomes averaged more than 6 percent during this period, and Asians enjoyed huge increases in cars, computers, and other consumer goods as well as vast improvements in health, life expectancy, and education.

During 1997–1999, however, turmoil erupted for the economies of Indonesia, South Korea, Malaysia, Thailand, and the Philippines. The crisis soon spread to Russia and Brazil. Moreover, the Japanese economy suffered a hangover from the bursting stock market and land bubbles at the end of the 1980s. Plunging currencies and stock markets put Asia's growth miracle in deep freeze, and minds concentrated simply on survival.

Asia's economic turmoil was worrisome to the United States. Asia was an important trading partner of the United States. If Asian economies stagnated, this could result in lost sales for U.S. exporters and declining economic activity in the United States. Because economies are interdependent, what happened in Asia might also occur in the United States.

As things turned out, the crisis did have an impact on the U.S. economy. One consequence was a marked decline in U.S. net exports and a widening of the trade deficit. The growing trade deficit was largely attributable to three factors:

(1) faster income growth in the United States than in most other industrial countries, which raises imports; (2) outright contraction in Japan and much of the rest of East Asia, which cut U.S. exports; and (3) a rise in the dollar's exchange value, which made U.S. exports more expensive to foreigners and U.S. imports from other countries cheaper for Americans.

Among the sectors of the U.S. economy most adversely affected by the crisis were agriculture and manufacturing. American farmers suffered from shrinking exports and low prices, attributable partly to the financial crisis. In manufacturing, both export industries and industries that compete with imports sustained damage. The commercial aircraft industry, headed by Boeing, suffered from the fall of exports to Asia. The steel industry and the textiles and apparel industry came under import pressure as the rise in the dollar's exchange value reduced the price of imports from the crisis countries. Also, U.S. financial markets felt the impact, and financial institutions suffered losses on their loans and investments in Asian economies.

However, the Asian crisis was not all bad for the U.S. economy. Thanks to foreign economic stagnation, Americans enjoyed cheap imports and weak commodity prices. All that contributed to spectacular economic growth and low inflation. The fact that foreign economies were weak also meant that foreigners parked their investment funds in the United States, which contributed to economic growth and a booming stock market. Put simply, the United States continued to enjoy strong economic growth despite Asia's economic crisis.

conferences are now recognizing and incorporating into their discussions the problems of the less developed nations. For resources such as energy and raw materials, the Western industrial nations rely on the less developed nations for a portion of their consumption requirements. However, this reliance varies among nations. For Europe and

Japan, dependence on foreign energy and materials is much more striking than for the United States. On the other hand, the livelihood of the developing nations' economies greatly depends on the exports of the industrial nations.

Recognizing that world economic interdependence is complex and its effects uneven, the economic community has made efforts toward *international cooperation*. Conferences devoted to global economic issues have explored the avenues through which cooperation could be fostered between the industrial and the less developed nations. The efforts of the less developed nations to reap larger gains from international trade and to participate more fully in international institutions have been hastened recently by the impact of the global recession on manufacturers, industrial inflation, and the burdens of high-priced energy.

Interdependence among nations also applies in the case of *foreign debt*. Throughout the 1970s, the growth of middle-income developing nations (such as Brazil) was widely viewed as a great success story. Of particular importance was their success in increasing exports of manufactured goods. However, much of this success was due to the availability of loans from industrial nations. Based on overly optimistic expectations about export earnings and interest rates, these nations borrowed excessively to finance growth. Then, with the impact of world recession on export demand, high interest rates, and tumbling oil prices, countries such as Argentina and Mexico found they had to make annual payments of principal and interest that exceeded their total exports of goods and services. The reluctance of creditor nations to lend as much as in the past meant that debtor nations were pressed to cut imports or expand exports, in spite of a worldwide recession. It was recognized that failure to repay the debt could result in a serious disruption of the international financial system.

During the past decade, the world's market economies have become integrated as never before. Exports and imports as a share of national output have reached unprecedented levels for most industrial nations, while foreign investment and international lending have expanded more rapidly than world trade. This closer linkage of economies can be mutually advantageous for trading nations. It permits producers in each nation to take advantage of specialization and economies of large-scale production. A nation can consume a wider variety of products at a cost less than that which could be achieved in the absence of trade. Despite these advantages, demands have grown for protection against imports. For industrial nations, protectionist pressures have been strongest during periods of rising unemployment caused by economic recession. Moreover, developing nations often maintain that the so-called liberalized trading system called for by industrial nations works to the disadvantage of developing nations. Their reason: The prices of developing-nation exports have not increased as much as the prices of developing-nation imports over the twentieth century as a whole.

Economic interdependence also has direct consequences for a student taking an introductory course in international economics. As consumers, we can be affected by changes in the international values of currencies. Should the Japanese yen or British pound appreciate against the U.S. dollar, it would cost us more to purchase Japanese television sets or British automobiles. As investors, we might prefer to purchase Swiss securities if overseas interest rates rise above U.S. levels. As members of the labor force, we might want to know whether the President plans to protect U.S. workers producing steel or automobiles from foreign competition.

In short, economic interdependence has become a complex issue in recent times, often resulting in strong and uneven impacts among nations and among sectors within a given nation. Business, labor, investors, and consumers all feel the repercussions of changing economic conditions and trade policies in other nations. Today's global economy requires cooperation on an international level to cope with the myriad issues and problems.

THE GLOBALIZATION OF ECONOMIC ACTIVITY

The last 50 years have seen world trade expand faster than world output by a significant margin, increasing the degree to which national economies rely on international trade in overall economic activity. On an annual average basis, merchandise exports grew by 6 percent in real terms from 1948 to 1999, compared to an annual average output growth of 3.7 percent. Put differently, trade multiplied by the factor 17, while gross domestic product grew approximately sixfold during this period. It follows from these statistics that countries typically rely on trade to a greater degree today that at any time since World War II, and probably at any other time in history.

What are the forces driving globalization?[1] The first and perhaps most profound influence is technological change. Since the industrial revolution of the late 1700s and early 1800s, technical innovations have led to an explosion of productivity and slashed transportation costs. The steam engine preceded the arrival of railways and the mechanization of a growing number of activities hitherto reliant on muscle power. Later discoveries and inventions such as electricity, the telephone, the automobile, container ships, and pipelines altered production, communication, and transportation in ways unimagined by earlier generations. More recently, rapid developments in computer information and communications technology have further shrunk the influence of time and geography on the capacity of individuals and enterprises to interact and transact around the world. As technical progress has extended the scope of what can be produced and where it can be produced, and advances in transport technology have continued to bring people and enterprises closer together, the boundary of tradable goods and services has been greatly extended.

Also, continuing liberalization of trade and investment has made for an ever more unencumbered policy environment for economic relations among nations. For example, the World Trade Organization system has made significant progress in the reduction or elimination of national barriers to trade through eight rounds of multilateral trade negotiations. Tariffs in industrial countries have come down from high double digits in the immediate postwar period to less than 10 percent in the late 1960s, and 5 percent at the turn of the millennium. At the same time, most quantitative restrictions (quotas) on trade, except for those imposed for health, safety, or other public policy reasons, have been removed. Globalization has also been promoted by the widespread liberalization of investment transactions and the development of international financial markets. These factors have facilitated international trade through the more ready availability and affordability of financing.

Lower trade barriers and financial liberalization have allowed more and more companies to globalize production structures through investment abroad, which in turn has provided a further stimulus to trade. On the technology side, increased information flows and the greater tradability of goods and services have profoundly influenced production location decisions. Businesses are increasingly able to locate different components of their production processes in various countries and regions and still maintain a single corporate identity. As firms subcontract part of their production processes to their affiliates or other enterprises abroad, jobs, technologies, capital, and skills are transferred around the globe.

Fewer and fewer products can be produced competitively today solely on the basis of national inputs. For the production of a particular car, for example, manufactured by one of the large U.S. auto firms, no fewer than nine countries are involved in some aspect of production, marketing, and selling. Thirty percent of the car's value goes to South Korea for assembly, $17\frac{1}{2}$ percent to Japan for components and advanced technology, $7\frac{1}{2}$ percent to Germany for design, 4 percent to Taiwan and Singapore for minor parts, $2\frac{1}{2}$ percent to the United Kingdom for advertising and marketing services, and $1\frac{1}{2}$ percent to Ireland and Barbados for data processing. This means that only 37 percent of the production value of this "American" car is generated in the United States.

How significant is production sharing in world trade? Researchers have estimated production

[1] This section draws from World Trade Organization, *Annual Report*, 1998, pp. 33–36.

sharing by calculating the share of components and parts in world trade. They conclude that global production sharing accounts for about 30 percent of world trade in manufactured goods. Moreover, trade in components and parts is growing significantly faster than trade in finished products, highlighting the increasing interdependence of countries through production and trade.[2]

THE UNITED STATES AS AN OPEN ECONOMY

It is generally agreed that the U.S. economy has become increasingly integrated into the world economy (become an open economy) in recent decades. Such integration involves a number of dimensions, including trade of goods and services, financial markets, the labor force, ownership of production facilities, and dependence on imported materials.

As a rough measure of the importance of international trade in a nation's economy, we can look at the nation's exports as a percentage of its gross domestic product (GDP). Table 1.1 shows these percentages for selected nations as of 1999. In that year, the United States exported about 12 percent of its GDP; in 1970, this figure was only 5 percent. Although the U.S. economy has been increasingly tied to international trade, this tendency is even more striking for many other nations. As shown in Table 1.1, the Netherlands exported a whopping 55 percent of its GDP in 1999! It may come as a surprise to find that in 1999 Japan exported only 10 percent of its GDP; from reading the newspapers, one might get the erroneous impression that Japan's exports constitute a much larger share of its national output than they actually do.

What underlies the variations in dependencies on trade as shown in Table 1.1? Many nations

Table 1.1	Exports of Goods and Services as a Percentage of Gross Domestic Product (GDP), 1999
Country	Exports as Percentage of GDP
Netherlands	55%
Norway	41
Canada	39
Mexico	31
South Korea	31
United Kingdom	29
Germany	25
France	25
United States	12
Japan	10

Source: International Monetary Fund, *International Financial Statistics*, June 2000.

with limited resource endowments and limited domestic markets cannot produce with reasonable efficiency the variety of products they desire to consume. Such nations realize that exports are required for obtaining imported products desired. As a result, exports may constitute 30 percent or more of their domestic outputs. Other nations, such as the United States, are endowed with rich and diverse resource bases and immense domestic markets; they are less dependent on world trade.

The significance of international trade for the U.S. economy is even more noticeable when specific products are considered. For example, we would have fewer personal computers without imported components, no aluminum if we did not import bauxite, no tin cans without imported tin, and no chrome bumpers if we did not import chromium. Students taking an 8 A.M. course in international economics might sleep through the class (do you really believe this?) if we did not import coffee or tea. Moreover, many of the products we buy from foreigners would be much more costly if we were dependent on our domestic production.

[2] Yeats, A. *Just How Big Is Global Production Sharing?* World Bank, Policy Research Working Paper No. 1871, 1998, Washington, DC.

With which nations does the United States conduct trade? As seen in Table 1.2, Canada Japan, and Mexico head the list. Other leading trading partners of the United States include Germany, the United Kingdom, China, South Korea, and Singapore.

The United States has become increasingly tied to the rest of the world in finance. Foreign ownership of U.S. financial assets has risen since the 1960s. During the 1970s, the OPEC nations recycled many of their oil dollars by making investments in U.S. financial markets. The 1980s also witnessed major flows of investment funds to the United States as Japan and other nations, with dollars accumulated from trade surpluses with the United States, acquired U.S. financial assets, businesses, and real estate. Consuming more than it was producing, by the late 1980s and 1990s, the United States had become a net borrower from the rest of the world to pay for the difference. Increasing concerns were raised about the interest cost of this debt to the U.S. economy and about the impact of this debt burden on the living standards of future U.S. generations.

The process of globalization has also increased in international banking. The average daily turnover in today's foreign-exchange market (where currencies are bought and sold) is estimated at more than $1.5 trillion, compared to $205 billion in 1986. The global trading day begins in Tokyo and Sydney and, in a virtually unbroken 24-hour cycle, moves around the world through Singapore and Hong Kong to Europe and finally across the United States before being picked up again in Japan and Australia. London remains the largest center for foreign-exchange trading, followed by the United States; significant volumes of currencies are also traded in the Asian centers, Germany, France, Scandinavia, Canada, and elsewhere.

In commercial banking, U.S. banks developed worldwide branch networks in the 1960s and 1970s for loans, payments, and foreign-exchange trading. Foreign banks also increased their presence in the United States throughout the 1980s and early 1990s, reflecting (1) the multinational population base of the United States, (2) the size and importance of U.S. markets, and (3) the role of the U.S. dollar as an international medium of exchange and reserve currency. Today, more than 250 foreign banks operate in the United States; in particular, Japanese banks have been the dominant group of foreign banks operating in the United States.

In the 1970s, U.S. securities firms began to establish operations in Europe and Tokyo. Foreign securities firms subsequently expanded into the United States. By the 1970s, foreign exchange became a 24-hour market, with major banks conducting business with one another in the United States, the Far East, the Middle East, and Europe. Table 1.3 profiles the world's top banks and securities firms.

By the 1980s, U.S. government securities were traded on virtually a 24-hour basis. Foreign investors purchased U.S. treasury bills, notes, and bonds, and many desired to trade during their own working hours rather than those of the United States. Primary dealers of U.S. government securities opened offices in such locations as Tokyo and London. Stock markets became increasingly internationalized, with companies listing their stocks on different exchanges throughout the world. Financial futures markets also spread throughout

Table 1.2 Leading Trading Partners of the United States, 1998		
Country	Value of U.S. Exports (in Billions of Dollars)	Value of U.S. Imports (in Billions of Dollars)
Canada	$154	$178
Japan	58	125
Mexico	79	96
China	14	75
Germany	27	51
United Kingdom	39	36
France	18	25
South Korea	17	25
Belgium	14	9
Netherlands	19	8

Source: International Monetary Fund, *Direction of Trade Statistics*, Washington, DC, December 1999, p. 244.

Table 1.3 Profiles of the World's Largest Banks and Financial-Services Firms, 1999

Banks	Assets
1. Deutsche Bank (Germany)	$706 billion
2. UBS (Switzerland)	683
3. Bank of Tokyo-Mitsubishi (Japan)	640
4. Bank of America (U.S.)	618
5. Fuji Bank (Japan)	513
6. ABN Amro (Netherlands)	505
7. HSBC Holdings (U.K./Hong Kong)	476
8. Credit Suisse Group (Switzerland)	474
9. Bayerische Hypotheken & Vereinsbank (Germany)	473
10. Sumitomo Bank (Japan)	466

Securities Firms	Capital
1. Merrill Lynch (U.S.)	$67.7 billion
2. Morgan Stanley Dean Witter (U.S.)	41.6
3. Lehman Brothers Holdings (U.S.)	32.8
4. Credit Suisse First Boston (U.S./Switzerland)	30.3
5. Salomon Smith Barney Holdings (U.S.)	28.9
6. Goldman Sachs (U.S.)	26.2
7. Bear Stearns (U.S.)	20.1
8. Nomura Securities (Japan)	17.3
9. Daiwa Securities (Japan)	9.2
10. PaineWebber Group (U.S.)	7.3

Source: "World Business," *The Wall Street Journal*, September 27, 1999, p. R–31.

the world, with market acronyms such as SIMEX for Singapore and LIFFE for London.

WHY IS INTERNATIONAL TRADE IMPORTANT?

Because of trade, individuals, firms, regions, and nations can specialize in the production of things they do well and use the earnings from these activities to purchase from others those items for which they are high-cost producers. Therefore, trading partners can produce a larger joint out-put and achieve a higher standard of living than would otherwise be possible. Economists refer to this as the law of comparative advantage, which will be further discussed in Chapter 2.

According to the **law of comparative advantage**, the citizens of each nation can gain by spending more of their time and resources doing those things where they have a relative advantage. If a good or service can be obtained more economically through trade, it makes sense to trade for it instead of producing it domestically. It is a mistake to focus on whether a good is going to be produced domestically or abroad. The central issue is how the available resources can be used to obtain each good at the lowest possible cost. When trading partners use more of their time and resources producing things they do best, they are able to produce a larger joint output, which provides the source for mutual gain.

International trade also results in gains from the competitive process. Competition is essential to both innovation and efficient production. International competition helps keep domestic producers on their toes and provides them with a strong incentive to improve the quality of their products. The experience of the U.S. auto industry illustrates this point. Faced with stiff competition from Japanese companies in the 1980s, U.S. automakers worked hard to improve the quality of their vehicles. Therefore, the reliability of the automobiles and light trucks available to American consumers—including those produced by domestic manufacturers—is almost certainly higher than would have been the case in the absence of competition from abroad.

COMMON FALLACIES OF INTERNATIONAL TRADE

Despite the gains derived from international trade, fallacies abound.[3] One fallacy is that trade

[3] This section draws from *Twelve Myths of International Trade*, U.S. Senate, Joint Economic Committee, June 1999, pp. 2–4.

is a zero-sum activity—if one trading party gains, the other must lose. In fact, just the opposite occurs—both partners gain from trade. Consider the case of trade between Brazil and the United States. These countries are able to produce a larger joint output when Brazilians supply coffee and Americans supply wheat. The larger production will make it possible for Brazilians to gain by using revenues from their coffee sales to purchase American wheat. At the same time, Americans will gain by doing the opposite, by using revenues from their wheat sales to purchase Brazilian coffee. In turn, the larger joint output provides the basis for the mutual gains achieved by both. By definition, if countries specialize in what they are comparatively best at producing, they must import goods and services that other countries produce best. The notion that imports are "bad" while exports are "good"—popular among politicians and the media—is incorrect.

Another fallacy is that imports reduce employment and act as a drag on the economy, while exports promote growth and employment. This fallacy stems from a failure to consider the link between imports and exports. For example, American imports of German machinery provide Germans with the purchasing power to buy our computer software. If Germans are unable to sell as much to Americans, then they will have fewer dollars with which to buy from Americans. Thus, when the volume of U.S. imports decreases, there will be an automatic secondary effect—Germans will have fewer dollars with which to purchase American goods. Therefore, sales, production, and employment will decrease in the U.S. export industries.

Finally, people often feel that tariffs, quotas, and other import restrictions will save jobs and promote a higher level of employment. Like the previous fallacy, this one also stems from the failure to recognize that a reduction in imports does not occur in isolation. When we restrict foreigners from selling to us, we are also restricting their ability to obtain the dollars needed to buy from us. Thus, trade restrictions that reduce the vol-

ume of imports will also reduce exports. As a result, jobs saved by the restrictions tend to be offset to jobs lost due to a reduction in exports.

Why don't we use tariffs and quotas to restrict trade among the 50 states? After all, think of all the jobs that are lost when, for example, Michigan "imports" oranges from Florida, apples from Washington, wheat from Kansas, and cotton from Georgia. All of these products could be produced in Michigan. However, the residents of Michigan generally find it cheaper to "import" these commodities. Michigan gains by using its resources to produce and "export" automobiles, and other goods it can produce economically, and then using the sales revenue to "import" goods that would be expensive to produce in Michigan. Indeed, most people recognize that free trade among the 50 states is a major source of prosperity for each of the states. Similarly, most recognize that "imports" from other states do not destroy jobs—at least not for long.

The implications are identical for trade among nations. Free trade among the 50 states promotes prosperity; so, too, does free trade among nations. Of course, sudden removal of trade barriers might harm producers and workers in protected industries. It may be costly to transfer quickly the protected resources to other, more productive activities. Gradual removal of the barriers would minimize this shock effect and the accompanying cost of relocation.

CONSEQUENCES OF INCREASED OPENNESS

What implications does increased international economic interdependence have for the domestic economy? Opening the economy to foreign trade tends to curtail *inflationary pressures* at home. From 1981 to 1985, for example, the U.S. dollar became more expensive in terms of foreign currencies. This was largely due to high interest rates in the United States, caused by a tight monetary policy, an expansionary fiscal policy, and a

FOREIGN COMPETITION AND THE U.S. AUTO INDUSTRY

U.S. Automobile Market: Market Shares, January 2000

Manufacturer	Percentage Share of U.S. Market	Manufacturer	Percentage Share of U.S. Market
General Motors*	28.4%	Mitsubishi	1.6%
Ford*	22.2	Hyundai	1.2
DaimlerChrysler*	15.2	Mazda	1.1
Toyota*	10.6	Subaru*	1.0
Honda*	6.2	Suzuki*	0.3
Nissan*	4.3	Other imports	7.9

*Vehicles built in the United States, Canada, and Mexico for sale in the United States.

Source: *The Wall Street Journal*, February 2, 2000, p. B–7. This table appears in *The Wall Street Journal* during the first week of the month, in section A or B.

The history of the U.S. automobile industry can be divided into the following distinct eras: the emergence of Ford Motor Company as a dominant producer in the early 1900s; the shift of dominance to General Motors in the 1920s; and the rise of foreign competition in the 1970s.

As a share of the U.S. market, foreign nameplate autos expanded from 0.4 percent in the late 1940s to more than 25 percent by the 1990s. Foreign producers have been effective competitors for the U.S. auto oligopoly, which used to be largely immune from market pressures (such as costs and product quality). Increased competitiveness has forced U.S. auto companies to alter price policies, production methods, work rules, and product quality. Japanese firms are the largest source of the competition.

The competitive success of foreign manufacturers in the U.S. market has led to the deconcentration of the domestic industry. Although the Big Three (GM, Ford, DaimlerChrysler) controlled more than 90 percent of the U.S. market in the 1960s, their collective market share has greatly diminished because of import competition. As of 2000, the Big Three accounted for about 66 percent of U.S. auto sales. In particular, foreign manufacturers have emphasized the small-car segment of the market; their impact on U.S. auto-company deconcentration has been greatest in this segment.

low domestic savings rate. The high interest rates attracted foreign investment to the United States, which increased the demand for the dollar and bid up its price. With the dollar more expensive in terms of foreign currencies, foreign imports into the United States became cheaper in terms of the dollar. Import prices fell by 14 percent between 1981 and 1985, which contributed to a lower inflation rate in the United States.

Increased foreign competition places constraints on those sectors (such as steel and autos) in which wages get out of line with the general wage level. The practice of *wage concessions*, or givebacks, has occurred in industries facing intense foreign competition. With their members becoming unemployed, unions feel compelled to renegotiate compensation levels and work rules in order to save jobs.

Another result of increased openness is the reduction or elimination of the *crowding out* of private investment that was predicted to occur as a result of undue growth in U.S. budget deficits in the 1980s. Budget deficits were expected to lead to increased money demand and higher interest rates. Because firms would find it more expensive to undertake investment projects, they would decrease investment spending. As it turned out, the expansionary fiscal policy and tight monetary policy of the early 1980s triggered flows of foreign investment funds into the United States. The investment inflow increased the supply of funds in U.S. financial markets and held domestic interest rates below expected levels, thus mitigating the crowding-out problem.

Increased openness makes the domestic economy *vulnerable to disturbances* initiated overseas, as seen in the skyrocketing gasoline prices of 2000. But increased openness also helps to dissipate the disturbances that occur in the domestic economy. During periods of domestic recession, the rest of the world may operate somewhat like a sink into which excess domestic output can be poured (although foreigners may initiate international dumping complaints). Conversely, the output of the rest of the world may satisfy domestic consumption during eras of shortages. This situation occurred in 1959, when a strike by U.S. steelworkers shut down domestic production for a number of months; an increase in steel imports fulfilled consumption requirements and greatly reduced the effects of the strike on the American economy.

Greater openness also affects *fiscal policy* (taxes and government spending). Suppose domestic residents spend more on imports out of each dollar of income earned. An expansionary fiscal policy, which increases the income and spending of domestic residents, will be transmitted overseas via increased imports more quickly, thus lessening the fiscal policy's impact on the domestic economy.

GLOBALIZATION AND THE BUSINESS CYCLE

At the turn of the millennium, the U.S. economy enjoyed the longest periods of growth in the postwar era. Indeed, some gurus postulated that the "bust" had been permanently separated from the boom-bust business cycle. That claim almost certainly is too optimistic. The nation is hardly insulated to external shocks such as an oil-related crisis or a financial sell-off that sends foreign investors fleeing en masse. Moreover, theorists who analyze business cycles simply maintain that there have always been recessions, so there will be another. Yet at the turn of the millennium, a growing body of opinion suggested that when another recession occurs in the United States, it could be milder and shorter than past downturns.

One reason for the optimism is that the U.S. economy has been restructured so that it is not nearly as vulnerable to major oscillations as it used to be. Perhaps the most powerful force transforming the economy is globalization. For decades, corporate giants such as Boeing and General Electric conducted business in a global environment. By the 1990s, many midsize companies had also emerged as global players: They obtained parts and materials from foreigners and sold their products worldwide. With more than a quarter of the U.S. economy depending on exports or imports, the result was a diversified economy that was more adaptable to changes in supply and demand.

Consider the case of Eaton, a U.S. manufacturer of truck and auto components. Foreign competition has forced the firm to become nimble and productive. During the 1990s, the firm paid out as much as 4 percent more each year for labor and materials, but raised prices by less than 1 percent. To remain in business, the firm had to continue driving down its overall costs through new technologies and management methods. In effect, foreign competition resulted in the firm's absorbing inflation.

Another example is Invacare, an Ohio-based manufacturer of wheelchairs and other health-care equipment. For the wheelchairs it sells in Germany, the electronic controllers come from the firm's New Zealand factories; the design is largely American, and the final assembly is done in Germany with parts shipped from the United States, France, and the United Kingdom. By purchasing parts and components worldwide, Invacare can resist suppliers' efforts to increase prices for aluminum, steel, rubber, and other materials. By selling its products in 80 nations, Invacare can maintain a more stable workforce in Ohio than if it were completely dependent on the U.S. market; if sales decline anytime in the United States, Invacare has an ace up its sleeve: exports.

Because this dynamism has unfolded in industry after industry throughout the United States, economists' concerns about factory bottlenecks are lessened. If DuPont or Dow attempts to increase prices, buyers can seek price quotes from suppliers in Europe or elsewhere. If a foreign competitor underbids a U.S. supplier, components can be airfreighted for delivery within 48 hours. Therefore, raising prices is difficult—and that implies that economic expansion may not result in the inflationary risks, and the resulting contractionary monetary policy, that it once did.

WHAT MAKES A COMPANY "AMERICAN"?

In recent years, many calls have been advanced for U.S. companies to revitalize their international competitiveness. But wait! What is an "American" company? Are General Motors, IBM, and Whirlpool American companies? What about Toyota, Honda, or Sony?

Consider two hypothetical corporations. First is ABC Computers, headquartered in San Francisco. Its managers, directors, and stockholders are U.S. citizens. However, most of ABC's employees are South Korean because the firm conducts its product design and manufacturing in South Korea. Many of these computers are exported to the United States. The second firm is XYZ Computers, headquartered in Germany. Its managers, directors, and stockholders are German citizens. But most of XYZ's employees are Californians who design and manufacture computers, many of which are exported to Germany. Which of these firms is the "American" corporation? Which is more important to the economic welfare of the United States?

As Robert Reich notes,[4] we have witnessed an increasing number of corporations like ABC and XYZ as the U.S. economy has become internationalized. Reich notes that the U.S. corporation is typically perceived as the main vehicle for improving U.S. competitiveness. He speculates that most people would designate ABC Computers as the "American" corporation.

But in recent years, the competitiveness of U.S.-owned corporations is no longer the same as "American" competitiveness. Consider International Business Machines. More than 40 percent of IBM's employees are foreign. Its Japanese subsidiary employs more than 18,000 Japanese workers and is one of Japan's leading exporters of computers. Or consider Whirlpool, which employees more than 43,000 people around the world in 45 countries. Another example is Texas Instruments, which conducts most of its research and development, product design, and manufacturing in East Asia.

Reich argues that in an economy of increasing international investment, foreign-owned XYZ Computers, with its manufacturing presence in the United States, is far more significant to U.S. economic welfare than U.S.-owned ABC Computers, with its staff of South Korean workers. Reich defines "American competitiveness" as the capacity of U.S. workers to add value to the international economy irrespective

[4] Robert Reich has served as a professor of political economy at Brandeis University and as U.S. Secretary of Labor. This section is based on his article "Who Is Us?" *Harvard Business Review*, January–February 1990, pp. 53–64.

EVEN THE BOEING 777 ISN'T ALL AMERICAN: NEITHER IS THE AIRBUS A330 ALL EUROPEAN

Boeing	U.S. Suppliers	Japanese Suppliers	Other International Suppliers*	
Nose section	Fixed trailing edge	Cargo doors	Radome	Aileron
Trailing edge panels	Floor beams	Fuselage panels	Dorsal fin	Wingtip assembly
Vertical fin	Spoilers	Wing-to-body fairing	Rudder	Main landing gear
Horizontal stabilizer	Inboard flaps	In-spar ribs	Elevator	Engine
Fixed leading edge	Leading edge flaps	Wing center section	Flaperon	Nose landing gear
Wing box	Engine	Main landing-gear doors	Flap-support	Nose landing-gear
Struts and fairings		Passenger doors	fairings	doors
			Outboard flap	

*France, Canada, China, Italy, Australia, South Korea, United Kingdom.

Economic interdependence is reflected in many products that embody worldwide production. In our global economy, it is increasingly difficult to say what is a "U.S." product. Years ago, products had distinct national identities. Regardless of where products were traded, their country of origin (the name of which was generally imprinted on them) was never in doubt. But in today's world, goods are produced efficiently in many different locations and combined in all sorts of ways to fulfill buyer needs in many places.

What is traded between nations is less often finished goods than research and development, management, design, marketing, advertising, and financial and legal services, as well as materials and components. When passengers travel in a Boeing 777, for example, they are riding in a global jetliner—about 35 percent of its parts are manufactured in foreign nations.

The same applies to the jetliners produced by Boeing's European competitor, Airbus Industrie. For example, about 40 percent of an Airbus A330 is provided by parts coming from the United States, and up to 80 percent of the costs of renewable items during maintenance of the A330 are expended in the United States. Thousands of U.S. citizens earn their livelihood working for more than 800 airbus suppliers in 40 states.

Source: Boeing news releases. See also Jeremy Main, "Betting on the 21st Century Jet," *Fortune*, April 20, 1992, pp. 102–117 and Airbus Industrie of North America, Inc., *The Last Frontier?* (Herndon, VA) 1998.

of the nationality of the company that employs them. U.S. competitiveness is thus not the profitability or market share of U.S.-owned corporations. Indeed, the interests of U.S.-owned firms may or may not coincide with those of the U.S. population.

So who represents the United States? Reich maintains that it is represented by the U.S. workforce, the people, but not necessarily the U.S.-owned corporation. U.S. ownership of a corporation is less significant for U.S. economic well-being than the training, skills, and knowledge attained by U.S. workers—workers who increasingly are hired by foreign-owned firms.

The policy implications of this view are clear. If the United States desires to revitalize its competitiveness, it must invest in people, not in nationally defined corporations. The United States must open its boundaries to foreign investors instead of favoring firms that may simply fly the U.S. flag. And government should increase investment in education, training, research, and infrastructure, so that the United States becomes a good location to set up shop for any international firm seeking talented employees.

Reich notes that, in reality, the U.S. government often does the opposite of what he advocates; namely, it identifies national interest with the self-interest of home-based corporations. For example, in 1989 the U.S. government criticized Japan for excluding Motorola from the Tokyo market for telephone equipment and speculated about retaliation. But Motorola designs and manufactures much of its telephone equipment in Kuala Lumpur; most of the U.S. workers who manufacture telephone equipment in the United States for export to Japan are hired by Japanese-owned firms. If Reich is correct, the U.S. allegiance to a Texas Instruments or an IBM should be conditional instead of merely patriotic, just as America's affection for Toyota and Honda should be based on what they bring to the United States.

INTERNATIONAL COMPETITIVENESS

International competitiveness is a hot issue these days. Intense debate has focused on how firms based in a particular nation can create and maintain competitiveness against the world's leaders in a particular industry. The United States has a Competitiveness Council, and Europe, a Competitiveness Advisory Group. Many governments around the world have embarked upon what appears to be a crusade for competitiveness. Let us consider the meaning of competitiveness and how it applies to firms, industries, and nations.[5]

[5] See Michael Porter, *The Competitive Advantage of Nations* (New York: The Free Press, 1990), Chapter 2.

FIRM (INDUSTRY) COMPETITIVENESS

Competitiveness refers to the extent to which the goods of a firm or industry can compete in the marketplace; this competitiveness depends on the relative prices and qualities of products. If Toyota can produce a better automobile at a lower price than General Motors, it is said to be more competitive; if the U.S. steel industry can produce better steel at a lower price than Brazil's steel industry, it is said to be more competitive. Governments are concerned about the competitiveness of their firms and industries because it is difficult for uncompetitive ones to survive.

The long-run trend in a firm's productivity (output per worker hour) relative to those of other firms is a key indicator of changing competitiveness. If the productivity of Honda workers increases at a faster rate than the productivity of Ford workers, then Honda's cost per unit of output will decrease over time relative to Ford's cost per unit. How much physical output a worker produces, on average, in an hour's work depends on (1) what the output is; (2) the worker's motivation and skill; (3) the technology, plant, and equipment in use, as well as the parts and raw materials; (4) the scale of production; (5) how easy the product is to manufacture; and (6) how the many tasks of production are organized in detail.

The structural characteristics of an economy also influence the competitiveness of a firm or industry. These characteristics include an economy's assets, such as infrastructure, and institutions such as the educational system. These factors determine whether a nation's business environment is fertile for developing competitiveness for its firms and industries.

A NATION'S COMPETITIVENESS Although one can assess the competitiveness of a firm or industry, assessing the competitiveness of a nation is more difficult. What criteria underlie a nation's international competitiveness? For a nation to be competitive, must all of its firms and industries be competitive? Even economic powerhouses like Japan and Germany have economies in which

large segments cannot keep pace with foreign competitors. Does a nation have to have a balance-of-trade surplus (exports exceeding imports) to be competitive? Nations such as the United States have realized increasing national income in spite of trade deficits (imports exceeding exports). Is a competitive nation one that creates jobs for its citizens? Although this ability is important, the creation of jobs in itself is not the critical issue; what matters most is the creation of high-paying jobs that improve a nation's standard of living. If the goal of domestic policy were to maximize jobs, today we would have thriving horse-drawn-carriage and blacksmith industries. By keeping the same jobs we have always had, we discourage the development of new high-skill jobs that add to the stock of knowledge and generate innovation and growth. Finally, is a competitive nation one in which wage rates are low? Low wages are not the key to exporting. If they were, nations such as Haiti and Bangladesh would be great exporters. The truth is exactly the opposite. High-wage nations such as Germany and the United States are the world's largest exporters. Clearly, none of these explanations for national competitiveness is fully satisfactory.

A primary economic objective of a nation is to generate a high and increasing standard of living for its people. Accomplishing this goal depends not on the vague notion of maintaining national competitiveness, but rather on achieving high productivity of its employed resources. Over time, productivity is a major determinant of a nation's standard of living because it underlies domestic per capita income. Besides supporting high incomes, high productivity allows people the option of choosing more leisure instead of working long hours. Productivity also creates the national income that can be taxed to pay for public services that enhance the standard of living.

International trade allows a nation to increase its productivity by eliminating the need to produce all goods and services within the nation itself. A nation can thus specialize in those industries in which its firms are relatively more productive than foreign rivals and can import the goods and services in which its firms are less productive. In this way, resources are channeled from low-productivity uses to high-productivity uses, thus increasing the economy's average level of productivity. Both imports and exports are necessary for rising productivity. This conclusion contradicts the sometimes popular notion that exports are good and imports are bad.

No nation can be competitive in, and thus be a net exporter of, everything; in spite of Japan's success as an exporter, it is hardly an exporter of all products. Because a nation's stock of resources is limited, the ideal is for these resources to be used in their most productive manner. The export success of industries having competitive advantage leads to increases in the demand for labor and capital in the nation, thus pushing up their costs. Rising input costs, in turn, worsen the competitiveness of other domestic industries. Rising exports of competitive industries also make the domestic currency more costly in foreign-exchange markets, thus making it more difficult for other domestic industries to export. Even those nations having high living standards, such as the United States and Japan, have many industries in which domestic producers are uncompetitive.

The process of importing products in those industries where the nation is relatively less productive and increasing exports in more productive industries is vital for improving a nation's standard of living. In this manner, international competition allows a nation to upgrade its productivity over time. This upgrading process, however, leads to a situation in which market positions in some industries are sacrificed as national economic prosperity increases. Implementing import restrictions or subsidies to protect uncompetitive industries detracts from the upgrading of the economy and thus lessens the nation's economic prosperity.

Recall that the principle of comparative advantage maintains that as long as *relative (comparative)* costs of two goods differ in two nations, there are gains to be made from specialization and trade; this occurs even if one nation is worse at making all goods than any other nation. A nation can benefit from specialization and trade by making a good in which its margin of disadvantage is smaller, or its margin of advantage is greater, according to the principle of comparative advantage.

The concept of comparative advantage is analogous to exchange between individuals. Suppose a lawyer can write ten briefs or type four pages of text in an hour, while a secretary can write two briefs or type two pages of text in an hour. Are there potential gains from specialization and trade between the lawyer and the secretary? Although the lawyer can write more briefs *and* also can type faster than the secretary, it is beneficial for the lawyer to specialize in writing briefs and for the secretary to do the typing. This is because the lawyer's margin of advantage is greater in writing briefs, and the secretary's margin of disadvantage is smaller in typing. The lawyer thus has a comparative advantage in writing briefs, while the secretary has a comparative advantage in typing. Specialization and trade between the secretary and the lawyer thus lead to higher output. The principle of comparative advantage also pertains to exchange between nations. Nations gain from trade because they obtain goods and services more cheaply by specializing in activities in which they have a comparative advantage.

We conclude that even nations that are desperately bad at making everything can expect to gain from international competition. By specializing according to their comparative advantage, nations can prosper through trade regardless of how inefficient, in absolute terms, they may be in their chosen specialty. The principle of comparative advantage is discussed further in the next chapter.

GLOBALIZATION AND COMPETITIVENESS

Does exposure to competition with the world leader in a particular industry improve a firm's productivity? The McKinsey Global Institute has addressed this question by examining labor productivity in manufacturing industries in Japan, Germany, and the United States. Its study concluded that global competitiveness is a bit like golf. You get better by playing against people who are better than you.[6]

Comparing the labor productivity of nine industries in 1990, the Institute found that Japan led in five industries: autos, auto parts, consumer electronics, metalworking, and steel. The United States led in four industries: computers, processed food, soap and detergent, and beer. In none of the industries surveyed was Germany the most productive. The weighted average of Japanese workers' productivity in these industries was 17 percent below that in the United States, and German workers' productivity was 21 percent below U.S. levels.

The McKinsey researchers analyzed the sources of productivity differences among these nations in the industries investigated. They found that conventional explanations such as economies of scale and different manufacturing technologies had a small role in explaining the productivity gaps in steel, metalworking, beer, and processed food. These factors, however, did not go very far in explaining the gaps in other industries. Neither did the factor of worker skill levels and education, which were similar in all three nations. Nor was it the cost of raw materials, which were essentially equally priced around the world. High productivity, it appeared, rested on the ability of managers to invent new and ever more efficient ways of making products and on the ability of engineers to design products that are easy to make.

The McKinsey Institute found that, whether in the auto industry in Japan or the food industry in the United States, managers and engineers do not achieve innovations because they are smarter, work harder, or are better educated than their peers. They do so because they are subjected to intense global competition, where improving labor productivity is the key to success. Conversely, government trade restrictions have

[6] See William Lewis, "The Secret to Competitiveness," *The Wall Street Journal*, October 22, 1993, p. A–14.

protected most productivity laggards from the painful rigors of global competition.

Exposure to global competition depends on the laws and regulations governing trade and investment and the structure of the market for corporate control. Of the three nations, the United States was the most exposed to international competition. Foreign transplant factories (for example, Japanese auto assembly plants) in the United States also led to U.S. productivity gains by introducing leading-edge technologies and stimulating competition.

Figure 1.1 summarizes the results of the McKinsey study. On the figure's horizontal axis, a globalization index measures the degree to which an industry is exposed to the world leader in that industry either through free and unprotected trade or through transplant factories from the leader nation. The vertical axis measures the productivity of a particular industry as a percentage of the productivity of the leading nation's industry. For example, in 1990 the Japanese food industry was 33 percent as productive as the U.S. food industry, the world leader.

The figure shows that relative productivity performance in industries is closely linked to globalization. When domestic industry is insulated from global competition, and thus faces only local or regional competition, the incentive to innovate is weak and productivity is low. This was the case with the Japanese food industry and the German beer industry in 1990. When industries are exposed to leading technologies of other nations, however, the pressure to innovate is high and productivity increases; the productivity gap with the leading nation is thus closed. For example, U.S. computer companies have located transplant factories in Europe; they are largely responsible for the fact that Germany's productivity in computers nearly equaled that of the United States and Japan, the world leaders, in the 1990s. The McKinsey study provides evidence that the surest path to high productivity, and thus to high living standards, is to open markets to trade, investment, and ideas from the most advanced nations and to permit vigorous competition with firms that have implemented leading-edge technologies.

Is International Trade an Opportunity or a Threat to Workers?

- Tom lives in Chippewa Falls, Wisconsin. His former job as a bookkeeper for a shoe company, where he was employed for many years, was insecure. Although he earned $100 a day, promises of promotion never panned out, and the company eventually went bankrupt as cheap imports from Mexico forced shoe prices down. Tom then went to a local university, earned a degree in management information systems, and was hired by a new machine-tool firm that exports to Mexico. He now enjoys a more comfortable living even after making the monthly payments on his government-subsidized student loan.
- Rosa and her family recently moved from a farm in southern Mexico to the country's northern border, where she works for a U.S.-owned electronics firm that exports to the United States. Her husband, José, operates a janitorial service and sometimes crosses the border to work illegally in California. Rosa and José and their daughter have improved their standard of living since moving out of subsistence agriculture. But Rosa's wage has not increased in the past year; she still earns about $2.25 per hour with no future gains in sight.

Workers around the globe are living increasingly intertwined lives. Most of the world's population now live in countries that either are integrated into world markets for goods and finance, or are rapidly becoming so. Are workers better off as a result of these globalizing trends? Stories about losers from international trade are often featured in newspapers: how Tom lost his job because of competition from poor Mexicans. But Tom currently has a better job, and the U.S. economy benefits from his company's exports to Mexico. Producing goods for export has led to an improvement in Rosa's living standard, and her daughter can hope for a better future. José is

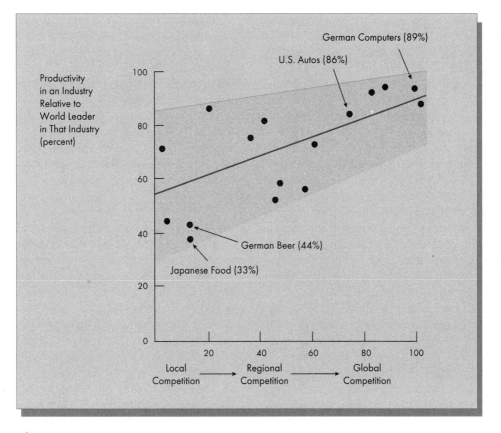

Figure 1.1 Productivity Gaps and Global Competitiveness

The relative productivity performance in industries is closely linked to globalization. When domestic industry is insulated from global competition, the incentive to innovate is weak and productivity is low. As domestic industry becomes exposed to competition from other nations, it must compete vigorously to survive, thus reducing the productivity advantage of the industry leader.

Source: McKinsey Global Institute, *Manufacturing Productivity*, Washington, DC, 1993, p. 3.

looking forward to the day when he will no longer have to travel illegally to California.

International trade benefits most workers. It enables them to shop for consumption goods that are cheapest and permits employers to purchase the technologies and equipment that best complement their workers' skills. Trade also allows most workers to become more productive as the goods they produce increase in value. Moreover, producing goods for export generates jobs and income for domestic workers. Workers

in exporting industries appreciate the benefits of an open trading system.

But not all workers gain from international trade. The world trading system, for example, has come under attack by some in industrial countries where rising unemployment and wage inequality have made people feel apprehensive about the future. Some workers in industrial countries are threatened with losing their jobs because of cheap exports produced by lower-cost, foreign workers. Others worry that firms are relocating abroad in search of low wages and lax environmental standards or fear that masses of poor immigrants will be at their company's door, offering to work for lower wages. Trade with low-wage developing countries is particularly threatening to unskilled workers in the import-competing sectors of industrial countries.

As an economy opens up to international trade, domestic prices become more aligned with international prices; wages tend to increase for workers whose skills are more scarce internationally than at home and to decrease for workers who face increased competition from foreign workers. As the economies of foreign nations open up to trade, the relative scarcity of various skills in the world marketplace changes still further, harming those countries with an abundance of workers who have the skills that are becoming less scarce. Increased competition also suggests that unless countries match the productivity gains of their competitors, the wages of their workers will deteriorate. It is no wonder that workers in import-competing industries often lobby for restrictions on the importation of goods so as to neutralize the threat of foreign competition. Slogans such as "Buy American" and "American goods create American jobs" have become rallying cries among many U.S. workers.

Keep in mind, however, that what is true for the part is not necessarily true for the whole. It is certainly true that imports of steel or automobiles can eliminate American steel or automobile jobs. But it is not true that imports decrease the total number of jobs in a nation. A large increase in U.S. imports will inevitably lead to a rise in U.S. exports or foreign investment in the United States. In other words, if Americans suddenly wanted more European autos, eventually American exports would have to increase to pay for these products. The jobs lost in one industry are replaced by jobs gained in another industry. The long-run effect of trade barriers is thus not to increase total domestic employment, but at best to reallocate workers away from export industries and toward less efficient, import-competing industries. This reallocation leads to a less efficient utilization of resources.

Simply put, international trade is just another type of technology. Think of it as a machine that adds value to its inputs. In the United States, trade is the machine that turns computer software, which the United States makes very well, into CD players, baseballs, and other things that it also wants, but does not make quite so well. International trade does this at a net gain to the economy as a whole. If somebody invented a device that could do this, it would be considered a miracle. Fortunately, international trade has been developed.

If international trade is squeezing the wages of the less skilled, so are other types of advancing technology, only more so. Yes, you might say, but to tax technological progress or put restrictions on labor-saving investment would be idiotic: that would only make everybody worse off. Indeed it would, and exactly the same goes for international trade—whether this superior technology is taxed (through tariffs) or overregulated (in the form of international efforts to harmonize labor standards).

This is not an easy thing to explain to American textile workers who compete with low-wage workers in China, Malaysia, and the like. However, free-trade agreements will be more easily reached if those who may lose by new trade are helped by all of the rest of us who gain.

HAS GLOBALIZATION GONE TOO FAR?

At the turn of the millennium, the U.S. economy was in the midst of a boom that was reinforced by globalization. Open borders permitted new ideas and technology to flow freely around the world, fueling productivity growth and helping U.S. firms to become more competitive than they had been in decades. Moreover, increased trade helped restrain U.S. consumer prices, so inflation became less likely to disrupt economic growth.

In spite of the advantages of globalization, critics maintained that U.S. policies primarily benefited large corporations rather than average citizens—of the United States or any other country. Environmentalists argued that elitist trade organizations, such as the World Trade Organization, made undemocratic decisions that undermined national sovereignty on environmental regulation. Also, unions maintained that unfettered trade permits unfair competition from countries that lack labor standards. Moreover, human rights activists contended that the World Bank and International Monetary Fund supported governments that allowed sweatshops and pursued policies that bailed out governmental officials at the expense of local economies. Put simply: A gnawing sense of unfairness and frustration emerged about trade policies' ignoring the concerns of the environment, American workers, and international labor standards. Table 1.4 summarizes the pros and cons of globalization.

Indeed, there are no easy solutions when it comes to helping people adapt to globalization. Constantly improving education and skills is the only real answer. In today's economy, life-long learning is essential. This should come as no surprise to students who are reading this textbook and completing their degrees at colleges and universities.

Throughout this text, we will examine the pros and cons of globalization. Let us first consider the principle of comparative advantage and the case for free trade as discussed in the next chapter.

THE PLAN OF THIS BOOK

This book examines the functioning of the international economy. Although it emphasizes the theoretical principles that govern international trade, it also gives considerable coverage to empirical evidence of world trade patterns and to trade policies of the industrial and developing nations. The book is divided into two major parts. Part One deals with international trade and commercial policy; Part Two stresses the balance of payments and adjustment in the balance of payments.

Table 1.4 Advantages and Disadvantages of Globalization

Advantages	Disadvantages
Productivity increases faster when countries produce goods and services in which they have a comparative advantage. Living standards can increase more rapidly.	Millions of Americans have lost jobs because of imports or shifts in production abroad. Most find new jobs that pay less.
Global competition and cheap imports keep a constraint on prices, so inflation is less likely to disrupt economic growth.	Millions of other Americans fear getting laid off, especially at those firms operating in import-competing industries.
An open economy promotes technological development and innovation, with fresh ideas from abroad.	Workers face demands of wage concessions from their employers, which often threaten to export jobs abroad if wage concessions are not agreed to.
Jobs in export industries tend to pay about 15 percent more than jobs in import-competing industries.	Besides blue-collar jobs, service and white-collar jobs are increasingly vulnerable to operations being sent overseas.
Unfettered capital movements provide the United States access to foreign investment and maintain low interest rates.	American employees can lose their competitiveness when companies build state-of-the-art factories in low-wage countries, making them as productive as those in the United States.

Source: "Backlash: Behind the Anxiety over Globalization," *Business Week*, April 24, 2000, p. 41.

COMPETITION IN THE WORLD STEEL INDUSTRY

Cost per Ton of Steel, March 1999

Cost Components*	United States	Japan	South Korea	Brazil	Mexico
Labor cost					
Labor hours per ton	4.24	4.05	5.0	6.6	7.88
Employee cost per hour	$37.50	$40	$12	$10	$8
Labor cost**	$159	$162	$60	$66	$63
Material costs	283	258	250	241	246
Depreciation expense	30	40	30	35	42
Interest expense	10	20	18	35	35
Total cost per ton	$482	$480	$358	$377	$386

*Dollar-cost calculations for Japan, South Korea, Brazil, and Mexico were made at the following exchange rates: 118 yen per dollar; 1,209 won per dollar; 1.76 real per dollar, and 9.69 pesos per dollar.

**The product of labor-hours-per-ton times employee-cost-per-hour.

Source: Peter F. Marcus and Karlis M. Kirsis, *Cost Monitor #21*, World Steel Dynamics, March 1999.

During the 1960s and 1970s, the relatively low production costs of foreign steelmakers encouraged their participation in the U.S. market. In 1982, the average cost per ton of steel for integrated U.S. producers was $685 per ton—52 percent higher than for Japanese producers, the highest of the Pacific Rim steelmakers. This cost differential was largely due to a strong U.S. dollar and higher domestic costs of labor and raw materials, which accounted for 25 percent and 45 percent, respectively, of total cost. Moreover, domestic operating rates were relatively low, resulting in high fixed costs of production for each ton of steel.

The cost disadvantage encouraged U.S. steelmakers to initiate measures to reduce production costs and regain competitiveness. Many steel companies closed obsolete and costly steel mills, coking facilities, and ore mines. They also negotiated long-term contracts permitting materials, electricity, and natural gas to be obtained at lower prices. Labor contracts were also renegotiated, with a 20- to 40-percent improvement in labor productivity.

By the turn of the millennium, the U.S. steel industry had substantially reduced its cost of producing a ton of steel, as seen in the above table. U.S. steelworker productivity was estimated to be higher than that of most foreign competitors, a factor that enhanced U.S. competitiveness. But semi-industrialized nations, such as South Korea and Brazil, had labor-cost advantages because of lower wages and other employee costs. Overall, the cost disadvantage of U.S. steel companies narrowed considerably from the 1980s to the 2000s.

Chapters 2 through 4 deal with the theory of comparative advantage, as well as theoretical extensions and empirical tests of this model. This topic is followed by a treatment of tariffs, nontariff trade barriers, and contemporary trade policies of the United States in Chapters 5 through 7. Discussions of trade policies for the developing nations, regional trading arrangements, and international factor movements in Chapters 8 through 10 complete the first part of the text.

The treatment of international financial relations begins with an overview of the balance of payments, the foreign-exchange market, and exchange-rate determination in Chapters 11 through 13. Balance-of-payments adjustment under alternate exchange-rate regimes is discussed in Chapters 14 through 16. Chapter 17 considers macroeconomic policy in an open economy, and Chapter 18 analyzes the international banking system.

S U M M A R Y

1. Throughout the post–World War II era, the world's economies have become increasingly interdependent in terms of the movement of goods and services, business enterprise, capital, and technology.
2. The United States has seen growing interdependence with the rest of the world in its trade sector, financial markets, ownership of production facilities, and labor force.
3. Largely owing to the vastness and wide diversity of its economy, the United States remains among the countries for which exports constitute a small fraction of national output.
4. Proponents of an open trading system contend that international trade results in higher levels of consumption and investment, lower prices of commodities, and a wider range of product choices for consumers. Arguments against free trade tend to be voiced during periods of excess production capacity and high unemployment.

S T U D Y   Q U E S T I O N S

1. What factors explain why the world's trading nations have become increasingly interdependent, from an economic and political viewpoint, during the post–World War II era?
2. What are some of the major arguments for and against an open trading system?
3. What significance does growing economic interdependence have for a country like the United States?
4. What factors influence the rate of growth in the volume of world trade?

NETLINK

1.1 *The Economic Report of the President* contains a wealth of information about the U.S. and world economies, as well as recent and historical international trade statistics. Set your browser to URL:
http://www.gpo.ucop.edu/catalog/erp00.html

1.2 The U.S. Census Bureau has extensive recent and historical data on U.S. exports, imports, and trade balances with individual countries. It has also developed a profile of U.S. exporting companies. Set your browser to URL:
http: //www.census.gov/ftp/pub/ foreign-trade/www

1.3 Toyota maintains both American and Japanese Web sites. For a better understanding of economic interdependence and the concept of what makes a company "American," visit and compare these Web sites by setting your browser to URL:
http://www.toyota.com (American site) and
http://www.toyota.co.jp/ (Japanese site)

1.4 The World Bank Briefing Papers on "Assessing Globalization" tries to answer three dominant questions: Is globalization increasing world poverty? Is it worsening world inequality by destroying jobs and lowering wages among the poor and unskilled? Is it causing deterioration in environmental standards? Set your browser to URL:
http://www.worldbank.org/html/extdr/pb/ globalization/index.htm

To access NetLink Exercises and the Virtual Scavenger Hunt, visit the Carbaugh Web site at http://carbaugh.swcollege.com.

part one

INTERNATIONAL
TRADE
RELATIONS

chapter 2

Foundations of Modern Trade Theory

Modern trade theory seeks to answer the following questions: (1) What constitutes the **basis for trade**—that is, why do nations export and import certain products? (2) At what **terms of trade** (relative prices) are products exchanged in the world market? (3) What are the **gains from international trade** in terms of production and consumption? This chapter addresses these questions, first by summarizing the historical development of modern trade theory and next by presenting the contemporary theoretical principles used in analyzing the effects of international trade.

HISTORICAL DEVELOPMENT OF MODERN TRADE THEORY

Modern trade theory is the product of an evolution of ideas in economic thought. In particular, the writings of the mercantilists, and later those of Adam Smith and David Ricardo, have been instrumental in providing the framework of modern trade theory.

THE MERCANTILISTS   During the period 1500–1800, a group of writers appeared in Europe who were concerned with the process of nation building. According to the **mercantilists**, the central question was how a nation could regulate its domestic and international affairs so as to promote its own interests. The solution lay in a strong foreign-trade sector. If a country could achieve a *favorable trade balance* (a surplus of

KEY CONCEPTS AND TERMS

- *Autarky*
- *Basis for trade*
- *Complete specialization*
- *Constant opportunity costs*
- *Exit barriers*
- *Free trade*
- *Gains from international trade*
- *Increasing opportunity costs*
- *Labor theory of value*
- *Marginal rate of transformation (MRT)*
- *Mercantilists*
- *Partial specialization*
- *Price-specie-flow doctrine*
- *Principle of absolute advantage*
- *Principle of comparative advantage*
- *Production gains from specialization*
- *Production possibilities schedule*
- *Terms of trade*
- *Trade triangle*
- *Trading possibilities line*

exports over imports), it would enjoy payments received from the rest of the world in the form of gold and silver. Such revenues would contribute to increased spending and a rise in domestic output and employment. To promote a favorable trade balance, the mercantilists advocated government regulation of trade. Tariffs, quotas, and other commercial policies were proposed by the mercantilists to minimize imports in order to protect a nation's trade position.[1]

By the eighteenth century, the economic policies of the mercantilists were under strong attack. According to David Hume's **price-specie-flow doctrine**, a favorable trade balance was possible only in the short run, for over time it would automatically be eliminated. To illustrate, suppose England were to achieve a trade surplus that resulted in an inflow of gold and silver. Because these precious metals would constitute part of England's money supply, their inflow would increase the amount of money in circulation. This would lead to a rise in England's price level relative to that of its trading partners. English residents would therefore be encouraged to purchase foreign-produced goods, while England's exports would decline. As a result, the country's trade surplus would eventually be eliminated. The Hume price-specie-flow mechanism thus showed that mercantilist policies could provide at best only short-term economic advantages.[2]

The mercantilists were also attacked for their *static* view of the world economy. To the mercantilists, the world's economic pie was of constant size. This meant that one nation's gains from trade came at the expense of its trading partners; not all nations could simultaneously enjoy the benefits of international trade. This view was challenged with the publication in 1776 of Adam Smith's *Wealth of Nations*. According to Smith (1723–1790), the world's economic pie is not a

fixed quantity. International trade permits nations to take advantage of specialization and the division of labor, which increase the general level of productivity within a country and thus increase world output. Smith's dynamic view of trade suggested that *both* trading partners could simultaneously enjoy higher levels of production and consumption with free trade. Smith's trade theory is further explained in the next section.

WHY NATIONS TRADE: ABSOLUTE ADVANTAGE

Adam Smith, a classical economist, was a leading advocate of **free trade** (open markets) on the grounds that it promoted the international division of labor. With free trade, nations could concentrate their production on goods they could make most cheaply, with all the consequent benefits of the division of labor.

Accepting the idea that *cost differences* govern the movement of goods among nations, Smith sought to explain why costs differ among nations. Smith maintained that *productivities* of factor inputs represent the major determinant of production cost. Such productivities are based on natural and acquired advantages. The former include factors relating to climate, soil, and mineral wealth, whereas the latter include special skills and techniques. Given a natural or acquired advantage in the production of a good, Smith reasoned that a nation would produce that good at lower cost, becoming more competitive than its trading partner. Smith thus viewed the determination of competitive advantage from the *supply side* of the market.[3]

Smith's concept of cost was founded upon the **labor theory of value**, which assumes that within each nation, (1) labor is the only factor of production and is homogeneous (of one quality) and (2) the cost or price of a good depends exclusively upon the amount of labor required to produce it. For example, if the United States uses less labor to manufacture a yard of cloth

[1] See E. A. J. Johnson, *Predecessors of Adam Smith* (New York: Prentice-Hall, 1937).

[2] David Hume, "Of Money," *Essays*, vol. 1, (London: Green and Co., 1912), p. 319. Hume's writings are also available in Eugene Rotwein, *The Economic Writings of David Hume* (Edinburgh: Nelson, 1955).

[3] Adam Smith, *The Wealth of Nations* (New York: Modern Library, 1937), pp. 424–426. For a discussion concerning the logical possibility of the absolute-advantage concept, see Royall Brandis, "The Myth of Absolute Advantage," *American Economic Review*, March 1967.

than the United Kingdom, U.S. production cost will be lower.

Smith's trading principle was the **principle of absolute advantage**: In a two-nation, two-product world, international trade and specialization will be beneficial when one nation has an absolute cost advantage (that is, uses less labor to produce a unit of output) in one good and the other nation has an absolute cost advantage in the other good. For the world to benefit from international division of labor, each nation must have a good that it is absolutely more efficient in producing than its trading partner. A nation will *import* those goods in which it has an absolute cost *disadvantage*; it will *export* those goods in which it has an absolute cost *advantage*.

An arithmetic example helps illustrate the principle of absolute advantage. Referring to Table 2.1, suppose workers in the United States can produce 5 bottles of wine or 20 yards of cloth in an hour's time, while workers in the United Kingdom can produce 15 bottles of wine or 10 yards of cloth in an hour's time. Clearly, the United States has an absolute advantage in cloth production; its cloth workers' productivity (output per worker hour) is higher than that of the United Kingdom, which leads to lower costs (less labor required to produce a yard of cloth). In like manner, the United Kingdom has an absolute advantage in wine production.

Table 2.1	A Case of Absolute Advantage When Each Nation Is More Efficient in the Production of One Good

World Output Possibilities in the Absence of Specialization

Nation	Output per Labor Hour	
	Wine	Cloth
United States	5 bottles	20 yards
United Kingdom	15 bottles	10 yards

According to Smith, each nation benefits by specializing in the production of the good that it produces at a lower cost than the other nation, while importing the good that it produces at a higher cost. Because the world uses its resources more efficiently as the result of specializing according to the principle of absolute advantage, there occurs an increase in world output, which is distributed to the two nations through trade.

WHY NATIONS TRADE: COMPARATIVE ADVANTAGE

According to Smith, mutually beneficial trade requires each nation to be the *least-cost producer* of at least one good that it can export to its trading partner. But what if a nation is more efficient than its trading partner in the production of *all* goods? Dissatisfied with this looseness in Smith's theory, David Ricardo (1772–1823) developed a principle to show that mutually beneficial trade can occur even when one nation is absolutely more efficient in the production of all goods.[4]

Like Smith, Ricardo emphasized the supply side of the market. The immediate basis for trade stemmed from cost differences between nations, which were underlaid by their natural and acquired advantages. Unlike Smith, who emphasized the importance of absolute cost differences among nations, Ricardo emphasized *comparative* (relative) cost differences. Ricardo's trade theory thus became known as the **principle of comparative advantage**. Indeed, countries often develop comparative advantages resulting from natural advantages and acquired advantages, as shown in Table 2.2.

According to Ricardo's comparative-advantage principle, even if a nation has an absolute cost disadvantage in the production of *both* goods, a basis for mutually beneficial trade may still exist. The less efficient nation should specialize in and export the good in which it is relatively less inefficient (where its absolute disadvantage is least). The more efficient nation should specialize in and export that good in which

[4] David Ricardo, *The Principles of Political Economy and Taxation* (London: Cambridge University Press, 1966), Chapter 7.

Table 2.2	Examples of Comparative Advantages in International Trade

Speciality Resulting from Natural Advantages

Canada	Lumber
Israel	Citrus fruit
Italy	Wine
Jamaica	Aluminum ore
Mexico	Tomatoes
Saudi Arabia	Oil
United States	Wheat, corn

Speciality Resulting from Acquired Advantages

Hong Kong	Textiles
Japan	Automobiles, consumer electronics
South Korea	Steel, ships
Switzerland	Watches
United States	Jetliners, computer software
United Kingdom	Financial services

which it is relatively more efficient (where its absolute advantage is greatest).

To understand the difference between absolute advantage and comparative advantage, consider the case of Mark McGwire, the home-run champion of major league baseball. Not only does McGwire have an absolute advantage in playing baseball, but he is likely better than most other people at other activities as well. For example, McGwire can probably mow his lawn faster than any gardener. Thus, McGwire also has an absolute advantage in lawn care. Just becasuse he can mow his lawn fast, does this suggest he should? Obviously, it is best for McGwire to pass up lawn care and stick to hitting home runs where his absolute advantage is greatest. Similarly, the United States may well be more productive than other countries in textiles as well as computer software, but it would do better to import those cheap shirts from China and ease the way for Microsoft to export software all over the world.

To demonstrate the principle of comparative advantage, Ricardo formulated a simplified model based on the following assumptions:

1. The world consists of two nations, each using a single input to produce two commodities.

2. In each nation, labor is the only input (the labor theory of value). Each nation has a fixed endowment of labor, and labor is fully employed and homogeneous.

3. Labor can move freely among industries within a nation, but is incapable of moving between nations.

4. The level of technology is fixed for both nations. Different nations may use different technologies, but all firms within each nation utilize a common production method for each commodity.

5. Costs do not vary with the level of production and are proportional to the amount of labor used.

6. Perfect competition prevails in all markets. Because no single producer or consumer is large enough to influence the market, all are price takers. Product quality does not vary among nations, implying that all units of each product are identical. There is free entry to and exit from an industry, and the price of each product equals the product's marginal cost of production.

7. Free trade occurs between nations; that is, no government barriers to trade exist.

8. Transportation costs are zero. Consumers will thus be indifferent between domestically produced and imported versions of a product if the domestic prices of the two products are identical.

9. Firms make production decisions in an attempt to maximize profits, whereas consumers maximize satisfaction through their consumption decisions.

10. There is no money illusion; that is, when consumers make their consumption choices and firms make their production decisions, they take into account the behavior of all prices.

WHERE DOES U.S. COMPARATIVE ADVANTAGE LIE?

U.S. Comparative Advantage, by Manufacturing Sector, 1998

Industry	Revealed Comparative-Advantage Ratio	
Civilian aircraft	+0.42	Greatest Comparative
Medical equipment	+0.24	Advantage
Chemicals	+0.21	
Telecommunications equipment	+0.19	
Food	+0.06	
Industrial supplies	−0.16	
Autos	−0.34	
Consumer goods	−0.46	
Steel	−0.57	Greatest Comparative
Energy	−0.63	Disadvantage

Source: U.S. Department of Commerce, *Survey of Current Business*, July 1999.

In which manufacturing industries does the United States enjoy a comparative advantage? The table above lists *revealed comparative advantage*, measured by the ratio of U.S. net exports (exports minus imports) in each product category to the sum of the U.S. exports and imports in that category. This ratio can take any value between 1 (greatest comparative advantage) and -1 (greatest comparative disadvantage). The larger the algebraic value for a product category *relative to the values for other product categories*, the greater the nation's comparative advantage (or the smaller its disadvantage) in that category. The magnitude of the ratio for a product category has little significance in and of itself, apart from comparison with the ratio magnitudes for other categories. Of course, protectionist barriers somewhat distort the ratios that would occur under free trade.

As seen in the table, a ranking of the product categories (industries) according to these ratios indicates that, as of 1998, civilian aircraft was the manufacturing sector in which the United States had the greatest comparative advantage; energy and steel were the U.S. industries of greatest comparative disadvantage. Although these rankings can and do change with underlying economic conditions, pronounced changes in the short run are unlikely.

11. Trade is balanced (exports must pay for imports), thus ruling out flows of money between nations.

Table 2.3 illustrates Ricardo's comparative-advantage principle when one nation has an absolute advantage in the production of both commodities. Assume that in one hour's time U.S. workers can produce 40 bottles of wine or 40 yards of cloth, while U.K. workers can produce 20 bottles of wine or 10 yards of cloth. According to Smith's principle of absolute advantage, there is no basis for mutually beneficial specialization and trade, because the United States is more efficient in the production of both goods.

Ricardo's principle of comparative advantage, however, recognizes that the United States is four

Table 2.3 A Case of Comparative Advantage When the United States Has an Absolute Advantage in the Production of Both Goods

World Output Possibilities in the Absence of Specialization

Nation	Output per Labor Hour	
	Wine	Cloth
United States	40 bottles	40 yards
United Kingdom	20 bottles	10 yards

times as efficient in cloth production (40 / 10 = 4) but only twice as efficient in wine production (40 / 20 = 2). The United States thus has a *greater absolute advantage* in cloth than in wine, while the United Kingdom has a *smaller absolute disadvantage* in wine than in cloth. Each nation specializes in and exports that good in which it has a *comparative advantage*—the United States in cloth, the United Kingdom in wine. The output gains from specialization will be distributed to the two nations through the process of trade.

Concerning U.S. trade patterns during the 1980s and 1990s, in which the United States realized large trade deficits (imports exceeded exports) with Japan, some doomsayers appeared to believe that Japan could outproduce the United States in virtually everything. Those who foresaw a flood of imports from Japan causing the United States to deindustrialize and become a nation of fast-food restaurants seemed to be suggesting that the United States did not have a comparative advantage in anything.

It is possible for a nation not to have an absolute advantage in anything; but it is not possible for one nation to have a comparative advantage in everything and the other nation to have a comparative advantage in nothing. That's because comparative advantage depends on relative costs. As we have seen, a nation having an absolute disadvantage in all goods would find it advantageous to specialize in the production of the good in which its absolute disadvantage is least. There is no reason for the United States to surrender and let Japan produce all of everything. The United States would lose and so would Japan, because world output would be reduced if U.S. resources were left idle. The idea that a nation has nothing to offer confuses absolute advantage and comparative advantage.

COMPARATIVE ADVANTAGE IN MONEY TERMS Although Ricardo's comparative-advantage principle is used to explain international trade patterns, people are not generally concerned with which nation has a comparative advantage when they purchase something. A person in a candy store does not look at Swiss chocolate and U.S. chocolate and say, "I wonder which nation has the comparative advantage in chocolate production?" The buyer relies on price, after allowing for quality differences, to tell which nation has the comparative advantage. It is helpful, then, to illustrate how the principle of comparative advantage works in terms of money prices.

Refer again to the Ricardian comparative-advantage example of Table 2.3, which assumes that labor is the only input and is homogeneous. Recall that (1) the United States has an absolute advantage in the production of both cloth and wine; and (2) the United States has a comparative advantage in cloth production, while the United Kingdom has a comparative advantage in wine production. This information is restated in Table 2.4. As we shall see, even though the United Kingdom is absolutely less efficient in producing both goods, it will export wine (the product of its comparative advantage) when its money wages are so much lower than those of the United States that it is cheaper to make wine in the United Kingdom. Let us see how this works.

Suppose the wage rate is $20 per hour in the United States, as indicated in Table 2.4. If U.S. workers can produce 40 yards of cloth in an hour, the average cost of producing a yard of cloth is $0.50 ($20 / 40 yards = $0.50 per yard);

Table 2.4 Ricardo's Comparative-Advantage Principle Expressed in Money Prices

Nation	Labor Input	Hourly Wage Rate	Cloth (Yards)		Wine (Bottles)	
			Quantity	Price	Quantity	Price
United States	1 hour	$20	40	$0.50	40	$0.50
United Kingdom	1 hour	£5	10	£0.50	20	£0.25
United Kingdom*	1 hour	$8	10	$0.80	20	$0.40

*Dollar prices of cloth and wine, when the prevailing exchange rate is $1.60 = £1. This exchange rate was chosen for this example because at other exchange rates it would not be possible to have balanced trade and balance in the foreign-exchange market.

similarly, the average cost of producing a bottle of wine in the United States is $0.50. Because Ricardian theory assumes that markets are perfectly competitive, in the long run a product's price equals its average cost of production. The prices of cloth and wine produced in the United States are shown in the table.

Suppose now that the wage rate is £5 (5 British pounds) per hour in the United Kingdom. Thus, the average cost (price) of producing a yard of cloth in the United Kingdom is £0.50 (£5 / 10 yards = £0.50 per yard), and the average cost (price) of producing a bottle of wine is £0.25. These prices are also shown in Table 2.4.

Is cloth less expensive in the United States or the United Kingdom? In which nation is wine less expensive? When U.S. prices are expressed in dollars and U.K. prices are expressed in pounds, we cannot answer this question. We must therefore express all prices in terms of one currency—say, the U.S. dollar. To do this, we must know the prevailing *exchange rate* at which the pound and the dollar trade for each other.

Suppose the dollar/pound exchange rate is $1.60 = £1. In Table 2.4, we see that the U.K. hourly wage rate (£5) is equivalent to $8 at this exchange rate (£5 × $1.60 = $8). The average dollar cost of producing a yard of cloth in the United Kingdom is $0.80 ($8 / 10 yards = $0.80 per yard), and the average dollar cost of producing a bottle of wine is $0.40 ($8 / 20 bottles = $0.40 per bottle). Compared to the costs of producing these products in the United States, we see that the United Kingdom

has lower costs in wine production but higher costs in cloth production. The United Kingdom thus has a comparative advantage in wine.

We conclude that even though the United Kingdom is not as efficient as the United States in the production of wine (or cloth), its lower wage rate (in terms of dollars) more than compensates for its inefficiency. At this wage rate, the U.K. average cost (in dollars) of producing wine is less than the U.S. average cost. With perfectly competitive markets, the U.K. selling price is lower than the U.S. selling price, and the United Kingdom exports wine to the United States.

PRODUCTION POSSIBILITIES SCHEDULES

Ricardo's law of comparative advantage suggested that specialization and trade can lead to gains for both nations when comparative advantage exists. His theory, however, depended on the restrictive assumption of the labor theory of value, in which labor was assumed to be the only factor input. In practice, however, labor is only one of several factor inputs.

Recognizing the shortcomings of the labor theory of value, modern trade theory provides a more generalized theory of comparative advantage. It explains the theory using a **production possibilities schedule**, also called a transformation schedule.[5] This schedule shows various alternative combinations of two goods that a nation can produce when all of its factor inputs (land, labor, capital, entrepreneurship) are used in their most efficient manner. The production possibilities

schedule thus illustrates the maximum output possibilities of a nation. Note that we are no longer assuming labor to be the only factor input, as Ricardo did.

Figure 2.1(a) illustrates hypothetical production possibilities schedules for the United States and Canada. By fully using all available inputs with the best available technology during a given time peri-

[5] See Gottfried Haberler, *The Theory of International Trade* (New York: Macmillan, 1950), Chapter 10.

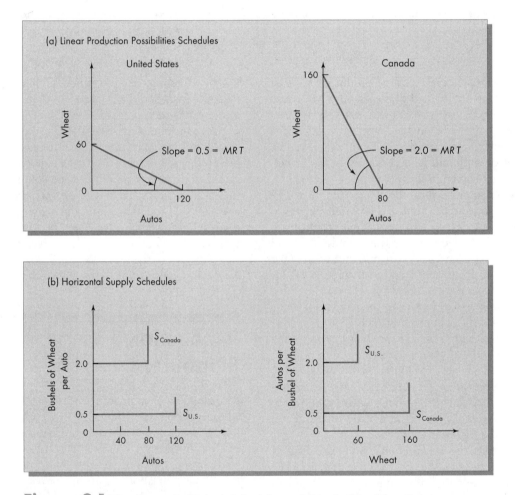

Figure 2.1 Production Possibilities Schedules and Supply Schedules: Constant Opportunity Costs

Given constant opportunity cost conditions, the relative cost of producing one good in terms of the other good remains the same no matter where a nation chooses to locate along its production possibilities schedule. Constant opportunity costs lead to linear production possibilities schedules and horizontal supply schedules.

od, the United States could produce either 60 bushels of wheat or 120 autos or certain combinations of the two products. Similarly, Canada could produce either 160 bushels of wheat or 80 autos or certain combinations of the two products.

Just how does a production possibilities schedule illustrate the concept of comparative cost? The answer lies in the slope of the production possibilities schedule, which is referred to as the **marginal rate of transformation (MRT)**. The *MRT* shows the amount of one product a nation must sacrifice to get one additional unit of the other product:

$$MRT = \frac{\Delta Wheat}{\Delta Autos}$$

This rate of sacrifice is sometimes called the *opportunity cost* of a product. Because this formula also refers to the slope of the production possibilities schedule, the *MRT* equals the absolute value of the production possibilities schedule's slope.

In Figure 2.1(a), the *MRT* of wheat into autos gives the amount of wheat that must be sacrificed for each additional auto produced. Concerning the United States, movement from the top endpoint on its production possibilities schedule to the bottom endpoint shows that the relative cost of producing 120 additional autos is the sacrifice of 60 bushels of wheat. This means that the relative cost of each auto produced is 0.5 bushel of wheat sacrificed (60 / 120 = 0.5)—that is, the *MRT* = 0.5. Similarly, Canada's relative cost of each auto produced is 2 bushels of wheat—that is, Canada's *MRT* = 2.

TRADING UNDER CONSTANT-COST CONDITIONS

This section illustrates the principle of comparative advantage under **constant opportunity costs**. Although the constant-cost case may be of limited relevance to the real world, it serves as a useful pedagogical tool for analyzing interna-

tional trade. The discussion focuses on two questions. First, what are the *basis for trade* and the *direction of trade*? Second, what are the potential *gains from free trade*, for a single nation and for the world as a whole?

CONSTANT COSTS Referring to Figure 2.1(a), notice that the production possibilities schedules for the United States and Canada are drawn as straight lines. The fact that the production possibilities schedules are linear indicates that the relative costs of the two products do not change as the economy shifts its production from all wheat to all autos, or anywhere in between. Figure 2.1(a) shows that for the United States the relative cost of an auto is 0.5 bushel of wheat as output expands or contracts; for Canada, the relative cost of an auto is 2 bushels of wheat as output expands or contracts.

There are *two reasons* for constant costs. First, the factors of production are perfect substitutes for each other. Second, all units of a given factor are of the same quality. As a country transfers resources from the production of wheat into the production of autos, or vice versa, the country will not have to resort to resources that are less well suited for the production of the commodity. Therefore, the country must sacrifice exactly the same amount of wheat for each additional auto produced, regardless of how many autos it is already producing.

The constant-cost concept can also be illustrated in terms of a *supply schedule*. Recall that the law of supply indicates that a producer's supply price rises as the producer offers more of the good for sale on the market. This means that the supply schedule slopes upward from the quantity axis. The factor underlying the law of supply is the tendency for marginal production costs to increase as the level of output rises. But what if a producer faces constant-cost conditions? What then would be the shape of the supply schedule?

Based on the production possibilities schedules in Figure 2.1(a), Figure 2.1(b) illustrates the supply schedules of autos and wheat for the United States and Canada. Note that on the vertical axes, the prices of the goods are measured in opportunity-cost terms rather than in monetary terms. The production possibilities schedules of the two countries suggest that the relative price (cost) of producing each extra auto is 0.5 bushel of wheat for the United States, whereas it is 2 bushels of wheat for Canada. Because constant-cost conditions imply that these prices do not change with the level of production, the supply schedules of autos are drawn as horizontal lines at the respective supply prices. Wheat production provides similar results. The production conditions are such that the relative price of producing an extra bushel of wheat is 2 autos for the United States and 0.5 auto for Canada.

THE BASIS FOR TRADE AND DIRECTION OF TRADE

Let us now examine trade under constant-cost conditions. Referring to Figure 2.2, assume that in **autarky** (the absence of trade) the United States prefers to produce and consume at point *A* on its production possibilities schedule, with 40 autos and 40 bushels of wheat. Assume also that Canada produces and consumes at point *A'* on its production possibilities schedule, with 40 autos and 80 bushels of wheat.

The *slopes* of the two countries' production possibilities schedules give the *relative cost* of one product in terms of the other. The relative cost of producing an additional auto is only 0.5 bushel of wheat for the United States but is 2 bushels of wheat for Canada. According to the principle of comparative advantage, this situation provides a basis for mutually favorable trade owing to the differences in the countries' relative costs. As for the direction of trade, we find the United States specializing in and exporting autos and Canada specializing in and exporting wheat.

PRODUCTION GAINS FROM SPECIALIZATION

The law of comparative advantage asserts that

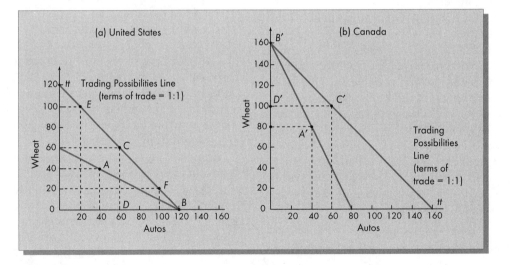

Figure 2.2 Trading Under Constant Opportunity Costs

With constant opportunity costs, a nation will specialize in the product of its comparative advantage. The principle of comparative advantage implies that with specialization and free trade, a nation enjoys production gains and consumption gains. A nation's trade triangle denotes its exports, imports, and terms of trade. In a two-nation, two-product world, the trade triangle of one nation equals that of the other nation; one nation's exports equal the other nation's imports, and there is one equilibrium terms of trade.

with trade each country will find it favorable to specialize in the production of the good of its comparative advantage and will trade part of this for the good of its comparative disadvantage. In Figure 2.2(a), the United States moves from production point A to production point B, totally specializing in auto production. Canada totally specializes in wheat production by moving from production point A' to production point B' in Figure 2.2(b). Taking advantage of specialization can result in **production gains** for both countries.

Looking at Figure 2.2(a), we find that prior to specialization, the United States produces 40 autos and 40 bushels of wheat. But with complete specialization, the United States produces 120 autos and no wheat. As for Canada, its production point in the absence of specialization is at 40 autos and 80 bushels of wheat, whereas its production point under complete specialization is at 160 bushels of wheat and no autos. Combining these results, we find that both nations together have experienced a net production gain of 40 autos and 40 bushels of wheat under conditions of complete specialization. Table 2.5(a) summarizes these production gains.

CONSUMPTION GAINS FROM TRADE In the absence of trade, the consumption alternatives of the United States and Canada are limited to points *along* their domestic production possibilities schedules. The exact consumption point for each nation will be determined by the tastes and preferences in each country. But with specialization and free trade, the two nations can achieve posttrade consumption points *outside* their domestic production possibilities schedules; that is, they can thus consume more wheat and more autos than they could consume in the absence of trade. Thus, trade can result in *consumption gains* for both countries.

The set of posttrade consumption points that a nation can achieve is determined by the rate at which its export product is traded for the other country's export product. This rate is known as the **terms of trade**. The terms of trade defines the relative prices at which two products are traded in the marketplace.

Table 2.5 Gains from Specialization and Trade: Constant Opportunity Costs

(a) Production Gains from Specialization

	Before Specialization		After Specialization		Net Gain (Loss)	
	Autos	Wheat	Autos	Wheat	Autos	Wheat
United States	40	40	120	0	80	-40
Canada	40	80	0	160	-40	80
World	80	120	120	160	40	40

(b) Consumption Gains from Trade

	Before Trade		After Trade		Net Gain (Loss)	
	Autos	Wheat	Autos	Wheat	Autos	Wheat
United States	40	40	60	60	20	20
Canada	40	80	60	100	20	20
World	80	120	120	160	40	40

Under constant-cost conditions, the slope of the production possibilities schedule defines the domestic rate of transformation (domestic terms of trade), which represents the relative prices at which two commodities can be exchanged at home. For a country to consume at some point *outside* its production possibilities schedule, it must be able to exchange its export good internationally at a terms of trade more favorable than the domestic terms of trade.

Assume that the United States and Canada achieve a terms-of-trade ratio that permits both trading partners to consume at some point outside their respective production possibilities schedules (Figure 2.2). Suppose that the terms of trade agreed on is a 1:1 ratio, whereby 1 auto is exchanged for 1 bushel of wheat. Based on these conditions, let line *tt* represent the international terms of trade for both countries. This line is referred to as the **trading possibilities line** (note that it is drawn with a slope having an absolute value of 1).

Suppose now that the United States decides to export, say, 60 autos to Canada. Starting at post-specialization production point *B* in Figure 2.2(a), the United States will slide along its trading possibilities line until point *C* is reached. At point *C*, 60 autos will have been exchanged for 60 bushels of wheat, at the terms-of-trade ratio of 1:1. Point *C* then represents the U.S. *posttrade consumption point*. Compared with consumption point *A*, point *C* results in a *net consumption gain* for the United States of 20 autos and 20 bushels of wheat. The triangle *BCD* showing the U.S. exports (along the horizontal axis), imports (along the vertical axis), and terms of trade (the slope) is referred to as the **trade triangle**.

Does this trading situation provide favorable results for Canada? Starting at postspecialization production point *B'* in Figure 2.2(b), Canada can import 60 autos from the United States by giving up 60 bushels of wheat. Canada would slide along its trading possibilities line until it reached point *C'*. Clearly, this is a more favorable consumption point than point *A'*. With free trade, Canada experiences a *net consumption gain* of

20 autos and 20 bushels of wheat. Canada's trade triangle is denoted by *B'C'D'*. Note that in our two-country model, the trade triangles of the United States and Canada are identical; one country's exports equal the other country's imports, which are exchanged at the equilibrium terms of trade. Table 2.5(b) summarizes the consumption gains from trade for each country and the world as a whole.

DISTRIBUTING THE GAINS FROM TRADE

Our trading example has assumed that the terms of trade agreed to by the United States and Canada will result in both trading partners' benefiting from trade; both will be able to achieve posttrade consumption points outside their domestic production possibilities schedules. Note that the consumption gains from trade are not always distributed equally between countries. The closer the international terms-of-trade line is located to the U.S. production possibilities schedule, the smaller are the U.S. consumption gains from trade. At the extreme, if the international terms of trade were to coincide with the U.S. domestic rate of transformation, the United States would not realize any gains from trade. This is because the U.S. posttrade consumption point would lie along its production possibilities schedule. The United States might trade at a terms of trade coinciding with its domestic rate of transformation, but at no terms of trade less favorable than that. The same reasoning also applies to Canada.

The domestic transformation rates of the United States and Canada clearly represent the *limits* within which the international terms of trade must fall. But where will the international terms of trade ultimately fall? As we explain in the next chapter, the actual location depends on the relative demand of the two nations for the products in question.

COMPLETE SPECIALIZATION

One implication of the foregoing trading example was that the United States produced only autos, whereas Canada produced only wheat. To see why **com-**

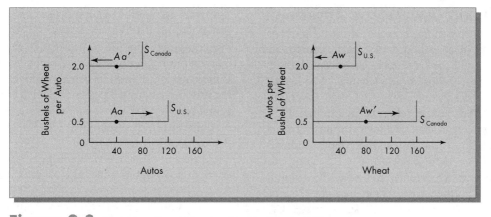

Figure 2.3 Complete Specialization Under Constant Costs

According to the principle of comparative advantage, complete specialization occurs under constant opportunity costs. Because production costs do not change with the level of output, a nation does not lose its comparative advantage (or disadvantage) as it produces more (or less) of a product.

plete **specialization** in production occurs under constant-cost conditions, consider Figure 2.3. The figure depicts the cost conditions and production points for the United States and Canada based on the trading example of Figure 2.2. The United States is assumed to have the cost advantage in auto production, whereas Canada is more efficient in wheat production.

As the United States increases and Canada decreases the production of autos, both countries' unit production costs remain constant. Since the relative costs never become equal, the United States does not lose its comparative advantage, nor does Canada lose its comparative disadvantage. The United States therefore produces only autos. Similarly, as Canada produces more wheat and the United States reduces its wheat production, both nations' production costs remain the same. Canada produces only without losing its advantage to the United States.

The only exception to complete specialization would occur if one of the countries, say Canada, is too small to supply the United States with all of the U.S. needs for wheat. Then Canada would be completely specialized in its export product, wheat, while the United States (large country) would produce both goods; however, the United States would still export autos and import wheat.

PRODUCTIVITY AND COMPARATIVE ADVANTAGE

The comparative advantage developed by manufacturers of a particular product can vanish over time when productivity growth falls behind that of foreign competitors. In the post–World War II era, for example, many U.S. steel companies produced steel in aging plants in which productivity increases lagged behind those of foreign manufacturers. This contributed to U.S. steel companies' loss of market share to foreign firms. Other U.S. industries that went the way of steel were automobiles, machine tools, and consumer electronics. By the 1990s, Japanese computer suppliers had begun to compete effectively with U.S. producers in markets including printers, floppy-disk drives, and dynamic random-access memory chips. This was particularly disturbing to those who considered computers to be a treasure of U.S. technology and a hallmark of U.S. competitiveness.

CHANGING COMPARATIVE ADVANTAGE

Our trade model has been based on the assumption that in each nation resource endowments are fixed and the set of technologies available to each nation is constant; each nation's production possibilities schedule is thus fixed in shape and location. Let us now relax this assumption.

If, as a result of technological improvements, productivity in the Japanese computer industry grows faster than it does in the U.S. computer industry, the opportunity cost of each computer produced in the United States increases relative to the opportunity cost of the Japanese. U.S. computers become less competitive in international markets because Japanese manufacturers can sell computers at lower prices.

Figure 2.4 illustrates the production possibilities schedules, for computers and automobiles, of the United States and Japan under conditions of constant opportunity cost. Note that the *MRT* of automobiles into computers initially equals 1.0 for the United States and 2.0 for Japan. The United States thus enjoys a comparative advantage in the production of computers and a comparative disadvantage in auto production.

Over a number of years, suppose both nations experience productivity increases in manufacturing computers but no productivity change in manufacturing automobiles. Assume that the United States increases its computer-manufacturing productivity by 50 percent (from 100 to 150 computers) but that Japan increases its computer-manufacturing productivity by 300 percent (from 40 to 160 computers).

As a result of these productivity gains, the production possibilities schedule of each country *rotates outward and becomes flatter.* More output can now be produced in each country with the same amount of resources. Referring to the new production possibilities schedules, the *MRT* of automobiles into computers equals 0.67 for the United States and 0.5 for Japan. The comparative cost of a computer in Japan has thus fallen below that in the United States. For the United States, the consequence of lagging productivity growth is that it loses its comparative advantage in computer production! But even after Japan achieves comparative advantage in computers, the United States still has a comparative advantage in autos; the change in manufacturing productivity thus

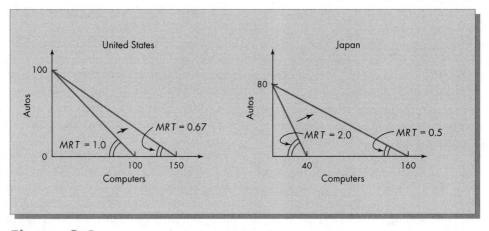

Figure 2.4 Changing Comparative Advantage

If productivity in the Japanese computer industry grows faster than it does in the U.S. computer industry, the opportunity cost of each computer produced in the United States increases relative to the opportunity cost of the Japanese. For the United States, comparative advantage shifts from computers to autos.

results in a change in the direction of trade. The lesson of this example is that producers who fall behind in research and development, technology, and equipment tend to find their competitiveness dwindling in world markets.

For domestic workers, what are the consequences of lost competitiveness in particular export markets? Not only do they lose jobs to foreign workers, but their wages tend to decrease relative to the wages of competing workers abroad. Some domestic workers with specialized skills that are not transferable to other industries may face lasting reductions in income.

It should be noted, however, that all countries enjoy a comparative advantage in some product or service. For the United States, the growth of international competition in industries such as steel and autos may make it easy to forget that the United States continues to be a major exporter of aircraft, paper, instruments, plastics, and chemicals. But putting the comparative-advantage principle into operation can be difficult, because workers are often reluctant to retrain and relocate to areas of the country where industries are expanding. Workers in import-competing industries often demand trade restrictions (such as tariffs or quotas) to preserve their jobs and wages.

U.S. MANUFACTURING PRODUCTIVITY

TRENDS The post–World War II era has been bruising for many U.S. manufacturers. During this era, the "Made in the USA" label vanished as foreign manufacturers came to dominate entire industries. In 1970, U.S. manufacturers produced 90 percent of the nation's machine tools, 88 percent of its automobiles, and 82 percent of its television sets; by the 1990s, they had given up almost one-third of the auto market, one-half of the domestic machine-tool market, and all of the television market. Although manufacturing comprised about one-fifth of total U.S. output, much of that reflected growing numbers of foreign-owned (transplant) plants in the United States. It was widely felt that the U.S. technological edge had been reduced, or eliminated, in many industries.

Available evidence suggests that the United States traditionally has been a leader in manufacturing productivity. During the 1950s and 1960s, countries in Europe and elsewhere complained that superior know-how due to scientific and technological achievement in the United States allowed U.S. manufacturers to penetrate European markets in electronics, aircraft, and computers. Other factors that supported the U.S. productivity edge included the U.S. educational system, high-quality management, research and development (R&D) expenditures, and the combining of R&D with production and marketing.

By the 1980s, the U.S. technological advantage had been reduced. Table 2.6 shows that manufacturing productivity growth in the United States tended to lag behind productivity growth in many of its trading partners during this era. In industries such as autos and steel, the United States yielded its technological advantage to other countries, especially Japan. Analysts maintained that part of the U.S. problem was that its companies did not imitate and build on the technological advances of their rivals as cheaply and

Table 2.6	Annual Indexes of Manufacturing Productivity		
	Output per Hour (1992 = 100)		
Country	1980	1990	1998
United States	71.9	97.8	127.0
Canada	75.3	95.3	111.7
Japan	63.9	95.4	120.5
Belgium	65.4	96.8	122.4
Denmark	90.3	99.1	104.5
France	66.7	93.5	127.5
Germany	77.2	99.0	127.1
Italy	64.1	92.5	113.6
Netherlands	69.2	98.6	132.8
Norway	76.7	96.6	104.1
Sweden	74.0	95.0	136.5
United Kingdom	56.2	88.4	104.8

Source: U.S. Department of Labor, Bureau of Labor Statistics, August 1999. See the BLS Internet site at http://stats.bls.gov/news. See also U.S. Department of Labor, *Monthly Labor Review*.

THE ANXIETY BEHIND GLOBALIZATION AND TRADE

If globalization, and the trade liberalization that is part of it, brings such benefits in terms of higher incomes and enhanced opportunity, why does controversy characterize key aspects of the globalization debate? The reason is that any process of change, including change that offers betterment and greater opportunity for society as a whole, carries with it anxieties and challenges.

First, globalization carries distributional consequences. Trade liberalization creates winners and losers, and it matters little to the losers that their losses may be temporary or that the winners gain more than they lose. The globalization process is also associated in the minds of some with the notion of marginalization. Not all countries share fully in the benefits of globalization, and the often unspoken assumption is that the marginalization of some countries is intrinsic to the globalization process itself.

Take the "dual economy" of the United States. By most measures, international trade has helped the U.S. economy to create enormous wealth—but not for everyone. Increased wealth has primarily occurred in "new economy" industries such as computer software and biotechnology. But global competition has squeezed workers in "old economy" industries such as textiles and electronics as jobs disappear to overseas countries that are more competitive. Dual economies also exist in many other industrial and developing countries. As globalization opens up economies, incomes for the millions working in export industries rise. But for the millions employed in import-competing industries that are

no longer competitive, real wages plummet and jobs disappear. In India, software writers are now part of America's labor pool, and their incomes are rising; but workers in once protected motorcycle and auto plants are suffering from new competition from Japanese imports as India opens its economy.

Second, by fostering growth and development, the globalization process can cause unintended collateral damage to the environment. If environmental quality and the environmental costs of economic activity are ignored, considerable damage may be done. In these circumstances, growth and development will become unsustainable in the longer run.

Third, globalization and trade are viewed by some as undesirably intrusive upon societies, attacking the diversity of social values among and within nations. One concern is that unbridled market forces will obligate countries to adopt lower standards in order to compete, and that regulatory permissiveness will replace sound public policy. This notion of a "race to the bottom" finds expression in the trade and environment debate, and in relation to labor standards. Fears of imposed uniformity also touch on matters of cultural diversity. In addition, there is the question of sovereignty, and the fear that globalization weakens nation governments, rendering them less effective in carrying out their economic and social responsibilities. Throughout this book, we will examine the anxieties behind globalization and trade and their possible solutions.

Source: World Trade Organization, *1998 Annual Report*, Geneva, Switzerland, p. 46.

quickly as Japanese firms did. By the 1990s, however, U.S. manufacturing productivity showed signs of revival.

Based on interviews with scores of U.S. business leaders, analysts have concluded that to survive in the competitive environment of the 2000s, U.S. companies must restructure their

managerial methods. Among the recommendations were these: Companies must (1) streamline factory processes to slash production costs, inventories, and material costs; (2) pare management layers to force designers, engineers, production workers, and marketers to work as teams; (3) harness computer technology to make small batches of customized products at low cost; (4) pounce on breakthrough discoveries, such as superconductivity, that will revolutionize entire businesses; (5) cultivate a workforce that is less specialized and is continuously learning; (6) accept labor representatives as valued partners in the innovation process; and (7) not be excessively concerned with short-term profits.

TRADE RESTRICTIONS

The principle of comparative advantage under constant costs suggests that trading nations will achieve the greatest possible gains from trade when they *completely specialize* in the production of the commodities of their comparative advantage. One factor that limits specialization is the restrictions governments impose on the movement of commodities among nations. By reducing the overall volume of trade, trade restrictions tend to reduce the gains from trade.

Assume that, for reasons of national security, the United States establishes restrictions on the amount of oil that can be imported from the Organization of Petroleum Exporting Countries (OPEC). Rather than importing all of its oil from OPEC, which is assumed to have a comparative advantage in oil production, suppose that the United States wishes to produce some oil itself. The United States chooses to produce some of the commodity of its *comparative disadvantage* in return for a greater degree of national security.

Figure 2.5 illustrates this trading situation between the United States and OPEC. Because the

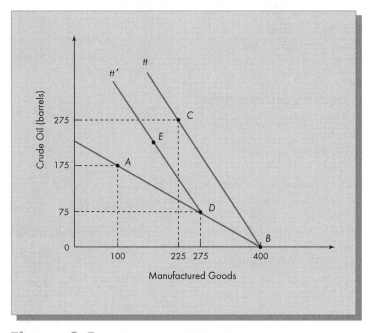

Figure 2.5 Trade Restrictions and the Gains from Trade

For a nation to achieve the greatest possible gains from trade, it must produce only the commodity of its comparative advantage. Trade restrictions reduce the production and consumption gains from specialization and trade by decreasing the extent of specialization and the volume of trade.

United States has the comparative advantage in the production of manufactured goods, it would benefit by specializing in the production of manufactured goods. The United States thus moves its production location from autarky point *A* to point *B*. By exporting, say, 175 manufactured goods at the international terms of trade *tt*, the United States would import 275 barrels of crude oil. At posttrade consumption point *C*, the U.S. consumption gains from trade total 125 manufactured goods and 100 barrels of crude oil.

Suppose instead that, for national security reasons, the United States wishes to produce some crude oil as well as some manufactured goods. Assume that the United States locates at point *D*, producing 75 barrels of crude oil and 275 manufactured goods. Given terms of trade *tt'* (assumed to be the same as terms of trade *tt*), the United States will achieve a lower posttrade consumption point than would exist under free trade. The U.S. posttrade consumption point will now lie along *tt'* (note that *tt'* is drawn parallel to *tt*), say, at point *E*. Clearly, point *E* is *inferior* to point *C*.

TRADING UNDER INCREASING-COST CONDITIONS

The preceding section illustrated the comparative-advantage principle under constant-cost conditions. But in the real world, a good's opportunity cost may increase as more of it is produced. The principle of comparative advantage must be illustrated in a slightly modified form.

INCREASING COSTS Increasing opportunity costs give rise to a production possibilities schedule that appears *concave*, or bowed outward from the diagram's origin. In Figure 2.6, with movement along the production possibilities schedule from *A* to *B*, the opportunity cost of producing autos becomes larger and larger in terms of wheat sacrificed. Because the real cost of producing autos rises as more autos are produced, the auto supply schedule is *positively* sloped. Auto producers will offer more autos on the market only if they are

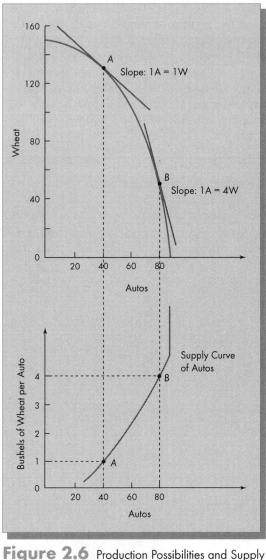

Figure 2.6 Production Possibilities and Supply Schedules Under Increasing-Cost Conditions

Increasing opportunity costs lead to a production possibilities schedule that is concave, viewed from the diagram's origin. The marginal rate of transformation equals the (absolute) slope of the production possibilities schedule. Under increasing costs, a product's supply schedule is upward sloping, suggesting that unit costs rise with the level of output. The vertical portion of the auto supply schedule corresponds to the endpoint of the production possibilities schedule at which all resources are devoted to auto production.

compensated for their rising costs of production. Changes in the quantity supplied and product price are therefore directly related. This is shown in the lower part of Figure 2.6.

Increasing costs mean that the *MRT* of wheat into autos *rises* as more autos are produced. Remember that the *MRT* is measured by the absolute slope of the production possibilities schedule at a given point. With movement from production point *A* to production point *B*, the respective tangent lines become *steeper*—their slopes increase in absolute value. The *MRT* of wheat into autos rises, indicating that each additional auto produced requires the sacrifice of increasing amounts of wheat.

Increasing costs represent the usual case in the real world. In the *overall economy*, increasing costs may result when inputs are imperfect substitutes for each other. As auto production rises and wheat production falls in Figure 2.6, inputs that are less and less adaptable to autos are introduced into that line of production. To produce more autos requires more and more of such resources and thus an increasingly greater sacrifice of wheat.

For a *particular product*, such as autos, increasing cost is explained by the principle of diminishing marginal productivity. The addition of successive units of labor (variable input) to capital (fixed input) beyond some point results in decreases in the marginal production of autos that is attributable to each additional unit of labor. Unit production costs thus rise as more autos are produced.

Under increasing costs, the slope of the concave production possibilities schedule varies as a nation locates at different points on the schedule. Because the domestic *MRT* equals the production possibilities schedule's slope, it will also be different for each point on the schedule. In addition to considering the *supply factors* underlying the production possibilities schedule's slope, we must also take into account the *role of tastes* and *preferences* (i.e., demand factors), for they will determine the point along the production possibilities schedule at which a country chooses to consume.

INCREASING-COST TRADING CASE Figure 2.7 shows the production possibilities schedules of

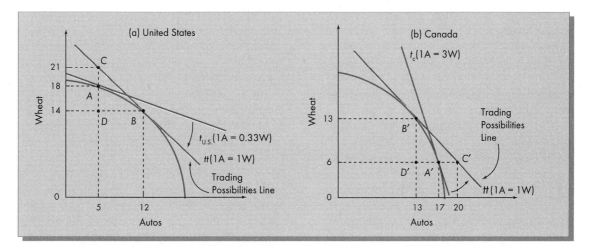

Figure 2.7 Trading Under Increasing Opportunity Costs

With increasing opportunity costs, comparative product prices in each country are determined by both supply and demand factors. This is unlike the case of production under constant opportunity costs, whereby comparative product prices are determined solely by supply factors; changes in demand do not affect unit production costs and prices under constant-cost conditions.

the United States and Canada under conditions of increasing costs. In Figure 2.7(a), assume that in the absence of trade the United States is located at point A along its production possibilities schedule; it produces and consumes 5 autos and 18 bushels of wheat. In Figure 2.7(b), assume that in the absence of trade Canada is located at point A' along its production possibilities schedule, producing and consuming 17 autos and 6 bushels of wheat. For the United States, the relative cost of wheat into autos is indicated by the slope of line $t_{U.S.}$, tangent to the production possibilities schedule at point A (1 auto = 0.33 bushels of wheat). In like manner, Canada's relative cost of wheat into autos is denoted by the slope of line t_C (1 auto = 3 bushels of wheat). Because line $t_{U.S.}$ is *flatter* than line t_C, autos are relatively cheaper in the United States and wheat is relatively cheaper in Canada. According to the law of comparative advantage, the United States will export autos and Canada will export wheat.

As the United States specializes in auto production, it slides downward along its production possibilities schedule from point A toward point B. The relative cost of autos (in terms of wheat) rises, as implied by the increase in the (absolute) slope of the production possibilities schedule. At the same time, Canada specializes in wheat. As Canada moves upward along its production possibilities schedule from point A' toward point B', the relative cost of autos (in terms of wheat) decreases, as evidenced by the decrease in the (absolute) slope of its production possibilities schedule.

The process of specialization continues in both nations until (1) the relative cost of autos is identical in both nations and (2) U.S. exports of autos precisely equal Canada's imports of autos, and conversely for wheat. Assume that this situation occurs when the domestic rates of transformation (domestic terms of trade) of both nations converge at the rate given by line *tt*. At this point of convergence, the United States produces at point B, while Canada produces at point B'. Line *tt* becomes the international terms-of-trade line for the United States and Canada; it coincides with each nation's domestic terms of trade. The international terms

of trade are favorable to both nations since *tt* is steeper than $t_{U.S.}$ and flatter than t_C.

What are the *production gains* from specialization for the United States and Canada? Comparing the amount of autos and wheat produced by the two nations at their points prior to specialization with the amount produced at their postspecialization production points, we see that there are gains of 3 autos and 3 bushels of wheat. The production gains from specialization are shown in Table 2.7(a).

What are the *consumption gains* from trade for the two nations? With trade, the United States can choose a consumption point along international terms-of-trade line *tt*. Assume that the United States prefers to consume the same number of autos as it did in the absence of trade. It will export 7 autos for 7 bushels of wheat, achieving a posttrade consumption point at C. The U.S. consumption gains from trade are 3 bushels of wheat, as shown in Figure 2.7 and also in Table 2.7(b). The U.S. *trade triangle*, showing its exports, imports, and terms of trade, is denoted by triangle BCD in Figure 2.7(a).

In like manner, Canada can choose to consume at some point along international terms-of-trade line *tt*. Assuming that Canada holds constant its consumption of wheat, it will export 7 bushels of wheat for 7 autos and wind up at posttrade consumption point C'. Its consumption gain of 3 autos is also shown in Table 2.7(b). Canada's *trade triangle* is depicted in Figure 2.7(b) by triangle B'C'D'. Note that Canada's trade triangle is identical to that of the United States.

PARTIAL SPECIALIZATION One feature of the increasing-cost model analyzed here is that trade generally leads each country to specialize only partially in the production of the good in which it has a comparative advantage. The reason for **partial specialization** is that increasing costs constitute a mechanism that forces costs in two trading nations to converge. When cost differentials are eliminated, the basis for further specialization ceases to exist.

Table 2.7 Gains from Specialization and Trade: Increasing Opportunity Costs

(a) Production Gains from Specialization

	Before Specialization		After Specialization		Net Gain (Loss)	
	Autos	Wheat	Autos	Wheat	Autos	Wheat
United States	5	18	12	14	7	-4
Canada	17	6	13	13	-4	7
World	22	24	25	27	3	3

(b) Consumption Gains from Trade

	Before Trade		After Trade		Net Gain (Loss)	
	Autos	Wheat	Autos	Wheat	Autos	Wheat
United States	5	18	5	21	0	3
Canada	17	6	20	6	3	0
World	22	24	25	27	3	3

Figure 2.8 assumes that prior to specialization the United States has a comparative cost advantage in producing autos, whereas Canada is relatively more efficient at producing wheat. With specialization, each country produces more of the commodity of its comparative advantage and less of the commodity of its comparative disadvantage. Given increasing-cost conditions, unit costs rise as both nations produce more of their export commodities. Eventually, the cost differentials are eliminated, at which point the basis for further specialization ceases to exist.

When the basis for specialization is eliminated, there exists a strong probability that both nations will produce some of each good. This is because costs often rise so rapidly that a country loses its comparative advantage vis-à-vis the other country before it reaches the endpoint of its production possibilities schedule. In the real world of increasing-cost conditions, partial specialization is a likely result of free trade.

COMPARATIVE ADVANTAGE EXTENDED TO MANY PRODUCTS AND COUNTRIES

In our discussion so far, we have used a trading model in which only two goods are produced and consumed and in which trade is confined to two countries. This simplified approach has permitted us to analyze many essential points about comparative advantage and trade. But the real world of international trade involves more than two products and two countries; each country produces thousands of products and trades with many countries. To move in the direction of realism, it is necessary to understand how comparative advantage functions in a world of many products and many countries. As we will see, the conclusions of comparative advantage hold when more realistic situations are encountered.

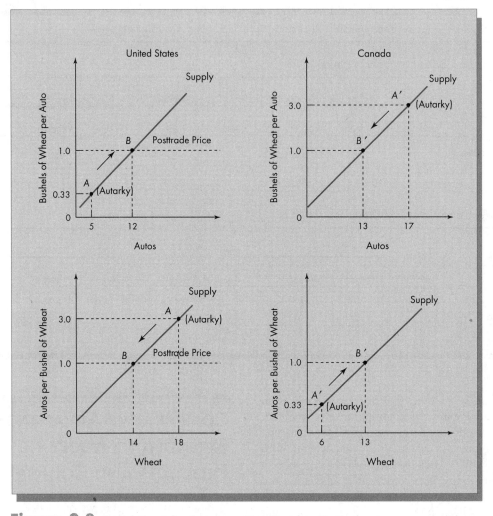

Figure 2.8 Partial Specialization: Increasing Opportunity Costs

Specialization in production tends to be partial in the case of increasing costs. This is because unit costs rise as each nation produces additional amounts of its export good. As the cost differentials among nations are eliminated, the basis for continued specialization disappears.

MORE THAN TWO PRODUCTS When a large number of goods are produced by two countries, operation of comparative advantage requires that the goods be ranked by the degree of comparative cost. Each country *exports* the product(s) in which it has the *greatest comparative advantage*. Conversely, each country *imports*

the product(s) in which it has *greatest comparative disadvantage*.

Figure 2.9 illustrates the hypothetical arrangement of six products—chemicals, jet planes, computers, autos, steel, and semiconductors—in rank order of the comparative advantage of the United States and Japan. The arrangement

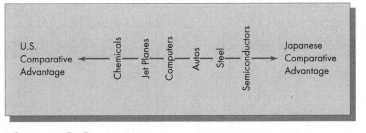

Figure 2.9 Hypothetical Spectrum of Comparative Advantages for the United States and Japan

When a large number of goods are produced by two countries, operation of the comparative-advantage principle requires the goods to be ranked by the degree of comparative cost. Each country exports the product(s) in which its comparative advantage is strongest. Each country imports the product(s) in which its comparative advantage is weakest.

implies that chemical costs are lowest in the United States relative to Japan, whereas the U.S. cost advantage in jet planes is not quite as pronounced. Conversely, Japan enjoys its greatest comparative advantage in semiconductors.

The product arrangement of Figure 2.9 clearly indicates that, with free trade, the United States will produce and export chemicals and that Japan will produce and export semiconductors. But where will the *cutoff point* lie between what is exported and what is imported? Between computers and autos? Or will Japan produce computers and the United States produce only chemicals and jet planes? Or will the cutoff point fall along one of the products rather than between them—so that computers, for example, might be produced in both Japan and the United States?

The cutoff point between what is exported and what is imported depends on the relative strength of international demand for the various products. One can visualize the products as beads arranged along a string according to comparative advantage. The strength of demand and supply will determine the cutoff point between U.S. and Japanese production. A rise in the demand for steel and semiconductors, for example, leads to price increases that move in favor of

Japan. This leads to rising production in the Japanese steel and semiconductor industries.

MORE THAN TWO COUNTRIES When many countries are included in a trading example, the United States will find it advantageous to enter into *multilateral trading relationships*. Figure 2.10 illustrates the process of multilateral trade for the United States, Japan, and OPEC. The arrows in the figure denote the directions of exports. The United States exports jet planes to OPEC, Japan imports oil from OPEC, and Japan exports semiconductors to the United States. The real world of international trade involves trading relationships even more complex than this triangular example.

This example casts doubt upon the idea that *bilateral balance* should pertain to any two trading partners. Indeed, there is no more reason to expect bilateral trade to balance between nations than between individuals. The predictable result is that a nation will realize a trade surplus (exports of goods exceed imports of goods) with trading partners that buy a lot of the things that we supply at low cost. Also, a nation will realize a trade deficit (imports of goods exceed exports of goods) with trading partners that are low-cost suppliers of goods that we import intensely.

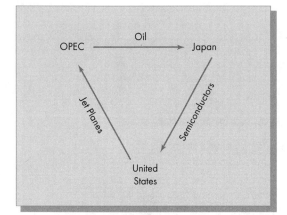

Figure 2.10 Multilateral Trade Among the United States, Japan, and OPEC

When many countries are involved in international trade, the home country will likely find it advantageous to enter into multilateral trading relationships with a number of countries. This figure illustrates the process of multilateral trade for the United States, Japan, and OPEC.

Consider the trade "deficits" and "surpluses" of a dentist who likes to snow ski. The dentist can be expected to run a trade deficit with ski resorts, sporting goods stores, and favorite suppliers of items like shoe repair, carpentry, and garbage collection. Why? The dentist is highly likely to buy these items from others. On the other hand, the dentist can be expected to run trade surpluses with his patients and medical insurers. These trading partners are major purchasers of the services provided by the dentist. Moreover, if the dentist has a high rate of saving, the surpluses will substantially exceed the deficits.

The same principles are at work across nations. A country can expect to run sizable surpluses with trading partners that buy a lot of the things the country exports, while trade deficits will be present with trading partners that are low-cost suppliers of the items imported. Table 2.8 shows the nations that the United States ran the largest trade surpluses and deficits in 1998.

What would be the effect if all countries entered into bilateral trade agreements that balanced exporters and imports between each pair of countries? The volume of trade and specialization would be greatly reduced, and resources would be hindered from moving to their highest productivity. Although exports would be brought into balance with imports, the gains from trade would be lessened.

EXIT BARRIERS

According to the principle of comparative advantage, an open trading system results in a channeling of resources from uses of low productivity to those of high productivity. Competition forces high-cost plants to exit, leaving the lowest-cost plants to operate in the long run. In practice, the restructuring of inefficient companies can take a long time because they often cling to capacity by nursing along antiquated plants. Why do companies delay plant closing when profits are subnormal and overcapacity exists? Part of the answer lies in the existence of **exit barriers**, various cost conditions that make lengthy exit a rational response by companies.

Consider the case of the U.S. steel industry. Throughout the 1980s and early 1990s, industry analysts maintained that overcapacity was a key problem facing U.S. steel companies. Overcapacity was caused by factors such as imports, reduced demand for steel, and installation of modern technology that allowed greater productivity and increased output of steel with fewer inputs of capital and labor. It was estimated that if steel capacity utilization could be increased, given existing prices, significant cost reductions would occur, bringing the industry to a position of profitability.

Traditional economic theory envisions hourly labor as a *variable cost* of production. However, the U.S. steel companies' contracts with the United Steelworkers of America, the labor union, make hourly labor a *fixed cost* instead of a variable cost, at least in part. The contracts call for

Table 2.8 Top Ten U.S. Trade Surpluses and Trade Deficit Countries in 1998 (Billions of Dollars)

Country	Trade Surplus	Country	Trade Deficit
Netherlands	$11.4	Japan	$-64.1
Australia	6.5	China	-56.9
Belgium-Lux.	5.7	Germany	-23.2
Brazil	5.0	Canada	-18.5
United Kingdom	4.3	Mexico	-15.7
Saudi Arabia	4.2	Taiwan	-15.0
Argentina	3.6	Italy	-12.0
Egypt	2.4	Malaysia	-10.0
Hong Kong	2.4	Thailand	-8.2
United Arab Emirates	1.7	South Korea	-7.4

Source: IMF Direction of Trade Statistics. Also, U.S. Department of Commerce, Bureau of Economic Analysis, *U.S. International Trade in Goods and Services*, June 1999. Web site http://www.bea.doc.gov.

employee benefits such as health and life insurance, pensions, and severance pay when a plant is shut down—as well as unemployment benefits. From a business perspective, if labor costs remain fixed, it may be rational to keep a plant operating even if it is losing money. For example, in 1980 Kaiser Steel decided to keep more than 11,000 workers employed because closing an aging plant would have cost the company more than $350 million in employee benefits!

Besides employee benefits, other exit costs tend to delay the closing of antiquated steel plants. These costs include penalties for terminating contracts to supply raw materials and expenses associated with writing off undepreciated plant assets. Steel companies also face environmental costs when they close plants: They are potentially liable for cleanup costs at their abandoned facilities for treatment, storage, and disposal costs that can easily amount to hundreds of millions of dollars. Furthermore, steel companies cannot realize much by selling their plants' assets. The equipment is unique to the steel industry and is of little value for any purpose other than producing steel. What's more, the equipment in a closed plant is generally in need of major renovation because the former owner allowed the plant to become antiquated prior to closing.

U.S. steel companies have maintained that they face cost disadvantages when they attempt to reduce plant capacity relative to their foreign competition. They point out that foreign companies often receive government assistance for closing obsolete plants. Japanese steel companies receive financing from the Bank of Japan to assist in restructuring, and European steel companies receive subsidies from their national governments for plant closures.

In summary, the existence of exit barriers delays the market adjustments that occur according to the principle of comparative advantage. Indeed, the movement of resources from uses of low productivity to those of high productivity may take considerable time.

EMPIRICAL EVIDENCE ON COMPARATIVE ADVANTAGE

Ricardo's theory of comparative advantage implies that each country will export goods for which its labor is relatively productive compared with that of its trading partners. Does his theory accurately predict trade patterns? A number of economists have put Ricardo's theory to empirical tests.

THE RACE IN RESEARCH AND DEVELOPMENT

National Research-and-Development Expenditures as a Percentage of Gross Domestic Product

	United States	France	Germany	Japan	United Kingdom
Total R&D					
1980	2.3	1.8	2.4	2.2	2.1
1985	2.8	2.3	2.8	2.8	2.3
1997	2.8	2.3	2.5	2.8	2.1
Nondefense R&D					
1980	1.7	1.4	2.3	2.2	1.5
1985	2.0	1.8	2.5	2.8	1.6
1997	2.1	1.9	2.3	2.7	1.9

Source: National Science Foundation, *National Patterns of R&D Resources*, October 4, 1999 (http://www.nsf.gov/sbe/srs/nprdr/start.htm) and Organization for Economic Cooperation and Development, *Main Science and Technology Indicators Database*. See also U.S. Department of Commerce, *Statistical Abstracts of the United States*.

During the 1980s, international competition forced the United States to learn anew how to compete on cost and quality in products such as steel, autos, and electronics. By the 1990s, the United States faced stiffer challenges in science and invention as well. The table above shows research and development (R&D) expenditures as a percentage of gross domestic product for selected nations.

The United States still spends the most on R&D by far in total dollar terms. Among the U.S. corporations with the largest R&D budgets are GM, IBM, AT&T, Digital Equipment, DuPont, Hewlett-Packard, Eastman Kodak, and United Technologies. In addition, U.S. law permits cooperative R&D ventures among U.S. companies. They range from the Electric Power Research Institute, dedicated to helping utilities generate and deliver electricity, to the Automotive Emissions Cooperative Research Program, established by U.S. auto companies and oil companies.

It is widely felt, however, that although the United States has been the source of many brilliant ideas—the big breakthroughs that win Nobel prizes—it has taken a beating when it comes to practical innovation, in which inventions are translated into products. In addition, Japan and Europe were spending more and more on R&D in the 1990s, reducing the U.S. advantage in science and technology.

The first test of the Ricardian model was made by the British economist G. D. A. MacDougall in 1951.[6] Comparing the export patterns of 25 separate industries for the United States and the United Kingdom for the year 1937, MacDougall tested the Ricardian prediction that nations tend to export goods in which their labor productivity is relatively high. His results strongly supported the Ricardian theory.

[6] G. D. A. MacDougall, "British and American Exports: A Study Suggested by the Theory of Comparative Costs," *Economic Journal* 61 (1951).

In each industry that MacDougall studied, U.S. labor productivity exceeded that of the United Kingdom, giving the United States an absolute cost advantage. However, the average U.S. wage rate was twice as high as the average U.K. wage rate, giving the United States an absolute cost disadvantage. MacDougall maintained that production costs would be lower in the United States in those industries where U.S. workers were *more than twice as productive* as British workers. These would be the industries in which the United States has a comparative advantage and undersells the United Kingdom in the world market. In those industries where British workers were *more than half as productive* as U.S. workers, the United Kingdom would have a comparative advantage and could undersell the United States in the world market.

Table 2.9 summarizes MacDougall's results. Of the 25 industries studied, 20 fit the predicted pattern; the United States had the larger share of world exports when its labor produc-

tivity was at least twice the British productivity. The MacDougall investigation thus supported the Ricardian theory of comparative advantage. Using different sets of data, subsequent studies by Balassa and Stern also confirmed Ricardo's conclusions.[7]

A more recent test of the Ricardian model comes from Stephen Golub, who examined the relationship between relative unit labor costs (the ratio of wages to productivity) and trade for the United States vis-à-vis the United Kingdom, Japan, Germany, Canada, and Australia. He found that relative unit labor cost helps to explain trade patterns for these nations. The U.S. and Japanese results lend particularly good support for the Ricardian model, as shown in Figure 2.11. The figure displays a scatter plot of

[7] B. Balassa, "An Empirical Demonstration of Classical Comparative Cost Theory," *Review of Economics and Statistics*, August 1963, pp. 231–238. See also R. Stern, "British and American Productivity and Comparative Costs in International Trade," *Oxford Economic Papers*, October 1962.

Table 2.9 United States and United Kingdom Output per Worker and Quantity of Exports to Third Countries in 1937

U.S. Output per Worker More Than Twice the U.K. Output	U.S. Exports Compared to U.K. Exports (Ratio)	U.S. Output per Worker Less Than Twice the U.K. Output	U.S. Exports Compared to U.K. Exports (Ratio)
Wireless sets/ valves	8:1	Cigarettes	1:2
Pig iron	5:1	Linoleum	1:3
Motor cars	4:1	Hosiery	1:3
Glass containers	$3^1/_2$:1	Leather footwear	1:3
Tin cans	3:1	Coke	1:5
Machinery	$1^1/_2$:1	Rayon weaving	1:5
Paper	1:1	Cotton goods	1:9
		Cement	1:11
		Rayon making	1:11
		Beer	1:18
		Men's/boy's coats	1:23
		Margarine	1:32
		Woolen and worsted	1:250

Exceptions (U.S. output per worker more than twice the U.K. output, but U.K exports exceed U.S. exports): electric lamps, rubber tires, soap, biscuits, watches.

Source: G. D. A. MacDougall, "British and American Exports: A Study Suggested by the Theory of Comparative Costs," *Economic Journal* 61, 1951.

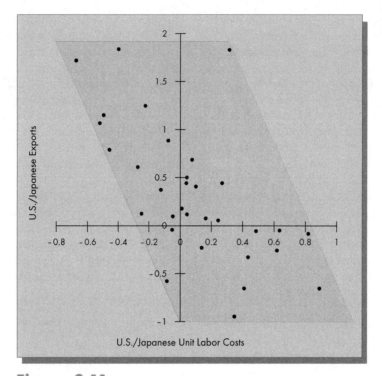

Figure 2.11 Relative Exports and Relative Unit Labor Costs: U.S./Japan, 1990

The figure displays a scatter plot of U.S./Japanese export data for 33 industries. It shows a clear negative correlation between relative exports and relative unit labor costs. A rightward movement along the figure's horizontal axis indicates a rise in U.S. unit labor costs relative to Japanese unit labor costs; this correlates with a decline in U.S. exports relative to Japanese exports, a downward movement along the figure's vertical axis.

Source: S. Golub, *Comparative and Absolute Advantage in the Asia–Pacific Region*, Center for Pacific Basin Monetary and Economic Studies, Economic Research Department, Federal Reserve Bank of San Francisco, October 1995, p. 46.

U.S.-Japan trade data showing a clear negative correlation between relative exports and relative unit labor costs for 33 industries investigated.[8]

Although there is empirical support for the Ricardian model, it is not without limitations.

Labor is not the only factor input. Allowance should be made where appropriate for production and distribution costs other than direct labor. Differences in product quality also explain trade patterns in industries such as automobiles and footwear. We should therefore proceed with caution in explaining a nation's competitiveness solely on the basis of labor productivity and wage levels.

[8] S. Golub, *Comparative and Absolute Advantage in the Asia–Pacific Region*, Center for Pacific Basin Monetary and Economic Studies, Economic Research Department, Federal Reserve Bank of San Francisco, October 1995, p. 46.

S U M M A R Y

1. Modern trade theory is primarily concerned with determining the basis for trade, the direction of trade, and the gains from trade.

2. Current explanations of world trade patterns are based on a rich heritage in the history of economic thought. Among the most important forerunners of modern trade theory were the mercantilists as well as Adam Smith and David Ricardo.

3. To the mercantilists, stocks of precious metals represented the wealth of a nation. The mercantilists contended that the government should adopt trade controls to limit imports and promote exports. One nation could gain from trade only at the expense of its trading partners because the stock of world wealth was fixed at a given moment in time and because not all nations could simultaneously have a favorable trade balance.

4. Smith challenged the mercantilist views on trade by arguing that, with free trade, international specialization of factor inputs could increase world output, which could be shared by trading nations. All nations could simultaneously enjoy gains from trade. Smith maintained that each nation would find it advantageous to specialize in the production of those goods in which it had an absolute advantage.

5. Ricardo argued that mutually gainful trade is possible even if one nation has an absolute disadvantage in the production of both commodities compared with the other nation. The less productive nation should specialize in the production and export of the commodity in which it has a comparative advantage.

6. Modern trade theory reasons that if in the absence of trade the comparative costs (prices) of two products differ between nations, both nations can benefit from international trade. The gains from trade stem from increased levels of production and consumption brought about by the international division of labor and specialization.

7. Comparative costs can be illustrated with the production possibilities schedule. This schedule indicates the maximum amount of any two products an economy can produce, assuming that all resources are used in their most efficient manner. The slope of the production possibilities schedule provides a measure of the marginal rate of transformation, which indicates the amount of one product that must be sacrificed per unit increase of another product.

8. Under constant-cost conditions, the production possibilities schedule is a straight line. Domestic relative prices are determined exclusively by a nation's supply conditions. Complete specialization of a country in the production of a single commodity may occur in the case of constant costs.

9. In the real world, nations tend to experience increasing-cost conditions. Thus, production possibilities schedules are drawn concave to the diagram's origin. Relative product prices in each country are determined by both supply and demand factors. Complete specialization in production is improbable in the case of increasing costs.

10. The comparative advantage accruing to manufacturers of a particular product in a particular country can vanish over time when productivity growth falls behind that of foreign competitors. Lost comparative advantages in foreign markets reduce the sales and profits of domestic companies as well as the jobs and wages of domestic workers.

11. When a large number of goods are produced by two countries, operation of comparative advantage requires that the goods be ranked by the degree of comparative cost. Each country exports the product(s) in which its comparative advantage is strongest, while importing the product(s) in which its comparative advantage is weakest. When many countries are involved in international trade, the home

country likely finds it advantageous to enter into multilateral trading relationships.

12. According to the comparative-advantage principle, competition forces high-cost producers to exit from the industry. In practice, the restructuring of an industry can take a long time because high-cost producers often cling to capacity by nursing along obsolete plants. Exit barriers refer to various cost conditions that make lengthy exit a rational response by high-cost producers.

13. The first empirical test of Ricardo's theory of comparative advantage was made by G. D. A. MacDougall. Comparing the export patterns of the United States and the United Kingdom, MacDougall found that wage rates and labor productivity were important determinants of international trade patterns. His findings supported Ricardo's theory. A more recent test of the Ricardian model, done by Stephen Golub, also supported Ricardo.

S T U D Y   Q U E S T I O N S

1. Identify the basic questions with which modern trade theory is concerned.

2. How did Smith's views on international trade differ from those of the mercantilists?

3. Develop an arithmetic example that illustrates how a nation could have an absolute disadvantage in the production of two goods and could still have a comparative advantage in the production of one of them.

4. Both Smith and Ricardo contended that the pattern of world trade is determined solely by supply conditions. Explain.

5. How does the comparative-cost concept relate to a nation's production possibilities schedule? Illustrate how differently shaped production possibilities schedules give rise to different opportunity costs.

6. What is meant by constant opportunity costs and increasing opportunity costs? Under what conditions will a country experience constant or increasing costs?

7. Why is it that the pretrade production points have a bearing on comparative costs under increasing-cost conditions but not under conditions of constant costs?

8. What factors underlie whether specialization in production will be partial or complete on an international basis?

9. The gains from specialization and trade are discussed in terms of *production gains* and *consumption gains*. What do these terms mean?

10. What is meant by the term *trade triangle*?

11. With a given level of world resources, international trade may bring about an increase in total world output. Explain.

12. The maximum amount of steel or aluminum that Canada and France can produce if they fully use all the factors of production at their disposal with the best technology available to them is shown (hypothetically) in Table 2.10.

   Assume that production occurs under constant-cost conditions. On graph paper, draw the production possibilities schedules for Canada and France; locate aluminum on the horizontal axis and steel on the vertical axis of each country's graph. In the absence of trade, assume that Canada produces and consumes 600 tons of aluminum and 300 tons of steel and that France produces and consumes 400 tons of aluminum and 600 tons of steel. Denote these autarky points on each nation's

Table 2.10 Steel and Aluminum Production

	Canada	France
Steel (tons)	500	1,200
Aluminum (tons)	1,500	800

production possibilities schedule.

a. Determine the *MRT* of steel into aluminum for each nation. According to the principle of comparative advantage, should the two nations specialize? If so, which product should each country produce? Will the extent of specialization be complete or partial? Denote each nation's specialization point on its production possibilities schedule. Compared to the output of steel and aluminum that occurs in the absence of trade, does specialization yield increases in output? If so, by how much?

b. Within what limits will the terms of trade lie if specialization and trade occur? Suppose Canada and France agree to a terms-of-trade ratio of 1:1 (1 ton of steel = 1 ton of aluminum). Draw the terms-of-trade line in the diagram of each nation. Assuming that 500 tons of steel are traded for 500 tons of aluminum, are Canadian consumers better off as the result of trade? If so, by how much? How about French consumers?

c. Describe the trade triangles for Canada and France.

13. The hypothetical figures in Table 2.11 give five alternate combinations of steel and autos that Japan and South Korea can produce if they fully use all factors of production at their disposal with the best technology available to them. On graph paper, sketch the production possibilities schedules of Japan and South Korea. Locate steel on the vertical axis and autos on the horizontal axis of each nation's graph.

a. The production possibilities schedules of the two countries appear concave, or bowed out, from the origin. Why?

b. In autarky, Japan's production and consumption points along its production possibilities schedule are assumed to be 500 tons of steel and 600 autos. Draw a line tangent to Japan's autarky point and from it calculate Japan's *MRT* of steel into autos. In autarky, South Korea's production and consumption points along its production possibilities schedule are assumed to be 200 tons of steel and 800 autos. Draw a line tangent to South Korea's autarky point and from it calculate South Korea's *MRT* of steel into autos.

c. Based on the *MRT* of each nation, should the two nations specialize according to the principle of comparative advantage? If so, in which product should each nation specialize?

d. The process of specialization in the production of steel and autos continues in Japan and South Korea until their relative product prices, or *MRTs*, become equal. With specialization, suppose the *MRTs* of the two nations converge at *MRT* = 1. Starting at Japan's autarky point, slide along its production possibilities schedule until the slope of the tangent line equals 1. This becomes Japan's production point under partial specialization. How many tons of steel and how many autos will Japan produce at this point? In like manner, determine South Korea's production point under partial specialization. How many tons of steel and how many autos will South Korea produce? For the two countries, do their combined production of steel and autos with partial specialization exceed their output in the absence of specialization? If so, by how much?

Table 2.11 Steel and Auto Production

Japan		South Korea	
Steel (Tons)	Autos	Steel (Tons)	Autos
520	0	1,200	0
500	600	900	400
350	1,100	600	650
200	1,300	200	800
0	1,430	0	810

e. With the relative product prices in each nation now in equilibrium at 1 ton of steel equal to 1 auto (*MRT* = 1), suppose 500 autos are exchanged at this terms of trade.

(1) Determine the point along the terms-of-trade line at which Japan will locate after trade occurs. What are Japan's consumption gains from trade?

(2) Determine the point along the terms-of-trade line at which South Korea will locate after trade occurs. What are South Korea's consumption gains from trade?

2.1 For a look at some international data from the United Nations' home page, set your browser to URL:

http://www.un.org/depts/unsd/mbsreg.htm

2.2 The Web site of the World Trade Organization offers a number of avenues to explore, including a brief biographical sketch of David Ricardo, information on recent world trade and output growth, and a summary of the arguments in favor of free trade. Set your browser to URL:

http://www.wto.org/

2.3 For a skeptical look at free trade, go to the United Auto Workers' home page and look at some of the articles in the online magazines. Also, Ralph Nader's organization has created a home page that supports this skepticism of free trade, the Public Citizen Global Trade Watch. These two sites can be found by setting your browser to URL:

http:/www.uaw.org/
and
http://www.citizen.org/pctrade/tradehome.html

To access NetLink Exercises and the Virtual Scavenger Hunt, visit the Carbaugh Web site at http://carbaugh.swcollege.com.

International Equilibrium

chapter **3**

Chapter 2 emphasized the role of international differences in the cost of producing tradable goods as the main determinant of international trade patterns. By considering only supply-side factors, however, we could not determine (1) the equilibrium point on each nation's production possibilities schedule, (2) the equilibrium value of the international terms of trade, or (3) the equilibrium consumption point of each nation under free trade. Let us now include the role of demand conditions in our trade model so that we can determine the magnitude of these items.

INDIFFERENCE CURVES

Modern trade theory contends that the pattern of world trade is governed by international differences in *supply conditions* and *demand conditions*. Therefore, the role of demand must be developed and introduced into the trade model. Economic theory reasons that an individual's demand curve is based on several underlying determinants, among them (1) the level of disposable income and (2) personal tastes and preferences. Discussion of income as a determinant of demand is undertaken in Chapter 4. Here we consider the role of personal tastes and preferences in demand analysis.

The role of tastes and preferences can be illustrated graphically by a consumer's indifference curve. An **indifference curve** depicts the various combinations of two commodities that are equally preferred in the eyes of the consumer—that is, yield the same level of satisfaction. The term *indifference curve* stems from the idea that the consumer is indifferent among the many possible

KEY CONCEPTS AND TERMS

- *Commodity terms of trade*
- *Community indifference curve*
- *Immiserizing growth*
- *Importance of being unimportant*
- *Indifference curve*
- *Indifference map*
- *Marginal rate of substitution (MRS)*
- *No-trade boundary*
- *Offer curve*
- *Outer limits for the equilibrium terms of trade*
- *Region of mutually beneficial trade*
- *Theory of reciprocal demand*

commodity combinations that provide identical amounts of satisfaction. Figure 3.1 illustrates a consumer's **indifference map**, which consists of a set of indifference curves. Referring to indifference curve I, a consumer is just as happy consuming, say, 6 bushels of wheat and 1 auto at point *A* as consuming 3 bushels of wheat and 2 autos at point *B*. All combination points along an indifference curve are equally desirable because they yield the same level of satisfaction. Besides this fundamental characteristic, indifference curves have several other features.

Inspection of Figure 3.1 reveals that an indifference curve tends to be negatively sloped—that is, sloped downward to the right. This is assured by the assumption that a consumer always desires more of a commodity than less of it. Because each combination of goods along an indifference curve provides the same level of sat-

isfaction, it follows that a consumer who increases auto holdings must decrease wheat intake by some amount if the initial level of satisfaction is to be maintained. If the wheat holdings are not decreased, the new market basket would include more of the combined amount of both commodities, resulting in a higher level of satisfaction. Because changes in the consumption of one commodity are inversely related to changes in the amount consumed of another for a given level of satisfaction to be maintained, it follows that an indifference curve slopes downward to the right.

Indifference curves are also generally convex (bowed in) to the diagram's origin. The negative slope of an indifference curve indicates that, for any given level of satisfaction, some amount of one good must be sacrificed if more of another is to be acquired. The rate at which the substitution occurs is called the **marginal rate of substitution**

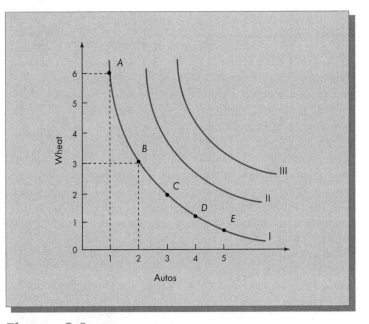

Figure 3.1 A Consumer's Indifference Map

An indifference map is a graph that illustrates an entire set of indifference curves. Each higher indifference curve represents a greater level of satisfaction for the consumer. A community indifference curve denotes various combinations of two goods that yield equal amounts of satisfaction to the nation as a whole.

(**MRS**). In terms of Figure 3.1, the marginal rate of substitution indicates the extent to which a consumer is willing to substitute autos for wheat (or vice versa) while maintaining a given level of satisfaction. The marginal rate of substitution of autos for wheat is expressed algebraically as

$$MRS = \frac{\Delta Wheat}{\Delta Autos}$$

The marginal rate of substitution is equal to an indifference curve's absolute slope. As we move downward along the indifference curve, autos become relatively plentiful while wheat becomes relatively scarce. With less wheat and more autos, each additional auto becomes less valuable to the consumer. For each additional auto consumed, the consumer is willing to sacrifice smaller amounts of wheat. This means that the marginal rate of substitution of autos for wheat decreases as more autos are consumed—hence, the convex nature of an indifference curve.

The indifference map in Figure 3.1 shows several of the consumer's indifference curves. Those indifference curves lying farther from the origin (the "higher" curves) represent greater levels of satisfaction. This is because any point on a higher indifference curve suggests at least the same amount of one commodity plus more of another commodity. Although the figure contains only three indifference curves, an infinite number can be drawn.

Having developed an indifference curve for one individual, can we assume that the preferences of all consumers in the entire nation could be added up and summarized by a **community indifference curve**? Strictly speaking, the answer is no, because it is impossible to make interpersonal comparisons of satisfaction. For example, person A may prefer a lot of coffee and little sugar, whereas person B prefers the opposite. The dissimilar nature of individuals' indifference curves results in their being noncomparable. Despite these theoretical problems, a community indifference curve can be used as a pedagogical device that depicts the role of consumer preferences in international trade.

EQUILIBRIUM IN THE ABSENCE OF TRADE

Beginning once again with the assumption of isolation, what is the optimal level of production and consumption for a nation? In other words, *at what point on its production possibilities schedule will a nation choose to locate in the absence of trade?*

Assuming that a nation wishes to maximize satisfaction, it will attempt to consume some combination of goods on the highest indifference curve that it can reach. But an indifference curve only tells what a nation would like to do. Given the availability and quality of resources and the level of technology, there is a constraint on how many goods will actually be available to consume. For a nation, this production constraint is represented by its production possibilities schedule. A nation in the absence of trade will maximize satisfaction if it can reach the highest attainable indifference curve, given the production constraint of its production possibilities schedule. This will occur when the production possibilities schedule is *tangent* to an indifference curve.

Figure 3.2 illustrates the production possibilities schedule and indifference map for a single nation. In the absence of trade, the nation will maximize satisfaction if it produces and consumes at point *E,* where indifference curve II is tangent to its production possibilities schedule. Any point on a higher indifference curve—say, *F*—is unattainable because it is beyond the economy's capacity to produce. Any point on a lower indifference curve, such as *G* or *H,* does not represent maximum satisfaction. This is because a higher indifference curve can be reached with the existing production possibilities schedule. Point *E,* then, represents the equilibrium of production and consumption in the absence of trade.

A RESTATEMENT: BASIS FOR TRADE, GAINS FROM TRADE

Using indifference curves, let us now develop a trade example to restate the basis-for-trade and

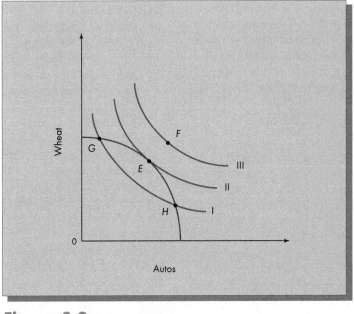

Figure 3.2 Indifference Curves and International Trade

In the absence of trade, a nation achieves equilibrium at the point where its community indifference curve is tangent to its production possibilities schedule. At this point, the nation experiences the highest attainable level of satisfaction given the constraint of its production possibilities schedule, which limits the amount of goods available for consumption.

the gains-from-trade issues. Figure 3.3 depicts the trading position of the United States. Assuming that the United States attempts to maximize satisfaction, its location of production and consumption will be at point *A*, where the U.S. production possibilities schedule is just tangent to indifference curve I. At point *A*, the U.S. relative price ratio is denoted by line $t_{U.S.}$ which equals the absolute slope of the production possibilities curve at that point.

Suppose that the United States has a comparative advantage vis-à-vis Canada in the production of autos. The United States will find it advantageous to specialize in auto production until the two countries' relative prices of autos equalize. Suppose this occurs at production point *B*, where the U.S. price rises to Canada's price, depicted by

line *tt*. Also suppose that *tt* becomes the international terms-of-trade line. Starting at production point *B*, the United States will export autos and import wheat, trading along line *tt*. The immediate problem the United States faces is to determine the *level of trade that will maximize its welfare*.

Suppose that the United States exchanges 6 autos for 50 bushels of wheat at terms-of-trade *tt*. This would shift the United States from production point *B* to posttrade consumption point *D*. But the United States would be no better off with trade than it was in the absence of trade. This is because in both cases the consumption points are located along indifference curve I. Trade volume of 6 autos and 50 bushels of wheat thus represents the *minimum* acceptable volume of trade for the United States. Any smaller vol-

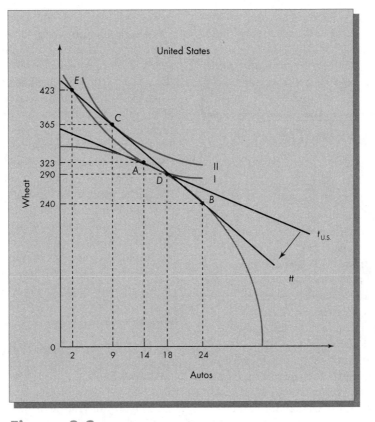

Figure 3.3 Basis for Trade, Gains from Trade

A nation benefits from international trade if it can achieve a higher level of satisfaction (indifference curve) than it can attain in the absence of trade. Maximum gains from trade occur at the point where the international terms-of-trade line is tangent to a community indifference curve.

ume would force the United States to locate on a lower indifference curve.

Suppose instead that the United States decides to trade 22 autos for 183 bushels of wheat. The United States would move from production point *B* to posttrade consumption point *E*. With trade, the United States would again locate on indifference curve I, resulting in no gains from trade. From the U.S. viewpoint, trade volume of 22 autos and 183 bushels of wheat therefore represents the *maximum* acceptable volume of

trade. Any greater volume would find the United States moving to a lower indifference curve.

Trading along terms-of-trade line *tt*, the United States can achieve *maximum welfare* if it exports 15 autos and imports 125 bushels of wheat. The U.S. posttrade consumption location would be at point *C* along indifference curve II, the highest attainable level of satisfaction. Comparing point *A* and point *C* reveals that with trade the United States consumes more wheat, but fewer autos, than it does in the absence of trade. Yet point *C* is clearly a preferable consumption location. This is because under indifference-curve analysis, the gains from trade are measured in terms of total satisfaction rather than in terms of number of goods consumed.

THE EQUILIBRIUM TERMS OF TRADE

A shortcoming of the Ricardian principle of comparative advantage was its inability to explain fully the *distribution* of the gains from trade among trading partners. The best description of the gains from trade that Ricardo could provide was only the *outer limits* within which the equilibrium terms of trade would fall. This is because the Ricardian theory relied solely on supply conditions in explaining trade patterns; it ignored the role of demand.

To visualize Ricardo's analysis of the terms of trade, recall our example of trade under constant opportunity costs in Chapter 2 (see Figure 2.2). It was assumed that for the United States the relative cost of producing an additional auto was 0.5 bushels of wheat ($MRT = 0.5$) whereas for Canada the relative cost of producing an additional auto was 2 bushels of wheat ($MRT = 2.0$). The United States had a comparative advantage in autos, whereas Canada had a comparative advantage in wheat. Figure 3.4 illustrates these domestic cost conditions of the United States and Canada. Note that we have translated the domestic cost ratio, given by the negatively sloped production possibilities schedule, into a *positively sloped* price-ratio line.

According to Ricardo, the domestic price ratios set the **outer limits for the equilibrium terms of trade.** If the United States is to export autos, it should not accept any terms of trade less than a ratio of 0.5:1, indicated by its domestic price line. Otherwise, the U.S. posttrade consumption point would lie inside its domestic production possibilities schedule. The United States would clearly be better off without trade than

with trade. The U.S. domestic price line therefore becomes its **no-trade boundary.** Similarly, Canada would require a minimum of 1 auto for every 2 bushels of wheat exported, as indicated by its domestic price line; any terms of trade less than this rate would be unacceptable to Canada. The no-trade boundary line for Canada is thus defined by its domestic price ratio line.

For gainful international trade to exist, a nation must achieve a posttrade consumption location at least equivalent to its point along its domestic production possibilities schedule. Any acceptable international terms of trade has to be more favorable than or equal to the rate defined by the domestic price line. The **region of mutually beneficial trade** is thus bounded by the cost ratios of the two countries. But where will the equilibrium terms of trade actually lie?

THEORY OF RECIPROCAL DEMAND

By bringing into the picture the relative strength of the trading partners' demands, John Stuart Mill (1806–1873) was able to formulate the **theory of reciprocal demand.**[1] This theory suggests that the actual price at which trade takes place depends on the trading partners' *interacting demands.*

Suppose Canada, which has a comparative advantage in the production of wheat, expresses an *enormous demand for autos*, both domestically produced and imported. Because the price that Canada is willing to pay for autos rises, the United States will realize most of the gains from trade. Starting at point *A* in Figure 3.4, where the gains from trade are evenly divided between the two nations, an improving U.S. terms of trade suggests that a given quantity of auto exports buys larger amounts of wheat imports. The United States will achieve a posttrade consumption point farther outside its production possibilities

---

[1] John Stuart Mill, *Principles of Political Economy* (New York: Longmans, Green, 1921), pp. 584–585.

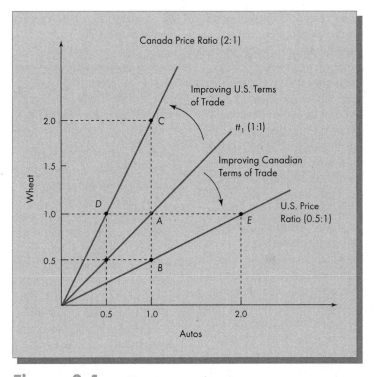

Figure 3.4 Equilibrium Terms-of-Trade Limits

The supply-side analysis of Ricardo describes the outer limits within which the equilibrium terms of trade must fall. The domestic price ratios set the outer limits for the equilibrium terms of trade. Mutually beneficial trade for both nations occurs if the equilibrium terms of trade lies between the two nations' domestic price ratios. According to the theory of reciprocal demand, the actual price at which trade occurs depends on the trading partners' interacting demands.

schedule. At the outer extreme, the Canadian auto demand could be so enormous that the terms of trade would settle along its domestic price-ratio line. The United States would then be the only country to gain from trade.

Again starting at point *A* in Figure 3.4, suppose the United States expresses an *enormous demand for wheat*, both domestically produced and imported. Because the price the United States is willing to pay for wheat rises, Canada will enjoy most of the gains from trade. An improving Canadian terms of trade suggests that a given amount of wheat exports buys increasing amounts

of auto imports. At the extreme, the terms of trade could settle at the U.S. domestic price ratio, in which case only Canada would gain from trade.

According to Mill's theory, the equilibrium terms of trade depends on both the Canadian demand for autos and wheat and the U.S. demand for the same products. The stronger the Canadian demand for autos relative to the U.S. demand for wheat, the closer the terms of trade will settle to the Canadian domestic price ratio. The reverse is equally true. The reciprocal demand theory thus contends that the equilibrium terms of trade depends on the relative strength of each nation's demand for the other nation's product.

The reciprocal-demand theory best applies when both nations are of *equal economic size*, so that the demand of each nation has a noticeable effect on market price. Given two nations of *unequal economic size*, it is possible that the relative demand strength of the smaller nation will be dwarfed by that of the larger nation. In this case, the domestic price ratio of the larger nation will prevail. Assuming the absence of monopoly elements working in the markets, the small nation can export as much of the commodity as it desires, enjoying large gains from trade.

Consider trade in crude oil and autos between Venezuela and the United States before the rise of the OPEC (Organization of Petroleum Exporting Countries) oil cartel. Venezuela, as a small nation, accounted for only a very small share of the U.S.–Venezuelan market, whereas the U.S. market share was overwhelmingly large. Because Venezuelan consumers and producers had no influence on market price levels, they were in effect price takers. In trading with the United States, no matter what the Venezuelan demand was for crude oil and autos, it was not strong enough to affect U.S. price levels. As a result, Venezuela traded according to the U.S. domestic price ratio, buying and selling autos and crude oil at the price levels existing within the United States.

The example just given implies the following generalization: if two nations of approximately the *same size* and with similar taste patterns participate in international trade, the gains from trade will be shared about *equally* between them. However, if one nation is significantly larger than the other, the *larger nation* attains *fewer gains* from trade while the *smaller nation* attains *most of the gains* from trade. This situation is characterized as the **importance of being unimportant**. What's more, when nations are very dissimilar in size, there is a strong possibility that the larger nation will continue to produce its comparative-disadvantage good because the smaller nation is unable to supply all of the world's demand for this product. A more detailed presentation of the

equilibrium terms of trade is contained in the appendix of this chapter.

ECONOMIC GROWTH AND THE TERMS OF TRADE

Does a nation necessarily become better off when it produces more? Does economic growth enhance domestic welfare?

Consider Brazil, heavily committed to coffee as an export crop. Suppose technological improvements lead to productivity increases in Brazil's coffee production, resulting in an excess supply of coffee at the prevailing international terms of trade. If Brazil is sufficiently large to be able to affect world price and if the foreign demand for coffee is relatively price-inelastic, the world price of coffee will fall substantially. *Export-biased growth thus worsens Brazil's terms of trade.*

Export-biased growth has two opposing effects for Brazil's welfare. Brazil gains because it can produce more, but it loses because it receives a lower price for its exports. Whether the benefits of rising output more than outweigh the losses due to the deterioration of the terms of trade will determine whether Brazil is better off or worse off as a result of growth. If the negative terms-of-trade effect outweighs the positive effect of increased output, the technological improvement that generated this outcome is known among economists as **immiserizing growth**.

Figure 3.5 illustrates the possibility of immiserizing growth. The figure shows Brazil's production possibilities schedules for coffee (export sector) and computers (import sector). Initially, Brazil produces at point A and exports coffee for computers at the terms-of-trade ratio denoted by tt_0. With trade, Brazil achieves a welfare level indicated by indifference curve I and attains a posttrade consumption point at B.

Because of the technological improvements in coffee production, Brazil's production possibilities schedule shifts rightward; as drawn, the growth is "biased" toward Brazil's export sector

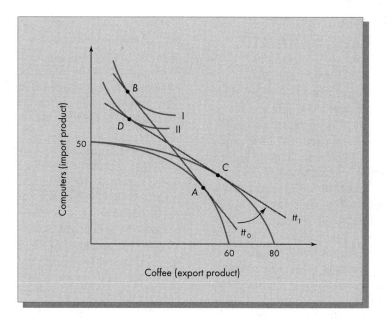

Figure 3.5 Immiserizing Growth

Prior to economic growth, Brazil achieves a posttrade consumption point B along indifference curve I. Export-biased growth shifts out Brazil's production possibilities schedule; as drawn, the growth is biased toward coffee. If the resulting increased volume of trade substantially reduces Brazil's terms of trade, the country's posttrade consumption point D may end up on indifference curve II, which lies below indifference curve I.

(coffee). Because Brazil is a large nation, compared to the world economy, the country's increased coffee output causes coffee prices to fall; Brazil's terms of trade thus decline to tt_1. At this exchange ratio, Brazil continues to export coffee, but it can only achieve a posttrade consumption point at D on the lower indifference curve, curve II. Brazil's economic growth thus leads to reduced Brazilian welfare! It should be noted that the conditions under which immiserizing growth could occur are extreme and that it is usually considered to be more of a theoretical possibility than an empirical reality.[2]

Before concluding that economic growth is undesirable, consider other possibilities, such as import-biased growth. Suppose Brazil's growth is

concentrated in computers, its import-competing product, rather than coffee. It can be shown that a technological advantage that occurs in the import-competing sector tends to raise the price of the export good relative to the price of the import-competing good and thus improve Brazil's terms of trade. It is left to more advanced texts to illustrate this point.

---

[2] The case of immiserizing growth is most likely to occur when (a) the nation's economic growth is biased toward its export sector; (b) the country is large relative to the world market, so that its export price falls when domestic output expands; (c) the foreign demand for the nation's export product is highly price-inelastic, which implies a large decrease in price in response to an increase in export supply; and (d) the nation is heavily engaged in international trade, so that the negative effects of the terms-of-trade deterioration more than offset the positive effects of increased production.

TERMS-OF-TRADE ESTIMATES

The gains a nation enjoys from its foreign trade consist of a larger income owing to a wider range of goods available to consumers and the favorable influence trade has on productivity levels. Estimating these gains at a particular time would be extremely difficult, for it would require knowledge of what a nation's imports would cost if it produced them itself instead of purchasing them from a less expensive foreign source. Instead, economists have attempted to measure the direction of these gains over time. This is accomplished by calculating changes in the terms of trade.

The **commodity terms of trade** (also referred to as the *barter terms of trade*) is the most frequently used measure of the direction of trade gains. It measures the relationship between the prices a nation gets for its exports and the prices it pays for its imports. This is calculated by dividing a nation's export price index by its import price index, multiplied by 100 to express the terms of trade in percentages:

$$Terms\ of\ Trade = \frac{Export\ Price\ Index}{Import\ Price\ Index} \times 100$$

An *improvement* in a nation's terms of trade requires that the prices of its exports rise relative to the prices of its imports over the given time period. A smaller quantity of export goods sold abroad is required to obtain a given quantity of imports. Conversely, a *deterioration* in a nation's terms of trade is due to a rise in its import prices relative to its export prices over a time period. The purchase of a given quantity of imports would require the sacrifice of a greater quantity of exports.

Table 3.1 gives the commodity terms of trade for selected countries. With 1995 as the base year (equal to 100), the table shows that by 1999 the U.K.'s index of export prices was 95, a decrease of 5 percent. During the same period, the index of U.K. import prices fell by 13 percent, to a level of 87. Using the terms-of-trade formula, we find that the U.K.'s terms of trade rose by 9 percent [(95 / 87) × 100 = 109] over the period 1995–1999. This means that to purchase a given quantity of imports, the U.K. had to sacrifice 9 percent fewer exports; conversely, for a given number of exports, the U.K. could obtain 9 percent more imports. Table 3.2 shows historical movements in the commodity terms of trade for the industrial countries, oil-exporting countries, and non–oil-exporting developing countries.

Although changes in the commodity terms of trade indicate the direction of movement of the gains from trade, their implications must be interpreted with caution. Suppose there occurs an increase in the foreign demand for U.S.

Table 3.1 Commodity Terms of Trade, 1999 (1995 = 100)

Country	Export Price Index	Import Price Index	Terms of Trade
United Kingdom	95	87	109
Switzerland	82	78	105
Japan	85	81	105
United States	95	92	103
China	93	90	103
France	91	91	100
Canada	95	97	98
Australia	82	87	94

Source: International Monetary Fund, *IMF Financial Statistics*, Washington, DC, May 2000.

Table 3.2 The Commodity Terms of Trade: Annual Changes, in Percentages

Year	Industrial Countries	Oil-Exporting Countries	Non-Oil-Exporting Developing Countries
1981–1990 (average)	1.0	−5.2	−0.6
1991–1999	0.8	−4.6	−0.4
1998	1.3	−18.0	−3.3
1999	0.5	−4.4	0.2
2000*	−0.1	6.7	0.3

*Estimate.

Source: International Monetary Fund, *World Economic Outlook*, World Economic and Financial Surveys, Washington, DC, October 1999. See also International Monetary Fund, *Annual Report*, Washington, DC, various issues.

exports, leading to higher prices and revenues for U.S. exporters. In this case, an improving terms of trade implies that the U.S. gains from trade have increased. However, suppose that the cause of the rise in export prices and terms of trade is falling productivity of U.S. workers. If this results in reduced export sales and less revenue earned from exports, we could hardly say that U.S. welfare has improved.[3] Despite its limitations, however, the commodity terms of trade is a useful concept. Over a long period, it illustrates how a country's share of the world gains from trade changes and gives a rough measure of the fortunes of a nation in the world market.[4]

[3] Other difficulties encountered when interpreting the commodity terms of trade include (a) allowing for changes in product quality and for new products, (b) determining methods of valuing exports and imports, and (c) determining methods to weight the products included in the price indexes.

[4] Other terms-of-trade measures include the *income terms of trade*, the *single-factorial terms of trade*, and the *double-factorial terms of trade*. A fuller discussion of terms-of-trade measurement can be found in J. Viner, *Studies in Theory of International Trade* (New York: Harper & Brothers, 1937). See also G. Meier, *The International Economics of Development* (New York: Harper & Row, 1968), Chapter 3.

S U M M A R Y

1. Demand and supply conditions determine the basis for trade and the direction of trade. Demand also helps establish the international terms of trade—that is, the relative prices at which commodities are exchanged between nations.

2. A community indifference curve depicts a nation's tastes or preferences. Community indifference curves illustrate the various combinations of two commodities that yield equal satisfaction to a nation. A higher indifference curve indicates more satisfaction. Community indifference curves are analogous to an individual's indifference curve. The slope of a community indifference curve at any point indicates the marginal rate of substitution between two goods in consumption. This shows the amount of one good a nation is willing to sacrifice in order to gain an additional unit of another good while still remaining on the same indifference curve.

3. The introduction of community indifference curves into the trade model permits a restatement of the basis for trade and the gains from trade.

4. In the absence of trade, a nation achieves equilibrium when its community indifference curve is tangent to its production possibilities sched-

ule. The domestic relative commodity price is denoted by the common slope of these two curves at their point of tangency. When the relative commodity prices of two nations differ, a basis for mutually beneficial trade exists.

5. A nation will benefit from trade when it is able to reach a higher indifference curve (level of satisfaction) than could be achieved without trade. Gains from trade will be maximized when a nation's posttrade consumption point is located where the international terms-of-trade line is tangent to a community indifference curve.

6. Because Ricardian trade theory relied solely on supply analysis, it was not able to determine precisely the equilibrium terms of trade. This limitation was addressed by John Stuart Mill in his theory of reciprocal demand. This theory suggests that before the equilibrium terms of trade can be established, it is necessary to know both nations' demands for both products. The theory of reciprocal demand can be analyzed by means of offer curves, which illustrate the determination of the equilibrium terms of trade.

7. The commodity terms of trade is often used to measure the direction of trade gains. It indicates the relationship between the prices a nation gets for its exports and the prices it pays for its imports over a given time period.

STUDY QUESTIONS

1. What advantages are provided by introducing community indifference curves into the trade model?

2. What is the difference between the marginal rate of transformation and the marginal rate of substitution?

3. Even though the production conditions of two nations are identical, gainful trade may still occur if demand conditions are dissimilar. Demonstrate this fact by using community indifference curves.

4. Why is it that the gains from trade could not be determined precisely under the Ricardian trade model?

5. What is meant by the theory of reciprocal demand? How does it provide a meaningful explanation of the international terms of trade?

6. How is the international terms of trade influenced by changing supply-and-demand conditions?

7. Why is it that the domestic cost ratios of two countries provide limits to the equilibrium terms of trade?

8. How does the commodity terms-of-trade concept attempt to measure the direction of trade gains?

9. What problems do we encounter when attempting to interpret the commodity terms of trade?

10. Table 3.3 gives hypothetical export price indexes and import price indexes (1990 = 100) for Japan, Canada, and Ireland. Compute the commodity terms of trade for each country for the period 1990–2000. Which country's terms of trade improved, worsened, or showed no change?

11. Will export-biased growth lead to improvements in the home country's welfare? Why or why not?

12. What is meant by *immiserizing growth*, and what implications does it have for a country's welfare?

Table 3.3 Export Price and Import Price Indexes

	Export Price Index		Import Price Index	
Country	1990	2000	1990	2000
Japan	100	150	100	140
Canada	100	175	100	175
Ireland	100	167	100	190

A P P E N D I X

OFFER CURVES AND THE EQUILIBRIUM TERMS OF TRADE

Offer curves can be used to demonstrate the determination of the terms of trade between two nations. Referring to Figure 3.6, the U.S. offer curve indicates the amount of autos (in which the United States has a comparative advantage) that it is willing to offer Canada for different amounts of wheat (in which Canada has a comparative advantage). Similarly, the Canadian offer curve indicates the amount of wheat that Canada is willing to offer the United States for different amounts of autos.

These offer curves bring together the supply characteristics embodied in a nation's production possibilities schedule and the demand preferences depicted in a nation's indifference curve. As a *supply schedule*, an offer curve shows that more of an export good will be supplied as its relative price rises; this is especially plausible if it is assumed that the nation produces under increasing-cost conditions. As a *demand schedule*, an offer curve shows that increasing amounts of an import good will be demanded as its relative price falls; this is plausible if it is assumed that additional imports yield progressively less satisfaction. In

this introductory textbook, we will not get into a formal derivation of offer curves.

Near the origin of Figure 3.6(a), the U.S. offer curve has a terms of trade that matches its domestic terms of trade. At this terms of trade, the United States is indifferent to trade with Canada. As the relative price of autos rises, the United States is able to obtain more imported wheat for each exported auto, making exporting more attractive. The curve also reveals the U.S. willingness to import larger quantities of wheat as the relative price of wheat falls. The falling price of wheat means wheat is less costly in terms of the amount of autos that must be exported in exchange. Each point on the curve represents the U.S. desired exports and imports for the terms of trade denoted by a ray from the origin through that point. In Figure 3.6(b), we see that as the relative price of wheat rises Canada is willing to export larger quantities of wheat; as the relative price of autos falls, Canada is willing to import larger quantities of autos.

If the actual terms of trade is to be the equilibrium terms of trade, the amount of a commodity that a nation wants to export must match the amount demanded as imports by another nation. In Figure 3.7(a), point *A* represents the market equilibrium for the United States and

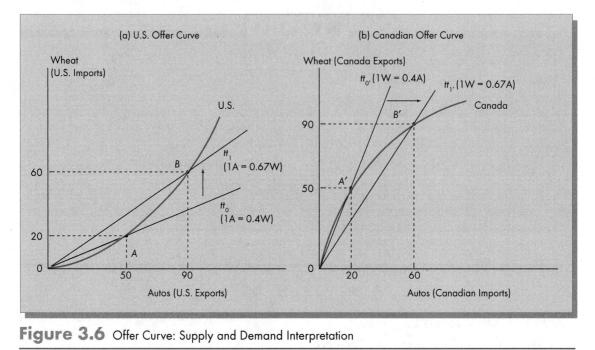

Figure 3.6 Offer Curve: Supply and Demand Interpretation

An offer curve shows the quantity of exports that a nation will have to provide in order to obtain imports at various terms of trade and the quantity of imports that a nation desires to purchase at various terms of trade.

Canada. At terms of trade tt_0, the quantity of autos the United States is willing to export (100 autos) equals the quantity of autos demanded by Canada as imports (100 autos). In like manner, Canada's wheat exports just match U.S. wheat imports.

However, what if market equilibrium does not exist? Are there forces that will automatically restore market balance? At terms of trade tt_1 in Figure 3.7(a), the number of autos that the United States is willing to supply (80 autos) falls short of the number of autos demanded by Canada (150 autos). Alternatively stated, the amount of wheat that Canada is willing to supply (113 units) exceeds the amount demanded by the United States (60 units) at terms of trade tt_1. In a competitive market, the relative price of autos will rise and the relative price of wheat will fall until all shortages and surpluses are eliminated. The equi-

librium terms of trade is thus restored at tt_0. Alternatively, a shortage of wheat and a surplus of autos will lead to a rise in the relative price of wheat and a fall in the relative price of autos until the equilibrium terms of trade is restored at tt_0.

We can now make a precise statement of Mill's principle of reciprocal demand. The equilibrium terms of trade between two nations will be established by the intersection of their respective offer curves.

Offer curves can also be used to illustrate the impact of a change in reciprocal demand. Starting at equilibrium point A in Figure 3.7(b), assume that the Canadian demand for autos increases while the U.S. demand for wheat remains constant. This change in reciprocal demand is illustrated by an upward shift in the Canadian offer curve from $Canada_0$ to $Canada_1$. The shift moves the intersection of the Canadian and U.S. offer

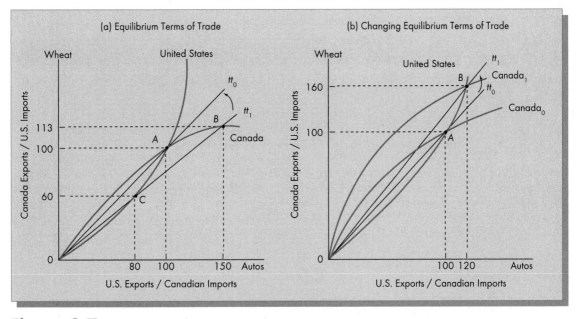

Figure 3.7 International Equilibrium with Offer Curves

At the equilibrium terms of trade, tt_0, the quantity of autos that the United States wishes to export equals the quantity of autos that Canada wishes to import and the amount of wheat that Canada wishes to export equals the amount of wheat that the United States wishes to import. At any other terms of trade, there is a surplus of one good and a shortage of the other good. An increase in the Canadian demand for autos leads to an upward shift in Canada's offer curve and a deterioration in its terms of trade.

curves from point *A* to point *B* and leads to a new terms of trade, tt_1. The terms of trade are now worse for Canada than before the shift, and its gains from trade are less. Alternatively, suppose we assumed that the U.S. demand for wheat increases while the Canadian demand remains constant; the terms of trade improve for Canada, and its gains from trade are greater.

chapter 4

Trade Model Extensions and Applications

Our analysis so far has stressed the importance of relative price differentials among nations as the immediate basis for trade. Because relative prices are underlaid by supply and demand conditions, an account should be made of factors such as resource endowments, technology, tastes and preferences, and income levels. In this chapter, we first consider the leading theories that attempt to explain what underlies relative price differentials. We then turn our attention to the role of transportation costs and their impact on trade flows.

FACTOR-ENDOWMENT THEORY

As discussed in Chapter 2, the Ricardian principle of comparative advantage explains why specialization and trade lead to gains for producers and consumers. It does not, however, in itself explain why the production possibilities schedules of different nations have different shapes, and thus why a nation's comparative advantage is in one product rather than another.

Ricardo thought that comparative advantage depended on comparative differences in labor productivity—that is, differences in technology. However, he did not explain the basis for these differences. Ricardo essentially assumed the existence of comparative advantage in his theoretical model. Moreover, Ricardo's assumption of a single factor of production (labor) ruled out an explanation of how trade affects the distribution of income within a nation and why

KEY CONCEPTS AND TERMS

- *Business services*
- *Distribution of income*
- *Dynamic comparative advantage*
- *Economies of scale*
- *Environmental regulation*
- *Factor-endowment theory*
- *Factor-price equalization*
- *Heckscher–Ohlin theory*
- *Industrial policy*
- *Interindustry specialization*
- *Interindustry trade*
- *Intraindustry specialization*
- *Intraindustry trade*
- *Leontief paradox*
- *Polluter-pays principle*
- *Product life cycle theory*
- *Specific-factors theory*
- *Theory of overlapping demands*
- *Transportation costs*

certain groups favor free trade, whereas other groups oppose it.

In the 1920s and 1930s, the Swedish economists Eli Heckscher and Bertil Ohlin formulated a theory addressing two questions left largely unexplained by Ricardo: (1) What determines comparative advantage? (2) What effect does international trade have on the earnings of various factors of production (distribution of income) in trading nations? Because Heckscher and Ohlin maintained that factor (resource) endowments underlie a nation's comparative advantage, their theory became known as the **factor-endowment theory**. It is also known as the **Heckscher–Ohlin theory**,[1] and Ohlin was awarded the 1977 Nobel prize in economics for his contribution to the theory of international trade.

The factor-endowment theory states that comparative advantage is explained exclusively by differences in relative national *supply conditions*. In particular, the theory highlights the role of nations' *resource endowments* (such as labor and capital) as the key determinant of comparative advantage. The theory implies that Brazil exports coffee because it has an abundance of the soil and climactic conditions required for coffee's production; the United States and Canada export wheat because they are endowed with an abundance of temperate-zone land, which is well suited for wheat production; and India and China are huge exporters of shoes and garments because they are heavily endowed with labor.

The factor-endowment theory relies on several simplifying assumptions: (1) nations have the same tastes and preferences (demand conditions); (2) they use factor inputs that are of uniform quality; and (3) they use the same technology. This last assumption is made explicitly to neutralize the possibility that trade is based on international technological variations in favor of the possibility that trade is based solely on differences in supplies of labor and capital.

According to the factor-endowment theory, relative price levels differ among nations because (1) the nations have different relative endowments of factor inputs and (2) different commodities require that the factor inputs be used with differing intensities in their production. Given these circumstances, a nation will *export* that commodity for which a large amount of the relatively *abundant* (cheap) input is used. It will *import* that commodity in the production of which the relatively *scarce* (expensive) input is used. That is why land-abundant nations (such as Australia) export land-intensive goods, such as meat, while labor-abundant nations (such South Korea) export labor-intensive goods, such as textiles.

The factor-endowment theory is illustrated in Figure 4.1, which shows the production possibilities schedules of France and Germany. Assume that auto production is capital-intensive, requiring much capital and little land; wheat production is assumed to be land-intensive, requiring much land and little capital. Suppose that capital is relatively abundant in Germany and that land is relatively abundant in France. The abundance of capital in Germany causes its production possibilities schedule to be biased toward the auto axis; the abundance of land in France causes its production possibilities schedule to be biased toward the wheat axis.

According to the factor-endowment theory, demand conditions are assumed to be identical for each nation. This is illustrated in Figure 4.1 by the community indifference curves (curve I and curve II), which are common for both France and Germany. In Figure 4.1(a), the points where community indifference curve I is tangent to the production possibilities schedules of Germany and France indicate the equilibrium locations for the two countries. In the absence of trade, Germany locates at point *G* on its production possibilities schedule and France at point *F* on its schedule. The relative price ratios at these points suggest that Germany has the comparative advantage in producing autos and France has the comparative advantage in producing wheat.

Figure 4.1(a) depicts the following assertion of the Heckscher–Ohlin theory: Given identical

[1] Eli Heckscher's explanation of the factor-endowment theory is outlined in his article "The Effects of Foreign Trade on the Distribution of Income," *Economisk Tidskrift* 21 (1919), pp. 497–512. Bertil Ohlin's account is summarized in his *Interregional and International Trade* (Cambridge, MA: Harvard University Press, 1933).

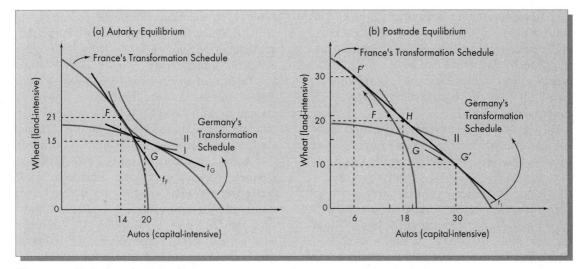

Figure 4.1 Comparative Advantage According to the Factor-Endowment Model

The factor-endowment model asserts that the pattern of trade is explained by differentials in resource endowments. A capital-abundant nation will have a comparative advantage in a capital-intensive product, while a labor-abundant nation will have a comparative advantage in a labor-intensive product.

demand conditions and input productivities, differences in the relative abundance of resources determine relative price levels and the pattern of trade. Capital is relatively cheaper in the capital-abundant country, and land is relatively cheaper in the land-abundant country. *The capital-abundant country thus exports the capital-intensive product, and the land-abundant country exports the land-intensive product.*

Refer now to Figure 4.1(b). With trade, each nation continues to specialize in the production of the commodity of its comparative advantage until its commodity price equalizes with that of the other nation. Specialization in production continues until France reaches F' and Germany reaches G', the points at which each nation's production possibilities schedule is tangent to the common relative price line t_1.

With trade, France maximizes its welfare by exchanging 10 bushels of wheat for 12 autos, and achieves posttrade consumption at point H along community indifference curve II. Similarly,

Germany exchanges 12 autos for 10 bushels of wheat and achieves posttrade consumption at point H. With trade, both nations achieve a higher level of satisfaction (community indifference curve II) than that which occurs in the absence of trade (community indifference curve I).

FACTOR-PRICE EQUALIZATION In Chapter 2 we learned that free trade tends to equalize commodity prices among trading partners. Can the same be said for factor prices?[2] A nation with trade finds output expanding in its comparative-advantage industry, which uses a lot of the cheap, abundant factor. As a result of the rise in demand for the abundant factor, its price increases. At the same time, the expensive, scarce factor is being released from the comparative-disadvantage industry; producers will not be induced to employ

[2] See Paul A. Samuelson, "International Trade and Equalization of Factor Prices," *Economic Journal*, June 1948, pp. 163–184, and "International Factor-Price Equalization Once Again," *Economic Journal*, June 1949, pp. 181–197.

this factor unless its price falls. Because this process occurs at the same time in both nations, each nation experiences a *rise in the price of the abundant factor* and a *fall in the price of the scarce factor*. Trade therefore leads toward an equalization of the relative factor prices in the two trading partners.

In the preceding example, the French demand for inexpensive German autos results in an increased German demand for its abundant factor, capital; the price of capital thus rises in Germany. As France produces fewer autos, its demand for capital decreases, and the price of capital falls. The effect of trade is thus to equalize the price of capital in the two nations. Similarly, the German demand for cheap French wheat leads to France's demanding more land, its abundant factor; the price of land thus rises in France. With Germany producing less wheat, its demand for land decreases, and the price of land falls. With trade, the price of land tends to equalize in the two trading partners. We conclude that by redirecting demand away from the scarce factor and toward the abundant factor in each nation, trade leads toward **factor-price equalization**. In each nation, the cheap factor becomes more expensive, and the expensive factor becomes cheaper.

In the real world, differences in factor prices do exist. For example, the average salary of unskilled labor in the United States is higher than in Korea. That resource prices may not fully equalize between trading partners can be explained in part by the fact that the assumptions underlying the factor-endowment theory are not completely borne out in the real world. For example, to the extent that different countries use different technologies or that markets are not perfectly competitive, factor prices may only partially equalize. Transportation costs and trade barriers may prevent product prices from becoming equal. Such market imperfections reduce the volume of trade, limiting the extent to which commodity prices and factor prices can become equal.

An example of the tendency toward factor-price equalization is provided by the U.S. auto

industry. By the early 1980s, the compensation of the U.S. autoworker was roughly double that of the Japanese autoworker. In 1981, the average General Motors worker earned hourly wages and benefits of $19.65, compared to the $10.70 earned by the average Japanese autoworker. Owing to the domestic (U.S.) recession, high gasoline prices, and other factors, the demand for U.S.-produced autos deteriorated. However, the U.S. consumer continued to purchase Japanese vehicles up to the limit permissible under the prevailing quota system. To save its members' jobs with struggling U.S. auto companies, the United Auto Workers (UAW) union reluctantly accepted wage cuts so that the companies could remain in business. It is no wonder that the UAW pushed for trade legislation to further restrict foreign autos entering the United States, thereby insulating the wages of domestic autoworkers from the market pressure created by foreign competition.

TRADE AND THE DISTRIBUTION OF INCOME

We have seen how free trade can increase the level of output and income for trading nations. Not only does trade affect a nation's aggregate income level, however; it also affects the internal **distribution of income** among the owners of resources.

The factor-endowment theory states that the export of commodities embodying large amounts of the relatively cheap, abundant factors makes those factors less abundant in the domestic market. The increased demand for the *abundant* factor leads to an *increase* in its return. At the same time, returns to the factor used intensively in the import-competing product (the *scarce factor*) *decrease* as its demand falls. The increase in the returns to each country's abundant factor thus comes at the expense of the scarce factor's returns.

In theory, increased trade could worsen inequalities in wages even while increasing national income. The U.S. economy, for example, has a relative abundance of skilled labor, and so its comparative advantage is in producing

THE HECKSCHER–OHLIN THEORY: U.S.–CHINA TRADE

Skill Group (Key Industries)	Percent of Chinese Exports to the United States	Percent of U.S. Exports to China
HIGHER SKILL Periodicals, office and computing machines	4.8	7.7
Aircraft and parts, industrial inorganic chemicals	2.6	48.8
Engines and turbines, fats and oils	3.9	21.3
Concrete, nonelectric plumbing and heating	11.5	4.3
Watches, clocks, toys, sporting goods	18.9	6.3
Wood buildings, blast furnaces, basic steel	8.2	1.3
Ship building and repair, furniture and fixtures	4.1	2.8
Cigarettes, motor vehicles, iron and steel foundries	5.2	1.8
Weaving, wool, leather tanning and finishing	17.2	0.4
LOWER SKILL Children's outerwear, nonrubber footwear	23.5	5.2

Source: Jeffrey Sachs and Howard Shatz, "Trade and Jobs in U.S. Manufacturing," *Brookings Papers on Economic Activity*, I (1994), pp. 18, 53.

According to the Heckscher–Ohlin theory, factor endowments are the source of comparative advantage among nations. As we have learned, human capital (skills) is abundant in the United States, but unskilled labor is scarce. Conversely, China is rich in unskilled labor. Thus, the Heckscher–Ohlin theory predicts that the United States will export to China goods embodying large amounts of skilled labor; China will export to the United States goods for which a large amount of unskilled labor is used.

The table shows the results of a study that tested the prediction of Heckscher–Ohlin for U.S.–China trade in 1990. The researchers divided up a sample of 131 industries into ten groups according to their skill intensity. The industries of group 1 embodied the highest amount of worker skill, and the industries of group 10 were the least skill-intensive.

The pattern of U.S.–China trade corresponds well to the predictions of Heckscher–Ohlin. U.S. exports to China were concentrated in the higher skilled industries; skill groups 1 through 3 included about 78 percent of U.S. exports to China. Conversely, Chinese exports to the United States fell into the lower skill industries; 41 percent of China's exports to the United States were located in skill groups 9 and 10.

skill-intensive goods. The factor-endowment model suggests that the United States will tend to export goods requiring relatively large amounts of skilled labor and import goods requiring relatively large amounts of unskilled labor. International trade in effect increases the supply of unskilled labor to the U.S. economy, lowering the wages of unskilled American workers relative to those of skilled workers. Skilled workers—

who are already at the upper end of the income distribution—find their incomes increasing as exports expand, while unskilled workers are forced into accepting even lower wages in order to compete with imports. According to the factor-endowment theory, then, international trade can aggravate income inequality, at least in a country such as the United States where skilled labor is relatively abundant.

From the perspective of an unskilled U.S. worker, it makes little difference whether her wages are driven down directly via relaxed immigration laws that let in more people from low-wage nations, or indirectly via the importation of products that make heavy use of unskilled labor. To the extent that free trade and import competition impose hardship on suppliers of the scarce factor, those suppliers may desire tariffs or quotas on imports. This may explain why segments of the U.S. labor force (such as steel-workers or autoworkers) favor protection against import competition; labor is scarce relative to capital in the United States, compared with the rest of the world.

The notion that the abundant factor gains from free trade and that the relatively scarce factor loses is founded on the assumption that resources are completely mobile among industries within a country and completely immobile among countries. In the short run, however, the mobility of factors may be imperfect and the results quite different. The appendix to this chapter discusses the effects of opening trade when resources are immobile in the short run.

DOES TRADE MAKE THE POOR EVEN POORER?

Are your wages set in Mexico or China? That question has underlined many Americans' fears about their economic future. They worry that the growth of trade with low-wage developing nations could reduce the demand for low-skilled workers in the United States and cause unemployment and wage decreases for U.S. workers.

The wage gap between skilled and unskilled workers widened in the United States between the 1970s and 1990s. This wider gap has destroyed the confidence of many Americans that the economic system works for them. For example, for every dollar that a high-school graduate earned in 1973, a college graduate would have made $1.48. By 2000, the college graduate was making about $1.78 for every dollar earned by the high-school graduate. Over the same period, imports increased as a percentage of gross domestic product. These facts raise the questions, Is trade harming low-skilled workers? If so, is this an argument for protectionism? Economists agree that some combination of trade, technology, education, immigration, and union weakness has held down wages for unskilled American workers; but apportioning the blame is tough, partly because income inequality is so pervasive.

Trade and immigration are obvious targets for criticism. It's easy to cite large U.S. firms that fire workers at home and set up shop abroad, or point to workers migrating from Mexico to the United States. However, several studies have found that the easily measured direct effects of trade on the wage distribution have been small, implying that the vast majority of wage dispersion is due to domestic factors. The many estimates of the worsening effect of trade on American wage inequality suggest that trade explains only 10 to 20 percent of the net change in income inequality, as shown in Figure 4.2.

Foreign workers do not compete with U.S. workers directly but instead through the products that they produce and sell. The view that imports force down wages for unskilled labor is predicated on a relationship between the relative prices of goods and the prices of the inputs used to produce them. If competition from developing nations reduces the prices of goods whose major content is unskilled labor, the wages of unskilled workers will be forced down, widening income disparities. During the 1980s, however, the average relative price of goods that embody substantial inputs of unskilled labor actually increased, thus raising questions about the validity of this argument.[3]

Moreover, trade and immigration have not been big enough, relative to the entire U.S. economy, to produce big effects on wages. As of 1999, immigrants represented about 9 percent of the labor force, and merchandise imports accounted

---

[3] Robert Lawrence and Matthew Slaughter, "International Trade and American Wages in the 1980s," *Brookings Papers on Economic Activity*, 1993.

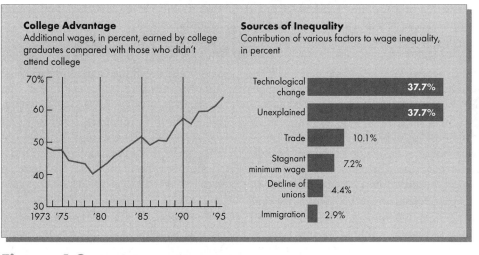

Figure 4.2 The Widening of the Wage Gap

Source: U.S. Census Bureau, "Historical Income Tables—Households," at the Internet site
http://www.census.gov/hhes/income/histinc/h13.html. See also William Cline, *Trade, Jobs, and Income Distribution*,
Institute for International Economics, Washington, DC, 1997.

for about 10 percent of gross domestic product. Also, about 60 percent of U.S. non-oil imports came from nations with higher labor costs, such as Germany and Japan, giving little incentive to cut wages in the United States to compete. Furthermore, most U.S. service workers—technicians, consultants, clerks—have not been noticeably affected by international trade. Finally, a low-wage rival can change, through trade, into a high-wage society. In the 1970s, Japanese manufacturing wages were less than half of U.S. levels; by 1999, they were higher.

The effects of trade on wages, however, may be larger if the internationalization of the U.S. economy also affects wages indirectly. For example, the threat of increased import competition or of the relocation of a factory to another nation may undermine workers' bargaining power. It is not known how important such effects have been.

If trade, or factors such as immigration that affect the relative supply of workers, were the main cause of wage disparities, one would expect to see domestic producers taking advantage of the lower cost of unskilled workers by using more of them. Yet just the opposite has occurred in the United States. In most industries, employment of skilled workers has increased relative to that of unskilled workers, despite the higher cost of skilled workers. This implies that factors influencing the demand for workers have been more in favor of skilled workers; these factors have been the more powerful force influencing relative wages.

Trade does have some effect on U.S. wage stagnation, but not nearly as great an effect as technological change, most economists maintain. They argue that within-industry shifts in labor demand, away from less educated workers, are the most important factors behind the eroding wages of the less educated. Such shifts appear to be the result of economy-wide technological and organizational changes in how work is performed. The use of computers in the workplace has increased significantly in recent years. Not only has computerization led to the replacement of rote jobs (typing letters on an electric typewriter), but workers who use computers are generally paid higher wages than those who do not.

The decline in the proportion of workers belonging to unions and the decrease in the real value of the minimum wage have also contributed to wage dispersion.

Even if the impact is small, trade indeed seems to have some adverse effect in aggravating wage inequality. In many ways, the effects of trade are similar to those of technological advance: both increase national income but can worsen inequality. Yet just as a crusade against technology is not the solution to increased inequality resulting from technological progress, most economists argue that neither is protectionism the answer to wage inequality. A better solution involves better education and increased training to allow low-income workers to take advantage of the technological changes that increase productivity.

ARE ACTUAL TRADE PATTERNS EXPLAINED BY THE FACTOR-ENDOWMENT THEORY?

The first attempt to investigate the factor-endowment theory empirically was undertaken by Wassily Leontief.[4] It had been widely recognized

[4] Wassily W. Leontief, "Domestic Production and Foreign Trade: The American Capital Position Reexamined," *Proceedings of the American Philosophical Society* 97, September 1953.

that in the United States capital was relatively abundant and labor was relatively scarce. According to the factor-endowment theory, *the United States should export capital-intensive goods and its import-competing goods should be labor-intensive.*

In 1954, Leontief tested this proposition by analyzing the capital/labor ratios for some 200 export industries and import-competing industries in the United States, based on trade data for 1947. As shown in Table 4.1, Leontief found that the capital/labor ratio for U.S. export industries was lower (about $14,000 per worker year) than that of its import-competing industries (about $18,000 per worker year). Leontief concluded that exports were *less* capital-intensive than import-competing goods! These findings, which contradicted the predictions of the factor-endowment theory, became known as the **Leontief paradox.**

Some economists maintained that 1947 was not a normal year, because the World War II reconstruction of the global economy had not been corrected by that time. To silence his critics, Leontief repeated his investigation in 1956, using 1951 trade data. Leontief again determined that U.S. import-competing goods were more capital-intensive than U.S. exports.

Since Leontief's time, many other studies have tested the predictions of the factor-endowment model. Although the tests conducted thus far are not conclusive, they seem to provide support for

Table 4.1   Factor Content of U.S. Trade: Capital and Labor Requirements per Million Dollars of U.S. Exports and Import Substitutes

Empirical Study	Import Substitutes	Exports	Import/Export Ratio
Leontief			
Capital	$3,091,339	$2,550,780	
Labor (person years)	70	182	
Capital/person years	$18,184	$14,015	1.30

Source: W. Leontief, "Domestic Production and Foreign Trade: The American Capital Position Reexamined," *Economia Internazionale*, February 1954, pp. 3–32. See also W. Leontief, "Factor Proportions and the Structure of American Trade: Further Theoretical and Empirical Analysis," *Review of Economics and Statistics*, November 1956, pp. 386–407.

a more generalized factor-endowment model that takes into account many subvarieties of capital, land, and human factors and recognizes that factor endowments change over time as a result of investment and technological advances.

The upshot of a generalized factor-endowment model can be seen by looking at some trading patterns of the United States. Table 4.2 shows the shares of world resources for the United States in 1980. Compared with its other productive inputs, physical capital is relatively abundant in the United States (33.6 percent of world capital). In like manner, the United States is relatively well endowed with research and development scientists (50.7-percent share) and arable land (29.3-percent share); relative scarcities occur in semiskilled labor (19.1-percent share) and unskilled labor (0.19-percent share).

Because the United States has a larger share of physical capital and R&D scientists than of world resources in total, the factor-endowment model predicts that the United States should have a comparative advantage in goods and services that embody more scientific know-how and physical capital. This prediction is consistent with the 1980 export/import ratios for the United States, which are also shown in Table 4.2. The U.S. export/import ratios are greater than unity (that is, the United States is a net exporter) for technologically intensive manufac-

tured goods (such as transportation equipment) and services (such as financial services and lending) that reflect U.S. technological know-how and past accumulation of physical capital. The United States is a net importer (the export/import ratio is less than unity) of standardized and labor-intensive manufactured goods (such as footwear and textiles). The situation represented in Table 4.2 is probably not much different today.

Early versions of the Heckscher–Ohlin model emphasized relative endowments of capital, labor, and natural resources as sources of comparative advantage. More recently, researchers have increasingly focused on the importance of worker *skills* in the creation of comparative advantage. Investments in skill, education, and training, which enhance a worker's productivity, create human capital in much the same manner that investments in machinery create physical capital. The United States is abundant in this human capital, including a well-educated and skilled labor force, relative to those of many other nations, as shown in Table 4.3. Therefore, the United States exports goods, such as jetliners and computer software, that use a highly skilled workforce intensively.

Researchers at the World Bank have analyzed the relationship between manufactures and primary products to relative supplies of skills and

---

Table 4.2 Applying the Factor-Endowment Theory to the United States

Resource	U.S. Share of World* Resource Endowment	Product	U.S. Export/Import Ratio
Physical capital	33.6%	Technology-intensive	1.52
Skilled labor	27.7	Standardized	0.39
Semiskilled labor	19.1	Labor-intensive	0.38
Unskilled labor	0.19	Services	1.50
Arable land	29.3	Primary products	0.55
R&D scientists	50.7		

*Computed from a set of the 34 largest economies of the world.

Source: John Mutti and Peter Morici, *Changing Patterns of U.S. Industrial Activity and Comparative Advantage*, National Planning Association, Washington, DC, 1983; and World Bank, *World Development Report 1984*, Washington, DC, 1984, appendix table I.

Table 4.3 U.S. Human Capital Relative to That of Other Nations

	School Enrollment as a Percent of Age Group*		
	Primary Education	Secondary Education	Tertiary** Education
United States	106	98	81
Germany	98	100	36
Russia	107	88	45
Chile	99	66	27
Ethiopia	23	12	1
Mali	31	8	1
India	101	30	5
China	118	55	4
El Salvador	80	29	15
Saudi Arabia	75	48	14

Although education captures only one aspect of human capital, it is the easiest to measure.

*Enrollment ratios may exceed 100 percent because some pupils are younger or older than the country's standard age for a particular level of education.

**Tertiary education includes all postsecondary schools such as technical schools, junior colleges, colleges, and universities.

Source: World Bank, *World Development Report 1997*, Washington, DC, 1997, pp. 226–227.

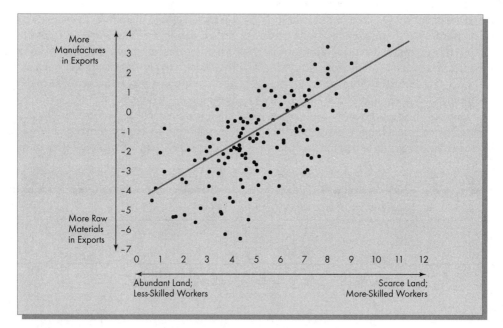

Figure 4.3 Heckscher–Ohlin, Skills, and Comparative Advantage

The regression line in the figure suggests that a nation endowed with more-skilled workers tends to have a comparative advantage in manufactures. Conversely, a land-abundant nation tends to have a comparative advantage in primary products.

Source: World Bank, *World Development Report 1995* (Geneva: World Bank, 1995), p. 59.

NIKE AND REEBOK RESPOND TO SWEATSHOP CRITICS: BUT WAGES REMAIN AT POVERTY LEVEL

Prodded by controversy over exploitation in foreign factories that make much of America's clothes and shoes, Nike, Reebok, and other U.S. corporations have pushed for sweatshop reforms. A sweatshop is characterized by the systematic violation of workers' rights that have been certified in law. These rights include the right to organize and bargain collectively and the prohibition of child labor. Too, employers must pay wages that allow workers to feed, clothe, and shelter themselves and their families.

For example, a 1997 audit by the firm of Ernst & Young, commissioned by Nike, was leaked to reporters. The audit found that employees in a large Vietnam factory were exposed to cancer-causing toluene and had a high incidence of respiratory problems. The audit also found that employees were required to work as long as 65-hour weeks, sometimes in unsafe conditions. Also, in 1999 Reebok released a study of two large Indonesian factories. The study uncovered substandard working conditions, sex bias, and health problems among workers.

Pressured by sweatshop critics, in 1999 Nike and Reebok initiated improvements in the wages and working conditions of its foreign workers. Nike and Reebok increased wages and benefits in their Indonesian footwear factories, which employed more than 100,000 workers, making base compensation 43 percent higher than the minimum wage. Also, Nike agreed to end health and safety problems at its 37 factories in Vietnam and other nations. Moreover, Reebok and Nike took unprecedented steps to defend labor rights activists who have long been their adversaries. However, critics argued that these reforms left much to be desired. For example, the Indonesia wage increases by Reebok and Nike put total minimum compensation at only 20 U.S. cents an hour, less than what is needed to support a family and well below the 27 cents per hour that Nike paid until Indonesia's economic crisis began in 1997.

In the late 1990s, dozens of U.S. universities jumped on the antisweatshop bandwagon, reacting to a growing student protest movement, and took steps to bar labor abuses in the manufacture of clothes that bear college logos. This led to a new White House-sponsored alliance, the Fair Labor Association (FLA), which consisted of 56 universities and corporations such as Nike, Reebok, Liz Claiborne, and Phillips-Van Hausen. The alliance is intended to set up an elaborate, worldwide factory-monitoring system to attempt to eliminate sweatshop abuses. Under its provisions, participating companies can use the FLA logo on their labels and in their advertising, helping portray the firms as ethical corporate citizens. Ethics-minded consumers, in turn, can look for the FLA logo while shopping to guarantee that what they purchase is free of moral stigma. Simply put, company executives hope that the FLA logo will improve their products' image and boost sales; critics of sweatshops hope that the logo will pressure nonparticipating companies into eliminating sweatshop abuses and join the FLA.

Source: Robert Collier, "U.S. Firms Reducing Sweatshop Abuses: But Wages Still at Poverty Level," *San Francisco Chronicle*, April 17, 1999 and "Reebok Finds Ills at Indonesian Factories," *The Wall Street Journal*, October 18, 1999.

land, as shown in Figure 4.3. Their study included export data for 126 industrial and developing nations in 1985. Values along the horizontal axis of the figure denote the ratio of a nation's average educational attainment to its land area; values along the vertical axis indicate the ratio of manufactured exports to exports of primary products. In the figure, the regression line relates the division of each nation's exports between manufactures and primary products to its relative supplies of skills and land. The regression line suggests that nations endowed with relatively large amounts of skilled workers tend to emphasize the export of manufactures. Conversely, land-abundant nations tend to emphasize exports of primary products.

In spite of the appeal of the factor-endowment theory, not all empirical tests support its predictions. Many empirical studies have raised questions about the validity of this theory. The consensus among economists appears to be that factor endowments explain only a portion of trade patterns. Other determinants of trade patterns include technology, economies of scale, and economic policies, which we will examine throughout this chapter.

ECONOMIES OF SCALE AND SPECIALIZATION

Another explanation of trade patterns involves efficiencies of large-scale production, which reduce a firm's per-unit costs. Such **economies of scale** are pronounced in industries that use mass-production techniques and capital equipment. The economic justification for economies of scale is that a large organization may reduce costs by specializing in machinery and labor, operating assembly-line production, using its by-products, and obtaining quantity discounts obtained on the purchase of inputs.

How do economies of scale underlie a nation's comparative advantage? Adam Smith gave the answer in his 1776 classic, *The Wealth of Nations*, which stated that the division of labor is limited by the size of the market. By widening the size of a firm's market, international trade permits the firm to take advantage of longer production runs, which lead to increasing efficiency. An example is Boeing, which has sold more than half of its jet planes overseas in recent years. Without exports, Boeing would have found it difficult to cover the large design and tooling costs of its jumbo jets, and the jets might not have been produced at all.

Figure 4.4 illustrates the effect of economies of scale on trade. Assume that a U.S. auto firm and a Mexican auto firm are each able to sell 100,000 vehicles in their respective countries. Also assume

that identical cost conditions result in the same long-run average cost curve for the two firms, *AC*. Note that scale economies result in decreasing unit costs over the first 275,000 autos produced.

Initially, there is no basis for trade, because each firm realizes a production cost of $10,000 per auto. Suppose that rising income in the United States results in demand for 200,000 autos, while the Mexican auto demand remains constant. The larger demand allows the U.S. firm to produce more output and take advantage of economies of scale. The firm's cost curve slides downward until its cost equals $8,000 per auto. Compared to the Mexican firm, the U.S. firm can produce autos at a lower cost. With free trade, the United States will now export autos to Mexico.

Economies of scale thus provide additional cost incentives for *specialization* in production. Instead of manufacturing only a few units of each and every product that domestic consumers desire to purchase, a country specializes in the manufacture of large amounts of a limited number of goods and trades for the remaining goods. Specialization in a few products allows a manufacturer to benefit from longer production runs, which lead to decreasing average costs.

How might trade operate with economies of scale? Figure 4.5 represents the production possibilities schedules of the United States and South Korea for computers and steel. Note that the two nations' production possibilities schedules are *bowed inward* (convex from the diagram's origin), indicating that the cost of producing steel becomes less and less in terms of computers sacrificed. At each point, the (absolute) slope of the production possibilities schedule reflects the cost of steel in terms of computers sacrificed.

Without trade, suppose South Korea and the United States desire both computers and steel. Both countries would have to manufacture some of each good at inefficient points, such as point *A* for South Korea and point *B* for the United States. Reflecting the (absolute) slopes of the production possibilities schedules at these points, South Korea has a comparative advantage in steel, while the United States has a comparative advantage in computers. The two countries

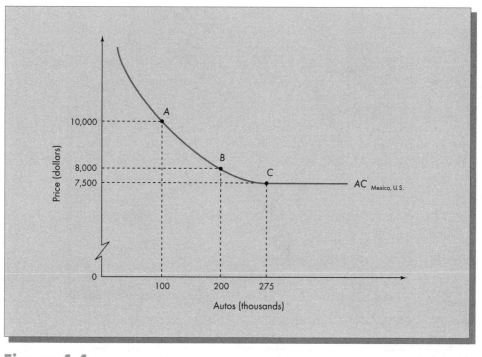

Figure 4.4 Economies of Scale as a Basis for Trade

By adding to the size of the domestic market, international trade permits longer production runs by domestic firms, which can lead to greater efficiency and reductions in unit costs.

should not remain for long at these inefficient production points. They can reduce costs by *specializing completely* in the production of the goods of their comparative advantage.

As South Korea moves to the right of point *A* along its production possibilities schedule, the relative cost of steel continues to decrease until South Korea totally specializes in steel production at point *C*. Similarly, as the United States moves to the left of point *B* along its production possibilities schedule, the relative cost of computers continues to fall until the United States totally specializes in computer production at point *D*. With trade, U.S. computers are exchanged for South Korean steel at the equilibrium terms of trade (not illustrated); both countries can attain consumption points that are superior to those attained in the absence of trade.

THEORY OF OVERLAPPING DEMANDS

The relationship between demand conditions and international trade patterns has been analyzed by Staffan Linder.[5] According to Linder, the factor-endowment theory has considerable explanatory power for trade in *primary products* (natural resources) and agricultural goods, not for trade in *manufactured goods*, because the main force influencing manufactured-good trade is domestic *demand conditions*. Because much of international trade involves manufactured goods, demand

[5] Staffan B. Linder, *An Essay on Trade and Transformation* (New York: Wiley, 1961), Chapter 3.

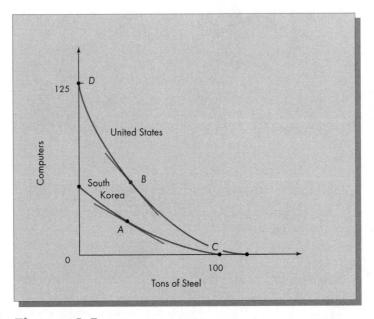

Figure 4.5 Trade and Specialization Under Decreasing Costs (Economies of Scale)

With decreasing costs, a country has the cost incentive to specialize completely in the product of its comparative advantage. Devoting additional resources to steel (computer) production results in economies of large-scale production and falling unit cost. With specialization, South Korea produces 100 tons of steel at point C, while the United States produces 125 computers at point D.

conditions play an important role in explaining overall trade patterns.

Linder states that firms within a country are generally motivated to manufacture goods for which there is a large domestic market. This market determines the set of goods that these firms will have to sell when they begin to export. The foreign markets with greatest export potential will be found in nations with consumer tastes similar to those of domestic consumers. A nation's exports are thus an extension of production for the domestic market.

Going further, Linder contends that tastes of consumers are conditioned strongly by their income levels. Thus, a country's average or *per capita income* will yield a particular pattern of tastes. Nations with high per capita incomes will

demand high-quality manufactured goods (luxuries), while nations with low per capita incomes will demand lower-quality goods (necessities). The Linder hypothesis explains which types of nations will most likely trade with each other. Nations with similar per capita incomes will have overlapping demand structures and will likely consume similar types of manufactured goods. Wealthy (industrial) nations will likely trade with other wealthy nations, and poor (developing) nations will likely trade with other poor nations. The Linder hypothesis is thus known as the **theory of overlapping demands**.

Linder does not rule out all trade in manufactured goods between wealthy and poor nations. Because of unequal income distribution within nations, there will always be some overlapping of demand structures; some people in poor nations are wealthy, and some people in wealthy nations are poor. However, the potential for trade in manufactured goods is small when the extent of demand overlap is small.

Linder's theory is in rough accord with the facts. A high proportion of international trade in manufactured goods takes place among the relatively high-income (industrial) nations: Japan, Canada, the United States, and the European nations. Moreover, much of this trade involves the exchange of similar products: Each nation exports products that are much like the products it imports. However, detailed empirical support for the theory has not been found.

INTRAINDUSTRY TRADE

The trade models considered so far have dealt with **interindustry trade**—the exchange between nations of products of different industries; examples include computers and aircraft traded for textiles and shoes, or finished manufactured items traded for primary materials. Interindustry trade involves the exchange of goods with *different* factor requirements. Nations having large supplies of skilled labor tend to export sophisticated manufactured products, while nations with large supplies of natural resources export resource-intensive goods. Much of interindustry trade is between nations having vastly different resource endowments (such as developing countries and industrial countries) and can be explained by the principle of comparative advantage (the Heckscher–Ohlin model).

Interindustry trade is based on **interindustry specialization**: Each nation specializes in a particular industry (say, steel) in which it enjoys a comparative advantage. As resources shift to the industry with a comparative advantage, certain other industries having comparative disadvantages (say, electronics) contract. Resources thus move geographically to the industry where comparative costs are lowest. As a result of specialization, a nation experiences a growing *dissimi-*

larity between the products that it exports and the products that it imports.

Although some interindustry specialization occurs, this generally has not been the type of specialization that industrialized nations have undertaken in the post–World War II era. Rather than emphasizing entire industries, industrial countries have adopted a narrower form of specialization. They have practiced **intraindustry specialization**, focusing on the production of particular products or groups of products within a given industry (for example, subcompact autos rather than autos). With intraindustry specialization, the opening up of trade does not generally result in the elimination or wholesale contraction of entire industries within a nation; however, the range of products produced and sold by each nation changes.

Advanced industrial nations have increasingly emphasized **intraindustry trade**—two-way trade in a similar commodity. For example, computers manufactured by IBM are sold abroad, while the United States imports computers produced by Hitachi of Japan. Table 4.4 provides examples of intraindustry trade for the United States. As the table indicates, the United States is involved in two-way trade in many manufactured goods such as chemicals and autos.

Table 4.4 Intraindustry Trade Examples: Selected U.S. Exports and Imports, 1998 (in Millions of Dollars)

Category	Exports	Imports
Autos	73,156	149,055
Computers	45,246	72,475
Chemicals	44,979	29,239
Paper	12,150	11,233
Machine tools	11,727	8,813
Meat	6,751	4,314
Fish	2,352	8,117
Telecommunications equipment	24,956	17,074
Household appliances	15,344	39,186
Trucks and buses	7,585	5,775

Source: U.S. Department of Commerce, "U.S. International Transactions, 1974–1998," *Survey of Current Business*, July 1999.

The existence of intraindustry trade appears to be *incompatible* with the models of comparative advantage previously discussed. In the Ricardian and Heckscher–Ohlin models, a country would not simultaneously export and import the same product. However, California is a major importer of French wines as well as a large exporter of its own wines; the Netherlands imports Löwenbrau beer while exporting Heineken. Intraindustry trade involves flows of goods with *similar* factor requirements. Nations that are net exporters of manufactured goods embodying sophisticated technology also purchase such goods from other nations. Much of intraindustry trade is conducted among industrial countries, especially those in Western Europe, whose resource endowments are similar. The firms that produce these goods tend to be oligopolies, with a few large firms constituting each industry.

Intraindustry trade includes trade in homogeneous goods as well as in differentiated products. For *homogeneous goods*, the reasons for intraindustry trade are easy to grasp. A nation may export and import the same product because of *transportation costs*. Canada and the United States, for example, share a border whose length is several thousand miles. To minimize transportation costs (and thus total costs), a buyer in New York may import cement from a firm in Quebec, while a manufacturer in Washington sells cement to a buyer in British Columbia. Such trade can be explained by the fact that it is less expensive to transport cement from Quebec to New York than to ship cement from Washington to New York.

Another reason for intraindustry trade in homogeneous goods is *seasonal*. The seasons in the Southern Hemisphere are opposite those in the Northern Hemisphere. Brazil may export seasonal items (such as agricultural products) to the United States at one time of the year and import them from the United States at another time during the same year. Differentiation in time also affects electricity suppliers. Because of heavy fixed costs in electricity production, utilities attempt to keep plants operating close to full capacity, meaning that it may be less costly to export electricity at off-peak times, when domestic demand is inadequate to ensure full-capacity utilization, and import electricity at peak times.

Although some intraindustry trade occurs in homogeneous products, available evidence suggests that most intraindustry trade occurs in *differentiated products*. Within manufacturing, the levels of intraindustry trade appear to be especially high in machinery, chemicals, and transportation equipment. A significant share of the output of modern economies consists of differentiated products within the same broad product group. Within the automobile industry, a Ford is not identical to a Honda, a Toyota, or a Chevrolet. Two-way trade flows can occur in differentiated products within the same broad product group.

For industrial countries, intraindustry trade in differentiated manufactured goods often occurs when manufacturers in each country produce for the "majority" consumer tastes within their country while ignoring "minority" consumer tastes. This unmet need is fulfilled by imported products. For example, most Japanese consumers prefer Toyotas to General Motors vehicles; yet some Japanese consumers purchase vehicles from General Motors, while Toyotas are exported to the United States. Intraindustry trade increases the range of choices available to consumers in each country, as well as the degree of competition among manufacturers of the same class of product in each country.

Intraindustry trade in differentiated products can also be explained by overlapping demand segments in trading nations. When U.S. manufacturers look overseas for markets in which to sell, they often find them in countries having market segments that are similar to the market segments in which they sell in the United States—for example, luxury automobiles sold to high-income buyers. Nations with similar income levels can be expected to have similar tastes, and thus sizable overlapping market segments, as envisioned by Linder's theory of overlapping demand; they would be expected to engage heavily in intraindustry trade.

Besides marketing factors, economies of scale associated with differentiated products also explain intraindustry trade. A nation may enjoy a cost advantage over its foreign competitor by specializing in a few varieties and styles of a product (for example, subcompact autos with a standard transmission and optional equipment), while its foreign competitor enjoys a cost advantage by specializing in other variants of the same product (subcompact autos with automatic transmission, air-conditioning, cassette player, and other optional equipment). Such specialization permits longer production runs, economies of scale, and decreasing unit costs. Each nation exports its particular type of auto to the other nation, resulting in two-way auto trade. In contrast to interindustry trade, which is explained by the principle of comparative advantage, intraindustry trade can be explained by product differentiation and economies of scale.

With intraindustry specialization, fewer adjustment problems are likely to occur than with interindustry specialization, because intraindustry specialization requires a shift of resources within an industry instead of between industries. Interindustry specialization results in a transfer of resources from import-competing to export-expanding sectors of the economy. Adjustment difficulties can occur when resources, notably labor, are occupationally and geographically immobile in the short run; massive structural unemployment may result. In contrast, intraindustry specialization often occurs without requiring workers to exit from a particular region or industry (as when workers are shifted from the production of large-size automobiles to subcompacts); the probability of structural unemployment is thus lessened.

PRODUCT CYCLES

The underlying explanations of international trade presented so far are similar in that they presuppose a *given* and unchanging state of technology. The basis for trade was ultimately attributed to such factors as differing labor productivities, factor endowments, and national demand structures. In a dynamic world, however, technological changes occur in different nations at different rates of speed. Technological innovations commonly result in new methods of producing existing commodities, in the production of new commodities, or in commodity improvements. These factors can affect comparative advantage and the pattern of trade.

Recognition of the importance of *dynamic* changes has given rise to another explanation of international trade in manufactured goods: the **product life cycle theory**. This theory focuses on the role of technological innovation as a key determinant of trade patterns in manufactured products.[6] According to this theory, many manufactured goods such as electronic products and office machinery undergo a predictable *trade cycle*. During this cycle, the home country initially is an exporter, then loses its competitive advantage vis-à-vis its trading partners, and eventually may become an importer of the commodity. The stages that many manufactured goods go through include the following:

1. Manufactured good is introduced to home market.
2. Domestic industry shows export strength.
3. Foreign production begins.
4. Domestic industry loses competitive advantage.
5. Import competition begins.

The introduction stage of the trade cycle begins when an innovator establishes a technological breakthrough in the production of a manufactured good. At the start, the relatively small local market for the product and technological uncertainties imply that mass production is not feasible. The manufacturer will likely operate close to the local market to gain quick feedback on the quality and overall appeal of the product.

---

[6] See Raymond Vernon, "International Investment and International Trade in the Product Life Cycle," *Quarterly Journal of Economics* 80, May 1966, pp. 190–207.

POCKET CALCULATORS AND THE INTERNATIONAL PRODUCT CYCLE

Pocket calculators provide an illustration of a product that has moved through the stages of the international product cycle. This product was invented in 1961 by engineers at Sunlock Comptometer, Inc., and was marketed soon after at a price of approximately $1,000. Sunlock's pocket calculator was more accurate than slide rules (widely used by high-school and college students at that time) and more portable than large mechanical calculators and computers that performed many of the same functions.

By 1970, several U.S. and Japanese companies had entered the market with competing pocket calculators; these firms included Texas Instruments, Hewlett-Packard, and Casio (of Japan). The increased competition forced the price down to about $400. As the 1970s continued, additional companies entered the market. Several began to assemble their pocket calculators in foreign countries, such as Singapore and Taiwan, to take advantage of lower labor costs. These calculators were then shipped to the United States. Steadily improving technologies resulted in product improvements and falling prices; by the mid-1970s, pocket calculators sold routinely for $10 to $20, sometimes even less. It appears that pocket calculators had reached the standardized-product stage of the product cycle by the late 1970s, with product technology available throughout the industry, price competition (and thus costs) of major significance, and product differentiation widely adopted. In a period of less than two decades, the international product cycle for pocket calculators was complete.

During the trade cycle's next stage, the domestic manufacturer begins to export its product to foreign markets having similar tastes and income levels. The local manufacturer finds that, during this stage of growth and expansion, its market becomes large enough to support mass-production operations and the sorting out of inefficient production techniques. The home-country manufacturer is therefore able to supply increasing amounts to the world markets.

As time passes, the manufacturer realizes that it must locate production operations closer to the foreign markets to protect its export profits. The domestic industry enters its mature stage as innovating businesses establish branches abroad. A reason for locating production operations abroad is that the cost advantage initially enjoyed by an innovator is not likely to last indefinitely. Over time, the innovating nation may find its technology becoming more commonplace and transportation costs and tariffs playing an increasingly important role in influencing selling costs. The innovator may also find that the foreign market is large enough to permit mass-production operations.

Although an innovating nation's monopoly position may be prolonged by legal patents, it will likely break down over time, because in the long run knowledge tends to be a free good. The benefits an innovating nation achieves from its technological gap are short-lived, as import competition from foreign producers begins. Once the innovative technology becomes fairly commonplace, foreign producers begin to imitate the production process. The innovating nation gradually loses its comparative advantage, and its export cycle enters a declining phase.

The trade cycle is complete when the production process becomes so standardized that it can be easily used by other nations. The technological breakthrough therefore no longer benefits only the innovating nation. In fact, the innovating nation may itself become a net importer of the product as its monopoly position is eliminated by foreign competition. Textiles and paper products are generally considered to have run the full course of the trade cycle. The spread of automobile production into many parts of the world implies that its production process is close to becoming standardized.

The experience of U.S. and Japanese radio manufacturers illustrates the product life cycle model. Following World War II, the radio was a well-established product. U.S. manufacturers dominated the international market for radios because vacuum tubes were initially developed in the United States. But as production technologies spread, Japan used cheaper labor and captured a large share of the world radio market. The transistor was then developed by U.S. companies. For a number of years, U.S. radio manufacturers were able to compete with the Japanese, who continued to use outdated technologies. Again, the Japanese imitated the U.S. technologies and were able to sell radios at more competitive prices.

DYNAMIC COMPARATIVE ADVANTAGE: INDUSTRIAL POLICY

David Ricardo's theory of comparative advantage has influenced international trade theory and policy for almost 200 years. It implies that nations are better off by promoting free trade and allowing competitive markets to determine what should be produced and how.

Ricardian theory emphasizes specialization and reallocation of existing resources found domestically. It is essentially a *static* theory that does not allow for a dynamic change in industries' comparative advantage or disadvantage over the course of several decades. The theory overlooks the fact that additional resources can be made available to the trading nation because they can be created or imported.

Ricardian theory also suffers from its assumption of increasing costs, in which additional use of limited resources results in rising unit costs as resources become fully used. Although this principle holds in the short run, empirical evidence suggests that unit costs may *decrease* over time—partly because firms learn to be more efficient and partly because of economies of large-scale production.

The remarkable postwar economic growth of the East Asian countries appears to be based on a modification of the static concept of comparative advantage. The Japanese were among the first to recognize that comparative advantage in a particular industry can be created through the mobilization of skilled labor, technology, and capital. They also realized that, in addition to the business sector, government can establish policies to promote opportunities for change through time. Such a process is known as **dynamic comparative advantage**. When government is actively involved in creating comparative advantage, the term **industrial policy** applies.

In its simplest form, industrial policy is a strategy to revitalize, improve, and develop an industry. Proponents maintain that government should enact policies that encourage the development of emerging, "sunrise" industries (such as high-technology). This strategy requires that resources be directed to industries in which productivity is highest, linkages to the rest of the economy are strong (as with semiconductors), and future competitiveness is important. Presumably, the domestic economy will enjoy a higher average level of productivity and will be more competitive in world markets as a result of such policies.

A variety of government policies can be used to foster the development and revitalization of industries; examples are antitrust immunity, tax incentives, R&D subsidies, loan guarantees, low-interest-rate loans, and trade protection. Creating comparative advantage requires government to identify (or target) the "winners" and encourage resources to move into industries with the highest growth prospects.

To better understand the significance of dynamic comparative advantage, we might think of it in terms of the classic example of Ricardo's theory of comparative advantage. His example showed that, in the eighteenth century, Portugal and England would each have gained by specializing respectively in the production of wine and cloth, even though Portugal might produce both cloth and wine more cheaply than England. According to static comparative-advantage theory, both nations would be better off by specializing in the product in which they had an existing comparative advantage.

By adhering to this prescription, however, Portugal would sacrifice long-run growth for short-run gains. Instead, if Portugal adopted a dynamic theory of comparative advantage, it would specialize in the growth industry of that time (cloth). The Portuguese government (or Portuguese textile manufacturers) would thus initiate policies to foster the development of its cloth industry. This strategy would require Portugal to think in terms of acquiring or creating strength in a "sunrise" sector instead of simply accepting the existing supply of resources and using that endowment as productively as possible.

Today, every industrialized country and many less-developed countries use industrial policies that encourage the development or revitalization of basic industries, including steel, autos, chemicals, transportation, and other important manufactures. Each of these industrial policies differs in character and approach; common to all is an active role for government in the economy. Usually, industrial policy is a strategy developed collectively by government, business, and labor through some sort of tripartite consultation process.

Advocates of industrial policy typically cite Japan as a nation that has been highly successful in penetrating foreign markets and achieving rapid economic growth. Following World War II, the Japanese were the high-cost producers in many basic industries (such as steel). In this situation, a static notion of comparative advantage would require the Japanese to look to areas of lesser disadvantage that were more labor-intensive (such as textiles). Such a strategy would have forced Japan into low-productivity industries that would eventually compete with other East Asian nations having abundant labor and modest living standards.

Instead, the Japanese invested in basic industries (steel, autos, and later electronics, including computers) that required intensive employment of capital and labor. From a short-run, static perspective, Japan appeared to pick the wrong industries. But from a long-run perspective, those were the industries in which technological progress was rapid, labor productivity rose fast, and unit costs decreased with the expansion of output. They were also industries in which one would expect rapid growth in demand as national income increased.

These industries combined the potential to expand rapidly, thus adding new capacity, with the opportunity to use the latest technology and thus promote a strategy of cost reduction founded on increasing productivity. Japan, placed in a position similar to that of Portugal in Ricardo's famous example, refused to specialize in "wine" and chose "cloth" instead. Within three decades, Japan became the world's premier low-cost producer of many of the products for which it initially started in a high-cost position.

Critics of industrial policy, however, contend that the causal factor in Japanese industrial success is unclear. They admit that some of the Japanese government's targeted industries—such as semiconductors, steel, shipbuilding, and machine tools—are probably more competitive than they would have been in the absence of government assistance. But they assert that Japan also targeted some losers, such as petrochemicals and aluminum, for which the returns on investment were disappointing and capacity had to be reduced. Moreover, there are examples of successful Japanese industries that did not receive government assistance—motorcycles, bicycles, paper, glass, and cement.

Industrial-policy critics contend that if all trading nations took the route of using a combination of trade restrictions on imports and subsidies on exports, a "beggar-thy-neighbor" process of trade-inhibiting protectionism would result. They also point out that the implementation of industrial policies can result in pork-barrel politics, in which politically powerful industries receive government assistance. Finally, it is argued that in a free market, profit-maximizing businesses have the incentive to develop new resources and technologies that change a country's comparative advantage. This raises the question of whether the government does a better job than the private sector in creating comparative advantage.

BOEING, AIRBUS, AND INDUSTRIAL POLICY

The world's manufacturers of large commercial jetliners operate in an imperfectly competitive market that has been dominated by Boeing of Seattle. The largest non-U.S. manufacturer is Airbus Industrie, which was created in 1966 by four European nations that pooled their resources to form an aircraft company to compete with the United States.

The members of the Airbus consortium are France's Aerospatiale (38-percent ownership), Germany's Messerschmitt, Boelkow and Bloom (38 percent), British Aerospace (20 percent), and Construcciones Aeronauticas of Spain (4 percent). These companies cooperate in the manufacturing of jetliners, although they compete against each other in other aircraft products. During the mid-1970s, Airbus sold less than 5 percent of the world's jetliners; by 1999, it had captured about 46 percent of the world market.

SUBSIDIES TO AN "INFANT" ENTERPRISE
Throughout the 1980s, the United States complained that Airbus received unfair subsidies from the governments of the four partners, placing the United States at a disadvantage. The Airbus consortium allegedly received loans from European governments for the development of new aircraft; these loans were made at below-market interest rates and amounted to 70 to 90 percent of an aircraft's development cost. Rather than repaying the loans according to a prescribed timetable, as typically would occur in a free market, Airbus was allowed to repay them as it delivered an aircraft. Airbus was also alleged to benefit from debt forgiveness when it suffered losses.

According to the U.S. Department of Commerce, Airbus received more than $13.5 billion in government subsidies between 1970

and 1990. In short, the United States maintained that Europe's treatment of Airbus was tantamount to an industrial policy in which a government targets a producer for subsidization to ensure its competitiveness. These subsidies allowed Airbus to set unrealistically low prices, to offer concessions and attractive financing terms to airlines, to write off development costs, and to use state-owned airlines to obtain orders.

Critics of these subsidies contended that conventional economic theory could not be used to analyze Airbus, because it was motivated by factors other than just profits. For example, Airbus had a stated objective of keeping its production lines in operation, irrespective of profits, to provide jobs for European workers. Because government subsidies lessened or eliminated financial risks for Airbus, the firm did not have to base its decisions to launch new aircraft types solely on profits/losses. Airbus's financial statements showed that it did not generate a profit from the 1970s to the 1990s; without subsidies, the firm would have gone bankrupt.

Airbus defended its subsidies on the grounds that they prevented the United States from holding a worldwide monopoly in commercial jet aircraft. In the absence of Airbus, European airlines would have to rely exclusively on U.S. companies as suppliers. Fears of dependence and the loss of autonomy in an area on the cutting edge of technology motivated European governments to subsidize Airbus. Simply put, Airbus argued that, as an infant enterprise, it was entitled to subsidies to help it compete against Boeing.

Airbus also argued that U.S. commercial aircraft producers benefited from government assistance. Rather than receiving direct governmental subsidies like Airbus, U.S. firms received indirect subsidies. For example, governmental research organizations (such as the National Aeronautics and Space Administration) supported aeronautics and propulsion research that was shared with U.S. aircraft manufacturers. Support for commercial aircraft innovation also came from military-sponsored research and military procurement. Research financed by the armed services yielded indirect but important technological spillovers to the commercial aircraft industry, most notably in aircraft engines and aircraft design. A 1991 study by the European Commission estimated that from 1976 to 1990 Boeing received $18 billion to $22 billion of indirect subsidies from the U.S. government.

As a result of the Boeing/Airbus conflict, in the late 1980s the United States and Europe negotiated the issue of aircraft subsidies. In 1992, the nations agreed on terms to curb subsidies for Airbus and its U.S. rivals. The principal element of the accord was a 33-percent cap on the amount of government subsidies that the United States and European aerospace industries could receive for product development. In addition, the indirect subsidies (spillover benefits from military contracts) would be limited, under a complicated formula, to 5 percent of a firm's civil-aeronautics revenue. The pact also required Europe and the United States to report more clearly what public funds are used to support civilian-aircraft development.

LAUNCH-AID SUBSIDIES Although the subsidy agreement helped calm trade tensions between the United States and Europe, in 2000 it appeared that the subsidy dispute was about to reemerge. The United States criticized the European Union for permitting subsidies of Airbus to continue and called for the European Union to renegotiate the 1992 deal. No longer was Airbus an infant enterprise, but rather a mature company that should no longer require any direct subsidies, according to the United States.

What inspired the United States to renew its efforts to force European compliance with the U.S. interpretation of the subsidy pact were plans by Airbus to develop a new "super-jumbo" airliner (the A3XX) capable of carrying 480 to 650 passengers. First deliveries were planned for 2005. The Airbus jumbo jet would challenge the market supremacy of the Boeing 747 (with about 400 seats), the only other jumbo jet available for sale.

To pay for the development costs of the A3XX, which could reach $15 billion, Airbus expected to get 40 percent of its funding from parts suppliers, 30 percent from government

loans arranged by its partners, and the final chunk from its own resources. Reorganizing Airbus to a fully private corporation would be necessary for Airbus to arrange this financing. The United States worried that as Airbus proceeded with its planned conversion to a private corporation, certain past loans might be "forgiven" as the new organization was set up. Also, as new subsidy loans for the A3XX are put into place, any renegotiation of subsidy limits or rules would be increasingly difficult to achieve.

Airbus suspected that Boeing was able to use its monopoly profits on the 747 to keep down its prices for smaller aircraft and so snatch away Airbus sales. Boeing denied this and argued that the A3XX would be a disaster, creating overcapacity and losses for manufacturers of jetliners. Boeing maintained that there is only a limited market for aircraft bigger than its 747, and that the best way of meeting that need is to enlarge it rather than build a new super-jumbo.

ENVIRONMENTAL REGULATORY POLICIES AND INTERNATIONAL COMPETITIVENESS

Beginning in the early 1960s, the U.S. government became increasingly concerned with the quality of life for its people—the conditions under which goods and services are produced, the effect of production on society, and the physical characteristics of the products themselves. This led to government regulations that promoted safer and better products, less pollution, better working conditions, and greater equality of opportunity. Although the objectives of these regulations were widely recognized as laudable, it was apparent that they added to a business's costs and prices.

Questions have arisen as to whether *differing efforts* by individual nations to improve the quality of life distort international trade patterns. It has been argued that because the United

States is a more litigious society than many of its foreign competitors, U.S. companies are burdened with relatively high regulatory costs that hinder their international competitiveness. Because most of the cost of U.S. social regulations has been attributed to environmental policy, it is worth examining the trade effects of **environmental regulation** separately.

Figure 4.6 illustrates the *trade consequences* of pollution regulations imposed on the production process. Assume a world of two steel producers, South Korea and the United States. The supply and demand schedules of South Korea and those of the United States are indicated by $S_{S.K._s}$ and $D_{S.K._0}$, and by $S_{U.S._0}$ and $D_{U.S._0}$. In the absence of trade, South Korean producers sell 5 tons of steel at $400 per ton, while 12 tons of steel are sold in the United States at $600 per ton. South Korea thus enjoys a cost advantage in steel production. With free trade, South Korea moves toward greater specialization in steel production, and the United States produces less steel. Under increasing-cost conditions, South Korea's costs and prices rise, while prices and costs fall in the United

States. The basis for further growth of trade is eliminated when prices in the two countries are equal at $500 per ton. At this price, South Korea produces 7 tons, consumes 3 tons, and exports 4 tons, and the United States produces 10 tons, consumes 14 tons, and imports 4 tons.

Now suppose that the production of steel results in discharges into waterways, leading the U.S. Environmental Protection Agency to impose pollution regulations on U.S. steel producers. Meeting these regulations adds to production costs, resulting in the U.S. supply schedule for steel shifting to $S_{U.S._1}$. If we assume that the South Korean government does not initiate environmental regulations, South Korean producers enjoy an additional competitive advantage. As South Korean producers expand steel production, say, to 9 tons, higher production costs result in a rise in prices to $600. At this price, South Korean consumers demand only 1 ton. The excess supply of 8 tons is earmarked for sale to the United States. As for the United States, 12 tons of steel are demanded at the price of $600, as determined by South Korea. Given supply schedule $S_{U.S._1}$, U.S.

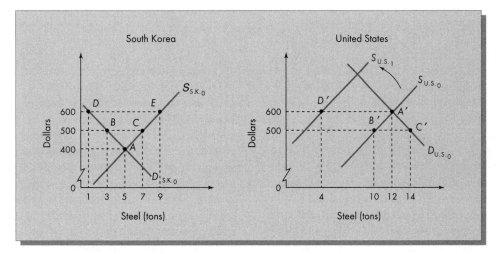

Figure 4.6 Trade Effects of Pollution-Control Regulations

The imposition of pollution-control regulations on U.S. steel companies leads to higher costs and a decrease in market supply. This detracts from the competitiveness of U.S. steel companies and reduces their share of the U.S. steel market.

firms now produce only 4 tons of steel at the $600 price. The excess demand, 8 tons, is met by imports from South Korea. For U.S. steel companies, the costs imposed by pollution regulations lead to further competitive disadvantage and a smaller share of the U.S. market.

During the early 1990s, the United States, Canada, and Mexico negotiated a North American Free Trade Agreement (NAFTA), designed to phase out trade barriers among the three nations (see Chapter 9). Environmental activists in these nations, however, expressed concerns that a free-trade agreement would encourage many U.S. companies that pollute to move to Mexico, where enforcement of environmental regulations was considered to be more lenient. They further argued that the competition for investment among the nations in a free-trade area could push environmental standards and enforcement to the lowest common denominator. Some environmental groups even asserted that NAFTA would encourage the importation into the United States of environmentally unsafe products (such as agricultural products with high levels of pesticides). Furthermore, there was concern about the impact of NAFTA on the border region between the United States and Mexico, which serves as a home to foreign-owned factories; it was feared that the increased volume of trade under NAFTA would lead to further degradation of this environment, as well as degradation of the overall environment of all three NAFTA nations.

In practice, the impact of environmental regulation on the locational decisions by firms is largely an empirical question. Studies typically confirm the nonexistent or very limited effect of environmental standards on locational decisions. Simply put, environmental regulatory costs are not large enough to negate the general findings of other researchers concerning the importance of capital, raw materials, labor skills and wages, and R&D as determinants of trade performance.[7]

Relative to the environmental standards of many *developing nations*, the standards of the United States (and other industrial nations) appear to be more stringent. Developing nations such as Mexico, South Korea, Brazil, and Taiwan have been criticized as being "pollution havens" with lenient environmental standards that encourage the production of pollution-intensive goods.

It should be noted, however, that most industrialized nations are greater polluters than less-industrialized nations. Developing nations contend that industrial nations, rather than undertaking radical domestic environmental policy changes that threaten their own economic growth, attempt to impose stringent environmental standards on developing nations without any assistance in paying for them; lack of compensation lessens the opportunity for less-industrialized nations to grow.

Why would less-industrialized, developing nations adopt less stringent environmental policies than industrial nations? Poorer nations may place a higher priority on the benefits of production (more jobs and income) relative to the benefits of environmental quality than wealthy nations; as income rises, however, demand for environmental quality tends to increase. Moreover, less-industrialized nations may have greater environmental capacities to reduce pollutants by natural processes (such as Latin America's rain-forest capacity to reduce carbon dioxide in the air) than do industrial nations that suffer from the effects of past pollution. Less-industrialized nations can thus tolerate higher levels of emissions without increasing pollution levels. Finally, the introduction of a polluting industry into a sparsely populated developing nation will likely have less impact on the capacity of the environment to reduce pollution by natural processes than it would have in a densely populated industrial nation.

Some experts maintain that trade and environmental concerns not only complement each other, but can actually be mutually beneficial. It is argued that stringent environmental standards can foster the creation and upgrading of competitive advantage. They force companies to improve quality, upgrade technology, and pro-

---

[7] World Trade Organization, *Annual Report*, 1998, pp. 54-55. See also D. Brack, ed., *Trade and Environment: Conflict or Compatibility?* (London: Earthscan Publications Ltd, 1998).

vide features in important areas of customer and social concern. Especially beneficial are stringent environmental regulations that lead to the adoption of similar standards in other nations.

To the extent that domestic producers lose competitiveness because of stringent environmental regulations, what might be done? Government could provide *subsidies* to domestic producers to offset production-cost disadvantages caused by environmental regulations. However, subsidies must be financed by higher taxes and may not be in the national interest. International differences in the cost of environmental regulations could also be neutralized through tariffs (taxes) applied to imports of goods produced by polluting industries overseas. Such a policy, however, could invite tariff retaliation by foreign governments.

The international environmental policy of the United States and other industrial nations is founded on the **polluter-pays principle**. It states that the cost of pollution prevention and control measures should be incorporated into the prices of goods and services that cause pollution in the production process or consumption. This approach is intended to give producers the incentive to develop more efficient pollution-control techniques and production processes that do not pollute as much and to find substitute goods whose use is less polluting. Subsidies for pollution control are seen as weakening these incentives. But exceptions to the polluter-pays principle do exist. All industrial countries, including the United States, have offered some government assistance to help domestic companies finance the cost of pollution abatement. The U.S. government, for example, has used industrial revenue bonds that allow companies to borrow money at subsidized interest rates.

TRADE IN BUSINESS SERVICES

The trading of products among countries is not confined to the exporting and importing of manufactured goods, but also includes a group of activities known as **business services**. In many cases, business services are nonstorable, in that they must be consumed as they are produced (for sexample, management consulting); unlike manufactured goods, business services cannot be maintained in inventories by producers. Examples of internationally traded business services include the following:

TRAVEL AND TRANSPORTATION
- Tourism
- Passenger transportation (for example, airlines)
- Shipping transportation (for example, freight and port facilities)

PROPRIETARY RIGHTS
- The use and sale of intangible property or rights (for example, fees and royalties paid for the use of technology, patents, and copyrights)

OTHER BUSINESS SERVICES
- Construction, architecture, engineering, consulting, brokerage, communications, management and technical services, R&D assessments, banking, finance, insurance, information management, medical, and legal

In recent years, business services have become an important item on national and international policy agendas; Table 4.5 shows the world's leading exporters and importers of business services. The reasons for this growing interest are easy to identify. In many countries, business-service activities account for the largest share of employment and national production. Most of the job creation in industrial countries in the past two decades has been in the service sector. Technological innovations are creating many new services and making many types of services tradable across national boundaries. These innovations have gone hand in hand with changes in the organization of production; the production and trade of goods and services have become increasingly linked.

Does the *theory of comparative advantage* apply to trade in business services? The theory suggests that trade between two countries creates

Table 4.5 Leading Exporters and Importers of Business Services, 1997 (Billions of Dollars)

Exporters	Value	Importers	Value
United States	$229.9	United States	$150.1
United Kingdom	85.5	Japan	122.1
France	80.3	Germany	120.1
Germany	75.4	Italy	70.1
Italy	71.7	United Kingdom	68.6
Japan	68.1	France	62.1
Netherlands	48.5	Netherlands	43.8
Spain	43.6	Canada	35.9
Hong Kong, China	37.3	Belgium-Luxembourg	32.1
Belgium-Luxembourg	34.0	China	30.1

Source: World Trade Organization, *Annual Report*, 1998, pp. 4–5.

mutual economic gains, provided that such trade is based on a competitive market. As a theoretical statement, the theory of comparative advantage should be equally valid whether the products involved are tradable merchandise (such as aircraft) or tradable services (such as accounting services). The wine and cloth in Ricardo's classic example of comparative advantage could easily have been replaced by wine and insurance policies without altering the validity of the comparative-advantage doctrine.

Similar to manufactured goods, business services are produced by combining resources to create something of value that can be bought or sold in the market. One would expect that the production and sale of services would follow a pattern of economic behavior similar to the production and sale of manufactured goods. The majority of researchers who have examined the applicability of the comparative-advantage principle to services have indicated that there is nothing in the theory that intrinsically makes it less applicable to services than to goods.

One problem of applying comparative-advantage theory to trade involving business services is that many services—being intangible, nonstorable, and nontransportable—cannot be traded without the physical relocation of providers or receivers. International trade in services (such as

construction) requires the consumer and the producer to be at the same place at the same time because the production and consumption activities are exactly the same process.

Applying the comparative-advantage principle to services is also difficult because they are such a *heterogeneous group*. The clear differences that exist among, say, banking services, air freight, and architecture services have led many to question whether the theory of comparative advantage can be a useful empirical guide for all service sectors. The heterogeneous nature of services makes it impossible to think of them as a single entity or for a nation to think of itself as having a competitive advantage in all services, any more than it can have a cost advantage in all manufactured goods.

It is unlikely that a single theory can encompass all the characteristics of international trade in services. But the same holds true for trade in goods. Some characteristics of trade in particular goods have led to the development of partial theories (such as overlapping demand theory, which applies to manufactured goods). In like manner, partial theories will likely have to be developed for single services or groups of services having common characteristics.

Although there is no single theory involving trade in business services, empirical research has identified a number of determinants underlying a nation's competitiveness in various services:

- Skills and capabilities of employees and employee wages
- A business's ability to organize a cooperative effort among workers with the right complementary skills
- Abundance of equipment, including communications facilities, data processing, and computers
- The institutional support provided by the legal system, practices, and traditions found in each nation
- The potential economies of scale afforded by a market's size

Of these determinants, the cost of capital and labor and physical proximity depend on a nation's current endowment of resources. The other determinants—institutional environment, organization, and personal skills—can be acquired.

The export advantage in many services, as revealed by existing patterns of trade in services, appear to lie with the developed countries. Empirical evidence suggests that many traded services tend to be intensive in the use of both technology and capital, whether human or physical. This seems to give the developed countries a competitive edge. The United States, for example, has often been characterized as having a comparative advantage in business services; this advantage reflects the longstanding position of the United States as a net exporter of technology and know-how.

TRANSPORTATION COSTS

Because the movement of goods among nations involves economic distance, the effects of transportation costs cannot be ignored. Indeed, new technological advances in transportation and telecommunications have reduced the economic distances among nations, as seen in Table 4.6. **Transportation costs** refer to the costs of moving goods, including freight charges, packing and handling expenses, and insurance premiums. These costs can modify international trade patterns.

TRADE EFFECTS The trade effects of transportation costs can be illustrated with a conventional supply and demand model based on increasing cost conditions. Figure 4.7(a) illustrates the supply and demand curves of autos for the United States and Canada. Reflecting the assumption that the United States has the comparative advantage in auto production, the U.S. and Canadian equilibrium locations are at points *E* and *F*, respectively. In the absence of trade, the

Table 4.6 Costs of Air Transportation and Telephone Calls (in 1990 U.S. Dollars)

Year	Average Air Transportation Revenue per Passenger Mile	Cost of a Three-Minute Call, New York to London
1930	$0.68	$244.65
1940	0.46	188.51
1950	0.30	53.20
1960	0.24	45.86
1970	0.16	31.58
1980	0.10	4.80
1990	0.11	3.32

Source: Richard Herring and Robert Litan, *Financial Regulation in the Global Economy*, Washington, DC, Brookings Institution, 1995, p. 14. See also International Monetary Fund, *World Economic Outlook*, 1997, p. 46.

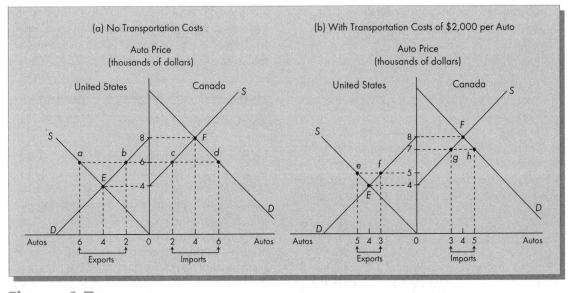

Figure 4.7 Free Trade Under Increasing-Cost Conditions

In the absence of transportation costs, free trade results in the equalization of the prices of the traded goods, as well as resource prices, in the trading nations. With the introduction of transportation costs, the low-cost exporting nation produces less, consumes more, and exports less; the high-cost importing nation produces more, consumes less, and imports less. The degree of specialization in production between the two nations decreases, as do the gains from trade.

U.S. auto price, $4,000, is lower than that of Canada, $8,000.

When trade is allowed, the United States will move toward greater specialization in auto production, whereas Canada will produce fewer autos. Under increasing-cost conditions, the U.S. cost and price levels rise, and Canada's price falls. The basis for further growth of trade is eliminated when the two countries' prices are equal, at $6,000. At this price, the United States produces 6 autos, consumes 2 autos, and exports 4 autos; Canada produces 2 autos, consumes 6 autos, and imports 4 autos. Thus, $6,000 becomes the equilibrium price for both countries because the excess auto supply of the United States just matches the excess auto demand in Canada.

The introduction of transportation costs into the analysis modifies the conclusions of this example. Suppose the per-unit cost of transporting an auto from the United States to Canada is $2,000, as shown in Figure 4.7(b). The United States would find it advantageous to produce autos and export them to Canada until its relative price advantage is eliminated. But when transportation costs are included in the analysis, the U.S. export price reflects domestic production costs *plus* the cost of transporting autos to Canada. The basis for trade thus ceases to exist when the U.S. auto price plus the transportation cost rises to equal Canada's auto price. This equalization occurs when the U.S. auto price rises to $5,000 and Canada's auto price falls to $7,000, the difference between them being the $2,000 per-unit transportation cost. Instead of a single price ruling in both countries, there will be two domestic auto prices, differing by the cost of transportation.

Compared with free trade in the absence of transportation costs, when transportation costs are included the high-cost importing country will produce more, consume less, and import less. The low-cost exporting country will produce less, consume more, and export less. *Transportation costs, therefore, tend to reduce the volume of trade, the degree of specialization in production among the nations concerned, and thus the gains from trade.*

The inclusion of transportation costs in the analysis modifies our trade-model conclusions. A product will be traded internationally as long as the pretrade price differential between the trading partners is greater than the cost of transporting the product between them. When trade is in equilibrium, the price of the traded product in the exporting nation is less than the price in the importing country by the amount of the transportation cost.

Transportation costs also have implications for the factor-price-equalization theory presented earlier in this chapter. Recall that this theory suggests that free trade tends to equalize commodity prices and factor prices so that all workers will earn the same wage rate and all units of capital will earn the same interest income in both nations. Free trade permits factor-price equalization to occur because factor inputs that cannot move to another country are implicitly being shipped in the form of commodities. Looking at the real world, however, we see U.S. autoworkers earning more than South Korean autoworkers. One possible reason for this differential is transportation costs. By making low-cost South Korean autos more expensive for U.S. consumers, transportation costs reduce the volume of autos shipped from South Korea to the United States. This reduced trade volume stops the process of commodity- and factor-price equalization before it is complete. In other words, the prices of U.S. autos and the wages of U.S. autoworkers do not fall to the levels of those in South Korea. Transportation costs thus provide some relief to high-cost domestic workers who are producing goods subject to import competition.

How important are transportation costs for U.S. imports? Since the 1960s, the cost of inter-national transportation has decreased significant-ly relative to the value of U.S. imports. From 1965 to the 1990s, transportation costs as a percentage of the import value of all U.S. imports decreased from 10 percent to less than 5 percent. This decline in the relative cost of international transportation has made imports more competitive in U.S. markets and contributed to a higher volume of trade for the United States. Falling transportation costs have been due largely to technological improvements, including the development of large dry-bulk containers, large-scale tankers, containerization, and wide-bodied jets.

Domestic transportation costs also affect the international competitiveness of import-competing industries. For example, U.S. steel and auto producers tend to concentrate production in the midwestern states. Because of the costs of transportation by land, import penetration for these industries increases as distance increases from the Midwest's production centers. Thus, foreign-auto sales in the United States have been strongest in the Pacific Coast states and weakest in states bordering the Great Lakes.

TRANSPORTATION COSTS AND THE U.S. STEEL INDUSTRY Transportation costs for steel products are an important factor affecting the competitive position of U.S. manufacturers and foreign companies that export steel to the United States. Because steel has a low value per unit, transportation costs are a significant part of the cost to end users. To minimize transportation costs, U.S. steel companies have generally located production close to either their main sources of raw materials or their large-volume customers.

The geographic pattern of steel consumption and production in the United States contributes to the high transportation costs faced by shippers of steel products. Most U.S. steel mills are located in Indiana, Ohio, Pennsylvania, and Illinois. The cost of transporting steel, via truck or rail, to other locations in the United States can be sizable. Customers in many locations may be closer to a foreign steel mill than to a U.S. steel mill. Steel imports from Brazil, Japan, South Korea,

Taiwan, and Germany are shipped to the United States by ocean freight. The cost of transporting steel within the United States via rail and truck—which is often high compared to ocean freight rates—may thus reduce the competitiveness of U.S. steel firms. This possibility is especially likely for West Coast steel manufacturers who compete with foreign firms for sales in the eastern part of the United States.

Steel transportation costs also vary by port of entry into the United States because of port facilities and the distance from the foreign steel mill. The exporting nations previously mentioned generally ship steel to the U.S. port where transportation costs will make up the lowest percentage of total costs. As seen in Table 4.7, Japan, South Korea, and Taiwan send the largest portion of their shipments to the West Coast; the United Kingdom and Germany ship the largest portion of their steel exports to the Great Lakes via the St. Lawrence Seaway; and Brazil ships the majority of its steel exports to the East Coast.

FALLING TRANSPORTATION COSTS FOSTER TRADE BOOM

If merchants everywhere appear to be selling imports, there is a reason. International trade has been growing at a startling pace. What underlies the expansion of international commerce? The worldwide decrease in trade barriers, such as tariffs and quotas, is certainly one reason. The economic opening of nations that have traditionally been minor players, such as Mexico and China, is another. But one factor behind the trade boom has largely been unnoticed: the declining costs of getting goods to the market.[8]

Today, transportation costs are a less severe obstacle than they used to be. One reason is that the global economy has become much less transport-intensive than it once was. In the early 1900s, for example, manufacturing and agriculture were the two most important industries in most nations. International trade thus emphasized raw materials, such as iron ore and wheat, or processed goods such as steel. These sorts of goods are heavy and bulky, resulting in a relatively high cost of transporting them compared with the value of the goods themselves. As a result, transportation costs had much to do with the volume of trade. Over time, however, world output has shifted into goods whose value is unrelated to their size and weight. Finished manufactured goods, not raw commodities, dominate the flow of trade. Therefore, less transportation is required for every dollar's worth of exports or imports.

Consider the business of manufacturing disk drives for computers. Most of the world's disk-drive manufacturing occurs in East Asia, a situation that is possible only because disk drives, although valuable, are small and light and there-

[8] Drawn from "Delivering the Goods," *The Economist,* November 15, 1997, pp. 85–86.

Table 4.7 Steel Transportation Costs, 1998

Exporting Nation	Primary Port of Entry into United States	Unit Value (dollars/ton)	Transportation Cost/Ton
Brazil	East Coast	$494	$62
Japan	West Coast	560	61
South Korea	West Coast	482	53
Taiwan	West Coast	518	60
Germany	Great Lakes	559	62
United Kingdom	Great Lakes	458	58

Source: WEFA Group, *Global Steel Outlook,* 1998, Bala Cynwyd, PA, fall 1998.

fore cost little to transport. Computer manufacturers in the United States or Japan will not face hugely bigger freight bills if they import drives from Malaysia rather than purchasing them domestically. Distance thus presents no hindrance to the globalization of the disk-drive industry.

That the cost of shipping has decreased dramatically also accounts for the growth of international trade. In the early 1900s, the physical process of importing or exporting was difficult. Imagine a British textile firm desiring to sell its product in the United States. First, at the firm's loading dock, workers would have lifted bolts of fabric into the back of a truck. The truck would have headed to a port and unloaded its cargo, bolt by bolt, into a dockside warehouse. As a vessel prepared to set sail, dockworkers would have removed the bolts from the warehouse and hoisted them into the hold, where other dockworkers would have stowed them in place. When the cargo reached the United States, the process would have been reversed. Indeed, this sort of shipment was a complicated task, requiring much effort and expense.

Indeed, falling transport costs provided a boost to trade. In 1868, for example, it cost 177.5 pence to ship eight bushels of wheat from Chicago to Liverpool. By 1902, it cost only 46.5 pence. Thanks to cheaper transport and lower tariffs, prices across the world converged. Whereas in 1870 wheat cost 58 percent more in Liverpool than in Chicago, by 1895 it cost only 18 percent more.

By the 1950s, changes occurred in the transportation of goods when American shippers developed more efficient methods of moving goods. Under their original scheme, a truck trailer, wheels and all, was unhitched from the driver's cab and hoisted onto the deck of a ship, thus eliminating the need for longshoremen to handle the individual items inside the cargo compartment. This method soon evolved into the use of metal containers that could be separated from the truck's trailer. With the trailer left at dockside, the containers could be stacked several high aboard the ship. As time passed, a container crane was invented, which made it possible to load and unload containers without capsizing a vessel. Moreover, the adoption of standard container sizes permitted almost any box to be transported on any vessel.

Although the shipping container transformed ocean shipping into a highly productive business, getting the cargo to and from the dock was another problem. National governments generally regulated the prices and shipping practices of domestic freight companies. New firms could enter the freight business only with great difficulty and were subject to tight restrictions. This situation started changing during the 1970s when the United States began to deregulate its transportation industry. First airlines, then road shippers and railroads, were freed from regulations on what they could carry, where they could haul it, and what price they could charge. Trucks were no longer forced to run empty because they were licensed to ship goods on only one leg of a round-trip journey. Railways were no longer forced to maintain unprofitable branch lines, but could emphasize the shipping of freight in large volumes over long distances. Deregulation of the transportation industry resulted in increased efficiency and lower costs.

The freight revolution intensified during the 1980s, as deregulation and new technology eliminated the boundaries between different modes of transportation. For example, an electronics manufacturer in, say, Taiwan could request an ocean freight company to deliver its exports to the American Midwest. The ocean freighter might negotiate a deal with a railroad to ship the container from Oakland to Kansas City; hire a trucking firm to haul it from Kansas City to Topeka; assume responsibility for fulfilling delivery schedules at each stage of the journey; and send a single invoice for the entire shipment. Such intermodalism has resulted in freight companies such as United Parcel Service and Federal Express, which specialize in using a combination of aircraft and trucks to deliver freight quickly. It has also resulted in railroads' building tracks at dockside, so containers can be shipped directly from ships onto trains.

STEELMAKERS COMPLAIN ABOUT REGULATORY BURDENS

According to the American Iron and Steel Institute, U.S. steel producers are today technologically advanced, low cost, environmentally responsible, and customer focused. Yet they continue to face economic policies of the U.S. government that impair their competitiveness and trade prospects, as seen in the following examples.

- **Alternative Minimum Tax.** The corporate alternative minimum tax (AMT) maintains slower depreciation methods than under the regular corporate tax. The AMT increases the cost of capital for steel by about 3.6 percent, acts as a disincentive to capital investment in steel, and harms the competitiveness of domestic steel companies.
- **Health Care.** U.S. steel companies spent more than $1.5 billion for health care in 1999—for workers, retirees, and dependents. This adversely affects the competitiveness of U.S. steel companies vis-à-vis foreign competitors, many of whose health-care costs are borne by government through general tax revenues.
- **OSHA.** The complexity and cost of compliance with Occupational Safety and Health Administration (OSHA) regulations continue to increase. Many OSHA rules do not have a sound scientific or medical basis and thus are impractical and cost-ineffective.

- **Electricity Policy.** Electricity is a major component of steel-manufacturing costs, but it cannot be purchased on a competitive basis as are other commodities.
- **Global Climate Change.** Efforts by the United States to achieve a 7-percent decrease in greenhouse gas emissions from 1990 levels by the year 2012, as dictated by the Kyoto Protocol, could result in $5 billion in extra annual energy costs for U.S. steel companies.
- **Clean Air.** Proposed tighter standards for pollutants could place much of the United States—including many steel industry sites—in nonattainment areas. The result would be enormous new costs for steel, with no comparable requirements for U.S. trading partners.
- **Cleanup Standards.** Cleanup standards of manufacturing sites, as mandated by the Resource Conservation and Recovery Act, are cost ineffective. No comparable program exists in other nations. Likewise, U.S. steel companies are often stymied in their efforts to return former industrial properties to productive, job-creating use.

Source: *Domestic Policies that Impact American Steel's International Competitiveness*, American Iron and Steel Institute, Washington, DC, 1999, pp. 1–2.

In the United States, the era of huge productivity gains in transportation appears to be dwindling after more than two decades of deregulation. In other nations, however, the process still has far to go. State ownership of airlines and railroads, regulation of freight rates, and the permission of ocean-shipping cartels and cargo-handling monopolies all keep the cost of shipping relatively high and thus hinder international trade. Bringing these barriers down would help bring the world's economies even closer.

S U M M A R Y

1. The immediate basis for trade stems from relative commodity price differences among nations. Because relative prices are determined by supply and demand conditions, such factors as resource endowments, technology, and national income are important determinants of the basis for trade.

2. The Heckscher–Ohlin theory suggests that differences in relative factor endowments among nations underlie the basis for trade. The theory asserts that a nation will export that commodity in the production of which a relatively large amount of its abundant and cheap resource is used. Conversely, it will import commodities in the production of which a relatively scarce and expensive resource is used. The theory also states that with trade, the relative differences in resource prices between nations tend to be eliminated.

3. Contrary to the predictions of the Heckscher–Ohlin model, the empirical tests of Wassily Leontief demonstrated that for the United States exports are labor-intensive and import-competing goods are capital-intensive. His findings became known as the Leontief paradox.

4. By widening the size of the domestic market, international trade permits firms to take advantage of longer production runs and increasing efficiencies (such as mass production). Such economies of large-scale production can be translated into lower product prices, which improve a firm's competitiveness.

5. Staffan Linder offers two explanations of world trade patterns. Trade in primary products and agricultural goods conforms well to the factor-endowment theory. But trade in manufactured goods is best explained by overlapping demand structures among nations. For manufactured goods, the basis for trade is stronger when the structure of demand in the two nations is more similar—that is, when the nations' per capita incomes are similar.

6. Besides interindustry trade, the exchange of goods among nations includes intraindustry trade—two-way trade in a similar product. Intraindustry trade occurs in homogeneous goods as well as in differentiated products.

7. One dynamic theory of international trade is the product life cycle theory. This theory views a variety of manufactured goods as going through a trade cycle, during which a nation initially is an exporter, then loses its export markets, and finally becomes an importer of the product. Empirical studies have demonstrated that trade cycles do exist for manufactured goods at some times.

8. Dynamic comparative advantage refers to the creation of comparative advantage through the mobilization of skilled labor, technology, and capital; it can be initiated by either the private or public sector. When government attempts to create comparative advantage, the term *industrial policy* applies. Industrial policy seeks to encourage the development of emerging, sunrise industries through such measures as tax incentives and R&D subsidies.

9. The environmental laws of national governments can affect the competitive position of their industries. These laws often result in cost-increasing compliance measures, such as the installation of pollution-control equipment, which can detract from the competitiveness of domestic industries.

10. International trade includes the flow of services between countries as well as the exchange of manufactured goods. As with trade in manufactured goods, the principle of comparative advantage applies to trade in services.

11. Transportation costs tend to reduce the volume of international trade by increasing the prices of traded goods. A product will be traded only if the cost of transporting it between nations is less than the pretrade difference between their relative commodity prices.

STUDY QUESTIONS

1. What are the effects of transportation costs on international trade patterns?

2. Explain how the international movement of products and of factor inputs promotes an equalization of the factor prices among nations.

3. How does the Heckscher–Ohlin theory differ from Ricardian theory in explaining international trade patterns?

4. The Heckscher–Ohlin theory demonstrates how trade affects the distribution of income within trading partners. Explain.

5. How does the Leontief paradox challenge the overall applicability of the factor-endowment model?

6. According to Staffan Linder, there are two explanations of international trade patterns—one for manufactures and another for primary (agricultural) goods. Explain.

7. Do recent world-trade statistics support or refute the notion of a product life cycle for manufactured goods?

8. How can economies of large-scale production affect world trade patterns?

9. Distinguish between intraindustry trade and interindustry trade. What are some major determinants of intraindustry trade?

10. What is meant by the term *industrial policy*? How do governments attempt to create comparative advantage in sunrise sectors of the economy? What are some problems encountered when attempting to implement industrial policy?

11. How can environmental regulatory policies affect an industry's international competitiveness?

12. International trade in services is determined by what factors?

13. Table 4.8 illustrates the supply and demand schedules for calculators in Sweden and Norway. On graph paper, draw the supply and demand schedules of each country.

    a. In the absence of trade, what are the equilibrium price and quantity of calculators produced in Sweden and Norway? Which country has the comparative advantage in calculators?

    b. Assume there are no transportation costs. With trade, what price brings about balance in exports and imports? How many calculators are traded at this price? How many calculators are produced and consumed in each country with trade?

Table 4.8 Supply and Demand Schedules for Calculators

	Sweden			Norway	
Price	Quantity Supplied	Quantity Demanded	Price	Quantity Supplied	Quantity Demanded
$ 0	0	1,200	$ 0	–	1,800
5	200	1,000	5	–	1,600
10	400	800	10	–	1,400
15	600	600	15	0	1,200
20	800	400	20	200	1,000
25	1,000	200	25	400	800
30	1,200	0	30	600	600
35	1,400	–	35	800	400
40	1,600	–	40	1,000	200
45	1,800	–	45	1,200	0

c. Suppose the cost of transporting each calculator from Sweden to Norway is $5. With trade, what is the impact of the transportation cost on the price of calculators in Sweden and Norway? How many calculators will each country produce, consume, and trade?

d. In general, what can be concluded about the impact of transportation costs on the price of the traded product in each trading nation? The extent of specialization? The volume of trade?

A P P E N D I X

SPECIFIC FACTORS: TRADE AND THE DISTRIBUTION OF INCOME IN THE SHORT RUN

The factor-price-equalization theory assumes that factor inputs are completely mobile among industries within a nation and completely immobile among nations. However, although factor mobility among industries may occur in the long run, many factors are immobile in the short run. Physical capital (such as factories and machinery), for example, is generally used for specific purposes; a machine designed for computer production cannot suddenly be used to manufacture jet aircraft. Similarly, workers often acquire certain skills suited to specific occupations and cannot immediately be assigned to other occupa-

tions. The so-called **specific-factors theory** analyzes the income-distribution effects of trade in the *short run* when factor inputs are *immobile* among industries—in effect, a short-run version of the factor-price-equalization theory.

Referring to Figure 4.8, suppose the United States produces steel and computers using labor and capital. Assume that labor is perfectly mobile between the steel and computer industries, but capital is industry-specific: Steel capital cannot be used in computer production, and computer capital cannot be used in steel production. Also assume that the total U.S. labor force equals 30 workers.

In each industry, labor is combined with a fixed quantity of the other factor (steel capital or computer capital) to produce the good. Labor is thus subject to diminishing marginal productivity, and the labor demand schedule in each industry is

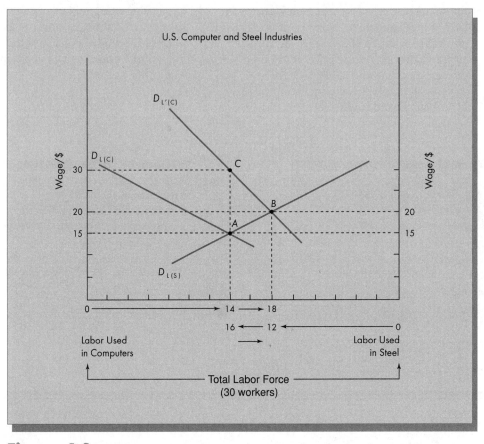

Figure 4.8 Relative Prices and the Specific Factors Model

The computer labor demand schedule increases in proportion to the rise in the price of computers (100 percent); however, the wage rate increases less than proportionately (33 percent). Labor is transferred from steel to computer production. Output of computers thus increases, while output of steel falls.

downward sloping.[9] The computer industry's labor demand schedule is denoted by $D_{L(C)}$,

[9] The value of marginal product (*VMP*) refers to the price of a product (*P*) times the marginal product of labor (*MP*). The *VMP* schedule is the labor demand schedule. This is because a business hiring under competitive conditions finds it most profitable to hire labor up to the point at which the price of labor (wage rate) equals its *VMP*. The *VMP* schedule is downward sloping because of the law of diminishing returns: As extra units of labor are added to capital, beyond some point the marginal product attributable to each additional unit of labor will decrease. Because $VMP = P \times MP$, falling *MP* means that *VMP* decreases as more units of labor are hired.

while $D_{L(S)}$ denotes the labor demand schedule in the steel industry. Because labor is assumed to be the mobile factor, it will move from the low-wage industry to the high-wage industry until wages are equalized. Let the equilibrium wage rate equal $15 per hour, seen at the intersection point *A* of the two labor demand schedules. At this wage, 14 workers are hired for computer production (reading from left to right) and 16 are used in steel production (reading from right to left).

Suppose the United States has a comparative advantage in computer production. With free trade and expanded output, the domestic price of computers increases, say, from $2,000 to $4,000 per unit, a 100-percent increase; the demand for labor in computer production increases by the same proportion as the computer price increase and is denoted by demand schedule $D_{L'(C)}$.[10] The result of the demand increase is a shift in equilibrium from point A to point B.

The increased demand for labor in computer production has two effects. First, the equilibrium wage rate rises, from $15 to $20, which is a lesser increase (33 percent) than the computer price increase (100 percent). Second, the increased labor demand in computer production draws workers away from steel production. At the new equilibrium point B, 18 workers are employed in computer production and 12 workers are employed in steel manufacturing; compared to equilibrium point A, 4 workers are shifted from steel to computers. Output of computers thus rises, and output of steel falls.

How does trade affect the *distribution of income* for the three groups: workers, owners of computer capital, and owners of steel capital? Workers find that although their nominal wages are higher than before, their real wages (that is, the purchasing power of the nominal wage) have fallen relative to the price of computers but have risen relative to the price of steel, which is assumed to be unchanged. Given this information, we are uncertain whether workers are better off or worse off. Their welfare will rise, fall, or remain the same depending on whether they purchase computers or steel or a combination of the two goods.

Owners of computer capital, however, are better off with trade. More computers are being manufactured, and the price received per computer has risen more than the wage cost per unit. The difference between the price and the wage rate is the income of capital owners for each computer sold. Conversely, owners of steel capital are worse off as the rise in computer prices decreases the purchasing power of any given income—that is, real income falls.[11] In general, owners of factors specific to *export* industries tend to *gain* from international trade, while owners of factors specific to *import-competing* industries *suffer*. International trade thus gives rise to potential conflict between different resource suppliers within a society.

The specific-factors theory helps to explain Japan's rice policy. Japan permits only small quantities of rice to be imported, even though rice production in Japan is more costly than in other nations such as the United States. It is widely recognized that Japan's overall welfare would rise if free imports of rice were permitted. However, free trade would harm Japanese farmers. Although rice farmers displaced by imports might find jobs in other sectors of Japan's economy, they would find changing employment to be time-consuming and costly. Moreover, as rice prices decrease with free trade, so would the value of Japanese farming land. It is no surprise that Japanese farmers and landowners strongly object to free trade in rice; their unified political opposition has influenced the Japanese government more than the interests of Japanese consumers.

---

[10] Because $VMP = P \times MP$, a 100-percent rise in computer prices (P) leads to a 100-percent increase in VMP. As a result, the labor demand schedule shifts upward by 100 percent from $D_{L(C)}$ to $D_{L'(C)}$ following the price increase. To visualize this shift, compare point A and point C along the two demand schedules. After the increase in demand, computer firms will be willing to hire a given amount of labor, say 14 workers, at a wage rate of up to $30 instead of $15, a 100-percent increase. In like manner, all points along $D_{L'(C)}$ are located at a wage rate that is 100-percent greater than the corresponding wage rate along $D_{L(C)}$.

[11] Not only do the real incomes of steel-capital owners fall, but so do their nominal incomes. Trade results in a decrease in their VMP due to a decline in their MP, even if the price of steel remains the same.

Tariffs

The conclusion of the trade models presented so far is that free trade leads to the most efficient use of world resources. When nations specialize according to the comparative-advantage principle, the level of world output is maximized. Not only does free trade enhance world welfare, but it can also benefit each participating nation. Every nation can overcome the limitations of its own productive capacity to consume a combination of goods that exceeds the best it can produce in isolation.

Despite the power of the free-trade argument, however, free-trade policies meet major resistance among those companies and workers who face losses in income and jobs because of import competition. Policy makers are torn between the appeal of greater global efficiency made possible by free trade and the needs of the voting public whose main desire is to preserve short-run interests such as employment and income. The benefits of free trade may take years to achieve and are spread out over wide segments of society, whereas the costs of free trade are immediate and fall on specific groups (for example, workers in the import-competing industry).

In today's world, restrictions on the flow of goods and services in international trade are widespread. This chapter considers one type of restriction, tariffs, and their impact on trade.

THE TARIFF CONCEPT

A **tariff** is simply a tax (duty) levied on a product when it crosses national boundaries. The most widespread tariff is the *import tariff*, which is a tax levied on an imported product. A less common tariff is an *export tariff*, which is a tax imposed on an exported product. Export tariffs have often

KEY CONCEPTS AND TERMS

- *Ad valorem tariff*
- *Beggar-thy-neighbor policy*
- *Bonded warehouse*
- *Compound tariff*
- *Consumer surplus*
- *Consumption effect*
- *Cost-insurance-freight (CIF) valuation*
- *Customs valuation*
- *Deadweight loss*
- *Domestic revenue effect*
- *Effective tariff rate*
- *Foreign-trade zone (FTZ)*
- *Free-on-board (FOB) valuation*
- *Free-trade argument*
- *Free-trade-biased sector*
- *Infant-industry argument*
- *Large nation*
- *Level playing field*
- *Nominal tariff rate*
- *Offshore-assembly provision (OAP)*
- *Optimum tariff*
- *Producer surplus*
- *Production sharing*
- *Protection-biased sector*
- *Protective effect*
- *Protective tariff*
- *Redistributive effect*
- *Revenue effect*
- *Revenue tariff*
- *Scientific tariff*
- *Small nation*
- *Specific tariff*
- *Tariff*
- *Tariff escalation*
- *Terms-of-trade effect*

been used by developing nations. For example, cocoa exports have been taxed by Ghana, and oil exports have been taxed by the Organization of Petroleum Exporting Countries (OPEC) in order to raise revenue or promote scarcity in global markets and hence increase the world price.

Did you know that the United States cannot levy export tariffs? When the U.S. Constitution was written, southern cotton-producing states feared that northern textile-manufacturing states would pressure the federal government into levying export tariffs to depress the price of cotton. An export duty would lead to decreased exports and thus a fall in the price of cotton within the United States. As the result of negotiations, the Constitution was worded so as to prevent export taxes: "No tax or duty shall be laid on articles exported from any state."

Tariffs may be imposed for protection or revenue purposes. A **protective tariff** is designed to insulate import-competing producers from foreign competition. Although a protective tariff generally is not intended to totally prohibit imports from entering the country, it does place foreign producers at a competitive disadvantage when selling in the domestic market. A **revenue tariff** is imposed for the purpose of generating tax revenues and may be placed on either exports or imports.

Over time, tariff revenues have decreased as a source of government revenue for industrial nations, including the United States. In 1900, tariff revenues constituted more than 41 percent of U.S. government receipts; by 1998, the figure stood at 1 percent. However, many developing nations currently rely on tariffs as a major source of government revenue. Table 5.1 shows the percentage of government revenue selected nations derive from tariffs.

TYPES OF TARIFFS

Tariffs can be specific, ad valorem, or compound. A **specific tariff** is expressed in terms of a fixed amount of money per physical unit of the imported product. For example, a U.S. importer

of a German computer may be required to pay a duty to the U.S. government of $100 per computer, regardless of the computer's price. An **ad valorem tariff**, much like a sales tax, is expressed as a fixed percentage of the value of the imported product. Suppose that an ad valorem duty of 15 percent is levied on imported trucks. A U.S. importer of a Japanese truck valued at $20,000 would be required to pay a duty of $3,000 to the government ($20,000 × 15% = $3,000). A **compound tariff** is a combination of specific and ad valorem tariffs. For example, a U.S. importer of a television might be required to pay a duty of $20 plus 5 percent of the value of the television. Table 5.2 lists U.S. tariffs on certain items.

What are the relative merits of specific, ad valorem, and compound tariffs?

SPECIFIC TARIFF As a fixed monetary duty per unit of the imported product, a specific tariff is relatively easy to apply and administer, particularly to standardized commodities and staple products where the value of the dutiable goods cannot be easily observed. A main disadvantage of a specific tariff is that the degree of protection it affords domestic producers varies inversely with changes in import prices. For example, a specific tariff of $1,000 on autos will discourage imports priced at $20,000 per auto to a greater degree than those priced at $25,000. During times of rising import prices, a given specific tariff loses some of its protective effect. The result is to encourage domestic firms to produce less expensive goods, for which the degree of protection against imports is higher. On the other hand, a specific tariff has the advantage of providing domestic producers more protection during a business recession, when cheaper products are purchased. Specific tariffs thus cushion domestic producers progressively against foreign competitors who cut their prices.

AD VALOREM TARIFF Ad valorem tariffs usually lend themselves more satisfactorily to manufactured goods, because they can be applied to products with a wide range of grade variations. As a percentage applied to a product's value, an

Table 5.1 Tariff Revenues as a Percentage of Government Revenues: Selected Countries

Developing Countries	Percentage	Industrial Countries	Percentage
Bahamas	59	Australia	3
Madagascar	53	New Zealand	2
Lebanon	46	Portugal	2
Sierra Leone	46	Canada	2
Ethiopia	42	United States	1
Gambia	41	Sweden	1
Maldives	35	Denmark	1
Rwanda	31	Finland	1
Belize	28	Switzerland	1

Source: International Monetary Fund, *Government Finance Statistics Yearbook*, Washington, DC, 1998.

Table 5.2 Selected U.S. Tariffs

Product	Duty Rate
Brooms	32 cents each
Fishing reels	24 cents each
Wrist watches (without jewels)	29 cents each
Ball bearings	2.4% ad valorem
Electrical motors	6.7% ad valorem
Bicycles	5.5% ad valorem
Wool blankets	1.8 cents/kg + 6% ad valorem
Electricity meters	16 cents each + 1.5% ad valorem
Auto transmission shafts	25 cents each + 3.9% ad valorem

Source: U.S. International Trade Commission, *Tariff Schedules of the United States*, Washington, DC, Government Printing Office, 2000, at Internet site http://www.usitc.gov/taffairs.htm.

ad valorem tariff can distinguish among small differentials in product quality to the extent that they are reflected in product price. Under a system of ad valorem tariffs, a person importing a $20,000 Honda would have to pay a higher duty than a person importing a $19,900 Toyota. Under a system of specific tariffs, the duty would be the same.

Another advantage of an ad valorem tariff is that it tends to maintain a constant degree of protection for domestic producers during periods of changing prices. If the tariff rate is 20 percent ad valorem and the imported product price is $200, the duty is $40. If the product's price increases, say, to $300, the duty collected rises to $60; if the product price falls to $100, the duty drops to $20. An ad valorem tariff yields revenues proportionate to values, maintaining a constant degree of relative protection at all price levels. An ad valorem tariff is similar to a proportional tax in that the real proportional tax burden or protection does not change as the tax base changes. In recent decades, in response to global inflation and the rising importance of world trade in manufactured products, ad valorem duties have been used more often than specific duties.

Determination of duties under the ad valorem principle at first appears to be simple, but in practice it has suffered from administrative complexities. The main problem has been trying to determine the value of an imported product, a process referred to as **customs valuation**. Import prices are estimated by customs appraisers, who may disagree on product values. Moreover, import prices tend to fluctuate over time, which makes the valuation process rather difficult.

Another customs-valuation problem stems from variations in the methods used to determine a commodity's value. For example, the United States has traditionally used **free-on-board (FOB)** valuation, whereby the tariff is applied to a product's value as it leaves the exporting country. But European countries have traditionally used a **cost-insurance-freight (CIF) valuation**, whereby ad valorem tariffs are levied as a percentage of the imported commodity's total value as it arrives at its final destination. The CIF price thus includes transportation costs, such as insurance and freight.

COMPOUND TARIFF Compound duties are often applied to manufactured products embodying raw materials that are subject to tariffs. In this case, the specific portion of the duty neutralizes the cost disadvantage of domestic manufactures that results from tariff protection granted to domestic suppliers of raw materials, and the ad valorem portion of the duty grants protection to the finished-goods industry. In the United States, for example, there is a compound duty on woven fabrics (48.5 cents per kilogram plus 38 percent). The specific portion of the duty (48.5 cents) compensates U.S. fabric manufacturers for tariff protection granted to U.S. cotton producers, while the ad valorem portion of the duty (38 percent) provides protection for their own woven fabrics.

EFFECTIVE RATE OF PROTECTION

A main objective of an import tariff is to protect domestic producers from foreign competition. By increasing the domestic price of an import, a tariff serves to make home-produced goods more attractive to resident consumers. Output in the import-competing industry can thus expand beyond what would exist in the absence of a tariff. The degree of protection afforded by a tariff reflects the extent to which domestic prices can rise above foreign prices before the home producers are priced out of the market.

The **nominal tariff rate** published in a country's tariff schedule gives us a general idea of the

level of protection afforded the home industry. But it may not always truly indicate the actual, or effective, protection given. For example, it is not necessarily true that a 25-percent import tariff on an automobile provides the domestic auto industry a protective margin of 25 percent against foreign producers. This is because the nominal tariff rates apply only to the total value of the final import product. But in the production process, the home import-competing industry may use imported material inputs or intermediate products that are subject to a different tariff than that on the final product; in this case, the **effective tariff rate** will differ from the nominal tariff rate.[1]

The effective tariff rate is an indicator of the actual level of protection that a nominal tariff rate provides the domestic import-competing producers. It signifies *the total increase in domestic productive activities (value added) that an existing tariff structure makes possible,* compared with what would occur under free-trade conditions. The effective rate tells us how much more expensive domestic production can be relative to foreign production and still compete in the market.

Assume that the domestic radio industry adds value to imported inputs by assembling component radio parts imported from abroad. Suppose the imported components can enter the home country on a duty-free basis. Suppose also that 20 percent of a radio's final value can be attributed to domestic assembly activities (value added), the remaining 80 percent reflecting the value of the imported components. Furthermore, let the cost of the radio components be the same for both the domestic country and the foreign country. Finally, assume that the foreign country can produce a radio for $100.

Suppose the home country imposes a nominal tariff of 10 percent on finished radios, so that the domestic import price rises from $100 to $110 per unit (see Table 5.3). Does this mean that home producers are afforded an effective rate of

---

[1] The effective tariff is a measure that applies to a single nation. In a world of floating exchange rates, if all nominal or effective tariff rates rose, the effect would be offset by a change in the exchange rate.

Table 5.3 The Effective Rate of Protection

Foreign Radio Import	Cost	Domestic Competing Radio	Cost
Component parts	$ 80	Component parts	$ 80
Assembly activity (value added)	20	Assembly activity (value added)	30 (?)
Nominal tariff	10	Domestic price	$110
Import price	$110		

protection equal to 10 percent? Certainly not! The imported component parts enter the country duty-free (at a nominal tariff rate less than that on the finished import product), so the effective rate of protection is 50 percent. Compared with what would exist under free trade, domestic radio producers can be 50 percent more costly in their assembly activities and still be competitive!

Table 5.3 shows the figures in detail. Under free trade (zero tariff), a foreign radio could be imported for $100. To meet this price, domestic producers would have to hold their assembly costs down to $20. But under the protective umbrella of the tariff, domestic producers can afford to pay up to $30 for assembly and still meet the $110 domestic price of imported radios. The result is that domestic assembly costs could rise to a level of 50 percent above what would exist under free-trade conditions: ($30 − $20) / $20 = 0.5.

In general, the effective tariff rate is given by the following formula:

$$e = \frac{(n - ab)}{(1 - a)}$$

where

- e = the effective rate of protection
- n = the nominal tariff rate on the final product
- a = the ratio of the value of the imported input to the value of the final product
- b = the nominal tariff rate on the imported input

When the values from the radio example are plugged into this formula, we obtain

$$e = \frac{0.1 - 0.8\,(0)}{1 - 0.8}$$
$$= 0.5.$$

The nominal tariff rate of 10 percent levied on the final import product thus affords domestic production activities an effective degree of protection equal to 50 percent—five times the nominal rate.

Two consequences of the effective-rate calculation are worthy of mention. First, the degree of effective protection increases as the value added by domestic producers declines (the ratio of the value of the imported input to the value of the final product increases). In the formula, the higher the value of a, the greater the effective-protection rate for any given nominal tariff rate on the final product. Second, a tariff on imports used in the production process reduces the level of effective protection. The higher the value of b, the lower the effective-protection rate for any given nominal tariff on the final product. In the formula, as b rises, the numerator of the formula decreases and hence e decreases. Note that is possible for the effective-tariff rate to assume a negative value, depending on the values of the components in the formula for the calculation of the effective-tariff rate.

Generalizing from this analysis, *when material inputs or intermediate products enter a country at a very low duty while the final imported commodity is protected by a high duty, the result tends to be a high protection rate for the domestic producers.* The nominal-tariff rate on finished goods thus understates the effective rate of protection. But should a tariff be imposed on imported inputs that exceeds that on the finished good, the nominal-tariff rate on the finished product would tend to overstate its protective effect. Such a situation might occur if the home government desired to protect suppliers of raw materials more than domestic manufacturers.

TARIFF ESCALATION

As illustrated in Table 5.4, in many industrialized nations the effective rate of protection is more than twice the nominal rate. An apparently low nominal tariff on a final import product may thus understate the effective rate of protection, which takes into account the effects of tariffs levied on raw materials and intermediate goods. In addition, the tariff structures of industrialized nations have generally been characterized by rising rates that give greater protection to intermediate and finished products than to primary commodities. This is commonly referred to as **tariff escalation**. Although raw materials are often imported at zero or low tar-

iff rates, the nominal and effective protection increases at each stage of production. Many industrialized nations afford a relatively high degree of protection to their manufacturing sector, as suggested in Table 5.5.

The tariff structures of the industrialized nations may indeed discourage the growth of processing and manufacturing industries in the less-developed nations. The industrialized nations' low tariffs on primary commodities encourage the developing nations to expand operations in these sectors, while the high protective rates levied on manufactured goods pose a significant entry barrier for any developing nation wishing to compete in this area. From the point of view of the less-developed nations, it may be in their best interest to discourage disproportionate tariff reductions on raw materials. The effect of these tariff reductions is to magnify the discrepancy between the nominal and effective tariffs of the industrialized nations, worsening the potential competitive position of the less-developed nations in the manufacturing and processing sectors.

Table 5.4   Nominal and Effective Tariff Rates*

Product	United States		Japan		European Union	
	Nominal Rate (%)	Effective Rate (%)	Nominal Rate (%)	Effective Rate (%)	Nominal Rate (%)	Effective Rate (%)
Agriculture, forestry, fish	1.8	1.9	18.4	21.4	4.8	4.1
Food, beverages, tobacco	4.7	10.6	25.4	50.3	10.1	17.8
Textiles	9.2	18.0	3.3	2.4	7.2	8.8
Wearing apparel	22.7	43.3	13.8	42.2	13.4	19.3
Leather products	4.2	5.0	3.0	-14.8	2.0	-2.2
Footwear	8.8	15.4	15.7	50.0	11.6	20.1
Wood products	1.6	1.7	0.3	-30.6	2.5	1.7
Furniture and fixtures	4.1	5.5	5.1	10.3	5.6	11.3
Paper and paper products	0.2	-0.9	2.1	1.8	5.4	8.3
Printing and publishing	0.7	0.9	0.1	-1.5	2.1	-1.0

*Following the completion of the Tokyo Round of Multilateral Trade Negotiations in 1979.

Source: Alan Deardorff and Robert Stern, "The Effects of the Tokyo Round on the Structure of Protection," in R. Baldwin and A. Krueger, *The Structure and Evolution of Recent U.S. Trade Policy*, Chicago, University of Chicago Press, 1984, pp. 368–377.

Table 5.5 Tariff Escalation on Industrial Countries' Imports from Developing Countries: Post–Uruguay Round Nominal Tariffs

	Nominal Tariff
All industrial products (excluding petroleum)	
Raw materials	0.8%
Semimanufactures	2.8
Finished products	6.2
All tropical industrial products	
Raw materials	0.0
Semimanufactures	3.5
Finished products	2.6
Natural-resource-based products	
Raw materials	2.0
Semimanufacturers	2.0
Finished products	5.9

Source: General Agreement on Tariffs and Trade, *Final Act Embodying the Results of the Uruguay Round of Multilateral Trade Negotiations*, Geneva, GATT Trade Negotiations Committee, 1994. See also World Economic and Financial Surveys, *International Trade Policies: The Uruguay Round and Beyond: Volume II, Background Papers*, Washington, DC, International Monetary Fund, 1994.

PRODUCTION SHARING AND OFFSHORE-ASSEMBLY PROVISION

Production sharing is a key aspect of our global economy. Production sharing occurs when certain aspects of a product's manufacture are performed in more than one country. For example, electronic components made in the United States are shipped to a regionally accessible country with low labor costs, say, Singapore, for assembly into television sets. The assembled sets are then returned to the United States for further processing or packaging and distribution. This *foreign assembly* type of production sharing has evolved into an important competitive strategy for many U.S. producers of low-cost, labor-intensive products. Market share, in the United States and abroad, can often be preserved as a result of improvements in cost competitiveness by way of foreign assembly, which allows firms to retain higher production and employment levels in the United States than might otherwise be possible.

In addition to the use of foreign assembly plants to reduce labor costs, production-sharing operations may be designed to penetrate foreign markets where high tariffs or other trade barriers restrict direct export of finished goods. Production sharing may also take advantage of a certain unique foreign production technology, labor skills, raw materials, or specialized components. Table 5.6 provides examples of production sharing for the United States.

U.S. trade policy includes an **offshore-assembly provision (OAP)** that provides favorable treatment to products assembled abroad from U.S.-manufactured components. Under OAP, when a finished component originating in the United States (such as a semiconductor) is sent overseas and there is assembled with one or more other components to become a finished good (such as a television set), the cost of the U.S. component is not included in the dutiable value of the imported assembled article into which it has been incorporated. U.S. import duties thus apply only to the *value added in the foreign assembly process*, provided that U.S.-made components are used by overseas companies in their assembly

Table 5.6	U.S. Production Sharing: Use of U.S. Components and Materials in Foreign Assembly Operations

Country	Products
Dominican Republic	Medical goods, apparel
El Salvador	Apparel
Honduras	Apparel
Hong Kong	Semiconductors
Malaysia	Semiconductors
Mexico	Apparel, autos and parts, wiring harnesses, internal combustion engines
Philippines	Semiconductors
South Korea	Semiconductors

Source: U.S. International Trade Commission, *Production Sharing: Use of U.S. Components and Materials in Foreign Assembly Operations, 1992–1995*, April 1997.

operations. Manufactured goods entering the United States under OAP have included motor vehicles, office machines, television sets, aluminum cans, and semiconductors.

The U.S. OAP pertains not only to U.S. firms, but to foreign companies as well. For example, a U.S. computer company could produce components in the United States, send them to Taiwan for assembly, and ship computers back to the United States under favorable OAP. Alternatively, a Japanese photocopier firm desiring to export to the United States could purchase U.S.-manufactured components, assemble them in Malaysia, and ship photocopiers to the United States under favorable OAP.

Suppose that the United States imports television sets from South Korea at a price of $300 per set. If the tariff rate on such televisions is 10 percent, a duty of $30 would be paid on each television entering the United States, and the price to the U.S. consumer would be $330.[2] Now, suppose that U.S. components are used in the televi-

sion sets assembled by the Koreans and that these components have a value of $200. Under OAP, the 10-percent U.S. tariff rate is levied on the value of the imported set minus the value of the U.S. components used in manufacturing the set. When the set enters the United States, its dutiable value is thus $300 − $200 = $100, and the duty is 0.1 × $100 = $10. The price to the U.S. consumer after the tariff has been levied is $300 + $10 = $310. With the OAP system, the consumer is better off because the effective tariff rate is only 3.3 percent ($10 / $300) instead of the 10 percent shown in the tariff schedule.

The OAP provides potential advantages for the United States. By reducing import tariffs on foreign-assembled sets embodying U.S. components, OAP provides incentives for Korean manufacturers desiring to export to the United States to purchase components from U.S. sources; this generates sales and jobs in the U.S. component industries. However, television-assembly workers in the United States object to OAP, which they claim exports jobs that rightfully belong to U.S. workers; it is in their interest to lobby for the abolition of OAP.

POSTPONING IMPORT DUTIES

Import duties may have unintended side effects for some businesses. For example, duties may discourage a company from importing goods in amounts large enough to take advantage of quantity discount pricing. Before imported goods are released by the U.S. Customs Service, import duties must be paid, or a bond must be posted to guarantee their payment. Up-front payment of these duties may impose financial hardships on importers.

Consider a U.S. assembler who uses imported components. By purchasing its annual requirement of components at one time and shipping it in bulk, the firm could reduce the cost of the imported components. Paying the import duty on the entire year's supply of components at one time, however, might be too expensive for the importer.

---

[2] This assumes that the United States is a "small" country, as discussed later in this chapter.

U.S. trade laws mitigate the effects of import duties by allowing U.S. importers to postpone and prorate over time their duty obligations through bonded warehouses and foreign-trade zones.

BONDED WAREHOUSE According to U.S. tariff law, dutiable imports can be brought into a customs territory and left in a **bonded warehouse**, duty-free. These storage facilities are operated under the lock and key of the U.S. Customs Service. Owners of storage facilities must be bonded to ensure that they will satisfy all customs duty obligations.

Imported goods can be stored, repacked, or further processed in the bonded warehouse. As long as the products are kept in the bonded warehouse, the duty obligation is postponed. The goods may later be sold duty-free overseas or withdrawn for domestic sale upon payment of import duties. When goods are processed in a bonded warehouse with additional domestic materials and enter the domestic market at a later date, only the imported portion of the finished good is subject to customs duties.

Bonded warehouses are sometimes used for reexportation. Imported goods are stored in the bonded warehouse until suitable foreign markets can be found. If these goods are not stored in a bonded warehouse, the importer must pay duty on them when they enter the country. The importer can then claim a refund of 99 percent of the duties paid, referred to as a *drawback*, after they have been reexported. By using a bonded warehouse, however, a business can avoid the delay and costs associated with customs clearance and drawback application connected with reexport.

FOREIGN-TRADE ZONE Because of inspection and surveillance by the U.S. Customs Service, storage in bonded warehouses is generally more costly than in ordinary storage facilities. As a less expensive alternative, the U.S. government permits importers to use a **foreign-trade zone (FTZ)**. FTZs enlarge the benefits of a bonded warehouse by eliminating the restrictive aspects of customs surveillance and by offering more suitable manufacturing facilities.

An FTZ is a site within the United States where foreign merchandise can be imported without formal U.S. customs entry (payment of customs duties) or government excise taxes. FTZs are intended to stimulate international trade, attract industry, and create jobs by providing an area that gives users tariff and tax breaks. Merchandise in the zone can be stored, used in manufacturing or assembling a final product, or handled in several other ways.

In 1970, there were 17 FTZs in the United States; as of 2000, there were more than 240 FTZs housing more than 2,500 firms. Many are situated at seaports, but some are located at inland distribution points. Despite their growing importance, FTZs account for only about 2 percent of the merchandise exports and imports of the United States. Among the businesses that enjoy FTZ status are Caterpillar, Chrysler, Eli Lilly and Co., General Electric, and International Business Machines (IBM).

By offering cost savings to U.S. importers and exporters, FTZs encourage international competitiveness. Companies importing merchandise into an FTZ enhance their cash flow because they do not pay customs duties or federal excise taxes until the goods are shipped out of the zone to U.S. markets. If a good is shipped from an FTZ to a foreign country, no U.S. import duty is imposed on the good. For example, in an FTZ located in Seattle, optical equipment is assembled using lenses from Japan, prisms from Germany, plastic castings from the United Kingdom, precision mechanisms from Switzerland, and control instruments from France. In an FTZ located in Kansas City, Kansas, pool tables and related equipment are produced using frames from the United States, slate from Italy, balls from Belgium, rubber from Japan, and cue sticks from Taiwan. U.S. Customs Service officials monitor the FTZs by performing audits and spot inspections.

Besides seeing FTZs as a mechanism to reduce costs on imported components through deferral of duty payment, manufacturers have sought FTZ status to obtain relief from "inverted" tariff schedules—those that place higher duty rates on imported inputs than on the industry's final product. Manufacturers in the FTZ can reduce their tariff liability on components or raw materials with higher duty rates by zone processing or assembly into finished goods that enter the U.S. market at a lower duty rate.

In short, the principal financial advantages of an FTZ include (1) improved cash flow through payment of duties at shipment out of the warehouse or factory instead of on receipt at the facility; (2) no payment of tariffs on scrap, waste, or obsolete materials; (3) the option of paying the tariff on the imported materials or on the final product shipped from the zone, whichever is less; (4) no tariff duty on the value of the labor, overhead, and profit incurred in zone processing in the United States; and (5) no tariff owed on exported merchandise.

TARIFF WELFARE EFFECTS: CONSUMER SURPLUS AND PRODUCER SURPLUS

To analyze the effect of trade policies on national welfare, it is useful to separate the effects on consumers from those on producers. For each group, a measure of welfare is needed; these measures are known as consumer surplus and producer surplus.

Consumer surplus refers to the difference between the amount that buyers would be willing and able to pay for a good and the actual amount they do pay. To illustrate, assume that the price of a Pepsi is $.50. Being especially thirsty, suppose you would have been willing to pay up to $.75 for a Pepsi. Your consumer surplus on this purchase is $.25 ($.75 – $.50 = $.25). For all Pepsis bought, consumer surplus is merely the sum of the surplus for each unit.

Consumer surplus can also be depicted graphically. Let us first remember that (1) the height of

the market demand curve indicates the maximum price that buyers are willing and able to pay for each successive unit of the good, and (2) in a competitive market, buyers pay a single price (the equilibrium price) for all units purchased. Referring now to Figure 5.1(a), assume the market price of gasoline is $2 per gallon. If buyers purchase 4 gallons at this price, they spend $8, represented by area *ACED*. For those 4 gallons, buyers would have been willing and able to spend $12, as shown by area *ABCED*. The difference between what buyers actually spend and the amount they were willing and able to spend is consumer surplus; in this case, it equals $4 and is denoted by area *ABC*.

The size of consumer surplus is affected by the market price. A decrease in the market price will lead to an increase in the quantity purchased and a larger consumer surplus. Conversely, a higher market price will reduce the amount purchased and shrink the consumer surplus.

Let us now consider the other side of the market: producers. **Producer surplus** is the revenue producers receive over and above the minimum amount required to induce them to supply the good. This minimum amount has to cover the producer's total variable costs. Recall that total variable cost equals the sum of the marginal cost of producing each successive unit of output.

In Figure 5.1(b), producer surplus is represented by the area above the supply curve of gasoline and below the good's market price. Recall that the height of the market supply curve indicates the lowest price at which producers will be willing to supply gasoline; this minimum price increases with the level of output because of rising marginal costs. Suppose that the market price of gasoline is $2 per gallon, and 4 gallons are supplied. Producers receive revenues totaling $8, represented by area *ACDB*. The minimum revenue they must receive to produce 4 gallons equals total variable cost, which equals $4 and is depicted by area *BsCD*. Producer surplus is the difference, $4 ($8 – $4 = $4), and is depicted by area *ABC*.

If the market price of gasoline rises, more gasoline will be supplied, and producer surplus will

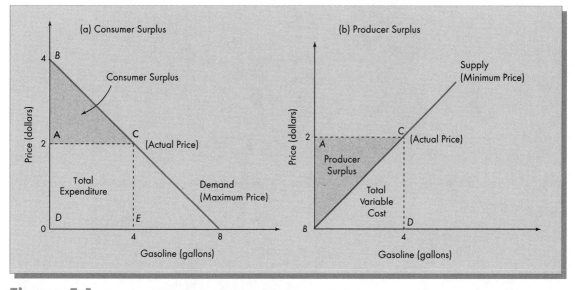

Figure 5.1 Consumer Surplus and Producer Surplus

Consumer surplus is the difference between the maximum amount buyers are willing to pay for a given quantity of a good and the amount actually paid. Graphically, consumer surplus is represented by the area under the demand curve and above the good's market price. Producer surplus is the revenue producers receive over and above the minimum necessary for production. Graphically, producer surplus is represented by the area above the supply curve and below the good's market price.

rise. It is equally true that if the market price of gasoline falls, producer surplus will fall. In the following sections, we will use the concepts of consumer surplus and producer surplus to analyze the effects of import tariffs on the nation's welfare.

TARIFF WELFARE EFFECTS: SMALL-NATION MODEL

To measure the effects of a tariff on a nation's welfare, consider the case of a nation whose imports constitute a very small portion of the world market supply. This **small nation** would be a *price taker*, facing a constant world price level for its import commodity. This is not a rare case; many nations are not important enough to influence the terms at which they trade.

In Figure 5.2, the small nation before trade produces at market equilibrium point E, as determined by the intersection of its domestic supply and demand schedules. At equilibrium price $9,500, the quantity supplied is 50 units, and the quantity demanded is 50 units. Now suppose that the economy is opened to foreign trade and that the world auto price is $8,000, less than the domestic price. Because the world market will supply an unlimited number of autos at price $8,000, the world supply schedule would appear as a horizontal (perfectly elastic) line. Line S_{d+w} shows the supply of autos available to the small-nation consumers from domestic and foreign sources combined. This overall supply schedule is the one that would prevail in free trade.

Free-trade equilibrium is located at point F in the figure. Here the number of autos demanded is 80 units, whereas the number produced

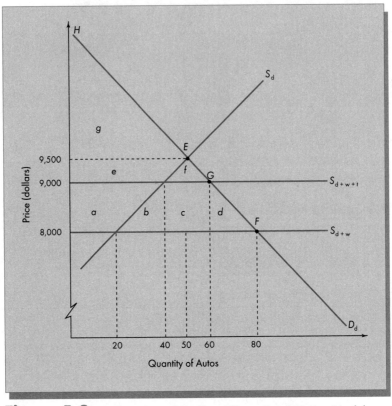

Figure 5.2 Tariff Trade and Welfare Effects: Small-Nation Model

For a small nation, a tariff placed on an imported product is shifted totally to the domestic consumer via a higher product price. Consumer surplus falls as a result of the price increase. The small nation's welfare decreases by an amount equal to the protective effect and consumption effect, the so-called deadweight losses due to a tariff.

domestically is 20 units. The excess domestic auto demand is fulfilled by imports of 60 autos. Compared with the situation before trade occurred, free trade results in a fall in the domestic auto price from $9,500 to $8,000. Consumers are better off because they can import more autos at a lower price. However, domestic producers now sell fewer autos at a lower price than they did before trade.

Under free trade, the domestic auto industry is being damaged by foreign competition. Industry sales and revenues are falling, and workers are losing their jobs. Suppose management and labor

unite and convince the government to levy a protective tariff on auto imports. Assume the small nation imposes a tariff of $1,000 on auto imports. Because this small nation is not important enough to influence world market conditions, the world supply price of autos remains constant, unaffected by the tariff. This means that the small nation's terms of trade remains unchanged. The introduction of *the tariff raises the home price of imports by the full amount of the duty, and the increase falls entirely on the domestic consumer.* The overall supply shifts upward by the amount of the tariff, from S_{d+w} to S_{d+w+t}.

CALCULATING THE WELFARE EFFECTS OF A TARIFF

Figure 5.2 presents the welfare effects of a tariff in dollar terms. For example, the dollar value of the consumption effect (area *d*) equals $10,000. It is easy to carry out the calculation of triangular area *d*. Recall from geometry that the area of a triangle equals (base × height) / 2. The height of the triangle ($1,000) equals the price increase in autos due to the tariff; the base (20 autos) equals the reduction in domestic consumption due to the tariff. The consumption effect is thus (20 × $1,000) / 2 = $10,000.

Similarly, the dollar value of the protective effect (area *b*) equals $10,000. The height of

the triangle equals the increase in price due to the tariff ($1,000); the triangle's base (20 autos) equals the increase in domestic auto production due to the tariff. The protection effect is thus (20 × $1,000) / 2 = $10,000.

The calculation of all such "triangular" welfare effects of tariffs (and other protectionist devices) is based on the same formula. The reader will find this formula useful for calculating the welfare effects of trade barriers in response to the study questions at the end of chapters.

The protective tariff results in a new equilibrium quantity at point *G*, where the domestic auto price is $9,000. Domestic production increases by 20 units, whereas domestic consumption falls by 20 units. Imports decrease from their pretariff level of 60 units to 20 units. This reduction can be attributed to falling domestic consumption and rising domestic production. The effects of the tariff are to impede imports and protect domestic producers. But what are the tariff's effects on the national welfare?

Figure 5.2 shows that before the tariff was levied, consumer surplus equaled areas *a* + *b* + *c* + *d* + *e* + *f* + *g*. With the tariff, consumer surplus falls to areas *e* + *f* + *g*, an overall loss in consumer surplus equal to areas *a* + *b* + *c* + *d*. This change affects the nation's welfare in a number of ways. The welfare effects of a tariff include a revenue effect, a redistribution effect, a protective effect, and a consumption effect. As might be expected, the tariff provides the government with additional tax revenue and benefits domestic auto producers; at the same time, however, it wastes resources and harms the domestic consumer.

The tariff's **revenue effect** represents the government's collections of duty. Found by multiplying the number of imports (20 units) times the tariff ($1,000), government revenue equals area *c*, or $20,000. This represents the portion

of the loss of consumer surplus, in monetary terms, that is transferred to the government. For the nation as a whole, the revenue effect does not result in an overall welfare loss; consumer surplus is merely shifted from the private to the public sector.

The **redistributive effect** is the transfer of consumer surplus, in monetary terms, to the domestic producers of the import-competing product. This is represented by area *a*, which equals $30,000. Under the tariff, domestic home consumers will buy from domestic firms 40 autos at a price of $9,000, for a total expenditure of $360,000. At the free-trade price of $8,000, the same 40 autos would have yielded $320,000. The imposition of the tariff thus results in home producers' receiving additional revenues totaling areas *a* + *b*, or $40,000 (the difference between $360,000 and $320,000). As the tariff encourages domestic production to rise from 20 to 40 units, however, producers must pay part of the increased revenue as higher costs of producing the increased output, depicted by area *b*, or $10,000. The remaining revenue, $30,000, area *a*, is a net gain in producer income. The redistributive effect, therefore, is a transfer of income from consumers to producers. Like the revenue effect, it does not result in an overall loss of welfare for the economy.

Area *b*, totaling $10,000, is referred to as the **protective effect** of the tariff. It illustrates the loss to the domestic economy resulting from wasted resources used to produce additional autos at increasing unit costs. As the tariff-induced domestic output expands, resources that are less adaptable to auto production are eventually used, increasing unit production costs. This means that resources are used less efficiently than they would have been with free trade, in which case autos would have been purchased from low-cost foreign producers. A tariff's protective effect thus arises because less efficient domestic production is substituted for more efficient foreign production. Referring to Figure 5.2, as domestic output increases from 20 to 40 units, the domestic cost of producing autos rises, as shown by supply schedule S_d. But the same increase in autos could have been obtained at a unit cost of $8,000 before the tariff was levied. Area *b*, which depicts the protective effect, represents a loss to the economy.

Most of the consumer surplus lost because of the tariff has been accounted for: *c* went to the government as revenue; *a* was transferred to home suppliers as income; and *b* was lost by the economy because of inefficient domestic production. The **consumption effect**, represented by area *d*, which equals $10,000, is the residual not accounted for elsewhere. It arises from the decrease in consumption resulting from the tariff's artificially increasing the price of autos from $8,000 to $9,000. A loss of welfare occurs because of the increased price and lower consumption. Like the protective effect, the consumption effect represents a real cost to society, not a transfer to other sectors of the economy. Together, these two effects equal the **deadweight loss** of the tariff (areas *b* + *d* in the figure).

As long as it is assumed that a nation accounts for a negligible portion of international trade, its levying an import tariff necessarily lowers its national welfare. This is because there is no favorable welfare effect resulting from the tariff that would offset the deadweight loss of consumer surplus. If a nation could impose a tariff that would improve its terms of trade vis-à-vis its trading partners, it would enjoy a larger share of the gains from trade. This would tend to increase its national welfare, offsetting the deadweight loss of consumer surplus. Because it is so insignificant relative to the world market, however, a small nation is unable to influence the terms of trade. Levying an import tariff, therefore, reduces a small nation's welfare.

TARIFF WELFARE EFFECTS: LARGE-NATION MODEL

Now consider the case of an importing nation that is large enough so that changes in the quantity of its imports, by means of tariff policy, influence the world price of the product. This **large-nation** case could apply to the United States, which is a large importer of autos, steel, oil, and consumer electronics, and to other economic giants such as Japan and the European Union.

If the United States imposes a tariff on automobile imports, prices increase for American consumers. The result is a decrease in the quantity demanded, which may be significant enough to force Japanese firms to reduce the prices of their exports. Because Japanese firms can produce and export smaller amounts at a lower marginal cost, they are likely to prefer to reduce their price to the United States to limit the decrease in their sales to the United States. The tariff incidence is thus shared between U.S. consumers, who pay a higher price than under free trade for each auto imported, and Japanese firms, which realize a lower price than under free trade for each auto exported. The difference between these two prices is the tariff duty. U.S. welfare rises when the United States can shift some of the tariff to Japanese firms via export price reductions. The terms of trade improves for the United States at the expense of Japan.

Table 5.7 illustrates the extent to which U.S. import tariffs can reduce world prices of imported goods. For example, an 11-percent increase in

Table 5.7 Effects of Increases in U.S. Tariffs on the World Price of Imported Goods

Product	Tariff (or Equivalent)	Increase in U.S. Price	Decrease in World Price
Ball bearings	11.0%	10.2%	0.8%
Chemicals	9.0	6.5	2.5
Footwear	20.0	16.1	3.9
Glassware	11.0	7.3	3.7
Jewelry	9.0	5.4	3.6
Luggage	16.5	11.0	5.5
Lumber	6.5	4.1	2.4
Orange juice	30.0	21.7	8.3
Resins	12.0	5.4	6.6

Source: G. Hufbauer and K. Elliot, *Measuring the Costs of Protection in the United States*, Washington, DC, Institute for International Economics, 1994, pp. 28–29.

the U.S. tariff on ball-bearing imports would increase the price to the American consumer by an estimated 10.2 percent. This leads to a decrease in the quantity of ball bearings demanded in the United States and a 0.8 percent decrease in the world price.

What are the economic effects of an import tariff for a large country? Referring to Figure 5.3, line S_d represents the domestic supply schedule, and line D_d depicts the home demand schedule. Autarky equilibrium occurs at point E. With free trade, the importing nation faces a total supply schedule of S_{d+w}. This schedule shows the number of autos that both domestic and foreign producers together offer domestic consumers. The total supply schedule is upward sloping rather than horizontal because the foreign supply price is not a fixed constant. The price depends on the quantity purchased by an importing country when it is a large buyer of the product. With free trade, our country achieves market equilibrium at point F. The price of autos falls to $8,000, domestic consumption rises to 110 units, and domestic production falls to 30 units. Auto imports totaling 80 units satisfy the excess domestic demand.

Suppose that the importing nation imposes a specific tariff of $1,000 on imported autos. By increasing the selling cost, the tariff results in a shift in the total supply schedule from S_{d+w}

to S_{d+w+t}. Market equilibrium shifts from point F to point G, while product price rises from $8,000 to $8,800. The tariff-levying nation's consumer surplus falls by an amount equal to areas $a + b + c + d$. Area a, totaling $32,000, represents the *redistributive effect*; this amount is transferred from domestic consumers to domestic producers. Areas $d + b$ depict the tariff's deadweight loss, the deterioration in national welfare because of reduced consumption (*consumption effect* = $8,000) and an inefficient use of resources (*protective effect* = $8,000).

As in the small-nation example, a tariff's *revenue effect* equals the import tariff multiplied by the quantity of autos imported. This yields areas $c + e$, or $40,000. Notice, however, that the tariff revenue accruing to the government now comes from foreign producers as well as domestic consumers. This differs from the small-nation case, in which the supply schedule is horizontal and the tariff's burden falls entirely on domestic consumers.

The tariff of $1,000 is added to the free-trade import price of $8,000. Although the price in the protected market will exceed the foreign supply price by the amount of the duty, it will not exceed the free-trade foreign supply price by this amount. Compared with the free-trade foreign supply price, $8,000, the domestic consumers

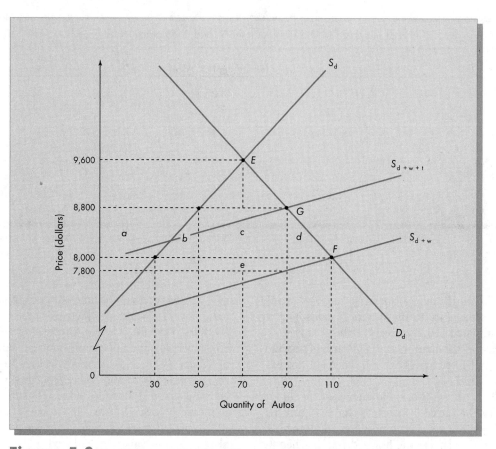

Figure 5.3 Tariff Trade and Welfare Effects: Large-Nation Model

For a large nation, a tariff on an imported product may be partially shifted to the domestic consumer via a higher product price and partially absorbed by the foreign exporter via a lower export price. The extent by which a tariff is absorbed by the foreign exporter constitutes a welfare gain for the home country. This gain offsets some (all) of the deadweight welfare losses due to the tariff's consumption effect and protective effect.

pay only an additional $800 per imported auto. This is the portion of the tariff shifted forward to the consumer. At the same time, the foreign supply price of autos falls by $200. This means that foreign producers earn smaller revenues, $7,800, for each auto exported. Because foreign production takes place under increasing-cost conditions, the reduction of imports from abroad triggers a decline in foreign production, and unit costs decline. The reduction in the foreign supply price, $200, represents that portion of the tariff

borne by the foreign producer. The levying of the tariff raises the domestic price of the import by only part of the duty, as foreign producers lower their prices in an attempt to maintain sales in the tariff-levying nation. The importing nation finds that its terms of trade has improved if the price it pays for auto imports decreases while the price it charges for its exports remains the same.

Thus, the *revenue effect* of an import tariff in the large-nation case includes two components. The first is the amount of tariff revenue shifted

COSTS TO THE CONSUMER OF PRESERVING A PRODUCTION WORKER'S JOB

Saving Jobs: Consumer Costs

Industry	Annual Cost to Consumers	
	Total (Millions of Dollars)	Per Job Saved (Dollars)
Specialty steel	520	1,000,000
Nonrubber footwear	700	55,000
Color TVs	420	42,000
Bolts, nuts, screws	110	550,000
Mushrooms	35	117,000
Automobiles	5,800	105,000
Textiles and apparel	27,000	42,000
Carbon steel	6,800	750,000
Motorcycles	104	150,000

Source: Gary Hufbauer et al., *Trade Protection in the United States: 31 Case Studies*, Washington, DC, Institute for International Economics, 1986, Tables 1.1 and 1.2.

Although import restrictions may provide benefits to domestic firms and workers, they are, in effect, a tax on the consumers of the protected products. Trade restraints result in an increase in the price and a decrease in the quantity of imported goods, which in turn increase the consumption of domestically produced goods as well as domestic prices.

A striking fact about protection to preserve jobs is that each job often ends up costing domestic consumers more than the worker's salary! As seen in the table, the consumer cost of protecting each job preserved in the auto industry in the United States is estimated to be $105,000 a year; this is far above the salary a production employee in that industry would receive. The fact that costs to consumers for each production job saved are so high underpins the argument that an alternative approach should be used to help workers, and that workers departing from an industry facing foreign competition should be liberally compensated (subsidized) for moving to new industries or taking early retirement.

from domestic consumers to the tariff-levying government; in Figure 5.3, this equals the level of imports (40 units) multiplied by the portion of the import tariff borne by domestic consumers ($800). Area c depicts the **domestic revenue effect**, which equals $32,000. The second element is the tariff revenue extracted from foreign producers in the form of a lower supply price. Found by multiplying auto imports (40 units) by the portion of the tariff falling on foreign producers ($200), the **terms-of-trade effect** is shown as area e, which equals $8,000. Note that the terms-of-trade effect represents a redistribution of income from the foreign nation to the tariff-levying nation because of the new terms of trade. The tariff's revenue effect thus includes the domestic revenue effect and the terms-of-trade effect.

A nation that is a major importer of a product is in a favorable trade situation. It can use its tariff policy to improve the terms at which it trades, and therefore its national welfare. But remember that the negative welfare effect of a tariff is the deadweight loss of consumer surplus that results from the protection and consumption effects.

Referring to Figure 5.3, to decide if a tariff-levying nation can improve its national welfare, we must compare the impact of the deadweight loss (areas $b + d$) with the benefits of a more favorable terms of trade (area e). The conclusions regarding the welfare effects of a tariff are as follows:

1. If $e > (b + d)$, national welfare is increased.
2. If $e = (b + d)$, national welfare remains constant.
3. If $e < (b + d)$, national welfare is diminished.

In the preceding example, the domestic economy's welfare would have declined by an amount equal to $8,000. This is because the deadweight welfare losses, totaling $16,000, more than offset the $8,000 gain in welfare attributable to the terms-of-trade effect.

We have seen that a large nation can improve its terms of trade by imposing a tariff on imports. However, a tariff causes the volume of imports to decrease, which lessens the nation's welfare by reducing its consumption of low-cost imports. There is thus a gain due to improved terms of trade and a loss due to reduced import volume. A nation optimizes its economic welfare by imposing a tariff rate at which the positive difference between the gain of improving terms of trade and the loss of declining import volume is maximized; an **optimum tariff** refers to such a tariff rate.

A likely candidate for a nation imposing an optimum tariff would be the United States; it is a large importer, compared with world demand, of autos, electronics, and other products. Note, however, that an optimum tariff is only beneficial to the importing nation. Because any benefit accruing to the importing nation through a lower import price implies a loss to the foreign exporting nation, imposing an optimum tariff is a **beggar-thy-neighbor policy** that could invite retaliation. After all, if the United States were to impose an optimal tariff of 25 percent on its imports, why should Japan and the European Union not levy tariffs of 40 or 50 percent on their imports? When all countries impose optimal tariffs, it is likely that everyone's economic welfare will decrease as impediments to free trade become great. The possibility of foreign retaliation may be a sufficient deterrent for any nation considering whether to impose higher tariffs.

A classic case of a tariff-induced trade war was the implementation of the Smoot-Hawley tariff by the U.S. government in 1930. The tariff was initially intended to provide relief to U.S. farmers. However, senators and members of Congress from industrial states used the technique of vote trading to obtain increased tariffs on manufactured goods. The result was a policy that increased tariffs on more than a thousand products, with an average nominal duty on protected goods of 53 percent! Viewing the Smoot-Hawley tariff as an attempt to force unemployment on its workers, 12 nations promptly increased their duties against the United States. U.S. farm exports fell to one-third of their former level, and between 1930 and 1933 total U.S. exports fell by almost 60 percent. Although the Great Depression accounted for much of that decline, the adverse psychological impact of the Smoot-Hawley tariff on business activity cannot be ignored.

TARIFF EXAMPLES

The previous section analyzed the welfare effects of import tariffs from a theoretical perspective. Now let us turn to some examples of import tariffs and examine estimates of their costs and benefits to the nation.

LAMB TARIFFS FLEECE U.S. CONSUMERS

In 1999, the U.S. government imposed stiff tariffs on imports of lamb to protect high-cost U.S. producers and provide stability to the domestic market. Consider the remarks on this matter of Douglas Irwin, a professor of economics at Dartmouth College.[3] Do you agree?

President Clinton dealt a serious blow to free trade last Wednesday, when he announced that the United States would impose stiff import tariffs on lamb from Australia and

[3] Douglas A. Irwin, "Lamb Tariffs Fleece U.S. Consumers, *The Wall Street Journal*, July 12, 1999, p. A28. Reprinted by permission.

New Zealand. His decision undercuts American leadership and makes a mockery of the administration's claims that it favors free and fair trade.

U.S. sheep producers have long been dependent on government. For more than half a century, until Congress enacted farm-policy reforms in 1995, they received subsidies for wool. Having lost that handout, saddled with high costs and inefficiencies, and facing domestic competition from chicken, beef, and pork, sheep producers sought to stop foreign competition by filing for import relief.

Almost all U.S. lamb imports come from Australia and New Zealand, major agricultural producers with a crushing comparative advantage. New Zealand has fewer than four million people but as many as 60 million sheep (compared with about seven million sheep in the United States). New Zealand's farmers have invested substantial resources in new technology and effective marketing, making them among the most efficient producers in the world. New Zealand also eliminated domestic agricultural subsidies in the free-market reforms of the 1980s and is a free-trading country, on track to eliminate all import tariffs by 2006.

Rather than emulate this example, the American Sheep Industry Association, among others, filed an "escape clause" petition under the Trade Act of 1974, which allows temporary "breathing space" protection to import-competing industries. Under the escape-clause provision, a petitioning industry is required to present an adjustment plan to ensure that it undertakes steps to become competitive in the future. The tariff protection is usually limited and scheduled to be phased out.

The U.S. International Trade Commission (ITC) determines whether imports are a cause of "serious injury" to the domestic industry and, if so, proposes a remedy, which the President has full discretion to adopt, change, or reject. In February, the ITC did not find that the domestic industry had suffered "serious injury" but rather adopted the weaker ruling that imports were a "substantial cause of threat of serious injury." The ITC did not propose to roll back imports, only to impose a 20-percent tariff (declining over four years) on imports above last year's levels.

The administration at first appeared to be considering less restrictive measures. Australia and New Zealand even offered financial assistance to the U.S. producers, and the administration delayed any announcement and appeared to be working toward a compromise. But these hopes were completely dashed with the shocking final decision, in which the administration capitulated to the demands of the sheep industry and its advocates in Congress.

The congressional charge was led by Sen. Max Baucus (Democrat, Montana), a member of the Agriculture Committee whose sister, a sheep producer, had appeared before the ITC to press for higher tariffs. The administration opted for far tighter trade restrictions than the ITC had proposed. On top of existing tariffs, the President imposed a 9-percent tariff on all imports in the first year (declining to 6 percent and then 3 percent in years two and three), and a whopping 40-percent tariff on imports above last year's levels (dropping to 32 percent and 24 percent).

These tariffs will roll back imports even though the ITC failed to find that the existing level of imports had caused the domestic industry any "serious injury." The American Sheep Industry Association's president happily announced that the move will "bring some stability to the market." Whenever producers speak of bringing stability to the market, you know that consumers are getting fleeced.

The lamb decision, while little noticed at home, has been closely followed abroad. The decision undercuts the administration's free-trade rhetoric and harms its efforts to get other countries to open up their markets. Some import relief had been expected, but not so clearly protectionist as what finally materialized. The extreme decision has outraged farmers in Australia and New Zealand, and *officials there have vowed to take the United States to a World Trade Organization (WTO) dispute settlement panel.*

The administration's timing could not have been worse. The decision came right after an Asia–Pacific Economic Cooperation summit reaffirmed its commitment to reduce trade barriers and a few months before the WTO's November meeting in Seattle, where the WTO hoped to launch a new round of multilateral trade negotiations. A principal U.S. objective at the summit was the reduction of agricultural protection in Europe and elsewhere.

In 1947, facing an election the next year, President Truman courageously resisted special interest pressure and vetoed a bill to impose import quotas on wool, which would have jeopardized the first postwar multilateral trade negotiations due to start later that year. In contrast, Mr. Clinton, though a lame duck, caved in to political pressure.

MOTORCYCLES There have been approximately 150 manufacturers of motorcycles in the United States since the first commercially produced motorcycle was manufactured in 1901. By the 1980s, there were one U.S.-owned firm, Harley-Davidson Motor Co., and two Japanese-owned firms, Kawasaki and Honda, operating in the United States. Harley specializes in the production of heavyweight motorcycles (1,000 and 1,300 cc).

In the early 1970s, Harley had 100 percent of the U.S. market for heavyweight motorcycles; by the early 1980s, its market share was less than 15 percent. During this decade, Harley continually lost ground to Japanese competitors such as Suzuki, Yamaha, Honda, and Kawasaki. Being used to tough competition, these Japanese firms were able to undercut Harley by $1,500 to $2,000 per motorcycle. Industry analysts maintained that Harley was plagued by inefficient production methods and poor management and that its per-unit costs were higher than those of the U.S. plants of Honda and Kawasaki.

During this period, Harley was the victim of a Honda–Yamaha struggle for domination of the motorcycle market. In the early 1980s, both Japanese motorcycle manufacturers flooded the U.S. market with a variety of new competitive models. Bloated Japanese inventories, stashed in U.S. dealerships and warehouses, estimated to be a year-and-a-half supply of new motorcycles, led to heavy price cuts and intense product promotion.

By 1982, Harley was rapidly approaching bankruptcy because of a recession and reduced demand for motorcycles, operating inefficiencies, and a massive debt problem. Harley was surviving on borrowed money from Citicorp, and the bank was becoming increasingly apprehensive about extending additional loans. Harley suffered a huge buildup in motorcycle inventories throughout 1982, which led to declines in profits, wages, and employment. In 1980, Harley had more than 4,000 employees; by the end of 1982, it had 2,200. Harley turned to the U.S. government for tariff protection that would result in reductions in Japanese motorcycle inventories and increases in the price of Japanese motorcycles. With massive layoffs of their members, union officials actively supported Harley's plea for protectionism. In hopes of forestalling possible trade restrictions, the Japanese motorcycle producers offered technical assistance and loan guarantees to Harley, which turned down the offers. Apparently, Harley felt that it could convince the government that import restrictions were justified.

In September 1982, Harley petitioned the U.S. government for protectionist relief from the importation of heavyweight motorcycles. The government concluded that rising motorcycle imports from Japan were a substantial cause of a threat of serious injury to Harley and that temporary protectionism was justified to permit Harley to recover from its injuries and provide it time to complete a comprehensive program to fully compete with the Japanese.

On April 1, 1983, the U.S. government implemented a five-year tariff program for heavyweight motorcycles (700 cc engines and larger). During the first year, the import tariff was raised from 4.4 percent to 49.4 percent; during the second year, the tariff was reduced to 39.4 percent; in the next three years, the tariff was cut by 15 percent, 5 percent, and 5 percent. After the fifth year, the tariff was to revert to 4.4 percent. The tariff hikes did not apply to motorcycle imports from Italy, Germany, and the United Kingdom, which accounted for less than 20 percent of U.S. imports of heavyweight motorcycles in 1982. The five-year tariff program was intended to allow Harley sufficient time to eliminate its excess inventories and to benefit from improved economies of scale obtained from increased sales and production.

The U.S. International Trade Commission (ITC) estimated the economic effects of the increased tariff on imported heavyweight motorcycles. During the first year of the tariff, motorcycle prices would increase 10 percent; prices would rise more than 12 percent during the second year as motorcycle inventories were reduced. The ITC felt that Harley would be restrained from raising prices to any significant degree by continued competition from motorcycles produced domestically by Honda and Kawasaki, as well as from imports. The ITC also estimated that during the first two years of the tariff program, overall motorcycle sales would fall by 20,000 units; however, sales of Harley-Davidson motorcycles would rise by more than 8,000 units. This would allow Harley to keep its plants operating.

But the substantial tariff looked much better on paper than it worked out in reality. Stung, Japanese motorcycle manufacturers reacted promptly to circumvent the tariff policy. They quickly downsized their 750-cc motorcycle engines to 699 cc, thus evading the tariff that applied to motorcycle imports having engines of 700 cc or more. The press dubbed these downsized models "tariff busters." The downsized engine wiped out approximately half of the tariff's value to Harley.

At the same time, Kawasaki and Honda quickly increased production of heavyweight motorcycles in their U.S. plants. That left only Suzuki and Yamaha motorcycles, with engines over 1,000 cc, subject to the tariff. And these manufacturers were permitted to ship 7,000 to 10,000 of these heavyweight motorcycles to the United States before they had to start paying the extra import duty.

Although the outcome of the tariff was disappointing to Harley, two of its important objectives were accomplished—ending the escalation of U.S. motorcycle inventories by Japanese firms and liquidating the large stock of motorcycles already in dealers' showrooms and warehouses. This liquidation, however, occurred at discounted prices, which put further competitive pressure on Harley.

As the 1980s continued, Harley's economic performance improved. By 1987, Harley enjoyed record profits of almost $18 million. It also enjoyed a 40-percent market share in the superheavyweight motorcycle class, 11 percentage points ahead of its closest rival, Honda, and 17 points above its 1983 low of 23 percent. In March 1987, Harley announced that it no longer needed special tariffs to compete with the Japanese motorcycle firms. Harley indicated that, given temporary relief from predatory import practices, it had become competitive in world markets.[4]

JAPANESE LUXURY CARS In 1995, the Clinton Administration threatened to increase tariffs on imported Japanese luxury cars from the existing 2.9 percent to fully 100 percent. The proposed tariff hike was an attempt to pressure the Japanese into opening their markets for U.S. autos and auto parts. U.S. officials contended that the Japanese discriminated against American-made products, which Washington felt were just as good as those manufactured in Japan; if the U.S. government shut down Japan's luxury-car business in the United States, the Japanese might change their objectionable practices.

Thirteen luxury models produced by Toyota, Nissan, Honda, Mazda, and Mitsubishi were targeted for increased duties. These models were critical to Japanese automakers: More than

---

[4] Daniel Klein, "Taking America for a Ride: The Politics of Motorcycle Tariffs," *Cato Institute Policy Analysis*, No. 32, January 1984. See also U.S. International Trade Commission, *Heavyweight Motorcycles, and Engines and Power Train Subassemblies Therefor*, Washington, DC, Government Printing Office, February 1983; and Peter Reid, *Well Made in America* (New York: McGraw-Hill, 1989).

200,000 units had been sold in the United States the previous year, and they provided higher profit margins than less-expensive models.

The higher tariff would dramatically increase the price of Japanese luxury cars compared with their U.S. and European competitors. Because such price increases would likely drive most U.S. consumers out of Japanese showrooms, Japanese automakers might attempt to swallow the increased tariffs and avoid raising prices; this action appeared unlikely given a sluggish Japanese auto market and an appreciating yen that had led to decreased profits in the U.S. market. The tariff's likely impact would be plummeting sales of Japanese luxury models. Table 5.8 illustrates the likely losers and winners from the punitive tariffs.

The Big Three Detroit automakers issued jubilant statements following the announcement of the proposed tariffs. The tariffs could

Table 5.8   Likely Losers and Winners from a 100-Percent Tariff Applied to Japanese Luxury Autos

Sanctions against Tokyo would have significantly increased the price of Japanese luxury cars in the U.S. market. Below are some of the American and European models that stood to profit from the sanctions.*

Japanese Loser	U.S./European Winner
Lexus LS400 $51,680 → $88,000	BMW 740i $57,900
Nissan Infiniti Q45 $52,850 → $89,000	Jaguar XJ6 $53,450
Lexus ES300 $31,980 → $54,000	Lincoln Mark VIII $38,800
Acura Legend $37,000 → $62,900	Oldsmobile Aurora $31,370
Mazda Millenia $26,435 → $45,000	Buick Riviera $27,632

*Estimated increase in price under higher tariffs were based on 70 percent of the current retail price.

Source: Bill Diem, *Automotive News*. See also "Trade Warrior," *Newsweek*, May 29, 1995, pp. 46-47.

fatten profits for General Motors, Ford, and DaimlerChrysler in the luxury-car segment, where they had lost market share to the Japanese. The Big Three promised the U.S. government they wouldn't be greedy and raise prices under the tariff umbrella. But history shows that whenever an artificial restriction is imposed on the market, consumers end up paying more. Moreover, industry analysts maintained that the tariffs would not significantly add to U.S. car sales. Consider the Lincoln Town Car, Ford's big luxury car, or the Cadillac Seville, GM's big luxury car. Both sold in the mid-$30,000 range in 1995. Market surveys showed that U.S. car buyers were reluctant to cross-shop when looking for a new vehicle; if they wanted to buy a $50,000 import like the Infiniti or Lexus, they were unlikely to consider a U.S.-made vehicle, despite price. They would likely switch to luxury European autos such as BMW and Mercedes, considered of similar quality to Japanese vehicles. With the tariff, however, European automakers would have the incentive to raise prices in the United States. The result would be higher prices for the U.S. consumer without increased production for the Big Three Detroit automakers.

In the end, the United States did not impose the 100-percent tariff on Japanese luxury automobiles. Instead, Japan and the United States negotiated an automobile pact that obligated Japan to open its automotive market to the United States.

WHO PAYS FOR IMPORT RESTRICTIONS?

Empirical studies often maintain that the total cost of trade restrictions can be high. Trade restrictions also affect the distribution of income within a society. A legitimate concern of government officials is whether the welfare costs of protectionism are shared uniformly by all people in a country, or whether some income groups absorb a disproportionate share of the costs.

EFFECTS OF ELIMINATING IMPORT TARIFFS

Eliminating Import Tariffs: Gains and Losses

Import-Competing Industry	Millions of Dollars			Job Loss (in Thousands)
	Consumer Gain	Producer Loss	Domestic Tax Loss	
Rubber footwear	$272.2	$44.1	$28.5	2.4
Women's footwear	325.1	54.6	38.0	3.5
Ceramic tile	90.0	10.0	11.6	0.4
Luggage	186.3	36.4	21.0	1.8
Women's handbags	134.4	25.7	15.5	1.6
Glasswear	185.8	77.2	14.8	2.5
Resins	93.1	45.1	5.8	1.1
Bicycles	38.1	10.0	4.0	0.6
Ball bearings	50.3	3.9	6.9	0.1
Canned tuna	61.3	35.0	3.2	0.8
Cedar shingles	25.3	11.5	6.1	0.1

Source: U.S. International Trade Commission, *The Economic Effects of Significant U.S. Import Restraints, Phase 1: Manufacturing*, Washington, DC, Government Printing Office, October 1989, Tables ES-1 and ES-2.

What would be the effects if the United States unilaterally removed tariffs on imported products? On the positive side, tariff elimination lowers the price of the affected imports and may lower the price of the competing U.S. good, resulting in economic gains to the U.S. consumer. On the negative side, the lower price to import-competing producers, as a result of eliminating the tariff, results in profit reductions; workers become displaced from the domestic industry that loses protection; and the U.S. government loses tax revenue as the result of eliminating the tariff. The table gives estimates of the short-run effects that would occur in the first year after tariff removals.

A Federal Reserve study considered the income-distribution effects of import restraints. It concluded that import restraints tend to be inequitable because they impose the most severe costs on *low-income families.* Tariffs, for example, are often applied to products at the lower end of the price and quality range. Basic products such as clothing are subject to tariffs, and these items constitute large shares of the budgets of low-income families. Import restraints thus can be likened to sales taxed on the products protected, and, as typically occurs with sales taxes, their effects are *regressive.*

The Federal Reserve study estimated the price increases caused by import restrictions on sugar, automobiles, and clothing. The calculations were then used to estimate the "income tax surcharge" equivalent (i.e., the amount of additional tax placed on consumers) of trade restrictions for various income groups in the United States. As shown in Table 5.9, for low-income families (below $9,350 a year), the price increases from trade restrictions are equivalent to a 66-percent income tax increase. But for high-income families ($58,500 a year), the identical price increases are equivalent to a 5-percent income tax increase.

Table 5.9   Tax Effect of U.S. Import Restrictions, 1984

Income Range	Income Tax Surcharge Equivalent (%)
$ 7,000–9,350	66
9,350–11,700	47
11,700–14,050	39
14,050–16,400	33
16,400–18,700	28
18,700–23,400	24
23,400–28,050	20
28,050–35,100	17
35,100–46,800	13
46,800–58,500	10
58,500 and over	5

Source: Susan Hickok, "The Consumer Cost of U.S. Trade Restraints," Federal Reserve Bank of New York, *Quarterly Review*, Summer 1985, pp. 10–11.

These figures help us understand why President Bill Clinton restricted the proposed punitive 100-percent tariff to luxury cars during the 1995 trade conflict between the United States and Japan. Lower-income households do not typically purchase an Infiniti or an Acura Legend. If imposed, Clinton's punitive restrictions would have had their primary effect on upper-income households.

HOW A TARIFF BURDENS EXPORTERS

The benefits and costs of protecting domestic producers from foreign competition, as discussed earlier in this chapter, are based on the direct effects of an import tariff. Import-competing businesses and workers can benefit from tariffs through increases in output, profits, jobs, and compensation. A tariff imposes costs on domestic consumers in the form of higher prices of protected products and reductions in consumer surplus. There is also a net welfare loss for the econ-omy because not all of the loss of consumer surplus is transferred as gains to domestic producers and the government (the protective effect and consumption effect).

A tariff carries additional burdens. In protecting import-competing producers, a tariff leads indirectly to a reduction in domestic exports. The net result of protectionism is to move the economy toward greater self-sufficiency, with lower imports and exports. For domestic workers, the protection of jobs in import-competing industries comes at the expense of jobs in other sectors of the economy, including exports. Although a tariff is intended to help domestic producers, the economy-wide implications of a tariff are adverse for the export sector. The welfare losses due to restrictions in output and employment in the economy's export industry may offset the welfare gains enjoyed by import-competing producers.

Because a tariff is a tax on imports, the burden of a tariff falls initially on importers, who must pay duties to the domestic government. However, importers generally try to shift increased costs to buyers through price increases. There are at least three ways in which the resulting higher prices of imports injure domestic exporters.

First, exporters often purchase imported inputs subject to tariffs that *increase the cost of inputs*. Because exporters tend to sell in competitive markets where they have little ability to dictate the prices they receive, they generally cannot pass on a tariff-induced increase in cost to their buyers. Higher export costs thus lead to higher prices and reduced overseas sales.

Consider the hypothetical case of Caterpillar, a U.S. exporter of tractors. In Figure 5.4, suppose the firm realizes constant long-run costs, suggesting that marginal cost equals average cost at each level of output. Let the production cost of a tractor equal $100,000, denoted by $MC_0 = AC_0$. Caterpillar maximizes profits by producing 100 tractors, the point at which marginal revenue equals marginal cost, and selling them at a price of $110,000 per unit. The firm's revenue thus totals $11 million (100 × $110,000) while its costs total $10 million (100 × $100,000); as a result, the firm realizes profits of $1 million.

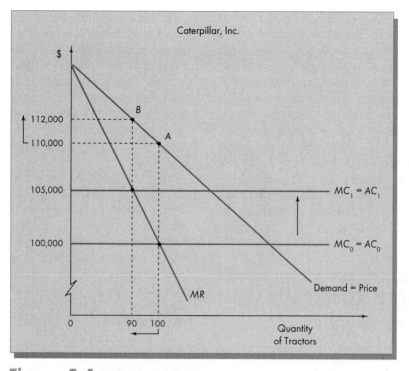

Figure 5.4 How an Import Tariff Burdens Domestic Exporters

A tariff placed on imported steel increases the costs of a steel-using manufacturer. This leads to a higher price charged by the manufacturer and a loss of international competitiveness.

Suppose now that the U.S. government levies a tariff on steel imports, while foreign nations allow steel to be imported duty-free. If the production of tractors uses imported steel, and competitively priced domestic steel is not available, the tariff leads to an increase in Caterpillar's costs to, say, $105,000 per tractor, as denoted by $MC_1 = AC_1$. Again the firm maximizes profits by operating where marginal revenue equals marginal cost. However, Caterpillar must charge a higher price, $112,000; the firm's sales thus decrease to 90 tractors and profits decrease to $630,000. The import tariff applied to steel represents a tax on Caterpillar that reduces its international competitiveness. Protecting domestic steel producers from import competition can thus lessen the export competitiveness of domestic steel-using producers.

Tariffs also *raise the cost of living* by increasing the price of imports. Workers thus have the incentive to demand correspondingly higher wages, resulting in higher production costs. Tariffs lead to expanding output for import-competing companies that in turn bid for workers, causing money wages to rise. As these higher wages pass through the economy, export industries ultimately face higher wages and production costs, which lessen their competitive position in international markets.

Finally, import tariffs have *international repercussions* that lead to reductions in domestic exports. Tariffs cause the quantity of imports to decrease, which in turn decreases other nations' export revenues and ability to import. The decline in foreign export revenues results in a smaller demand for a nation's exports and leads to falling output and employment in its export industries.

If domestic export companies are damaged by import tariffs, why don't they protest such policies more vigorously? One problem is that tariff-induced increases in costs for export companies are subtle and invisible. Many exporters may not be aware of their existence. Also, the tariff-induced cost increases may be of such magnitude that some potential export companies are incapable of developing and have no tangible basis for political resistance.

ARGUMENTS FOR TRADE RESTRICTIONS

The **free-trade argument** is, in principle, persuasive. It states that if each nation produces what it does best and permits trade, over the long run all will enjoy lower prices and higher levels of output, income, and consumption than could be achieved in isolation. In a dynamic world, comparative advantage is constantly changing owing to shifts in technologies, input productivities, and wages, as well as tastes and preferences. A free market compels adjustment to take place. Either the efficiency of an industry must improve, or else resources will flow from low-productivity uses to those with high productivity. Tariffs and other trade barriers are viewed as tools that prevent the economy from undergoing adjustment, resulting in economic stagnation.

Although the free-trade argument tends to dominate in the classroom, virtually all nations have imposed restrictions on the international flow of goods, services, and capital. Often, proponents of protectionism say that free trade is fine in theory, but that it does not apply in the real world. Modern trade theory assumes perfectly competitive markets whose characteristics do not reflect real-world market conditions. Moreover, even though protectionists may concede that economic losses occur with tariffs and other restrictions, they often argue that noneconomic benefits such as national security more than offset the economic losses. In seeking protection from imports, domestic industries and labor unions attempt to secure their economic welfare. Over the years, a number of arguments have been advanced to pressure the President and Congress to enact restrictive measures.

JOB PROTECTION The issue of jobs has been a dominant factor in motivating government officials to levy trade restrictions on imported goods. During periods of economic recession, workers are especially eager to point out that cheap foreign goods undercut domestic production, resulting in a loss of domestic jobs to foreign labor. Alleged job losses to foreign competition historically have been a major force behind the desire of most U.S. labor leaders to reject free-trade policies.

This view, however, has a serious omission: It fails to acknowledge the dual nature of international trade. Changes in a nation's imports of goods and services are closely related to changes in its exports. Nations export goods because they desire to import products from other nations. When the United States imports goods from abroad, foreigners gain purchasing power that will eventually be spent on U.S. goods, services, or financial assets. U.S. export industries then enjoy gains in sales and employment, whereas the opposite occurs in U.S. import-competing industries. Rather than promoting overall unemployment, imports tend to generate job opportunities in some industries as part of the process by which they decrease employment in other industries. However, the job gains due to open trade policies tend to be less visible to the public than the readily observable job losses stemming from foreign competition. The more conspicuous losses have led many U.S. business and labor leaders to combine forces in their opposition to free trade.

Trade restraints raise employment in the protected industry (such as steel) by increasing the price (or reducing the supply) of competing import goods. Industries that are primary suppliers of inputs to the protected industry also gain jobs. However, industries that purchase the protected product (such as auto manufacturers) face higher costs. These costs are then passed on to the consumer through higher prices, resulting in decreased sales. Thus employment falls in these related industries.

Economists at the Federal Reserve Bank of Dallas have examined the effects on U.S. employment of trade restrictions on textiles and apparel, steel, and automobiles. They conclude that in an economy near full employment, trade protection will have little or no positive effect on the level of employment in the long run. Trade restraints tend to provide job gains for only a few industries, while they result in job losses spread across many industries.

Table 5.10 illustrates the effects of U.S. restrictions on steel imports in 1984. The restraints provided additional jobs for U.S. steelworkers; the mining industry, a primary supplier to the steel industry, also experienced significant employment increases. The restraints, however, resulted in job losses for steel-using industries, including motor vehicles and equipment, furniture and fixtures, transportation equipment, and fabricated metal products. Comparing the job gainers and losers, the economists at the Federal Reserve Bank of Dallas found that trade restraints provided negligible employment gains for the U.S. economy.

The researchers drew similar conclusions concerning the employment effects of trade restrictions in the textiles and apparel industry and the automobile industry.

PROTECTION AGAINST CHEAP FOREIGN LABOR

One of the most common arguments used to justify the protectionist umbrella of trade restrictions is that tariffs are needed to defend domestic jobs against cheap foreign labor. As indicated in Table 5.11, production workers in the United States have been paid much higher wages, in terms of the U.S. dollar, than workers in countries such as Mexico and Sri Lanka. So it could be argued that low wages abroad make it difficult for U.S. producers to compete with producers using cheap foreign labor and that unless U.S. producers are protected from imports, domestic output and employment levels will decrease.

Indeed, there is a widely held view that competition from goods produced in low-wage countries is unfair and harmful to American workers. Moreover, it is thought that companies that produce goods in foreign countries to take advantage of cheap labor should not be allowed to dictate the wages paid to American workers. A solution: Impose a tariff or tax on goods brought into the United States equal to the wage differential between foreign workers and U.S. workers in

Table 5.10 Employment Effects of U.S. Trade Restrictions on Steel Imports

Job-Gaining Industries	Number of Jobs	Job-Losing Industries	Number of Jobs
Steel	31,003	Motor vehicles/equipment	11,311
Mining	3,280	Furniture and fixtures	3,417
Utilities	1,244	Machinery	16,914
Finance and insurance	6,108	Transportation equipment	6,497
Printing and publishing	1,234	Construction	15,763
Wholesale and retail trade	12,720	Other	23,538
Services	16,177	Total	77,440
Other	5,679		
Total	77,455		

Source: Linda Hunter, "U.S. Trade Protection: Effects on the Industrial and Regional Composition of Employment," Federal Reserve Bank of Dallas, *Economic Review*, January 1990, pp. 1–13.

Table 5.11 Hourly Compensation Costs in U.S. Dollars for Production Workers in Manufacturing, 1998

Country	Hourly Compensation (Dollars per Hour)
Germany	$27.99
Switzerland	24.38
Norway	23.70
Belgium	23.11
United States	18.56
Japan	18.05
Canada	15.69
Ireland	13.33
Taiwan	5.24
Korea	5.03
Mexico	1.83
Sri Lanka	.47

Source: U.S. Department of Labor, Bureau of Labor Statistics, *Foreign Labor Statistics: Hourly Compensation Costs in U.S. Dollars,* January 2000, at Internet site http://stats.bls.gov/news/release/ichcc.02.htm.

the same industry. That way, competition would be confined to who makes the best product, not who works for the least amount of money. Therefore, if Calvin Klein wants to manufacture sweatshirts in Pakistan, his firm would be charged a tariff or tax equal to the difference between the earnings of a Pakistani worker and a U.S. apparel worker.

Although this viewpoint may have widespread appeal, it fails to recognize the links among efficiency, wages, and production costs. Even if domestic wages are higher than those abroad, if domestic labor is more productive than foreign labor, domestic labor costs may still be competitive. Total labor costs reflect not only the wage rate but output per labor hour. If the productive superiority of domestic labor more than offsets the higher domestic wage rate, the home nation's labor costs will actually be less than they are abroad.

Figure 5.5 shows wages, labor productivity (output per worker), and unit labor costs in man-

ufacturing, relative to the United States, for several nations: India, Philippines, Malaysia, Mexico, and Korea. We see that in 1990, wages in these nations were only fractions of U.S. wages; however, labor productivity levels in these nations were also fractions of U.S. labor productivity. Even if wage rates in, say, Malaysia are lower than in the United States, Malaysia still could have higher unit labor costs if its productivity is lower than U.S. productivity. The figure also shows labor cost per unit of output (the ratio of wages to productivity) relative to the United States in 1990. For the five nations, we see that international differences in unit labor costs, relative to the United States, were invariably much smaller than differences in wages suggest. For example, Mexican wages in manufacturing were about 23 percent that of the United States, while Mexico's unit labor costs in manufacturing were about 75 percent that of the United States. In fact, unit labor cost in India and the Philippines were higher than those of the United States—the productivity gap exceeded the wage gap. These data show that low wages, by themselves, do not guarantee low production costs.

Another limitation of the cheap-foreign-labor argument is that low-wage nations tend to have a competitive advantage only in the production of goods requiring much labor and little of the other factor inputs—that is, only when the wage bill is the largest component of the total costs of production. It is true that a high-wage nation may have a relative cost disadvantage compared with its low-wage trading partner in the production of labor-intensive commodities. But this does not mean that foreign producers can undersell the home country across the board in all lines of production, causing the overall domestic standard of living to decline. Foreign nations should use the revenues from their export sales to purchase the products in which the home country has a competitive advantage—products requiring a large share of the factors of production that are abundant domestically.

The Heckscher–Ohlin theory of factor endowments suggests that as economies become integrated through trade, there is a ten-

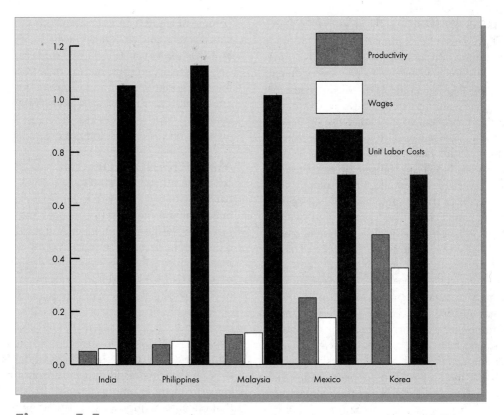

Figure 5.5 Productivity, Wages, and Unit Labor Costs, Relative to the United States: Total Manufacturing, 1990

Low wages by themselves do not guarantee low production costs. To the degree that low wages reflect low labor productivity, any cost advantage of employing low-wage workers is neutralized.

Source: Stephen Golub, "Comparative and Absolute Advantage in the Asia–Pacific Region," Pacific Basin Working Paper Series, Federal Reserve Bank of San Francisco (October, 1995).

dency for resource payments to become equal in different nations, given competitive markets. A nation with expensive labor will tend to import products embodying large amounts of labor. As imports rise and domestic output falls, the resulting decrease in demand for domestic labor will cause domestic wages to fall to the foreign level.

In automobile manufacturing, for example, there has been sufficient international competition to warrant such a process. This was seen in the 1980s, when high unemployment in the U.S. auto industry permitted General Motors and Ford to scale down the compensation levels of their employees as a means of offsetting their cost disadvantages against the Japanese. The adverse implications of resource-price equalization for the wages of U.S. workers could explain why the United Auto Workers (UAW) supports protectionism. By shielding U.S. wage levels from market pressures created by foreign competition, protectionism would result in the U.S. government's validating the high wages and benefits of UAW members.

FAIRNESS IN TRADE: A LEVEL PLAYING FIELD

Fairness in trade is another reason given for protectionism. Business firms and workers often argue that foreign governments play by a different set of rules than the home government, giving foreign firms unfair competitive advantages. Domestic producers contend that import restrictions should be enacted to offset these foreign advantages, thus creating a **level playing field** on which all producers can compete on equal terms.

U.S. companies often allege that foreign firms are not subject to the same government regulations regarding pollution control and worker safety as U.S. companies; this is especially true in many developing nations (such as Mexico and South Korea), where environmental laws and enforcement have been lax. Moreover, foreign firms may not pay as much in corporate taxes and may not have to comply with employment regulations such as affirmative action, minimum wages, and overtime pay. Also, foreign governments may erect high trade barriers that effectively close their markets to imports, or they may subsidize their producers so as to enhance their competitiveness in world markets.

These fair-trade arguments are often voiced by organized lobbies that are losing sales to foreign competitors. They may sound appealing to the voters because they are couched in terms of fair play and equal treatment. However, there are several arguments against levying restrictions on imports from nations that have high trade restrictions or that place lower regulatory burdens on their producers.

First, there is a benefit to the domestic economy from trade even if foreign nations impose trade restrictions. Although foreign restrictions that lessen our exports may decrease our welfare, retaliating by levying our own import barriers—which protect inefficient domestic producers—decreases our welfare even more.

Second, the argument does not recognize the potential impact on global trade. If each nation were to increase trade restrictions whenever foreign restrictions were higher than domestic restrictions, there would occur a worldwide escalation in restrictions; this would lead to a lower

volume of trade, falling levels of production and employment, and a decline in welfare. There may be a case for threatening to levy trade restrictions unless foreign nations reduce their restrictions; but if negotiations fail and domestic restrictions are employed, the result is undesirable. Other countries' trade practices are seldom an adequate justification for domestic trade restrictions.

MAINTENANCE OF THE DOMESTIC STANDARD OF LIVING

Advocates of trade barriers often contend that tariffs are useful in maintaining a high level of income and employment for the home nation. It is argued that by reducing the level of imports, tariffs encourage home spending, which stimulates domestic economic activity. As a result, the home nation's level of employment and income will be enhanced.

Although this argument appears appealing on the surface, it merits several qualifications. It is apparent that all nations together cannot levy tariffs to bolster domestic living standards. This is because tariffs result in a redistribution of the gains from trade among nations. To the degree that one nation imposes a tariff that improves its income and employment, it does so at the expense of its trading partner's living standard. Nations adversely affected by trade barriers are likely to impose retaliatory tariffs, resulting in a lower level of welfare for all nations. It is little wonder that tariff restrictions designed to enhance a nation's standard of living at the expense of its trading partner are referred to as *beggar-thy-neighbor policies*.

EQUALIZATION OF PRODUCTION COSTS

Proponents of a **scientific tariff** seek to eliminate what they consider to be unfair competition from abroad. Owing to such factors as lower wage costs, tax concessions, or government subsidies, foreign sellers may enjoy cost advantages over domestic firms. To offset any such advantage, tariffs equivalent to the cost differential should be imposed. Such provisions were actually part of the U.S. Tariff Acts of 1922 and 1930.

In practice, the scientific tariff suffers from a number of problems. Because within a given industry costs differ from business to business, how can costs actually be compared? Suppose that all U.S. steelmakers were extended protection from all foreign steelmakers. This would require the costs of the most efficient foreign producer to be set equal to the highest costs of the least efficient U.S. company. Given today's cost conditions, prices would certainly rise in the United States. This would benefit the more efficient U.S. companies, which would enjoy economic profits, but the U.S. consumer would be subsidizing inefficient production. Because the scientific tariff approximates a prohibitive tariff, it completely contradicts the notion of comparative advantage and wipes out the basis for trade and gains from trade.

INFANT-INDUSTRY ARGUMENT One of the more commonly accepted cases for tariff protection is the **infant-industry argument**. This argument does not deny the validity of the case for free trade. However, it contends that for free trade to be meaningful, trading nations should temporarily shield their newly developing industries from foreign competition. Otherwise, mature foreign businesses, which are at the time more efficient, can drive the young domestic businesses out of the market. Only after the young companies have had time to become efficient producers should the tariff barriers be lifted and free trade take place.

Although there is some truth in the infant-industry argument, it must be qualified in several respects. First, once a protective tariff is imposed, it is very difficult to remove, even after industrial maturity has been achieved. Special-interest groups can often convince policy makers that further protection is justified. Second, it is very difficult to determine which industries will be capable of realizing comparative-advantage potential and thus merit protection. Third, the infant-industry argument generally is not valid for mature, industrialized nations such as the United States, Germany, and Japan. Finally, there may be other ways of insulating a developing industry from cutthroat competition. Rather than adopt a protective tariff, the government could grant a subsidy to the industry. A subsidy

has the advantage of not distorting domestic consumption and relative prices; its drawback is that instead of generating revenue, as an import tariff does, a subsidy spends revenue.

NONECONOMIC ARGUMENTS Noneconomic considerations also enter into the arguments for protectionism. One such consideration is *national security*. The national-security argument contends that a country may be put in jeopardy in the event of an international crisis or war if it is heavily dependent on foreign suppliers. Even though domestic producers are not as efficient, tariff protection should be granted to ensure their continued existence. A good application of this argument involves the major oil-importing nations, which saw several Arab nations impose oil boycotts on the West to win support for the Arab position against Israel during the 1973 Middle East conflict. The problem, however, is stipulating what constitutes an essential industry. If the term is defined broadly, many industries may be able to win import protection, and the argument loses its meaning.

Another noneconomic argument is based on *cultural and sociological considerations*. New England may desire to preserve small-scale fishing; West Virginia may argue for tariffs on hand-blown glassware, on the grounds that these skills enrich the fabric of life; certain products such as narcotics may be considered socially undesirable, and restrictions or prohibitions placed on their importation. These arguments constitute legitimate reasons and cannot be ignored. All the economist can do is point out the economic consequences and costs of protection and identify alternative ways of accomplishing the same objective.

In Canada, many nationalists maintain that Canadian culture is too fragile to survive without government protection. The big threat: U.S. cultural imperialism. To keep the Yanks in check, Canada has long maintained some restrictions on sales of U.S. publications and textbooks. By the 1990s, the envelop of Canada's cultural protectionism was expanding. The most blatant example was a 1994 law that levied an 80-percent tax on Canadian ads in Canadian editions of U.S. magazines—in effect, an effort to kill off the U.S. intruders. Without protections for the Canadian media, the cultural nationalists feared that U.S. magazines such as *Sports Illustrated*, *Time*, and *Business Week* could soon deprive Canadians of the ability to read about themselves in *Maclean's* and *Canadian Business*. Although U.S. protests of the tax ultimately led to its abolishment, the Canadian government continued to examine other methods of preserving the culture of its people.

It is important to note that most of the arguments justifying tariffs are based on the assumption that the national welfare, as well as the individual's welfare, will be enhanced. The strategic importance of tariffs for the welfare of import-competing producers is one of the main reasons that reciprocal tariff liberalization has been so gradual. It is no wonder that import-competing producers make such strong and politically effective arguments that increased foreign competition will undermine the welfare of the nation as a whole as well as their own. Although a liberalization of tariff barriers may be detrimental to a particular group, we must be careful to differentiate between the individual's welfare and the national welfare. If tariff reductions result in greater welfare gains from trade and if the adversely affected party can be compensated for the loss it has faced, the overall national welfare will increase. However, proving that the gains more than offset the losses in practice is very difficult.

THE POLITICAL ECONOMY OF PROTECTIONISM

Recent history indicates that increasing dependence on international trade yields uneven impacts across domestic sectors. The United States has enjoyed comparative advantages in such products as agricultural commodities, industrial machinery, chemicals, and scientific instruments. However, some of its industries have lost their comparative advantage and suffered from international trade—among them apparel and textiles, motor vehicles, electronic goods, basic iron and steel, and footwear. Formulating international trade policy in this environment is difficult. Free trade can yield substantial benefits for the overall economy through increased productivity and lower prices, but specific groups may benefit if government provides them some relief from import competition. Government officials must consider these opposing interests when setting the course for international trade policy.

Considerable attention has been devoted to what motivates government officials when formulating trade policy. As voters, we do not have the opportunity to go to the polls and vote for a trade bill. Instead, formation of trade policy rests in the hands of elected officials and their appointees. It is generally assumed that elected officials form policies to maximize votes and thus remain in office. The result is a bias in the political system that favors protectionism.

The **protection-biased sector** of the economy generally consists of import-competing companies, the labor unions representing workers in that industry, and the suppliers to the companies in the industry. Seekers of protectionism are often established firms in an aging industry that have lost their comparative advantage. High costs may be due to lack of modern technology, inefficient management procedures, outmoded work rules, or high payments to domestic workers. The **free-trade-biased sector** generally comprises exporting companies, their workers, and their suppliers. It also consists of consumers, including wholesalers and retail merchants of imported goods.

Government officials understand that they will likely lose the political support of, say, the UAW if they vote against increases in tariffs on auto imports. They also understand that their vote on this trade issue will not be the key factor underlying the political support provided by many other citizens. Their support can be retained by appealing to them on other issues while voting to increase the tariff on auto imports to maintain UAW support.

U.S. protection policy is thus dominated by special-interest groups that represent producers.

Consumers generally are not organized, and their losses due to protectionism are widely dispersed, whereas the gains from protection are concentrated among well-organized producers and labor unions in the affected sectors. Those harmed by a protectionist policy absorb individually a small and difficult-to-identify cost. Many consumers, though they will pay a higher price for the protected product, will not associate the higher price with the protectionist policy and thus are unlikely to be concerned about trade policy. Special-interest groups, however, are highly concerned about protecting their industries against import competition. They provide support for government officials who share their views and lobby against the election of those who do not. Clearly, government officials seeking reelection will be sensitive to the special-interest groups representing producers.

The political bias favoring domestic producers is seen in the tariff escalation effect, discussed earlier in this chapter. Recall that the tariff structures of industrial nations often result in lower import tariffs on intermediate goods and higher tariffs on finished goods. For example, U.S. imports of cotton yarn have traditionally faced low tariffs, while higher tariffs have been applied to cotton fabric imports. The higher tariff on cotton fabrics appears to be the result of ineffective lobbying efforts of diffused consumers, who lose to organized U.S. fabric producers lobbying for protectionism. But for cotton yarn, the protectionist outcome is less clear. Purchasers of cotton yarn are U.S. manufacturers who want low tariffs on imported inputs. These companies form trade associations and can pressure Congress for low tariffs as effectively as U.S. cotton suppliers, who lobby for high tariffs. Protection applied to imported intermediate goods, such as cotton yarn, is thus less likely.

Not only does the interest of the domestic producer tend to outweigh that of the domestic consumer in trade policy deliberations, but import-competing producers tend to exert stronger influence on legislators than do export producers. A problem faced by export producers is that their gains from international trade are often in addition to their prosperity in the domestic market; producers that are efficient enough to sell overseas are often safe from foreign competition in the domestic market. Most deliberations on trade policy emphasize protecting imports, and the indirect damage done by import barriers to export producers tends to be spread over many export industries. But import-competing producers can gather evidence of immediate damage caused by foreign competition, including falling levels of sales, profits, and employment. Legislators tend to be influenced by the more clearly identified arguments of the import-competing industry and see that a greater number of votes are at stake among their constituents than among the constituents of the export producers.

The political economy of import protection can be analyzed in terms of supply and demand. Protectionism is supplied by the domestic government, while domestic companies and workers are the source of demand. The supply of protection depends on (1) the costs to society, (2) the political importance of the import-competing industry, (3) adjustment costs, and (4) public sympathy.

Enlightened government officials realize that although protectionism provides benefits to the domestic industry, society as a whole pays costs. These *costs* include the losses of consumer surplus because of higher prices and the resulting deadweight losses as import volume is reduced, lost economies of scale as opportunities for further trade are foregone, and the loss of incentive for technological development provided by import competition. The higher the costs of protection to society, the less likely it is that government officials will shield an industry from import competition.

The supply of protectionism is also influenced by the *political importance* of the import-competing industry. An industry that enjoys strong representation in the legislature is in a favorable position to win import protection. It is more difficult for politicians to disagree with one million autoworkers than with 20,000 copper workers. The national security argument for protection is

PETITION OF THE CANDLE MAKERS

Free-trade advocate Frederic Bastiat presented the French Chamber of Deputies with a devastating satire of protectionists' arguments in 1845. His petition asked that a law be passed requiring people to shut all windows, doors, and so forth so that the candle industry would be protected from the "unfair" competition of the sun. He argued that this would be a great benefit to the candle industry, creating many new jobs and enriching suppliers. Consider the following excerpts from his satire:

We are subjected to the intolerable competition of a foreign rival, who enjoys, it would seem, such superior facilities for the production of light, that he is flooding the domestic market with it at an incredibly low price. From the moment he appears, our sales cease, all consumers turn to him, and a branch of French industry whose ramifications are innumerable is at once reduced to complete stagnation. This rival is no other than the sun.

We ask you to be so good as to pass a law requiring the closing of all windows, dormers, skylights, shutters, curtains, and blinds—in short, all openings, holes, chinks, and fissures through which the light of the sun is wont to enter houses, to the detriment of our industries.

By shutting out as much as possible all access to natural light, you create the necessity for artificial light. Is there in France an industry which will not, through some connection with this important object, be benefitted by it? If more tallow be consumed, there will arise a necessity for an increase of cattle and sheep. If more oil be consumed, it will cause an increase in the cultivation of the olive tree. Navigation will profit as thousands of vessels would be employed in the whale fisheries. There is, in short, no market which would not be greatly developed by the granting of our petitions.

While it is undoubtedly true that the French candle industry would benefit from a lack of sunlight, consumers would obviously not be happy about being forced to pay for light that they could get for free were there no government intervention.

Source: Frederic Bastiat, *Economic Sophisms*, edited and translated by Arthur Goddard, New York, D. Van Nostrand, 1964.

---

a variant on the consideration of the political importance of the industry. Thus, for example, the U.S. coal and oil industries were successful in obtaining a national-security clause in U.S. trade law permitting protection if imports threaten to impair domestic security.

The supply of protection also tends to increase when domestic businesses and workers face large costs of adjusting to rising import competition (for example, unemployment or wage concessions). This protection is seen as a method of delaying the full burden of *adjustment*.

Finally, as *public sympathy* for a group of domestic businesses or workers increases (for example, if workers are paid low wages and have few alternative work skills), a greater amount of protection against foreign-produced goods tends to be supplied.

On the demand side, factors that underlie the domestic industry's demand for protectionism are (1) comparative disadvantage, (2) import penetration, (3) concentration, and (4) export dependence.

The demand for protection rises as the domestic industry's *comparative disadvantage* intensifies. This is seen in the U.S. steel industry, which has vigorously pursued protection against low-cost Japanese and South Korean steel manufacturers in recent decades.

Higher levels of *import penetration*, suggesting increasing competitive pressures for domestic producers, also trigger increased demands for protection. A significant change in the nature of the support for protectionism occurred in the late 1960s, when the AFL-CIO abandoned its long-held belief in the desirability of open markets and supported protectionism. The shift in the union's position was due primarily to the rapid rise in import-penetration ratios that occurred during the 1960s in such industries as electrical consumer goods and footwear.

Another factor that may affect the demand for protection is *concentration* of domestic production. The U.S. auto industry, for example, is dominated by the Big Three. Support for import protection can be financed by these firms without fear that a large share of the benefits of protectionism will accrue to nonparticipating firms. Conversely, an industry that comprises many small producers (for example, meat packing) realizes that a substantial share of the gains from

protectionism may accrue to producers who do not contribute their fair share to the costs of winning protectionist legislation. The demand for protection thus tends to be stronger the more concentrated the domestic industry.

Finally, the demand for protection may be influenced by the degree of *export dependence.* One would expect that companies whose foreign sales constitute a substantial portion of total sales (for example, Boeing) would not be greatly concerned about import protection. Their main fear is that the imposition of domestic trade barriers might invite retaliation overseas, which would ruin their export markets.

SUMMARY

1. Even though the free-trade argument has strong theoretical justifications, trade restrictions are widespread throughout the world. Trade barriers consist of tariff restrictions and nontariff trade barriers.

2. There are several types of tariffs. A specific tariff represents a fixed amount of money per unit of the imported commodity. An ad valorem tariff is stated as a fixed percentage of the value of an imported commodity. A compound tariff combines a specific tariff with an ad valorem tariff.

3. Concerning ad valorem tariffs, several procedures exist for the valuation of imports. The free-on-board (FOB) measure indicates a commodity's price as it leaves the exporting nation. The cost-insurance-freight (CIF) measure shows the product's value as it arrives at the port of entry.

4. The effective tariff rate tends to differ from the nominal tariff rate when the domestic import-competing industry uses imported resources whose tariffs differ from those on the final commodity. Developing nations have traditionally argued that many advanced nations escalate the tariff structures on industrial commodities to yield an effective rate of protection several times the nominal rate.

5. U.S. trade laws mitigate the effects of import duties by allowing U.S. importers to postpone and prorate over time their duty obligations by means of bonded warehouses and foreign trade zones.

6. The welfare effects of a tariff can be measured by its protective effect, consumption effect, redistributive effect, revenue effect, and terms-of-trade effect.

7. If a nation is small compared with the rest of the world, its welfare necessarily falls by the total amount of the protective effect plus the consumption effect if it levies a tariff on imports. If the importing nation is large relative to the world, the imposition of an import tariff may improve its international terms of trade by an amount that more than offsets the welfare losses associated with the consumption effect and the protective effect.

8. Although tariffs may improve one nation's economic position, any gains generally come at the expense of other nations. Should tariff retaliations occur, the volume of international trade decreases, and world welfare suffers. Tariff liberalization is intended to promote freer markets so that the world can benefit from expanded trade volumes and international specialization of inputs.

9. Tariffs are sometimes justified on the grounds that they protect domestic employment and wages, help create a level playing field for international trade, equate the cost of imported products with the cost of domestic import-competing products, allow domestic industries to be insulated temporarily from foreign competition until they can grow and develop, or protect industries necessary for national security.

S T U D Y   Q U E S T I O N S

1. Describe a specific tariff, an ad valorem tariff, and a compound tariff. What are the advantages and disadvantages of each?

2. What are the methods that customs appraisers use to determine the values of commodity imports?

3. Under what conditions does a nominal tariff applied to an import product overstate or understate the actual, or effective, protection afforded by the nominal tariff?

4. Less-developed nations sometimes argue that the industrialized nations' tariff structures discourage the less-developed nations from undergoing industrialization. Explain.

5. Distinguish between consumer surplus and producer surplus. How do these concepts relate to a country's economic welfare?

6. When a nation imposes a tariff on the importation of a commodity, economic inefficiencies develop that detract from the national welfare. Explain.

7. What factors influence the size of the revenue, protective, consumption, and redistributive effects of a tariff?

8. A nation that imposes tariffs on imported goods may find its welfare improving should the tariff result in a favorable shift in the terms of trade. Explain.

9. Which of the arguments for tariffs do you feel are most relevant in today's world?

10. Although tariffs may improve the welfare of a single nation, the world's welfare may decline. Under what conditions would this be true?

11. What impact does the imposition of a tariff normally have on a nation's terms of trade and volume of trade?

12. Suppose that the production of $1 million worth of steel in Canada requires $100,000 worth of taconite. Canada's nominal tariff rates for importing these goods are 20 percent for steel and 10 percent for taconite. Given this information, calculate the effective rate of protection for Canada's steel industry.

13. Would a tariff imposed on U.S. oil imports promote energy development and conservation for the United States?

14. What is meant by the terms *bonded warehouse* and *foreign-trade zone*? How does each of these help importers mitigate the effects of domestic import duties?

15. Assume the nation of Australia is "small," unable to influence world price. Its demand and supply schedules for TV sets are shown in Table 5.12. Using graph paper, plot the demand and supply schedules on the same graph.

   a. Determine Australia's market equilibrium for TV sets.

   (1) What are the equilibrium price and quantity?

Table 5.12 Demand and Supply: TV Sets (Australia)

Price of TV Sets	Quantity Demanded	Quantity Supplied
$500	0	50
400	10	40
300	20	30
200	30	20
100	40	10
0	50	0

(2) Calculate the value of Australian consumer surplus and producer surplus.

b. Under free-trade conditions, suppose Australia imports TV sets at a price of $100 each. Determine the free-trade equilibrium, and illustrate graphically.

   (1) How many TV sets will be produced, consumed, and imported?

   (2) Calculate the dollar value of Australian consumer surplus and producer surplus.

c. To protect its producers from foreign competition, suppose the Australian government levies a specific tariff of $100 on imported TV sets.

   (1) Determine and show graphically the effects of the tariff on the price of TV sets in Australia, the quantity of TV sets supplied by Australian producers, the quantity of TV sets demanded by Australian consumers, and the volume of trade.

   (2) Calculate the reduction in Australian consumer surplus due to the tariff-induced increase in the price of TV sets.

   (3) Calculate the value of the tariff's consumption, protective, redistributive, and revenue effects.

   (4) What is the amount of deadweight welfare loss imposed on the Australian economy by the tariff?

16. Assume that the United States, as a steel-importing nation, is large enough so that changes in the quantity of its imports influence the world price of steel. The U.S. supply and demand schedules for steel are illustrated in Table 5.13, along with the overall amount of steel supplied to U.S. consumers by domestic and foreign producers.

Using graph paper, plot the supply and demand schedules on the same graph.

a. With free trade, the equilibrium price of steel is $ _____ per ton. At this price, _____ tons are purchased by U.S. buyers, _____ tons are supplied by U.S. producers, and _____ tons are imported.

Table 5.13 Supply and Demand: Tons of Steel (United States)

Price per Ton	Quantity Supplied (Domestic)	Quantity Supplied (Domestic & Imports)	Quantity Demanded
$100	0	0	15
200	0	4	14
300	1	8	13
400	2	12	12
500	3	16	11
600	4	20	10
700	5	24	9

b. To protect its producers from foreign competition, suppose the U.S. government levies a specific tariff of $250 per ton on steel imports.

   (1) Show graphically the effect of the tariff on the overall supply schedule of steel.

   (2) With the tariff, the domestic price of steel rises to $ _____ per ton. At this price, U.S. buyers purchase _____ tons, U.S. producers supply _____ tons, and _____ tons are imported.

   (3) Calculate the reduction in U.S. consumer surplus due to the tariff-induced price of steel, as well as the consumption, protective, redistributive, and domestic revenue effects. The deadweight welfare loss of the tariff equals $ _____ .

   (4) By reducing the volume of imports with the tariff, the United States forces the price of imported steel down to $ _____ . The U.S. terms of trade thus (improves/worsens), which leads to (an increase/ a decrease) in U.S. welfare. Calculate the terms-of-trade effect.

   (5) What impact does the tariff have on the overall welfare of the United States?

NETLINK

5.1 The International Trade Commission Web site contains information about U.S. tariffs, as well as many documents that address contemporary issues in international economics. Examine the searchable version of the "Harmonized Tariff Schedule of the United States" or various "Reports and Publications" on international economics by setting your browser to URL:

http://www.usitc.gov/

5.2 The Web site of the U.S. Department of Commerce/Bureau of Export Administration provides information on U.S. export controls, including restrictions on exports of nuclear weapons and financial services encryption products. Set your browser to URL:

http: //www.bxa.doc.gov/

5.3 U.S. embassy staffs prepare the Country Commercial Guides once a year. It reports the business and economic situation of foreign countries and the political climate as it affects U.S. business. To get information on topics such as marketing, trade regulations, investment climate, and business travel, set your browser to URL:

http://www1.usatrade.gov/Website/ccg.nsf

5.4 Reports issued by the Office of the United States Trade Representative (OUSTR) and related entities on the National Trade Estimate Report on Foreign Trade Barriers can be found at the Web site:

http://www.ustr.gov/reports/index.shtml

5.5 The Sectoral and Trade Barriers Database of selected countries prepared by the European Union can be accessed by setting the browser to URL:

http://mkaccdb.eu.int/

To access NetLink Exercises and the Virtual Scavenger Hunt, visit the Carbaugh Web site at http://carbaugh.swcollege.com.

chapter 6

Nontariff Trade Barriers

This chapter considers policies other than tariffs that restrict international trade. Referred to as **nontariff trade barriers (NTBs)**, such measures have been on the rise since the 1960s and have become the most widely discussed topics at recent rounds of international trade negotiations. Indeed, the post–World War II success in international negotiations for the reduction of tariffs has made remaining NTBs even more visible.

NTBs encompass a variety of measures. Some have unimportant trade consequences; for example, labeling and packaging requirements can restrict trade, but generally only marginally. Other NTBs significantly affect trade patterns; examples include import quotas, voluntary export restraints, subsidies, and domestic content requirements. These NTBs are intended to reduce imports and thus benefit domestic producers.

Table 6.1 shows the NTB trade coverage ratios for major industrial nations. This ratio indicates the percentage of industrial-nation imports (by value) subject to NTBs; for example, 7.7 percent of U.S. imports were subject to NTBs in 1996.

IMPORT QUOTA

An **import quota** is a physical restriction on the quantity of goods that may be imported during a specific time period; the quota generally limits imports to a level below that which would occur under free-trade conditions. For example, a quota might state that no more than 1 million kilograms of cheese or 20 million kilograms of wheat can be imported during some specific time period. Table 6.2 gives examples of import

KEY CONCEPTS AND TERMS

- Antidumping duty
- Buy-national policies
- Corporate average fuel economy standards (CAFÉ)
- Cost-based definition of dumping
- Domestic content requirement
- Domestic subsidy
- Dumping
- Export credit subsidy
- Export quota
- Export-revenue effect
- Export subsidy
- Foreign sourcing
- Global quota
- Import quota
- Margin of dumping
- Nonrestrained suppliers
- Nontariff trade barriers (NTBs)
- Orderly marketing agreement (OMA)
- Persistent dumping
- Predatory dumping
- Price-based definition of dumping
- Selective quota
- Social regulation
- Sporadic dumping
- Subsidies
- Tariff-rate quota
- Trade-diversion effect
- Voluntary export restraints (VER)

| **Table 6.1** | Import Coverage Ratios of Nontariff Trade Barriers* Applied by Major Industrial Nations |

	Import Coverage Ratio (Percent)		
	1988	1993	1996
United States	16.7	17.0	7.7
European Union	13.2	11.1	6.7
Japan	8.6	8.1	7.4
Canada	5.7	4.5	4.0
Norway	13.8	11.1	3.0
Switzerland	13.2	13.2	9.8
Australia	8.9	0.4	0.6
New Zealand	11.5	0.2	0.2
Mexico	18.6	17.4	6.9

*Includes variable levies, voluntary export restraints, import quotas, import surveillance, and automatic licensing.

Source: Organization for Economic Cooperation and Development, *Indicators of Tariff and Nontariff Trade Barriers*, Paris, OECD, 1997.

| **Table 6.2** | Examples of U.S. Import Quotas |

Imported Article	Quota Quantity (Yearly)
Condensed milk (Australia)	91,625 kg
Condensed milk (Denmark)	605,092 kg
Evaporated milk (Germany)	9,997 kg
Evaporated milk (Netherlands)	548,393 kg
Blue-mold cheese (Argentina)	2,000 kg
Blue-mold cheese (Chile)	80,000 kg
Cheddar cheese (New Zealand)	8,200,000 kg
Italian cheese (Poland)	1,325,000 kg
Italian cheese (Romania)	500,000 kg
Swiss cheese (Switzerland)	1,850,000 kg

kg = kilograms

Source: U.S. International Trade Commission, *Tariff Schedules of the United States*, Washington, DC, Government Printing Office, 2000.

quotas that have been used by the United States. For several reasons that we will soon investigate, import quotas are considered more restrictive than tariffs.

Import quotas on manufactured goods have been outlawed by the World Trade Organization. Where import quotas have been used by advanced countries such as Japan and the United States is to protect agricultural producers. However, recent trade negotiations have called for countries to convert their quotas to equivalent tariffs.

One way of administering import limitations is through a **global quota**. This technique permits a specified number of goods to be imported each year, but does not specify where the product is shipped from or who is permitted to import. When the specified amount has been imported (the quota is filled), additional imports of the product are prevented for the remainder of the year.

In practice, the global quota becomes unwieldy because of the rush of both domestic importers and foreign exporters to get their goods shipped into the country before the quota is filled. Those who import early in the year get their goods; those who import late in the year may not. Moreover, goods shipped from distant locations tend to be discriminated against because of the longer transportation time. Smaller merchants, without good trade connections, may also be at a disadvantage relative to large merchants. Global quotas are thus plagued by accusations of favoritism against merchants fortunate enough to be the first to capture a large portion of the business.

To avoid the problems of a global quota system, import quotas are usually allocated to specific countries; this type of quota is known as a **selective quota**. For example, a country might impose a global quota of 30 million apples per year, of which 14 million must come from the United States, 10 million from Mexico, and 6 million from Canada. Customs officials in the importing nation monitor the quantity of a particular good that enters the country from each source; once the quota for that source has been filled, no more goods are permitted to be imported.

Selective quotas suffer from many of the same problems as global quotas. Consider the case of K-mart, which ordered more than a million dollars' worth of wool sweaters from China in the 1980s. Before the sweaters arrived in the United States, the Chinese quota was filled for the year; K-mart could not bring them into the country until the following year. By that time, the sweaters were out of style and had to be sold at discounted prices. The firm estimated that it recovered only 60 cents on the dollar on these sweater sales.

Another feature of quotas is that their use may lead to domestic monopoly of production and higher prices. Because a domestic firm realizes that foreign producers cannot surpass their quotas, it may raise its prices. Tariffs do not necessarily lead to monopoly power, because no limit is established on the amount of goods that can be imported into the nation.

TRADE AND WELFARE EFFECTS Like a tariff, an import quota affects an economy's welfare. Figure 6.1 represents the case of cheese, involving the United States in trade with the European Union. Suppose the United States is a "small" country in terms of the world cheese market. Assume that $S_{U.S.}$ and $D_{U.S.}$ denote the supply and demand schedules of cheese for the United States. S_{EU} denotes the supply schedule of the European Union. Under free trade, the price

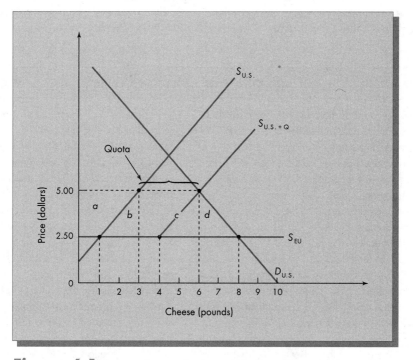

Figure 6.1 Import Quota: Trade and Welfare Effects

By restricting available supplies of an imported product, a quota leads to higher import prices. This price umbrella allows domestic producers of the import-competing good to raise prices. The result is a decrease in consumer surplus. Of this amount, the welfare loss to the importing nation consists of the protective effect, the consumption effect, and that portion of the revenue effect that is captured by the foreign exporter.

of European Union cheese and U.S. cheese equals $2.50 per pound. At this price, U.S. firms produce 1 pound, U.S. consumers purchase 8 pounds, and imports from the European Union total 7 pounds.

Suppose the United States limits its cheese imports to a fixed quantity of 3 pounds by imposing an import quota. Above the free-trade price, the total U.S. supply of cheese now equals U.S. production plus the quota. In Figure 6.1, this is illustrated by a shift in the supply curve from $S_{U.S.}$ to $S_{U.S.+Q}$. The reduction in imports from 7 pounds to 3 pounds raises the equilibrium price to $5; this leads to an increase in the quantity supplied by U.S. firms from 1 pound to 3 pounds and a decrease in U.S. quantity demanded from 8 pounds to 6 pounds.

Import quotas can be analyzed in terms of the same welfare effects identified for tariffs in the preceding chapter. Because the quota in our example results in a price increase to $5 per pound, U.S. consumer surplus falls by an amount equal to area $a + b + c + d$ ($17.50). Area a ($5) represents the *redistributive effect*, area b ($2.50) represents the *protective effect*, and area d ($2.50) represents the *consumption effect*. The *deadweight loss* of welfare to the economy resulting from the quota is depicted by the protective effect plus the consumption effect.

But what about the quota's *revenue effect*, denoted by area c ($7.50)? This amount arises from the fact that U.S. consumers must pay an additional $2.50 for each of the 3 pounds of cheese imported under the quota, as a result of the quota-induced scarcity of cheese. Where does this revenue go?

One outcome occurs when U.S. importers (for example, Safeway grocery stores) organize as buy-

ALLOCATING QUOTA LICENSES

Because an import quota restricts the quantity of imports, usually below the free-trade quantity, not all domestic importers can obtain the same number of imports that they could under free trade. Governments thus allocate the limited supply of imports among domestic importers.

In oil and dairy products, the U.S. government has issued import licenses, which are rights to a stipulated quantity of imports, to U.S. importers on the basis of their historical share of the import market. But this method discriminates against importers seeking to import goods for the first time. In other cases, the U.S. government has allocated import quotas on a pro rata basis, whereby U.S. importers receive a fraction of their demand equal to the ratio of the import quota to the total quantity demanded collectively by U.S. importers.

The U.S. government has also considered using another method of allocating licenses among domestic importers: the auctioning of import licenses to the highest bidder in a competitive market. This technique has been used in Australia and New Zealand.

Consider a hypothetical quota on U.S. imports of textiles. The quota pushes the price of textiles in the United States above the world price, making the United States an unusually profitable market. Windfall profits can be captured by U.S. importers (for example, Sears, Wal-Mart) if they buy textiles at the lower world price and sell them to U.S. buyers at the higher price made possible because of the quota. Given these windfall profits, U.S. importers would likely be willing to pay for the rights to import textiles. By auctioning import licenses to the highest bidder in a competitive market, the government could capture the windfall profits (the revenue effect shown as area c in Figure 6.1). Competition among importers to obtain the licenses would drive up the auction price to a level at which no windfall profits would remain, thus transferring the entire revenue effect to the government. The auctioning of import licenses would turn a quota into something akin to a tariff, which generates tax revenue for the government.

ers. Such importers might bargain favorably with European Union exporters and purchase cheese at the prevailing world price of $2.50 per pound, reselling the cheese to U.S. consumers at a price of $5 per pound. In this case, the quota's revenue accrues to the U.S. importers as profits. Alternatively, European Union exporters might organize as sellers and drive up the delivered price of cheese to $5 per pound, thereby capturing the quota's revenue effect. Still another outcome results if the U.S. government auctions import licenses to the highest bidder in a competitive market. Such auctions are intended to permit the government to recoup the quota revenue that would have accrued to importers in the form of monopoly profits (see box on page 154).

SUGAR IMPORT QUOTAS

The U.S. sugar industry provides an example of the impact of an import quota on a nation's welfare. Traditionally, U.S. sugar growers have received government subsidies in the form of price supports. Under this system, domestic sugar producers are provided a higher price than the free-market price; the difference between these two prices is the deficiency payment of the U.S. government. If the market price of sugar falls (or rises), the government's deficiency payment rises (or falls). To keep the market price of sugar close to the support price, and thus minimize its deficiency payments, the government has relied on import tariffs and quotas.

The price-support program ran into trouble when a glut of sugar in the world market sent the commercial price of sugar plunging to 6 cents a pound in 1982, compared with 41 cents a pound in 1980. This price was well below the 17-cents-a-pound support price of the federal government. Unless the government took action to prop up the commercial price paid to U.S. growers, the cost to the government of maintaining the support price of sugar would amount to an extra $800 million.

One way of boosting the U.S. commercial price of sugar was to raise the tariff on sugar imports. But, according to U.S. tariff codes, import duties could not exceed 50 percent of the world price of sugar. Although import duties

were raised to their legal maximum, the import duty system was deemed inadequate to protect U.S. growers from cheap foreign sugar as world prices fell throughout 1982. However, the government did impose quotas on imported sugar as a means of boosting domestic prices.

In 1982, the United States announced an import quota system that fixed nation-by-nation import allocations for 24 countries. Each nation's quota was based on its average sugar exports to the United States between 1975 and 1981, excluding the highest and lowest years. The total amount any nation could export to the United States was adjusted on a quarterly basis in light of changing market conditions. The quota for the first year of the system was 2.98 million tons, well below the 4.4 to 5.4 million tons that had entered the United States each year from 1976 to 1981. By reducing sugar supplies, the quota was intended to force up the commercial price of sugar in the United States. The quota program thus transferred the cost of sugar support from the U.S. taxpayer to the U.S. sugar consumer.

Figure 6.2 illustrates the effects of the sugar quota during 1983, as estimated by the Federal Trade Commission. Note that the United States is assumed to be a "small" country with regard to the world sugar market. The world price of sugar, including transportation charges to the United States, was 15 cents a pound during 1983, denoted by curve S_W. In addition, the U.S. duty on sugar that year was 2.8 cents per pound. Therefore, the domestic market price was 17.8 cents, denoted by schedule S_{W+T}. At this price, the United States imported 5.06 million tons of sugar $(9.356 - 4.296 = 5.06)$.

Under the quota program, U.S. sugar imports were cut from 5.06 million tons to 2.98 million tons. The quota-induced scarcity of sugar drove the domestic price up from 17.8 cents per pound to 21.8 cents per pound. This price increase reduced the cost of maintaining sugar price supports for the U.S. government. It also led to a decrease in U.S. consumer surplus equal to area *a+b+c+d* ($735.2 million). Of this loss, the *redistributive effect* (area *a*) and the *protective effect* (area *b*) totaled $483.6 million, while the

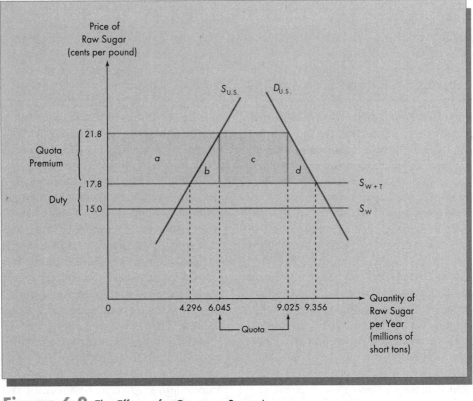

Figure 6.2 The Effects of a Quota on Sugar Imports

By forcing up the market price of sugar, an import quota reduces the costs to the U.S. government of maintaining price supports for domestic sugar producers. The higher market price of sugar, however, leads to decreases in welfare for U.S. consumers.

Source: David Tarr and Morris Morkre, *Aggregate Costs to the United States of Tariffs and Quotas on Imports*, Washington, DC: Federal Trade Commission, 1984.

consumption effect (area *d*) equaled $13.2 million. The quota's *revenue effect* (area *c*) equaled $238.4 million. Because the sugar quota was administered by the exporting countries and U.S. importers operated as competitive buyers, the lion's share of the revenue effect was captured by foreign exporters.

The sugar price increases under the quota program hastened the development of sugar substitutes in the United States. In particular, high-fructose corn syrup and various artificial sweeteners were produced and sold to former U.S. sugar-using industries.

The sugar quotas also had international repercussions. About half of the U.S. sugar requirements are fulfilled with imported sugar, much of which comes from poorer, developing nations. The restricted market created financial problems for nations such as the Dominican Republic, where sugar accounted for almost 40 percent of its exports to the United States.

Like most regulations, the sugar quotas had loopholes waiting to be discovered. It turns out that when sugar comes into the United States blended with at least 65 percent of another sweetener, flavoring, or food, the government does not consider it sugar. Thus, the sugar quota does not apply. In 1981, the year before the implementation of the sugar program, only 300 tons of "blended sugar" were imported by the United States. In 1982, however, the amount rose to 13,000 tons, and by 1983, some 75,000 tons found their way into U.S.-made soft drinks, ice cream, and candy bars. The majority of blended-sugar imports came from Canada, because Canadian refiners could import sugar at low world prices and, despite U.S. tariffs, export to the United States at roughly 8 cents below the U.S. domestic refined price. Because of its proximity to the United States, Canada also enjoyed the advantage of lower transportation costs compared with most other sugar-exporting nations.

QUOTAS VERSUS TARIFFS Previous analysis suggests that the revenue effect of import quotas differs from that of import tariffs. These two

commercial policies can also differ in the impact they have on the volume of trade. The following example illustrates how, during periods of growing demand, an import quota restricts the volume of imports by a greater amount than does an equivalent import tariff.

Figure 6.3 represents a hypothetical trade situation of the United States in autos. The U.S. supply and demand schedules for autos are given by $S_{U.S._0}$ and $D_{U.S._0}$, and S_{J_0} represents the Japanese auto supply schedule. Suppose the U.S. government has the option of levying a tariff or a quota on auto imports to protect U.S. companies from foreign competition.

In Figure 6.3(a), a tariff of $1,000 would raise the price of Japanese autos from $6,000 to $7,000; auto imports would fall from 7 million units to 3 million units. In Figure 6.3(b), an import quota of 3 million units would put the United States in a trade position identical to that

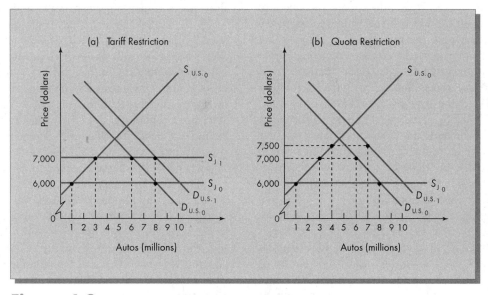

Figure 6.3 Trade Effects of Tariffs Versus Quotas

In a growing market, an import tariff is a less restrictive trade barrier than an equivalent import quota. With an import tariff, the adjustment that occurs in response to an increase in domestic demand is an increase in the amount of the product that is imported. With an import quota, an increase in demand induces an increase in product price. The price increase leads to a rise in production and a fall in consumption of the import-competing good, while the level of imports remains constant.

which occurs under the tariff: the quota-induced scarcity of autos results a rise in the price from $6,000 to $7,000. So far, it appears that the tariff and the quota are equivalent with respect to their restrictive impact on the volume of trade.

Now suppose the U.S. demand for autos rises from $D_{U.S._0}$ to $D_{U.S._1}$. Figure 6.3(a) shows that, despite the increased demand, the price of auto imports remains at $7,000. This is because the U.S. price cannot differ from the Japanese price by an amount exceeding the tariff duty. Auto imports rise from 3 million units to 5 million units. Under an import tariff, then, domestic adjustment takes the form of an increase in the quantity of autos imported rather than a rise in auto prices.

In Figure 6.3(b), an identical increase in demand induces a rise in domestic auto prices. Under the quota, there is no limit on the extent to which the U.S. price can rise above the Japanese price. Given an increase in domestic auto prices, U.S. companies are able to expand production. The domestic price will rise until the increased production plus the fixed level of imports are commensurate with the domestic demand. Figure 6.3(b) shows that an increase in demand from $D_{U.S._0}$ to $D_{U.S._1}$ forces auto prices up from $7,000 to $7,500. At the new price, domestic production equals 4 million units, and domestic consumption equals 7 million units. Imports total 3 million units, the same amount as under the quota before the increase in domestic demand. Adjustment thus occurs in domestic prices rather than in the quantity of autos imported.

During periods of growing demand, then, an import quota is a more restrictive trade barrier than an equivalent import tariff. Under a quota, the government arbitrarily limits the quantity of imports. Under a tariff, the domestic price can rise above the world price only by the amount of the tariff; domestic consumers can still buy unlimited quantities of the import if they are willing and able to pay that amount. You might test your understanding of the approach used here by working out the details of two other hypothetical situations: (1) a reduction in the domestic supply of autos caused by rising pro-

duction costs and (2) a reduction in domestic demand due to economic recession.

Besides differing in their revenue effects and restrictive impacts on the volume of trade, tariffs and quotas have several other notable differences. Quotas are administratively easier to manage than tariffs, but they normally do not provide government tax revenues. Quotas are relatively easy to enact for emergency purposes, whereas enactment of tariffs is a time-consuming process requiring Congress to enact legislation.

TARIFF-RATE QUOTA: A TWO-TIER TARIFF

Another restriction used to insulate a domestic industry from foreign competition is the **tariff-rate quota**. The U.S. government has imposed tariff-rate quotas on imports such as stainless steel flatware, brooms, cattle, fish, sugar, and milk.

As its name suggests, a tariff-rate quota displays both tariff-like and quota-like characteristics. This device allows a specified number of goods to be imported at one tariff rate (the *within-quota rate*), whereas any imports above this level face a higher tariff rate (the *over-quota rate*). A tariff-rate quota is thus a *two-tier tariff*. For example, in 1995 the U.S. tariff-rate quota quantity for cotton was set at 2.1 million kilograms; imports within this limit faced a duty of 4.4 cents per kilogram, but a duty of 36 cents per kilogram pertained to any imports over this limit.

Figure 6.4 illustrates the welfare effects of a hypothetical tariff-rate quota on sugar. Assume that the U.S. demand and supply schedules for sugar are given by $D_{U.S.}$ and $S_{U.S.}$, and the equilibrium (autarky) price of sugar is $540 per ton. Assuming free trade, suppose the United States faces a constant world price of sugar equal to $400 per ton. At the free-trade price, U.S. production equals 5 tons, U.S. consumption equals 40 tons, and imports equal 35 tons.

To protect its producers from foreign competition, suppose the United States enacts a tariff-rate import quota of 5 tons. Imports within this

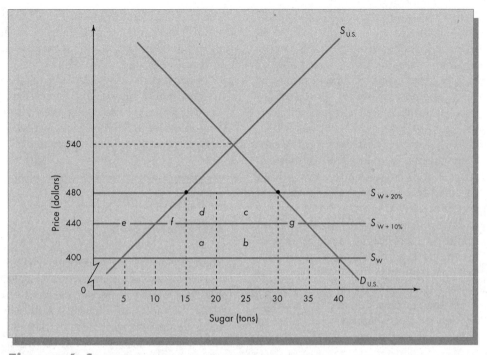

Figure 6.4 Tariff-Rate Quota: Trade and Welfare Effects

A tariff-rate quota is a two-tier tariff levied on imports. Its imposition leads to higher product prices and a decrease in consumer surplus for domestic buyers. Of the tariff-rate quota's revenue effect, a portion accrues to the domestic government, while the remainder accrues to domestic importers or foreign exporters as windfall profits.

limit face a 10-percent tariff, but a 20-percent tariff applies to imports in excess of the limit.

Because the United States initially imports an amount exceeding the limit as defined by the tariff-rate quota, both the within-quota rate and the over-quota rate apply. This two-tier tariff causes the price of sugar sold in the United States to rise from $400 to $480 per ton. Domestic production increases to 15 tons, domestic consumption falls to 30 tons, and imports fall to 15 tons. Increased sales allow the profits of U.S. sugar producers to rise by an amount equal to area *e* ($800). The deadweight losses to the U.S. economy, in terms of production and consumption inefficiencies, equal areas *f* ($400) and *g* ($400), respectively.

An interesting feature of the tariff-rate quota is the revenue it generates. Some of it accrues to the domestic government as tariff revenue, but the remainder is captured by business as windfall profits—a gain to business resulting from sudden or unexpected government policy.

In this example, after enactment of the tariff quota, imports total 15 tons of sugar. The U.S. government collects area *a* ($200), found by multiplying the within-quota duty of $40 times 5 tons. Area *b* + *c* ($800), found by multiplying the remaining 10 tons of imported sugar times the over-quota duty of $80, also accrues to the government.

Area *d* ($200) in the figure represents windfall profits. Under the tariff-rate quota, the domestic price of the first 5 tons of sugar imported is $440, reflecting the foreign supply price of $400 plus the import duty of $40. Suppose U.S. import companies can obtain foreign sugar at $440 per ton. By reselling the 5 tons to U.S. consumers at $480 per ton, the price of over-quota sugar, U.S. importers would capture area *d* as windfall profits. But this opportunity will not last long, because foreign sugar suppliers will want to capture the windfall gain. To the extent that they can restrict sugar exports to the United States, foreign producers could force up the price of sugar and expropriate profits from U.S. importing companies. Foreign producers conceivably could capture the entire area *d* by raising their supply price to $480 per ton. The portion of the windfall profit captured by foreign sugar producers represents a welfare loss to the U.S. economy.

As part of the Uruguay Round of multilateral trade negotiations (see Chapter 7), members of the World Trade Organization (WTO) changed their systems of import protection for those agricultural products helped by government farm programs. The trade pact required WTO countries to convert to tariffs or tariff-rate quotas all nontariff trade barriers (import quotas, variable levies, discretionary licensing, outright import bans) applicable to imports from other WTO countries; existing nontariff barrier restrictions could continue to apply to non-WTO countries. The trade pact thus put all nontariff barriers on a common standard—tariffs—that any exporter could readily measure and understand. It also resulted in the establishment by WTO countries of low within-quota tariff rates to ensure that agricultural imports would account for at least 3 percent of base-period domestic consumption in 1995 and 5 percent by the year 2000; higher tariff rates would help shield domestic producers against imports exceeding the within-quota threshold. Table 6.3 provides examples of U.S. tariff-rate quotas applied to agricultural imports.

ORDERLY MARKETING AGREEMENTS

An **orderly marketing agreement (OMA)** is a market-sharing pact negotiated by trading partners. Its main purpose is to moderate the intensity of international competition, allowing less efficient domestic producers to participate in markets that would otherwise have been lost to foreign producers that sell a superior product at a lower price. OMAs involve trade negotiations between importing and exporting nations, generally for a variety of labor-intensive manufactured goods.

A typical OMA consists of voluntary quotas applied to exports. These controls are known as **voluntary export restraints (VERs)**; they are sometimes supplemented by backup import controls to ensure that the restraints are effective. For example, Japan may impose limits on steel exports to Europe, or Taiwan may agree to cutbacks on shoe exports to the United States.

Table 6.3 Examples of U.S. Tariff-Rate Quotas

Product	Within-Quota Rate	Import-Quota Threshold	Over-Quota Tariff Rate
Peanuts	9.35 cents/kg	30,393 tons	187.9 percent ad valorem
Beef	4.4 cents/kg	634,621 tons	31.1 percent ad valorem
Milk	3.2 cents/L	5.7 million L	88.5 cents/L
Blue cheese	10 cents/kg	2.6 million kg	$2.60/kg
Cotton	4.4 cents/kg	2.1 million kg	36 cents/kg

Source: U.S. International Trade Commission, *Harmonized Tariff Schedule of the United States, 2000*, Washington, DC, U.S. Government Printing Office.

CATERPILLAR OPPOSES STEEL QUOTAS

From 1984 to 1992, the U.S. government nego-tiated export quota agreements with foreign steel-producing nations in order to provide relief for a declining U.S. steel industry. These agree-ments were widely opposed by steel-using firms in the United States. Consider why Caterpillar, Inc., one of the nation's largest steel users, opposed the steel quotas.

> We believe more protection for the U.S. steel indus-try is unnecessary and carries tremendous costs. Prices of the primary steel products used by Caterpillar—plate and hot rolled bar—have risen approximately 20 percent from January 1988 to April 1989. By artificially restricting the supply of steel, quotas would create additional availability problems and provide U.S. steel producers increased leverage to demand higher prices. Caterpillar and its workers, dealers, and customers will be forced to "pay the price" for this protection.
>
> For many Caterpillar products—including large tractors and off-highway trucks—steel comprises at least 20 percent of product cost. Since January

1988, prices for the primary steel products used by Caterpillar—plate and hot rolled bar—have increased approximately 20 percent. This price increase took place even though the cost to pro-duce steel in the United States has dropped sharply in recent years.

Did quotas contribute to this price increase? Caterpillar believes the answer is clearly yes. At the time the company negotiated its 1988 plate price, U.S. mills were running flat out; the plate quota was 99.8 percent filled. Plate lead times in the United States were 14 to 16 weeks. Yet outside the United States, plate was in ample supply.

Besides causing higher prices, steel shortages have hurt Caterpillar in other ways. In late 1987, for example, the company's U.S. facilities ran out of the large special section steel used to manufacture crawler-tractor track shoes. The consequence was incomplete products and inefficient factory opera-tions. Because there were no U.S. producers of this type of steel . . . and quotas prevented Caterpillar from importing enough steel to satisfy its needs...the shortage was clearly quota-induced.

Source: Excerpts from *Steel Import Quotas: Update*, April 1989, Caterpillar, Inc. Reprinted Courtesy of Caterpillar Inc.

Because OMAs are reached through negotia-tions, on the surface they appear to be less one-sided than unilateral protectionist devices such as import tariffs and quotas. In practice, the distinc-tion between negotiated versus unilateral trade curbs becomes blurred. Trade negotiations are often carried out with the realization that the importing nations may adopt more stringent protectionist devices should the negotiators be unable to reach an acceptable settlement. An exporting nation's motivation to negotiate OMAs may thus stem from its desire to avoid a more costly alternative—that is, a full-fledged trade war. OMAs have covered trade in such commodities as television sets, steel, textiles, autos, and ships, as seen in Table 6.4.

Recent rounds of trade negotiations have restricted the use of OMAs. Under the provisions of the Uruguay Round of 1986–1993 (see Chapter

7), nations cannot enact new OMAs in response to escape-clause claims of injury by domestic firms and workers. Moreover, existing OMAs were phased out in 1998, except for the Japan–European Union auto agreement, which ran until its scheduled close in 1999.

EXPORT QUOTA EFFECTS

A typical OMA involves limitations on export sales adminis-tered by one or more exporting nations or industries. What are the trade and welfare effects of **export quotas**?

Figure 6.5 illustrates these effects in the case of trade in autos among the United States, Japan, and Germany. Assume that $S_{U.S.}$ and $D_{U.S.}$ depict the sup-ply and demand schedules of autos for the United States. S_J denotes the supply schedule of Japan, assumed to be the world's low-cost producer, and S_G denotes the supply schedule of Germany.

Table 6.4 Orderly Marketing Agreement Examples

Manufactured Good	Principal Nations	Accord Provisions
Specialty steel	United States, European Union, Sweden, Japan, Canada	Japan negotiates export quota in U.S. market; United States imposes import quota on others
Television sets	Japan, Benelux, Britain	Japan voluntarily limits exports to Britain and Benelux
Ships	Japan, European Union	Japan enters into agreement with European Union to curb price competition
Garments and textiles	41 exporting and importing nations	Export and import quotas; annual growth rates
Autos	Japan, United States	Japan voluntarily restrains exports to the United States

Source: *Annual Report of the President of the United States on the Trade Agreements Program*, Washington, DC, Government Printing Office, various issues.

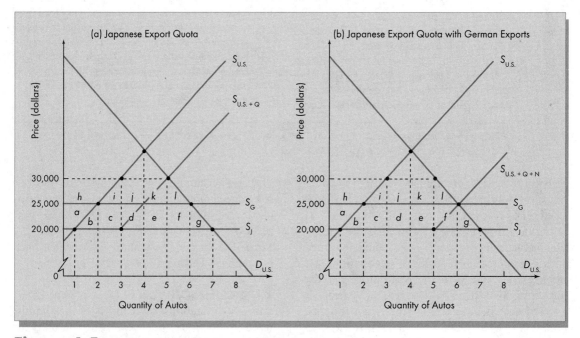

Figure 6.5 Trade and Welfare Effects of a Voluntary Export Quota

By reducing available supplies of a product, an export quota (levied by the foreign nation) leads to higher prices in the importing nation. The price increase induces a decrease in consumer surplus. Of this amount, the welfare loss to the importing nation equals the protective effect, the consumption effect, and the portion of the revenue effect that is captured by the foreign exporter. To the extent that nonrestrained countries augment shipments to the importing nation, the welfare loss of an export quota decreases.

Referring to Figure 6.5(a), the price of autos to the U.S. consumer is $20,000 under free trade. At that price, U.S. firms produce 1 auto, and U.S. consumers purchase 7 autos, with imports from Japan totaling 6 autos. Note that German autos are too costly to be exported to the United States at the free-trade price.

Suppose that Japan, responding to protectionist sentiment in the United States, decides to restrain auto shipments to the United States rather than face possible mandatory restrictions on its exports. Assume that the Japanese government imposes an export quota on its auto firms of 2 units, down from the free-trade level of 6 units. Above the free-trade price, the total U.S. supply of autos now equals U.S. production plus the export quota; the auto supply curve thus shifts from $S_{U.S.}$ to $S_{U.S.+Q}$ in Figure 6.5(a). The reduction in imports from 6 autos to 2 autos raises the equilibrium price to $30,000. This leads to an increase in the quantity supplied by U.S. firms from 1 auto to 3 autos and a decrease in the U.S. quantity demanded from 7 autos to 5 autos.

The export quota's price increase causes consumer surplus to fall by area $a + b + c + d + e + f + g + h + i + j + k + l$, an amount totaling $60,000. Area $a + h$ ($20,000) represents the transfer to U.S. auto companies as *profits*. The export quota results in a deadweight welfare loss for the U.S. economy equal to the *protective effect*, denoted by area $b + c + i$ ($10,000), and the *consumption effect*, denoted by area $f + g + l$ ($10,000). The export quota's *revenue effect* equals area $d + e + j + k$ ($20,000), found by multiplying the quota-induced increase in the Japanese price times the volume of autos shipped to the United States.

Remember that under an import quota, the disposition of the revenue effect is indeterminate: It will be shared between foreign exporters and domestic importers, depending on the relative concentration of bargaining power. But under an export quota, it is the foreign exporter who is able to capture the larger share of the quota revenue. In our example of the auto export quota, the Japanese exporters, in compliance with their government, self-regulate shipments to the United States. This supply-side restriction, resulting from Japanese firms' behaving like a monopoly, leads to a scarcity of autos in the United States. Japanese automakers then are able to raise the price of their exports, capturing the quota revenue. For this reason, it is not surprising that exporters might prefer to negotiate a voluntary restraint pact in lieu of facing other protectionist measures levied by the importing country. As for the export quota's impact on the U.S. economy, the expropriation of revenue by the Japanese represents a welfare loss in addition to the deadweight losses of production and consumption.

Another characteristic of a voluntary export agreement is that it typically applies only to the most important exporting nation(s). This is in contrast to a tariff or import quota, which generally applies to imports from all sources. When voluntary limits are imposed on the chief exporter, the exports of the **nonrestrained suppliers** may be stimulated. Nonrestrained suppliers may seek to increase profits by making up part of the cutback in the restrained nation's shipments. They may also want to achieve the maximum level of shipments against which to base any export quotas that might be imposed on them in the future. For example, Japan was singled out by the United States for restrictions in textiles during the 1950s and in color television sets during the 1970s. Other nations quickly increased shipments to the United States to fill in the gaps created by the Japanese restraints. Hong Kong textiles replaced most Japanese textiles, and TV sets from Taiwan and Korea supplanted Japanese sets.

Referring to Figure 6.5(b), let us start again at the free-trade price of $20,000, with U.S. imports from Japan totaling 6 autos. Assume that Japan agrees to reduce its shipments to 2 units. However, suppose Germany, a nonrestrained supplier, exports 2 autos to the United States in response to the Japanese cutback. Above the free-trade price, the total U.S. supply of autos now equals U.S. production plus the Japanese export quota plus the nonrestrained exports coming from Germany. In Figure 6.5(b), this is illustrated by a shift in the supply curve from $S_{U.S.}$ to $S_{U.S.+Q+N}$. The reduction in imports from 6 autos to 4 autos raises equilibrium price to \$25,000. The resulting deadweight losses of production and consumption inefficiencies equal area $b + g$ (\$5,000), less than the deadweight losses under Japan's export quota in the absence of nonrestrained supply. Assuming that Japan administers the export restraint program, Japanese companies would be able to raise the price of their auto exports from \$20,000 to \$25,000 and earn profits equal to area $c + d$ (\$10,000). Area $e + f$ (\$10,000) represents a **trade-diversion effect**, which reflects inefficiency losses due to the shifting of 2 units from Japan, the world's low-cost producer, to Germany, a higher-cost source. Such trade diversion results in a loss of welfare to the world because resources are not being used in their most productive manner. The overall welfare of the United States thus decreases by area $b + c + d + e + f + g$ under the export-quota policy.

When increases in the nonrestrained supply offset part of the cutback in shipments that occurs under an export quota, the overall inefficiency loss for the importing nation (deadweight losses plus revenue expropriated by foreign producers) is less than that which would have occurred in the absence of nonrestrained exports. In the preceding example, this reduction amounts to area $i + j + k + l$ (\$15,000). The next section will consider the effects of voluntary export quotas on the U.S. auto industry.

JAPANESE AUTO RESTRAINT In 1981, as domestic auto sales fell, protectionist sentiment gained momentum in the U.S. Congress, and legislation was introduced calling for import quotas. This momentum was a major factor in the administration's desire to negotiate a voluntary restraint pact with the Japanese. Japan's acceptance of this agreement was apparently based on its view that voluntary limits on its auto shipments would derail any protectionist momentum in Congress for more stringent measures.

The restraint program called for self-imposed export quotas on Japanese auto shipments to the United States for three years, beginning in 1981. First-year shipments were to be held to 1.68 million units, 7.7 percent below the 1.82 million units exported in 1980. In subsequent years, auto shipments were to be held to the same number plus 16.5 percent of any increase in domestic U.S. auto sales recorded in 1981. As it turned out, falling U.S. sales caused Japanese auto exports to be limited to 1.68 million units in 1982 and 1983. Still facing a weak auto industry, the United States was able to negotiate an export restraint pact with Japan for 1984, during which Japanese firms would limit auto shipments to the United States to 1.85 million units. In 1984, the United States released Japan from its formal commitment to the export agreement, but the Japanese government thought it imprudent to permit its automakers to export freely to the United States. The Japanese government has imposed its own export quotas on its auto manufacturers since the termination of the export agreement.

The purpose of the export agreement was to help U.S. automakers by diverting U.S. customers from Japanese to U.S. showrooms. As domestic sales increased, so would jobs for American autoworkers. It was assumed that Japan's export quota would assist the U.S. auto industry as it went through a transition period of reallocating production toward smaller, more fuel-efficient autos and adjusting production to become more cost-competitive. The restraint program would provide U.S. auto companies temporary relief from foreign competition so they could restore profitability and reduce unemployment.

Not all Japanese auto manufacturers were equally affected by the export quota. By requiring Japanese auto companies to form an export cartel against the U.S. consumer, the quota allowed the large, established firms (Toyota, Nissan, and Honda) to increase prices on autos sold in the United States. To derive more revenues from a limited number of autos, Japanese firms shipped autos to the United States with fancier trim, bigger engines, and more amenities such as air-conditioners and deluxe stereos as standard equipment. Product enrichment also helped the Japanese broaden their hold on the U.S. market and enhance the image of their autos. As a result, the large Japanese manufacturers earned record profits in the United States.

The export quota was unpopular, however, with smaller Japanese automakers, including Suzuki and Isuzu. Under the restraint program, as administered by the Japanese government, each company's export quota was based on the number of autos sold in the United States three years prior to initiation of the quota. Smaller producers claimed that the quota forced them to freeze their U.S. dealer networks and abandon plans to introduce new models. It was argued that the quotas helped Nissan, which was floundering before the restraints, to become a dominant force in the U.S. market at the expense of smaller Japanese automakers. Table 6.5 depicts the estimated welfare effects for the United States of the Japanese export quota.

Table 6.5 Effects of Japanese Export Quota in Autos*

Effect	Amount
Price of Japanese autos sold in the United States (increase)	$1,300
Price of U.S. autos sold in the United States (increase)	$660
Cost to U.S. consumers (increase)	$15.7 million
Number of Japanese autos sold in the United States (decrease)	1 million units
Japanese share of U.S. auto market (decrease)	9.6%
Sales of U.S.-produced autos (increase)	618,000 units
U.S. auto industry jobs (increase)	44,000

*These estimates apply to 1984, the fourth year of the export quota.

Source: U.S. International Trade Commission, *A Review of Recent Developments in the U.S. Automobile Industry Including an Assessment of the Japanese Voluntary Restraint Agreements*, Washington, DC, Government Printing Office, 1985.

DOMESTIC CONTENT REQUIREMENTS

Today, many products, such as autos and aircraft, embody worldwide production. Domestic manufacturers of these products purchase resources or perform assembly functions outside the home country, a practice known as **foreign sourcing** (outsourcing) or production sharing. For example, General Motors has obtained engines from its subsidiaries in Mexico, DaimlerChrysler has purchased ball joints from Japanese producers, and Ford has acquired cylinder heads from European companies. Firms have used foreign sourcing to take advantage of lower production costs overseas, including lower wage rates. Domestic workers often challenge this practice, maintaining that foreign sourcing means that cheap foreign labor takes away their jobs and imposes downward pressure on the wages of those workers who are able to keep their jobs.

To limit the practice of foreign sourcing, organized labor has lobbied for the use of **domestic content requirements**. These requirements stipulate the minimum percentage of a product's total value that must be produced domestically. The effect of content requirements is to force both domestic and foreign firms who sell products in the home country to use domestic inputs (workers) in the production of those products. The demand for domestic inputs thus increases, contributing to higher input prices. Manufacturers generally lobby against domestic content requirements, because they prevent manufacturers from obtaining inputs at the lowest cost, thus contributing to higher product prices and loss of competitiveness.

Worldwide, local content requirements have received most attention in the automobile industry. Developing countries have often used content requirements to foster domestic automobile production, as shown in Table 6.6.

HOW "FOREIGN" IS YOUR CAR?

Did you know that U.S. buyers of cars and light trucks can learn how American or foreign their new vehicle is? On cars and trucks weighing 8,500 pounds or less, the law requires content labels telling buyers where the parts of the vehicle were made. Content is measured by the dollar value of components, not the labor cost of assembling vehicles. The percentages of North American (U.S. and Canadian) and foreign parts must be listed as an average for each car line. Manufacturers are free to design the label, which can be included on the price sticker or fuel economy sticker or can be separate. Below are some examples of the domestic and foreign content of vehicles sold in the United States for the 2000 model year. The data was collected from automobile stickers at dealers' lots.

	Assembly	North American Parts Content (Percent)	Foreign Parts Content (Percent)
Ford Focus	United States	75	25
Ford Windstar	United States	95	5
Ford Mustang	United States	90	10
GMC Sierra	United States	90	10
Dodge Intrepid	Canada	86	14
Dodge Alero	United States	76	24
Oldsmobile Intrigue	United States	85	15
Buick Regal	Canada	85	15
Chevrolet Impala	Canada	85	15
Chevrolet Cavalier	United States	85	15

Table 6.6 Domestic Content Requirements Applied to Automobiles in Selected Countries

Country	Minimum Domestic Content Required (Percent)
Argentina	76
Brazil	60
Malaysia	60
South Africa	55
Thailand	54
Chinese Taipei	50
Venezuela	41
China	40
Pakistan	40

Source: U.S. Department of Commerce, International Trade Administration, Office of Automotive Affairs, *Vehicle Import Requirements*, 2000, at the Internet site http://www.ita.doc.gov/auto/impreq.html.

Figure 6.6 illustrates possible welfare effects of an Australian content requirement on automobiles. Assume that D_A denotes the Australian demand schedule for Toyota automobiles while S_J depicts the supply price of Toyotas exported to Australia, $24,000. With free trade, Australia imports 500 Toyotas. Japanese resource owners involved in manufacturing this vehicle realize incomes totaling $12 million, denoted by area $c + d$.

Suppose the Australian government imposes a domestic content requirement on autos. This policy causes Toyota to establish a factory in Australia to produce vehicles replacing the Toyotas previously imported by Australia. Assume that the transplant factory combines Japanese management with Australian resources (labor and materials) in vehicle production. Also assume that high Australian resource prices (wages) cause the transplant's supply price to be $33,000, denoted by S_T. Under the content

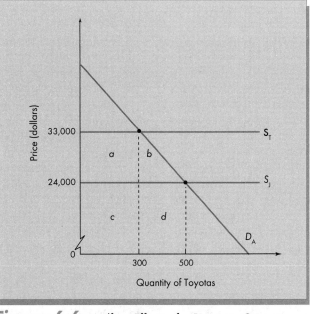

Figure 6.6 Welfare Effects of a Domestic Content Requirement

A domestic content requirement leads to rising production costs and prices to the extent that manufacturers are "forced" to locate production facilities in a high-cost nation. Although the content requirement helps preserve domestic jobs, it imposes welfare losses on domestic consumers.

requirement, Australian consumers demand 300 vehicles. Because production has shifted from Japan to Australia, Japanese resource owners lose $12 million of income. Australian resource owners gain $9.9 million of income (area $a+c$) minus the income paid to Japanese managers and the return to Toyota's capital investment (factory) in Australia.

However, the income gains of Australian resource owners inflict costs on Australian consumers. Because the content requirement causes the price of Toyotas to increase by $9,000, Australian consumer surplus decreases by area a + b ($3,600,000). Of this amount, area b ($900,000) is a deadweight welfare loss for Australia. Area a ($2,700,000) is the consumer cost of employing higher-priced Australian

resources instead of lower-priced Japanese resources; this amount represents a redistribution of welfare from Australian consumers to Australian resource owners. Similar to other import restrictions, content requirements lead to the subsidizing by domestic consumers of the domestic producer.

Throughout the early 1980s, as unemployment increased among U.S. autoworkers, the UAW pressured the U.S. government for protection against foreign-produced autos. Defending the interests of its members, the UAW maintained that domestic content legislation was needed to ensure that all companies selling autos in the United States would build a portion of each vehicle with U.S. parts and assembly. In 1982, the U.S. House of Representatives passed a domestic content bill titled the Fair Practices in Automotive Products Act. The proposed legislation would have required all domestic and foreign manufacturers producing more than 100,000 vehicles for sale in the U.S. market to achieve minimal domestic content requirements on a scale graduating to the level of U.S. sales. General Motors and Ford, for example, would have faced minimum content requirements (U.S.-added domestic value as a percentage of wholesale price) of 90 percent, whereas the requirement for Toyota would have been 71 percent. The bill was never passed by the U.S. Senate and did not become part of U.S. trade policy. However, it pressured Japanese automakers to locate transplant factories in the United States; such sites became numerous by the late 1980s.

SUBSIDIES

National governments sometimes grant **subsidies** to domestic producers to help improve their trade position. Such devices are an indirect form of protection provided to home businesses, whether they be import-competing producers or exporters. By providing domestic firms a cost advantage, a subsidy allows them to market their products at prices lower than warranted by their actual cost or profit considerations. Governments wanting

to see certain domestic industries expand may provide subsidies to encourage their development. Governmental subsidies assume a variety of forms, including outright cash disbursements, tax concessions, insurance arrangements, and loans at below-market interest rates. Table 6.7 provides examples of governmental subsidies for several nations.

For purposes of our discussion, two types of subsidies can be distinguished: a **domestic subsidy**, which is sometimes granted to producers of import-competing goods, and an **export subsidy**, which goes to producers of goods that are to be sold overseas. In both cases, the recipient producer views the subsidy as tantamount to a negative tax: The government adds an amount to the price the purchaser pays rather than subtracting from it. The net price actually received by the producer equals the price paid by the purchaser plus the subsidy. The subsidized producer is thus able to supply a greater quantity at each consumer's price. Let us use Figure 6.7 to analyze the effects of these two types of subsidies.

DOMESTIC SUBSIDY Figure 6.7(a) illustrates the trade and welfare effects of a production subsidy granted to import-competing manufacturers. Assume that the initial supply and demand schedules of the United States for steel are depicted by curves $S_{U.S._0}$ and $D_{U.S._0}$, so that the

---

Table 6.7 Examples of Governmental Subsidies

Country	Subsidy Policy
Australia	Export market development grants extended to Australian exporters to seek out and develop overseas markets.
Canada	Rail transportation subsidies granted to Canadian exporters of wheat, barley, oats, and alfalfa.
European Union	Export subsidies provided to many agricultural products such as wheat, beef, poultry, fruits, and dairy products. Financial assistance extended to Airbus.
Japan	Financial assistance extended to Japanese aerospace producers, including loans at low interest rates and assistance with R&D costs.
United States	Export subsidies provided to U.S. producers of agricultural and manufactured goods through the Commodity Credit Corporation and the Export Import Bank

Source: Office of the U.S. Trade Representative, *Foreign Trade Barriers*, Washington, DC, U.S. Government Printing Office, various issues.

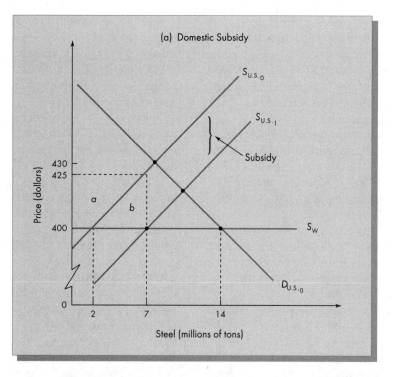

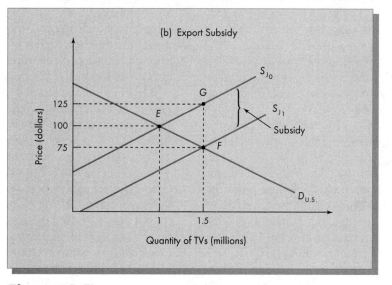

Figure 6.7 Trade and Welfare Effects of Subsidies

A government subsidy granted to import-competing producers leads to increased domestic production and reduced imports. The subsidy revenue accruing to the producer is absorbed by producer surplus and high-cost production (protective effect). A government subsidy granted to exporters results in an export revenue effect and a terms-of-trade effect.

market equilibrium price is $430 per ton. Assume also that, because the United States is a small buyer of steel, changes in its purchases do not affect the world price of $400 per ton. Given a free-trade price of $400 per ton, the United States consumes 14 tons of steel, produces 2 tons, and imports 12 tons.

To partially insulate domestic producers from foreign competition, suppose the U.S. government grants them a production subsidy of $25 per ton of steel. The cost advantage made possible by the subsidy results in a shift in the U.S. supply schedule from $S_{U.S._0}$ to $S_{U.S._1}$. Domestic production expands from 2 to 7 million tons, and imports fall from 12 to 7 million tons. These changes represent the subsidy's trade effect.

The subsidy also affects the national welfare of the United States. According to Figure 6.7(a), the subsidy permits U.S. output to rise to 7 million tons. Note that, at this output, the net price to the steelmaker is $425—the sum of the price paid by the consumer ($400) plus the subsidy ($25). To the U.S. government, the total cost of protecting its steelmakers equals the amount of the subsidy ($25) times the amount of output to which it is applied (7 million tons), or $175 million.

Where does this subsidy revenue go? Part of it is redistributed to the more efficient U.S. producers in the form of *producer surplus*. This amount is denoted by area *a* ($112.5 million) in the figure. There is also a *protective effect*, whereby more costly domestic output is allowed to be sold in the market as a result of the subsidy. This is denoted by area *b* ($62.5 million) in the figure. To the United States as a whole, the protective effect represents a deadweight loss of welfare.

To encourage production by its import-competing manufacturers, a government might levy tariffs or quotas on imports. But tariffs and quotas involve larger sacrifices in national welfare than would occur under an equivalent subsidy. Unlike subsidies, tariffs and quotas distort choices for domestic consumers (resulting in a decrease in the domestic demand for imports), in addition to permitting less efficient home production to occur. The result is the familiar consumption effect of protection, whereby a dead-

weight loss of consumer surplus is borne by the home nation. This welfare loss is absent in the subsidy case. Thus, a subsidy tends to yield the same result for domestic producers as does an equivalent tariff or quota, but at a lower cost in terms of national welfare.

Subsidies are not free goods, however, for they must be financed by someone. The direct cost of the subsidy is a burden that must be financed out of tax revenues paid by the public. Moreover, when a subsidy is given to an industry, it is often in return for accepting government conditions on key matters (such as wage and salary levels). Thus a subsidy may not be as superior to other types of commercial policies as this analysis suggests.

EXPORT SUBSIDY Besides attempting to protect import-competing industries, many national governments grant subsidies, including special tax exemptions and the provision of capital at favored rates, to increase the volume of exports. By providing a cost advantage to domestic producers, such subsidies are intended to encourage a nation's exports by reducing the price paid by foreigners. Foreign consumers are favored over domestic consumers to the extent that the foreign price of a subsidized export is less than the product's domestic price.

The granting of an export subsidy yields two direct effects for the home economy: a *terms-of-trade effect* and an **export-revenue effect**. Because subsidies tend to reduce the foreign price of home-nation exports, the home nation's terms of trade is worsened. But lower foreign prices generally stimulate export volume. Should the foreign demand for exports be relatively elastic, so that a given percentage drop in foreign price is more than offset by the rise in export volume, the home nation's export revenues will increase.

Figure 6.7(b) illustrates the case of an export subsidy applied to television sets in trade between Japan and the United States. Under free trade, market equilibrium exists at point *E*, where Japan exports 1 million television sets to the United States at a price of $100 per unit. Suppose the Japanese government, to encourage export sales, grants to its exporters a subsidy of $50 per set.

The Japanese supply schedule shifts from S_{J_0} to S_{J_1}, and market equilibrium moves to point *F*. The terms of trade thus turns against Japan, because its export price falls from $100 to $75 per television set exported. Whether Japan's export revenue rises depends on how U.S. buyers respond to the price decrease. If the percentage increase in the number of television sets sold to U.S. buyers more than offsets the percentage decrease in price, Japan's export revenue will rise. This is the case in Figure 6.7b, which shows Japan's export revenue rising from $100 million to $112.5 million as the result of the decline in the price of its export good.

Although export subsidies may benefit industries and workers in a subsidized industry by increasing sales and employment, the benefits may be offset by certain costs that fall on the society as a whole. Consumers in the exporting nation suffer as the international terms of trade moves against them. This situation comes about because, given a fall in export prices, a greater number of exports must be exchanged for a given dollar amount in imports. Domestic consumers also find they must pay higher prices than foreigners for the goods they help subsidize. Furthermore, to the extent that taxes are required to finance the export subsidy, domestic consumers find themselves poorer. In the previous example, the total cost of the subsidy to Japanese taxpayers is $75 million ($50 subsidy times 1.5 million television sets).

One type of export subsidy is the **export credit subsidy**. To encourage exporting by domestic producers, governments frequently extend loans to foreign customers. These loans are often awarded when private banks are unwilling to grant credit to importing businesses viewed as high risk. The interest rates charged on export credits have traditionally been lower than those demanded by private banks on similar loans. Export credit subsidies transfer money from domestic taxpayers to the subsidized export industry, foreign purchasers, or both. To prevent nations from attaining unfair competitive advantage through export subsidies, industrial nations have established guidelines that stipulate the interest rate, term, and down payment for credit programs.

DUMPING

The case for protecting import-competing producers from foreign competition is bolstered by the antidumping argument. **Dumping** is recognized as a form of international price discrimination. It occurs when foreign buyers are charged lower prices than domestic buyers for an identical product, after allowing for transportation costs and tariff duties. Selling in foreign markets at a price below the cost of production is also considered dumping.

FORMS OF DUMPING Commercial dumping is generally viewed as sporadic, predatory, or persistent in nature. Each type is practiced under different circumstances.

Sporadic dumping (distress dumping) occurs when a firm disposes of excess inventories on foreign markets by selling abroad at lower prices than at home. This form of dumping may be the result of misfortune or poor planning by foreign producers. Unforeseen changes in supply and demand conditions can result in excess inventories and thus in dumping. Although sporadic dumping may be beneficial to importing consumers, it can be quite disruptive to import-competing producers, who face falling sales and short-run losses. Temporary tariff duties can be levied to protect home producers, but because sporadic dumping has minor effects on international trade, governments are reluctant to grant tariff protection under these circumstances.

Predatory dumping occurs when a producer temporarily reduces the prices charged abroad to drive foreign competitors out of business. When the producer succeeds in acquiring a monopoly position, prices are then raised commensurate with its market power. The new price level must be sufficiently high to offset any losses that occurred during the period of cutthroat pricing. The firm would presumably be confident in its ability to prevent the entry of potential competitors long enough for it to enjoy economic profits. To be successful, predatory dumping would have to be practiced on a massive basis to provide consumers with sufficient opportunity for bargain shopping. Home governments are generally concerned about predatory pricing for monopolizing purposes and may retaliate with antidumping duties that eliminate the price differential. Although predatory dumping is a theoretical possibility, economists have not found empirical evidence that supports its existence.

Persistent dumping, as its name suggests, goes on indefinitely. In an effort to maximize economic profits, a producer may consistently sell abroad at lower prices than at home. The rationale underlying persistent dumping is explained in the next section.

INTERNATIONAL PRICE DISCRIMINATION

Consider the case of a domestic seller that enjoys market power as a result of barriers that restrict competition at home. Suppose this firm sells in foreign markets that are highly competitive. This means that the domestic consumer response to a change in price is less than that abroad; the home demand is less elastic than the foreign demand. A profit-maximizing firm would benefit from international price discrimination, charging a higher price at home, where competition is weak and demand is less elastic, and a lower price for the same product in foreign markets to meet competition. The practice of identifying separate groups of buyers of a product and charging different prices to these groups results in increased revenues and profits for the firm as compared to what would occur in the absence of price discrimination.

Figure 6.8 illustrates the demand and cost conditions of South Korean Steel Inc. (SKS), which sells steel to buyers in South Korea (less elastic market) and in Canada (more elastic market); the total steel market consists of these two submarkets. Let D_{SK} be the South Korean steel demand and D_C be the Canadian demand, with the corresponding marginal revenue schedules represented by MR_{SK} and MR_C, respectively. D_{SK+C} denotes the market demand schedule, found by adding horizontally the demand schedules of the two submarkets; similarly, MR_{SK+C} depicts the market marginal revenue schedule. The marginal cost and average total cost schedules of SKS are denoted respectively by MC and ATC.

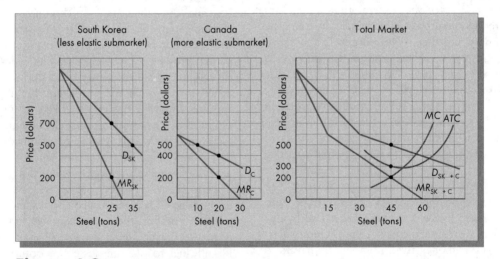

Figure 6.8 International Price Discrimination

A price-discriminating firm maximizes profits by equating marginal revenue, in each submarket, with marginal cost. The firm will charge a higher price in the less-elastic-demand (less competitive) market and a lower price in the more-elastic-demand (more competitive) market. Successful dumping leads to additional revenue and profits for the firm compared to what would be realized in the absence of dumping.

SKS maximizes total profits by producing and selling 45 tons of steel, at which marginal revenue equals marginal cost. At this output level, $ATC =$ $300 per ton, and total cost equals $13,500 ($300 $\times$ 45 tons). The firm faces the problem of how to distribute the total output of 45 tons, and thus set price, in the two submarkets in which it sells. Should the firm sell steel to South Korean and Canadian buyers at a uniform (single) price, or should the firm practice differential pricing?

As a *nondiscriminating seller*, SKS sells 45 tons of steel to South Korean and Canadian buyers at the single price of $500 per ton, the maximum price permitted by demand schedule D_{SK+C} at the $MR = MC$ output level. To see how many tons of steel are sold in each submarket, construct a horizontal line in Figure 6.8 at the price of $500. The optimal output in each submarket occurs where the horizontal line intersects the demand schedules of the two nations. SKS thus sells 35 tons of steel to South Korean buyers at a price of $500 per ton and receives revenues totaling $17,500. The firm sells 10 tons of steel to Canadian buyers at a price of $500 per ton and realizes revenues of $5,000. Sales revenues in both submarkets combined equal $22,500. With total costs of $13,500, SKS realizes profits of $9,000.

Although SKS realizes profits as a nondiscriminating seller, its profits are not optimal. By engaging in price discrimination, the firm can increase its total revenues without increasing its costs, and thus increase its profits. The firm accomplishes this by charging higher prices to South Korean buyers, who have less elastic demand schedules, and lower prices to Canadian buyers, who have more elastic demand schedules.

As a price-discriminating seller, SKS again faces the problem of how to distribute the total output of 45 tons of steel, and thus set price, in the two submarkets in which it sells. To accomplish this, the firm follows the familiar $MR = MC$ principle, whereby the marginal revenue of each submarket equals the marginal cost at the profit-maximizing output. This can be shown in Figure 6.8 by first constructing a horizontal line from $200, the point where $MC = MR_{SK+C}$. The optimal output and price in each submarket is then found where

this horizontal line intersects the MR schedules of the submarkets. SKS thus sells 25 tons of steel to South Korean buyers at a price of $700 per ton and receives revenues totaling $17,500. The firm sells 20 tons of steel to Canadian buyers at a price of $400 per ton and collects revenues of $8,000. The combined revenues of the two submarkets equal $25,500, a sum $3,000 greater than in the absence of price discrimination. With total costs of $13,500, the firm realizes profits of $12,000, compared to $9,000 under a single pricing policy. As a price-discriminating seller, SKS thus enjoys higher revenues and profits.

Notice that the firm took advantage of its ability to price-discriminate, charging different prices in the two submarkets: $700 per ton to South Korean steel buyers and $400 per ton to Canadian buyers. For international price discrimination to be successful, certain conditions must hold. First, to ensure that at any price the demand schedules in the two submarkets have different demand elasticities, the submarkets' demand conditions must differ. Domestic buyers, for example, may have income levels or tastes and preferences that differ from those of buyers abroad. Second, the firm must be able to separate the two submarkets, preventing any significant resale of commodities from the lower-priced to the higher-priced market. This is because any resale by consumers will tend to neutralize the effect of differential prices and will narrow the discriminatory price structure to the point at which it approaches a single price to all consumers. Because of high transportation costs and governmental trade restrictions, markets are often easier to separate internationally than nationally.

EXCESS CAPACITY Another reason for sporadic or distress dumping is that producers sometimes face reductions in demand that leave them with idle productive capacity. This *excess capacity* is of particular concern to a nation such as Japan, which has guaranteed lifetime employment to much of its industrial labor force. For many Japanese companies, therefore, labor comes close to being a fixed cost because wages must be paid regardless of the company's production, sales, or profitability. Management thus has the incentive to compete vigorously for sales and to keep output high to generate revenues.

Should a firm find that its productive capacity exceeds the requirements of the domestic market, it may consider it more profitable to use the capacity to fulfill export orders at low prices rather than to allow the capacity to go idle. If necessary to keep exports high, a firm may be willing to sell abroad at a loss. Any profits generated by higher-priced domestic sales can help subsidize the goods that are dumped in foreign markets.

Consider the case of a radio producer under the following assumptions: (1) The producer's physical capacity is 150 units of output over the given time period. (2) The domestic market's demand for radios is price-inelastic, whereas foreign demand is price-elastic. Refer to Table 6.8. Suppose that the producer charges a uniform price (no dumping) of $300 per unit to both domestic and foreign consumers. With domestic demand inelastic, domestic sales total 100 units. But with elastic demand conditions abroad, suppose the producer cannot market any radios at the prevailing price. Sales revenues would equal $30,000, with variable costs plus overhead costs totaling $30,000. Without dumping, the firm would find itself with excess capacity of 50 radios. Moreover, the firm would just break even on its domestic market operations.

Suppose this producer decides to dump radios abroad at lower prices than at home. As long as all variable costs are covered, any price that contributes to overhead costs will permit larger prof-its (smaller losses) than those realized with idle plant capacity at hand. According to Table 6.8, by charging $300 to home consumers, the firm can sell 100 units. Suppose that by charging a price of $250 per unit, the firm is able to sell an additional 50 units abroad. The total sales revenue of $42,500 would not only cover variable costs plus overhead costs, but would permit a profit of $2,500.

With dumping, the firm is able to increase profits even though it is selling abroad at a price less than full cost (full cost = $40,000 / 150 = $267). Firms facing excess productive capacity may thus have the incentive to stimulate sales by cutting prices charged to foreigners—perhaps to levels that just cover variable production costs. Of course, domestic prices must be sufficiently high to keep the firm operating profitably over the relevant time period.

ANTIDUMPING REGULATIONS Despite the benefits that dumping may offer to importing consumers, governments have often levied stiff penalty duties against commodities they believe are being dumped into their markets from abroad. U.S. antidumping law is designed to prevent price discrimination and below-cost sales that injure U.S. industries. Under U.S. law, an **antidumping duty** is levied when the U.S. Department of Commerce determines a class or kind of foreign merchandise is being sold at *less than fair value* (LTFV) and the U.S. International Trade Commission (ITC) determines that LTFV imports are causing or threatening material injury

---

Table 6.8 Dumping and Excess Capacity

	No Dumping	Dumping
Home sales	100 units @ $300	100 units @ $300
Export sales	0 units @ $300	50 units @ $250
Sales revenue	$30,000	$42,500
Less variable costs of $200 per unit	-$20,000	-$30,000
	$10,000	$12,500
Less overhead costs of $10,000	-$10,000	-$10,000
Profit	$0	$2,500

(such as unemployment and lost sales and profits) to a U.S. industry. Such antidumping duties are imposed in addition to the normal tariff in order to neutralize the effects of price discrimination or below-cost sales.

The **margin of dumping** is calculated as the amount by which the foreign market value exceeds the U.S. price. Foreign market value is defined in one of two ways. According to the **priced-based definition**, dumping occurs whenever a foreign company sells a product in the U.S. market at a price below that for which the same product sells in the home market. When a home-nation price of the good is not available (for example, if the good is produced only for export and is not sold domestically), an effort is made to determine the price of the good in a third market.

In cases where the price-based definition cannot be applied, a **cost-based definition** of foreign market value is permitted. Under this approach, the Commerce Department "constructs" a foreign market value equal to the sum of (1) the cost of manufacturing the merchandise, (2) general expenses, (3) profit on home-market sales, and (4) the cost of packaging the merchandise for shipment to the United States. The amount for general expenses must equal at least 10 percent of the cost of manufacturing, and the amount for profit must equal at least 8 percent of the manufacturing cost plus general expenses.

Antidumping cases begin with a complaint filed concurrently with the Commerce Department and the International Trade Commission. The complaint comes from within an import-competing industry (for example, from a firm or labor union) and consists of evidence of the existence of dumping and data that demonstrate material injury or threat of injury.

The Commerce Department first makes a preliminary determination as to whether or not dumping has occurred, including an estimate of the size of the dumping margin. If the preliminary investigation finds evidence of dumping, U.S. importers must immediately pay a special tariff (equal to the estimated dumping margin) on all imports of the product in question. The Commerce Department then makes its final determination as to whether or not dumping has taken place, as well as the size of the dumping margin. If the Commerce Department rules that dumping did not occur, special tariffs previously collected are rebated to U.S. importers. Otherwise, the International Trade Commission determines whether or not material injury has occurred as the result of the dumping.

If the International Trade Commission rules that import-competing firms were not injured by the dumping, the special tariffs are rebated to U.S. importers. But if both the International Trade Commission and the Commerce Department rule in favor of the dumping petition, a permanent tariff is imposed that equals the size of the dumping margin calculated by the Commerce Department in its final investigation.

U.S. PUTS SQUEEZE ON CHINESE APPLE JUICE

Imagine owning and operating an apple juice company in Small Town, USA. For years you have run a tight ship: You track your costs with a keen eye, and consider your company the most efficient producer of apple juice—bar none—either in the United States or worldwide. However, despite your efficient operations and fair prices, you find that you are consistently being underpriced by a foreign competitor. Knowing the market as you do, you know that your competitor is charging far less than it costs to produce apple juice and is charging more for it in its home market. Simply put, the lack of a level playing field makes it difficult for your firm to compete.

Such was the situation faced by several U.S. producers of apple juice who alleged that the U.S. industry was being injured by reason of imports of apple juice from China that were being sold in the United States at less than fair value. In 1999, the U.S. apple juice industry filed an antidumping complaint, contending that the dumping of juice at low prices had damaged domestic producers and caused losses of $135 million.

The apple industry based its argument on the 1,200-percent increase in juice imports between 1995 and 1998. Imports rose from 3,000 metric tons to 40,000 metric tons and resulted in an increase in the Chinese share of the U.S. market from 1 to 18 percent. During the same period,

SMITH CORONA FINDS ANTIDUMPING VICTORIES ARE HOLLOW

Although antidumping duties are intended to protect domestic producers from unfairly priced imports, they can be an inconclusive weapon. Consider the case of Smith Corona, Inc., which won several antidumping cases from the 1970s to the 1990s but had little to show for it.

Trouble erupted for Smith Corona in the 1970s when it encountered ferocious competition from Brother Industries Ltd. of Japan, which flooded the U.S. market with its portable typewriters. Responding to Smith Corona's dumping complaint, in 1980 the U.S. government imposed antidumping duties of 49 percent on Brother portables. Smith Corona's antidumping victory proved to be hollow, however, because Brother realized that the antidumping ruling applied only to typewriters without a memory or calculating function. Through the tactic of *product evolution*, Brother evaded the duties by upgrading its typewriter to include a tiny computer memory. It took until 1990 for Smith Corona to get this loophole plugged by the federal court of appeals in Washington, DC. By that time, Brother had found a more permanent method of circumventing antidumping duties: It began assembling portable typewriters in the United States from components manufactured in Malaysia and Japan. These typewriters were no longer "imported," and thus the 1980s duties did not apply.

Then competition shifted to another product, the personal word processor. By 1990, Smith Corona complained that Brother and other Japanese manufacturers were dumping word processors in the United States. This led the U.S. government to impose import duties of almost 60 percent on Japanese word processors in 1991. But that victory was also hollow, because it applied only to word processors manufactured in Japan; the Japanese firms assembled their word processors in the United States.

Undeterred, Smith Corona filed another complaint, invoking a provision in U.S. trade law that was designed to deter foreign firms from evading antidumping duties by importing components and assembling them in the United States. But the provision assumed that imported components would come from domestic (Japanese) factories, so it did not cover components produced in third countries. Recognizing this loophole, Brother demonstrated that its imported components came from third countries, and therefore its word processors were not subject to antidumping duties. All in all, obtaining relief from foreign dumped goods was a difficult process for Smith Corona!

Source: Eduardo Lachica, "Antidumping Pleas Are Almost Useless, Smith Corona Finds," *The Wall Street Journal*, June 18, 1992, pp. A–1, A–11.

---

the price that U.S. importers paid for Chinese juice dropped from $7.65 per gallon to $3.57. With the flood of Chinese juice, the price paid to U.S. growers for their processing apples fell 64 percent, to $55 per ton as compared to a price of $153 per ton three years earlier.

The sale of juice to the United States from China came at a time when China was increasing its apple production. In 1999, there was an estimated 4 million acres of apple orchards in China. Simply put, the dumping of juice was a major cause for low prices on U.S. apples, These low prices drove small family apple farms in the United States out of business. Apple-industry representatives maintained that an antidumping duty was needed to level the playing field and help domestic growers recoup through the market some of what they had lost.

Agreeing with the U.S. apple industry's complaint, the U.S. Department of Commerce ruled that Chinese juice had been sold in the United States at 52 percent below its cost of production. This ruling was supported by the U.S. International Trade Commission's determination that U.S. apple growers were economically injured by China's dumping of apple-juice concentrate on the U.S. market. Therefore, the Commerce Department imposed a 52-percent duty on imported juice. A gallon of apple juice that initially cost $4 wound up costing about $6.08 after the imposition of the duty. The duty was to remain in effect for five years. Following the imposition of the duty, imports of Chinese juice dropped by more than 60 percent. The U.S. apple industry was pleased that the antidumping duty corrected the injustice of the Chinese dumping.

CANADIANS PRESS WASHINGTON APPLE PRODUCERS FOR LEVEL PLAYING FIELD

Not only have foreign producers dumped products in the United States, but U.S. firms have sometimes dumped goods abroad. In 1989, the Canadian government ruled that U.S. Delicious apples, primarily those grown in Washington, had been dumped on the Canadian market, causing injury to 4,500 commercial apple growers. As a result of the ruling, a 42-pound box of Washington apples could not be sold in Canada for less than $11.87, the "normal value" (analogous to the U.S. concept of "fair value") established by the Canadian government for regular-storage apples. Canadian importers purchasing U.S. apples at below-normal value had to pay an antidumping duty to the Canadian government so that the total purchase price equaled the established value. The antidumping order was for the five years 1989 to 1994.

The Canadian apple growers' complaint alleged that extensive tree plants in the United States during the late 1970s and early 1980s resulted in excess apple production. In 1987 and 1988, Washington growers experienced a record harvest and inventories that exceeded storage facilities. The growers dramatically cut prices in order to market their crop, leading to a collapse of the North American price of Delicious apples.

When Washington apple growers failed to provide timely information, the Canadian government estimated the normal value of a box of U.S. apples using the best information available. As seen in Table 6.9, the normal value for a box of apples in the crop-year 1987–1988 was $11.87. During this period, the U.S. export price to Canada was about $9 a box. Based on a comparison of the export price and the normal value of apples, the weighted-average dumping margin was determined to be 32.5 percent.

The Canadian government determined that the influx of low-priced Washington apples into the Canadian market displaced Canadian apples and resulted in losses to Canadian apple growers

Table 6.9   Normal Value and the Margin of Dumping: Delicious Apples, Regular Storage, 1987–1988*

U.S. FOB per Packed Box (42 pounds)	Normal Value (in Dollars)
Growing and harvesting costs	5.50
Packing, marketing, and storing costs	5.49
Total costs	10.99
Profit (8% margin)	.88
Total normal value	11.87

Margin of Dumping	Percentage
Range	0–63.44
Weighted-average margin	32.53

*The weighted-average dumping margin for controlled atmosphere-storage apples was 23.86 percent.

Source: *Statement of Reasons: Final Determination of Dumping Respecting Delicious Apples Originating in or Exported from the United States of America*, Revenue Canada, Customs and Excise Division, December 1988.

of $1 to $6.40 (Canadian dollars) per box during the 1987–1988 growing season. The Canadian government ruled that the dumped apples injured Canadian growers, and thus imposed antidumping duties on Washington apples.

OTHER NONTARIFF TRADE BARRIERS

Other NTBs consist of governmental codes of conduct applied to imports. Even though such provisions are often well disguised, they remain important sources of commercial policy. Let's consider three such barriers: government procurement policies, social regulations, and sea transport and freight regulations.

GOVERNMENT PROCUREMENT POLICIES

Because government agencies are large buyers of goods and services, they are attractive customers for foreign suppliers. If governments purchased goods and services only from the lowest-cost suppliers, the pattern of trade would not differ significantly from that which occurs in a competitive market. Most governments, however, favor domestic suppliers over foreign ones in the procurement of materials and products. This is evidenced by the fact that the ratio of imports to total purchases in the public sector is much smaller than in the private sector.

Governments often extend preferences to domestic suppliers in the form of **buy-national policies**. The U.S. government, through explicit laws, openly discriminates against foreign suppliers in its purchasing decisions. Although most other governments do not have formally legislated preferences for domestic suppliers, they often discriminate against foreign suppliers through hidden administrative rules and practices. Such governments utilize closed bidding systems that restrict the number of companies allowed to bid on sales, or they may publicize government contracts in such a way as to make it difficult for foreign suppliers to make a bid.

To stimulate domestic employment during the Great Depression, in 1933 the U.S. government passed the Buy American Act. This act requires federal agencies to purchase materials and products from U.S. suppliers if their prices are not "unreasonably" higher than those of foreign competitors. A product, to qualify as domestic, must have at least a 50-percent domestic component content and must be manufactured in the United States. As it stands today, U.S. suppliers of civilian agencies are given a 6-percent preference margin. This means that a U.S. supplier receives the government contract as long as the U.S. low bid is no more than 6 percent higher than the competing foreign bid. This preference margin rises to 12 percent if the low domestic bidder is situated in a labor-surplus area, and to 50 percent if the purchase is made by the Department of Defense. These preferences are waived when it is determined that the U.S.-produced good is not available in sufficient quantities or is not of satisfactory quality.

By discriminating against low-cost foreign suppliers in favor of domestic suppliers, buy-national policies are a barrier to free trade. Domestic suppliers are given the leeway to use less efficient production methods and to pay resource prices higher than those permitted under free trade. This yields a higher cost for government projects and deadweight welfare losses for the nation in the form of the protective effect and consumption effect.

The buy-American restrictions of the U.S. government have been liberalized with the adoption of the Tokyo Round of Multilateral Trade Negotiations in 1979. However, the pact does not apply to the purchase of materials and products by state and local government agencies. More than 30 states currently have buy-American laws, ranging from explicit prohibitions on purchases of foreign products to loose policy guidelines favoring U.S. products. Advocates of state buy-American laws usually maintain that the laws provide direct local economic benefit in the form of jobs; moreover, the threat of foreign retaliation is minimal at the state level.

The adoption of Minnesota's buy-American legislation provides an example of state feelings toward foreign competition. In 1978, the Minnesota Department of Transportation awarded a $3.7 million contract to a local firm to build a portion of a bridge. The winning firm's bid was lower than that of its nearest competitor largely because it embodied lower-cost Japanese steel instead of the U.S. steel contained in the second-place bid. The Minnesota AFL-CIO estimated that the award decision cost Minnesota steel fabricators some $750,000 in wages, a portion of which would have been paid back as taxes to the state. Local labor unions pressured the state government to prevent future occurrences of such losses. Three months later, the Minnesota legislature passed a tough buy-American law by a 91-to-33 vote.[1]

SOCIAL REGULATIONS Since the 1950s, nations have assumed an ever-increasing role in regulating the quality of life for society. **Social regulation** attempts to correct a variety of undesirable side effects in an economy that relate to health, safety, and the environment—effects that markets, left to themselves, often ignore. Social regulation applies to a particular issue, say environmental quality, and affects the behavior of firms in many industries such as automobiles, steel, and chemicals.

CAFÉ STANDARDS Although social regulations may advance health, safety, and environmental goals, they can also serve as barriers to international trade. Consider the case of fuel economy standards imposed by the U.S. government on automobile manufacturers.

Originally enacted in 1975, **corporate average fuel economy standards (CAFÉ)** represent the foundation of U.S. energy conservation policy. Applying to all passenger vehicles sold in the United States, the standards are based on the average fuel efficiency of all vehicles sold by all manufacturers. Since 1990, the CAFÉ require-

ment for passenger cars has been 27.5 miles a gallon. Manufacturers whose average fuel economy falls below this standard are subject to fines.

During the 1980s, CAFÉ requirements were used not only to promote fuel conservation but also to protect jobs of U.S. autoworkers. The easiest way for U.S. car manufacturers to improve the average fuel efficiency of their fleets would have been to import smaller, more fuel-efficient vehicles from their subsidiaries in Asia and Europe. However, this would have decreased employment in an already depressed industry. The U.S. government thus enacted separate but identical standards for domestic and imported passenger cars. Therefore, General Motors, Ford, and DaimlerChrysler, which manufactured vehicles in the United States and also sold imported cars, would be required to fulfill CAFÉ targets for both categories of vehicles. U.S. firms thus could not fulfill CAFÉ standards by averaging the fuel economy of their imports with their less fuel-efficient, domestically produced vehicles. By calculating domestic and imported fleets separately, the U.S. government attempted to force domestic firms not only to manufacture more efficient vehicles but to produce them in the United States! In short, government regulations sometimes place effective import barriers on foreign commodities, whether they are intended to do so or not, thus aggravating foreign competitors.

HORMONES IN BEEF PRODUCTION The European Union's ban on hormone-treated meat is another case where social regulations can lead to a beef. Growth-promoting hormones are used widely by livestock producers to speed up growth rates and produce leaner livestock more in line with consumer preferences for diets with reduced fat and cholesterol. However, critics of hormones maintain that they can cause cancer for consumers of meat.

In 1989, the European Union enacted its ban on production and importation of beef derived from animals treated with growth-promoting hormones. The European Union justified the ban as needed to protect the health and safety of consumers.

---

[1] John Kline, *State Government Influence in U.S. International Economic Policy* (Lexington, MA: Heath, 1983), pp. 87–91.

The ban was immediately challenged by U.S. producers who used the hormones in about 90 percent of their beef production. According to the United States, there was no scientific basis for the ban that restricted beef imports on the basis of health concerns. Instead, the ban was merely an attempt to protect the relatively high-cost European beef industry from foreign competition. U.S. producers noted that when the ban was imposed, European producers had accumulated large, costly-to-store beef surpluses that resulted in enormous political pressure to limit imports of beef. The European Union's emphasis on health concerns was thus a smokescreen for protecting an industry with comparative disadvantage, according to the United States.

The trade dispute eventually went to the World Trade Organization (WTO) (see Chapter 7), which ruled that the European Union's ban on hormone-treated beef was illegal and resulted in lost annual U.S. exports of beef to the European Union in the amount of $117 million. Nonetheless, the European Union, citing consumer preference, refused to lift its ban. Therefore, the WTO authorized the United States to impose tariffs high enough to prohibit $117 million of European exports to the United States. The United States exercised its right and slapped 100-percent tariffs on a list of European products that included tomatoes, roquefort cheese, prepared mustard, goose liver, citrus fruit, pasta, hams, and other products. The U.S. hit list focused on products from Denmark, France, Germany and Italy—the biggest supporters of the European Union's ban on hormone-treated beef. By effectively doubling the prices of the targeted products, the 100-percent tariffs pressured the Europeans to liberalize their imports of beef products.

Sea Transport and Freight Restrictions

During the 1990s, U.S. shipping companies serving Japanese ports complained of a highly restrictive system of port services. They contended that Japan's association of stevedore companies (companies that unload cargo from ships) used a system of prior consultations to control competition,

allocate harbor work among themselves, and frustrate the implementation of any cost cutting by shipping companies.

In particular, shipping companies contended that they were forced to negotiate with the Japanese stevedore-company association on everything from arrival times to choice of stevedores and warehouses. Because port services were controlled by the stevedore-company association, foreign shippers could not negotiate with individual stevedore companies about prices and schedules. Moreover, U.S. shippers maintained that the Japanese government approved these restrictive practices by refusing to license new entrants into the port service business and by supporting the requirement that foreign shippers negotiate with Japan's stevedore-company association.

A midnight trip to Tokyo Bay illustrates the frustration of U.S. shipping companies. The lights are dimmed and the wharf is quiet, even though the *Sealand Commerce* has just docked. At 1 A.M., lights turn on, cranes swing alive, and trucks appear to unload the ship's containers, which carry paper plates, computers, and pet food from the United States. At 4 A.M., however, the lights shut off and the work ceases. Longshoremen won't return until 8:30 A.M. and will take three more hours off later in the day. They have unloaded only 169 of 488 containers that they must handle before the ship sails for Oakland. At this rate, the job will take until past noon; but at least it isn't Sunday, when docks close altogether.

When the *Sealand Commerce* reaches Oakland, however, U.S. dockworkers will unload and load 24 hours a day, taking 30 percent less time for about half the price. To enter Tokyo Bay, the ship had to clear every detail of its visit with Japan's stevedore-company association; to enter the U.S. port, it will merely notify port authorities and the Coast Guard. According to U.S. exporters, this unequal treatment on waterfronts is a trade barrier because it makes U.S. exports more expensive in Japan.

In 1997, the United States and Japan found themselves on the brink of a trade war after the U.S. government decided to direct its Coast

Guard and Customs Service to bar Japanese-flagged ships from unloading at U.S. ports. The U.S. government demanded that foreign shipping companies be allowed to negotiate directly with Japanese stevedore companies to unload their ships, thus giving shippers a way around the restrictive practices of Japan's stevedore-company association. After consultation between the two governments, an agreement was reached to liberalize port services in Japan. As a result, the United States rescinded its ban against Japanese ships.

S u m m a r y

1. With the decline in import tariffs in the past two decades, nontariff trade barriers have gained in importance as a measure of protection. Nontariff trade barriers include such practices as (a) import quotas, (b) orderly marketing agreements, (c) domestic content requirements, (d) subsidies, (e) antidumping regulations, (f) discriminatory government procurement practices, (g) social regulations, and (h) sea transport and freight restrictions.

2. An import quota is a government-imposed limit on the quantity of a product that can be imported. Quotas are imposed on a global (worldwide) basis or a selective (individual country) basis. Although quotas have many of the same economic effects as tariffs, they tend to be more restrictive. A quota's revenue effect generally accrues to domestic importers or foreign exporters, depending on the degree of market power they possess. If government desired to capture the revenue effect, it could auction import quota licenses to the highest bidder in a competitive market.

3. A tariff-rate quota is a two-tier tariff placed on an imported product. It permits a limited number of goods to be imported at a lower tariff rate, whereas any imports beyond this limit face a higher tariff. Of the revenue generated by a tariff-rate quota, some accrues to the domestic government as tariff revenue and the remainder is captured by producers as windfall profits.

4. Orderly marketing agreements are market-sharing pacts negotiated by trading nations. They generally involve quotas on exports and imports. Proponents of orderly marketing agreements contend that they are less disruptive of international trade than unilaterally determined tariffs and quotas.

5. Because an export quota is administered by the government of the exporting nation (supply-side restriction), its revenue effect tends to be captured by sellers of the exporting nation. For the importing nation, the quota's revenue effect is a welfare loss in addition to the protective and consumption effects.

6. Domestic content requirements try to limit the practice of foreign sourcing and encourage the development of domestic industry. They typically stipulate the minimum percentage of a product's value that must be produced in the home country for that product to be sold there. Local content protection tends to impose welfare losses on the domestic economy in the form of higher production costs and higher-priced goods.

7. Government subsidies are sometimes granted as a form of protection to domestic exporters and import-competing companies. They may take the form of direct cash bounties, tax concessions, credit extended at low interest rates, or special insurance arrangements. Direct production subsidies for import-competing producers tend to involve a smaller loss in economic welfare than do equivalent tariffs and quotas. The imposition of export subsidies results in a terms-of-trade effect and an export-revenue effect.

8. International dumping occurs when a firm sells its product abroad at a price that is (1) less than average total cost or (2) less than that charged to domestic buyers of the same

product. Dumping can be sporadic, predatory, or persistent in nature. Idle productive capacity may be the reason behind dumping. Governments often impose stiff penalties against foreign commodities that are believed to be dumped in the home economy.

9. Government rules and regulations in areas such as safety and technical standards and marketing requirements can have significant impacts on world trade patterns.

STUDY QUESTIONS

1. In the past two decades, nontariff trade barriers have gained in importance as protectionist devices. What are the major nontariff trade barriers?
2. How does the revenue effect of an import quota differ from that of a tariff?
3. What are the major forms of subsidies that governments grant to domestic producers?
4. What is meant by voluntary export restraints, and how do they differ from other protective barriers?
5. Should U.S. antidumping laws be stated in terms of full production costs or marginal costs?
6. Which is a more restrictive trade barrier—an import tariff or an equivalent import quota?
7. Differentiate among sporadic, persistent, and predatory dumping.
8. A subsidy may provide import-competing producers the same degree of protection as tariffs or quotas but at a lower cost in terms of national welfare. Explain.
9. Rather than generating tax revenue as do tariffs, subsidies require tax revenue. Therefore, they are not an effective protective device for the home economy. Do you agree?
10. In 1980, the U.S. auto industry proposed that import quotas be imposed on foreign-produced cars sold in the United States. What would be the likely benefits and costs of such a policy?
11. Why did the U.S. government in 1982 provide import quotas as an aid to domestic sugar producers?
12. Which tends to result in a greater welfare loss for the home economy: (a) an import quota

levied by the home government or (b) a voluntary export quota imposed by the foreign government?
13. What would be the likely effects of export restraints imposed by Japan on its auto shipments to the United States?
14. Why might U.S. steel-using firms lobby against the imposition of quotas on foreign steel sold in the United States?
15. Concerning international dumping, distinguish between the price-based and cost-based definitions of foreign market value.
16. Table 6.10 illustrates the demand and supply schedules for television sets in Venezuela, a "small" nation that is unable to affect world prices. On graph paper, sketch Venezuela's demand and supply schedules of TV sets.
    a. Suppose Venezuela imports TV sets at a price of $150 each. Under free trade, how many TV sets does Venezuela produce, consume, and import? Determine Venezuela's consumer surplus and producer surplus.

Table 6.10 Venezuelan Supply of and Demand for Television Sets

Price per TV Set	Quantity Demanded	Quantity Supplied
$100	900	0
200	700	200
300	500	400
400	300	600
500	100	800

b. Assume that Venezuela imposes a quota that limits imports to 300 TV sets. Determine the quota-induced price increase and the resulting decrease in consumer surplus. Calculate the quota's redistributive effect, consumption effect, protective effect, and revenue effect. Assuming that Venezuelan import companies organize as buyers and bargain favorably with competitive foreign exporters, what is the overall welfare loss to Venezuela as a result of the quota? Suppose that foreign exporters organize as a monopoly seller. What is the overall welfare loss to Venezuela as a result of the quota?

c. Suppose that, instead of a quota, Venezuela grants its import-competing producers a subsidy of $100 per TV set. In your diagram, draw the subsidy-adjusted supply schedule for Venezuelan producers. Does the subsidy result in a rise in the price of TV sets above the free-trade level? Determine Venezuela's production, consumption, and imports of TV sets under the subsidy. What is the total cost of the subsidy to the Venezuelan government? Of this amount, how much is transferred to Venezuelan producers in the form of producer surplus, and how much is absorbed by higher production costs due to inefficient domestic production? Determine the overall welfare loss to Venezuela under the subsidy.

17. Table 6.11 illustrates the demand and supply schedules for computers in Ecuador, a "small" nation that is unable to affect world prices. On graph paper, sketch Ecuador's demand and supply schedules of computers.

a. Assume that Hong Kong and Taiwan can supply computers to Ecuador at a per-unit price of $300 and $500, respectively. With free trade, how many computers does Ecuador import? From which nation does it import?

Table 6.11 Computer Supply and Demand: Ecuador

Price per Computer	Quantity Demanded	Quantity Supplied
$ 0	100	—
200	90	0
400	80	10
600	70	20
800	60	30
1,000	50	40
1,200	40	50
1,400	30	60
1,600	20	70
1,800	10	80
2,000	0	90

b. Suppose Ecuador and Hong Kong negotiate a voluntary export agreement in which Hong Kong imposes on its exporters a quota that limits shipments to Ecuador to 40 computers. Assume Taiwan does not take advantage of the situation by exporting computers to Ecuador. Determine the quota-induced price increase and the reduction in consumer surplus for Ecuador. Determine the quota's redistributive effect, protective effect, consumption effect, and revenue effect. Because the export quota is administered by Hong Kong, its exporters will capture the quota's revenue effect. Determine the overall welfare loss to Ecuador as a result of the quota.

c. Again assume that Hong Kong imposes an export quota on its producers that restricts shipments to Ecuador to 40 computers, but now suppose that Taiwan, a nonrestrained exporter, ships an additional 20 computers to Ecuador. Ecuador thus imports 60 computers. Determine the overall welfare loss to Ecuador as a result of the quota.

d. In general, when increases in nonrestrained supply offset part of the cutback in shipments that occur under an export quota, will the overall welfare loss for the importing country be greater or smaller than that which occurs in the absence of nonrestrained supply? Determine this amount in example of Ecuador.

18. Figure 6.9 illustrates the practice of international dumping by British Toys, Inc. (BTI). Figure 6.9(a) shows the domestic demand and marginal revenue schedules faced by BTI in the United Kingdom, and Figure 6.9(b) shows the demand and marginal revenue schedules faced by BTI in Canada. Figure 6.9(c) shows the combined demand and marginal revenue schedules for the two markets, as well as BTI's average total cost and marginal cost schedules.

   a. In the absence of international dumping, BTI would charge a uniform price to U.K. and Canadian customers (ignoring trans-

portation costs). Determine the firm's profit-maximizing output and price, as well as total profit. How much profit accrues to BTI on its U.K. sales and on its Canadian sales?

   b. Suppose now that BTI engages in international dumping. Determine the price that BTI charges its U.K. buyers and the profits that accrue on U.K. sales. Also determine the price that BTI charges its Canadian buyers and the profits that accrue on Canadian sales. Does the practice of international dumping yield higher profits than the uniform pricing strategy? If so, by how much?

19. Why is a tariff-rate quota viewed as a compromise between the interests of the domestic consumer and those of the domestic producer? How does the revenue effect of a tariff-rate quota differ from that of an import tariff?

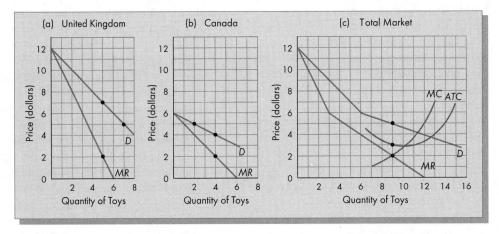

Figure 6.9 International Dumping Schedules

NETLINK

6.1 The Department of State reports on the history, politics, and economic and trade policies of the regions and countries with which the United States regularly trades. Look at the background notes on regions after setting our browser to URL:

http://www.state.gov/www/about_state/business/

6.2 For another country's perspective on foreign trade and tariffs, examine the New Zealand Ministry of Foreign Affairs and Trade Web page. Their foreign trade policy, bilateral and regional relationships, and trade and investment are available at URL:

http://www.mft.govt.nz/for.html

6.3 The Canadian Trade Commissioner Service serving Canadian business abroad provides their market reports and services abroad by sector and by country at URL:

http://www.infoexport.gc.ca/menu-e.asp

To access NetLink Exercises and the Virtual Scavenger Hunt, visit the Carbaugh Web site at http://carbaugh.swcollege.com

chapter 7

Trade Regulations and Industrial Policies

Previous chapters have examined the benefits and costs of tariff and nontariff trade barriers. This chapter discusses the major trade regulations of the United States. It also considers the various industrial policies implemented by the United States and other nations to enhance the competitiveness of their producers.

THE SMOOT–HAWLEY ACT

As Table 7.1 makes clear, U.S. tariff history can be likened to a roller coaster. This was especially true until the early 1930s; since then, the overall trend of U.S. tariffs has been downward.

The high point of U.S. protectionism occurred with the passage of the **Smoot–Hawley Act** in 1930, under which U.S. average tariffs were raised to 53 percent on protected imports. As the Smoot-Hawley bill moved through the U.S. Congress, formal protests from foreign nations flooded Washington, eventually adding up to a document of some 200 pages. Nevertheless, both the House of Representatives and the Senate approved the bill. Although about a thousand U.S. economists beseeched President Herbert Hoover to veto the legislation, he did not do so, and the tariff was signed into law on June 17, 1930. Simply put, the Smoot–Hawley Act tried to divert national demand away from imports and toward domestically produced goods.

KEY CONCEPTS AND TERMS

- Commodity Credit Corporation
- Countervailing duty
- Economic sanctions
- Escape clause
- Export-Import Bank
- Fast-track authority
- General Agreement on Tariffs and Trade (GATT)
- Intellectual property rights (IPRs)
- Kennedy Round
- Knowledge-based growth policy
- Ministry of International Trade and Industry (MITI)
- Most-favored-nation (MFN) clause
- Normal trade relations
- Reciprocal Trade Agreements Act
- Section 301
- Smoot–Hawley Act
- Strategic trade policy
- Tokyo Round
- Trade adjustment assistance
- Uruguay Round
- World Trade Organization (WTO)

Table 7.1 U.S. Tariff History: Average Tariff Rates	
Tariff Laws and Dates	Average Tariff Rate* (%)
McKinley Law, 1890	48.4
Wilson Law, 1894	41.3
Dingley Law, 1897	46.5
Payne–Aldrich Law, 1909	40.8
Underwood Law, 1913	27.0
Fordney–McCumber Law, 1922	38.5
Smoot–Hawley Law, 1930	53.0
1930–1939	43.6
1940–1949	24.1
1950–1959	12.0
1960–1969	11.8
1970–1979	7.4
1980–1989	5.3
1990–1997	5.2

*Ratio of duties collected to FOB value on dutiable imports.

Source: U.S. Census Bureau, *Statistical Abstract of the United States,* Washington, DC, Government Printing Office, various issues.

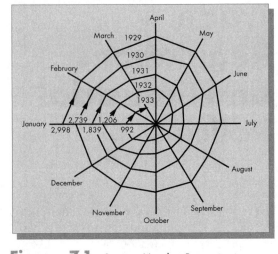

Figure 7.1 Smoot–Hawley Protectionism and World Trade, 1929–1933 (Millions of Dollars)

The figure shows the pattern of world trade from 1929 to 1933. Following the Smoot–Hawley Act of 1930, which raised U.S. tariffs to an average level of 53 percent, other nations retaliated by increasing their own import restrictions, and the volume of world trade decreased as the global economy fell into the Great Depression.

Source: League of Nations, *Monthly Bulletin of Statistics,* February 1934. See also Charles Kindleberger, *The World in Depression,* Berkeley, CA, University of California Press, 1973, p. 170.

The legislation provoked retaliation by 25 trading partners of the United States. Spain implemented the Wais tariff in reaction to U.S. tariffs on cork, oranges, and grapes. Switzerland boycotted U.S. exports to protest new tariffs on watches and shoes. Canada increased its tariffs threefold in reaction to U.S. tariffs on timber, logs, and many food products. Italy retaliated against tariffs on olive oil and hats with tariffs on U.S. automobiles. Mexico, France, Cuba, Australia, France, and New Zealand also participated in tariff wars. Other beggar-thy-neighbor policies, such as foreign-exchange controls and currency depreciations, were also implemented. The effort by several nations to run a trade surplus by reducing imports led to a breakdown of the international trading system. Within two years after the Smoot–Hawley Act, U.S. exports decreased by nearly two-thirds. Figure 7.1 shows the decline of world trade as the global economy fell into the Great Depression.

How did President Hoover fall into such a protectionist trap? The President felt compelled to honor the 1928 Republican platform calling for tariffs to aid the weakening farm economy. The stock market crash of 1929 and the imminent Great Depression further led to a crisis atmosphere. Republicans had been sympathetic to protectionism for decades. Now they viewed import tariffs as a method of fulfilling demands that government should initiate positive steps to combat domestic unemployment.

President Hoover felt bound to tradition and to the platform of the Republican party. Henry Ford spent an evening with Hoover requesting a presidential veto of what he referred to as "economic stupidity." Other auto executives sided with Ford. However, tariff legislation had never before been vetoed by a president, and Hoover was not about to set a precedent. Hoover remarked that "with returning normal conditions, our foreign trade will continue to expand."

By 1932, U.S. trade with other nations had collapsed. Presidential challenger Franklin Roosevelt denounced the trade legislation as ruinous. Hoover responded that Roosevelt would have U.S. workers compete with peasant labor overseas. Following Hoover's defeat in the presidential election of 1932, the Democrats dismantled the Smoot–Hawley legislation. But they used caution, relying on reciprocal trade agreements instead of across-the-board tariff concessions by the United States. Sam Rayburn, the Speaker of the House of Representatives, insisted that any party member who wanted to be a member of the House Ways and Means Committee had to support trade reciprocity instead of protectionism. The Smoot–Hawley approach was discredited, and the United States pursued trade liberalization via reciprocal trade agreements.

THE RECIPROCAL TRADE AGREEMENTS ACT

The combined impact on U.S. exports of the Great Depression and the foreign retaliatory tariffs imposed in reaction to the Smoot–Hawley Act resulted in a reversal of U.S. trade policy. In 1934, Congress passed the **Reciprocal Trade Agreements Act**, which set the stage for a wave of *trade liberalization*. Specifically aimed at tariff reduction, the act contained two features: (1) negotiating authority and (2) generalized reductions.

Under this law, the President was given the unprecedented authority to negotiate bilateral tariff-reduction agreements with foreign governments (for example, between the United States and Sweden). Without congressional approval, the President could lower tariffs by up to 50 percent of the existing level. Enactment of any tariff reductions was dependent on the willingness of other nations to reciprocally lower their tariffs on U.S. goods. From 1934 to 1947, the United States entered into 32 bilateral tariff

agreements, and over this period the average level of tariffs on protected products fell to about half of the 1934 levels.

The Reciprocal Trade Agreements Act also provided for generalized tariff reductions through the **most-favored-nation (MFN) clause**. This clause is an agreement between two nations to apply tariffs to each other at rates as low as those applied to any other nation. For example, if the United States extends MFN treatment to Brazil and then grants a low tariff on imports of machinery from France, the United States is obligated to provide the identical low-tariff treatment on imports of machinery from Brazil. Brazil thus receives the same treatment as the initially most favored nation, France. The advantage to Brazil of MFN status is that it can investigate all of the tariff policies of the United States concerning imported machinery to see if treatment to some nation is more favorable than that granted to it; if any more favorable terms are found, Brazil can call for equal treatment. In 1998, the U.S. government replaced the term *most-favored nation* with **normal trade relations**, which will be used throughout the rest of this textbook.

According to the provisions of the World Trade Organization (see next section), there are two exceptions to the normal trade relations clause: (1) Industrial nations can grant preferential tariffs to imports from developing nations that are not granted to imports from other industrial nations; and (2) Nations belonging to a regional trading arrangement (for example, the North American Free Trade Agreement) can eliminate tariffs applied to imports of goods coming from other members while maintaining tariffs on imports from nonmembers.

Granting normal trade relation status or imposing differential tariffs has been used as an instrument of foreign policy. For example, a nation may punish unfriendly nations with high import tariffs on their goods and reward friendly nations with low tariffs. The United States has granted normal trade relation status to most of the nations with which it trades. As of 2000, the United States did not grant normal trade relation status to the following countries: Afghanistan,

Cuba, Laos, North Korea, and Vietnam. U.S. tariffs on imports from these countries are often three or four (or more) times as high as those on comparable imports from nations receiving normal trade relation status, as seen in Table 7.2.

THE GENERAL AGREEMENT ON TARIFFS AND TRADE

Partly in response to trade disruptions during the Great Depression, the United States and some of its allies sought to impose order on trade flows after World War II. The first major postwar step toward liberalization of world trade was the **General Agreement on Tariffs and Trade (GATT)**, signed in 1947. GATT was crafted as an agreement among contracting parties, the member nations, to decrease trade barriers and to place all nations on an equal footing in trading relationships. GATT was never intended to become an organization; instead, it was set of bilateral agreements among countries around the world to reduce trade barriers.

In 1995, GATT was transformed into the **World Trade Organization (WTO)**. The WTO embodies the main provisions of GATT, but its role was expanded to include a mechanism intended to improve GATT's process for resolving trade disputes among member nations. Let us first discuss the operation of the original GATT system.

THE GATT SYSTEM GATT was based on several principles designed to foster more liberalized trade. One was *nondiscrimination*, embodying the principles of *normal trade relations* and *national treatment*. Under the normal trade relations principle, all member nations are bound to grant to each other treatment as favorable as they give to any nation with regard to trade matters. This allows comparative advantage to be the main determinant of trade patterns, which promotes global efficiency. There have been exceptions to the normal trade relations principle; for example, regional trade blocs (European Union, North American Free Trade Agreement) have been allowed. Under the national-treatment principle, member nations must treat other nations' industries no less favorably than they do their own domestic industries, once foreign goods have entered the domestic market; thus, in principle, domestic regulations and taxes cannot be biased against foreign products.

Table 7.2   U.S. Tariffs on Imports from Nations Granted, and not Granted, Normal Trade Relation Status: Selected Examples

	Tariff (Percent)	
Product	With Normal Trade Relation Status	Without Normal Trade Relation Status
Hams	1.2 cents/kg	7.2 cents/kg
Sour cream	3.2 cents/liter	15 cents/liter
Butter	12.3 cents/liter	30.9 cents/liter
Fish	3% ad valorem	25% ad valorem
Saws	4% ad valorem	30% ad valorem
Cauliflower	10% ad valorem	50% ad valorem
Coffee	10% ad valorem	20% ad valorem
Woven fabrics	15.7% ad valorem	81% ad valorem
Babies' shirts	20.2% ad valorem	90% ad valorem
Gold necklaces	5% ad valorem	80% ad valorem

Source: U.S. International Trade Commission, *Harmonized Tariff Schedule of the United States*, Washington, DC, Government Printing Office, 2000.

The GATT principle of nondiscrimination made trade liberalization a *public good*: What was produced by one nation in negotiation with another was available to all. This gave rise to the coordination problem shared by all public goods: that of getting each party to participate rather than sit back and let others do the liberalizing, thus free-riding on their efforts. A weakness of GATT trade negotiations from the 1940s to the 1970s was the limited number of nations that were actively negotiating participants; many nations—especially the developing nations—remained on the sidelines as free riders on others' liberalizations: They maintained protectionist policies to support domestic producers while realizing benefits from trade liberalization abroad.

Another aspect of GATT was its role in the settlement of trade disputes. Historically, trade disputes consisted of matters strictly between the disputants; no third party was available to which they might appeal for a favorable remedy. As a result, conflicts often remained unresolved for years, and when they were settled the stronger country generally won at the expense of the weaker country. GATT improved the dispute-resolution process by formulating complaint procedures and providing a conciliation panel to which a victimized country could express its grievance.

GATT's dispute-settlement process, however, did not include the authority to enforce the conciliation panel's recommendations—a weakness that inspired the formation of the World Trade Organization.

GATT also obligated its members to use tariffs rather than quotas to protect their domestic industry. GATT's presumption was that quotas were inherently more trade distorting than tariffs because they allowed the user to discriminate between suppliers, were not predictable and transparent to the exporter, and imposed a maximum ceiling on imports. Here, too, there were exceptions to GATT's prohibition of quotas. Member nations could use quotas to safeguard their balance of payments, promote economic development, and allow the operation of domestic agricultural-support programs. Voluntary export-restraint agreements, which used quotas, also fell outside the quota restrictions of GATT because the agreements were voluntary.

MULTILATERAL TRADE NEGOTIATIONS

GATT has also sponsored a series of negotiations, or rounds, to reduce tariffs and nontariff trade barriers, as summarized in Table 7.3. The first round of GATT negotiations, completed in 1947, achieved tariff reductions averaging 21 percent.

Table 7.3 GATT Negotiating Rounds

Negotiating Round and Coverage	Dates	Number of Participants	Tariff Cut Achieved (Percent)
Addressed Tariffs			
Geneva	1947	23	21
Annecy	1949	13	2
Torquay	1951	38	3
Geneva	1956	26	4
Dillon Round	1960–1961	26	2
Kennedy Round	1964–1967	62	35
Addressed Tariff and Nontariff Barriers			
Tokyo Round	1973–1979	99	33
Uruguay Round	1986–1993	125	34
Millennium Round	1999–	135	

However, tariff reductions were much smaller in the GATT rounds of the late 1940s and 1950s. During this period, protectionist pressures intensified in the United States as the war-damaged industries of Japan and Europe were reconstructed. Moreover, GATT negotiations emphasized *bilateral* bargaining (for example, between Canada and France) for tariff cuts on particular products, carried out concurrently by all of the participating nations. The process was slow and tedious, and nations often were unwilling to consider tariff cuts on many goods. A new approach to trade negotiations was thus considered desirable.

During the period 1964–1967, GATT members participated in the so-called **Kennedy Round** of trade negotiations, named after U.S. President John F. Kennedy, who issued an initiative calling for the negotiations. A *multilateral* meeting of GATT participants occurred at which the form of negotiations shifted from a product-by-product format to an across-the-board format. Tariffs were negotiated on broad categories of goods, and a given rate reduction applied to the entire group—a more streamlined approach. The Kennedy Round cut tariffs on manufactured goods by an average of 35 percent, to an average ad valorem level of 10.3 percent.

The GATT rounds from the 1940s to the 1960s focused almost entirely on tariff reduction. As average tariff rates in industrial nations decreased during the postwar period, the importance of nontariff barriers increased. In response to these changes, negotiators shifted emphasis to the issue of nontariff distortions in international trade.

At the **Tokyo Round** of 1973 to 1979, signatory nations agreed to tariff cuts that took the across-the-board form initiated in the Kennedy Round. The average tariff on manufactured goods of the nine major industrial countries was cut from 7.0 percent to 4.7 percent, a 40-percent decrease. Tariff reductions on finished products were deeper than those on raw materials, thus tending to decrease the extent of tariff escalation. After the Tokyo Round, tariffs were so low that they were not a significant barrier to trade in industrial countries. A second accomplishment of the Tokyo Round was the agreement to remove or lessen many nontariff

barriers. Codes of conduct were established in six areas: customs valuation, import licensing, government procurement, technical barriers to trade (such as product standards), antidumping procedures, and countervailing duties.

In spite of the trade liberalization efforts of the Tokyo Round, during the 1980s, world leaders felt that the GATT system was weakening. GATT members had increasingly used bilateral arrangements, such as voluntary export restraints, and other trade-distorting actions, such as subsidies, that stemmed from protectionist domestic policies. World leaders also felt that GATT needed to encompass additional areas, such as trade in intellectual property, services, and agriculture. They also wanted GATT to give increasing attention to the developing countries, who had felt bypassed by previous GATT rounds of trade negotiations.

These concerns led to the **Uruguay Round** from 1986 to 1993. As seen in Table 7.4, the Uruguay Round achieved across-the-board tariff cuts for industrial countries averaging 40 percent. Tariffs were eliminated entirely in several sectors, including steel, medical equipment, construction equipment, pharmaceuticals, and paper. Also, many nations agreed for the first time to bind, or cap, a significant portion of their tariffs, giving up the possibility of future rate increases above the bound levels. Significant progress was also made by the Uruguay Round in decreasing or eliminating nontariff barriers. The government-procurement code opened a wider range of markets for signatory nations. The Uruguay Round made extensive efforts to eliminate quotas on agricultural products and required nations to rely instead on tariffs. In the apparel and textile sector, various bilateral quotas were to be phased out by 2005. The safeguards agreement prohibited the use of voluntary export restraints. Moreover, the Uruguay Round called for the transformation of the GATT into a permanent international institution, the World Trade Organization, responsible for governing the conduct of trade relations among its members (see next section).

Although completion of the Uruguay Round was a notable achievement, many serious trade

Table 7.4 Uruguay Round Tariff Reductions on Industrial Products by Selected Countries

Country	Average Tariff Rate (Percent)	
	Pre-Uruguay Round	Post-Uruguay Round
Industrial Countries		
Australia	20.1	12.2
Canada	9.0	4.8
European Union	5.7	3.6
Japan	3.9	1.7
United States	5.4	3.5
Developing Countries		
Argentina	38.2	30.9
Brazil	40.7	27.0
Chile	34.9	24.9
Colombia	44.3	35.3
India	71.4	32.4

Source: "Uruguay Round Outcome Strengthens Framework for Trade Relations," *IMF Survey*, November 14, 1994, p. 355.

problems remained. The pact did not explicitly address the interface of trade policies with environmental and labor standards or the trade effects of domestic policies, such as competition and investment policy. Moreover, there was the tendency for the global economy to become segregated into three major trading blocs: the European Union; the North American Free Trade Area; and a bloc that included Southeast Asian countries, Japan, and possibly Australia. Although regional trading blocs promote free trade among member countries, potentially they can lead to additional bilateral deals and interbloc trade disputes.

THE WORLD TRADE ORGANIZATION

On January 1, 1995, the day on which the Uruguay Round took effect, GATT was trans-

formed into the World Trade Organization. This transformation turned GATT from a trade accord into a membership organization, responsible for governing the conduct of trade relations among its members. GATT obligations remain at the core of the WTO. However, the WTO Agreement requires that its members adhere not only to GATT rules, but also to the broad range of trade pacts that have been negotiated under GATT auspices in recent decades. This undertaking ends the free ride of many GATT members (especially developing countries) that benefited from, but refused to join, new agreements negotiated in GATT since the 1970s.

How different is the WTO from the old GATT? The WTO is a full-fledged international organization, headquartered in Geneva, Switzerland; the old GATT was basically a provisional treaty serviced by an ad hoc secretariat. The WTO has a far wider scope than the old GATT, bringing into the multilateral trading system, for the first time, trade in services, intellectual property, and investment. The WTO also administers a unified package of agreements to which all members are committed; in contrast, the GATT framework included many side agreements (for example, antidumping measures and subsidies) whose membership was limited to a few nations. Moreover, the WTO reverses policies of protection in certain "sensitive" areas (for example, agriculture and textiles) that were more or less tolerated in the old GATT. The WTO is not a government; individual nations remain free to set their own appropriate levels of environment, labor, health, and safety protections.

Through various councils and committees, the WTO administers the many agreements contained in the Uruguay Round, plus agreements on government procurement and civil aircraft. It oversees the implementation of the tariff cuts and reduction of nontariff measures agreed to in the negotiations. It is also a watchdog of international trade, regularly examining the trade regimes of individual members. In its various bodies, members flag proposed or draft measures by others that can cause trade conflicts. Members are also required to update various trade measures and statistics, which are maintained by the WTO in a large database.

SETTLING TRADE DISPUTES A major objective of the WTO was strengthening the GATT mechanism for settling trade disputes. The old GATT dispute mechanism suffered from long delays, the ability of accused parties to block decisions of GATT panels that went against them, and inadequate enforcement. The dispute-settlement mechanism of the WTO addresses each of these weaknesses. It guarantees the formation of a dispute panel once a case is brought and sets time limits for each stage of the process. The decision of the panel may be taken to a newly created appellate body, but the accused party can no longer block the final decision. The dispute-settlement issue was especially important to the United States because this nation was the most frequent user of the GATT dispute mechanism.

During the first five years of the WTO's operation, this framework proved useful to the United States. As a complaining party, the United States prevailed in 22 out of 24 cases, having favorably settled 10 without litigation and having won 12 in litigation. Yet the WTO also handed the United States several major defeats. One such defeat involved a dispute with the European Union over a $2.2 billion U.S. tax break for exporters. Under the U.S. Foreign Sales Corporation program, U.S. companies set up offshore subsidiaries that were partially exempt from U.S. taxes on profits from the sale of certain goods. In 2000, the WTO ruled that the tax break constituted an illegal subsidy for U.S. exporters.

DOES THE WTO REDUCE NATIONAL SOVEREIGNTY? Do WTO rules or dispute settlements reduce the sovereignty of the United States or other countries? The United States benefits from WTO dispute settlement by having a set of rules to hold other countries accountable for their trade actions. At the same time, the U.S. government was careful to structure the WTO dispute-settlement rules to preserve the rights of Americans.

The findings of a WTO dispute-settlement panel cannot force the United States to change its laws. Only the United States determines exactly how it will respond to the recommendations of a WTO panel, if at all. If a U.S. measure is found to be in violation of a WTO provision, the United States may on its own decide to change the law; compensate a foreign country by lowering our trade barriers of equivalent amount in another sector; or do nothing and possibly undergo retaliation by the affected country in the form of increased barriers to U.S. exports of an equivalent amount. But America retains full sovereignty in its decision of whether or not to implement a panel recommendation. Simply put, WTO agreements do not preclude the United States from establishing and maintaining its own laws or limit the ability of the United States to set its environmental, labor, health, and safety standards at the level it considers appropriate. However, the WTO does not allow a nation to use trade restrictions to enforce its own environmental, labor, health, and safety standards when they have selective and discriminatory effects against foreign producers.

Economists generally agree that the real issue raised by the WTO is not whether it decreases national sovereignty, but whether the specific obligations that it imposes on a nation are greater or less than the benefits the nation receives from applying the same requirements to others (along with itself). According to this standard, the benefits of the United States of joining the WTO greatly exceed the costs. By granting the United States the status of normal trade relations with all 135 members, the agreement improves U.S. access to foreign markets. Moreover, it reduces the ability of other nations to impose restrictions to limit access to their markets. If the United States withdrew from the WTO, it would lose the ability to use the WTO mechanism to induce other nations to decrease their own trade barriers, and thus would harm U.S. exporting firms and their workers. Simply put, economists generally contend that the WTO puts some constraints on the decision making of the private and public sectors. But the costs of these constraints are outweighed by the economic benefits that citizens derive from freer trade.

DOES THE WTO HARM THE ENVIRON-MENT? In recent years, the debate has intensified on the links between trade and the environment, and the role the WTO should play in promoting environment-friendly trade. A central concern of those who have raised the profile of this issue in the WTO is that there are circumstances where trade and the pursuit of trade liberalization may have harmful environmental effects. Indeed, these concerns were voiced when thousands of environmentalists descended on the World Trade Organization summit in Seattle in 1999. They protested the WTO's influence on everything from marine destruction to global warming. Let us consider the opposing views on the links between trade and the environment.[1]

HARMING THE ENVIRONMENT. Three main arguments are forwarded as to how trade liberalization may harm the environment. First, trade liberalization leads to a "race to the bottom" in environmental standards. If some countries have low environmental standards, industry is likely to shift production of environment-intensive or highly-polluting products to such pollution havens. Trade liberalization can make the shift of smokestack industries across borders to pollution havens even more attractive. If these industries then create pollution with global adverse effects, trade liberalization can, indirectly, promote environmental degradation. Worse, trade-induced competitive pressure may force countries to lower their environmental standards, thus encouraging trade in products creating global pollution.

A second concern of environmentalists about the role of trade relates to social preferences. Some practices may simply be unacceptable for certain people or societies, so they oppose trade in products that encourage such practices. These can include killing dolphins in the process of catching tuna and using leghold traps for catching animals for their furs. During the 1990s, relations between environmentalists and the WTO clashed when the WTO ruled against a U.S. ban on imports of shrimp from countries using nets that trap turtles, after complaints by India, Malaysia, Pakistan, and Thailand. Also, the United States was found guilty of violating world trade law when it banned imports of Mexican tuna caught in ways that drown dolphins. Indeed, critics maintained that the free-trade policies of the WTO contradicted the goal of environmental quality (see box essay).

The third argument linking trade to the environment is that trade liberalization encourages trade in products creating global pollution. Consider Accelerated Tariff Liberalization, proposed by the United States and some other WTO members in 1999. This proposal calls for the elimination of tariffs on lumber and other logging products by 2004. Such trade liberalization would permit a flood of new forestry products to enter markets across the world, including countries such as Japan and China, where tariffs as high as 40 percent have kept most logging imports out.

To most economists, any measure that liberalizes trade enhances productivity and growth, puts downward pressure on inflation by increasing competition, and creates jobs. In Japan, tariffs are so high on imported finished-wood products that U.S. firms don't have much market there. And high local prices limit domestic demand in Japan. But if tariffs were abolished, demand for lumber products from the United States could surge, creating additional logging jobs in the United States and additional import-related jobs in Japan.

But environmentalists view the tariff elimination differently. Their main concern is that a non-tariff market, which would result in lower prices, will stimulate so much demand that logging will intensify in the world's remaining ancient forests, which they say serve as habitat for complex ecosystems that otherwise cannot survive intact in forests that have been cut into fragments. Such old forests still exist across much of Alaska, Canada, and Russia's Siberian region. Environmentalists note that in Pennsylvania, New York, and other states in the Northeast, the forests have been so

---

[1] World Trade Organization, *Annual Report*, Geneva, Switzerland, 1998, pp. 54-55 and "Greens Target WTO's Plan for Lumber," *The Wall Street Journal*, November 24, 1999, pp. A2 and A4.

WTO RULINGS OUTRAGE ENVIRONMENTALISTS

The protection of dolphins and sea turtles, which are playful and harmless, has received much sympathy in the United States. However, protecting these creatures has threatened the methods used to catch tuna and shrimp. Let's see how the environmentalists' goal of protecting dolphins and sea turtles clashed with the free-trade goal of the WTO.

For many years, fisheries in the Eastern Tropical Pacific have found tuna by looking for dolphins—surface-swimming dolphins that travel above schools of tuna. A net drawn around the dolphins catches the tuna and the dolphins. However, as the nets draw tight underwater, the dolphins, being mammals, drown.

To environmentalists, saving the dolphins is a matter of environmental and moral consciousness. As a result, the United States passed the Marine Mammals Protection Act of 1972. The act outlawed the setting of nets on dolphins by U.S. tuna fisheries anywhere in the world; it also outlawed this method for foreign fisheries in U.S. waters, out to a 200-mile limit. However, the law did not apply to foreigners catching tuna outside U.S. waters.

Across the border in Mexico, saving dolphins meant losing business and jobs for tuna fisheries.

They maintained that they had to catch enough tuna to justify a fishing expedition. To do so required them to use the most efficient methods of fishing, even if they were unsafe for dolphins. Mexican fisheries were thus unwilling to refrain from setting nets on dolphins.

To convince Mexico to use dolphin-safe methods of catching tuna, the U.S. government pressured three major tuna retailing firms in the United States (Bumble Bee, Chicken of the Sea, and StarKist) to refuse to purchase tuna from fisheries using dolphin-unsafe methods. These tuna retailers responded with "dolphin-safe" tuna labels to steer concerned shoppers to tuna caught without setting nets on dolphins. But the force of the marketplace, said environmentalists, wasn't enough. They insisted on the force of law.

In 1991, the U.S. government slapped an embargo on tuna imports from Mexico and four other countries. Mexico immediately complained to the WTO (then known as GATT). The U.S. embargo, Mexico argued, violated WTO policies against restricting trade through discriminatory action. Application of the embargo was against the free-trade principles of the WTO,

chopped up that many large predators have been driven from the land, leaving virtually no check on the deer population. Therefore, deer are in a state of overpopulation.

However, trade liberalization proponents play down the adverse impacts, arguing that reduced tariffs would boost world economies by decreasing the cost of housing, paper, and other products made from wood, while actually helping forest conditions. For example, timber officials in the United States say they could go into a country like Indonesia and persuade local firms to adopt more conservation-minded techniques.

IMPROVING THE ENVIRONMENT. On the other hand, it is argued that trade liberalization may improve the quality of the environment

rather than promote degradation. First, trade stimulates economic growth, and growing prosperity is one of the key factors in societies' demand for a cleaner environment. As people get richer, they want a cleaner environment—and they acquire the means to pay for it. Granted, trade can increase the cost of the wrong environmental policies. If farmers freely pollute rivers, for instance, higher agricultural exports will increase pollution. But the solution to this is not to shut off exports: it is to impose tougher environmental laws that make polluters pay.

Second, trade and growth can encourage the development and dissemination of environment-friendly production techniques as the demand for cleaner products grows and trade increases the

WTO RULINGS OUTRAGE ENVIRONMENTALISTS *(continued)*

according to Mexico. But the United States denied that the tuna embargo discriminated against Mexico. Even though the United States was embargoing certain countries, and not embargoing others, the United States was embargoing on objective criteria that applied to all countries, according to the United States.

In 1991, the WTO decided in favor of Mexico and upheld its prohibition of policies that exclude imports according to how they are produced. The WTO ruled that the United States, by levying an embargo only against Mexico and four other countries, was in the breach of the rule of nondiscrimination. The embargo, said the WTO, hurt not only the tuna industry but the ultimate beneficiary of free trade, the consumer, as well. Simply put, WTO does not allow a nation to use trade restrictions to enforce its own environmental laws when they have selective and discriminatory effects on foreign producers.

Another case involves sea turtles, an endangered specie. Nations such as Thailand, Malaysia, India, and Pakistan have often caught shrimp with nets that trap and kill an estimated 150,000 sea turtles each year. The U.S. Endangered Species Act, passed in 1989, mandated that shrimpers in U.S. waters include devices in their nets to exclude turtles; it also placed embargoes on imports of shrimp from nations that do not protect sea turtles from deadly entrapment in nets. Four Asian nations, who were unwilling to equip their nets, filed a complaint with the WTO in 1997 that claimed that the U.S. Endangered Species Act was an illegal trade barrier. Ruling in favor of these nations, the WTO said that the United States could not use trade policy to force other nations to adopt environmental policies to protect endangered species. Following this decision, the United States reached agreements with these nations to use turtle-excluding nets, and the United States provided financial and technical assistance in how to use them.

Indeed, environmentalists have been outraged by some decisions of the WTO. They maintain that too often the WTO is blindly for free trade at any cost.

---

size of markets. International companies may also contribute to a cleaner environment by using the most modern and environmentally clean technology in all their operations. This is less costly than using differentiated technology based on the location of production and helps companies to maintain a good reputation.

Finally, the costs of meeting environmental regulations often account for only a small fraction of total production costs, so that this factor is unlikely to be at the basis of relocation decisions. The U.S. Census Bureau finds that even the most polluting industries spend no more than 2 percent of their revenues on abating pollution. Other factors such as labor costs and the adequacy of infrastructure are much more important. For all the talk of a race to the bottom, no governments are rushing to lower environmental standards.

THE BATTLE IN SEATTLE: WTO MEETINGS OF 1999

Shattered storefront windows. Looting. Lingering wafts of tear gas. Pepper spray. Rubber bullets. Shock grenades. Midnight to dawn curfew. Police in riot gear dispersing unruly crowds. National Guard called in to help restore order. A flashback to the 1960s and 1970s during the Vietnam War? Nope. It's a snapshot of downtown Seattle as the World Trade Organization attempted to start a four-day summit meeting in 1999. What led to the battle in Seattle?

In 1998, WTO members accepted President Bill Clinton's invitation to come to Seattle, Washington, in 1999 and kick off a new round of trade negotiations for a new century. The participants attempted to establish a new approach to global trade negotiations, including:

- An accelerated negotiation framework designed to deliver new commercial opportunities in agriculture, manufactured goods, and services over a three-year timetable.
- Reforms to broaden participation in the WTO and increase openness and accountability; help lesser-developed countries become integrated in the global economy; and broaden the trade agenda to include labor and environmental matters.
- Work on issues such as electronic commerce, expanding membership of the WTO, and improvement of the dispute settlement process.

As the WTO's negotiations unfolded, there were conflicting agendas of participants. For example, the United States accused developing nations of trying to escape from prior commitments to such free-trade principles as lower tariffs and Japan for leading an assault on the long-accepted WTO ban on the dumping of subsidized goods. On the other hand, developing countries were dead set against a U.S. push to include protections for labor rights and the environment in trade agreements. A prohibition on imports made with child labor, they said, was really protectionism masquerading as concern over human rights. Table 7.5 shows the trade agendas of selected participants.

When the Seattle meetings convened, however, trade ministers met stiff resistance. As many as 100,000 antiglobalization demonstrators swamped Seattle to vocalize their opposition to WTO policies. These demonstrators included trade unionists, environmentalists, consumer-rights campaigners, and human-rights activists. Peaceful demonstrations evolved into anarchy and vandalism. In general, protesters were unhappy with the WTO, charging that it too often only considers the profits of giant multinational corporations at the expense of protecting the environment and workers' rights.

Table 7.5	Conflicting Agendas at the WTO's Millennium Round

U.S. Objectives

- Add environmental protections to trade agreements
- Terminate European farm subsidies
- Reduce tariffs on goods and services
- Protect e-commerce from regulations and taxes
- Protect biotech products from labeling requirements
- Promote labor rights

Japan's Objectives

- End European farm subsidies
- Maintain subsidies for Japan's fleet of fishing trawlers
- Allow China into the World Trade Organization

Europe's Objectives

- Maintain current farm subsidies
- Promote stronger enforcement of antitrust laws
- Promote labor rights
- Retain current rules for investment
- Restrict labeling requirements for bioengineered food

Developing Countries' Objectives

- Limit intellectual-property safeguards
- Relax antidumping enforcement
- Create special trade rules for developing nations
- Open more export markets for farm goods, textiles, and clothing

Source: "Bracing for a Battle in Seattle," *Business Week*, November 8, 1999, pp. 38–39 and U.S. Trade Representative, *America and the World Trade Organization*, 1999.

The WTO has become a magnet for resistance to globalization by old-fashioned protectionists and newer critics of free trade. Protectionists include American steelworkers who complain that the free-trade policies of the WTO allow cheap Russian steel to flood the U.S. market, resulting in Russian workers taking away their jobs. Also, critics of free trade are incensed that, as economies become more closely intertwined, trade policy is increasingly impinging on such sensitive issues as social justice, product safety, and the environment.

For example, U.S. labor unions insist that Indonesian firms must pay livable wages to their workers and improve the working conditions in their "sweatshop" factories if they are to sell their goods in the United States. Moreover, human rights proponents demand that China not be allowed to join the WTO until it treats its citizens with dignity. Finally, church leaders declare that the international debts of poor nations must be forgiven.

The Seattle meetings also marked the debut of the developing nations as highly organized and assertive participants pursuing their own trade agendas. Believing that they had been taken to the cleaners in previous rounds of trade negotiations, the developing nations were determined not to allow that to occur again. Coalitions formed among developing country delegations. Indeed, developing nations as a block will have to be taken more seriously by the industrial countries in future rounds of trade negotiations. Industrial countries will not be able to strike a deal and expect the rest of the world to succumb to its terms.

As things turned out, the WTO meetings broke down and were unable to reach a compromise on a negotiating agenda within the allotted time. Behind the meetings' collapse was the complicated nature of the trade issues under discussion. Past rounds of trade negotiations had resolved the easy issues: Tariffs were slashed, and quotas were eliminated on most manufactured goods. Future negotiations, however, must focus on agriculture and services, politically sensitive sectors. Moreover, the WTO's multilateral approach to trade talks, involving 135 participants in a comprehensive agenda requiring bargains across several sectors, may have outlived its usefulness. And the WTO's secretive ways of making decisions were also troublesome to many participants.

In spite of pressure for reform, the WTO has remained a centerpiece of the world trading system. Its policies are based on the notion that when countries can trade freely with each other, without import tariffs or other measures aimed at protecting the domestic market from competition, the world economy grows and everyone in general benefits. However, free trade can impose costs on firms and workers in import-competing industries.

The protesters at Seattle were a reminder that the policies of the WTO must be weighed in a broader context of the world community and social justice, not just increased economic growth.

The economic stakes of the future trade negotiations are enormous. Will tariff-cutting be extended to more industrial products? Will the negotiations address the harmful economic effects of proliferating national antidumping regimes, which are threats to exporters everywhere? What about the prospects of significant tariff reductions on textiles and clothing, which would give importers and consumers a break? Will there be new, more liberal, global investment rules? Will agricultural subsidies finally be curbed? Concerning biotechnology, will genetically-modified organisms be treated the same as other products, or will they be subject to additional protectionism? Will old-fashioned protectionist measures like taxes be applied to electronic commerce—everything from the Internet to smart cards that change the traditional meaning of money? Indeed, the World Trade Organization faces major challenges and an uncertain outcome.

FAST TRACK, WORKERS' RIGHTS, AND THE ENVIRONMENT

If international trade agreements were subject to congressional amendments, achieving such pacts would be arduous, if not hopeless. The provisions that had been negotiated by the President would soon be modified by a deluge of congressional amendments, which would quickly meet the disapproval of the trading partner, or partners, that had accepted the original terms.

To prevent this scenario, the mechanism of **fast-track authority** was devised in 1974. Under this provision, the President must formally notify Congress of his/her intent to enter trade negotiations with another country. This notification starts a clock in which Congress has 60 legislative days to permit or deny "fast-track" authority. If fast-track authority is approved, the President has a limited time period in which to complete the trade negotiations; extensions of this time period are permissible with congressional approval. Once the negotiations are completed, their outcome is subject only to a straight up-or-down vote (without amendment) in both houses of the Congress within 90 legislative days of submission. In return, the President agrees to consult actively with Congress and the private sector throughout the negotiation of the trade agreement.

Fast-track authority, which was extended several times through 1994, was instrumental in negotiating and implementing major trade agreements such as the Uruguay Round Agreements Act of 1994 and the North American Free Trade Agreement of 1993. Most analysts contend that the implementation of future trade agreements will require fast-track authority for the President.

In 1994, fast-track authority expired. Since that time, efforts to renew fast-track authority have faced stiff opposition, largely due to congressional concerns about delegating too much discretionary authority to the President and disagreements over the goals of U.S. trade negotiations. In particular, labor unions and environmentalists have sought to ensure that trade agreements will address their concerns. They believe that high labor and environmental standards in the United States put

American producers at a competitive disadvantage and that increased trade with countries with lax standards may lead to pressure to lower U.S. standards. If other countries are to trade with the United States, shouldn't they have similar labor and environmental standards?

Supporters of fast-track authority have generally argued that, although labor and environmental standards are important, they do not belong in a trade agreement. Instead, these issues should be negotiated through secondary agreements that accompany a trade agreement. However, labor leaders and environmentalists contend that past secondary agreements have lacked enforcement provisions and thus have done little to improve the quality of life abroad.

TRADE REMEDY LAWS

In addition to the WTO's examination of unfair trade practices and conflicts, the United States itself has adopted a series of trade remedy laws designed to produce a fair trading environment for all parties engaging in international business. Table 7.6 summarizes the provisions of the U.S. trade remedy laws, which are discussed in the following sections.

Table 7.6 Trade Remedy Law Provisions

Statute	Focus	Criteria for Action	Response
Fair trade (escape clause)	Increasing imports	Increasing imports are substantial cause of injury	Duties, quotas, tariff-rate quotas, orderly marketing arrangements, adjustment assistance
Subsidized imports (countervailing duty)	Manufacturing production, or export subsidies	Material injury or threat of material injury	Duties
Dumped imports (antidumping duty)	Imports sold below cost of production or below foreign market price	Material injury or threat of material injury	Duties
Unfair trade (Section 301)	Foreign practices violating a trade agreement or injurious to U.S. trade	Unjustifiable, unreasonable, or discriminatory practices, burdensome to U.S. commerce	All appropriate and feasible action

THE ESCAPE CLAUSE The **escape clause** is intended to provide relief to U.S. firms and workers desiring protection from *fairly traded imports*. It allows the President to terminate or make modifications in trade concessions granted foreign nations and to levy restrictions on imports of any product that causes or threatens serious injury to the domestic industry manufacturing a like or directly competitive product. Relief provided by the escape clause is temporary: Trade restrictions can be enacted for a five-year period and are to be phased down over this period in the transition to open markets.

An escape-clause action is usually initiated by a petition from an American industry to the U.S. International Trade Commission (ITC), which investigates and recommends a response to the President. All of the following conditions must be met for the ITC to recommend that import relief should be extended:

- Imports are *increasing*, either actually or relative to domestic production.
- A domestic industry producing an article like or directly competitive with the imported article is being *seriously injured* or threatened with such injury.
- The increased imports are a *substantial cause* of serious injury or threat to the domestic industry producing a like or directly competitive article.

An affirmative decision by the ITC is reported to the President, who determines what remedy, if any, is in the national interest. Table 7.7 provides examples of relief granted to U.S. businesses under the escape clause.

COUNTERVAILING DUTIES As consumers, we tend to appreciate the low prices of foreign subsidized steel. But foreign export subsidies are resented by import-competing producers, who must charge higher prices because they do not receive such subsidies. From their point of view, the export subsidies give foreign producers an unfair competitive advantage.

As viewed by the World Trade Organization, export subsidies constitute unfair competition. Importing countries can retaliate by levying a **countervailing duty**. The size of the duty is limited to the amount of the foreign export subsidy. Its purpose is to increase the price of the imported good to its fair market value.

Upon receipt of a petition by a U.S. industry or firm, the U.S. Department of Commerce conducts a preliminary investigation as to whether or not an export subsidy was given to a foreign supplier. If the preliminary investigation finds a reasonable indication of an export subsidy, U.S. importers must immediately pay a special tariff (equal to the estimated subsidy margin) on all imports of the product in question. The Commerce Department then conducts a final investigation to determine

Table 7.7 Escape Clause Relief: Selected Examples

Product	Type of Relief
Porcelain-on-steel cookware	Additional duties imposed for four years of 20 cents, 20 cents, 15 cents, and 10 cents per pound in the first, second, third, and fourth years, respectively
Prepared or preserved mushrooms	Additional duties imposed for three years of 20%, 15%, and 10% ad valorem in the first, second, and third years, respectively
High-carbon ferrochromium	Temporary duty increase
Color TV receivers	Orderly marketing agreements with Taiwan and Korea
Footwear	Orderly marketing agreements with Taiwan and Korea

Source: *Annual Report of the President of the United States on the Trade Agreements Program*, Washington, DC, Government Printing Office, various issues.

whether an export subsidy was in fact granted, as well as the amount of the subsidy. If it determines that there was no export subsidy, the special tariff is rebated to the U.S. importers. Otherwise, the case is investigated by the U.S. International Trade Commission, which determines if the import-competing industry suffered material injury as a result of the subsidy.[2] If both the Commerce Department and the International Trade Commission rule in favor of the subsidy petition, a permanent countervailing duty is imposed that equals the size of the subsidy margin calculated by the Commerce Department in its final investigation. Once the foreign nation stops subsidizing exports of that product, the countervailing duty is removed.

LUMBER QUOTAS HAMMER HOME BUYERS

Let us consider a countervailing-duty case involving the U.S. lumber industry. During the 1980s and 1990s, the United States and Canada quarreled over softwood lumber. The stakes were enormous: Canadian firms exported more than $7 billion worth of lumber annually to U.S. customers. This dollar value of U.S. lumber imports from Canada almost equaled that of its steel imports from the rest of the world!

The lumber dispute followed a repetitive pattern. First, some U.S. lumber producers accused their Canadian rivals of receiving government subsidies. In particular, they alleged that the Canadians paid unfairly low tree-cutting fees to harvest timber from lands owned by the Canadian government. In the United States, companies bid years in advance for the right to cut trees in government forests. Because the tree-cutting fees are fixed, the companies must forecast their prices accurately in order to ensure profitability. By contrast, Canadian regulations permit provincial governments to reduce their tree-cutting fees when lumber prices decline so as

to keep their sawmills profitable. U.S. sawmill operators maintain that this practice subsidizes the Canadian lumber mills. However, the Canadians responded that their timber-pricing policies were not market-distorting, and they generally won on the technical merits. Despite losing those battles, the American lumber lobby usually ended up winning the war: Their relentless political pressure forced Canada to accept some form of trade restraint just to ensure commercial peace.

For example, in 1996, the Coalition for Fair Lumber Imports, a group of U.S. sawmill companies, filed a countervailing-duty petition with the U.S. government charging that domestic producers were hurt by subsidized lumber exports from Canada. The complaint ultimately led to the Softwood Lumber Agreement of 1996, which established a tariff-rate quota to protect U.S. producers. Up to 14.7 billion board feet of Canadian softwood lumber exports from Canada to the United States could enter duty free. The next 0.65 billion board feet of exports was subject to a tariff of $50 per thousand board feet. The Canadian government also agreed to raise the tree-cutting fees it charged provincial producers. As a result of the trade agreement, lumber imports to the United States fell about 14 percent.

Proponents of the accord maintained that it created a "level playing field" in which American lumber companies and Canadian lumber companies could compete. However, critics argued that the trade pact failed to take into account the interests of American lumber users in the lumber-dealing, homebuilding, and home-furnishing industries. It also overlooked the interests of American buyers of new homes and home furnishings, according to the critics.

In the United States, a coalition of lumber users—including Home Depot, the National Association of Home Builders, and the National Lumber and Building Material Dealers Association—banded together to protest the lumber quotas. They noted that the trade restrictions increased the price of lumber between 20 percent and 35 percent, or $50-$80 per thousand board feet. Therefore, the cost of the average

---

[2] For those nations that are signatories to the WTO Subsidy Code, the International Trade Commission must determine that their export subsidies have injured U.S. producers before countervailing duties are imposed. The export subsidies of nonsignatory nations are subject to countervailing duties immediately following the Commerce Department's determination of their occurrence; the International Trade Commission does not have to make an injury determination.

new home increased between $800 and $1,300 because of the restrictions. Moreover, every $1,000 increase in housing prices means that an additional 300,000 families are unable to buy a home. The lumber quotas thus served as a tax that kept the dream of home ownership out of reach for many lower-income Americans.

Critics acknowledged that barriers against Canadian lumber imports would benefit some U.S. lumber producers and their workers. But in 2000, there were only 217,000 American jobs in logging and sawmills. That figure compared to 510,000 jobs in lumber-using manufacturing industries; 744,000 jobs in the wholesale and retail lumber trade; and more than 4.7 million jobs in homebuilding. Lumber-using workers thus outnumbered lumber-producing workers by more than 25 to 1.[3] Simply put, critics maintained that workers in the lumber-using industries stood to lose far more than workers in the lumber-producing industries would gain.

ANTIDUMPING DUTIES The objective of U.S. antidumping policy is to offset two unfair trading practices by foreign nations: (1) export sales in the United States at prices below the average total cost of production; and (2) price discrimination, in which foreign firms sell in the United States at a price less than that charged in the exporter's home market. Both practices can inflict economic hardship on U.S. import-competing producers; by reducing the price of the foreign export in the U.S. market, they encourage U.S. consumers to buy a smaller quantity of the domestically produced good.

Antidumping investigations are initiated upon a written request by the import-competing industry that includes evidence of (1) dumping; (2) material injury, such as lost sales, profits, or jobs; and (3) a link between the dumped imports and the alleged injury. Antidumping investigations commonly involve requests that foreign exporters and domestic importers fill out detailed question-

naires. Parties that elect not to complete questionnaires can be put at a disadvantage with respect to case decisions; findings are made on the best information available, which may simply be information supplied by the domestic industry in support of the dumping allegation.

If investigators determine that dumping is occurring and is causing material injury to the domestic industry, then the U.S. response is to impose an antidumping duty (tariff) on dumped imports equal to the margin of dumping. The effect of the duty is to offset the extent to which the dumped goods' prices fall below average total cost, or below the price at which they are sold in the exporter's home market.

SECTION 301: UNFAIR TRADING PRACTICES Section 301 of the Trade Act of 1974 gives the United States Trade Representative (USTR) authority, subject to the approval of the President, and means to respond to unfair trading practices by foreign nations. Included among these unfair practices are foreign-trade restrictions that hinder U.S. exports and foreign subsidies that hinder U.S. exports to third-country markets. The USTR responds when he or she determines that such practices result in "unreasonable" or "discriminatory" burdens on U.S. exporters. The legislation was primarily a congressional response to dissatisfaction with GATT's ineffectiveness in resolving trade disputes. Table 7.8 provides examples of Section 301 cases.

Section 301 investigations are usually initiated on the basis of petitions by adversely affected U.S. companies and labor unions; they also can be initiated by the President. If, after investigation, it is determined that a foreign nation is engaging in unfair trading practices, the USTR is empowered to (1) impose tariffs or other import restrictions on products and services and (2) deny the foreign country the benefits of trade-agreement concessions.

Although the ultimate sanction available to the United States is retaliatory import restrictions, the purpose of Section 301 is to obtain successful resolution of conflicts. In a large majority

[3] Brink Lindsey, Mark Groombridge, and Prakash Loungani, *Nailing the Homeowner: The Economic Impact of Trade Protection of the Softwood Lumber Industry*, CATO Institute, July 6, 2000, pp. 5–8.

Table 7.8 Section 301 Investigations of Unfair Trading Practices: Selected Examples

U.S. Petitioner	Product	Unfair Trading Practice
Heilman Brewing Co.	Beer	Canadian import restrictions
Amtech Co.	Electronics	Norwegian government procurement code
Great Western Sugar Co.	Sugar	European Union subsidies
National Soybean Producers Association	Soybeans	Brazilian subsidies
Association of American Vintners	Wine	South Korean import restrictions

Source: U.S. International Trade Commission, *Operation of the Trade Agreements Program*, Washington, DC, Government Printing Office, various issues.

of cases, Section 301 has been used to convince foreign nations to modify or eliminate what the United States has considered to be unfair trading practices; only in a small minority of cases has the United States retaliated against foreign producers by means of tariffs or quotas. However, foreign nations have often likened Section 301 to a "crowbar" approach for resolving trade disputes, which invites retaliatory trade restrictions. At least two reasons have been advanced for the limitations of this approach to opening foreign markets to U.S. exports: (1) Nationalism unites the people of a foreign nation against U.S. threats of trade restrictions; (2) The foreign nation reorients its economy toward trading partners other than the United States. The next section considers Section 301 cases involving bananas and automotive products.

EUROPE SLIPS IN BANANA DISPUTE

In 1993, the European Union (EU) implemented a single EU-wide regime on banana imports. The regime gave preferential entry to bananas from EU's former colonies, including parts of the Caribbean, Africa, and Asia. They also restricted entry from other countries, including several in Latin America where U.S. companies predominate.

The EU implemented the banana regime as part of its move toward a single, unified market that was inaugurated in 1992. Before the regime, individual countries imported bananas under an assortment of national practices. For example, Spain imported bananas exclusively from the Canary Islands; other EU countries imposed a 20-percent tariff on banana imports, and Germany allowed tariff-free entry. The banana regime was also justified on the grounds that European nations were obligated by treaty to protect their former colonies' banana industries from foreign competition.

The banana regime entered into force in 1993 and resulted in a maze of import quotas, licenses, and preferential tariffs that favored bananas from former European colonies. Under the banana regime, a modest tariff was applied to EU banana imports from its former colonies while substantial tariff and nontariff restrictions were applied to imports from other suppliers in Latin America. The EU's system of tariffs and quotas divided the banana world into haves and have-nots—those who have licenses allowing them to import bananas into the protected European market, and those who don't.

The root of the economic problem of the banana regime was that producers in the former Caribbean colonies of the EU were too small to be efficient in the global market. Due to the small size of farms and lack of economies of scale, as well as difficulties of terrain and climate, it was impossible for them to compete on equal terms with the vast plantations of Latin America. Without protection, the Caribbean industries could be destroyed. Moreover, the entire economies of some Caribbean states depended on banana trade. In Dominica, for example, banana trade accounted for around 70 percent of all export earnings, and there was hardly a family in the country that was not dependent to some degree on it. In seeking to safeguard these fragile economies, the banana regime was on moral high ground, according to the EU.

Because the amount of bananas Europe allowed in was far less than the amount consumers wanted to purchase, the price of bananas in Europe was inflated to about twice the U.S. level. In 1999, a pound of bananas sold for about 50 cents in the United States but went for about a dollar in Europe. Therefore, bananas were lucrative for holders of the licenses that allowed selling under Europe's higher prices. Analysts estimated that of the $2 billion the arrangement cost European consumers, only about $150 million found their way into the hands of banana farmers in former colonies. More than $1 billion wound up in the pockets of the companies that imported the bananas.

According to the United States, the EU's banana regime resulted in unfair treatment for American companies. U.S. trade officials maintained that Chiquita Brands International and Dole Food Co., which handle and distribute bananas of Latin American nations, lost half of their business because of EU's banana regime. Put simply, the United States contended that the EU must adopt a single trade policy for bananas that applies the same set of criteria for all suppliers of the world.

As a result, the United States, Mexico, Ecuador, Honduras, and Guatemala brought this issue to the World Trade Organization and successfully argued their case. The WTO ruled that the EU's banana regime discriminated against U.S. and Latin American distribution companies and banana exports from Latin American countries. Also, the WTO found that the banana regime caused $191 million in lost U.S. exports on an annual basis.

This decision gave the United States the right to apply 100-percent tariffs on a list of selected European products equivalent in value to the loss in U.S. exports caused by the EU's banana regime. The hit list of European products included candles, cashmere sweaters, bed linen, coffee and tea makers, cheese, plastic handbags, and so forth. Such high tariffs would presumably foreclose the U.S. market to these European products, because few U.S. consumers want to pay double and thus force the EU to abandon its banana regime. The only time that such high tariffs didn't foreclose the U.S. market to imports was in 1992, when the United States slapped 100-percent duties on Canadian beer and people kept buying the stuff. The United States had to increase the duties to 120 percent before the flow abated. The punitive duties on beer have been removed.

To many free-traders, the U.S.–Europe banana war was the ultimate sign of a world-trading system gone nuts: a power fight between two antagonists, neither of which grows bananas. Both sides, critics maintained, were defending the worst of their systems—colonial pretensions on the part of the Europeans, and political-campaign donations from Chiquita and Dole Food Co. on the part of the United States.

U.S.–JAPANESE AUTOMOTIVE TRADE DISPUTE

Since 1971, in good times and bad, the United States has realized a merchandise trade deficit with Japan. The composition of this deficit has disproportionately represented imbalances in trade in motor vehicles and parts. These persistent deficits have led to U.S. allegations that certain policies and practices have barred market access for autos and auto parts in Japan for more than three decades:

- Only a small minority of Japanese auto dealers sell American vehicles alongside Japanese-label cars, in contrast to the United States where most U.S. auto dealers sell imported cars alongside American-label vehicles.

- A complex system of regulations, surpassing what is essential for environmental protection or safety, has restricted the Japanese market for replacement auto parts supplied by foreigners.
- Japan's market for original equipment parts has involved closed-purchasing relationships between Japanese automakers and their suppliers, thus preventing U.S. suppliers from penetrating the Japanese market.

The Japanese, however, maintained that their automotive market was not closed. They noted that the U.S. Big Three had made negligible efforts to penetrate Japan's market, whereas Japanese automakers had made an enormous effort and spent large sums of money to crack the U.S. market. The Japanese pointed out that European automakers had made greater inroads in the Japanese market, commanding a market share of 4.9 percent, as opposed to a 3.2 percent share for U.S. automakers in 1995. European automakers had introduced 154 models of standard right-hand drive cars into the Japanese market, while the U.S. Big Three had introduced only 3 right-hand drive models. Finally, Japan maintained that almost four-fifths of the cars sold in Japan were compact models, while the U.S. Big Three concentrated their marketing strategies almost exclusively on large vehicles.

Prompted by threats of 100-percent tariffs on imports of certain Japanese luxury cars, Japan reached a trade agreement with the United States to further open its automotive market to imported products in 1995. The pact obligated Japan's major automakers to increase their parts purchases in North America and increase the number of vehicles manufactured in their North American plants.

The agreement also obligated the Japanese government to confirm the right of Japanese auto dealers to sell foreign motor vehicles, facilitate contracts between foreign vehicle manufacturers and Japanese vehicle dealers, and encourage foreign auto companies to pursue market opportunities in Japan. Further, the Japanese government pledged to initiate deregulation measures aimed at improving market access for competitive foreign parts suppliers in the Japanese auto-parts replacement market.

The clearest winner in the U.S.–Japan automotive trade agreement was the U.S. auto-parts industry. The trade pact's provisions, giving U.S. automakers greater access to Japanese dealers, would help U.S. parts manufacturers because much of the replacement market in Japan is handled through car dealers. The Japanese automakers' pledge to increase their factory purchases of original-equipment parts would lead to increased capital investment and employment at U.S. factories.

The biggest loser was the Japanese parts-making industry. Before the 1995 automotive agreement, Japanese parts manufacturers were struggling with a dwindling market: Japanese automakers were moving more production to North America, Europe, Latin America, and Southeast Asia. The 1995 agreement to purchase more U.S. auto parts resulted in further sales losses for Japanese parts suppliers.

REMEDIES AGAINST DUMPED AND SUBSIDIZED IMPORTS

Recall that the direct effect of dumping and subsidizing imports is to lower import prices, an effect that provides benefits and costs for the importing country. There are benefits to consumers if imports are finished goods and to consuming industries that use imports as intermediate inputs into their own production (*downstream* industry). Conversely, there are costs to the import-competing industry, its workers, and other domestic industries selling intermediate inputs to production of the import-competing industry (*upstream* industry). Dumping at prices below fair market value and subsidizing exports are considered unfair trade practices under international trade law; they can be neutralized by the imposition of antidumping or countervailing duties on dumped or subsidized imports.

U.S. STEEL COMPANIES LOSE AN UNFAIR TRADE CASE AND STILL WIN

For years, the U.S. steel industry has dominated at the complaint department of the U.S. International Trade Commission (USITC). During the 1980s and 1990s, it accounted for almost half of the nation's unfair-trade complaints, even though steel constituted less than 5 percent of U.S. imports. Year after year, the steel industry swamped the USITC with petitions alleging that foreign steel was being subsidized or dumped into the U.S. market. However, the steel industry was not very successful in its petitions against cheap imports. During the 1990s, for example, it lost more than half its cases.

To the steel industry, however, winning isn't everything. Filing and arguing its cases is part of the competitive strategy of the Big Steel consortium—U.S. Steel, Bethlehem, AK Steel, LTV Corp., Inland Steel Industries Inc., and National Steel. The consortium knows that it can use the trade laws to influence the supply of steel in the marketplace and thus limit foreign competition. Whenever the market gets weak, for whatever reason, the consortium files an unfair trade case.

Here's how the strategy works. The market gets soft, and the consortium files trade cases alleging foreign subsidization or dumping, and then imports from the target companies' decrease. The case proceeds for a year or so, allowing domestic steelmakers to increase market share and raise prices. Even if the USITC rules against the case, the market gets time to recover.

Once a case is filed, it takes months to proceed through a four-stage legal process, and time benefits domestic steelmakers. U.S. steelmakers usually win the first round, in which the industry has to show the USITC a "reasonable indication" of harm from imports. Armed with that finding, the U.S. Department of Commerce can set preliminary duties on the imports. Importers must post a financial bond to cover those duties. Then, the Commerce Department determines the final duties, based on the extent of foreign subsidization or dumping, and the case goes back to the USITC for a final determination of injury. If the U.S. companies lose, the duty is never collected, and the bond is lifted. If they win, however, the importer may be liable for the full amount.

During this process, U.S. importers have the right to continue importing. They might continue to import if they feel strongly that the U.S. steelmakers will lose the case. However, the USITC is a political body, with some of its presidentially appointed commissioners free-traders and others more protectionist. Because U.S. importers realize that they run a big risk if they are wrong, the response is usually to stop importing when a case is filed.

In 1997, Trinidad was hit with a complaint on steel wire rod, which is used to make wire. Wire-rod producers in Trinidad cut their U.S. shipments by 40 percent after the preliminary ruling, even though Trinidad's steelmakers eventually won the case.

Put simply, just by filing unfair trade cases, the U.S. steel industry may win. Whatever they spend on legal fees, they may recoup many times over in extra revenue. That's the great thing about filing: Even if you lose, you win.

Source: "U.S. Steelmakers Win Even When They Lose an Unfair-Trade Case," *The Wall Street Journal*, March 27, 1998, pp. A1, A6.

Figure 7.2 illustrates the effects of unfair trade practices on Canada, a nation too small to influence the foreign price of steel; for simplicity, the figure assumes that Canada's steel, iron ore, and auto companies operate in competitive markets. In Figure 7.2(a), S_C and D_C represent the Canadian supply and demand for steel. Suppose that South Korea, which has a comparative advantage in steel, supplies steel to Canada at the fair-trade price of $600 per ton. At this price, Canadian production equals 200 tons, Canadian consumption equals 300 tons, and imports equal 100 tons.

Now suppose that as a result of South Korean dumping and subsidizing practices, Canada

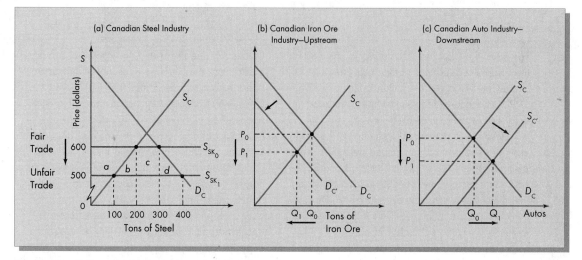

Figure 7.2 Effects of Dumped and Subsidized Imports and Their Remedies

Dumped or subsidized imports provide benefits to consumers if imports are finished goods and to consuming industries that use the imports as intermediate inputs into their own production; they inflict costs on the import-competing domestic industry, its workers, and other domestic industries selling intermediate inputs to the import-competing industry. An antidumping or countervailing duty inflicts costs on consumers if imports are finished goods and on consuming industries that use the imports as intermediate inputs into their own production; benefits are provided to the import-competing domestic industry, its workers, and other domestic industries selling intermediate inputs to the protected industry.

imports steel at a price of $500 per ton; the margin of dumping and subsidization thus equals $100 ($600 − $500 = $100). The unfair trade practice reduces Canadian production from 200 tons to 100 tons, increases Canadian consumption from 300 tons to 400 tons, and increases Canadian imports from 100 tons to 300 tons. Falling prices and quantities, in turn, lead to falling investment and employment in the Canadian steel industry. Although the producer surplus of Canadian steelmakers decreases by area a due to unfair trade, Canadian buyers find their consumer surplus rising by area $a + b + c + d$. The Canadian steel market as a whole benefits from unfair trade because the gains to its consumers exceed the losses to its producers by area $b + c + d$!

Unfair trade also affects Canada's upstream and downstream industries. If the Canadian iron-ore industry (upstream) supplies mainly to Canadian

steelmakers, the demand for Canadian iron ore will decrease as their customers' output falls due to competition from cheaper imported steel. As illustrated in Figure 7.2(b), without unfair trade, the quantity of iron ore demanded by Canadian steelmakers is Q_0 tons at a price of P_0 per ton. Because of unfair trade in the steel industry, the demand for iron ore decreases from D_C to $D_{C'}$; production thus falls as do revenues and employment in this industry. In autos (downstream), production will increase as manufacturing costs decrease because of the availability of cheaper imported steel. As illustrated in Figure 7.2(c), Canadian auto production increases from Q_0 units to Q_1 units, as the supply curve shifts downward from S_C to $S_{C'}$, with accompanying positive effects on revenues and employment; the decrease in production costs also improves the Canadian auto industry's competitiveness in international markets.

Suppose that unfair trade in steel results in the imposition by the Canadian government of an antidumping duty or countervailing duty on imported steel equal to the margin of dumping or subsidization ($100). The effect of an exactly off-setting duty in the steel industry is a regaining of the initial prices and quantities in Canada's steel, iron-ore, and auto industries, as seen in Figure 7.2. The duty raises the import price of unfairly traded steel in Canada, leading to increased steel production by Canadian steelmakers; this results in increased demand, and therefore higher prices, for Canadian iron ore, but also implies increased production costs, higher prices, and lower sales for Canadian automakers. With the import duty, the decrease in consumer surplus more than off-sets the increase in producer surplus in the Canadian steel market.

The U.S. International Trade Commission estimated the economic effects of antidumping duties and countervailing duties for U.S. petitioning industries and their upstream suppliers and downstream consumers for the year 1991. The study concluded that these duties typically benefited successful petitioning industries by raising prices and improving output and employment. However, the costs to the rest of the economy were far greater. The study estimated that the U.S. economy would have experienced a net welfare gain of $1.59 billion in the year 1991 had U.S. antidumping duties and countervailing duties *not* been in effect. In other words, these duties imposed costs on consumers, downstream industries, and the economy as a whole at least $1.59 billion greater than the benefits enjoyed by the successful petitioning industries and their employees.[4] Remember, however, that the purpose of antidumping and counter-vailing duty laws is not to protect consumers, but rather to discourage unfairly traded imports that cause harm to competing domestic industries and workers.

[4] U.S. International Trade Commission, *The Economic Effects of Antidumping and Countervailing Duty Orders and Suspension Agreements* (Washington, D.C.: International Trade Commission, June 1995), Chapter 10.

PROTECTION OF INTELLECTUAL PROPERTY RIGHTS

In the 1800s, Charles Dickens criticized U.S. publishers for printing unauthorized versions of his works without paying him one penny. But U.S. copyright protection did not apply to foreign (British) authors, so Dickens's popular fiction could be pirated without punishment. In recent years, it is U.S. companies whose profit expectations have been frustrated. Publishers in South Korea run off copies of bootlegged U.S. textbooks without providing royalty payments. U.S. research laboratories find themselves in legal tangles with Japanese electronics manufacturers concerning patent infringement.

Certain industries and products are well-known targets of pirates, counterfeiters, and other infringers of **intellectual property rights (IPRs)**. Counterfeiting has been widespread in industries such as automobile parts, jewelry, sporting goods, and watches. Piracy of audio and videotapes, computer software, and printed materials has been widespread throughout the world. Industries in which product life cycles are shorter than the time necessary to obtain and enforce a patent are also subject to thievery; examples are photographic equipment and telecommunications. Table 7.9 provides examples of IPR violations in China.

Intellectual property is an invention, idea, product, or process that has been registered with the government and that awards the inventor (or author) exclusive rights to use the invention for a given time period. Governments use several techniques to protect intellectual property. *Copyrights* are awarded to protect works of original authorship (for example, music compositions, textbooks); most nations issue copyright protection for the remainder of the author's life plus 50 years. *Trademarks* are awarded to manufacturers and provide exclusive rights to a distinguishing name or symbol (for example, "Coca Cola"). *Patents* secure to an inventor for a term, usually

Table 7.9 Intellectual Property Right Violations in China

Affected Firm	Violation in China
Epson	Copying machines and ink cartridges are counterfeited.
Microsoft	Counterfeiting of Windows and Windows NT, with packaging virtually indistinguishable from the real product and sold in authorized outlets.
Yamaha	Five of every six JYM150-A motorcycles and ZY125 scooters bearing Yamaha's name are fake in China. Some state-owned factories manufacture copies four months following the introduction of a new model.
Gillette	Up to one-fourth of its Parker pens, Duracell batteries, and Gillette razors sold in China are pirated.
Anheuser-Busch	Some 640 million bottles of fake Budweiser beer are sold annually in China.
Nike	Replicas of its T-shirts and sport shoes are widely sold throughout China.
Bestfoods	Bogus versions of Knorr bouillon and Skippy Peanut Butter lead to tens of millions of dollars in forgone sales each year.
Procter & Gamble	About 15 percent of the detergents and soaps bearing its Tide, Vidal Sassoon, Safeguard, and Head and Shoulders brands are bogus, costing $150 million annually in forgone sales.
DaimlerChrysler	Fake windshields, oil filters, brake disks, and shock absorbers for Mercedes cars are manufactured and sold in China.

Source: "Will China Follow WTO Rules?" *Business Week*, June 5, 2000, pp. 42–48.

15 years or more, the exclusive right to make, use, or sell the invention.

In spite of efforts to protect IPRs, competing firms sometimes infringe on the rights of others by making a cheaper imitation of the original product. In 1986, the courts ruled that Kodak had infringed on Polaroid's patents for instant cameras and awarded Polaroid more than $900 million in damages. Another infringement would occur if a company manufactured an instant camera similar to Polaroid's and labeled and marketed it as a Polaroid camera; this is an example of a counterfeit product.

The lack of effective international procedures for protecting IPRs becomes a problem when the expense of copying an innovation (including the cost of penalties if caught) is less than the cost of purchasing or leasing the technology. Suppose that Warner-Lambert Drug Co. develops a product that cures the common cold, called "Cold-Free," and that the firm plans to export it to Taiwan. If Cold-Free is not protected by a patent in Taiwan, either because Taiwan

does not recognize IPRs or Warner-Lambert has not filed for protection, cheaper copies of Cold-Free could legally be developed and marketed. Also, if Warner-Lambert's trademark is not protected, counterfeit cold remedies that are indistinguishable from Cold-Free could be legally sold in Taiwan. These copies would result in reduced sales and profits for Warner-Lambert. Moreover, if "Cold-Free" is a trademark that consumers strongly associate with Warner-Lambert, a counterfeit product of noticeably inferior quality could adversely affect Warner-Lambert's reputation and thus detract from the sales of both Cold-Free and other Warner-Lambert products.

Although most nations have regulations protecting IPRs, there have been many problems associated with trade in products affected by IPRs. One problem is differing IPR regulations across nations. For example, the United States uses a first-to-invent rule when determining patent eligibility, whereas most other nations employ a first-to-file rule. Another problem is lack of enforcement of international IPR agreements. These problems stem largely from differing incentives to protect intellectual property, especially between nations that are innovating, technological exporters and those that are noninnovating, technological importers. Developing nations, lacking in research and development and patent innovation, sometimes pirate foreign technology and use it to produce goods at costs lower than could be achieved in the innovating country. Poorer developing nations often find it difficult to pay the higher prices that would prevail if innovated products (such as medical supplies) were provided patent protection. Thus, they have little incentive to provide patent protection to the products they need.

As long as the cost of pirating technology, including the probability and costs of being caught, is less than the profits captured by the firm doing the pirating, technology pirating tends to continue. Pirating, however, reduces the rate of profitability earned by firms in the innovating nations, which in turn deters them from investing in research and development. Over time, this leads to fewer products and welfare losses for the people of both nations.

The United States has faced many obstacles in trying to protect its intellectual property. Dozens of nations lack adequate legal structures to protect the patents of foreign firms. Others have consciously excluded certain products (such as chemicals) from protection to support their industries. Even in advanced countries, where legal safeguards exist, the fast pace of technological innovation often outruns the protection provided by the legal system.

TRADE ADJUSTMENT ASSISTANCE

According to the free-trade argument, in a dynamic economy in which trade proceeds according to the comparative-advantage principle, resources flow from uses with lower productivity to those with higher productivity. The result is a more efficient allocation of the world's

resources over time. In the short run, however, painful adjustments may occur as less efficient companies go out of business and workers lose their jobs. These displacement costs can be quite severe to affected parties.

Many industrial nations in recent years have enacted programs for giving **trade adjustment assistance** to those who incur short-run hardships because of displaced domestic production. The underlying rationale comes from the notion that if society in general enjoys welfare gains from the increased efficiency stemming from trade liberalization, some sort of compensation should be provided for those who are temporarily injured by import competition. As long as free trade generates significant gains to the nation, the winners can compensate the losers and still enjoy some of the gains from free trade.

The 1962 Trade Expansion Act resulted in trade adjustment assistance being granted U.S. workers and businesses. Whenever the U.S. Tariff Commission found that tariff concessions were resulting in severe import competition, it could recommend adjustment assistance. Injured workers were entitled to job-training programs, cash payments, and relocation allowances. To businesses, the program offered technical aid in moving into new lines of production, market research assistance, and low-interest loans.

The adjustment assistance program, however, did not live up to full expectations during the 1960s because eligibility requirements were very strict, with the result that labor and business became frustrated at not being able to obtain relief. The eligibility requirements were loosened with the passage of the 1974 Trade Act. Either the secretary of labor or the secretary of commerce could determine whether aid should be extended to workers, businesses, and communities affected by increased imports. With the eligibility criteria liberalized, the number of grants rose.

Enactment of adjustment assistance programs is considered a significant innovation in trade policy. But even though it is often recognized that such programs are a political necessity in today's world, not all interested parties are enthusiastic about implementation of these programs. Adjustment assistance is intended to help domestic businesses become more competitive by switching to superior technologies and developing new products. But in practice, such programs can allegedly be manipulated to financially sustain a losing concern rather than help it become competitive. Proponents of adjustment assistance argue that it is preferable to help domestic labor and business become more productive or move into new occupations or product lines than to curb import competition through tariffs and quotas. In this way, the societal welfare gains arising from a competitive market are still attainable.

INDUSTRIAL POLICIES OF THE UNITED STATES

Besides enacting regulations intended to produce a fair trading environment for all parties engaging in international business, the United States has implemented *industrial policies* to enhance the competitiveness of domestic producers. As discussed in Chapter 4, such policies involve government channeling of resources into specific, targeted industries that it views as important for future economic growth. Among the methods used to channel resources are tax incentives, loan guarantees, and low-interest loans.

Today, almost all nations implement some kinds of industrial policies. Although industrial policies are generally associated with formal, explicit efforts of governments (as in Japan and France) to enhance the development of specific industries (such as steel or electronics), other traditionally free-enterprise nations (such as Germany and United States) also have less formal, implicit industrial policies.

Economic growth policies have deep roots in U.S. economic history. In the nineteenth century, the federal government backed the development of a transcontinental railroad by ceding huge tracts of land to get the job done. The government also sponsored a network of universities, extension services, and research to help U.S. farmers successfully reap the riches of a fertile land. During the twentieth century, government financing nurtured industries such as airlines and electronics. In spite of these examples, the United States does not have a full-blown industrial policy; the policy has been de facto rather than de jure. Put simply, calls for an explicit industrial policy in the United States have contradicted the dominant free-market ideology that precludes active government direction of the economy.

What has been the U.S. approach to industrial policy? The U.S. government has attempted to provide a favorable climate for business, given the social, environmental, and safety constraints imposed by modern society. Rather than formulating a coordinated industrial policy to affect particular industries, the U.S. government has generally emphasized macroeconomic policies (such as fiscal and monetary policies) aimed at such objectives as economic stability, growth, and the broad allocation of the gross domestic product.

There is no doubt, however, that the U.S. government uses a number of measures to shape the structure of the economy that would be called "industrial policies" in other nations. The most notable of these measures is agricultural policy. In agriculture, a farmer who initiates a major innovation can be imitated by many other farmers, who capture the benefits without sharing the risks. To rectify this problem, the U.S. government is involved in research in agricultural techniques and in the dissemination of this information to farmers through its agricultural extension service, as well as the fostering of large-scale projects such as irrigation facilities. The U.S. government has also provided support for the shipping and shipbuilding industries, primarily on the grounds of national security.

Energy is another sector of the U.S. economy that has received government assistance. Subsidies have been provided for decades to promote the development of the nuclear power industry. The extraction of oil from shale and sand has also received government support. Subsidy critics contend that these industries have become expensive failures that serve as a warning to advocates of government targeting of specific industries for subsidies.

U.S. government defense spending is often cited as an industrial policy. As the world's largest market for military goods, it is no wonder that the United States dominates their production. U.S. spending on military goods supports domestic manufacturers and permits them to achieve large economies of scale. U.S. defense spending has provided spillover benefits to civilian industries, especially commercial aircraft, computers, and electronics. And military research and development provides U.S. companies with expertise that they can apply elsewhere.

In manufacturing, the U.S. government has provided assistance to financially troubled industries. In automobiles, for example, the government provided a $1.5 billion loan guarantee in 1979 and 1980 to bail out Chrysler Corporation. It also negotiated voluntary export restrictions with the Japanese on autos in the 1980s to ease the burden of import competition. In return, recipient firms and workers were expected to reduce labor costs and reorganize production. These measures had elements of industrial policy, but lacked an overt attempt on the part of the government to make public assistance conditional on the industry's performance. The steel and textile industries have also been major recipients of trade protection.

EXPORT PROMOTION AND FINANCING
Another element of U.S. industrial policy is export promotion. The U.S. government maintains a variety of export programs to encourage businesses to expand their sales overseas. A primary objective of these programs is to offset or minimize deficiencies in the market system. Because of high costs of obtaining information, for example, many foreign buyers might remain unaware of prospective U.S. sellers were it not for U.S. promotion programs. U.S. exporters might likewise remain ignorant of foreign sales possibilities through lack of knowledge about foreign markets and exporting procedures. The U.S. government furnishes exporters with marketing information and technical assistance, in addition to trade missions that help expose new exporters to foreign customers. The government also promotes exports by sponsoring exhibits of U.S. goods at international trade fairs and establishing overseas trade centers that enable U.S. businesses to exhibit and sell machinery and equipment.

The U.S. government also encourages exports by allowing its manufacturers to form export trade associations to facilitate the marketing of U.S. products abroad. Moreover, U.S. manufacturers and financial institutions are permitted to combine their resources into joint export trading companies to export their own products or to act as an export service for other producers. Sears, Rockwell, General Electric, Control Data, and General Motors are examples of firms that have formed export trading companies.

The United States also provides export subsidies to its producers in the form of low-cost credit. The maintenance of competitive credit terms for U.S. exporters is a function of the U.S. Export-Import Bank and the Commodity Credit Corporation. The **Export-Import Bank** (*Eximbank*) is an independent agency of the U.S. government established to encourage exports of U.S. businesses. The Eximbank provides:

- Guarantees of working capital loans for U.S. exporters to cover pre-export costs.
- Export credit insurance that protects U.S. exporters or their lenders against commercial or political risks of nonpayment by foreign buyers.
- Guarantees of commercial loans to creditworthy foreign buyers of U.S. goods and services.
- Direct loans to these foreign buyers when private financing is unavailable.
- Special programs to promote U.S. exports of environmentally beneficial goods and services.
- Asset-based financing for large commercial aircraft and other appropriate exports.
- Project financing to support U.S. exports to international infrastructure projects.

In offering competitive interest rates in financing exports, Eximbank has sometimes been criticized because part of its funds are borrowed from the U.S. Treasury. Critics question whether U.S. tax revenues should subsidize exports to foreign countries at interest rates lower than could be obtained from private institutions. To this extent, it is true that tax funds distort trade and redistribute income toward exporters.

Table 7.10 provides examples of direct loans and loan guarantees made by the Eximbank. Major beneficiaries of Eximbank credit have included aircraft, telecommunications, power-generating equipment, and energy developments. Firms such as Boeing, McDonnell Douglas, and Westinghouse have enjoyed substantial benefits from these programs.

Officially supported lending for U.S. exports is also provided by the **Commodity Credit Corporation** (CCC), a government-owned corporation administered by the U.S. Department of Agriculture. The CCC makes available export credit financing for eligible agricultural commodities. The interest rates charged by the CCC are usually slightly below prevailing rates charged by private financial institutions.

KNOWLEDGE-BASED GROWTH POLICY

Critics of industrial policy claim that government officials cannot consistently pick winners among products and firms and thus encourage labor and capital to move into the industries with the highest growth prospects. This is because the develop-ment of commercially successful technology requires a knowledge of scientific possibilities, an awareness of market demand for new or improved products, and a good sense of timing. Critics argue that the free market is better at picking winners than politicians and bureaucrats.

Instead of targeting particular manufacturers for subsidization, an alternative is for government to sponsor the development of technologies that can be used by manufacturers to improve their competitiveness. For some years, the most competitive firms in the United States have been its brainiest, the ones producing cellular phones, supercomputers, synthetic drugs, and spreadsheets. These firms rely on ideas—ideas for raw materials, product designs, manufacturing processes, and ultimately, for commercial products. In this environment, knowledge counts more than capital and labor. A **knowledge-based growth policy** recognizes that knowledge is king in the world economy; those nations that excel at creating new knowledge and transforming it into new technologies and products will prosper in the years ahead.

Unlike industrial policies in manufacturing, a knowledge-based growth policy does not require government to pick winning and losing products and firms; it's the market that picks the winners and losers. The function of government is to

Table 7.10 Examples of Loans Provided by Eximbank of the United States (in Millions of Dollars)

Foreign Borrower/U.S. Exporter	Purpose	Loan or Long-Term Guarantee
Banco Santander Noroeste of Brazil/General Electric	Locomotives	87.7
Government of Bulgaria/Westinghouse	Instruments	81.8
Air China/Boeing	Aircraft	69.8
Government of Croatia/Bechtel International	Highway construction	228.7
Government of Ghana/Wanan International	Electrical equipment	21.1
Government of Indonesia/IBM	Computer hardware	20.2
Japan Airlines/Boeing	Aircraft	212.3
Fevisa Industrial of Mexico/Pennsylvania Crusher Inc.	Glass-manufacturing equipment	17.7
Delta Communications of Mexico/Motorola	Communications equipment	11.5

Source: Export-Import Bank of the United States, *Annual Report*, 1999, http://www.exim.gov/.

support the development of technological breakthroughs that encourage economic growth. It is true that investment in plant and equipment raises the growth rate of real income. But throw in technological breakthroughs, such as a jet turbine or a new software program, and opportunities arise.

INDUSTRIAL POLICIES OF JAPAN

Although the United States has generally not used explicit industrial policies to support specific industries, such policies have been used elsewhere. Consider the case of Japan.

Japan has become a technological leader in the post–World War II era. During the 1950s, Japan's exports consisted primarily of textiles and other low-tech products. By the 1960s and 1970s, its exports emphasized capital-intensive products such as autos, steel, and ships. By the 1980s and 1990s, Japan had become a major world competitor in high-tech goods, such as optical fibers and semiconductors.

Advocates of industrial policy assert that government assistance for emerging industries has helped transform the Japanese economy from low-tech to heavy industry to high-tech. They claim that protection from imports, R&D subsidies, and the like fostered the development of Japanese industry. Clearly, the Japanese government provided assistance to shipbuilding and steel during the 1950s, to autos and machine tools during the 1960s, and to high-tech industries beginning in the early 1970s. Japanese industrial policy has had two distinct phases: From the 1950s to the early 1970s, the Japanese government assumed strong control over the nation's resources and the direction of the economy's growth. Since the mid-1970s, the government's industrial policy has been more modest and subtle.

Japanese officials in charge of industrial policy maintain that since the 1970s, Japan's comparative advantage in international trade has shifted from capital-intensive industries to high-tech industries. They argue that the free market does not generate sufficient incentives to invest in emerging, high-tech industries, for at least two reasons: (1) The risks of creating a new technology may be too great for competitive firms to absorb by themselves, and (2) The benefits of new technologies to other firms and industries may be very widespread, so that the societal value of investing in emerging industries may be greater than the profits generated by the private firm undertaking the risks.

Japanese officials further contend that capital and labor do not flow smoothly out of declining industries any more than they flow smoothly into emerging industries; firms and workers are reluctant to abandon once-profitable investments and careers for uncertain investments and careers in emerging industries. As a result, Japanese officials feel that government should assist declining industries in adapting to structural changes in their economy.

To implement its industrial policies in manufacturing, the Japanese government has created the **Ministry of International Trade and Industry (MITI)**. MITI attempts to facilitate the shifting of resources into high-tech industries by targeting specific industries for support. With the assistance of consultants from leading corporations, trade unions, banks, and universities, MITI forms a consensus on the best policies to pursue. The next step of industrial policy is to increase domestic R&D, investment, and production. Targeted industries have received support in the form of trade protection, allocations of foreign exchange, R&D subsidies, loans at below-market interest rates, loans that must be repaid only if a firm becomes profitable, favorable tax treatment, and joint government-industry research projects intended to develop promising technologies.

Although government subsidies have enhanced Japanese industrial development, most of the funds for R&D projects and production facilities have come from private firms and commercial banks. The Japanese economy is very capitalistic and competitive, with none of the central planning that historically existed in Eastern Europe. Moreover, only a modest fraction of government subsidies go to emerging

HAS INDUSTRIAL POLICY HELPED JAPAN?

Relative Levels of Economic Growth Rates and Targeting of Japanese Industries, 1955–1990

Industry	Growth Rate	Low-Interest-Rate Loans	Net Subsidies*	Trade Protection	Tax Breaks
Electrical machinery	1	8	9	8	8
General machinery	2	12	4	11	8
Transportation equipment	3	7	11	4	8
Fabricated metal	4	10	6	12	7
Petroleum and coal	5	2	13	7	3
Precision instruments	6	13	10	6	8
Ceramics, stone, and glass	7	5	8	9	3
Pulp and paper	8	6	5	10	13
Chemicals	9	3	7	5	3
Basic metals	10	4	2	3	6
Processed food	11	9	12	1	12
Mining	12	1	1	13	1
Textiles	13	11	3	2	2

*Subsidies less indirect taxes.

Source: Richard Beason and David Weinstein, "Growth, Economies of Scale, and Targeting in Japan: 1955–1990," *Review of Economics and Statistics*, May 1996, p. 288.

It is commonly argued that the Japanese government has provided assistance to high-growth or high-productivity-growth industries to improve their international competitiveness. Moreover, the alleged success of Japanese targeting is often used as the justification for industrial policy in the United States. What is the evidence concerning Japanese industrial policy?

Contrary to the popular wisdom, recent research has found that a disproportionate amount of Japanese targeting has occurred in *low-growth industries* rather than high-growth industries. Moreover, evidence does not support the contention that industrial policy measures have fostered Japanese productivity.

The table shows the relative levels of economic growth and government assistance granted to 13 Japanese industries from 1955 to 1990. Column 1 ranks these industries according to their growth rates. Electrical machinery,

for example, was the fastest-growing industry, and textiles realized the slowest growth. Columns 2–5 show the usage of various industrial-policy tools. The industry that received the most government assistance in a category ranked first, and the industry that received the least ranked thirteenth. Mining, for example, received the most low-interest-rate loans, net subsidies, and tax breaks, but received the least amount of trade protection (tariffs and quotas).

The figures in the table do not provide strong support for Japan's industrial policy. In fact, it appears that the Japanese government targeted many laggard industries for assistance. For each of the industrial policy tools, the correlation between an industry's growth and the amount of government aid it received was negative. Therefore, the Japanese government provided more backing to losers than to winners.

industries as compared to the subsidies granted to other sectors of the economy, such as agriculture, transportation, and the environment.

Without government support, it is improbable that Japanese semiconductor, telecommunications equipment, fiber optics, and machine-tool industries would be as competitive as they are. Not all Japanese industrial policies have been successful, however, as seen in the cases of computers, aluminum, and petrochemicals. Even industries in which Japan is competitive in world markets, such as shipbuilding and steel, have witnessed prolonged periods of excess capacity. Moreover, some of Japan's biggest success stories (TVs, stereos, and VCRs) were not the industries most heavily targeted by the Japanese government.

The inability of governments to pick winners is evidenced by some of Japan's failures:

- MITI first wanted the Japanese automobile industry to produce only trucks and later wanted to limit the number of automobile companies to a few giants, in particular attempting to keep Honda out of the car business. Of course, market forces eventually led MITI to abandon these plans, but the intervention generated costs that could have been avoided. Had MITI been successful, Japan would have paid an enormous price for this policy.
- The Japanese heavily targeted an analog version of high-definition television (HDTV), but it appears that digital HDTV—the product of U.S. research and development—has become the industry standard.

The extent to which industrial policy has contributed to Japan's economic growth since World War II is unclear. Japan has benefited from a high domestic savings rate, an educated and motivated labor force, good labor-management relations, a shift of labor from low-productivity sectors (such as agriculture) to high-productivity manufacturing, entrepreneurs willing to assume risks, and the like. These factors have enhanced Japan's transformation from a low-tech nation to a high-tech nation. It is debatable how rapidly this transformation would have occurred in the absence of an industrial policy. Although Japan has the most visible industrial policy of the industrial nations, the importance of that policy to Japan's success should not be exaggerated.

STRATEGIC TRADE POLICY

Beginning in the 1980s, a new argument for industrial policy gained prominence. The theory behind **strategic trade policy** is that government can assist domestic companies in capturing economic profits from foreign competitors.[5] Such assistance entails government support for certain "strategic" industries (such as high-technology) that are important to future domestic economic growth and that provide widespread benefits (externalities) to society.

IMPERFECT COMPETITION AND GOVERNMENT SUBSIDIES The essential notion underlying strategic trade policy is *imperfect competition*. Many industries participating in trade, the argument goes, are dominated by a small number of large companies—large enough for each company to significantly influence market price. Such market power gives these companies the potential to attain long-run economic profits. According to the strategic-trade policy argument, government policy can alter the terms of competition to favor domestic companies over foreign companies and shift economic profits in imperfectly competitive markets from foreign to domestic companies.

A standard example is the aircraft industry. With high fixed costs of introducing a new aircraft and a significant learning curve in production that leads to decreasing unit production costs, this industry can support only a small number of man-

[5] The argument for strategic trade policy was first presented in J. Brander and B. Spencer, "International R&D Rivalry and Industrial Strategy," *Review of Economic Studies* 50 (1983), pp. 707–722. See also P. Krugman, ed., *Strategic Trade Policy and the New International Economics* (Cambridge, MA: MIT Press, 1986).

ufacturers. It is also an industry that typically is closely associated with national prestige.

Assume that two competing manufacturers, Boeing (representing the United States) and Airbus (a consortium owned jointly by four European governments), are considering whether to construct a new aircraft. If either firm manufactures the aircraft by itself, it will attain profits of $100 million. If both firms manufacture the aircraft, they will each suffer a loss of $5 million.

Now assume the European governments decide to subsidize Airbus production in the amount of $10 million. Even if both companies manufacture the new aircraft, Airbus is now certain of making a $5 million profit. But the point is this: Boeing will cancel its new aircraft project. The European subsidy thus ensures not only that Airbus will manufacture the new aircraft but also that Boeing will suffer a loss if it joins in. The result is that Airbus achieves a profit of $110 million and can easily repay its subsidy to the European governments. If we assume that the two manufacturers produce entirely for export, the subsidy of $10 million results in a transfer of $100 million in profits from the United States to Europe. Table 7.11 summarizes these results.

Consider another example. Suppose the electronics industry has just two companies, one in

Japan and one in the United States. In this industry, learning-by-doing reduces unit production costs indefinitely with the expansion of output. Suppose the Japanese government considers its electronics industry to be "strategic" and imposes trade barriers that close its domestic market to the U.S. competitor; assume the United States keeps its electronics market open. The Japanese manufacturer can expand its output and thus reduce its unit cost. Over a period of time, this competitive advantage permits it to drive the U.S. manufacturer out of business. The profits that the U.S. company had extracted from U.S. buyers are transferred to the Japanese.

Advocates of strategic trade policy recognize that the classical argument for free trade considered externalities at length. The difference, they maintain, is that the classical theory was based on *perfect competition* and thus could not appreciate the most likely source of the externality, whereas modern theories based on imperfect competition can. The externality in question is the ability of companies to capture the fruits of expensive innovation. Classical theory based on perfect competition neglected this factor because large fixed costs are involved in innovation and research and development, and such costs ensure that the number of competitors in an industry will be small.

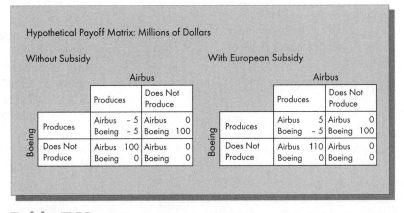

Table 7.11 Effects of a European Subsidy Granted to Airbus

Source: Paul Krugman, "Is Free Trade Passé?" *Economic Perspectives*, Fall 1987, pp. 131–144.

The strategic-trade policy concept has been criticized on several grounds. From a political perspective, there is danger that special-interest groups will dictate who will be the recipients of government support. Also, if a worldwide cycle of activist trade-policy retaliation and counter retaliation were to occur, all nations would be worse off. Moreover, governments lack the information to intervene intelligently in the marketplace. In our Boeing–Airbus example, the activist government must know how much profit it would be achieved as a result of proceeding with the new aircraft, both with and without foreign competition. Minor miscalculations could result in an intervention that makes the home economy worse off, instead of better off. Finally, the mere existence of imperfect competition does not guarantee that there is a strategic opportunity to be pursued, even by an omniscient government. There must also be a continuing source of economic profits, with no potential competition to erase them. But continuing economic profits are probably less common than governments think.

The case of the European subsidization of aircraft during the 1970s provides an example of the benefits and costs encountered when applying the strategic-trade policy concept. During the 1970s, Airbus received a government subsidy of $1.5 billion. The subsidy was intended to help Airbus offset the 20-percent cost disadvantage it faced on the production of its A300 aircraft compared to that of its main competitor, the Boeing 767. Did the subsidy help the European nations involved in the Airbus consortium? The evidence suggests no. Airbus itself lost money on its A300 plane and continued to face cost disadvantages relative to Boeing. There were benefits to European airlines and passengers because the subsidy kept Airbus prices lower; however, the amount of Airbus's losses roughly matched this gain. Because the costs of the subsidy had to be financed by higher taxes, Europe was probably worse off with the subsidy. The United States also lost, because Boeing's profits were smaller and were not fully offset by lower prices accruing to U.S. aircraft users; but the European sub-

sidy did not drive Boeing out of the market. The only obvious gainers were other nations, whose airlines and passengers enjoyed benefits from lower Airbus prices at no cost to themselves.[6]

WELFARE EFFECTS OF STRATEGIC TRADE POLICY

What are the effects on national welfare (consumers, business firms, and taxpayers) of a strategic trade policy that targets a domestic industry for subsidies so as to help it capture monopoly profits on foreign sales? Note that strategic behavior by firms takes place in international markets in which the number of firms is small enough to permit some degree of market power. In designing a profit-maximizing strategy, a firm must take account of reactions of rival firms and their governments.

Let us consider the hypothetical case of high-definition television (HDTV), a sophisticated blend of video and computer technology that produces images as sharp as 35-millimeter film and sound worthy of compact-disc players.

Most analysts agree that HDTV fits the requirements for strategic trade policy. The HDTV industry is likely to be highly concentrated, with only a few dominant European and Japanese producers (imperfect competition). Also, the industry is expected to provide spillover benefits to a number of sectors of the economy. Its technology will not only enhance television for home use, but also computer memory, chip manufacturing, computer-screen designs, and defense radar systems. The production of HDTV will provide a domestic market for other high-technology goods such as semiconductors. Moreover, the bulk of the cost of producing HDTV comes in the early research, development, and design stages. These costs occur irrespective of the number of television sets manufactured; the cost per set decreases substantially as more sets are manufactured, spreading the fixed costs over a larger number of units.

[6] R. Baldwin and P. Krugman, "Industrial Policy and International Competition in Wide-Bodied Jet Aircraft," in R. Baldwin, ed., *Trade Policy Issues and Empirical Analysis* (Chicago: University of Chicago Press, 1988), pp. 45–77.

Suppose that Europe and Japan vie for monopoly profits in the U.S. HDTV market. Assume that these nations have government-sponsored R&D programs and antitrust laws that permit consortiums among their producers. Figure 7.3 illustrates several possible outcomes of the rivalry between these nations for monopoly profits. These outcomes depend on which producers first penetrate the U.S. market, how much government assistance is granted to producers, and the reaction of the producers' rivals.

Assume that a consortium of European firms is the first to develop and market HDTV sets;

this group of firms becomes a monopoly seller in the United States. Suppose these firms realize a constant marginal production cost of $3,400 per set, denoted by schedule MC_0.[7] As a monopoly, the European consortium maximizes profit by selling that output at which marginal revenue equals marginal cost; 4 sets are sold at a price of $3,800 per set. On those 4 sets, the consortium realizes a profit of $400 per set and a total prof-

[7] For production with constant marginal cost, average variable cost and marginal cost are identical. Marginal cost always lies below average total cost for such processes. The average total cost schedule is downsloping because of declining average fixed cost.

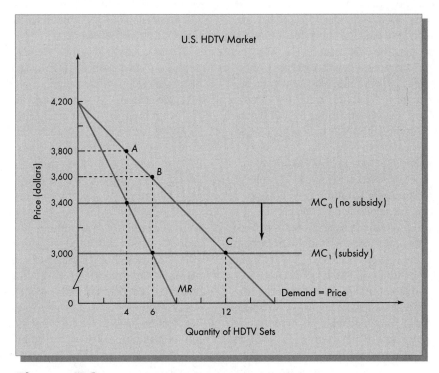

Figure 7.3 Welfare Effects of Strategic Trade Policy

A subsidy granted by the Japanese government to its HDTV exporters improves their competitiveness in the U.S. market; a sufficiently large Japanese subsidy will convince European exporters to retreat from the U.S. market, assuming that no retaliatory subsidies are granted by the European government. Japanese exporters thus enjoy increased export profits; however, Japanese taxpayers pick up the tab for the subsidy. If these export profits exceed the subsidy's cost to the Japanese taxpayer, Japan enjoys net gains. Consumers in the United States enjoy consumer surplus gains resulting from lower-priced HDTV sets due to the subsidy.

it of $1,600 (minus the fixed costs of becoming established in the United States). U.S. consumers also realize a consumer surplus of $800 (the area under the demand schedule down to the price of $3,800) from the availability of HDTV. World welfare thus rises by these amounts, as seen in Table 7.12, situation *a*.

Suppose now that a consortium of Japanese firms develops HDTV and that its marginal costs are identical to those of the Europeans, $3,400 per set. To enhance international competitiveness, suppose the Japanese government grants a permanent subsidy of $400 on each set manufactured by the Japanese consortium. The consortium's marginal costs now equal $3,400 less the $400 subsidy, or $3,000, as shown by MC_1. With the help of its government, the Japanese consortium is in a position to export to the United States even if the price of HDTV sets falls to low levels. If the subsidy policy convinces European producers that they can no longer compete with the Japanese, they will exit the U.S. market; the Japanese will become the monopoly seller of HDTV sets in the United States. The subsidy thus facilitates the Japanese consortium's success in the U.S. market!

The Japanese consortium maximizes profits by selling 6 sets, where marginal revenue equals marginal cost, at a price of $3,600 per set. The consortium realizes a profit of $600 per set and a total profit of $3,600 on the 6 sets (minus fixed costs). Japanese taxpayers lose the $2,400 granted to the Japanese producers as a subsidy ($400 × 6 sets). However, Japan enjoys overall gains equal to the amount by which its export profits (less fixed costs) exceed the taxpayer cost of the subsidy, or $1,200. At the price of $3,600, U.S. consumers enjoy consumer surplus of $1,800 from the availability of HDTV. The welfare gains to the world thus total $3,000 as seen in Table 7.12, situation *b*.

This example assumes that if Japan provides a permanent subsidy to its producers, it will drive the European producers out of the U.S. market, thus capturing their sales and profits. Suppose, however, that Europe retaliates and provides a permanent subsidy to its producers. In this case, the welfare of Japan and Europe tend to decrease, while U.S. welfare increases.

Assume that Japanese and European HDTV consortiums have identical marginal production costs of $3,400 and that each nation provides a $400 subsidy to its consortium; the subsidy-adjusted marginal costs are now $3,000. With government support, neither consortium will back down and exit the U.S. market. With open competition and intense price cutting, the Japanese

Table 7.12 Welfare Effects of Strategic Trade Policy: High-Definition Television

Situation	Gains (Losses)			
	European– Japanese Consortium*	European– Japanese Government	U.S. Consumer	World*
a. European consortium is the first to penetrate the U.S. market, and thus becomes a monopoly seller.	$1,600	_____	$800	$2,400
b. Japanese government grants a subsidy to its consortium, which now monopolizes the U.S. market.	3,600	–$2,400	1,800	3,000
c. European and Japanese governments grant offsetting subsidies to their consortiums; both nations compete in the U.S. market.	0	–4,800	7,200	2,400

*Minus fixed costs.

and European firms reduce their prices to $3,000, at which price 12 sets are sold and no profits are realized by either exporting nation.[8] The total cost of the subsidy to the Japanese and European governments is $4,800 ($400 × 12 sets). Japan and Europe are clearly worse off than in the case of no subsidies: Their taxpayers bear the burdens of the subsidy, but their firms do not realize the profits that come with increased market share. On the other hand, the U.S. consumer realizes consumer surplus of $7,200 (the area under the demand schedule down to the price of $3,000). To the extent that the gains to the U.S. consumer exceed the losses of Europe and Japan, the subsidy enhances world welfare. These results are summarized in Table 7.12, situation *c*.

ECONOMIC SANCTIONS

Instead of promoting exports, governments may restrict exports for domestic and foreign-policy objectives. **Economic sanctions** are government-mandated limitations placed on customary trade or financial relations among nations. They have been used to protect the

[8] Because the European and Japanese consortiums compete with each other, each must accept a price no higher than marginal cost. Both consortiums lose the fixed costs of becoming established in the United States. Over time, one or both consortiums may go bankrupt.

domestic economy, reduce nuclear proliferation, set compensation for property expropriated by foreign governments, combat international terrorism, preserve national security, and protect human rights. The nation initiating the economic sanctions, the *imposing nation*, hopes to impair the economic capabilities of the target nation to such an extent that the *target nation* will succumb to its objectives.

The imposing nation can levy several types of economic sanctions. *Trade sanctions* involve boycotts on imposing-nation exports. The United States has used its role as a major producer of grain, military hardware, and high-technology goods as a lever to win overseas compliance with its foreign-policy objectives. Trade sanctions may also include quotas on imposing-nation imports from the target nation. *Financial sanctions* can entail limitations on official lending or aid. During the late 1970s, the U.S. policy of freezing the financial assets of Iran was seen as a factor in the freeing of the U.S. hostages. Table 7.13 provides examples of economic sanctions levied by the United States for foreign-policy objectives.

Figure 7.4 can be used to illustrate the goal of economic sanctions levied against a target country, say, Iraq. The figure shows the hypothetical production possibilities curve of Iraq for machines and oil. Prior to the imposition of sanctions, suppose that Iraq is able to operate at maximum efficiency

Table 7.13 Selected Economic Sanctions of the United States

Year	Target Country	Objectives
1998	Pakistan	Discourage nuclear proliferation
1998	India	Discourage nuclear proliferation
1993	Haiti	Improve human rights
1992	Serbia	Terminate civil war in Bosnia-Herzegovina
1990	Iraq	Terminate Iraq's military takeover of Kuwait
1985	South Africa	Improve human rights
1983	Soviet Union	Retaliate for downing of Korean airliner
1981	Soviet Union	Terminate martial law in Poland; impair Soviet economic and military potential
1981	Nicaragua	Cease support for El Salvador rebels; destabilize Sandinista government
1979	Iran	Release U.S. hostages; settle expropriation claims

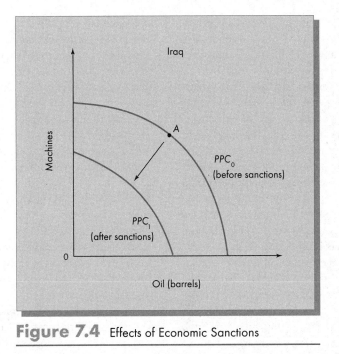

Figure 7.4 Effects of Economic Sanctions

Economic sanctions placed against a target country have the effect
of forcing it to operate inside its production possibilities curve.
Economic sanctions can also result in an inward shift in the target
nation's production possibilities curve.

as shown by point *A* along production possibilities curve PPC_0. Under the sanctions program, a refusal of the imposing nations to purchase Iraqi oil leads to idle wells, refineries, and workers in Iraq. Unused production capacity thus forces Iraq to move inside PPC_0. If imposing nations also impose export sanctions on productive inputs, and thus curtail equipment sales to Iraq, the output potential of Iraq would decrease. This is shown by an inward shift of Iraq's production possibilities curve to PPC_1. Economic inefficiencies and reduced production possibilities, caused by economic sanctions, are thus intended to inflict hardship on the people and government of Iraq. Over time, sanctions may cause a reduced growth rate for Iraq. Even if short-run welfare losses from sanctions are not large, they can appear in inefficiencies in the usage of labor and capital, deteriorating

domestic expectations, and reductions in savings, investment, and employment. Thus, sanctions do reduce the Iraq's output potential.

FACTORS INFLUENCING THE SUCCESS OF SANCTIONS The historical record of economic sanctions provides some insight into the factors that govern their effectiveness. Among the most important determinants of the success of economic sanctions are (1) the number of nations imposing sanctions, (2) the degree to which the target nation has economic and political ties to the imposing nation(s), (3) the extent of political opposition in the target nation, and (4) cultural factors in the target nation.

Although unilateral sanctions may have some success in achieving intended results, it helps if sanctions are imposed by a large number of nations. Multilateral sanctions generally result in greater economic pressure on the target nation than unilateral measures. Multilateral measures also increase the probability of success by demonstrating that more than one nation disagrees with the target nation's behavior, thus enhancing the political legitimacy of the effort. International ostracism can have a significant psychological impact on the people of a target nation. Failure to get strong multilateral cooperation, however, can result in sanctions' becoming counterproductive; disputes among the imposing nations over sanctions can be interpreted by the target nation as a sign of disarray and weakness.

Sanctions tend to be more effective if the target nation had substantial economic and political relationships with the imposing nation(s) before the sanctions were imposed. Then the potential costs to the target nation are very high if it does not comply with the wishes of the imposing nation(s). For example, the Western sanctions against South Africa during the 1980s helped convince the government to reform its apartheid system, in part because South Africa conducted four-fifths of its trade with six Western industrial nations and obtained almost all of its capital from the West.

Strength of political opposition within the target nation also affects the success of sanctions. When the target government faces substantial domestic opposition, economic sanctions can lead powerful business interests (such as companies with international ties) to pressure the government to conform to the imposing nation's wishes. Selected, moderate sanctions, with the threat of more severe measures to follow, inflict some economic hardship on domestic residents, while providing an incentive for them to lobby for compliance to forestall more severe sanctions; thus, the political advantage of levying graduated sanctions may outweigh the disadvantage of giving the target nation time to adjust its economy. If harsh, comprehensive sanctions are imposed immediately, domestic business interests have little incentive to pressure the target government to modify its policy; the economic damage has already been done.

When the people of the target nation have strong cultural ties to the imposing nation(s), they are likely to identify with the imposing nation's objectives, thus enhancing the effectiveness of sanctions. For example, South African whites have generally thought of themselves as part of the Western community. When economic sanctions were imposed on South Africa in the 1980s because of its apartheid practices, many liberal whites felt isolated and morally ostracized by the Western world; this encouraged them to lobby the South African government for political reforms.

IRAQI SANCTIONS In August 1990, the Iraqi military crossed into Kuwait and within six hours occupied the whole country. Iraqi President Saddam Hussein maintained that his forces had been invited into Kuwait by a revolutionary government that had overthrown the Kuwaiti emir and his government.

In response to Iraq's aggression, a United Nations resolution resulted in economic sanctions against Iraq. Sanctions were applied by virtually the entire international community, with only a few hard-line Iraqi allies refusing to cooperate. Under the sanctions program, imposing nations placed embargoes on their exports to Iraq, froze Iraqi bank accounts, terminated purchases of Iraqi oil, and suspended credit granted to Iraq. To enforce the sanctions, the United States supplied naval forces to prevent ships from leaving or arriving in Iraq or occupied Kuwait. The sanctions were intended to convince Iraq that its aggression was costly and that its welfare would be enhanced if it withdrew from Kuwait. If Saddam Hussein could not be convinced to leave Kuwait, it was hoped the sanctions would pressure the Iraqi people or military into removing him from office.

The sanctions were intended to have both short- and long-term consequences for Iraq. By blocking Iraqi imports of foodstuffs, the sanctions forced Iraq to adopt food rationing within several weeks of their initiation; although Iraq is self-sufficient in fruits and vegetables, shortages of flour, rice, sugar, and milk developed immediately following the imposition of sanctions. Over the longer term, the sanctions were intended to force Iraq to deindustrialize, interfering with its goal of becoming a regional economic power.

Despite the widespread application of sanctions against Iraq, it was widely felt that they would not bite hard enough to quickly destabilize the regime of Saddam Hussein. Over the short term, Iraq's ability to survive under the sanctions depended on how it rationed its existing stocks. One advantage Iraq had was a highly disciplined and authoritarian society and a people inured to shortages during its previous eight-year war with Iran; to enforce its rationing program, Saddam Hussein declared that black marketers would be executed. It was also widely believed that prior to the invasion of Kuwait, Saddam Hussein had spent some $3 billion from hidden funds to stockpile goods for domestic consumers. A plentiful agricultural harvest was also predicted for 1991.

Smuggled goods represented another potential source of supplies for Iraq. Although the United Nations pressured the governments of Jordan and Turkey, Iraq's neighbors, to comply with the sanctions, the potential rewards to smugglers increased as scarcities intensified and prices rose in Iraq. Reports indicated that families and tribes that straddled the Turkey–Iraq and Jordan–Iraq borders smuggled foodstuffs into Iraq. In addition, commodities flowed into Iraq from two of its traditional enemies, Iran and Syria. Such "leakages" detracted from the restrictive impact of the sanctions.

The sanctions also resulted in costs for the imposing nations. The closing down of the Iraqi and Kuwaiti oil trade removed some 5 million barrels of oil per day from the world marketplace, which led to price increases. From August to October 1990, oil prices jumped from $18 a barrel to $40 a barrel; oil prices subsequently decreased as other oil producers announced they would increase their production. In addition, nations dependent on Iraq for trade, especially neighboring countries, were hard hit by the embargoes. Turkey, for example, lost an estimated $2.7 billion as a result of the embargoes in 1990. Jordan's economy, much smaller and more dependent on Iraq's, faced a crisis even more severe. When the embargoes were initially imposed, most estimates suggested it would take up to two years before they would force Iraq to alter its policies. Therefore, the Bush

Administration concluded that sanctions would not succeed in a timely manner and a military strike against Iraq was necessary.

Following the ouster of the Iraqi army from Kuwait in 1990, the United Nations continued to impose sanctions against Iraq. The sanctions were to be kept in place until Iraq agreed to scrap its nuclear and biological weapons programs. However, Saddam Hussein dug his heels in and refused to make concessions. Therefore, the sanctions program continued throughout the 1990s into the new millennium.

Sanctions have been devastating for Iraq. Analysts estimate that Iraq's economy has shrunk more than two-thirds because of the sanctions. Moreover, that figure understates the extent of contraction. Every sector of the Iraqi economy depended to some degree on imports. The simplest textile mills could not operate without foreign-made parts; farmers needed imported pumps to run their irrigation systems, and the government could not repair war-damaged telephone, electricity, water, road, and sewage networks without material from abroad. As a result, factories and businesses shut down, forcing people out of work. Government employees remained on the job, but inflation reduced the purchasing power of their salaries to a pittance. Scientists, engineers, and academics abandoned their professions to drive taxis, sell liquor and cigarettes, and fish for a living. Crime and prostitution flourished. Moreover, the people of Iraq suffered from lack of food and medicine. Indeed, sanctions have affected the lives of all Iraqis every moment of the day, yet Saddam Hussein and his army remained as defiant as ever.

INDIAN AND PAKISTANI SANCTIONS In May 1998, India conducted a total of five nuclear tests, breaking its self-imposed 24-year moratorium on nuclear testing and setting off a storm of protest around the world. These nuclear tests were soon followed by Pakistan, who matched India with a series of nuclear-bomb tests. Immediately, U.S. President Bill Clinton announced that he was imposing wide-ranging sanctions on the two nations, remarking that the surprise nuclear testing "recalls the very worst events of the 20th century." Noting that 149 nations had signed the Comprehensive Test Ban Treaty, the President called on India and Pakistan to define their greatness "in 21st-century terms, not in terms that everybody else had already decided to reject."

Countries around the world joined the United States in expressing dismay and condemnation of the nuclear tests, although the strength of their concrete actions varied greatly. The major aspects of the U.S. sanctions included

- Termination of U.S. development assistance to India and Pakistan
- Termination of U.S. government sales of defense articles and service
- Denial of credit, credit guarantee, or other financial assistance by U.S. government agencies
- Opposition to assistance by any international financial institution, such as the World Bank
- Prohibition on U.S. commercial bank loans or credit to India and Pakistan
- Prohibition on exports of high-technology products to India and Pakistan

Soon after the nuclear blasts, the Indian government began wooing multinational enterprises. The government awarded 18 oil-exploration contracts, 11 of them to U.S. firms whose projects had been in limbo for two years. It cleared 34 exploration licenses for on-shore minerals in four states. Moreover, three foreign investments in power projects, which had been languishing for want of a government guarantee, were suddenly approved.

The Indian government apparently believed that wooing multinationals would limit the impact of the sanctions in several ways. First, private capital would replace help from the World Bank and Asian Development Bank. Second, by soothing foreign apprehension, India would circumvent a currency panic of the sort that hit East Asia in 1997. Finally, India needed U.S. companies to help lobby their government to terminate the sanctions in exchange for India's negotiating partial adherence to the comprehensive test-ban treaty.

Analysts predicted that the U.S. sanctions would have only a minor impact on the Indian economy. What India would no longer get from the United States, other nations would supply. If India must reduce, for example, its purchases of Boeing jetliners because it was refused financing from the U.S. Export-Import Bank, Europe's Airbus would step in to provide planes. If U.S. banks were forced to curtail their operation in India, European banks would take their place. Indian workers who left the United States because they could no longer remit money home could and would find work in other advanced nations.

Though the sanctions would likely hurt India little, some U.S. banks and companies would forgo lucrative opportunities. Major U.S. financial institutions such as Chase Manhattan, Citicorp, BankAmerica, and American Express worried that sanctions might force them to shutter their operations in India. At the very least, the sanctions could drive them out of the lucrative business of lending to state-owned Indian companies.

However, some analysts noted that this loss might not be a bad thing for the overall U.S. economy. To the extent that the lost business was the result of decreases in U.S. aid and subsidized-loan programs to India, U.S. economic efficiency would improve while U.S. taxpayer dollars were saved. Aid and subsidized loans are a form of disguised protectionism. Artificial increases in U.S. business abroad created by foreign and subsidized loans are not less harmful than artificial increases in domestic businesses due to tariffs.

Based on analysis of economic and trade data, the economic sanctions had a relatively minimal overall impact on the economies of India and Pakistan. The United States was a relatively small provider of aid, trade, and investment for these economies before the sanctions were activated; thus, the sanctions did not greatly affect the economies.[9] However, the sanctions represented a symbol of the resolve of the United States to convince India and Pakistan to terminate nuclear testing.

[9] U.S. International Trade Commission, *Overview and Analysis of the Economic Impact of U.S. Sanctions with Respect to India and Pakistan*, Washington, DC, September 1999.

S U M M A R Y

1. The trade policies of the United States have reflected the motivations of many groups, including government officials, labor leaders, and business management.

2. U.S. tariff history has been marked by ups and downs. Many of the traditional arguments for tariffs (revenue, jobs) have been incorporated into U.S. tariff legislation.

3. The Smoot–Hawley Act of 1930 raised U.S. tariffs to an all-time high, with disastrous results. Passage of the Reciprocal Trade Act of 1934 resulted in generalized tariff reductions by the United States, as well as the enactment of most-favored-nation provisions.

4. The purposes of the General Agreement on Tariffs and Trade were to decrease trade barriers and place all nations on an equal footing in trading relationships. In 1995, GATT was transformed into the World Trade Organization, which embodies the main provisions of GATT and provides a mechanism intended to improve the process of resolving trade disputes among member nations. The Tokyo Round and Uruguay Round of multilateral trade negotiations went beyond tariff reductions to liberalize various nontariff trade barriers.

5. Trade remedy laws can help protect domestic firms from stiff foreign competition. These laws include the escape clause, provisions for antidumping and countervailing duties, and Section 301 of the 1974 Trade Act, which addresses unfair trading practices of foreign nations.

6. The escape clause provides temporary protection to U.S. producers who desire relief from foreign imports that are fairly traded.

7. Countervailing duties are intended to offset any unfair competitive advantage that foreign producers might gain over domestic producers because of foreign subsidies.

8. Economic theory suggests that if a nation is a net importer of a product subsidized or dumped by foreigners, the nation as a whole gains from the foreign subsidy or dumping.

This is because the gains to domestic consumers of the subsidized or dumped good more than offset the losses to domestic producers of the import-competing goods.

9. U.S. antidumping duties are intended to neutralize two unfair trading practices: (1) export sales in the United States at prices below average total cost; and (2) international price discrimination, in which foreign firms sell in the United States at a price lower than that charged in the exporter's home market.

10. Section 301 of the 1974 Trade Act allows the U.S. government to levy trade restrictions against nations that are practicing unfair competition, if trade disagreements cannot be successfully resolved.

11. Intellectual property includes copyrights, trademarks, and patents. Foreign counterfeiting of intellectual property has been a significant problem for many industrial nations.

12. Because foreign competition may displace import-competing businesses and workers, the United States and other nations have initiated programs of trade adjustment assistance involving government aid to adversely affected businesses, workers, and communities.

13. The United States has been reluctant to formulate an explicit industrial policy in which government picks winners and losers among products and firms. Instead, the U.S. government has generally taken a less activist approach in providing assistance to domestic producers (such as the Export-Import Bank and export trade associations).

14. According to the strategic-trade policy concept, government can assist firms in capturing economic profits from foreign competitors. The strategic-trade policy concept applies to firms in imperfectly competitive markets.

15. Economic sanctions consist of trade and financial restraints imposed on foreign nations. They have been used to preserve national security, protect human rights, and combat international terrorism.

S T U D Y   Q U E S T I O N S

1. To what extent have the traditional arguments that justify protectionist barriers actually been incorporated into U.S. trade legislation?
2. At what stage in U.S. trade history did protectionism reach its high point?
3. What is meant by the most-favored-nation clause, and how does it relate to the tariff policies of the United States?
4. The GATT and its successor, the World Trade Organization, have established a set of rules for the commercial conduct of trading nations. Explain.
5. What are trade remedy laws? How do they attempt to protect U.S. firms from unfairly (fairly) traded goods?
6. What is intellectual property? Why has intellectual property become a major issue in recent rounds of international trade negotiations?
7. How does the trade adjustment assistance program attempt to help domestic firms and workers who are displaced as a result of import competition?
8. Under the Tokyo Round of trade negotiations, what were the major policies adopted concerning nontariff trade barriers? What about the Uruguay Round?
9. Describe the industrial policies adopted by the U.S. government. How have these policies differed from those adopted by Japan?
10. If the United States is a net importer of a product that is being subsidized or dumped by Japan, not only do U.S. consumers gain, but they gain more than U.S. producers lose from the Japanese subsidies or dumping. Explain why this is true.
11. What is the purpose of strategic trade policy?
12. What is the purpose of economic sanctions? What problems do they pose for the nation initiating the sanctions? When are sanctions most successful in achieving their goals?

13. Assume that the nation of Spain is "small," unable to influence the Brazilian (world) price of steel. Spain's supply and demand schedules are illustrated in Table 7.14. Assume Brazil's price to be $400 per ton. Using graph paper, plot the demand and supply schedules of Spain and Brazil on the same graph.
   a. With free trade, how many tons of steel will be produced, purchased, and imported by Spain? Calculate the dollar value of Spanish producer surplus and consumer surplus.
   b. Suppose the Brazilian government grants its steel firms a production subsidy of $200 per ton. Plot Brazil's subsidy-adjusted supply schedule on your graph.
      (1) What is the new market price of steel? At this price, how much steel will Spain produce, purchase, and import?
      (2) The subsidy helps/hurts Spanish firms because their producer surplus rises/falls by $ _____ ; Spanish steel users realize a rise/fall in consumer surplus of $ _____ . The Spanish economy as a whole benefits/suffers from the subsidy by an amount totaling $ _____ .

Table 7.14 Steel Supply and Demand for Spain

Price	Quantity Supplied	Quantity Demanded
$ 0	0	12
200	2	10
400	4	8
600	6	6
800	8	4
1,000	10	2
1,200	12	0

NetLink

7.1 The Export–Import Bank is a government-held corporation that encourages the sale of U.S. goods in foreign markets. For more information on its activities, set your browser to URL:

http://www.exim.gov/

7.2 The Canadian International Trade Tribunal considers cases of dumping. Examine some recent cases at its Web site by setting your browser to URL:

http://www.citt.gc.ca/

7.3 An in-depth look at R&D expenditures and the extent of government support in the United States can be found at the National Science Foundation's Web site at:

http://www.nsf.gov/sbe/srs/fedfunds/start.htm

Compare that to R&D expenditures in Japan by visiting the Statistics Bureau and Statistics Center, Management and Coordination Agency of Japan, at the Web site:

http://www.stat.go.jp/english/1.htm

7.4 Evaluation of industrial policy in cases of Japan and Korea can be found in *The World Bank Research Observer*, Volume 15, Number 1, February 2000 issue at the Web site:

http://www.worldbank.org/research/journals/wbro/obsfeb00/art3.htm

To access NetLink Exercises and the Virtual Scavenger Hunt, visit the Carbaugh Web site at http://carbaugh.swcollege.com.

chapter 8

Trade Policies for the Developing Nations

It is a commonly accepted practice to array all nations according to real income and then to draw a dividing line between the advanced and the developing ones. Included in the category of **advanced nations** are those of North America and Western Europe, plus Australia, New Zealand, and Japan. Most nations of the world are classified as developing, or less developed, nations. The **developing nations** are most of those in Africa, Asia, Latin America, and the Middle East. Table 8.1 provides economic and social indicators for selected nations as of 1998. In general, advanced nations are characterized by relatively high levels of gross domestic product per capita, longer life expectancies, and higher levels of adult literacy.

Although international trade can provide benefits to domestic producers and consumers, some economists maintain that the current international trading system hinders economic development in the developing nations. They believe that conventional international trade theory based on the principle of comparative advantage is irrelevant for these nations. This chapter examines the reasons some economists provide to explain their misgivings about the international trading system. The chapter also considers policies aimed at improving the economic conditions of the developing nations.

KEY CONCEPTS AND TERMS

- *Advanced nations*
- *Buffer stock*
- *Cartel*
- *Developing nations*
- *East Asian tigers*
- *Export controls*
- *Export-led growth*
- *Export-oriented policy*
- *Flying-geese pattern of economic growth*
- *Generalized system of preferences (GSP)*
- *Import substitution*
- *International commodity agreements (ICAs)*
- *Multilateral contract*
- *New international economic order*
- *Organization of Petroleum Exporting Countries (OPEC)*
- *Primary products*
- *Production controls*
- *United Nations Conference on Trade and Development (UNCTAD)*

Table 8.1 Basic Economic and Social Indicators for Selected Nations, 1998

	Gross National Product per Capita*	Life Expectancy (Years)	Adult Illiteracy (Percent)
United States	$29,340	78	Under 5%
Switzerland	26,620	70	"
Japan	23,180	80	"
Sweden	19,480	79	"
Chile	12,890	75	5
Mexico	8,190	72	10
Malaysia	6,990	72	15
Algeria	4,380	70	36
Indonesia	2,790	65	21
Guinea	2,680	46	76
Chad	980	48	52
Mozambique	850	46	59

*At purchasing power parity.

Source: The World Bank Group, *Development Data*, http://www.worldbank.org/data. See also the World Bank, *World Development Report 1999–2000*.

DEVELOPING-NATION TRADE CHARACTERISTICS

If we examine the characteristics of developing-nation trade, we find that developing nations are highly dependent on the advanced nations. A majority of developing-nation exports go to the advanced nations, and most developing-nation imports originate in the advanced nations. Trade among the developing nations is relatively minor.

Another characteristic is the composition of developing-nation exports, with its emphasis on **primary products** (agricultural goods, raw materials, and fuels). Of the manufactured goods that are exported by the developing nations, many (such as textiles) are labor intensive and include only modest amounts of technology in their production. Table 8.2 presents the structure of output for selected advanced nations and developing nations.

It is significant, however, that in the past three decades the dominance of primary products in developing-nation trade has been diminishing.

Table 8.2 Structure of Output for Selected Advanced Nations and Developing Nations, 1998

Economy	Value Added as a Percent of GDP		
	Agriculture, Forestry, and Fishing	Industry	Services
Advanced Nations			
United States	2	27	71
Japan	4	42	54
Canada	4	38	58
France	2	26	72
Italy	3	31	66
Developing Nations			
Albania	63	18	19
Chad	39	15	46
Pakistan	25	25	50
Tanzania	46	14	40
Mali	45	21	34

Source: The World Bank, *World Development Report 1999–2000*, pp. 252–253.

Developing nations have been able to increase their exports of manufactured goods relative to primary products. Compared with the advanced nations, however, the absolute value of manufactured goods produced by the developing nations is low. Note also that the rise in exports of manufactured goods has not accrued evenly to all developing nations. Instead, a handful of newly industrializing nations, such as South Korea and Hong Kong, have accounted for much of the increase in manufactured-goods production by developing nations.

TRADE PROBLEMS OF THE DEVELOPING NATIONS

The theory of comparative advantage maintains that all nations can enjoy the benefits of free trade if they specialize in production of those goods in which they have a comparative advantage and exchange some of these goods for goods produced by other nations. Policy makers in the United States and many other advanced nations maintain that the market-oriented structure of the international trading system furnishes a setting in which the benefits of comparative advantage can be realized. They claim that the existing international trading system has provided widespread benefits and that the trading interests of all nations are best served by pragmatic, incremental changes in the existing system. Advanced nations also maintain that to achieve trading success, they must administer their own domestic and international economic policies.

On the basis of their trading experience with the advanced nations, some developing nations have become dubious of the *distribution* of trade benefits between them and the advanced nations. They have argued that the protectionist trading policies of advanced nations hinder the industrialization of many developing nations. Accordingly, developing nations have sought a new international trading order with improved access to the markets of advanced nations. Among the problems that have plagued developing nations in their role as producers of primary products have been *unstable export markets* and *worsening terms of trade*.

UNSTABLE EXPORT MARKETS One characteristic of many developing nations is that their exports are concentrated in only one or a few primary products. This situation is shown in Table 8.3, which illustrates the dependence of selected developing nations on a single primary product. A poor harvest or a decrease in market demand for that product can significantly reduce export revenues and seriously disrupt domestic income and employment levels.

Many observers maintain that a key factor underlying the instability of primary-product prices and export receipts is the low price elasticity of the demand and supply schedules for products such as tin, copper, and coffee, as indicated in Table 8.4. Recall that the price elasticity of demand (supply) refers to the percentage change in quantity demanded (supplied) resulting from a 1-percent change in price. To the extent that com-

Table 8.3 Developing-Nation Dependence on Primary Products

Country	Major Export Product	Major Export Product as a Percentage of Total Exports
Nigeria	Oil	98%
Saudi Arabia	Oil	86
Burundi	Coffee	80
Ethiopia	Coffee	70
Venezuela	Oil	69
Mauritania	Iron ore	59
Chad	Cotton	54
Zambia	Copper	51
Rwanda	Coffee	44

Source: The World Bank Group, *Regions and Countries*, January 2000, http://www.worldbank.org/html/extdr/regions.htm.

Table 8.4	Long-Run Price Elasticities of Supply and Demand for Selected Commodities	

Commodity	Supply Elasticity (Developing Countries)	Demand Elasticity (Industrialized Countries)
Coffee	0.3	0.2
Cocoa	0.3	0.3
Tea	0.2	0.1
Sugar	0.2	0.1
Wheat	0.6	0.5
Copper	0.1	0.4
Rubber	0.4	0.5

Source: Jere Behrman, "International Commodity Agreements: An Evaluation of the UNCTAD Integrated Commodity Program," in William Cline, ed., *Policy Alternatives for a New International Economic Order*, New York, Praeger, 1979, pp. 118–121.

modity demand and supply schedules are relatively inelastic, suggesting that the percentage change in price exceeds the percentage change in quantity, a small shift in either schedule can induce a large change in price and export receipts.

Figure 8.1 illustrates the export market of Costa Rica, a producer of coffee. In Figure 8.1(a), once coffee has been planted, the quantity supplied is fixed for the following marketing period, irrespective of how the price of coffee may fluctuate. Let the supply of coffee be perfectly inelastic (vertical), as shown in the figure. Because of changing preferences, suppose the world demand for coffee falls from D_0 to D_1. The decrease in demand causes the price of coffee to decline from $6 to $3 per pound; this price decrease is larger than would occur if Costa Rica's supply schedule were upward-sloping (that is, if it exhibited greater price elasticity). As a result of the price

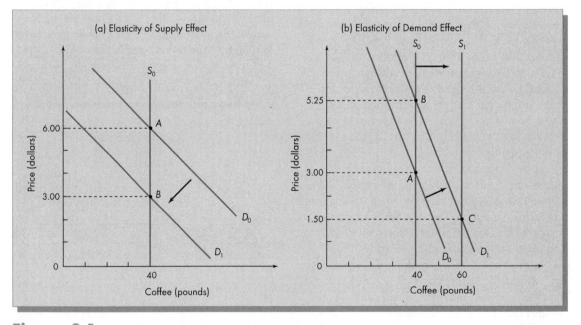

Figure 8.1 Export Price Instability for a Developing Country

When the supply of a commodity is highly price-inelastic, decreases (or increases) in demand will generate wide variations in price. When the demand for a commodity is highly price-inelastic, increases (or decreases) in supply will generate wide variations in price.

decline, Costa Rica's export receipts fall from $240 to $120. Conversely, an increase in the world demand for coffee would lead to higher prices and export receipts for Costa Rica. We conclude that export prices and earnings can be extremely volatile when supply is inelastic and there occurs a change in demand.

Not only do changes in demand induce wide fluctuations in price when supply is inelastic, but changes in supply induce wide fluctuations in price when demand is inelastic. The latter situation is illustrated in the two-period framework of Figure 8.1(b). Costa Rica's export supply schedule, S_0, is portrayed as perfectly inelastic, while the world demand schedule, D_0, is relatively price-inelastic. In equilibrium, the price of coffee equals $3 per pound, and Costa Rica's export receipts total $120.

In time period 1, suppose the world demand for coffee increases so that the demand schedule shifts from D_0 to D_1. This results in a substantial increase in price, from $3 to $5.25 per pound, and an increase in Costa Rica's export receipts from $120 to $210. Suppose that, because of the price increase, growers in Costa Rica plant additional coffee in the next time period, shifting the supply schedule from S_0 to S_1. With a relatively inelastic demand, the ensuing decrease in price will be substantial; the price of coffee falls from $5.25 to $1.50 per pound, and Costa Rica's export receipts fall to $90. Again we see that export prices and receipts can be very volatile when supply and demand conditions are price-inelastic.

WORSENING TERMS OF TRADE How the gains from international trade are distributed among trading partners has been controversial, especially among developing nations whose exports are concentrated in primary products. These nations generally maintain that the benefits of international trade accrue disproportionately to the industrial nations.

Developing nations complain that their commodity terms of trade has deteriorated in the past century or so, suggesting that the prices of their exports relative to their imports have fallen.

Worsening terms of trade has been used to justify the refusal of many developing nations to participate in trade-liberalization negotiations. It also has underlain the developing nations' demands for preferential treatment in trade relations with the advanced nations.

Observers maintain that the monopoly power of manufacturers in the industrial nations results in higher prices. Gains in productivity accrue to manufacturers in the form of higher earnings rather than price reductions. Observers further contend that the export prices of the primary products of developing nations are determined in competitive markets. These prices fluctuate downward as well as upward. Gains in productivity are shared with foreign consumers in the form of lower prices. The developing nations maintain that market forces cause the prices they pay for imports to rise faster than the prices commanded by their exports, resulting in a deterioration in their commodity terms of trade. Moreover, as income rises there is a tendency for people to spend more on manufactured goods than primary goods, thus contributing to a worsening in the developing nations' terms of trade.

The developing nations' assertion of worsening commodity terms of trade was supported by a United Nations study in 1949.[1] The study concluded that from the period 1876–1880 to 1946–1947, the prices of primary products compared with those of manufactured goods fell by 32 percent. However, because of inadequacies in data and the problems of constructing price indexes, the UN study was hardly conclusive. Other studies led to opposite conclusions about terms-of-trade movements. A 1983 study confirmed that the commodity terms of trade of developing nations deteriorated from 1870 to 1938, but much less so than had been maintained previously; by including data from the late 1940s up to 1970, the study found no evidence of deterioration.[2] Consistent with these findings,

---

[1] United Nations Commission for Latin America, *The Economic Development of Latin America and Its Principal Problems*, 1950.

[2] J. Sporas, *Equalizing Trade?* (Oxford: Clarendon Press, 1983).

FAIR-TRADE MOVEMENT HELPS POOR COFFEE FARMERS

Nicaraguan coffee farmer Santiago Rivera has traveled far beyond his mountain home to publicize what is known as the "fair trade" coffee movement. Have you heard of fair-trade coffee? You soon may. Started in Europe in the early 1990s and just making its way across the America States, the objective of the fair-trade coffee movement is to increase the incomes of poor farmers in developing countries by implementing a system where the farmers can sell their beans directly to roasters and retailers, bypassing the traditional practice of selling to middlemen in their own countries.

This arrangement permits farmers—who farm mainly in the mountainous regions of Latin America and other tropical regions where high-flavor, high-priced beans sold to gourmet stores are grown—to earn as much as $1.26 per pound for their beans, compared with the 40 cents per pound they were getting from middlemen.

Under the fair-trade system, farmers organize in cooperatives of as many as 2,500 members, which set prices and arrange for export directly to brokerage firms and other distributors. Middlemen—known as "coyotes" in Nicaragua—previously handled this role. So far, 500,000 of the developing world's four million coffee farmers have joined the fair-trade movement. However, the movement has led to incidents of violence in some places in Latin America, mostly involving middlemen who are being bypassed.

The fair-trade coffee movement is the latest example of how social activists are using free-market economics to foster social change. Organizers of the movement say they have signed up eight gourmet roasters and about 120 stores, including big chains like Safeway, Inc. Fair-trade coffee carries a logo identifying it as such.

Fair trade achieved much success in Europe, where fair-trade coffee sells in 35,000 stores and has sales of $250 million a year. In some countries like the Netherlands and Switzerland, fair-trade coffee accounts for as much as 5 percent of total coffee sales. Based on those achievements, organizers in Europe are expanding their fair-trade efforts to include other commodity items, including sugar, tea, chocolate, and bananas. But fair-trade activists admit that selling Americans on the idea of buying coffee with a social theme will be more challenging than it was in Europe. Americans, they note, tend to be less aware of social problems in the developing world than Europeans.

The fair-trade movement has yet to get the support of major U.S. coffee houses such as Maxwell and Folgers. Nevertheless, organizers are trying to nudge Seattle's two big coffee giants, Starbuck's Coffee Co. and Seattle Coffee Co., into agreeing to purchase some of the fair-trade coffee. In Oakland, Mayor Jerry Brown is persuading his colleagues to give more thought to how they purchase coffee. "I would hope that the people sipping their cappuccinos would take a moment to reflect on the sweat and labor of those who provided it."

Source: "A Global Effort for Poor Coffee Farmers," *The Wall Street Journal*, November 23, 1999, pp. A2 and A4.

a 1984 study concluded that the terms of trade of developing nations actually improved somewhat from 1952 to 1970.[3] Table 8.5 illustrates changes in the developing nations' commodity terms of trade during the period 1981–1999.

It is difficult to conclude whether the developing nations as a whole have experienced a deterioration or an improvement in their terms of trade. Conclusions about terms-of-trade movements become clouded by the choice of the base year used in comparisons, by the problem of making allowances for changes in technology and productivity as well as for new products and

[3] M. Michaely, *Trade Income Levels and Dependence* (Amsterdam: North-Holland, 1984).

Table 8.5 Developing Nations' Commodity Terms of Trade, by Predominant Export (Annual Percentage Change)

Period	Fuel	Nonfuel Exports	Manufactures	Primary Products
1981–1990	–4.4	5.1	8.7	1.5
1991–1999	0.9	9.5	10.7	7.2
1998	–20.9	–0.8	–2.7	–4.0
1999*	0.2	3.3	1.7	7.8

*Forecasted.

Source: International Monetary Fund, *World Economic Outlook: World Economic and Financial Surveys*, Washington, DC, May, 1999.

product qualities, and by the methods used to value exports and imports and to weight the commodities used in the index.

CALL FOR A NEW INTERNATIONAL ECONOMIC ORDER

Dissatisfied with their economic performance and convinced that many of their problems are due to shortcomings of the existing international trading system, developing nations have pressed collective demands on the advanced nations for institutions and policies that improve the climate for economic development in the international trading system. The developing nations' call for a **new international economic order** led to the convening of the **United Nations Conference on Trade and Development (UNCTAD)** in 1964. UNCTAD has since become a permanent agency of the United Nations and conducts meetings every four years to address the trading relations of developing and industrialized nations.

In its attempt to implement a new international economic order, UNCTAD has focused primarily on tariff preferences for developing-nation exports to advanced nations, international commodity agreements intended to stabilize prices of primary products, and advanced-nation

aid to developing nations. But success in these areas has been modest. The foreign aid of advanced nations has remained at low levels, and efforts to stabilize commodity prices have often failed. Although advanced nations have reduced conventional tariff protection, they have raised other nontariff trade barriers to products from developing nations.

The effectiveness of UNCTAD has been limited partly because its resolutions are not binding on nations that do not concur. Although developing nations feel the proposals for a new international economic order are justified, many advanced nations consider them a plea for massive redistribution of world income, which is not feasible. Advanced nations often argue that there is no quick fix for economic development; developing nations must pursue a gradual process of capital formation over many decades, as the advanced nations did. This view has led to strained dialogues between advanced nations and developing nations at UNCTAD conferences.

By the late 1980s, attention was increasingly focused on the need for developing nations to initiate policies aimed at enhancing domestic economic growth. These would include *macroeconomic policies* designed to increase domestic savings, reduce inflation, and foster capital formation, as well as *structural policies* to allocate resources more efficiently. It has been widely argued that many developing nations need to make public enterprises more efficient or, otherwise, to proceed with privatization. They should also eliminate price distortions through more market-oriented pricing mechanisms and should phase out administrative controls over goods, labor, and financial markets. Moreover, they should initiate tax reforms, including a broadening of the tax base and more effective enforcement, reduce government subsidies, extend the influence of markets over exchange rates, and eliminate exchange and trade restrictions.

STABILIZING COMMODITY PRICES

In an attempt to attain export market stability, developing nations have pressed for **international commodity agreements (ICAs)**. ICAs are typically agreements between leading producing and consuming nations about matters such as stabilizing commodity prices, assuring adequate supplies to consumers, and promoting the economic development of producers.

Both producers and consumers desire *stable* commodity markets. For producers, volatile commodity prices may disrupt the flow of export earnings (needed to pay for imports) and also cre-ate an unfavorable climate for investment in additional productive facilities. Consumers have also been motivated to form ICAs. During the 1970s, consuming nations were concerned by the sharp rise in commodity prices and by the questions raised about the longer-term availability of commodities. Consumers were also alarmed by the example of OPEC—that is, by the possibility that commodity supplies might be restricted through collusion among producing nations.

Table 8.6 gives examples of ICAs among producing and consuming nations. To promote stability in commodity markets, ICAs have relied on production and export controls, buffer stocks, and multilateral contracts.

PRODUCTION AND EXPORT CONTROLS

If an ICA accounts for a large share of total world output (or exports) of a commodity, its members may agree on **export controls** to stabilize export revenues. The idea behind such measures is to offset a decrease in the market demand for the primary commodity by assigning cutbacks in the market supply. If successful, the rise in price due to the curtailment in supply will be sufficient to compensate for the reduction in demand, so that total export earnings will remain at the original level.

Table 8.6 International Commodity Agreements

Agreement	Membership	Principal Stabilization Tools
International Cocoa Organization	26 consuming nations 18 producing nations	Buffer stock, export quota
International Tin Agreement	16 consuming nations 4 producing nations	Buffer stock, export controls
International Coffee Organization	24 consuming nations 43 producing nations	Export quota
International Sugar Organization	8 consuming nations 26 producing nations	Buffer stock, export quota
International Wheat Agreement	41 consuming nations 10 producing nations	Multilateral contract

Source: *Annual Report of the President of the United States on the Trade Agreements Program*, Washington, DC, Government Printing Office, various issues.

Figure 8.2 illustrates the process by which export receipts can be maintained at target levels for members of the International Coffee Agreement. Assume initial market equilibrium at point E. With the equilibrium price at $1 per pound and sales of 60 million pounds, the association's export receipts total $60 million. Let this figure be the target that the association wishes to maintain.

Suppose the market demand for coffee decreases from D_0 to D_1 because of a global economic downturn. The association's export revenues would now fall below the target level. To prevent this from occurring, the coffee producers could artificially hold back the supply of coffee to S_1. Market equilibrium would be at point F, where 40 million pounds of coffee would be sold at a price of $1.50 per pound. Total export receipts would again be at $60 million, the association's target figure. This stabilization technique is contrary to what we might expect because it is based on efforts to increase prices during eras of worsening demand conditions.

In their efforts to stabilize export receipts, producers' associations have adopted export quotas to regulate market supply. Over the longer run, however, export quotas must be accompanied by **production controls** to be effective. If production

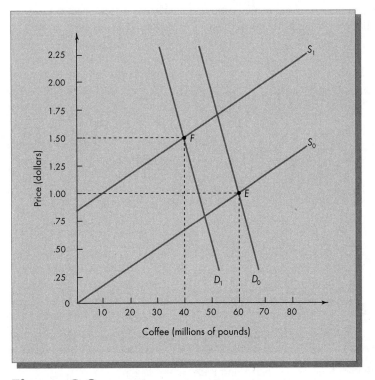

Figure 8.2 Production and Export Controls

Production controls and export restrictions are used to offset decreases in market demand and increases in market supply so as to stabilize commodity prices. These restrictions, however, are often associated with cheating on the part of participating nations.

is not controlled, expanding surpluses of the member nations will lead to a greater likelihood that prices will be cut and that the association will eventually fail.

BUFFER STOCKS Another technique for limiting commodity price swings is the **buffer stock**, in which a producers' association (or international agency) is prepared to buy and sell a commodity in large amounts. The buffer stock consists of supplies of a commodity financed and held by the producers' association. The buffer stock manager buys from the market when supplies are abundant and prices are falling below acceptable levels, and sells from the buffer stock when supplies are tight and prices are high.

Figure 8.3 illustrates the hypothetical price-stabilization efforts of the International Tin Agreement.

Assume that the association sets a price range, with a floor of $3.27 per pound and a ceiling of $4.02 per pound to guide the stabilization operations of the buffer-stock manager. Starting at equilibrium point A in Figure 8.3(a), suppose the buffer-stock manager sees the demand for tin rising from D_0 to D_1. To defend the ceiling price of $4.02, the manager must be prepared to sell 20,000 pounds of tin to offset the excess demand for tin at the ceiling price. Conversely, starting at equilibrium point E in Figure 8.3(b), suppose the supply of tin rises from S_0 to S_1. To defend the floor price of $3.27, the buffer-stock manager must purchase the 20,000-pound excess supply that exists at that price.

Proponents of buffer stocks contend that the scheme offers the primary producing nations several advantages. A well-run buffer stock can

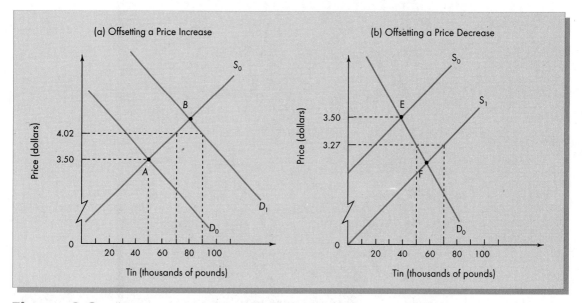

Figure 8.3 Buffer Stock: Price Ceiling and Price Support

During periods of rising tin demand, the buffer-stock manager sells tin to prevent the price from rising above the ceiling level. Prolonged defense of the ceiling price, however, may result in depletion of the tin stockpile, undermining the effectiveness of this price-stabilization tool and lending to an upward revision of the ceiling price. During periods of abundant tin supplies, the manager purchases tin to prevent the price from falling below the floor level. Prolonged defense of the price floor, however, may exhaust the funds to purchase excess supplies of tin at the floor price and may lead to a downward revision of the floor price.

promote economic efficiency because primary producers can plan investment and expansion if they know that prices will not gyrate. It is also argued that soaring commodity prices invariably ratchet industrial prices upward, whereas commodity price decreases exert no comparable downward pressure. By stabilizing commodity prices, buffer stocks can moderate the price inflation of the industrialized nations. Buffer stocks in this context are viewed as a means of providing primary producers more stability than is allowed by the free market.

Setting up and administering a buffer-stock program is not without costs and problems. The basic difficulty in stabilizing prices with buffer stocks is agreeing on a target price that reflects long-term market trends. If the target price is set too low, the buffer stocks will become depleted as the stock manager sells the commodity on the open market in an attempt to hold market prices in line with the target price. If the target price is set too high, the stock manager must purchase large quantities of the commodity in an effort to support market prices. The costs of holding the stocks tend to be high, for they include transportation expenses, insurance, and labor costs. In their choice of price targets, buffer-stock officials have often made poor decisions. Rather than conduct massive stabilization operations, buffer-stock officials will periodically revise target prices should they fall out of line with long-term price trends.

MULTILATERAL CONTRACTS Multilateral contracts are another method of stabilizing commodity prices. Such contracts generally stipulate a *minimum price* at which importers will purchase guaranteed quantities from the producing nations and a *maximum price* at which producing nations will sell guaranteed amounts to the importers. Such purchases and sales are designed to hold prices within a target range. Trading under a multilateral contract has often occurred among several exporters and several importing nations, as in the case of the International Sugar Agreement and the International Wheat Agreement.

One possible advantage of the multilateral contract as a price-stabilization device is that, in comparison with buffer stocks or export controls, it results in less distortion of the market mechanism and the allocation of resources. This result is because the typical multilateral contract does not involve output restraints and thus does not check the development of more efficient low-cost producers. If target prices are not set near the long-term equilibrium price, however, discrepancies will occur between supply and demand. Excess demand would indicate a ceiling too low, whereas excess supply would suggest a floor too high. Multilateral contracts also tend to furnish only limited market stability, given the relative ease of withdrawal and entry by participating members.

COMMODITY AGREEMENT EXPERIENCE

Commodity-producing nations face the fact that imbalances between demand and supply on the commodity markets tend to trigger large fluctuations in prices. This is true for agricultural commodities as well as for metals and other raw materials. The desire to achieve orderly marketing during the 1920s and 1930s led to the establishment of producers' associations for tin, sugar, rubber, tea, and wheat. But it was not until the 1960s that an international mechanism was formally initiated by the United Nations so that commodity agreements, among both producers and consumers, could be implemented under the auspices of a world body. Efforts to enact commodity agreements gained momentum following the stunning success of the Organization of Petroleum Exporting Countries (OPEC), which was able to raise prices fourfold in 1973 and 1974.

The goals of the various commodity agreements have generally included one or more of the following: (1) guarding against gyrating commodity prices, (2) stabilizing incomes or export revenues rather than prices, and (3) bidding prices significantly above their long-term trend. Part of the problem facing commodity agreements is that these objectives sometimes conflict with one another. The goal of stabilizing income, for example, may conflict with the goal of moderating price fluctuations for the pact nations. If a drought were to destroy part of the sugar crop, sales from a buffer stockpile might cushion price increases, but the result would be falling revenues for sugar exporters.

The International Tin Agreement is generally regarded as the commodity agreement with the best track record. Started in 1956, it used buffer stocks and export controls to limit price swings. The Tin Council periodically determined upper and lower price limits to guide the activities of the buffer-stock manager. When the buffer-stock operations could not moderate price decreases, they were sometimes supplemented by export controls.

After the International Tin Agreement went into operation in 1956, prices remained within the target limits set by the Tin Council. However, strong demand conditions forced the buffer-stock manager to sell tin. By 1961, the stocks were exhausted, and prices pushed above the ceiling. In the face of strong demand, the upper and lower price limits were raised several times during the 1960s to keep pace with current market conditions. During the commodity boom of the 1970s, tin prices shot through the ceiling. However, during the early 1980s, the weakening of demand caused by recession led to a progressively lower price. In 1981 the price fell to the bottom of the target limit, triggering price-support actions by the buffer stock.

In 1982, the International Tin Agreement was extended for a five-year period. Consuming and producing nations agreed to set the target price range of tin equal to $5.67 per pound at the lower limit and $6.81 per pound at the upper limit. Defense of price floors and ceilings would be facilitated by export controls and a buffer stock. The nations participating in the pact accounted for 79 percent of the world tin output and 50 percent of tin consumption. The United States, however, chose not to sign the 1982 agreement, contending that the target price range benefited inefficient producers. Moreover, the U.S. government had a tin stockpile of 200,000 tons, equal to four years of domestic use.

In 1987, the International Tin Agreement collapsed. The pact's support of prices at artificially high levels encouraged increases in tin mining by nonmember nations, such as Brazil, which refused to honor production quotas. Meanwhile, consumers economized on the use of overpriced tin. Tin content was reduced in some products, and plastic and aluminum substitutes were designed (including the development of the aluminum beverage can).

THE OPEC OIL CARTEL

Recall that commodity agreements involve cooperation among producing and consuming nations for the purpose of stabilizing the price of a particular commodity. Another method used by developing nations to stabilize the prices of their export commodities is to form cartels. Unlike commodity agreements, cartels involve unilateral attempts by the exporting nations to stabilize or increase the price of a product by exerting their collective power. One of the most successful cartels in recent history has been the Organization of Petroleum Exporting Countries.

The **Organization of Petroleum Exporting Countries (OPEC)** is a group of nations that sells petroleum on the world market. The OPEC nations attempt to support prices higher than would exist under more competitive conditions to maximize member-nation profits. After operating in obscurity throughout the 1960s, OPEC was able to capture control of petroleum pricing in 1973 and 1974, when the price of oil rose from approximately $3 to $12 per barrel. Triggered by the Iranian revolution in 1979, oil prices doubled from early 1979 to early 1980. By 1981, the price of oil averaged almost $36 per barrel. Largely because of world recession and falling demand, oil prices fell to $11 per barrel in 1986, only to rebound thereafter.

Prior to OPEC, oil-producing nations behaved like individual competitive sellers. Each nation by itself was so unimportant relative to the overall market that changes in its export levels did not significantly affect international prices over a sustained period of time. By agreeing to restrict competition among themselves via production quotas, the oil-exporting nations found that they could exercise considerable control over world oil prices, as seen in the price hikes of the 1970s. Table 8.7 illustrates OPEC's production quotas as of 2000.

MAXIMIZING CARTEL PROFITS A cartel attempts to support prices higher than they would be under more competitive conditions, thus increasing the profits of its members. Let us consider some of the difficulties encountered by a cartel in its quest for increased profits.

Assume that there are ten suppliers of oil, of equal size, in the world oil market and that oil is a standardized product. As a result of previous price wars, each supplier charges a price equal to minimum average cost. Each supplier is afraid to raise its price because it fears that the others will not do so and all of its sales will be lost.

Table 8.7 OPEC Production Quotas

Country	Production Quota (Million Barrels per Day)
Saudi Arabia	7.44
Iran	3.34
Venezuela	2.72
United Arab Emirates	2.00
Kuwait	1.84
Nigeria	1.89
Libya	1.23
Indonesia	1.19
Algeria	0.73
Iraq	1.31
Qatar	0.59
	24.28

Source: *OPEC Fact Sheet*, U.S. Department of Energy, Energy Information Administration, January 2000. See the EIA's Internet site at **http://www.eia.doe.gov**.

Rather than engage in cutthroat price competition, suppose these suppliers decide to collude and form a cartel. How will a cartel go about maximizing the collective profits of its members? The answer is, by behaving like a profit-maximizing monopolist: restrict output and drive up price.

Figure 8.4 illustrates the demand and cost conditions of the ten oil suppliers as a group [Figure 8.4(a)] and the group's average supplier [Figure 8.4(b)]. Before the cartel is organized, the market price of oil under competition is $20 per barrel. Because each supplier is able to achieve a price that just covers its minimum average cost, economic profit equals zero. Each supplier in the market produces 150 barrels per day. Total industry output equals 1,500 barrels per day (150 × 10 = 1,500).

Suppose the oil suppliers form a cartel whose objective is to maximize the collective profits of its members. To accomplish this objective, the cartel must first establish the profit-maximizing level of output; this output is where marginal revenue equals marginal cost. The cartel then divides up the cartel output among its members by setting up production quotas for each supplier.

In Figure 8.4(a), the cartel will maximize group profits by restricting output from 1,500 barrels per day to 1,000 barrels per day. This means that each member of the cartel must decrease its output from 150 barrels to 100 barrels per day, as shown in Figure 8.4(b). This production quota results in a rise in the market price of a barrel of oil from $20 to $30. Each member realizes a profit of $8 per barrel ($30 – $22 = $8) and a total profit of $800 on the 100 barrels of oil produced (area *a*).

The next step is to ensure that no cartel member sells more than its quota. This is a difficult task, because each supplier has the incentive to sell more than its assigned quota at the cartel price. But if all cartel members sell more than their quotas, the cartel price will fall toward the competitive level, and profits will vanish. Cartels thus attempt to establish penalties for sellers that cheat on their assigned quotas.

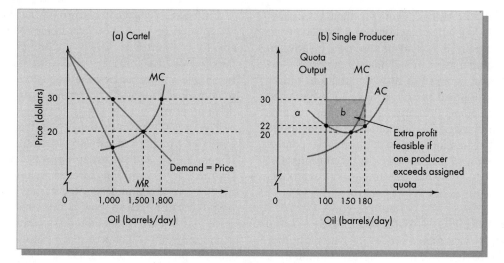

Figure 8.4 Maximizing OPEC Profits

As a cartel, OPEC can increase the price of oil from $20 to $30 per barrel by assigning production quotas for its members. The quotas decrease output from 1,500 to 1,000 barrels per day and permit producers that were pricing oil at average cost to realize a profit. Each producer has the incentive to increase output beyond its assigned quota, to the point at which the OPEC price equals marginal cost. But if all producers increase output in this manner, there will be a surplus of oil at the cartel price, forcing the price of oil back to $20 per barrel.

In Figure 8.4(b), each cartel member realizes economic profits of $800 by selling at the assigned quota of 100 barrels per day. However, an *individual* supplier knows that it can increase its profits if it sells more than this amount at the cartel price. Each individual supplier has the incentive to increase output to the level at which the cartel price, $30, equals the supplier's marginal cost; this occurs at 180 barrels per day. At this output level, the supplier would realize economic profits of $1,440, represented by area *a* + *b*. By cheating on its agreed-upon production quota, the supplier is able to realize an increase in profits of $640 ($1,440 − $800 = $640), denoted by area *b*. Note that this increase in profits occurs if the price of oil does not decrease as the supplier expands output; that is, if the supplier's extra output is a negligible portion of the industry supply.

A single supplier may be able to get away with producing more than its quota without significantly decreasing the market price of oil. But if each member of the cartel increases its output to 180 barrels per day to earn more profits, total output will be 1,800 barrels (180 × 10 = 1,800). To maintain the price at $30, however, industry output must be held to only 1,000 barrels per day. The excess output of 800 barrels puts downward pressure on price, which causes economic profits to decline. If economic profits fall back to zero (the competitive level), the cartel will likely break up. Besides the problem of cheating, there are several other obstacles to forming a cartel:

NUMBER OF SELLERS. Generally speaking, the larger the number of sellers, the more difficult it is to form a cartel. Coordination of price and output policies among three sellers that dominate the market is more easily achieved than when there are ten sellers each having 10 percent of the market.

COST AND DEMAND DIFFERENCES. When cartel members' costs and product demands differ, it is more difficult to agree on price. Such differences result in a different profit-maximizing price for each member, so there is no single price that can be agreed upon by all members.

POTENTIAL COMPETITION. The increased profits that may occur under a cartel may attract new competitors. Their entry into the market triggers an increase in product supply, which leads to falling prices and profits. A successful cartel thus depends on its ability to block the market entry of new competitors.

ECONOMIC DOWNTURN. Economic downturn is generally problematic for cartels. As market sales dwindle in a weakening economy, profits fall. Cartel members may conclude that they can escape serious decreases in profits by reducing prices, in expectation of gaining sales at the expense of other cartel members.

SUBSTITUTE GOODS. The price-making ability of a cartel is weakened when buyers can substi-

tute other goods (coal and natural gas) for the good that it produces (oil).

OPEC AS A CARTEL OPEC has generally disavowed the term *cartel*. But its organization is composed of a secretariat, a conference of ministers, a board of governors, and an economic commission. OPEC has repeatedly attempted to formulate plans for systematic production control among its members as a way of firming up oil prices. However, OPEC's production agreements have not always lived up to expectations because too many member nations have violated the agreements by producing more than their assigned quotas.

Since 1983, when production quotas were first assigned to members, OPEC's actual production levels have almost always been greater than its target levels, meaning that countries have been selling more oil than they're supposed to—in other words, they've been cheating, as shown in Figure 8.5.

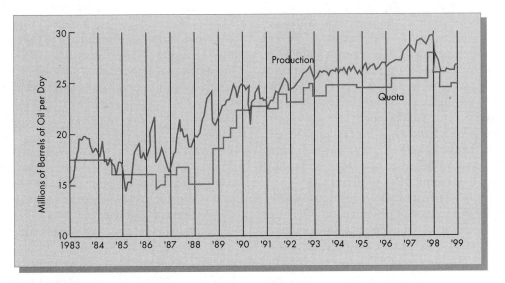

Figure 8.5 OPEC Production and Quotas: Blowing the Tops Off Oil Caps

Since quotas were first assigned to members, OPEC's actual production levels have almost always been greater than its target levels. In other words, the cartel members have been cheating.

Source: "Cartels: Breaking Up Ain't Hard to Do," *The Regional Economist*, Federal Reserve Bank of St. Louis, July 1999, p. 11. See also, Energy Information Administration, U.S. Department of Energy, *OPEC Fact Sheet* at Internet site http://www.eia.doe.gov.

The burden of production cutbacks has not been shared equally among OPEC nations. Saudi Arabia has generally served as the dominant adjuster in OPEC. Its eligibility for this role is based on its large oil reserves, small population, and limited need for oil revenues. This is not to say that OPEC has remained free from internal conflicts. For example, Saudi Arabia has sometimes increased output considerably to prevent other OPEC nations from achieving their goal of higher prices. During the world oil glut of 1982, Saudi Arabia was pressured by other OPEC nations to stop flooding the market with more oil than the market could absorb. Both Iran and Libya openly threatened to destroy the Saudis' oil fields or their government if the Saudis didn't lower production.

Most of the world's cartels have been short-lived. This is because the success of a cartel depends on several factors that are often difficult to achieve. Cartel members must control a very large share of the world market for their product and should agree on a common set of price and output policies. The length of time a cartel survives depends in part on the elasticity of supply of noncartel nations. If the noncartel supply is inelastic over the relevant price range, so that a significant increase in the cartel price calls forth only a small increase in output by noncartel nations, the cartel will face only minor competitive pressures. Similarly, the less elastic the demand for the cartel's product, the higher the cartel price can be raised without significantly reducing the amount demanded.

During the 1970s, OPEC was successful in increasing the revenues of its members. One reason is that the long-run price elasticity of oil supply in non-OPEC nations is inelastic. Estimates in the 1970s put the non-OPEC supply elasticity between 0.33 and 0.67, suggesting that a 1-percent increase in the OPEC price will induce only a 0.5-percent increase in non-OPEC output. The demand for gasoline in the United States was also estimated to be inelastic, having a long-run price elasticity coefficient of 0.8. Moreover, OPEC was able to dominate the world oil market, accounting for more than two-fifths of world production,

two-thirds of world reserves, and more than four-fifths of world exports.

By the 1980s, however, OPEC increasingly faced the pressures that often lead to the demise of cartels. The OPEC price hikes had induced non-OPEC nations to develop new production techniques and initiate new discoveries. The result was a fall in the OPEC share of the world market from 56 percent in 1973 to 33 percent in 1986. The OPEC price hikes also led to decreases in demand owing to increased usage of smaller autos and insulation and the switch to substitute energy sources, including coal and nuclear power. Furthermore, the recession of 1981–1983 led to weakening demand and a glut of oil on the world market.

OPEC's response to weakening demand conditions, with the exception of a small price cut in 1982, was to make large reductions in output via production quotas assigned to each member nation. Although the cutbacks succeeded for a time in keeping oil prices relatively stable, they were unable to withstand the pressures of falling demand. By 1986, a global oil-price war had broken out, causing oil prices to fall to less than $11 per barrel. Again the OPEC cartel attempted to defy market forces by assigning production quotas that would stabilize oil prices at $18 per barrel. In 1990, oil prices skyrocketed to more than $41 per barrel in response to Iraq's military invasion of Kuwait; this was followed by a decline in oil prices to $10 a barrel as peace was restored in the Middle East. By February 2000, however, oil prices surged to $34 a barrel in response to strong demand and tight supplies.

The surge in oil prices brought sharp criticism from President Bill Clinton. According to Clinton, in an open, competitive global economy, the OPEC cartel simply has no legitimate place. OPEC was tolerated by the West as a geopolitical tool during the cold war. Saudi Arabia and the Gulf states warded off communism and guaranteed a steady flow of oil to the United States, although at a high price at times. By 2000, communism was gone, and the geopolitical incentive to tolerate a cartel was over.

OPEC's Price Band Responding to criticism from importing countries about skyrocketing oil prices, in March 2000 OPEC announced a scheme to restore stability to the market. Under the scheme, OPEC pledged to keep the price of oil within a target band of $22–$28 a barrel. If the price of a basket of seven OPEC crudes stayed below $22 for 20 trading days, then the cartel would reduce production by 500,000 barrels a day. If it stayed above $28 for such a period, it would increase production by the same amount. The target zone scheme was a sharp departure from the past. Previously, OPEC met every six months and adjusted production in search of unspecified prices.

Although importing countries applauded the target zone scheme, skeptics maintained that a disjointed group such as OPEC would have trouble acting with the unity necessary to make it work. They noted that the price band was strictly a "gentleman's agreement" among OPEC members that might not be maintained when tested. OPEC has a history of indecision, infighting, and ineptitude which has led to cheating on previous agreements. Moreover, poor data makes it hard to establish what qualifies as a breach of the oil price limits. Ironically, the most serious problem for OPEC could emerge if the price band actually works. Stable oil prices might provide non-OPEC producers the confidence to boost their output, thus eroding the market share of OPEC.

Tapping the Strategic Oil Reserve

Although OPEC pledged to keep the price of oil within a band of $22–$28 a barrel, tight markets resulted in oil prices surging to more than $37 a barrel by September 2000. To moderate price increases, President Bill Clinton released 30 million barrels oil from the country's strategic oil reserve—the United States had 570 million barrels of crude oil sitting idle in salt caverns in Texas and Louisiana, enough to cover all U.S. imports for more than 2 months. The strategic oil reserve was originally intended as an insurance policy for sudden disruption of oil supplies or for war. According to Clinton, however,

what's wrong with pumping some oil out, knocking some wind out of OPEC, and relieving U.S. consumers? A release of oil could stabilize demand until market forces lower prices, according to the President.

However, critics of tapping the reserve maintained that such a policy would not help the long-term welfare of the country. They noted that crude oil was only one factor in high gasoline and heating oil prices. The main bottleneck was at the refineries, which were running out of capacity to produce gasoline and home heating oil. If there isn't enough refining capacity, releasing oil from the reserve isn't going to make a huge difference according to the critics. Also, tapping the reserve might backfire—it could discourage refiners from building their inventories because oil markets would be pricing crude oil cheaper in future months. If refiners think that the price of crude oil or heating oil is going to be lower, there is no incentive for them to increase their inventories of either crude oil or heating oil.

Because the amount of oil released from the reserve was tiny compared to the nation's needs, exactly what would happen to the price of oil was up to OPEC. A backlash from OPEC nations might occur, which could reduce supplies enough to neutralize any release of oil from the reserve. That would result in the worst of all worlds for the United States: If the United States failed, it would signal to the markets that the United States is unable to influence prices and thus diminish the power of future threats. At the writing of this textbook, the stability of oil prices remained a question.

Generalized System of Preferences

Entering world markets in manufactured goods is a problem that has plagued many developing nations. These nations often find it difficult to become cost-efficient enough to compete in a wide range of manufactured goods against industrial-nation producers. Also, industrialized

ARE INTERNATIONAL LABOR STANDARDS NEEDED TO PREVENT SOCIAL DUMPING?

A U.S. presidential task force composed of apparel industry representatives, unions, and human rights activists recently agreed to codes of conduct for labor practices by multinational corporations. In response to negative publicity, Nike, the athletic shoe and apparel company, hired former U.S. ambassador Andrew Young to conduct an independent investigation of its labor practices. Moreover, the Federation of International Football Associations announced it would not purchase soccer balls made with child labor. These events point to a growing concern about labor standards in the developing world.

High unemployment rates in Western Europe and stagnant wages of unskilled workers in the United States have contributed to a new ambivalence in the industrial countries about the benefits of trade with developing countries. Labor unions and human right activists in industrial countries fear that industrial-country wages and benefits are being forced down by unfair competition from countries with much lower labor costs—so-called "social dumping." They also maintain that market access in the industrial countries should be conditioned on raising labor standards in developing countries to prevent a "race to the bottom" in wages and benefits. Trade sanctions imposed in response to violations of labor standards are sometimes referred to as a "social clause."

There are two main arguments for the international harmonization of labor standards. The economic argument suggests that low wages and labor standards in developing countries threaten the living standards of workers in developed countries. The moral argument asserts that low wages and labor standards violate the human rights of workers in the developing countries. Human rights activists believe that raising labor standards in developing countries will benefit workers in these countries and that some labor practices are morally intolerable, such as the exploitation of working children and discrimination based on gender.

Proponents of the international harmonization of labor standards will not usually admit openly to any protectionist intent. However, developing countries remain deeply suspicious that disguised protectionism motivates many of the calls for compliance with labor standards of industrial countries, especially if the latter are to be enforced with trade sanctions. Some unions and human rights groups in the United States continue to insist that conditions on wages and benefits should be attached to agreements on labor standards.

That fairness should be observed in international competition seems indisputable. What constitutes fairness is not so obvious. Does the abundance of cheap labor in China render it an unfair competitor in the production of goods requiring relatively large amounts of unskilled labor? If so, do the plentiful coconut trees in the Philippines render it an unfair competitor in the production of coconut oil?

Another question concerns the implementation of international labor standards. Most industrial-county labor standards are not feasible for many developing countries. Concerning child labor, for example, it is indeed disturbing that young children in developing countries toil under harsh conditions for low pay. But the earnings of these children may be important to their families'—and their own—survival. Moreover, setting strict standards in a developing country's regulated sector may consign children to even more degrading, less renumerative work in the unregulated sector. Moreover, if the goal is to enhance the welfare of developing countries, perhaps a more effective way would be to allow free international migration from low- to high-standard countries, an argument rarely made by proponents of harmonization of labor standards.

Nonobservance of international labor standards may impair, rather than enhance, overall competitiveness. To be sure, exploitative child labor and forced labor may suppress wage rates, but such practices also prevent those victimized from shifting readily into activities that best match their skills and goals, and thus reduce their productivity.

Source: Stephen Golub, "Are International Labor Standards Needed to Prevent Social Dumping?" *Finance and Development*, December 1997, pp. 20–23.

nations have often levied low tariffs on raw materials and high tariffs on manufactured goods, discouraging industrial growth in developing nations.

To help developing nations strengthen their international competitiveness and expand their industrial base, many industrialized nations since the early 1970s have extended nonreciprocal tariff preferences to exports of developing nations. Under this **generalized system of preferences (GSP)**, major industrial nations temporarily reduce tariffs on designated manufactured imports from developing nations below the levels applied to imports from other industrial nations. The GSP is not a uniform system, however, because it consists of many individual schemes that differ in the types of products covered and extent of tariff reduction.

Since its origin in 1976, the U.S. GSP program has extended duty-free treatment to about 3,000 items. Beneficiaries of the U.S. program include some 150 developing nations and their dependent territories. Like the GSP programs of other industrial nations, the U.S. program excludes certain import-sensitive products from preferential tariff treatment. These products include electronics items, glass, certain steel and iron products, watches, and some types of footwear. Limits also exist on the amount of a particular product each beneficiary can export to the United States. Table 8.8 provides examples of U.S. imports under the GSP program.

Table 8.8	U.S. Imports Under the GSP from Leading Beneficiaries, 1998 (Billions of Dollars)	
Beneficiary	Total Imports	GSP Duty-Free Imports
Thailand	13.4	2.7
Brazil	9.9	2.2
Indonesia	9.3	1.9
Angola	2.2	1.6
India	8.2	1.4
Philippines	11.9	1.2
South Africa	3.1	.6
Venezuela	8.4	.5
Russia	5.7	.4
Poland	.8	.4

Source: U.S. International Trade Commission, *The Year in Trade: Operation of the Trade Agreements Program, 1998*, Washington, DC, Government Printing Office, July 1999.

ECONOMIC GROWTH STRATEGIES: IMPORT SUBSTITUTION VERSUS EXPORT-LED GROWTH

Developing countries have debated the merits of two competing strategies for industrialization: (1) an inward-looking strategy (import substitution), in which industries are established largely to supply the domestic market, and foreign trade is assigned negligible importance; (2) an outward-looking strategy (export-led growth) of encouraging the development of industries in which the country enjoys comparative advantage, with heavy reliance on foreign nations as purchasers of the increased production of exportable goods.

IMPORT SUBSTITUTION During the 1950s and 1960s, the industrialization strategy of **import substitution** became popular in developing nations such as Argentina, Brazil, and Mexico; some countries still use it today. Import substitution involves extensive use of trade barriers to protect domestic industries from import competition. The strategy is inward-oriented in that trade and industrial incentives favor production for the domestic market over the export market. For example, if fertilizer imports occur, import substitution calls for establishment of a domestic fertilizer industry to produce replacements for fertilizer imports. In the extreme, import-substitution policies could lead to complete self-sufficiency.

The rationale for import substitution arises from the developing countries' perspective on trade. Many developing countries feel that they cannot export manufactured goods because they cannot compete with established firms of the industrial countries, especially in view of the high trade barriers maintained by industrial countries. Given the need for economic growth and development, developing countries have no choice but to manufacture for themselves some of the goods they now import. The use of tariffs and quotas restricts imports, and the domestic market is reserved for domestic manufacturers. This rationale is often combined with the infant-industry argument: Protecting start-up industries will allow them to grow to a size where they can compete with the industries of the developed countries.

In one respect, import substitution appears logical: If a good is demanded and imported, why not produce it domestically? The economist's answer is that it may be more costly to produce it domestically and cheaper to import it; comparative advantage should decide which goods are imported and which are exported.

Encouraging economic development via import substitution has several advantages:

- The risks of establishing a home industry to replace imports are low because the home market for the manufactured good already exists.
- It is easier for a developing nation to protect its manufacturers against foreign competitors than to force industrial nations to reduce their trade restrictions on products exported by the developing nations.
- To avoid the import tariff walls of the developing country, foreigners have an incentive to locate manufacturing plants in the country, thus providing jobs for local workers.

In contrast to these advantages are several disadvantages:

- Because trade restrictions shelter domestic industries from international competition, they have no incentive to increase their efficiency.
- Given the small size of the domestic market in many developing countries, manufacturers

cannot take advantage of economies of scale and thus have high unit costs.
- Because the resources employed in the protected industry would otherwise have been employed elsewhere, protection of import-competing industries automatically discriminates against all other industries, including potential exporting ones.

IMPORT-SUBSTITUTION LAWS BACKFIRE ON BRAZIL

Although import-substitution laws have often been used by developing nations in their industrialization efforts, they sometimes backfire. Let us consider the example of Brazil.

In 1991, Enrico Misasi was the president of the Brazilian unit of Italian computer-maker Olivetti Inc., but he did not have an Olivetti computer. The computer behind his desk was instead manufactured by two Brazilian firms; it cost three times more than an Olivetti, and its quality was inferior. Rather than manufacturing computers in Brazil, Olivetti Inc. was permitted to manufacture only typewriters and calculators.

This anomaly was the result of import-substitution policies practiced by Brazil until 1991. From the 1970s until 1991, importing a foreign personal computer—or a microchip, a fax, or dozens of other electronic goods—was prohibited. Not only were electronic imports prohibited, but foreign firms willing to invest in Brazilian manufacturing plants were banned. Joint ventures were deterred by a law that kept foreign partners from owning more than 30 percent of a local business. These restrictions were intended to foster a home-grown electronics industry. Instead, even the law's proponents came to admit that the Brazilian electronics industry was uncompetitive and technologically outdated.

The costs of the import ban were clearly apparent by the early 1990s. Almost no Brazilian automobiles were equipped with electronic fuel injection or antiskid brake systems, both widespread throughout the world. Products such as Apple Computer's Macintosh computer were not permitted to be sold in Brazil. Brazil chose to allow Texas Instruments Inc. to shut down its Brazilian semiconductor plant, resulting in a loss of 250 jobs, rather than permit Texas Instruments to invest $133 million to modernize its product line. By adhering to its import-substitution policy, Brazil wound up a largely computer-unfriendly nation: by 1991, only 12 percent of small- and medium-sized Brazilian companies were at least partially computerized, and only 0.5 percent of Brazil's classrooms were equipped with computers. Many Brazilian companies postponed modernization because computers available overseas were not manufactured in Brazil and could not be imported. Some Brazilian companies resorted to smuggling in computers and other electrical equipment; those companies that adhered to the rules wound up with outdated and overpriced equipment.

Realizing that the import-substitution policy had backfired on its computer industry, in 1991 the Brazilian government scrapped a cornerstone of its nationalistic approach by lifting the electronics import ban—though continuing to protect domestic industry with high import duties. The government also permitted foreign joint-venture partners to raise their ownership shares from 30 percent to 49 percent and to transfer technology into the Brazilian economy.

EXPORT-LED GROWTH Another development strategy is **export-led growth,** or **export-oriented policy.** The strategy is outward-oriented because it links the domestic economy to the world economy. Instead of pursuing growth through the protection of domestic industries suffering comparative disadvantage, the strategy involves promoting growth through the export of manufactured goods. Trade controls are either nonexistent or very low, in the sense that any disincentives to export resulting from import barriers are counterbalanced by export subsidies. Industrialization is viewed as a natural outcome of development instead of being an objective pursued at the expense of the economy's efficiency. By the 1970s, many developing countries were abandoning their import-substitution strategies and shifting emphasis to export-led growth.

Export-oriented policies have a number of advantages: (1) They encourage industries in which developing countries are likely to have a comparative advantage, such as labor-intensive manufactured goods; (2) By providing a larger market in which to sell, they allow domestic manufacturers greater scope for exploiting economies of scale; (3) By maintaining low restrictions on imported goods, they impose a competitive discipline on domestic firms that forces them to increase efficiency.

However, against these advantages is a major problem: export-led growth depends on the willingness and ability of industrial countries to go on absorbing large amounts of manufactured goods from developing countries. Export-led growth policies were successful in the 1960s and early 1970s, when the markets of the industrial nations were growing and open. Increasingly, however, industrialized nations have become apprehensive of foreign competition, especially during eras of high unemployment.

South Korea is an example of a nation that has used an export-oriented strategy. During the 1960s, South Korea initiated measures encouraging exports of manufactures. Tariffs and quotas were eliminated on inputs imported for use in exported goods. Tax laws were modified to encourage foreign investment and to favor production that earned a profit on exports. The South Korean unit of currency, the *won*, was devalued. Furthermore, the labor market was unregulated, with no labor unions and no minimum-wage laws. From 1963 to 1975, manufacturing employment in South Korea grew 10.7 percent per year. Exports as a percentage of South Korean gross national product rose from 3 percent in 1960 to 36 percent in 1977. Export growth accounted for 10 percent of South Korea's overall growth during 1955 to 1963; the figure was 22 percent from 1963 to 1970, and 56 percent from 1970 to 1973.

The relationship between trade strategies and economic performance has been analyzed by economists for the period 1963–1992. Their research demonstrates that trade strategies had a significant impact on manufactured exports, industrial performance, and real gross domestic product. Figure 8.6 shows that the growth rate of real gross domestic product was higher for the strongly outward-oriented nations than for the strongly inward-oriented nations.

The evidence of Figure 8.6 strongly suggests that the economic performance of nations implementing outward-oriented trade policies has been superior to that of nations using inward-oriented trade policies. Outward-oriented policies introduce international competition to domestic markets, which encourages efficient firms and discourages inefficient ones. By creating a more competitive environment, they also promote higher productivity and hence faster economic growth. Conversely, inward-oriented policies relying on trade protection switch

demand to products produced domestically. Exporting is then discouraged by both the increased cost of imported inputs and the increased cost of domestic inputs relative to the price received by exporters.

EAST ASIAN ECONOMIES

East Asia has realized a remarkable record of high and sustained economic growth. As seen in Table 8.9, from the 1970s to 1998, the major economies of East Asia grew more rapidly than the rich industrial countries. This is unusual among developing countries; others have realized rapid growth

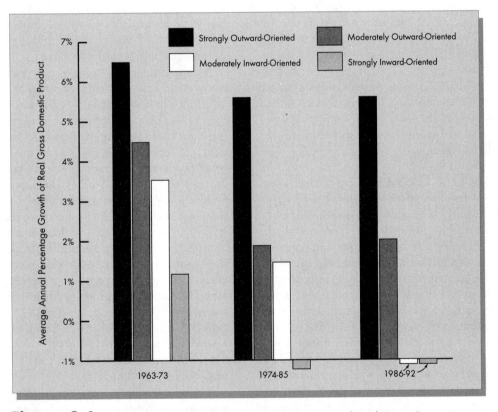

Figure 8.6 The Rewards of Openness: Trade Orientation and Real Gross Domestic Product in Developing Nations, 1963–1992.

Source: The World Bank, *World Bank Development Report*, Washington, DC, 1987, and various issues of International Monetary Fund, *World Economic Outlook*, Washington, DC. See also Organization for Economic Cooperation and Development, *Open Markets Matter: The Benefits of Trade and Investment Liberalization*, OECD Policy Brief, No. 6, 1998.

rates but not over the course of several decades. Moreover, the East Asian countries are unique in that they combined this rapid, sustained growth with highly equal income distributions. In particular, the East Asian economies became known as the **East Asian tigers**, a tribute to their strong economic growth rates.

EAST ASIA'S GROWTH STRATEGY The East Asian tigers are highly diverse in natural resources, populations, cultures, and economic policies. However, they have in common several characteristics underlying their economic success: (1) high rates of investment and (2) high and increasing endowments of human capital due to universal primary and secondary education.

To foster competitiveness, East Asian governments have invested in their people and provided a favorable competitive climate for private enterprise. They have also kept their economies open to international trade. The East Asian economies have actively sought foreign technology, such as licenses, capital-good imports, and foreign training.

The East Asian economies have generally discouraged the organization of trade unions—whether by deliberate suppression (South Korea

and Taiwan), by government paternalism (Singapore), or by a laissez-faire policy (Hong Kong). The outcome has been the prevention of minimum-wage legislation and the maintenance of free and competitive labor markets.

In the post–World War II era, trade policies in the East Asian economies (except Hong Kong) began with a period of import substitution. To develop their consumer-good industries, these countries levied high tariffs and quantitative restrictions on imported goods. They also subsidized some manufacturing industries such as textiles. Although these policies initially led to increased domestic production, as time passed they inflicted costs on the East Asian economies. Because import-substitution policies encouraged the importing of capital and intermediate goods and discouraged the exporting of manufactured goods, they led to large trade deficits for the East Asian economies. To obtain the foreign exchange necessary to finance these deficits, the East Asian economies shifted to a strategy of outward orientation and export promotion.

Export-push strategies were enacted in the East Asian economies by the late 1950s and 1960s. Singapore and Hong Kong set up trade regimes that were close to free trade. Japan, South

Table 8.9 East Asian Economies' Growth Rates

| | GNP per Capita*
1998 $ | GNP Growth, Annual Average % | | |
		1970–1979	1980–1989	1990–1998
Singapore	22,600	9.4	7.2	6.6
Hong Kong	22,000	9.2	7.5	6.9
Taiwan	14,590	10.2	8.1	6.3
South Korea	12,770	9.3	8.0	9.4
Malaysia	6,990	8.0	5.7	5.3
Thailand	5,840	7.3	7.2	7.3
Indonesia	2,790	7.8	5.7	6.1
Philippines	3,540	6.1	1.8	1.0
China	3,220	7.5	9.3	10.2
Rich industrial countries	23,440	3.4	2.6	3.1

*At purchasing power parity.

Source: The World Bank Group, *Development Data*, http://www.worldbank.org/data. See also the World Bank, *World Development Report 1999–2000*.

Korea, and Taiwan initiated policies to promote exports while protecting domestic producers from import competition. Indonesia, Malaysia, and Thailand adopted a variety of policies to encourage exports while gradually reducing import restrictions. These measures contributed to an increase in the East Asian economies' share of world exports, with manufactured exports accounting for most of this growth.

The stunning success of the East Asian economies has created problems, however. The industrialize-at-all-costs emphasis has left many of the East Asian economies with major pollution problems. Whopping trade surpluses have triggered a growing wave of protectionist sentiment overseas, especially in the United States, which sees the East Asian economies depending heavily on the U.S. market for future export growth.

FLYING-GEESE PATTERN OF GROWTH It is widely recognized that East Asian economies have followed a **flying-geese pattern of economic growth**, in which countries gradually move up in technological development by following in the pattern of countries ahead of them in the development process. For example, Taiwan and Malaysia take over leadership in apparel and textiles from Japan as Japan moves into the higher-technology sectors of automotive, electronic, and other capital goods. A decade or so later, Taiwan and Malaysia are able to upgrade to automotive and electronics products, while the apparel and textile industries move to Thailand, Vietnam, and Indonesia.

To some degree, the flying-geese pattern is a result of market forces: Labor-abundant nations will become globally competitive in labor-intensive industries, such as footwear, and will graduate to more capital- or skill-intensive industries as savings and education deepen the availability of capital and skilled workers. However, as the East Asian economies have demonstrated, more than just markets are necessary for flying-geese development. Even basic labor-intensive products, such as electronics assembly, are increasingly determined by multinational enterprises and technologies created in industrial nations.

For East Asian economies, a strong export platform has underlain their flying-geese pattern of development. East Asian governments have utilized several versions of an export platform, such as bonded warehouses, free-trade zones, joint ventures, and strategic alliances with multinational enterprises. Governments supported these mechanisms with economic policies that aided the incentives for labor-intensive exports.

Although East Asia's export platform strategy began with apparel and textiles, it shifted to electronics in the 1970s. U.S. firms, such as Texas Instruments and Hewlett-Packard, began a search for low-wage production sites that could house low-tech processes, such as chip assembly. The East Asian countries thus began to compete vigorously for footloose electronics firms. By the mid-1970s, East Asia employed more than 90 percent of global offshore electronics assembly workers. The flying geese of East Asia were swept into the updraft of global electronics production, which carried them through two decades of rapid economic growth. In this one sector lay much of the manufacturing export "miracle" of East Asia.

The flying-geese pattern of growth assumes that the sophistication of domestic production will advance one position at a time. Therefore, a nation assembling footwear is not likely to remain at that stage; education, learning by doing, and additional investment will lead from footwear to simple electronics assembly and from there to more sophisticated automotive parts and perhaps to high-technology goods. All of the early export-platform graduates, such as Singapore and South Korea, were able to develop higher levels of local technology and sophistication, typically by entering into joint ventures and strategic alliances with more sophisticated multinational enterprises. For example, Samsung advanced from chip assembly to world leadership in 64k random access memory chip production allied with International Business Machines, Inc., and other electronics firms.

INDUSTRIAL POLICIES East Asia's growth strategy has also involved industrial policy to support selected sectors of the economy. For example, in the 1950s, Japan targeted the steel, shipbuilding, coal, power, and fertilizer industries. Inputs to these industries could be imported duty-free, and firms in these sectors received preferential loans from government banks. During the 1950s, the automobile industry was targeted, while computers became the focus in the 1960s. Although industrial targeting declined in the 1970s and 1980s, the Japanese government has continued to promote the development of certain sectors, such as computer technology and high-definition television.

In the 1960s and 1970s, the Korean government targeted infant industries, typically by supporting the creation of large-scale enterprises that were given temporary monopolies. Notable examples include fertilizer, cement, petroleum refining, steel, petrochemicals, and shipbuilding. More recently, preferential treatment has been given to medium- and small-sized firms, especially in the electronics sector. Taiwan and Singapore have also provided preferential support to certain strategic industries since the early 1980s.

In spite of East Asia's strong economic performance, the net benefits of industrial policies targeting particular sectors are uncertain. Clearly, government intervention policies appear to have allowed firms to establish themselves in imperfectly competitive industries, such as automobiles, steel, and shipbuilding, where the costs of entry are high. However, there were problems associated with these policies. For example, Japan's industrial policies in the 1970s and 1980s were generally not directed toward the higher-growth industries. In Korea, support for bankrupt firms in the 1980s required the write-off or rescheduling of billions of dollars of loans. East Asian industrial policy thus appeared to be most successful when governments tried to encourage rather than pick winners individually to compete in world markets, with the marketplace being the ultimate arbiter of whether continued support of an industry was warranted.

WILL THE EAST ASIAN MIRACLE CONTINUE? Although East Asia enjoyed rapid economic growth from the 1970s to the mid-1990s,

it paid a steep price for that success. By the first half of the 1990s, every country across East Asia was blowing huge financial bubbles. The large inflows of capital led to dizzying rises in asset prices, particularly for real estate, and increased risk for banks and finance companies that forked out loans for the purchase of these assets. The boom ended in 1995 when the U.S. dollar, against which East Asian currencies were tied, began to recover against the yen. Asia's exports suddenly became too expensive, resulting in falling sales. Financial plagues then joined commercial ones that led to a wave of currency devaluations for the East Asian economies.

Reactions to East Asia's economic downturn fell into two broad categories. In the first were the pessimists who felt that the slowdown was *structural*. They were unsurprised by the downturn and felt that East Asia's rapid expansion was unsustainable all along because it was underlaid by heavy investment and a big shift of labor from farms into factories, rather than from productivity gains based on technological advance or organizational change. To the degree that growth is driven by capital accumulation rather than productivity gains, the marginal productivity of capital is likely to decline as capital per worker in the East Asian economies increases to the level of Western economies.

The optimists, on the other hand, gave little credence to the view that something was structurally wrong with the East Asian tigers. Instead, they believed that the past growth of East Asia was underlaid by the wise policies of the governments and the profit-seeking behavior of the people. As for the slowdown of the late 1990s, they explained that away as *cyclical*. Sooner or later, the optimists felt, the cycle would turn, and the Asian miracle would resume. The optimists maintained that on most structural issues, the East Asian economies had many things right: prudent monetary and fiscal policies, openness to most trade, high savings, secure property rights, and investment in education. Moreover, they contended that the pessimists' argument that growth is merely the result of heavy capital spending missed the point. East Asia's tigers imported the same technology that was available to the rest of the world, but they imported more of it and used it much more efficiently than other developing countries, thanks to a collection of sound policies. As the tiger economies mature, their growth rates will, naturally, tend to slow. But most of the tigers could grow at least as fast as the industrial economies for years to come.

At the turn of the millennium, the economies of East Asia showed signs of revitalization. The recession appeared to be ending for the reasons that recessions usually end: because households, investors, and firms began to consume and invest again. The turnaround was also aided by the impressive resilience of the U.S. economy, which absorbed many Asian exports of electronics, automobiles, and the like. Moreover, the International Monetary Fund credited its financial rescue packages for Indonesia, South Korea, and Thailand as being instrumental in their economic recovery.

Despite these economic improvements, skeptics maintained that it did not mean that regions' leaders should distinguish the impact of the business cycle from Asia's collection of structural challenges. They argued that East Asia should especially be concerned with using its resources more efficiently. That means stronger banking systems with more foreign involvement; less interference with the local price of capital; more transparent dealings between government and the private sector; a better system for administering bankruptcy; and incentives for people to learn more and make less wasteful use of natural resources. The most pressing changes involved capital markets. Because East Asian economies had outgrown their existing financial systems, reforms were needed to fix the banks so they could become more reliable and create a broader array of mechanisms for bringing and savers and borrowers together.

At the writing of this textbook, the future of East Asia's economy was unclear. Indeed, the debate concerning the performance of Asia's economy will continue into the new millennium.

CHINA AS A HIGH-PERFORMING ECONOMY

In the early 1970s, the People's Republic of China was an insignificant participant in the world market for goods. The value of its exports and imports was less than $15 billion, and it was only the 30th largest exporting country. China was also a negligible participant in world financial markets.

By the turn of the millennium, China had totally transformed its role in the world economy. In 2000, China's exports and imports exceeded $200 billion, and China was the world's 10th largest exporter, lagging behind only the major industrial countries. What caused this transformation?

Modern China began in 1949, when a revolutionary communist movement captured control of the nation. Soon after the communist takeover, China instituted a Soviet model of central planning with emphasis on rapid economic growth, particularly industrial growth. The state took over urban manufacturing industry, collectivized agriculture, eliminated household farming, and established compulsory production quotas.

In the late 1950s, China departed from the Soviet model and shifted from large-scale, capital-intensive industry to small-scale, labor-intensive industry scattered across the countryside. Little attention was paid to linking individual reward to individual effort. Instead, a commitment to the success of the collective plans was relied on as the motivation for workers. This system proved to be an economic failure. Although manufacturing output rose following the reforms, product quality was low and production costs were high. Because China's agricultural output was insufficient to feed its people, China became a large importer of grains, vegetable oils, and cotton. As a result of this domestic economic deterioration, plant managers, scientists, engineers, and scholars, who favored material incentives and reform, were denounced and sent to work in the fields.

By the 1970s, China could see its once-poor neighbors—Japan, Singapore, Taiwan, and South Korea—enjoying extraordinary growth and prosperity. This led to China's "marketizing" its economy through small, step-by-step changes to minimize economic disruption and political opposition. In agriculture and industry, reforms were made to increase the role of the producing unit, to increase individual incentives, and to reduce the role of state planners. Most goods were sold for market-determined—not state-controlled—prices. Greater competition was allowed both between new firms and between new firms and state firms; by the year 2000, nonstate firms manufactured about 75 percent of China's industrial output. Moreover, China opened its economy to foreign investment and joint ventures. The Chinese government's monopoly over foreign trade was also disbanded; in its place, economic zones were established in which firms could keep foreign exchange earnings and hire and fire workers.

At the turn of the millennium, China had made all of the easy economic adjustments in its transition toward capitalism: letting farmers sell their own produce and opening its doors to foreign investors and salespeople. Other reforms still needed addressing: (1) a massive restructuring of state-owned industries, which were losing money; (2) a cleanup of bankrupt state banks; (3) the creation of a social security system in a society that once guaranteed a job for life; and (4) establishment of a monetary system with a central bank free of Communist Party or government control. If China were to shut down money-losing enterprises, millions of workers would be laid off with no benefits; their addition to the 100 million-plus workers already adrift in China could be volatile. In addition, banks that lent the state companies cash would require cash infusions if bankruptcies increased in the state sector. Such loans could render a central bank monetary policy ineffective and could fuel inflation.

Although China has dismantled much of its centrally planned economy and has permitted free enterprise to replace it, political freedoms have not increased. Recall the Chinese government's use of military force to end a pro-democracy demonstration in Beijing's Tiananmen Square in 1989, which led to loss of life and demonstrated the Communist Party's determination to maintain its political power. China's evolution toward capitalism has thus consisted of expanded use of market forces under a communist political system. Today, China describes itself as a *socialist market economy.*

Important differences exist between China and the other East Asian economies. Public ownership and the share of public investment are much higher in China than in other East Asian economies. A significant share of China's state-owned enterprises has required government subsidies to remain in existence. Also, China has been more dependent on foreign capital to generate exports of manufactured products than other East Asian economies. Foreign-owned firms, or foreign-owned firms having joint ventures with Chinese firms, produce most of China's manufactured exports. A large portion of Chinese industry is thus not participating in China's export expansion. Finally, China is characterized by substantial income inequalities, especially between urban and rural living standards, which could undermine support for continued capitalistic reforms.

Concerning international trade, China has followed a pattern consistent with the principle of comparative advantage. On the export side, China has supplied a growing share of the world's demand for relatively inexpensive sporting goods, toys, footwear, garments, and textiles. These goods embody labor-intensive production methods and reflect China's abundance of labor. On the import side, China is a growing market for machinery, transportation equipment, and other capital goods that require higher levels of technologies than China can produce domestically. Most of China's economic expansion since 1978 has been driven by rapid growth in exports and investment spending. Table 8.10 illustrates China's direction of trade in 1998.

Table 8.10 Direction of China's Trade in 1998

Area	Exports (Billions of Dollars)	Imports (Billions of Dollars)
Industrial Countries	105.6	72.5
Japan	29.7	28.3
United States	38.0	17.0
Other	37.9	27.2
Developing Countries	81.7	64.7
Africa	3.4	1.4
Asia	63.4	52.7
Europe	5.0	4.5
Western Hemisphere	5.2	2.9
Other	4.7	3.2

Source: International Monetary Fund, *Direction of Trade Statistics Yearbook* Washington, DC, December, 1999.

How will future trading patterns evolve for China? As seen in Table 8.11, among major developing nations, China is the most poorly endowed with land except for Singapore. Therefore, China's specialization in labor-intensive manufacturing relative to agriculture is expected to be the greatest. This will result in China's importing food and moving into manufacturing exports to feed and generate employment for an expanding population. Its high savings rate allows the buildup of capital necessary to make the transition. At the same time, China will likely lose market shares in primary products.

What manufactured goods China exports will also depend on the quality of the labor force. With more people educated up to the secondary-school level than to the tertiary level, and with low capital per worker, China is more likely to emphasize low-skilled manufactures and light industry. With its weaker higher-education base, China is unlikely to emerge as a major source of knowledge-based and complementary skilled-labor products.

CHINA'S FAILURE TO PROTECT U.S. INTELLECTUAL PROPERTY

Enforcement of laws to protect intellectual property rights of foreigners has been a problem in China. Among the largest and most obvious offenders in China have been factories producing CDs, audiocassettes, videos, and video games.

Although China passed laws in 1991 that were supposed to protect intellectual property rights, enforcement of the laws has been selective. National copyright offices, located in China's provinces, have often lacked authority to take effective action against bootleggers. Also, the courts have been reluctant to issue substantial judgments in civil cases against Chinese defendants or criminal convictions for major copyright infringers. Furthermore, factories that make pirated goods have often been owned, or run by, powerful members of the provincial governments who hold themselves above the law. These factors have led to U.S. threats of trade sanctions unless China enforce its laws to protect intellectual property rights.

Responding to U.S. pressure, the Chinese government has agreed to improve its protection of intellectual property rights by (1) establishing antipiracy task forces and stepping up raids on retail establishments; (2) inspecting factories alleged by the United States to be producing pirated goods and imposing penalties against factories caught pirating intellectual property; and (3) opening its market for audiovisual and published products, and making the censorship process more transparent. In spite of these pledges, there have been numerous U.S. complaints over lackadaisical enforcement by the Chinese government.

CHINA AND PERMANENT NORMAL TRADE RELATIONS

Recall from Chapter 7 that if the United States grants normal trade relations to another country, it agrees to apply import tariffs to the country's goods as low as those applied to any other country. Normal trade relations can be granted to a nonmarket-economy country only if that country permits free and unrestricted emigration. The law was originally intended to encourage the Soviet Union to allow the emigration of Soviet Jews. The nonmarket-economy country's normal trade relation status must be renewed annually.

Table 8.11 Factor Endowments in China and Selected Other Countries*

Country	Cropland (Hectares per Worker) 1995	Labor Force (Millions) 1995	Labor Force (Millions) 2020	Physical Capital (Thousands of 1995 U.S. Dollars per Worker) 1995	Physical Capital (Thousands of 1995 U.S. Dollars per Worker) 2020	Tertiary Education (Years per Capita) 1995	Tertiary Education (Years per Capita) 2020
China	0.12	808.3	988.6	1.6	13.2	0.2	0.4
Indonesia	0.19	119.7	174.9	2.7	21.9	0.5	1.6
South Korea	0.07	31.8	35.9	21.5	115.2	3.0	6.8
Malaysia	0.42	11.6	19.7	15.8	139.6	0.5	2.2
Philippines	0.20	40.1	72.1	3.0	27.2	2.7	5.0
Singapore	0.00	2.1	2.6	62.7	384.9	0.5	2.7
Thailand	0.58	39.9	53.9	7.9	73.2	1.3	3.1
Brazil	0.61	101.4	145.9	9.6	31.2	1.1	2.1
India	0.30	561.3	886.2	1.7	8.2	0.5	1.3
Japan	0.05	87.0	75.1	131.4	397.8	0.8	1.8
U.S.	1.09	172.3	200.0	73.0	—	2.1	3.5

*Estimate for the year 2020.

Source: The World Bank, *China Engaged: Integration with the Global Economy,* Washington, DC, 1997, p. 34.

In 1979, the United States and China signed a bilateral trade agreement providing mutual normal trade relations. As a nonmarket-economy country, China's normal trade relation status was reviewed each year. Renewal of this status was routine throughout the 1980s, given China's willingness to allow as many as 10 million of its people to emigrate to the United States.

Since the suppression of the Tiananmen Square demonstrations in 1989, however, renewal of China's normal trade relation status has been controversial. Widespread concern has existed about China's treatment of dissidents and political prisoners. China has also been accused of using prison labor to produce and export products including diesel engines, tea, socks, machine presses, and wrenches. Importing such products is illegal under U.S. trade law. Other concerns have involved China's proliferation of weapons, its failure to enforce intellectual property rights, and the restrictions that it applies to imports from the United States and other countries.

These concerns have resulted in proposals that the United States use its economic leverage to promote improvements in China's policies in areas such as human rights, trade, and weapons nonproliferation. Proponents of these proposals maintain that the United States should not extend normal trade relation status to China unless China improves its behavior in these areas.

As one of China's largest export markets, the United States purchases almost one-third of its exports. Revoking U.S. normal trade relation status for China would make duties on Chinese products extremely high. For example, tariffs on toys would increase from 6.8 to 70 percent, those on cotton T-shirts would increase from 21 to 90 percent, and those on silk apparel would increase from 6.9 percent to 65 percent. Such tariff increases would diminish China's ability to provide certain products to the U.S. market at competitive prices; it would give the Chinese incentive to become a responsible member of the world community.

Not everyone agrees that trade sanctions are effective devices to force progress on human rights and democracy in China. U.S. business leaders fear potential economic losses were China to retaliate against a U.S. withdrawal of normal trade relations by raising its own tariffs or taking other measures to limit U.S. access to the Chinese market. Such retaliation would especially hurt U.S. producers of aircraft, power stations, machine tools, and communications systems. Revoking China's normal trade relation status would also hurt U.S. retailers relying on Chinese goods (sporting goods, textiles) for their livelihood, and employees of these enterprises would stand to lose their jobs. As tariffs increase, the U.S. consumer would bear the cost of price increases for Chinese imports or their alternatives. Finally, it is questionable whether trade sanctions would be effective in forcing a large, diversified nation such as China to modify its political behavior.

Proponents of granting normal trade relations status to China also contend that it promotes improving human rights. This is because increased foreign trade contributes to China's integration into the world community; as the Chinese economy grows and becomes increasingly decentralized, a new business society develops that is independent of the state. Moreover, with greater wealth and access to foreign goods and modern telecommunications, Chinese citizens are increasingly exposed to a broader set of ideas, undermining the government's monopoly on information. The result is a diffusion of economic power and information, creating the preconditions for a civil society, and with it more pluralistic forms of governance and a greater respect for human life.

A key question was whether to grant China normal trade relations on a permanent basis or subject the status to annual reviews. Proponents of permanent normal trade relations maintained that lasting status would provide China the stability needed to integrate into the world community. However, opponents argued that annual reviews of normal trade relations were necessary to pressure China on human rights, the environment, and labor conditions.

In 1999, the United States and China reached a bilateral trade agreement that resulted in China's agreeing to cut tariffs and remove nontariff barriers on trade in agriculture, industrial products and services; eliminate various restrictions on foreign investment in China; and accept U.S. use of safeguard measures to temporarily guard against possible import surges that might harm certain U.S. industries, such as textiles. This agreement led to the U.S. government's considering whether to permanently normalize trade relations with China. After intense debate, the U.S. government granted permanent normal trade relation status to China in 2000.

CHINA AND THE WORLD TRADE ORGANIZATION An important goal of the economic reforms that were initiated by the Chinese government in the late 1970s was to open the economy to international trade and investment flows. To further the policy of opening, the Chinese government applied to become a member of the World Trade Organization. China has made its accession to the WTO a major priority for a number of reasons:

- It would represent international recognition of China's growing economic power.
- It would enable China to play a major role in the development of new international rules on trade in the WTO.
- It would give China access to the dispute-resolution process in the WTO, reducing the threat of unilaterally imposed restrictions on Chinese exports.
- It would make it easier for reformers in China to push for liberalization policies if they could argue that such steps are necessary to fulfill China's international obligations.

Most analysts felt that it was important to include such a major trading nation in the multilateral trading system. Allowing China to become a member of the WTO, they maintained, would further open China's economy to imports and ensure that Chinese exporters operate by the rules of the multilateral system. However, some analysts maintained that China's trade regime, which is heavily regulated by the central government, is incompatible with the multilateral system. The principles that underlie the WTO—nondiscrimination, national treatment, and adherence to negotiated tariff rates at fixed maximum levels—imply trade based on market forces rather than central planning in which government directly regulates what is produced, exported, and imported. Therefore, in the past, the centrally planned economic systems of China and other nonmarket-economy nations have been considered incompatible with the WTO. Simply put, to accede to the WTO, China must change many laws, institutions, and policies to bring them into conformity with international trade rules. However, placing too many conditions on China's accession could lead to the exclusion of China, and thus a significant part of world trade, from the discipline of multilateral rules.

For 30 years, the United States has worked to bring China more fully into the community of nations and to promote both economic development and a more liberal society. The policy has been working. Anyone who saw China in the early 1980s and compared it with the turn of the millennium must be amazed. Drab Mao suits and bicycles have morphed into bright fashions and traffic jams; the freedom and the range of individual choices available to the average citizen have increased dramatically.

China's transition, however, is far from complete. Despite recent reforms intended to encourage the remaining state-owned firms to operate on a commercial basis, many of them are either making no profits or losing money. The central government has been reluctant to allow bankruptcies because of fear that unemployment may lead to unrest. Consequently, the state-owned firms are supported with subsidies from the state budget. Moreover, while the reforms have allowed a greater role for market prices, the government continues to play a role in fixing some prices. Furthermore, China lacks the kind of legal system necessary to support a market economy, a shortcoming that has created uncertainty in the enforcement of contracts and an environment conducive to corruption and criminal influence in business.

Another important issue concerning China's application for WTO membership is the pace at which China will conform to WTO laws. The measures required to gain membership will adversely affect domestic Chinese firms that currently rely on trade protection and government subsidies to survive. As a result, China wants WTO status as a developing economy and some flexibility in the time it will take to conform to WTO standards. The United States, however, does not view China as a typical developing nation, given its status as one of the world's major exporters, and thus presses for a relatively short time period for substantial trade liberalization.

The conclusion of the U.S.–China bilateral trade agreement of 1999 and the U.S. government's decision in 2000 to permanently normalize trade relations with China gave new momentum towards China's accession to the WTO—due in part to the important role the United States plays in the WTO, and because Chinese officials in the past complained that the U.S. position on China's WTO's accession was the main obstacle to China's admission. China's accession into the WTO was also supported by a bilateral trade agreement reached with China and the European Union in 2000. Final approval of China's accession would require China to complete talks with the WTO over the nature of its trade regime, before a final vote could be taken in the WTO on China's accession.

DOES THE U.S. ECONOMY GAIN FROM CHINA'S ACCESSION TO THE WORLD TRADE ORGANIZATION? Accession to the WTO requires numerous policy changes in China, including significant reductions in China's tariff and nontariff barriers that impede U.S. exports to China, the opening up of China's service sector, further protection of intellectual property rights, and the elimination of many barriers to trade in agricultural products.

As seen in Table 8.12, many sectors of the U.S. economy would benefit from China's accession to the WTO as Beijing removed certain trade barriers: agriculture, beverages, chemicals, plastics, electronic equipment, and the like. However, trade liberalization would foster efficiency gains for China because of further investment in China's economy, thereby expanding production.

CHINA AND WTO: UNIONS ARE WRONG

On April 12, 2000, Jagdish Bhagwati, an economics professor at Columbia University, published an essay that argued on behalf of China's entry into the World Trade Organization. Do you agree with his remarks?

Today the AFL-CIO plans to send more than 10,000 workers into the streets of Washington to protest China's entry into the World Trade Organization. Congress will soon vote on whether to grant China permanent normal trade status, which would pave the way for WTO membership.

This should be no contest. The economic case against China's entry into the WTO is laughable. The case for America opposing China's entry is weaker still if other nations vote for admission. Even the human rights case for barring China's entry is not compelling.

China, a major player in trade, belongs in the superstructure of international institutions whose implicit objective is universal membership. China's splendid economic performance reflects a steady shift toward functioning markets; their absence cannot be alleged to bar WTO entry.

China's exclusion would also mean that while America would continue to trade with it, it would lose the substantial gains U.S. Trade Representative Charlene Barshefsky has negotiated as "sweeteners" for our favorable vote on WTO entry. As with the North American Free Trade Agreement, in which the U.S. got far more than it gave to Mexico, China is giving much and getting little directly by way of trade concessions.

Without WTO, the United States would be forced to rely on bilateral treaties that are invariably narrower in scope and harder to enforce without stoking nationalist resentments. By contrast, the WTO imposes wide-ranging disciplines accompanied by a dispute-settlement mechanism that greatly enhances enforceability because of its multilateral nature, its impartiality, and its built-in retribution for noncompliance.

Skeptics fear that instead of being disciplined by the WTO, China will wreck the WTO. That is far-fetched. Large as it is, China is nowhere near big enough to have any clout by itself; nor should we assume that many countries, even the poor ones, would ally themselves with China to undermine the working of the WTO. Far more likely, the WTO will be the bull in China's shop, aiding the proponents of globalization and the rule of law.

Far more foolish than keeping China out of the WTO would be opposing its entry when others are ready to vote it in. If we did so, the United States would suffer discriminatory treatment in the Chinese market relative to other WTO members.

The only argument against China's entry that has at least superficial plausibility is that denial of entry would keep the pressure on China to improve its human rights performance. If only this were true. But what makes anyone think the 800-pound gorilla that is Beijing will be any easier to move through trade sanctions than the gnat that is Fidel Castro's Cuba? Congress has tried repeatedly to influence China's behavior with its annual debates about trade status, but to no avail. And as in Cuba, it's unlikely that any other country would join the U.S. in an effort to isolate China.

A better approach than trade sanctions is a full-throated condemnation of Chinese human rights abuses at all possible forums, such as the Human Rights Commission in Geneva. The rulers of China have expressed loud distaste for such criticism, proving that they are vulnerable to it. As China integrates into the world economy, and its prosperity grows, trade will have an eventual, beneficial effect on human rights. Meanwhile, such a human rights policy would keep the pressure on China's rulers, reinforcing what economics can contribute.

Table 8.12 China's Entry into the World Trade Organization: Examples of Predicted Export Gains for the United States in 1999

Product	Amount	Percentage Increase*
Wheat	$33.0 million	15.5
Vegetable oil	288.5	145.8
Cotton	230.1	59.2
Beverages and tobacco	222.9	124.5
Footwear and leather	126.7	21.3
Chemicals and plastics	102.2	2.8
Iron and steel	10.0	3.0
Electronic equipment	283.6	14.1
Machinery	515.6	11.0
Other manufacturing	205.6	114.0

*Estimates compared to base year 1998.

Source: U.S. International Trade Commission, *Assessment of the Economic Effects on the United States of China's Accession to the WTO*, August 1999, p. xiii.

Also, China would benefit from increased imports of capital goods, which would improve its productivity. Therefore, some U.S. industries would lose ground to imports of Chinese goods: footwear, wearing apparel, wood products, and other light manufacturers. In general, analysts concluded that an agreement with China would provide positive but minor benefits for the U.S. economy. This result is consistent with the fact that U.S. trade with China accounted for less than 1 percent of U.S. gross domestic product in 1999.

S U M M A R Y

1. Developing nations have attempted to enact trade policies—such as commodity agreements and cartels—to increase their level of income and standard of living.

2. Among the alleged problems facing the developing nations are (a) nondiversified economies, (b) unstable export markets, and (c) worsening terms of trade.

3. International commodity agreements have been formed by producers and consumers of primary products to stabilize export receipts, production, and prices. The methods used to attain these objectives are buffer stocks, export controls, and multilateral contracts.

4. Past efforts to form viable international commodity agreements have suffered from a number of limitations. Because production is labor-intensive, output cutbacks are often socially unacceptable to workers. Agreeing on a target price that reflects existing economic conditions is also troublesome. Agricultural products often face high storage costs and are perishable. Stockpiles of commodities in importing nations can be used to offset controls on production and export. Substitute products exist for many commodities.

5. The OPEC oil cartel was established in 1960 in reaction to the control that the major international oil companies exercised over the posted price of oil. OPEC has used production quotas to support prices and earnings above what could be achieved in more competitive conditions.

6. To help developing nations gain access to world markets, many industrial nations offer assistance known as a generalized system of preferences.

7. Besides attempting to stabilize commodity prices, developing nations have promoted internal industrialization through policies of import substitution and export promotion. Countries emphasizing export promotion have tended to realize higher rates of economic growth than countries emphasizing import-substitution policies.

8. The East Asian economies have realized remarkable economic growth. The foundation of such growth has included high rates of investment, the increasing endowments of an educated workforce, and the use of export-promotion policies. By the late 1990s, East Asia's economies showed signs of fatigue, and observers were asking whether the Asian miracle would continue.

9. By the 1990s, China had become a high-performing Asian economy. Although China has dismantled much of its centrally planned economy and permitted free enterprise to replace it, political freedoms have not increased. Today, China describes itself as a socialist market economy. Being heavily endowed with labor, China specializes in labor-intensive manufacturing.

S T U D Y   Q U E S T I O N S

1. What are the major reasons for the skepticism of many developing nations regarding the comparative-advantage principle and free trade?

2. Stabilizing commodity prices has been a major objective of many primary-product nations. What are the major methods used to achieve price stabilization?

3. What are some examples of international commodity agreements? Why have many of them broken down over time?

4. Why are the less-developed nations concerned with commodity-price stabilization?

5. The average person probably never heard of the Organization of Petroleum Exporting Countries until 1973 or 1974, when oil prices skyrocketed. In fact, OPEC was founded in 1960. Why is it that OPEC did not achieve worldwide prominence until the 1970s? What factors contributed to OPEC's problems in the 1980s?

6. Why is cheating a typical problem for cartels?

7. The generalized system of preferences is intended to help developing nations gain access to world markets. Explain.

8. How are import-substitution and export-promotion policies used to aid in the industrialization of developing nations?

9. Describe the strategy that East Asia used from the 1970s to the 1990s to achieve high rates of economic growth. Can the Asian miracle continue into the new millennium?

10. How has China achieved the status of a high-performing Asian economy? Why is China's most-favored-nation trade status a source of controversy in the United States? To date, why has China not been accepted as a member of the Word Trade Organization?

NETLINK

8.1 The United Nations Conference on Trade and Development (UNCTAD) assists developing nations to compete successfully in world markets. A description of UNCTAD's operations and a discussion of the problems of developing countries can be found by setting your browser to URL:

http://www.unctad.org/en/enhome.htm. To get to its publications, click Guide to Publication button.

8.2 For information on individual developing nations, the CIA's annual *World Factbook* provides comprehensive information on many countries and territories, including geography, natural resources,

demographics, government, and economic statistics. The CIA's *Handbook of International Economic Statistics* also contains much useful information on countries and regions. Set your browser to URL:

http://www.odci.gov/cia/publications/pubs.html

8.3 To get a glimpse of U.S. foreign policy and U.S. relations with the countries in the Asia–Pacific region, log onto the Web sites of the Bureau of East Asian and Pacific Affairs at:

http://www.state.gov/www/regions/eap/index.html

To access NetLink Exercises and the Virtual Scavenger Hunt, visit the Carbaugh Web site at http://carbaugh.swcollege.com.

Regional Trading Arrangements

Since World War II, advanced nations have significantly lowered their trade restrictions. Such trade liberalization has stemmed from two approaches. The first is a reciprocal reduction of trade barriers on a nondiscriminatory basis. Under the General Agreement on Tariffs and Trade—and its successor, the World Trade Organization—member nations acknowledge that tariff reductions agreed on by any two nations will be extended to all other members. Such an international approach encourages a gradual relaxation of tariffs throughout the world.

A second approach to trade liberalization occurs when a small group of nations, typically on a regional basis, forms a **regional trading arrangement**. Under this system, member nations agree to impose lower barriers to trade within the group than to trade with nonmember nations. Each member nation continues to determine its domestic policies, but the trade policy of each includes preferential treatment for group members. Regional trading arrangements (free-trade areas and customs unions) have been an exception to the principle of nondiscrimination embodied in the World Trade Organization. This chapter investigates some of the theoretical and empirical aspects of regional trading arrangements.

TYPES OF REGIONAL TRADING ARRANGEMENTS

Since the mid-1950s, the term **economic integration** has become part of the vocabulary of econ-

KEY CONCEPTS AND TERMS

- Asia–Pacific Economic Cooperation (APEC)
- Benelux
- Common agricultural policy
- Common market
- Convergence criteria
- Council for Mutual Economic Assistance (CMEA. COMECON)
- Countertrade
- Customs union
- Dynamic effects of economic integration
- Economic integration
- Economic union
- Euro
- European Economic Area
- European Monetary Union (EMU)
- European Union (EU)
- Export subsidies
- Free-trade area
- Free Trade Area of the Americas (FTAA)
- Maastricht Treaty
- Market economy
- Monetary union
- Nonmarket economy
- North American Free Trade Agreement (NAFTA)
- Optimum currency area
- Regional trading arrangement
- Static effects of economic integration
- Trade-creation effect
- Trade-diversion effect
- Transition economies
- U.S.–Canada Free Trade Agreement
- Variable levies

omists. Economic integration is a process of eliminating restrictions on international trade, payments, and factor mobility. Economic integration thus results in the uniting of two or more national economies in a regional trading arrangement. Before proceeding, let us distinguish the types of regional trading arrangements.

A **free-trade area** is an association of trading nations whose members agree to remove all tariff and nontariff barriers among themselves. Each member, however, maintains its own set of trade restrictions against outsiders. An example of this stage of integration is the *North American Free Trade Agreement (NAFTA)*, consisting of Canada, Mexico, and the United States. Another free-trade agreement occurred in 1999 when the European Union and Mexico reached a deal that will end all tariffs on their bilateral trade in industrial goods by 2007.

Like a free-trade association, a **customs union** is an agreement among two or more trading partners to remove all tariff and nontariff trade barriers among themselves. In addition, however, each member nation imposes identical trade restrictions against nonparticipants. The effect of the common external trade policy is to permit free trade within the customs union, whereas all trade restrictions imposed against outsiders are equalized. A well-known example is **Benelux** (Belgium, the Netherlands, and Luxembourg), formed in 1948.

A **common market** is a group of trading nations that permits (1) the free movement of goods and services among member nations, (2) the initiation of common external trade restrictions against nonmembers, and (3) the free movement of factors of production across national borders within the economic bloc. The common market thus represents a more complete stage of integration than a free-trade area or a customs union. The **European Union (EU)**[1]

achieved the status of a common market in 1992 (in 1999, 11 members of the EU formed a monetary union).

Beyond these stages, economic integration could evolve to the stage of **economic union**, in which national, social, taxation, and fiscal policies are harmonized and administered by a supranational institution. Belgium and Luxembourg formed an economic union during the 1920s. The task of creating an economic union is much more ambitious than achieving the other forms of integration. This is because a free-trade area, customs union, or common market results primarily from the abolition of existing trade barriers, but an economic union requires an agreement to transfer economic sovereignty to a supranational authority. The ultimate degree of economic union would be the unification of national monetary policies and the acceptance of a common currency administered by a supranational monetary authority. The economic union would thus include the dimension of a **monetary union**.

The United States serves as an example of a monetary union. Fifty states are linked together in a complete monetary union with a common currency, implying completely fixed exchange rates among the 50 states. Also, the Federal Reserve serves as the single central bank for the nation; it issues currency and conducts the nation's monetary policy. Trade is free among the states, and both labor and capital move freely in pursuit of maximum returns. The federal government conducts the nation's fiscal policy and deals in matters concerning retirement and health programs, national defense, international affairs, and the like. Other programs, such as police protection and education, are conducted by state and local governments so that states can keep their identity within the union.

---

[1] Founded in 1957, the European Community was a collective name for three organizations: the European Economic Community, the European Coal and Steel Community, and the European Atomic Energy Commission. In 1994, the European Community was replaced by the European Union following ratification of the Maastricht Treaty by the 12 member countries of the European Community. For simplicity, the name European Union is used throughout this chapter in discussing events that occurred before and after 1994.

THE IMPETUS FOR REGIONALISM

Regional trading arrangements are pursued for a variety of reasons. A motivation of virtually every regional trading arrangement has been the prospect of enhanced economic growth. An expanded regional market can allow economies of large-scale production, foster specialization and learning-by-doing, and attract foreign investment. Regional initiatives can also foster a variety of noneconomic objectives, such as managing immigration flows and promoting regional security. Moreover, regionalism may enhance and solidify domestic economic reforms. East European nations, for example, have viewed their regional initiatives with the European Union as a means of locking in their domestic policy shifts toward privatization and market-oriented reform.

Smaller nations may seek safe-haven trading arrangements with larger nations when future access to the larger nations' markets appears uncertain. This was an apparent motivation for the formation of NAFTA. In North America, Mexico was motivated to join NAFTA partially by fear of changes in U.S. trade policy toward a more managed or strategic trade orientation. Canada's pursuit of a free-trade agreement was significantly motivated by a desire to discipline the use of countervailing duties and antidumping duties by the United States.

As new regional trading arrangements are formed, or existing ones are expanded or deepened, the opportunity cost of remaining outside an arrangement increases. Nonmember exporters could realize costly decreases in market share if their sales are diverted to companies of the member nations. This prospect may be sufficient to tip the political balance in favor of becoming a member of a regional trading arrangement, as exporting interests of a nonmember nation outweigh its import-competing interests. The negotiations between the United States and Mexico to form a free-trade area appeared to have strongly influenced Canada's decision to join NAFTA, and thus not get left behind in the movement toward free trade in North America.

EFFECTS OF A REGIONAL TRADING ARRANGEMENT

What are the possible welfare implications of *regional trading arrangements*? We can delineate the theoretical benefits and costs of such devices from two perspectives. First are the **static effects of economic integration** on productive efficiency and consumer welfare. Second are the **dynamic effects of economic integration,** which relate to member nations' long-run rates of growth. Because a small change in the growth rate can lead to a substantial cumulative effect on national output, the dynamic effects of trade-policy changes can yield substantially larger magnitudes than those based on static models. Combined, these static and dynamic effects determine the overall welfare gains or losses associated with the formation of a regional trading arrangement.

STATIC EFFECTS The static welfare effects of lowering tariff barriers among members of a trade bloc are illustrated in the following example. Assume a world composed of three countries: Luxembourg, Germany, and the United States. Suppose that Luxembourg and Germany decide to form a customs union, and the United States is a nonmember. The decision to form a customs union requires that Luxembourg and Germany abolish all tariff restrictions between themselves while maintaining a common tariff policy against the United States.

Referring to Figure 9.1, assume the supply and demand schedules of Luxembourg to be S_L and D_L. Assume also that Luxembourg is very small relative to Germany and to the United States. This means that Luxembourg cannot influence foreign prices, so that foreign supply schedules of grain are perfectly elastic. Let Germany's supply price be $3.25 per bushel and that of the United States, $3 per bushel. Note that the United States is assumed to be the more efficient supplier.

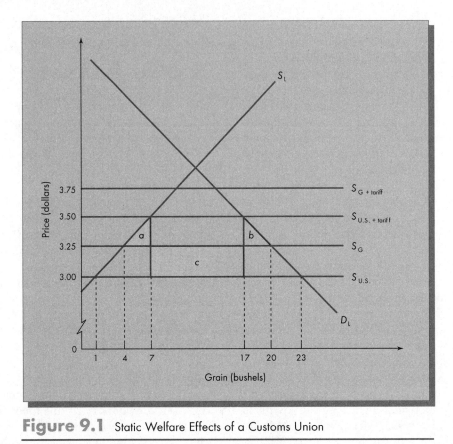

Figure 9.1 Static Welfare Effects of a Customs Union

The formation of a customs union leads to a welfare-increasing trade-creation effect and a welfare-decreasing trade-diversion effect. The overall effect of the customs union on the welfare of its members, as well as on the world as a whole, depends on the relative strength of these two opposing forces.

Before the formation of the customs union, Luxembourg finds that under conditions of free trade, it purchases all of its import requirements from the United States. Germany does not participate in the market because its supply price exceeds that of the United States. In free-trade equilibrium, Luxembourg's consumption equals 23 bushels, production equals 1 bushel, and imports equal 22 bushels. If Luxembourg levies a tariff equal to 50 cents on each bushel imported from the United States (or Germany), then imports will fall from 22 bushels to 10 bushels.

Suppose that, as part of a trade liberalization agreement, Luxembourg and Germany form a customs union. Luxembourg's import tariff against Germany is dropped, but it is still maintained on imports from the nonmember United States. This means that Germany now becomes the low-price supplier. Luxembourg now purchases all of its imports, totaling 16 bushels, from Germany at $3.25 per bushel, while importing nothing from the United States.

The movement toward freer trade under a customs union affects world welfare in two opposing ways: a welfare-increasing **trade-creation effect** and a welfare-reducing **trade-diversion effect**. The overall consequence of a customs union on the welfare of its members, as well as on the world as a whole, depends on the relative strengths of these two opposing forces.

Trade creation occurs when some domestic production of one customs-union member is replaced by another member's lower-cost imports. The welfare of the member countries is increased by trade creation because it leads to increased production specialization according to the principle of comparative advantage. The trade-creation effect consists of a *consumption effect* and a *production effect*.

Before the formation of the customs union and under its own tariff umbrella, Luxembourg imports from the United States at a price of $3.50 per bushel. Luxembourg's entry into the customs union results in its dropping all tariffs against Germany. Facing a lower import price of $3.25, Luxembourg increases its consumption of grain by 3 bushels. The welfare gain associated with this increase in consumption equals triangle *b* in Figure 9.1.

The formation of the customs union also yields a production effect that results in a more efficient use of world resources. Eliminating the tariff barrier against Germany means that Luxembourg producers must now compete against lower-cost, more efficient German producers. Inefficient domestic producers drop out of the market, resulting in a decline in home output of 3 bushels. The reduction in the cost of obtaining this output equals triangle *a* in the figure. This represents the favorable production effect. The overall trade-creation effect is given by the sum of triangles *a* + *b*.

Although a customs union may add to world welfare by way of trade creation, its trade-diversion effect generally implies a welfare loss. Trade diversion occurs when imports from a low-cost supplier outside the union are replaced by purchases from a higher-cost supplier within the union. This suggests that world production is reorganized less efficiently. In Figure 9.1,

although the total volume of trade increases under the customs union, part of this trade (10 bushels) has been diverted from a low-cost supplier, the United States, to a high-cost supplier, Germany. The increase in the cost of obtaining these 10 bushels of imported grain equals area *c*. This is the welfare loss to Luxembourg, as well as to the world as a whole. Our static analysis concludes that the formation of a customs union will increase the welfare of its members, as well as the rest of the world, if the positive trade-creation effect more than offsets the negative trade-diversion effect. Referring to the figure, this occurs if *a* + *b* is greater than *c*.

This analysis illustrates that the success of a customs union depends on the factors contributing to trade creation and diversion. Several factors that bear on the relative size of these effects can be identified. One factor is the kinds of nations that tend to benefit from a customs union. Nations whose preunion economies are quite competitive are likely to benefit from trade creation because the formation of the union offers greater opportunity for specialization in production. Also, the larger the size and the greater the number of nations in the union, the greater the gains are likely to be, because there is a greater possibility that the world's low-cost producers will be union members. In the extreme case in which the union consists of the entire world, there can exist only trade creation, not trade diversion. In addition, the scope for trade diversion is smaller when the customs union's common external tariff is lower rather than higher. Because a lower tariff allows greater trade to take place with nonmember nations, there will be less replacement of cheaper imports from nonmember nations by relatively high-cost imports from partner nations.

DYNAMIC EFFECTS Not all welfare consequences of a regional trading arrangement are static in nature. There may also be dynamic gains that influence member-nation growth rates over the long run. These dynamic gains stem from the creation of larger markets by the movement to

DID BRITAIN GAIN FROM ENTERING THE EUROPEAN UNION?
TRADE CREATION VERSUS TRADE DIVERSION

In 1973, life in Britain changed. Prices of agricultural goods increased sharply. It cost families more to keep food on the table. It wasn't an accident. A government decision pushed prices up. Britain turned away from cheaper produce from its former colony, Australia. Instead, it increased farm output and purchased rural commodities from its more expensive European neighbors. But why was that decision made? Was there gain to offset the pain?

Britain's trading relationship with Australia was bound by the tradition of empire. The former colony had supplied food to the plates of Mother England. In 1950, a third of Australia's exports wound up in Britain. But in 1973, that tradition was broken. Britain signed an agreement to join its neighbors and enter the European Union (formerly the European Community). Although the British generally believed that it was the right thing to do, they had to accept the economic consequences.

Those economics hit Australian farmers hard. Their traditional trade with Britain ended almost overnight. In joining the EU, Britain had to comply with its common agriculture policy, which set common barriers against agricultural producers outside the EU. Tariffs and quotas increased the price of non-EU produce to British consumers. Therefore, Australia's preferential access to the British market ended. It was shut out as Britain fell in line with other more costly European producers. Upon entering the EU, Britain's imports of Australian beef fell more than 75 percent, and the 800,000 tons of imported Australian wheat stopped almost instantly.

British consumers paid a high price for the change. Before joining the EU, the British food bills were the cheapest in Europe. Australia's beef, wheat, and other agricultural goods were efficiently produced and comparatively cheap. When Britain joined the EU, however, more expensive goods from Europe pushed its food prices up 25 percent on average; that increased its overall rate of inflation by 3 to 4 percent. Simply put, Britain lost because trade was diverted from a low- to high- cost producer; it had to pay more for agricultural goods.

But there's another side to this story. Trade in manufactured goods from Europe increased significantly as Britain entered the EU and thus abolished tariffs and quotas placed on imports of these goods from European nations. This allowed lower-priced imports from European trading partners to replace higher-priced British output, thus increasing welfare.

Evaluating whether entering the EU was good or bad for the British became an empirical question. Did the welfare-expanding effect of trade creation in manufactured goods more than offset the welfare-contracting effect of trade diversion in agricultural products? Many empirical studies have been conducted on the effects of Britain's entrance into the EU. They generally support the conclusion that significant trade diversion occurred in agriculture and significant trade creation occurred in manufacturing. The overall effect between trade creation and trade diversion is still being debated.

Source: Richard Pomfret, *Unequal Trade: The Economics of Discriminatory International Trade Policies*, New York, Blackwell Publishers, 1988.

freer trade under customs unions. The benefits associated with a customs union's dynamic gains may more than offset any unfavorable static effects. Dynamic gains include *economies of scale*, *greater competition*, and a *stimulus of investment*.

Perhaps the most noticeable result of a customs union is market enlargement. Being able to penetrate freely the domestic markets of other member nations, producers can take advantage of economies of scale that would not have occurred in smaller markets limited by trade restrictions. Larger markets may permit efficiencies attributable to greater specialization of workers and machinery, the use of the most efficient equipment, and the more complete use of by-products. There is evidence that significant economies of scale have been achieved by the EU in such products as steel, automobiles, footwear, and copper refining.

The European refrigerator industry provides an example of the dynamic effects of integration. Prior to the formation of the EU, each of the major European nations that produced refrigerators (Germany, Italy, and France) supported a small number of manufacturers that produced primarily for the domestic market. These manufacturers had production runs of fewer than 100,000 units per year, a level too low to permit the adoption of automated equipment. Short production runs translated into high per-unit cost. The EU's formation resulted in the opening of European markets and paved the way for the adoption of large-scale production methods, including automated press lines and spot welding. By the late 1960s, the typical Italian refrigerator plant manufactured 850,000 refrigerators annually. This volume was more than sufficient to meet the minimum efficient scale of operation, estimated to be 800,000 units per year. The late 1960s also saw German and French manufacturers averaging 570,000 units and 290,000 units per year, respectively.[2]

Broader markets may also promote greater competition among producers within a customs union. It is often felt that trade restrictions promote monopoly power, whereby a small number of companies dominate a domestic market. Such companies may prefer to lead a quiet life, forming agreements not to compete on the basis of price. But with the movement to more open markets under a customs union, the potential for successful collusion is lessened as the number of competitors expands. With freer trade, domestic producers must compete or face the possibility of

financial bankruptcy. To survive in expanded and more competitive markets, producers must undertake investments in new equipment, technologies, and product lines. This will have the effect of holding down costs and permitting expanded levels of output. Capital investment may also rise if nonmember nations decide to establish subsidiary operations inside the customs unions to avoid external tariff barriers.

EUROPEAN UNION

In the years immediately after World War II, the countries of Western Europe suffered balance-of-payments deficits in response to reconstruction efforts. To shield its firms and workers from external competitive pressures, they initiated an elaborate network of tariff and exchange restrictions, quantitative controls, and state trading. In the 1950s, however, these trade barriers were generally viewed to be counterproductive. Therefore, Western Europe began to dismantle its trade barriers in response to successful tariff negotiations under the auspices of GATT.

It was against this background of trade liberalization that the European Union (EU), then known as the European Community, was created by the Treaty of Rome in 1957. The EU initially consisted of six nations: Belgium, France, Italy, Luxembourg, the Netherlands, and West Germany. By 1973, the United Kingdom, Ireland, and Denmark had joined the trade bloc. Greece became the tenth member in 1981, and the entry of Spain and Portugal in 1987 raised the membership to 12 nations. In 1995, Austria, Finland, and Sweden were admitted into the EU. Table 9.1 gives an economic profile of the union's members.

PURSUING ECONOMIC INTEGRATION

According to the Treaty of Rome of 1957, the EU agreed in principle to follow the path of economic integration and eventually become an economic union. In pursuing this goal, members of the EU first dismantled tariffs and established a free-trade area by 1968. This liberalization of trade was accompanied by a fivefold increase in

[2] Nicholas Owen, *Economies of Scale, Competitiveness, and Trade Patterns Within the European Community* (New York: Oxford University Press, 1983), pp. 119–139.

Table 9.1 European Union: Economic Profile, 1998

Country	Population (Millions)	Area (Thousands of Sq. Km)	Per Capita Gross National Product* (Dollars)
Austria	8.1	84	22,740
Belgium	10.2	31	23,480
Denmark	5.3	43	23,830
Finland	5.2	338	20,270
France	58.8	552	22,320
Germany	82.1	357	20,810
Greece	10.5	132	13,010
Ireland	3.7	70	18,340
Italy	57.6	301	20,200
Luxembourg	0.5	3	37,420
Netherlands	15.7	37	21,620
Portugal	10.0	92	14,380
Spain	39.3	505	16,060
Sweden	8.9	450	19,480
United Kingdom	59.1	245	20,640

*At purchasing power parity.

Source: The World Bank, *World Development Report 1999–2000*. See also The World Bank, *World Bank Atlas*.

the value of industrial trade—higher than world trade, in general. The success of the free-trade area inspired the EU to continue its process of economic integration. In 1970, the EU became a full-fledged customs union when it adopted a common external tariff system for its members.

Several studies have been conducted on the overall impact of the EU on its members' welfare during the 1960s and 1970s. In terms of static welfare benefits, one study concluded that trade creation was pronounced in machinery, transportation equipment, chemicals, and fuels, whereas trade diversion was apparent in agricultural commodities and raw materials.[3] The broad conclusion can be drawn that trade creation in the manufactured-goods sector during the 1960s and 1970s was significant: 10 percent to 30 percent of total EU imports of manufactured goods. Moreover, trade creation exceeded trade diversion by a wide margin, estimated at 2 percent to 15 percent. In addition, analysts also noted that

the EU realized dynamic benefits from integration in the form of additional competition and investment and also economies of scale. For instance, it has been determined that many firms in small nations, such as the Netherlands and Belgium, realized economies of scale by producing both for the domestic market and for export. However, after becoming members of the EU, sizable additional economies of scale were gained by individual firms, reducing the range of products manufactured and increasing the output of the remaining products.[4]

After forming a customs union, the EU made little progress toward becoming a common market until 1985. The hostile economic climate (recession and inflation) of the 1970s led EU members to shield their people from external forces rather than dismantle trade and investment restrictions. By the 1980s, however, EU

[3] Mordechai E. Kreinin, *Trade Relations of the EEC: An Empirical Approach* (New York: Praeger, 1974), Chapter 3.

[4] Richard Harmsen and Michael Leidy, "Regional Trading Arrangements," in International Monetary Fund, World Economic and Financial Surveys, *International Trade Policies: The Uruguay Round and Beyond, Volume II*, 1994, p. 99.

members were increasingly frustrated with barriers that hindered transactions within the bloc. European officials also feared that the EU's competitiveness was lagging behind that of Japan and the United States.

In 1985, the EU announced a detailed program for becoming a common market. Plans called for the elimination of remaining nontariff trade barriers to intra-EU transactions by 1992. Examples of these barriers included border controls and customs red tape, divergent standards and technical regulations, conflicting business laws, and protectionist procurement policies of governments. The elimination of these barriers resulted in the formation of a European common market and turned the trade bloc into the second largest economy in the world, almost as large as the U.S. economy.

While the EU was becoming a common market, its heads of government agreed to pursue much deeper levels of integration. Their goal was to begin a process of replacing their central banks with a European Central Bank and replacing their national currencies with a single European currency (the euro). The **Maastricht Treaty**, signed in 1991, set January 1, 1999, as the date at which this process would begin. A full-fledged monetary union would emerge at the completion of this process.

When the Maastricht Treaty was signed, economic conditions in the various EU members differed substantially. The treaty specified that to be considered ready for monetary union, a country's economic performance would have to be similar to the performance of other members. Countries cannot, of course, pursue different rates of money growth, have different rates of economic growth, and different rates of inflation while having currencies that don't move up or down relative to each other. So the first thing the Europeans had to do was align their economic and monetary policies.

This effort, called *convergence*, has led to a high degree of uniformity in terms of price inflation, money supply growth, and other key economic factors. The specific **convergence criteria** as mandated by the Maastricht Treaty are as follows:

- **Price stability.** Inflation in each prospective member is supposed to be no more than 1.5 percent above the average of the inflation rates in the three countries with lowest inflation rates
- **Low long-term interest rates.** Long-term interest rates are to be no more than 2 percent above the average interest rate in those countries
- **Stable exchange rates.** The exchange rate is supposed to have been kept within the target bands of the monetary union with no devaluations for at least two years prior to joining the monetary union
- **Sound public finances.** One fiscal criterion is that the budget deficit in a prospective member should be at most 3 percent of GDP; the other is that the outstanding amount of government debt should be no more than 60 percent of a year's GDP.

In 1999, 11 of the EU's 15 members fulfilled the economic tests as mandated by the Maastricht Treaty and became the founding members of the **European Monetary Union (EMU)**. Greece was keen on joining, but had to wait until it could pass the economic tests. Only Britain, Sweden, and Denmark decided not to participate in EMU at this time.

An important motivation for EMU was the momentum it provides for political union, a long-standing goal of many European policy makers. France and Germany took the initiative towards EMU. Monetary union was viewed as an important way to anchor Germany securely in Europe. Moreover, it provided the French a larger role in determining monetary policy for Europe, which they would achieve with a common central bank. Prior to EMU, Europe's monetary policy was mainly determined by the German Bundesbank.

THE EMU PRESENTS DIFFERENT FACES TO PORTUGAL AND SWEDEN The year 1999 marked the advent of the historic EMU. European economies had to meet strict monetary and fiscal criteria before joining. Although Portugal and Sweden both met these criteria, only Portugal decided to exercise its option to become a member of the EMU. Consider the differing views of the two countries.[5]

In Lisbon, businessman Jorge Cruz Morais explains why Portugal supports the European Monetary Union (EMU). "We have to be in the first boat," he says. "If monetary union started without us, we'd fall off the map." In Stockholm, however, economist Roland Spant explains why Sweden shouldn't participate. "It is a giant step into the unknown," he says. "It's like jumping from the Empire State Building and inventing the parachute on the way down."

Situated at the opposite extremes of Europe, the countries of Portugal and Sweden were at the opposite ends of the debate over the EMU prior to its inception in 1999. Portugal wanted to be part of the common currency; Sweden wanted to stay out. Indeed, depending on whose eyes it was viewed through, EMU either meant Europe's boldest postwar move toward closer units or a major gamble with clear advantages but also significant risks.

It is easy to understand Portugal's preference for further European integration. Until its dictatorship disintegrated in the early 1970s, Portugal was long ostracized by Europe, and it looked for a place in the world. When Portugal joined the European Union in the 1980s, the move was not motivated only by economics: It was also an attempt to gain respectability. By the 1990s, Portugal feared that exclusion from the EMU would cause it to be an outsider once again. Another reason for membership was that prior to 1999, Portugal received a significant portion of funds paid to the European Union by member nations for infrastructure and other projects, far more than it paid in. Also, Portugal's exports to fulfill the strict monetary and fiscal criteria to qualify for the euro brought interest rates down sharply in the 1990s. This produced a boom rather than the pain felt in other European countries, and Portugal looked to EMU to lock in fiscal discipline.

On the downside, some business leaders felt that Portuguese industry was not fully prepared for the post-EMU onslaught of competition. Although Portugal had relatively low labor costs in 1997, they could boomerang into a big risk: A common currency could unleash a wave of demands by Portuguese workers for wages that would equal average European wages. However, the productivity of the average Portuguese was half that of the average German worker. Higher wages would thus result in relatively higher production costs for many Portuguese firms and a loss of competitiveness.

Although Sweden qualified for the common currency with flying colors, it decided not to join. The reason lay partly in Sweden's historic preference for neutrality with regard to the rest of Europe. Also, Sweden's decision to join the European Union in 1995 coincided with budgetary reductions that hurt the country's welfare state. Many Swedes thus associated the European Union with hardship and felt that monetary union could only make things worse by increasing pressure for tax harmonization, thus making it more difficult to finance welfare programs.

Moreover, Swedes maintained that by linking itself into a common currency, Sweden could no longer use a floating exchange to compensate for its high wage costs—and with a jobless rate of more than 12 percent, this might further increase unemployment. Finally, Swedish business leaders felt that such key domestic industries as mining, paper, and pulp were more sensitive to the dollar than to European currencies, so Sweden needed to retain monetary sovereignty to be able to react to events across the Atlantic ocean.

Most important, Swedes argued that Europe simply was not prepared for a monetary union. They contended that Europe, unlike the United States, was not a homogeneous market: Its economic structures and cycles were too different to justify tying the countries into a rigid arrangement. Put simply, it was not workable to have 15 governments and one central bank. If Italy has 6-percent inflation and Germany 1 percent, what should the European Central Bank do?

Indeed, both Portugal and Sweden had good reasons to join the EMU, and good reasons not to join. Their decisions involved balancing things that could not be measured as well as broad political goals. Later in this chapter, we will consider the economic costs and benefits of a common currency as applied to the European Monetary Union.

AGRICULTURAL POLICY

Besides providing for free trade in industrial goods among its members, the EU has abolished restrictions on agricultural products traded internally. A **common agricultural policy** has replaced the agricultural-stabilization policies of individual member nations, which differed widely before the formation of the EU. A substantial element of the common agricultural policy has been the support of prices received by farmers for their produce. Schemes involving deficiency payments, output controls, and direct income payments have been used for this purpose. In addition, the common agricultural policy has supported EU farm prices through a system of **variable levies**, which applies tariffs to agricultural imports entering the EU. Exports of any surplus quantities of EU produce have been assured through the adoption of **export subsidies**.

One problem confronting the EU's price-support programs is that agricultural efficiencies differ among EU members. Consider the case of grains. German farmers, being high-cost producers, have sought high support prices to maintain their existence. The more efficient French farmers do not need as high a level of support prices as the Germans do to keep them in operation; nevertheless, French farmers have found it in their interest to lobby for high price supports. In recent years, high price supports have been applied to products such as beef, grains, and butter. The common agricultural policy has thus encouraged inefficient farm production by EU farmers and has restricted food imports from more efficient nonmember producers. Such trade diversion has been a welfare-decreasing effect of the EU.

VARIABLE LEVY. Figure 9.2 illustrates the operation of a system of variable levies and export subsidies. Assume that S_{EU_0} and D_{EU_0} represent the EU's supply and demand schedules for wheat and that the world price of wheat equals $3.50 per bushel. Referring to Figure 9.2(a), assume that the EU wishes to guarantee its high-cost farmers a price of $4.50 per bushel. This price cannot not be sustained as long as imported wheat is allowed to enter the EU at the free-market price of $3.50 per bushel. Suppose the EU, to validate the support price, initiates a variable levy. Given an import levy of $1 per bushel, EU farmers are permitted to produce 5 million bushels of wheat, as opposed to the 3 million bushels that would be produced under free trade. At the same time, the EU imports total 2 million bushels instead of 6 million bushels.

Suppose now that, owing to increased productivity overseas, the world price of wheat falls to $2.50 per bushel. Under a variable-levy system, the levy is determined daily and equals the difference between the lowest price on the world market and the support price. The sliding-scale nature of the variable levy results in the EU's increasing its import tariff to $2 per bushel. The support price of wheat is sustained at $4.50, and EU production and imports remain unchanged. EU farmers are thus insulated from the consequences of variations in foreign supply. Should EU wheat production decrease, the import levy could be reduced to encourage imports. EU consumers would be protected against rising wheat prices.

The variable import levy tends to be more restrictive than a fixed tariff. It discourages foreign producers from absorbing part of the tariff and cutting prices to maintain export sales. This would only trigger higher variable levies. For the same reason, variable levies discourage foreign producers from subsidizing their exports in order to penetrate domestic markets.

EXPORT SUBSIDY. The EU has also used a system of export subsidies to ensure that any surplus agricultural output will be sold overseas. The high price supports of the common agricul-

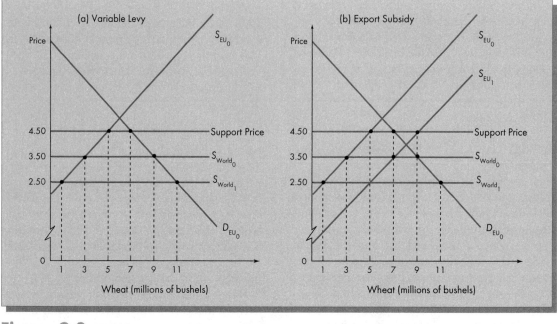

Figure 9.2 Variable Levies and Export Subsidies

The common agricultural policy of the EU has used variable levies to protect EU farmers from low-cost foreign competition. During periods of falling world prices, the sliding-scale nature of the variable levy results in automatic increases in the EU's import tariff. Export subsidies have also been used by the EU to make its agricultural products more competitive in world markets.

tural policy have given EU farmers the incentive to increase production, often in surplus quantities. But the world price of agricultural commodities has generally been below the EU price. The EU pays its producers export subsidies so they can sell surplus produce abroad at the low price but still receive the higher, international support price.

In Figure 9.2(b), let the world price of wheat be $3.50 per bushel. Suppose that improving technologies result in a shift in the EU supply schedule from S_{EU_0} to S_{EU_1}. At the internal support price, $4.50, EU production exceeds EU consumption by 2 million bushels. To facilitate the export of this surplus output, the EU provides its producers an export subsidy of $1 per bushel. EU wheat would be exported at a price of $3.50, and EU producers would receive a

price (including the subsidy) of $4.50. The EU export subsidies are also characterized by a sliding scale. Should the world price of wheat fall to $2.50, the $4.50 support price would be maintained through the imposition of a $2 export subsidy.

The EU's policy of assuring a high level of income for its farmers has been costly. High support prices for products including milk, butter, cheese, and meat have led to high internal production and low consumption. The result has often been huge surpluses that must be purchased by the EU to defend the support price. To reduce these costs, the EU has sold surplus produce in world markets at prices well below the cost of acquisition. These subsidized sales have met with resistance from farmers in other countries.

Virtually every industrial country subsidizes its agricultural products. As seen in Table 9.2, government programs accounted for 42 percent of the value of agricultural products in the EU in 1998. This amount is even higher in certain countries such as Japan, but it is much lower in others, including the United States, Australia, and New Zealand. Countries with relatively low agricultural subsidies have criticized the high-subsidy countries as being too protectionist.

URUGUAY ROUND MODIFICATIONS. The completion of the Uruguay Round of trade negotiations in 1994 brought rules to bear on the use of export subsidies and variable levies. Industrial nations were required to cut their spending on export subsidies by 36 percent over six years. At the same time, subsidized export quantities had to be reduced at least 21 percent on a commodity-specific basis. The few developing nations that subsidized exports had until 2005 to cut spending by 24 percent and subsidized quantities by 14 percent. The percentage reductions were taken from each nation's average subsidy levels during the years 1986 to 1990. The Uruguay Round also required that all nontariff import barriers, includ-ing variable levies, be converted to bound (fixed) tariffs over the period 1995 to 2000. This action eliminated the sliding-scale nature of the EU's system of protection against agricultural imports.

GOVERNMENT PROCUREMENT POLICIES

Another sensitive issue confronting the EU has been government procurement policies. Governments are major purchasers of goods and services, ranging from off-the-shelf items such as paper and pencils to major projects such as nuclear power facilities and defense systems. Government procurement has been used by EU nations to support national and regional firms and industries for several reasons: (1) national security (for example, aerospace); (2) compensation for local communities near environmentally damaging public industries (such as nuclear fuels); (3) support for emerging high-tech industries (for example, lasers); and (4) politics (as in assistance to highly visible industries, such as automobiles).

Although there may be sound justifications for purchasing locally, by the 1980s it was widely recognized that EU public procurement policies served as formidable barriers to foreign competitors; individual EU nations permitted only a minor fraction, often about 2 percent, of government contracts to be awarded to foreign suppliers. By downplaying intra-EU competition, governments paid more than they should for the products they needed and, in so doing, supported suboptimal producers within the community.

When the EU became a common market in 1992, it removed discrimination in government procurement by permitting all EU competitors to bid for public contracts. The criteria for awarding public contracts are specified as either the lowest price or the most economically advantageous tender that includes such factors as product quality, delivery dates, and reliability of supplies.

It was believed that savings from a more competitive government procurement policy would come from three sources: (1) EU governments would be able to purchase from the cheapest foreign suppliers (static trade effect). (2) Increased

Table 9.2	Government Support for Agriculture, 1997

Country	Producer-Subsidy Equivalents* as a Percent of Farm Prices
Australia	9
Canada	20
European Union	42
Japan	69
New Zealand	3
United States	16
OECD Average	**35**

*The producer-subsidy equivalent represents the total assistance to producers in the form of market price support, direct payments, and transfers that indirectly benefit producers.

Source: Organization of Economic Cooperation and Development (OECD), *Agricultural Policies in OECD Countries 1998*, Paris. See also "Producer Price Equivalents" at Internet site http://www.maf.govt.nz/MAFnet/publications/sonzaf98/agstats9.htm.

competition would occur as domestic suppliers decreased prices to compete with foreign competitors that had previously been shut out of the home market (competition effect). (3) Industries would be restructured over the long run, permitting the surviving companies to achieve economies of scale (restructuring effect).

These three sources of savings are illustrated in Figure 9.3, which represents public procurement of computers. Suppose a liberalized procurement policy permits the British government to buy computers from the cheapest EU supplier, assumed to be Germany. The result is a reduction in average costs from $AC_{U.K.}$ to AC_G. At the same time, increased competition results in falling prices and decreased profit margins. At an output of 10,000 computers, unit prices are reduced from \$10,000 to \$7,000, and profit margins

from $Profit_0$ to $Profit_1$. What's more, exploitation of economies of scale gives rise to further decreases in unit costs and prices, as output expands from 10,000 to 25,000 computers along cost schedule AC_G.

It is estimated that liberalizing government procurement markets has generated savings of 0.5 percent of EU gross domestic product. In the process, some 350,000 additional jobs have been created. The price savings from open competition (trade and competition effects) are estimated at 40 to 50 percent for pharmaceuticals in Germany and the United Kingdom; 60 to 70 percent for telecommunications equipment in Germany and Belgium; and about 10 percent for automobiles in the United Kingdom and Italy. In sectors where companies were too small to compete internationally, additional savings arose from mergers

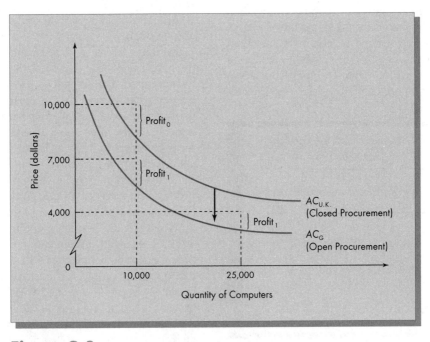

Figure 9.3 Opening Up of Government Procurement

Procurement liberalization allows the U.K. government to import computers from Germany, the low-cost EU producer. Cost savings result from the trade effect, the competition effect, and the restructuring (economies-of-scale) effect.

that resulted in a smaller number of EU companies able to exploit economies of scale. Examples included electric locomotives, turbine generators, and boilers, where decreases in units of costs of 12 to 20 percent were possible.[6]

ECONOMIC COSTS AND BENEFITS OF A COMMON CURRENCY: THE EUROPEAN MONETARY UNION

As we have learned, the formation of the EMU in 1999 resulted in the creation of a single currency (the euro) and a European Central Bank. Switching to a new currency is extremely difficult. Just imagine the task if each of the 50 U.S. states had its own currency and its own central bank, and then had to agree with the other 49 states on a single currency and a single financial system. That's exactly what the Europeans have done.

The European Central Bank is located in Frankfurt, Germany, and is responsible for the monetary policy and exchange-rate policy of the EMU. The European Central Bank alone controls the supply of euros, sets the short-term euro interest rate, and maintains permanently fixed exchange rates for the member countries. With a common central bank, the central bank of each participating nation performs operations similar to those of the 12 regional Federal Reserve Banks in the United States.

How is the value of the euro set? There are fixed conversion rates between the national currencies of the 11 members of the EMU and the euro. Between January 1, 1999, and June 30, 2002, one euro will be equivalent to the following amounts of each of the 11 currencies:

[6] European Union, *Public Procurement: Regional and Social Aspects* (Brussels: Commission of the European Communities, July 1989). See also Keith Hartley, "Public Purchasing," in *Economic Policy After 1992*, ed. D. Gowland and S. James (Brookfield, VT: Dartmouth Publishing Co, 1991) pp. 114–125.

Austrian schilling 13.7603
Belgian franc 40.3399
Finnish markka 5.94573
French franc 6.55957
German mark 1.95583
Irish punt 0.787564
Italian lire 1936.27
Luxembourg franc 40.3399
Netherlands guilder 2.20371
Portuguese escudo 200.482
Spanish pesata 166.386

In this basket of currencies, a German mark is a bit over half a euro. This reflects the economic and political importance of Germany relative to the 11 member countries.

In the transition period—January 1, 1999, to December 31, 2001—a consumer can use the euro for noncash transactions, but euro notes and coins will not yet circulate. To buy something with euros during the transition period, a consumer can use a credit card or traveler's check, or she can make an electronic funds transfer or write a check. Euro-denominated bank accounts, credit cards, and traveler's checks have been available since January 1, 1999. By July 1, 2002, national currency notes and coins will be withdrawn from circulation, and only euro notes and coins will circulate as legal tender.

For Americans, the benefits of a common currency are easy to understand. Americans know they can walk into a McDonald's or Burger King anywhere in the United States and purchase hamburgers with dollar bills in their purses and wallets. The same was not true in European countries prior to the formation of the EMU. Because each was a distinct nation with its own currency, a French person could not buy something at a German store without first exchanging his French francs for German marks. This would be like someone from St. Louis having to exchange her Missouri currency for Illinois currency each time she visits Chicago. To make matters worse, because marks and francs floated against each other within a range, the number of marks the French traveler receives today would probably differ from the number he would have received yesterday or tomorrow. On top of exchange-rate uncertainty, the traveler also had to pay a fee to exchange the currency, making a trip across the border a costly proposition indeed. Although the costs to individuals can be limited because of the small quantities of money involved, firms can incur much larger costs. By replacing the various European currencies with a single currency, the euro, the EMU can avoid such costs. Simply put, the euro will lower the costs of goods and services, facilitate a comparison of prices within the EU, and thus promote more uniform prices.

OPTIMUM CURRENCY AREA Much of the analysis of the benefits and costs of a common currency is based on the theory of optimum currency areas.[7] An area is an **optimum currency area** if the additional gains from monetary union exceed the additional costs.

According to the theory of optimum currency areas, there are gains to be had from sharing a currency across countries' boundaries. These gains include more uniform prices, lower transaction costs, greater certainty for investors, and enhanced competition. Also, a single monetary policy, run by an independent central bank, should promote price stability.

However, a single policy can also entail costs, especially if interest-rate changes affect different economies in different ways. Also, the broader benefits of a single currency must be compared against the loss of two policy instruments: an independent monetary policy and the option of changing the exchange rate. Losing these is particularly acute if a country or region is likely to suffer from "asymmetric shocks" that affect it differently from the rest of the single-currency area, because it will no longer be able to respond by adopting a more expansionary monetary policy or adjusting its currency.

Optimum currency theory then considers various reactions to asymmetric shocks, noting three. The first is the mobility of labor: Workers in the affected country must be able and willing to move freely to other countries. The second is the flexibility of prices and wages: The country must be able to adjust these in response to a disturbance. The third is some automatic mechanism for transferring fiscal resources to the affected country.

The theory of optimal currency areas concludes that for a currency area to have the best chance of success, asymmetric shocks should be rare, suggesting that the countries involved should have similar business cycles and similar economic structures. Also, the single monetary policy should affect all the participating countries in the same manner. Moreover, there should be no legal, cultural, or linguistic barriers to labor mobility across borders; there should be wage flexibility; and there should be some system of stabilizing transfers.

It does not take a Ph.D. in economics to realize that none of these conditions is fulfilled in the EMU. There are cyclical and structural differences among member economies, and interest rates operate in different ways. Europe has suffered from several major asymmetric shocks in the 1980s and 1990s, including the unification of Germany and the collapse of Finland's trade with the former Soviet Union. Also, there is little or no labor mobility among the participating nations, and wages are inflexible.

EUROPE AS A SUBOPTIMAL CURRENCY AREA Although Europe may not be an ideal currency area, forming a monetary union has some advantages. A monetary union may improve economic efficiency through lowering transaction costs of exchanging one currency for another. Tourists are familiar with the time and expense of changing one currency into another while traveling in Europe. Eliminating the transaction costs would benefit both consumers and businesses. A single currency would also facilitate genuine comparison of prices within Europe. Another advantage is the elimination of exchange-rate risk; businesses would more readily trade and invest in other European countries if they did not have to consider what the future exchange rate would be. EMU would also stimulate competition and would facilitate the broadening and deepening of European financial markets.

---

[7] The theory of "optimum currency areas" was first analyzed by Robert Mundell, who won the 1999 Nobel Price in Economics. See Robert Mundell, "A Theory of Optimum Currency Areas," *American Economic Review*, Vol. 51, September 1961, pp. 717–725.

The overall magnitudes of these gains appear to be relatively small. The European Commission estimates that savings in transaction costs will be about 0.4 percent of the EU's gross domestic product.[8] Even though small, the efficiency gains are greater the more a country trades with other countries in the monetary union. For example, the Netherlands, whose trade with Germany has typically exceeded 20 percent of its total trade, would benefit considerably by a monetary union with Germany. In contrast, only about 2 percent of the total trade of the Netherlands has typically been with Spain, making the benefits of monetary union with Spain much smaller.

A main disadvantage of EMU is that each participating European country loses the use of monetary policy and the exchange rate as a tool in adjusting to external shocks. If one country experiences a recession, it can no longer relax monetary policy or allow its currency to depreciate to stimulate its economy. The use of fiscal policy, too, may be limited by the need to keep budget deficits under control under EMU. Economic revival depends on wage flexibility and perhaps the ability and willingness of labor to move to new locations. Because wage rigidity in Europe is considerable and labor mobility is low, recovering from a recession could be difficult, leading to political pressure for an eas-

ing of the single monetary policy, or increased government debt of the country in recession.

Are the 15 members of the EU an optimum currency area? In other words, do the microeconomic gains of greater efficiency outweigh the macroeconomic costs of the loss of the exchange rate as an adjustment tool? Several economists have suggested that the costs exceed the gains for the 15 countries as a whole, and thus monetary union is not a good idea for all 15 countries.[9] For a smaller set of countries, however, the gains may exceed the costs, and monetary union makes sense. Trade among the smaller set of countries is much higher than trade with all 15 countries, so that the efficiency gains are higher.

In spite of these problems, countries are preparing to join the EMU. Cyprus, the Czech Republic, Estonia, Hungary, Poland, and Slovenia began detailed entry negotiations with the EMU in 1998 and hope to join in 2003 or soon after. The EMU has worried that its convergence criteria for eruozone entry will deny the relatively poor candidate countries the flexibility needed to rebuild and restructure their economies. However, the candidates see the convergence criteria as a small price to pay for the exchange-rate stability and the low interest rates that come with full entry into the monetary union. Table 9.3 shows the progress these countries made in meeting the convergence criteria in 1999.

[8] Commission of the European Communities, Directorate-General for Economic and Financial Affairs. "One Market, One Money: An Evaluation of the Potential Benefits and Costs of Forming an Economic and Monetary Union," *European Economy*, No. 44, October 1990, p. 11.

[9] Paul DeGrauwe, *The Economics of Monetary Integration* (New York: Oxford University Press, 1994), pp. 89–94.

Table 9.3 Meeting the EMU's Convergence Criteria, 1999

Country	Inflation Rate (Percent)	Government Budget Deficit as a Percent of GDP	Government Debt as a Percent of GDP
EMU Criteria	**3.2**	**3.0**	**60.0**
Cyprus	1.8	6.0	63.5
Czech Republic	2.5	4.9	46.4
Estonia	3.5	0.7	6.0
Hungary	10.0	3.8	60.6
Poland	7.1	2.5	45.3
Slovenia	6.0	0.7	37.0

Source: European Commission, press release. See also International Monetary Fund, *World Economic Outlook*, Washington, DC, October 1999.

EUROPE CAN'T HANDLE THE EURO

In 2000, Martin Feldstein, former chairman of President Reagan's Council of Economic Advisors and now a professor of economics at Harvard, wrote an essay describing why Europe can't handle the euro. Below are his reasons.

When leaders of the 11 European nations that agreed to combine their currencies gathered in 1999, they predicted great things: the single currency would shift global portfolios to euro assets, depressing the value of the dollar relative to the euro, and the new eurozone would be a strong player in the global economy, reflecting the size of an integrated European market. Instead the euro plummeted, Europe's economy remains weak, and unemployment is more than twice the U.S. level.

The European Central Bank (ECB) will be judged by whether it achieves low inflation and does so without increasing cyclical unemployment. I am not optimistic about either part of this goal. Maintaining low inflation will depend on avoiding political pressure to over-expand demand. During the past two decades, Germany has set the standard with virtual price stability, and the other countries of Europe limited demand in order to bring down their inflation rates because a failure to do so meant the embarrassment of devaluing relative to the mark. That discipline will disap-

pear when the mark is gone and each EMU country has a vote on monetary policy.

The ECB must make monetary policy for "Europe as a whole," which in practice means doing what is appropriate for Germany, France, and Italy, the eurozone's three largest countries. Last year, demand conditions in those countries were relatively weak, while demand conditions in Spain and Ireland were very strong. That meant a monetary policy that was too expansionary for Spain and Ireland, causing a substantial acceleration of their inflation and threatening their competitiveness. Such disparities of demand conditions will undoubtedly persist in the future because European countries differ substantially in industrial composition and in a variety of economic policies.

Europeans look to the success of the American economy and mistakenly assume that our single-currency system should work equally well there. But the response to a cyclical fall in demand in a U.S. region is very different from the response in Europe. In the United States, a fall in regional demand leads to lower wages, which help to maintain employment; to movements of labor to regions where demand is stronger; and to a net fiscal transfer from Washington (because lower regional income means lower federal tax liability). None of this

---

CHALLENGES FOR EMU The economic effect of EMU on Europe and on the United States will depend mostly on the policy decisions that are made in Europe in the years ahead. The actual move to a single currency, by itself, will likely have only a relatively small effect.

Perhaps the most important monetary policy challenge for EMU is the ability of the European Central Bank to focus on price stability over the long term. Some are concerned that, over time, monetary policy may become too expansionary, given the large number of countries voting on

monetary policy, and the fact that strong anti-inflationary actions are not well ingrained in countries such as Portugal, Spain, and Italy.

The operation of monetary policy may also present some challenges. If there is wide difference in economic growth rates among EMU countries, it may be difficult to decide on appropriate short-term interest rates. Tightening monetary policy to reduce inflationary pressures may be appropriate for some countries, while loosening monetary policy to stimulate activity may be appropriate for other countries. Therefore, deter-

EUROPE CAN'T HANDLE THE EURO (continued)

happens in Europe, where wages are inflexible, mobility is severely limited by language and custom, and there are no significant fiscal transfers.

Most of today's high unemployment in Europe is not cyclical but structural, reflecting bad welfare policies, bad regulations, and high taxes. The ability to solve these problems should be separate from the monetary arrangement. But the single currency will be a political impediment to reform. Politicians can now blame the ECB for high unemployment and complain that it is a powerful force beyond national control. Instead of seeking to make labor markets more flexible, European governments are talking more about "social wages," about mandatory 35-hour workweeks, and about rolling back even the small reductions in social benefits that Germany achieved under Helmut Kohl's government. Worse yet, there are attempts to eliminate differences in labor practices and even differences in wages among the EMU countries.

This makes Europe even less suited to a single currency and exacerbates the structural problems that keep unemployment so high. Moreover, these policies reduce the international competitiveness of many European industries and encourage the adoption of protec-

tionist policies to keep out non-European products. If labor standards and environmental regulations become acceptable subjects for international trade discussion, it's easy to imagine Europeans arguing that they should not have to compete with American companies that don't give their employees European-level social benefits, have longer working hours, and are subject to less restrictive environmental regulations.

The attempt to achieve Europe-wide policies will itself be a major force of discord within Europe. Forcing a single monetary policy on all of Europe will cause the countries that suffer what they regard as unnecessarily high unemployment to resent the actions of others. Attempts to force a Europe-wide tax system, especially if taxes are used to redistribute incomes among European countries, will compound the potential for conflict.

One way for European governments to create greater unity is to have a common adversary. With the Soviet Union gone, I worry that Europe will come to see the United States in the role—as a politically convenient opponent that can be used to advance the agenda of political and economic unification despite the tensions that it creates among the countries of Europe.

Source: Martin Feldstein, "Europe Can't Handle the Euro," *The Wall Street Journal*, February 9, 2000, p. A–26. Reprinted by permission. All rights reserved.

mining monetary policy for the eurozone as a whole, which the European Central Bank is required to do, may be difficult at times.

Although fiscal policy remains the province of national governments, avoidance of excessive budget deficits is important for the success of EMU. Because large budget deficits can lead to high interest rates and lower economic activity, budgetary restraint is desirable by itself. Most countries had considerable difficulty in reducing budget deficits and debts to meet the convergence criteria of EMU. Cutting government expenditures, especially on well-established social programs, was (and is) politically difficult. In the face

of aging populations in most countries, pressures on budgets may grow even stronger.

Finally, the need for structural reform in European countries presents a challenge for EMU countries. Labor-market flexibility is probably the most important structural issue. Real (inflationary adjusted) wage flexibility in Europe is estimated to be half that of the United States. Moreover, labor mobility is quite low in Europe, not only between countries, but also within them. Incentives to work and to acquire new skills are inadequate. Regulations that limit employers' ability to dismiss workers make them unwilling to hire and train new workers. Also, high taxes and generous unemployment benefits provided by European governments contribute to sluggish economies.

Analysts note that structural reforms are necessary for several reasons. First, they would lower the EU's persistently high structural unemployment rate. Second, firms would provide needed flexibility in adjusting to recessions, especially those that affected one or a few countries in the eurozone. If prices and wages were flexible downward, for example, a decline in demand would be followed by lower prices, tending to raise demand. Increased labor mobility would be particularly useful in adjusting to recessions.

EMU AND THE UNITED STATES

Is EMU good for the United States? At present, the U.S. dollar is by far the most widely used currency in international trade and finance. Many internationally-traded goods, such as oil, are priced, and paid for, in dollars. Bank loans and securities often are denominated in dollars. The dollar's international role is based on the strength of the U.S. economy and financial markets and also the large size of U.S. international trade and investment flows.

Many analysts agree that EMU, if successful, will eventually lead to decline in the dollar's role as an international payments and reserve currency. However, this decline would likely occur slowly, not suddenly, for several reasons. First, the dollar is the predominant currency in Asia and Latin America; it is unlikely the euro will replace the dollar in those areas any time in the near future. Second, the dollar serves as a safe haven at times of political and economic uncertainty. Simply put, European financial markets are unlikely to be transformed overnight; the U.S. financial market will probably remain the most liquid in the world for a long period of time.

Over the years, the U.S. government, which has a strong interest in a prosperous and stable Europe, has supported European efforts at economic integration. The policy on EMU has generally been that if it is good for Europe, it will be good for the United States. And it will be good for Europe if the conditions for sustained economic growth, particularly monetary policy credibility, sustainable fiscal deficits, and structural reforms, are achieved by European governments. If these concerns are addressed, EMU will likely stimulate economic growth and competitiveness in Europe, which should benefit the United States. Since U.S. trade with the eurozone is small relative to the size of the U.S. economy, the effect of EMU on bilateral trade flows is expected to be fairly low.

U.S.–CANADA FREE-TRADE AGREEMENT

The success of Europe in forming the European Union has inspired the United States to launch several regional trade agreements. During the 1980s and early 1990s, the United States negotiated three free-trade agreements: (1) U.S.–Israel Free Trade Agreement of 1985; (2) U.S.–Canada Free Trade Agreement of 1989; and the (3) North American Free Trade Agreement (NAFTA) of 1992, encompassing Mexico, Canada, and the United States. Given the economic importance of Canada and Mexico to the United States, let us consider the last two agreements.

The concept of a U.S.–Canadian free-trade area has a long tradition. During the 1800s and early 1900s, the two nations considered the free-trade issue several times. But because of the exigencies of nation building and apprehensions concerning political sovereignty, the nations maintained restrictionist stances. With the weakening of its position of world leadership by the 1980s, the United States appeared more willing to pursue bilateral trade negotiations with Canada. At the same time, Canada had grown increasingly dependent on the United States. By 1987, Canada exported more than 25 percent of its national output, and more than 73 percent of its exports were destined for the United States. Canadian business leaders also realized the difficulty of achieving economies of large-scale production without assured access to a large market.

These and other concerns led to the negotiation of the **U.S.–Canada Free Trade Agreement,** which became effective in 1989. The agreement, which fell short of establishing completely free trade between the United States and Canada, called for the elimination of all import tariffs and many nontariff barriers over a ten-year period.

CANADIAN ECONOMIES OF SCALE. Because trade between the two nations has been so much more important for Canada than for the United States, most of the theoretical work and empirical studies on the effects of a free-trade agreement have been done on Canada. Proponents of

the U.S.–Canada Free Trade Agreement generally cite economies of large-scale production as a major benefit to Canada, as illustrated in the following example.

Figure 9.4 represents the Canadian auto market, in which Canada is assumed to be a net exporter to the United States. Assume that prior to the elimination of U.S. trade restrictions, the U.S. demand for Canadian autos is $D_{U.S._0}$. Also assume that the Canadian auto demand is D_C. The overall demand schedule is thus denoted by $D_C + D_{U.S._0}$. Economies of scale are denoted in the downward-sloping cost schedule AC. For

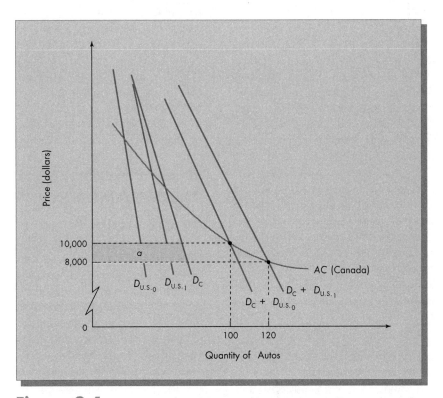

Figure 9.4 Economies of Scale in Canadian Auto Manufacturing: Benefits to Canada of Abolishing U.S. Trade Restrictions

With bilateral free trade, competing U.S. automakers may undercut Canadian manufacturers who maintain prices at $10,000. But longer production runs for Canadian manufacturers, made possible by the opening of the U.S. auto market, can result in cost reductions with economies of scale.

simplicity, assume that Canadian manufacturers price their automobiles at average cost. In the absence of a free-trade agreement, the total number of autos demanded is 100 units, and the price received by Canadian manufacturers is $10,000 per unit.

Under bilateral free trade with the United States, Canadian auto companies encounter a danger and an opportunity. The danger is that competing U.S. manufacturers may undercut Canadian companies that maintain prices at $10,000. But bilateral free trade also provides the Canadian companies an opportunity. The elimination of U.S. trade restrictions results in a shift in the export demand schedule faced by Canadian manufacturers from $D_{U.S._0}$ to $D_{U.S._1}$; thus, the overall demand schedule is now $D_C + D_{U.S._1}$. The total number of autos supplied by Canadian manufacturers increases to 120 units, and the resulting cost reductions permit the price charged by Canadian manufacturers to decrease to $8,000. Economies of large-scale production thus permit Canadian firms to adopt more competitive price policies.

For Canadian consumers, the $2,000 price reduction results in an increase in consumer surplus equal to area *a*, located under demand schedule D_C. Note that the gain to the Canadian consumer does *not* come at the expense of the Canadian manufacturer! The Canadian manufacturer can afford to sell autos at a lower price without any decrease in unit profits because economies of scale lead to reductions in unit costs. Economies of large-scale production therefore can provide benefits for both the producer and the consumer.

A WIN-WIN AGREEMENT. The U.S.–Canada Free Trade Agreement was described as a win-win situation, good for both nations. For Canada, bilateral free trade with the United States raised its real income by an estimated 1 to 3 percent above existing levels. It was also estimated that Canadian production costs would decrease by an average of 2.1 percent because of the exploitation of economies of scale. With bilateral free trade, a number of Canadian industries expanded, including forestry products,

paper, and transportation equipment. Because of increased competition from U.S. firms, a number of Canadian industries contracted: chemicals, electrical equipment, furniture, and miscellaneous manufacturing. The United States was expected to achieve modest economic gains from the free-trade agreement; it was estimated that the gain in U.S. real income would be a small fraction of 1 percent.

Some trade diversion was expected to occur as a result of the free-trade agreement. Canadian exports to the United States and U.S. exports to Canada were expected to expand at the expense of goods from Germany, Japan, and other countries that faced trade restrictions. Welfare losses would exist to the degree that tariff-free partner exports replaced low-cost, third-country exports encumbered by trade restrictions. Because Canada and the United States were each other's most important trading partner, however, and because their average tariff duties were low prior to the pact's implementation, the scope and cost of trade diversion were expected to be modest.[10]

NORTH AMERICAN FREE TRADE AGREEMENT (NAFTA)

The notion of a free-trade agreement negotiated by the United States and Mexico evolved from a distant objective to a reality in a short period of time. In the mid-1980s, Mexico was mired in debt and tied to an interventionist economic policy that limited imports and discouraged foreign participation in the Mexican economy. Realizing that such a policy could not revitalize its economy, by the 1990s Mexico had reduced governmental intervention in the economy and opened its market to foreign goods, services, and investment. This paved the way for the presidents of the two nations to endorse a comprehensive, bilateral free-trade agreement as the best means

---

[10] Canadian Department of Finance, *The Canada–U.S. Free Trade Agreement: An Economic Assessment* (Ottawa: Author, 1989), p. 32.

to strengthen economic relations and meet the challenges of international competition.

Subsequently, Canada, which already had a free-trade agreement with the United States, asked to participate in the negotiations. These trilateral negotiations resulted in a **North American Free Trade Agreement (NAFTA)** that went into effect in 1994.

The establishment of NAFTA was expected to provide each member nation better access to the others' markets, technology, labor, and expertise. In many respects, there were remarkable fits between the nations: The United States would benefit from Mexico's pool of cheap and increasingly skilled labor, while Mexico would benefit from U.S. investment and expertise. However, negotiating the free-trade agreement was difficult because it required meshing two large advanced industrial economies (United States and Canada) with that of a sizable developing nation (Mexico). The huge living-standard gap between Mexico, with its miserable wage scale and booming population, and the United States and Canada was a politically sensitive issue.

NAFTA's Benefits for Mexico and Canada

NAFTA's benefits to Mexico would be proportionately much greater than for the United States and Canada, because Mexico would be integrating with economies many times larger than its own. Eliminating trade barriers would presumably lead to increases in the production of goods and services for which Mexico has a comparative advantage. Mexico's gains would come largely at the expense of other low-wage countries, such as Korea, Taiwan, and Ireland. Generally, Mexico would produce more goods that benefit from a low-wage, low-skilled work force, such as fruits, vegetables, processed foods, sugar, tuna, and glass; labor-intensive manufactured exports, such as appliances and economy automobiles, would also increase. A free-trading Mexico, bordering on the world's largest and wealthiest market, would divert the flow of U.S. money and technology that previously had moved to low-cost havens in Asia and Eastern Europe.

Rising investment spending in Mexico would increase wage incomes and employment, national output, and foreign-exchange earnings; it would also facilitate the transfer of technology. Most studies suggested that Mexico's national output would rise between 3 percent and 10 percent as a result of NAFTA. A richer Mexico would demand additional exports from the United States and Canada. However, many Mexicans feared a loss of national sovereignty that might occur by integrating with North American partners that dwarf its economy; they did not wish to become the 51st state of the United States.

Canada's benefits from NAFTA were mostly in the form of safeguards: maintenance of its status in international trade, no loss of its current free-trade preferences in the U.S. market, and equal access to Mexico's market. Canada also desired to become part of any process that would eventually broaden market access to Central and South America. Although Canada hoped to benefit from trade with Mexico in the long run, most researchers predicted relatively small short-run gains because of the small amount of existing Canada–Mexico trade.

NAFTA's Benefits for the United States

NAFTA proponents maintained that the agreement would benefit the U.S. economy overall by expanding trade opportunities, reducing prices, increasing competition, and enhancing the ability of U.S. firms to attain economies of large-scale production. The United States would produce more goods that benefit from large amounts of physical capital and a highly-skilled work force, including chemicals, plastics, cement, sophisticated electronics and communications gear, machine tools, and household appliances. U.S. insurance companies would also benefit from fewer restrictions on foreign insurers operating in Mexico. U.S. companies, particularly larger ones, would get better access to cheaper labor and parts. Moreover, the United States would benefit from a more reliable source of petroleum; less illegal Mexican immigration, as new jobs became available in Mexico and wages increased; and enhanced Mexican political stability as a result of the nation's increasing wealth.

There was an additional benefit of NAFTA for the United States: New rules that give trade benefits only to products with high percentages of North American-made parts would make it unprofitable for Japanese and European multinationals to assemble finished products in Mexico from foreign-made parts. That meant increased investment in U.S. manufacturing facilities by foreigners, creating jobs for U.S. workers.

In spite of these benefits, the overall economic gains for the United States were estimated to be modest, because the U.S. economy was 25 times the size of the Mexican economy and many U.S.–Mexican trade barriers had previously been dismantled. Most studies suggested that U.S. output would increase by no more than 0.1 or 0.2 percent under the free-trade agreement.

U.S. Concerns About NAFTA

But even ardent proponents of NAFTA acknowledged that it would inflict pain on some segments of the U.S. economy. On the business side, the most likely losers would be industries such as citrus growing and sugar that rely on trade barriers to limit imports of low-priced Mexican goods. Other major losers would be unskilled workers, such as those in the apparel industry, whose jobs are most vulnerable to competition from low-paid workers abroad. It was estimated that NAFTA would result in the creation of 240,000 new jobs in the United States, but also in the loss of 110,000 existing jobs as a result of increased Mexican competition.

U.S. labor unions were especially concerned that Mexico's low wage scale would encourage U.S. companies to locate in Mexico, resulting in job losses in the United States. Cities such as Muskegon, Michigan, which has thousands of workers cranking out such basic auto parts as piston rings, appeared especially vulnerable to low-wage Mexican competition. Indeed, the hourly manufacturing compensation for Mexican workers has been a small fraction of that paid to U.S. and Canadian workers, as seen in Table 9.4. Although studies have shown that

wages are not necessarily the driving factor in business-location decisions, the huge disparity between U.S. and Mexican wages could not be ignored.

Another concern was Mexico's environmental regulations, criticized as being less stringent than those of the United States. U.S. labor and environmental activists feared that polluting Mexican plants might cause plants in the United States, which are cleaner but more expensive to operate, to close down. Environmentalists also feared that increased Mexican growth would bring increased air and water pollution. However, NAFTA advocates countered that a more prosperous Mexico would be more able and more willing to enforce its environmental regulations; more economic openness is also associated with production closer to state-of-the-art technology, which tends to be cleaner.

NAFTA was also concerned about domestic-content requirements (rules of origin). Recall that content requirements stipulate the minimum percentage of a product's value that must be produced or transformed domestically. The Big Three

Table 9.4 Hourly Manufacturing Compensation Costs for Production Workers (in U.S. Dollars)

Year	United States	Canada	Mexico
1985	13.01	10.94	1.59
1987	13.52	12.04	1.04
1989	14.32	14.77	1.43
1991	15.58	17.16	1.84
1993	16.51	16.43	2.40
1994	16.86	15.87	2.47
1995	17.20	16.03	1.51*
1996	17.74	16.68	1.53
1998	18.56	15.69	1.83

*From 1994 to 1995, the Mexican peso depreciated against the U.S. dollar from 3.3 pesos per dollar to 6.4 pesos per dollar, thus reducing Mexican labor compensation expressed in dollars.

Source: U.S. Department of Labor, Bureau of Labor Statistics, *Foreign Labor Statistics: Hourly Compensation Costs in U.S. Dollars,* January 2000, at Internet site http://stats.bls.gov/newsrels.htm.

DO DEVELOPED COUNTRIES GAIN FROM TRADE LIBERALIZATION WITH DEVELOPING COUNTRIES?

Potential Winners and Losers in the United States Under Trade with Mexico

	U.S. Winners	U.S. Losers
Potential Effects of Trade Liberalization (Example: NAFTA)	Higher-skill, higher-tech businesses could benefit from reduced trade barriers.	Labor-intensive, lower-wage, import-competing businesses could lose from reduced protections (tariffs) on competing imports.
	Labor-intensive businesses that relocate to Mexico could benefit by reducing production costs.	Workers in import-competing businesses could lose if their businesses close or relocate.
	Domestic businesses that use imports as components in the production process may save on production costs.	
Potential Effects of Trade Liberalization Modified by Worker-Rights Adherence in Mexico	Adherence to worker-rights requirements in Mexico could raise Mexican labor costs, making U.S. exports more competitive in Mexico.	On the other hand, some U.S. firms wanting to relocate to Mexico to save on labor costs could be discouraged from doing so because worker-rights adherence could increase their production costs.
	Consequently, workers in U.S. import-competing business could be under less pressure to either give back wages or have their worker-rights protections threatened.	

Critics of NAFTA maintain that the United States as a *developed country* has little to gain from trade liberalization with Mexico, a *developing country*. Indeed, the income per capita, wage levels, workers' rights, environmental regulations, and other factors differ for the two countries.

Trade liberalization with Mexico tends to result in three groups of *winners* for the United States, as shown in the table. The first group typically consists of higher-skill, higher-tech businesses that produce a given good or service relatively more efficiently and thus more cheaply than their Mexican trading partners can produce it. These are the exporters. The second group is labor-intensive businesses that relocate to Mexico to save on production costs. Theoretically, such businesses could produce in Mexico for both domestic consumption and for export. The third group is U.S. businesses that use imports from Mexico as components in their production processes.

However, liberalized trade with Mexico can impose losses on the United States. In particular, labor-intensive, low-wage, import-competing firms and their workers may lose market share from cheaper imports from Mexico.

How do these conclusions change when worker-rights protections (pertaining to minimum wages, collective bargaining, child labor, and occupational safety and health) are added to a trade agreement? Adherence to worker-rights provisions by Mexico tends to result in an increase in the cost of producing goods in that country. As a result, U.S. exports to Mexico would increase, and workers in the United States would be under less pressure to either give back wages or have their worker-rights provisions threatened. However, U.S. firms would be less inclined to relocate to Mexico because worker-rights adherence could increase their production costs.

auto firms of the United States feared that Japanese companies would assemble Japanese-made parts in Mexico, which would be exported as finished autos to the United States, duty-free. To prevent this practice, NAFTA imposed local-content requirements that ensured that a substantial portion of the value of each auto manufactured in Mexico and exported to the United States would involve North American production.

Proponents of NAFTA viewed it as an opportunity to create an enlarged productive base for the entire region through a new allocation of productive factors that would permit each nation to contribute to a larger pie. However, an increase in U.S. and Canadian trade with Mexico resulting from the reduction of trade barriers under NAFTA would partly displace U.S. and Canadian trade with other nations, including those in Central and South America, the Caribbean, and Asia. Some of this displacement would be expected to result in a loss of welfare associated with trade diversion—the shift from a lower-cost supplier to a higher-cost supplier. But because the displacement was expected to be small, it was projected to have a minor negative effect on the U.S. and Canadian economies.

In order to make the NAFTA treaty more agreeable to a skeptical U.S. Congress, the President negotiated side agreements with Mexico and Canada dealing with environmental and labor issues raised by the pact:

- **Environment.** An agency would be established in Canada to investigate environmental abuses in any of the three countries. Fines or trade sanctions could be levied on countries that failed to enforce their own environmental laws.
- **Labor.** An agency would be established in the United States to investigate labor abuses if two of the three countries agreed. Fines or trade sanctions would be imposed if countries failed to enforce minimum-wage standards, child-labor laws, or worker-safety rules.

The U.S. government also pledged: (1) to spend up to $90 million to retrain and aid workers who lost their jobs because of NAFTA in the first 18 months, (2) to establish a border environmental commission with Mexico that would spend up to $8 billion on various environmental cleanup projects, and (3) to establish a development bank with Mexico that would lend up to $3 billion to aid communities hurt by NAFTA.

NAFTA's Effects After 5½ Years

The North American Free Trade Agreement has been one of the most hotly debated trade pacts in recent history. NAFTA's critics envision U.S. jobs lost in a flood of goods from a country with an average wage about one-tenth that of the United States. Others see NAFTA as a boon to U.S. employment and living standards through greater trade and investment opportunities.

Now that NAFTA is in operation, how has it actually affected trade and employment? Researchers at the Federal Reserve Bank of Dallas have estimated the effects of NAFTA over its first 5½ years of operation, as summarized next.[11]

TRILATERAL TRADE. It is clear that during NAFTA's first 5 years, the agreement's main objective—of increasing trade among the United States, Mexico, and Canada—was met: Trilateral trade was substantially higher in 1999 than in 1993, before the start of the agreement. Concerning U.S.–Mexican trade, U.S. exports grew by 90 percent while imports from Mexico were up 140 percent during this period. Simply put, NAFTA appears to have increased both imports and exports for the two nations according to the principle of comparative advantage. By this criterion, NAFTA has been a success for the United States and Mexico.

Moreover, as overall duties on U.S.–Mexican trade have dropped, this has lowered the average tariff each country applies to goods from the other country. Thus, the average Mexican tariff on U.S. products dropped to 1.6 percent in 1999, down from 10 percent in 1993. The average U.S. tariff on Mexican goods—which, at 4 percent,

---

[11] See Lucinda Vargas, "NAFTA's First Five Years: Part I," *Business Frontier*, Federal Reserve Bank of Dallas, Issue 2, 1999, pp.1–8, and Congressional Research Service, the Library of Congress, *NAFTA: Estimated U.S. Job Gains and Losses by State Over 5½ Years*, February 2, 2000.

was low even before NAFTA—dropped to 0.4 percent in 1999. Because the reduction in the average Mexican tariff on U.S. goods was greater than the reduction in the average U.S. tariff on Mexican goods, the United States has especially benefited from NAFTA.

U.S. trade with Canada also grew during the 1993–1998 period. U.S. exports to Canada showed a 55-percent increase, while U.S. imports from Canada also grew by 56 percent. Notice that because the United States and Canada already had a free-trade agreement when NAFTA started in 1994, the increase in bilateral trade may be attributable to both agreements.

Trade between Canada and Mexico was not significant before NAFTA, but it increased considerably after the agreement's implementation. In 1999, Canada's imports from Mexico were up about 80 percent from their 1993 level, while Canada's exports to Mexico showed an increase of almost 40 percent. Despite these noteworthy increases, however, Canada represented only about 2 percent of Mexico's world trade in 1993 and throughout NAFTA's first 5½ years.

EMPLOYMENT. These days, international trade increasingly takes the form of trade in intermediate products, but the basic gains from trade are unaffected. U.S. firms locate the simpler parts of their production processes in developing countries, while the more sophisticated components are produced at home. For example, 21 months after NAFTA went into effect, the Key Tronic company, a large manufacturer of computer keyboards, laid off 277 workers in Spokane, Washington, as it relocated some of its assembly jobs to a plant in Ciudad Juarez, Mexico. However, Key Tronic's management reported that employment in its Spokane plant actually increased overall because many of the components used in the keyboards are made in Washington, and the lower costs of assembly in Mexico allowed the firm to reduce prices and increase sales.

Has NAFTA destroyed U.S. jobs? Clearly, NAFTA has neither spelled the death of the U.S. workforce, nor has it generated a dramatic increase in the number of jobs. During NAFTA's first 5½ years, approximately 260,000 job losses were certified by the U.S. Department of Labor in more than 1,100 plants as having resulted from increased imports from or plant relocations to Mexico or Canada—see Table 9.5. Of this, about 41 percent were in the apparel and electronics industries. The 260,000 workers covered by certification was relatively small—about three-tenths of total U.S. employment of 132.5 million as of 1999. From another perspective, the average number of jobs created per month between 1991 and 1999 was about 165,000. Also, from 1994 to 1999 the U.S. economy was near, if not at, what economists consider to be full employment, suggesting that displaced workers may have found jobs elsewhere (or dropped out of the labor force). Simply put, what dominates the employment picture in any year are movements in a country's own business cycle, not trade.

Table 9.5   Major U.S. Industries Facing Job Losses Because of Increased Imports from or Plant Relocations to Mexico or Canada, 1994–1999

Industry	Number of Job Losses	Percent of Job Losses
Apparel	73,568	28.3
Electronics	33,684	13.0
Transportation equipment	17,090	6.6
Fabricated metals	15,372	5.9
Textiles	14,150	5.5
Nonelectrical machinery	11,747	4.5
Lumber	9,826	3.8
Scientific instruments	9,433	3.6
Paper products	8,982	3.5
Rubber	7,722	3.0
Leather	7,521	2.9
Other manufacturing	35,171	13.5
Nonmanufacturing	15,352	5.9
	259,618	100

Source: Congressional Research Service, The Library of Congress, *NAFTA: Estimated U.S. Job Gains and Losses by State Over 5½ Years*, February 2, 2000, p. 9.

INVESTMENT. During the NAFTA debate, much concern was expressed that U.S. firms might relocate plants to Mexico to take advantage of its low wages. Others argued that wages are only one factor in the decision to invest abroad. In particular, productivity in most industries in Mexico is lower than in the United States, and Mexico's transportation and infrastructure are not as well developed as those of the United States.

The available data suggest that U.S. direct investment in Mexico is small relative to total U.S. investment. In 1998 (the latest data available), U.S. direct investment in Mexico was only 3 percent of the U.S. direct investment position in all countries. Moreover, U.S. investment in Mexico was less than 1 percent of all U.S. domestic investment in plant and equipment in 1997. This suggests that the investment effect of NAFTA was very small.

POLITICAL ALLY. It is in politics, not economics, that NAFTA has had its biggest impact. The trade agreement has come to symbolize a close and perhaps irreversible embrace between the United States and Mexico. Given the history of hostility between the two countries, this embrace is remarkable. Its cause was the realization by U.S. officials that their chance of curbing the flow of illegal immigrants and illegal drugs would be far greater were their southern neighbors wealthy instead of poor. Put simply, the United States bought itself an ally with NAFTA.

With NAFTA, Mexico's actions towards U.S. exports were sharply different during its 1995 recession than during its financial and economic crisis in the early 1980s. Then, Mexico imposed quotas and duties of up to 100 percent on American products, prompting U.S. exports to Mexico to plunge by 50 percent. It took nearly seven years for U.S. exports to return to their 1981 levels. Despite its worst recession since the 1930s, Mexico continued to lower its tariffs on U.S. and Canadian imports, as NAFTA required, even though it raised tariffs on products from other countries. Thus, although Mexican GDP contracted by more than 6 percent in 1995 when the recession took effect, U.S. exports to Mexico recovered in 18 months to reach record levels.

U.S. exports dropped only 9 percent in 1995, compared to a 25-percent drop for Japanese and European exports to Mexico.

In short, NAFTA is not the solution to all the economic problems of North America, but it is not the disaster that critics claimed it would be.

FREE TRADE AREA OF THE AMERICAS

Attempting to widen the scope of North American economic integration, in 1994 the United States convened the Summit of the Americas, which was attended by 34 nations in North and South America. The cornerstone of the conference was a call for the creation of a **Free Trade Area of the Americas** (FTAA) by 2005. This would create a market of more than 850 million consumers with a combined income of more than $13 trillion. It also would level the playing field for U.S. exporters who, in the mid-1990s, faced trade barriers more than $3\frac{1}{2}$ times higher those of the United States. The United States tangibly demonstrated its commitment to this objective by announcing that it, along with its NAFTA partners, Canada and Mexico, would initiate negotiations with Chile on accession to NAFTA. The inclusion of Chile would increase the total population of NAFTA to 381 million and its combined income to 30 percent of the world's total. The FTAA would attempt to expand its membership to include 34 nations that would stretch from northern Canada to the southern tip of Chile. It would also tie together the various regional trade agreements that exist throughout the Americas, as shown in Table 9.6.

Over the past two decades, Latin America has embraced progressively more open trade policies, intraregionally and with the world, as part of its overall economic platform. The larger economies of Latin America, once known for their collective indebtedness, are considered among the more promising emerging markets for trade and investment opportunities now in the 2000s. Three economic-policy shifts in Latin America paved the

Table 9.6   Major Western-Hemisphere Regional Trade Agreements

Agreement	Members	Year Effective
Free Trade Area of the Americas	34 countries	Negotiating
North American Free Trade Agreement (NAFTA)	Canada, Mexico, United States	1994
Southern Cone Common Market (MERCOSUR)	Argentina, Brazil, Paraguay, Uruguay	1991
Caribbean Community and Common Market	Antigua, Bahamas, Barbados, Barbuda, Belize, Dominica, Grenada, Guyana, Haiti, Jamaica, Montserrat, St. Kitts, Nevis, St. Lucia, St. Vincent, Surinam, Trinidad, and Tobago	1973
Andean Community	Bolivia, Colombia, Ecuador, Peru, Venezuela	1969
Central American Common Market	Costa Rica, El Salvador, Guatemala, Honduras, Nicaragua	1961

way for this new perspective: (1) reduced roles for government in managing the economies, with greater reliance placed on markets, private ownership, and deregulation; (2) use of conventional and generally restrictive macroeconomic policies to promote economic growth and stability; and (3) the movement away from protectionism, often by way of unilateral reductions in tariffs and other trade barriers.

In spite of these policy shifts, U.S. trade policy is squarely at a crossroads regarding whether—and if so, how—to proceed formally with an FTAA. Trade-policy debates have been contentious in the aftermath of NAFTA and the turbulent fallout from Mexico's 1994 peso devaluation. Also, issues raised by labor, environmental groups, and import-competing industries, which were central to the NAFTA debate, continue to be concerns in the FTAA context.

ASIA–PACIFIC ECONOMIC COOPERATION

Since 1989, the United States has been a member of **Asia–Pacific Economic Cooperation (APEC)**, which also includes Australia, Brunei, Canada, Chile, China, Indonesia, Japan, Malaysia, Mexico, New Zealand, Papua New Guinea, the Philippines, Singapore, South Korea, Taiwan, and Thailand. In 1993, leaders of the APEC countries put forth their vision of an Asia–Pacific economic community in which barriers to trade and investment in the region would be eliminated by the year 2020. All countries would begin to liberalize at a common date, but the pace of implementation would take into account the differing levels of economic development among APEC economies: The industrialized countries would achieve free trade and investment no later than 2010, and the developing economies no later than 2020. Table 9.7 shows the tariff rates of Asia–Pacific Economic Cooperation Members.

REGIONAL INTEGRATION VERSUS MULTILATERALISM

Traditionally, economists have expressed concerns that increasing the emphasis on regional integration might detract from multilateralism. Are regional trading arrangements building blocks or stumbling blocks to a multilateral trading system?

Table 9.7	Tariff Rates of Asia–Pacific Economic Cooperation Members

Country	Tariff Rate
Australia	6.1%
Brunei	2.0
Canada	6.7
Chile	10.9
China	23.0
Chinese Taipei (Taiwan)	8.6
Indonesia	13.1
Japan	9.0
Malaysia	9.0
Mexico	12.5
New Zealand	7.0
Philippines	15.6
Singapore	0.0
South Korea	7.9
Thailand	17.0
United States	6.4

Source: Office of the U.S. Trade Representative, *Foreign Trade Barriers*, Washington, DC, Government Printing Office, 1999.

Trade liberalization under a regional trading arrangement is very different from the multilateral liberalization embodied in the World Trade Organization. Under regional trading arrangements, nations reduce trade barriers only for a small group of partner nations, thus discriminating against the rest of the world. Under the World Trade Organization, trade liberalization by any one nation is extended to all WTO members (more than 135 nations) on an unconditional most-favored-nation basis; here, there is essentially no discrimination.

In general, regional trading blocs that decrease the discretion of member nations to pursue trade liberalization with outsiders are more likely to become stumbling blocks to multilateralism. For example, members of a customs union or common market are unable either to negotiate tariff reductions with nonmembers individually or to reduce external tariffs unilaterally. Moreover, as a regional trade bloc expands, its bargaining power in international negotiations and its market power

in international commerce grows, especially if it imposes a common external tariff. The trade bloc may thus consider it beneficial to increase barriers to outsiders, raising a stumbling block to multilateral trade liberalization.

Two other factors suggest that the members of a regional trading arrangement may not be greatly interested in global liberalization. First, trade-bloc members may not realize additional economies of scale from global trade liberalization, which often provides only modest opening of foreign markets. Regional trade blocs, which often provide more extensive trade liberalization, may allow domestic firms sufficient production runs to exhaust scale economies. Second, trade-bloc members may want to invest their time and energy in establishing strong regional linkages rather than invest them in global negotiations. That was true for the European Union in the 1980s, when it wanted to complete the common-market stage of integration and considered the Uruguay Round of multilateral trade negotiations to be of secondary importance.

Proponents of regional trading arrangements maintain that blocs of nations with many similar interests are more likely to liberalize trade dramatically than the large, heterogeneous groups of nations involved in multilateral negotiations. That may be true. Keep in mind, however, that regional trading arrangements may be beneficial or harmful to their members as well as to outsider nations; a regional trading arrangement is unlikely to be beneficial unless it has significant trade-creating effects.

When structured according to principles of openness and inclusiveness, regional blocs can be building blocks rather than stumbling blocks for global free trade and investment. There are several ways in which regional blocs can foster global market opening. First, regional agreements may achieve deeper economic integration among members than do multilateral accords, because of greater commonality of interests and simpler negotiating processes. Second, a self-reinforcing process is set in place by the establishment of a free-trade area: As the market encompassed by a free-trade area enlarges, it becomes increasingly attractive for nonmembers to join to receive the same trade preferences as member nations. Third, regional liberalization encourages partial adjustment of workers out of import-competing industries in which the nation's comparative advantage is weak and into exporting industries in which its comparative advantage is strong. As adjustment proceeds, the portion of the labor force that benefits from liberalized trade rises, and the portion that loses falls; this promotes political support for trade liberalization in a self-reinforcing process. For all of these reasons, when regional agreements are formed according to principles of openness, they tend to overlap and expand, thus promoting global free trade from the bottom up.

THE TRANSITION ECONOMIES

Trade preferences have also been extended to commercial and financial practices involving nations making the transition from a centrally planned economy to a market economy; such economies are known as the **transition economies**. Prior to the economic reforms in

Eastern European nations in the 1990s, these nations were classified as nonmarket economies; the Western nations, including the United States, were classified as market economies. Table 9.8 shows the GDP per capita for the transition economies as of 1998. Let us consider the major features of these economic systems.

In a **market economy**, the commercial decisions of independent buyers and sellers acting in their own interest govern both domestic and international trade. Market-determined prices value alternatives and allocate scarce resources. This means that prices play rationing and signaling roles that make the availability of goods consistent with buyer preferences and purchasing power.

In a **nonmarket economy** (one that is centrally planned), there is less regard for market considerations. State planning and control govern foreign and sometimes domestic trade. The central plan often controls the prices and output of goods bought and sold, with small recognition given to considerations of cost and efficiency. The state fixes prices to ration arbitrary quantities among buyers, and these prices are largely insulated from foreign-trade influences. Given these different pricing mechanisms, trade between market economies and

Table 9.8   GNP per Capita* for the Transition Economies, 1998

Former Republics of the Soviet Union		Central and Eastern European Countries	
Estonia	$6,050	Slovenia	$12,890
Latvia	4,950	Czech Republic	8,190
Belarus	4,610	Hungary	7,500
Lithuania	4.310	Croatia	7,500
Russia	3,950	Poland	6,740
Kazakstan	3,400	Slovakia	6,620
Uzbekistan	2,790	Romania	3,970
Ukraine	2,680	Former Yugoslav Republic of Macedonia	3,660
Kyrgyz Republic	2,200	Bulgaria	3,120
Azerbaijan	1,820	Albania	2,320
Armenia	1,660	Boznia-Herzegovina	390
Moldova	1,480		
Tajikistan	1,350		

*At purchasing power parity.

Source: The World Bank Group, *Development Data*, http://www.worldbank.org/data. See also World Bank, *World Development Report*.

centrally planned economies can be difficult. Because market-determined prices underlie the basis for trade according to the theory of comparative advantage, the theory has little to say about how nonmarket economies carry out their international trade policies.

The nonmarket nations of Eastern Europe and Asia historically have experienced only modest trade flows with the Western world. By the 1970s and 1980s, however, the nonmarket nations were increasingly looking to Western markets. In terms of the volume and composition of East–West trade, Western Europe has accounted for the largest share, whereas the U.S. share has been minor. Political considerations largely explain the small amount of U.S. trade with the East. The United States historically has placed controls on strategic exports of technology and goods to communist countries; it has also imposed restrictions on the credit terms extended to them.

What are some of the major issues currently affecting East–West trade? Among the most important are financing limitations and industrial cooperation, each of which will be discussed in turn.

FINANCING LIMITATIONS Throughout the 1980s and 1990s, the Eastern European nations have run up significant trade deficits with the West. The basic problem has been that the Eastern European countries cannot increase their exports commensurate with the rise in their imports. Eastern European imports must be paid for either with hard currency generated from the exports of goods and services or by the accumulation of debt. Loans from Western banks and governments have financed many Eastern European deficits.

One major impediment that Eastern European countries face in obtaining financing for imports from the United States is the absence of U.S. government credit. Most lending has come from commercial banks instead of the government's export institutions—the Export–Import Bank and the Commodity Credit Corporation.

East–West trade is also limited by legal lending restrictions on the amount of commercial bank funds available to finance exports. Another check is the Johnson Debt Default Act of 1934, which prevents U.S. institutions from making additional loans to foreign governments that are in default on debt obligations to the U.S. government.

INDUSTRIAL COOPERATION Until recently, East–West trade was relatively simple: Exports to and imports from Eastern European countries were settled in hard currency or credit. But with the expansion of East–West trade has come *countertrade*, which establishes a greater degree of interdependence between the private corporations of Western economies and the state enterprises of the Eastern European countries.

Countertrade refers to all international trade in which goods are exchanged for goods—a kind of barter. If swapping goods for goods sounds less efficient than using cash or credit, that's because it is. During tough economic times, however, shortages of hard currency and tight credit can hinder East–West trade. Instead of facing the possibility of reduced foreign sales, Western producers have viewed countertrade as the next best alternative.

Many Western nations conduct countertrade with the Eastern European countries, as shown in Table 9.9. In the United States, General Motors, Sears, and General Electric have established trading companies that conduct countertrade. A simple form of countertrade occurs when an Eastern European country agrees to pay for the delivery of plant, machinery, or equipment with the goods produced by the plant. For example, Germany has sold Russia steel pipe in exchange for deliveries of natural gas; Austria has supplied Poland with technological expertise and equipment in exchange for diesel engines and truck components. With the opening of the economies of the former Soviet Union, the role of countertrade has diminished in recent years.

Industrial cooperation has also resulted in *coproduction agreements*, by which Western companies establish production facilities in an

Table 9.9 Examples of Eastern European Countertrade Agreements with the West

Western Country (Supplier)	Type of Eastern European Import	Type of Eastern European Export
Germany	Polyethylene plant	Polyethylene
Italy	Detergent plant	Organic chemicals
United States	Fertilizer plant	Ammonia
Japan	Forestry handling equipment	Timber products
United Kingdom	Methanol plant	Methanol
France	Pulp paper plant	Wood pulp
Austria	Large-diameter pipe	Natural gas

Source: U.S. Department of Commerce, International Trade Administration.

Eastern European country. Because most Eastern European countries do not allow foreign ownership of such operations, an agreement is made whereby ownership is held by Eastern European nationals. Coproduction agreements are widely used in the areas of machine building, chemical products, electrical and electronic devices, and pharmaceutical goods.

Industrial cooperation may assume several other forms. Western companies have often made *joint R&D agreements* with Eastern European countries, particularly in industrial processes and technical areas. The findings of such activities are patented jointly, and license royalties are shared between the partners. Also popular are *contract manufacturing agreements*: Western nations supply materials and design specifications to Eastern European enterprises, which produce the goods and ship them back to the Western nations.

The motivations for industrial cooperation vary. For a Western company, such agreements get around the hard-currency scarcities of the Eastern European countries and permit access to the markets of Eastern Europe. Western companies can also tap additional supplies of raw materials and intermediate goods, or possibly maximize revenues by selling obsolete equipment. The Eastern European partner typically views industrial cooperation as a means of obtaining new technologies and expanding industrial capacity with small sacrifices of hard currency.

THE COUNCIL FOR MUTUAL ECONOMIC ASSISTANCE From 1949 to 1991, the communist countries in Eastern Europe attempted to overcome their trade problems with the West by forming their own regional trade bloc, the **Council for Mutual Economic Assistance (CMEA or COMECON)**. CMEA members included the Soviet Union, Bulgaria, Czechoslovakia, East Germany, Hungary, Mongolia, Poland, and Romania. For the Soviet Union, economic integration was a means of exercising economic and political control over other CMEA members; for the more developed member countries, the CMEA was a means of achieving further industrialization and realizing economic gains from trade and cooperation. Because these nonmarket economies usually did not use market-determined prices as a basis for international trade, analysis of the CMEA differs from that of other economic integration schemes.

Trade between Eastern Europe and the Soviet Union was conducted essentially through bilateral barter arrangements governed by the CMEA. The unit of account was the Soviet Union's "transferable ruble," which could not be exchanged for any other currency. Trade was thus conducted at nonmarket prices, and trade surpluses were merely reflected in accumulation of transferable ruble balances. Over time, the effect was to reinforce central planning and make the Eastern European countries and the Soviet Union more dependent on each other. CMEA trade consisted largely of Eastern Europe's receipt of oil and natural gas from the Soviet Union in exchange for manufactured capital goods and consumer goods. CMEA members attempted to keep their trade positions in approximate balance with each other.

The CMEA viewed trade with nonmember countries as a residual. Such trade could occur when intrabloc trade could not produce enough output to meet the needs of CMEA consumers. Rather than viewing international trade as a means of achieving economic gains through specialization, the CMEA considered internal self-sufficiency as a priority. Much of CMEA external trade, like the Soviet grain deals with the West, was induced by events that disrupted domestic production operations or by the lack of technological solutions for problems in such areas as electronics, automobiles, and machine tools.

Under the CMEA, member countries diverted trade away from nonmember countries and toward one another. When the CMEA was established in 1949, member countries conducted only 30 percent of their trade with one another. By the 1980s, this figure exceeded 60 percent for most CMEA countries, suggesting less trade with the outside world. The diversion of trade away from low-cost suppliers outside the CMEA resulted in welfare losses for CMEA members.

Following the political revolutions that swept through Eastern Europe and the Soviet Union between 1989 and 1991, the CMEA was disbanded as member countries shifted to more democratic political systems and more market-oriented economies.

The 1990s brought important changes to trade arrangements between the EU and countries in Eastern Europe and the former Soviet Union. In 1990, the EU concluded an agreement on trade, commercial, and economic cooperation with Russia and other members of the former Soviet Union that gave the latter most-favored-nation status and established a timetable for the removal of general quantitative restrictions on exports to the EU. By 1993, the EU gave Russia and other countries of the former Soviet Union access to the generalized system of preferences (GSP). The EU

also negotiated free-trade agreements with Estonia, Latvia, and Lithuania, providing preferential treatment on imports from these countries. Regional trading arrangements were also being negotiated among Eastern European nations and members of the former Soviet Union.

THE TRANSITION TOWARD A MARKET-ORIENTED ECONOMY In 1989, the world began to witness unprecedented developments in Eastern Europe, as many countries moved toward democracy and economic reform. Countries such as Hungary, Poland, Czechoslovakia, and the Soviet Union discarded their centrally controlled state economies and moved toward systems in which private ownership of property predominated and most resources were allocated through markets. These transitions reflected the failure of central planning systems to provide either political freedom or a decent standard of living.

In 1990, for example, per capita real income in the Soviet Union was less than one-tenth of per capita real income in the United States. Another example is the case of the two Germanys. Starting from the same point at the end of World War II and sharing a common culture, East Germany and West Germany followed two different paths. East Germany became an industrial wasteland with rundown, outmoded factories and a polluted environment, while West Germany achieved one of the highest living standards in the world.

The fundamental motivation for change in Eastern Europe was the failure of the economies there to generate a high standard of living for their people. The economic policies pursued in these countries failed because they were unable to provide adequate incentives for producers to supply efficiently the goods and services that consumers wanted to purchase. Widespread use of price controls, reliance on inefficient public enterprises, extensive barriers to competition with the rest of the world, and government regulation of production and investment all obstructed the normal operation of markets. The lack of enforceable property rights severely restricted incentives for entrepreneurs.

In Eastern Europe, central plans decided production levels. As a result, there was no reason to expect that the output produced would meet the wants or needs of the people. Shortages and surpluses occurred frequently, but managers had little motivation to modify their output as long as quotas were realized. Government investment choices led to underproduction of consumer goods and widespread rationing. Incentives to innovate were almost completely absent, except in the defense sector; but the European countries were unable to transfer their high levels of defense technology into improvements for consumers. Inefficient state-owned enterprises were common, and public funds were channeled into favored industries irrespective of the economic consequences.

Over time, the weaknesses of the political and economic systems of Eastern Europe and the contrasting success of the market-oriented systems became obvious. This created pressure that led to the collapse of Eastern Europe's communist governments.

As the economies of the communist countries deteriorated, piecemeal reforms occurred. Many Eastern European countries attempted to combine economic decentralization with partial price decontrol; however, the removal of price controls has often led to destabilizing bouts of inflation. It was hoped that with reduced central control, state-owned enterprises would operate as if they were part of well-functioning markets. Although national planning objectives were still stipulated, individual firms could establish their own goals and be responsible for production decisions. The system of price controls became more flexible and some small-scale enterprise was allowed. These piecemeal reforms, however, were doomed to failure. Private property rights were generally absent, which limited profit incentives and discouraged entrepreneurship, and state-owned monopolies were maintained. Apparently, widespread economic reforms were needed to revitalize the Eastern European economies.

Economists generally agree that Eastern Europe's transition toward a healthy market economy requires major restructuring of their economies: Sound fiscal and monetary policies must be established, domestic price controls must be removed, economies must be opened to international market forces, private property rights must be established along with a legal system to protect these rights, domestic competition must be promoted, and government's involvement in the economy must be reduced.

Although there is general agreement on what the former communist economies need to do, much debate exists about the sequence and timing of specific reforms. Advocates of *shock therapy* (the "big bang" approach) maintain that the economies in transition should proceed immediately on all fronts. That is, they should privatize, abandon price controls, liberalize trade, develop market institutions, and so on as quickly as possible. Although the initial economic pain may be severe, it will subside as the transition to a market economy leads to rising living standards. Poland and East Germany, starting from different circumstances, are undergoing rapid transformations to a market economy. Although the output and employment costs of the transition have been greater than initially expected, the measures are seen as a basis for a significant improvement in living standards over the longer term.

Advocates of a *gradualist* approach fear that the big-bang approach will cause too great a shock to the economic system and that organizations cannot change so quickly; the initial economic disruptions might create excessive burdens for the people and even lead to a return to the former communist system. Gradualists maintain that the best approach is to build up market institutions, gradually decontrol prices, and privatize only the most efficient government enterprises at first. Hungary, the Czech Republic, and Russia are examples of former communist countries that have adopted more gradual economic reforms. Table 9.10 shows the 2000 Index of Economic Freedom for selected transition economies as well as Hong Kong, Singapore, and the United States. The higher the score factor, the greater the level of government interference in the economy and the less economic freedom.

Table 9.10 Economies in Transition: 2000 Index of Economic Freedom*

Economy	Composite Index	
Hong Kong	1.30	Less Government Interference
Singapore	1.45	
Bahrain	1.80	
United States	1.80	
Estonia	2.20	
Czech Republic	2.20	
Hungary	2.55	
Latvia	2.65	
Poland	2.80	
Romania	3.30	
Bulguria	3.40	
Ukrane	3.60	
Russia	3.70	
Turkmenistan	4.30	
Uzbekistan	4.40	More Government Interference

*Based on ten broad economic factors in 161 economies: trade, taxation, government intervention, monetary policy, foreign investment, banking, wages and prices, property rights, regulation, black market.

Source: The Heritage Foundation, *2000 Index of Economic Freedom Rankings* at Internet site http://www.heritage.org/index.

S U M M A R Y

1. Trade liberalization has assumed two main forms. One involves the reciprocal reduction of trade barriers on a nondiscriminatory basis, as seen in the operation of the World Trade Organization. The other approach involves the establishment by a group of nations of regional trading arrangements among themselves. The European Union and the North American Free Trade Agreement are examples of regional trading arrangements.

2. The term *economic integration* refers to the process of eliminating restrictions on international trade, payments, and factor input mobility. The stages of economic integration are (a) free-trade area, (b) customs union, (c) common market, (d) economic union, and (e) monetary union.

3. The welfare implications of economic integration can be analyzed from two perspectives. First are the static welfare effects, resulting from trade creation and trade diversion.

Second are the dynamic welfare effects that stem from greater competition, economies of scale, and the stimulus to investment spending that economic integration makes possible.

4. From a static perspective, the formation of a customs union yields net welfare gains if the consumption and production benefits of trade creation more than offset the loss in world efficiency owing to trade diversion.

5. Several factors influence the extent of trade creation and trade diversion: (a) the degree of competitiveness that member-nation economies have prior to formation of the customs union, (b) the number and size its members, and (c) the size of its external tariff against nonmembers.

6. The European Union was originally founded in 1957 by the Treaty of Rome. Today it consists of 15 members with a combined population approximately equal to that of the United States and a production output almost as large. By 1992, the EU had essentially reached

the common-market stage of integration. Empirical evidence suggests that the EU has enjoyed welfare benefits in trade creation that have outweighed the losses from trade diversion. One of the stumbling blocks confronting the EU has been its common agricultural policy, which has required large government subsidies to support European farmers. The Maastricht Treaty of 1991 called for the formation of a monetary union for eligible EU members, which was initiated in 1999.

7. The formation of the European Monetary union in 1999 resulted in the creation of a single currency (the euro) and a European Central Bank. With a common central bank, the central bank of each participating nation performs operations similar to those of the 12 regional Federal Reserve Banks in the United States.

8. Much of the analysis of the benefits and costs of Europe's common currency is based on the theory of optimum currency areas. According to this theory, the gains to be had from sharing a currency across countries' boundaries include more uniform prices, lower transactions costs, greater certainty for investors, and enhanced competition. These gains must be compared against the loss of an independent monetary policy and the option of changing the exchange rate.

9. In 1989, the United States and Canada successfully negotiated a free-trade agreement under which free trade between the two nations would be phased in over a 10-year period. This agreement was followed by negotiation of the North American Free Trade Agreement (NAFTA) by the United States, Mexico, and Canada.

10. By the 1990s, nations of Eastern Europe and the former Soviet Union were making the transition from centrally planned economies to market economies. These transitions reflected the failure of central planning systems to provide either political freedom or a decent standard of living.

11. It is widely agreed that the transition of economies of Eastern Europe and the former Soviet Union into healthy market economies will require major restructuring: (a) establishing sound fiscal and monetary policies; (b) removing price controls; (c) opening economies to competitive market forces; (d) establishing private property rights and a legal system to protect those rights; and (e) reducing government's involvement in the economy.

STUDY QUESTIONS

1. How can trade liberalization exist on a nondiscriminatory basis versus a discriminatory basis? What are some actual examples of each?

2. What is meant by the term *economic integration*? What are the various stages that economic integration can take?

3. How do the static welfare effects of trade creation and trade diversion relate to a nation's decision to form a customs union? Of what importance to this decision are the dynamic welfare effects?

4. Why has the so-called common agricultural policy been a controversial issue for the European Union?

5. What are the welfare effects of trade creation and trade diversion for the European Union, as determined by empirical studies?

6. Table 9.11 depicts the supply and demand schedules of gloves for Portugal, a small nation that is unable to affect the world price. On graph paper, draw the supply and demand schedules of gloves for Portugal.

   a. Assume that Germany and France can supply gloves to Portugal at a price of $2 and $3, respectively. With free trade, which nation exports gloves to Portugal? How many gloves does Portugal produce, consume, and import?

Table 9.11 Supply and Demand for Gloves: Portugal

Price ($)	Quantity Supplied	Quantity Demanded
0	0	18
1	2	16
2	4	14
3	6	12
4	8	10
5	10	8
6	12	6
7	14	4
8	16	2
9	18	0

imports. Which nation exports gloves to Portugal? How many gloves will Portugal produce, consume, and import?

c. Suppose Portugal forms a customs union with France. Determine the trade-creation effect and the trade-diversion effect of the customs union. What is the customs union's overall effect on the welfare of Portugal?

d. Suppose instead that Portugal forms a customs union with Germany. Is this a trade-diverting or trade-creating customs union? By how much does the customs union increase or decrease the welfare of Portugal?

b. Suppose Portugal levies a 100-percent nondiscriminatory tariff on its glove

NETLINK

9.1 The home page of the proposed Free Trade Area of the Americas, a plan to integrate the economies of North and South America, can be found by setting your browser to URL:
http://www.alca-ftaa.org/

9.2 The Asia–Pacific Economic Cooperation is a regional organization of 18 countries that promotes free trade and economic cooperation. Visit its Web site by setting your browser to URL:
http: //www.apecsec.org.sg/

9.3 Information about the European Union can be found by visiting its home page, along with that of the Government and Social Science Information Service, administered by the University of California,

Berkeley. To find these two sites, set your browser to URL:
http://europa.eu.int/
and
http://www.lib.berkeley.edu/GSSI/eugde.html

9.4 To get information on NAFTA, log onto the Web page of The North American Integration and Development Center of the University of California at Los Angeles at:
http://naid.sppsr.ucla.edu/

9.5 The Association of ten Southeast Asian Nations (ASEAN) was established on August 8, 1967, to promote economic growth, social progress, and cultural development. Visit its Web site at:
http://www.aseansec.org/

To access NetLink Exercises and the Virtual Scavenger Hunt, visit the Carbaugh Web site at http://carbaugh.swcollege.com.

chapter 10

International Factor Movements and Multinational Enterprises

Our attention so far has been on international flows of goods and services. However, some of the most dramatic changes in the world economy have been due to international flows of factors of production, including labor and capital. In the 1800s, European capital and labor (along with African and Asian labor) flowed to the United States and fostered its economic development. In the 1960s, the United States sent large amounts of investment capital to Canada and Western Europe; in the 1980s and1990s, investment flowed from Japan to the United States. Today, workers from southern Europe find employment in northern European factories, while Mexican workers migrate to the United States. The tearing down of the Berlin Wall in 1990 triggered a massive exodus of workers from East Germany to West Germany.

The economic forces underlying international movements in factors of production are virtually identical to those underlying international flows of goods and services. Productive factors move, when they are permitted to, from nations where they are abundant (low productivity) to nations where they are scarce (high productivity). Productive factors flow in response to differences in returns (such as wages and yields on capital) as long as these are large enough to more than outweigh the cost of moving from one country to another.

KEY CONCEPTS AND TERMS

- Brain drain
- Conglomerate integration
- Foreign direct investment
- Guest workers
- Horizontal integration
- International joint ventures
- Labor mobility
- Maquiladoras
- Migration
- Multinational enterprise (MNE)
- Technology transfer
- Transfer pricing
- Transplants
- Vertical integration

A nation in which labor is scarce can either import labor-intensive products or import labor itself; the same applies to capital. Thus, *international trade in goods and services and flows of productive factors are substitutes for each other.* One cannot conduct a satisfactory study of international trade without also analyzing the international mobility of labor and capital.

This chapter considers the role of international capital flows (investment) as a substitute for trade in capital-intensive products. Special attention is given to the multinational enterprise that carries on the international reallocation of capital. The chapter also analyzes the international mobility of labor as a substitute for trade in labor-intensive products.

THE MULTINATIONAL ENTERPRISE

Although the term *enterprise* can be precisely defined, there is no universal agreement on the exact definition of a **multinational enterprise (MNE)**. But a close look at some representative MNEs suggests that these businesses have a number of identifiable features. Operating in many host countries, MNEs often conduct research and development (R&D) activities in addition to manufacturing, mining, extraction, and business-service operations. The MNE cuts across national borders and is often directed from a company planning center that is distant from the host country. Both stock ownership and company management are typically multinational in character. A typical MNE has a high ratio of foreign sales to total sales, often 25 percent or more. Regardless of the lack of agreement as to what constitutes an MNE, there is no doubt that the multinational phenomenon is massive in size. Table 10.1 provides a glimpse of some of the world's largest corporations.

MNEs may diversify their operations along vertical, horizontal, and conglomerate lines within the host and source countries. **Vertical integration** often occurs when the parent MNE decides to establish foreign subsidiaries to produce intermediate goods or inputs that go into the production of the finished good. For industries such as oil refining and steel, such *backward integration* may include the extraction and processing of raw materials. Most manufacturers tend to extend operations backward only to the production of component parts. The major international oil companies represent a classic case of backward vertical integration on a worldwide basis. Oil-production subsidiaries are located in areas such as the Middle East, whereas the refining and marketing operations occur in the industrial

Table 10.1 The World's Largest Corporations, 1999

Firm	Headquarters	Revenues ($ Billions)	Profits ($ Billions)	Employees
General Motors	United States	161.3	3.0	594,000
DaimlerChrysler	Germany	154.9	5.7	441,502
Ford Motor	United States	144.4	22.1	345,175
Wal-Mart Stores	United States	139.2	4.4	910,000
Mitsui	Japan	109.4	0.2	32,961
Itochu	Japan	108.7	-0.3	5,775
Mitsubishi	Japan	107.2	0.2	36,000
Exxon	United States	100.7	6.4	79,000
General Electric	United States	100.5	9.3	293,000
Toyota Motor	Japan	99.7	2.8	183,879

Source: "The World's Largest Corporations," *Fortune*, August 2, 1999, p. F11.

nations of the West. MNEs may also practice *forward integration* in the direction of the final consumer market. Automobile manufacturers, for example, may establish foreign subsidiaries to market the finished goods of the parent company. In practice, most vertical foreign investment is backward. MNEs often wish to integrate their operations vertically to benefit from economies of scale and international specialization.

Horizontal integration occurs when a parent company producing a commodity in the source country sets up a subsidiary to produce the identical product in the host country. These subsidiaries are independent units in productive capacity and are established to produce and market the parent company's product in overseas markets. Coca-Cola and Pepsi-Cola, for example, are bottled not only in the United States but also throughout much of the world. MNEs sometimes locate production facilities overseas to avoid stiff foreign tariff barriers, which would place their products at a competitive disadvantage. Parent companies also like to locate close to their customers because differences in national preferences may require special designs for their products.

Besides making horizontal and vertical foreign investments, MNEs may diversify into nonrelated markets, in what is known as **conglomerate integration**. For example, in the 1980s, U.S. oil companies stepped up their nonenergy acquisitions in response to anticipated declines of future investment opportunities in oil and gas. Exxon acquired a foreign copper-mining subsidiary in Chile, and Tenneco bought a French company producing automotive exhaust systems.

To carry out their worldwide operations, MNEs rely on **foreign direct investment**—acquisition of a controlling interest in an overseas company or facility. Foreign direct investment typically occurs when (1) the parent company obtains sufficient common stock in a foreign company to assume voting control (the U.S. Department of Commerce defines a company as directly foreign owned when a "foreign person" holds a 10-percent interest in the company); (2) the parent company acquires or constructs new plants and equipment overseas; (3) the parent company shifts funds abroad to finance an expansion of its foreign subsidiary; or (4) earnings of the parent company's foreign subsidiary are reinvested in plant expansion.

Table 10.2 summarizes the position of the United States with respect to foreign direct investment in 1998. Data are provided concern-

Table 10.2 Direct Investment Position of the United States, 1998 (Book Value)*

Country	U.S. Direct Investment Abroad		Foreign Direct Investment in United States	
	Amount (Billions of Dollars)	Percentage	Amount (Billions of Dollars)	Percentage
Canada	103.9	10.6	74.8	9.2
Europe	489.5	49.9	539.9	66.5
Latin America	196.7	20.1	32.2	4.0
Africa	13.5	1.4	0.8	0.0
Middle East	10.5	1.0	7.8	1.0
Asia and Pacific	161.8	17.0	156.1	19.3
	975.9	100.0	811.6	100.0

*Book value refers to the historical value of an investment; valuation is based on the time the investment occurred, with no adjustment for price changes.

Source: U.S. Department of Commerce, *U.S. Direct Investment Position Abroad and Foreign Direct Investment Position in the United States on a Historical-Cost Basis, 1982-1998* at http://www.bea.doc.gov. See also U.S. Department of Commerce, *Survey of Current Business*, Washington, DC, Government Printing Office.

ing U.S. direct investment abroad and foreign direct investment in the United States. In recent years, the majority of U.S. foreign direct investment has flowed to Europe and Canada, especially in the manufacturing sector. Most foreign direct investment in the United States has come from Europe, Japan, and Canada—areas that have invested heavily in U.S. manufacturing, petroleum, and wholesale trade facilities.

MOTIVES FOR FOREIGN DIRECT INVESTMENT

The case for opening markets to foreign direct investment is compelling as it is for trade. More open economies enjoy higher rates of private investment, which is a major determinant of economic growth and job creation. Foreign direct investment is actively courted by countries, not least because it generates spillovers such as improved management and better technology. As is true with firms that trade, firms and sectors where foreign direct investment is intense tend to have higher average labor productivity and pay higher wages. Outward investment allows firms to remain competitive and thus supports employment at home. Investment abroad stimulates exports of machinery and other capital goods.

New MNEs do not pop up haphazardly in foreign nations; they develop as a result of conscious planning by corporate managers. Both economic theory and empirical studies support the notion that foreign direct investment is conducted in anticipation of *future profits*. It is generally assumed that investment flows from regions of low anticipated profit to those of high anticipated profit, after allowing for risk. Although expected profits may ultimately explain the process of foreign direct investment, corporate management may emphasize a variety of other factors when asked about their investment motives. These factors include market-demand conditions, trade restrictions, investment regulations, labor costs, and transportation costs. All these factors have a bearing on cost and revenue conditions and hence on the level of profit.

DEMAND FACTORS   The quest for profits encourages MNEs to search for new markets and sources of demand. Some MNEs set up overseas subsidiaries to tap foreign markets that cannot be maintained adequately by export products. This sometimes occurs in response to dissatisfaction over distribution techniques abroad. Consequently, a business may set up a foreign marketing division and, later, manufacturing facilities. This incentive may be particularly strong when it is realized that local taste and design differences exist. A close familiarity with local conditions is of utmost importance to a successful marketing program.

The location of foreign manufacturing facilities may be influenced by the fact that some parent companies find their productive capacity already sufficient to meet domestic demands. If they wish to enjoy growth rates that exceed the expansion of domestic demand, they must either export or establish foreign production operations. General Motors, for example, has felt that the markets of such countries as Britain, France, and Brazil are strong enough to permit the survival of GM manufacturing subsidiaries. But Boeing Aircraft has centralized its manufacturing operations in the United States and exports abroad because an efficient production plant for jet planes is a large investment relative to the size of most foreign markets.

Market competition may also influence a firm's decision to set up foreign facilities. Corporate strategies may be defensive in nature if they are directed at preserving market shares from actual or potential competition. The most certain method of preventing foreign competition from becoming a strong force is to acquire foreign businesses. For the United States, the 1960s and early 1970s witnessed a tremendous surge in acquisition of foreign businesses. Approximately half of the foreign subsidiaries operated by U.S. MNEs were originally acquired through purchase of already existing concerns during this era. Once again, General Motors exemplifies this practice, purchasing and setting up auto producers around the globe. GM has been successful in gaining control of many larger-foreign-model firms, including Monarch (GM Canada) and Opel (GM

DO LOW WAGES ATTRACT FOREIGN INVESTMENT?

U.S. Direct Investment Abroad

	Value of Investment, 1995		Employment, 1993	
	$(Billions)	Percent of Total	Thousands	Percent of Total
United Kingdom	120	17	866	13
Canada	81	11	875	13
Germany	43	6	569	8
Japan	39	6	411	6
France	33	5	403	6
Italy	17	2	164	2
All Industrial*	509	72	4,379	65
Mexico	14	2	666	10
Total, All	712	100	6,731	100

*Includes Western Europe, Canada, Japan, Australia, and New Zealand.

Source: U.S. Department of Commerce, Bureau of Economic Analysis.

Foreign direct investment by U.S. companies—the establishment or expansion of a foreign subsidiary—grew at a rate of 10 percent per year between 1982 and 1995. A common explanation for this rise is that U.S. firms are lured overseas by low wages in developing countries, where they produce goods for exports to the United States.

An examination of the data suggests that such claims are exaggerated. As seen in the table, 72 percent of the stock of U.S. direct investment abroad was in high-wage, industrialized countries in 1995. Employment data presents a similar picture. Foreign affiliates of U.S. companies employed 6.7 million workers in 1993. About 65 percent of these workers held jobs in industrialized countries. Moreover, nearly half of the 6.7 million jobs are found in six major economies: Canada, France, Germany, Italy, Japan, and the United Kingdom.

Market access is one explanation for the preponderance of foreign direct investment in industrialized countries. When locating abroad, firms choose stable and prosperous markets. Furthermore, the presence of trade barriers may make direct investment preferable to exporting.

Though these data show that access to cheap labor is not the driving force for most foreign direct investment, U.S. companies do have a strong presence in some developing countries. Brazil and Mexico, for example, rank among the top ten recipients of U.S. direct investment based on employment data.

Source: "Low Wages and Foreign Investment," *National Economic Trends*, The Federal Reserve Bank of St. Louis, October 1996, p. 1.

Germany). It did not acquire smaller-model firms such as Toyota, Datsun, and Volkswagen, all of which have become significant competitors for General Motors.

COST FACTORS MNEs often seek to increase profit levels through reductions in production costs. Such cost-reducing foreign direct investments may take a number of forms. The pursuit of essential raw materials may underlie a company's intent to go multinational. This is particularly true of the extractive industries and certain agricultural commodities. United Fruit, for example, has established banana-producing facilities in Honduras to take advantage of the natural trade advantages afforded by the weather and growing conditions. Similar types of natural trade advantages explain why Anaconda has set up mining operations in Bolivia and why Shell produces and refines oil in Indonesia. Natural supply advantages such as resource endowments or climatic conditions may indeed influence a company's decision to invest abroad.

Production costs include factors other than material inputs, notably labor. *Labor costs* tend to differ among national economies. MNEs may be able to hold costs down by locating part or all of their productive facilities abroad. Many U.S. electronics firms, for instance, have had their products produced or at least assembled abroad to take advantage of cheap foreign labor. (The mere fact that the United States may pay higher wages than those prevailing abroad does not necessarily indicate higher costs. High wages may result from U.S. workers' being more productive than their foreign counterparts. Only when high U.S. wages are not offset by superior U.S. labor productivity will foreign labor become relatively more attractive.)

MNE location can also be affected by transportation costs, especially in industries where transportation costs are a high fraction of product value. When the cost of transporting raw materials used by a MNE is significantly higher than the cost of shipping its finished products to markets, the MNE will generally locate production facilities closer to its raw material sources than to its markets; lumber, basic chemicals, aluminum, and steel are among the products that fit this description. Conversely, when the cost of transporting finished products is significantly higher than the cost of transporting the raw materials that are used in their manufacture, MNEs locate production facilities close to their markets. Beverage manufacturers, such as Coca-Cola and Pepsi-Cola, transport syrup concentrate to plants all over the world, which add water to the syrup, bottle it, and sell it to consumers. When transportation costs are a minor fraction of product value, MNEs tend to locate where the availability and cost of labor and other inputs provide them the lowest manufacturing

cost. MNEs producing electronic components, garments, and shoes offer examples of such locational mobility.

Government policies may also lead to foreign direct investment. Some nations seeking to lure foreign manufacturers to set up employment-generating facilities in their countries may grant subsidies, such as preferential tax treatment or free factory buildings, to MNEs. More commonly, direct investment may be a way of circumventing import tariff barriers. The very high tariffs that Brazil levies on auto imports means that foreign auto producers wishing to sell in the Brazilian market must locate production facilities in that country. Another example is the response of U.S. business to the formation of the European Union, which imposed common external tariffs against outsiders while reducing trade barriers among member nations. U.S. companies were induced to circumvent these barriers by setting up subsidiaries in the member nations. Another example is Japanese businesses that apparently located additional auto-assembly plants in the United States in the 1980s and 1990s to defuse mounting protectionist pressures.

SUPPLYING PRODUCTS TO FOREIGN BUYERS: WHETHER TO PRODUCE DOMESTICALLY OR ABROAD

Once a firm knows that foreign demand for its goods exists, it must ascertain the least-cost method of supplying these goods abroad. Suppose Anheuser-Busch (A-B) of the United States wants to sell its Budweiser beer in Canada. A-B can do this in one of three ways: (1) brew Bud in the United States and export it to Canada (direct exporting); (2) establish its own production subsidiary in Canada (foreign direct investment); or (3) license the rights to a Canadian brewery to produce and market Bud in Canada. The method A-B chooses depends on the extent of economies of scale, transportation and distribution costs, and international trade barriers. These considerations are discussed in the following sections.

DIRECT EXPORTING VERSUS FOREIGN DIRECT INVESTMENT/LICENSING

Let us consider A-B's decision to supply Bud to Canada via direct exports versus foreign direct investment or licensing. We will first analyze the influence of economies of scale on A-B's decision. One would expect economies of scale to encourage A-B to export Bud to Canada when the quantity of beer demanded in Canada is relatively small, and to encourage Canadian production, via either licensing agreements or foreign direct investment, when a relatively large quantity of beer is demanded in Canada.

To illustrate this principle, assume that A-B, a Canadian brewery, and a Canadian subsidiary of A-B all have identical production functions exhibiting economies of scale and that the firms pay the same price for their inputs. As illustrated in Figure 10.1, their average cost schedules are identical and are denoted by *AC*.

Suppose U.S. consumers demand 200 cases per year of Bud at the going price. Producing this output permits A-B to realize economies of scale and a cost of $8 per case. Suppose that Canadians demand a smaller quantity of Bud, say 100 cases. Because this quantity is too small to permit efficient production in Canada, the Canadian brewery or A-B's production subsidiary realizes a higher cost of $11 per case. A-B thus minimizes cost by increasing its U.S. production to meet the additional Canadian demand. By brewing 300 cases, A-B achieves a longer production run and the resulting economies of scale so that costs fall to $6 per case. Canadian consumers are thus supplied 100 cases of Bud via direct export. As long as the cost of transporting Bud

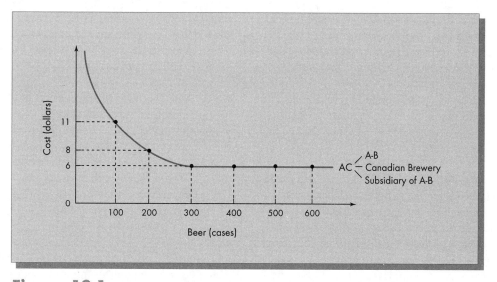

Figure 10.1 The Choice Between Direct Exporting and Foreign Direct Investment/Licensing

When the Canadian market's size is large enough to permit efficient production in Canada, a U.S. firm increases profits by establishing a Canadian production subsidiary or licensing the rights to a Canadian firm to produce and market its product in Canada. The U.S. firm increases profits by exporting its product to Canada when the Canadian market is too small to permit efficient production.

from the United States to Canada is less than $5 a case, A-B increases its profit by exporting beer to Canada.

If the quantity of Bud demanded by Canadians is 300 cases or more, it may be more profitable for A-B to locate production in Canada, either by licensing production technology to a Canadian brewery or by investing in a production subsidiary. Referring to Figure 10.1, suppose Canadians demand 400 cases of Bud whereas Bud sales in the United States remain at 200 cases. With economies of scale exhausted at 300 cases, the larger Canadian demand does not permit A-B to brew Bud at a cost lower than $6 per case. By increasing output from 100 to 400 cases, however, the Canadian brewery or production subsidiary of A-B could match A-B's efficiency since they realize the least possible cost of $6 per case. Given equal production costs, A-B minimizes total cost by avoiding the additional costs of transporting beer to Canada. A-B thus increases profits by either licensing its beer technology to a Canadian brewer or investing in a production subsidiary in Canada.

Similar to transportation costs, trade restrictions can neutralize production-cost advantages. If Canada has high import tariffs, production-cost advantages in the United States may be offset, so that foreign direct investment or licensing is the only feasible way of penetrating the Canadian market.

Foreign Direct Investment Versus Licensing

Once a firm chooses foreign production as a method of supplying goods abroad, it must decide whether it is more efficient to establish a foreign production subsidiary or license the technology to a foreign firm to produce its goods. In the United Kingdom, there are KFC establishments that are owned and run by local residents. The parent U.S. organization merely provides its name and operating procedures in return for royalty fees paid by the local establishments. Although licensing is widely used in practice, it presupposes that local firms are capable of adapting their operations to the production process or technology of the parent organization.

Figure 10.2 portrays the hypothetical cost conditions confronting A-B as it contemplates whether to license Bud production technology to a Canadian brewery or invest in a Canadian production subsidiary. Curve $AVC_{Subsidiary}$ represents the average variable cost (such as labor and materials) of A-B's production subsidiary, and AVC_{Canada} represents the average variable cost of a Canadian brewery. The establishment of a foreign production subsidiary also entails fixed costs denoted by curve $AFC_{Subsidiary}$. These include expenses of coordinating the subsidiary with the parent organization and the sunk costs of assessing the market potential of the foreign country. The total unit costs that A-B faces when establishing a foreign subsidiary are given by $ATC_{Subsidiary}$.

Comparing $ATC_{Subsidiary}$ with AVC_{Canada}, for a relatively small market of less than 400 cases of beer, the Canadian brewery has an absolute cost advantage. Licensing Bud production technology to a Canadian brewery in this case is more profitable for A-B. But if the Canadian market for Bud exceeds 400 cases, A-B's production subsidiary has an absolute cost advantage; A-B increases profits by supplying beer to Canadians via foreign direct investment.

Several factors influence the output level at which A-B's production subsidiary begins to realize an absolute cost advantage vis-à-vis the Canadian brewery (400 cases in Figure 10.2). To the extent that production is capital-intensive and A-B's production subsidiary can acquire capital at a lower cost than that paid by the Canadian brewery, the variable cost advantage of the subsidiary is greater. This neutralizes the influence of a fixed-cost disadvantage for the subsidiary at a lower level of output. The amount of the production subsidiary's fixed costs also has a bearing on this minimum output level. Smaller fixed costs lower the subsidiary's average total costs, again resulting in a smaller output at which the subsidiary first begins to have an absolute cost advantage.

As noted, international business decisions are influenced by such factors as production costs, fixed costs of locating overseas, the relative importance of labor and capital in the produc-

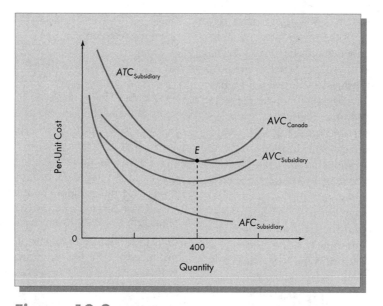

Figure 10.2 The Choice Between Foreign Direct Investment
and Licensing

The decision to establish foreign operations through direct investment or licensing depends on (1) the extent to which capital is used in the production process, (2) the size of the foreign market, and (3) the amount of fixed cost a business must bear when establishing an overseas facility.

tion process, and the size of the foreign market. Another factor is the element of risk and uncertainty. When determining where to locate production operations, management is concerned with possibilities such as currency fluctuations and subsidiary expropriations.

INTERNATIONAL TRADE THEORY AND MULTINATIONAL ENTERPRISE

Perhaps the main explanation of the development of MNEs lies in the strategies of corporate management. The reasons for engaging in international business can be outlined in terms of the comparative-advantage principle. Corporate managers see advantages they can exploit in the forms of access to factor inputs, new technologies and products, and managerial know-how. Organizations establish overseas subsidiaries largely because profit prospects are best enhanced by foreign production.

From a trade-theory perspective, the multinational-enterprise analysis is fundamentally in agreement with the predictions of the comparative-advantage principle. Both approaches contend that a given commodity will be produced in the low-cost country. The major difference between the multinational-enterprise analysis and the conventional trade model is that the former stresses the international movement of factor inputs, whereas the latter is based on the movement of merchandise among nations.

International trade theory suggests that the aggregate welfare of both the source and host countries is enhanced when MNEs make foreign direct investments for their own benefit. The presumption is that if businesses can earn a higher return on overseas investments than on those at home, resources are transferred from lower to higher productive uses, and on balance the world allocation of resources will improve. Thus, *analysis of MNEs is essentially the same as conventional trade theory, which rests on the movement of products among nations.*

Despite the basic agreement between conventional trade theory and the multinational-enterprise analysis, there are some notable differences. The conventional model presupposes that goods are exchanged between independent organizations on international markets at competitively determined prices. But MNEs are generally vertically integrated companies whose subsidiaries manufacture intermediate goods as well as finished goods. In an MNE, sales become *intrafirm* when goods are transferred from subsidiary to subsidiary. Although such sales are part of international trade, their value may be determined by factors other than a competitive pricing system.

JAPANESE TRANSPLANTS IN THE U.S. AUTOMOBILE INDUSTRY

During the 1980s, the growth of Japanese direct investment in the U.S. auto industry was widely publicized. From 1980 to 1990, Japanese automakers invested more than $5 billion in U.S.-based assembly facilities, known as **transplants**. Eight Japanese-affiliated auto manufacturers and more than a hundred Japanese parts suppliers operated or constructed facilities in the United States. By 1990, Japanese transplants built more than 15 percent of the passenger cars produced in the United States. Table 10.3 provides examples of Japanese transplant automakers in the United States.

Establishing transplants in the United States provided a number of benefits to Japanese automakers, including opportunities to:

- silence critics who insist that autos sold in the United States must be built there.
- avoid export restraints imposed by the Japanese government and potential import barriers of the United States.

Table 10.3 Japanese Auto Plants in the United States

Plant Name/Parent Company	Location/Date Open
Honda of America, Inc. (Honda)	Marysville, Ohio (1982) East Liberty, Ohio (1989)
Nissan Motor Manufacturing Corp. (Nissan)	Smyrna, Tennessee (1983)
New United Motor Manufacturing, Inc. (Toyota/General Motors)	Fremont, California (1984)
Toyota Motor Manufacturing, USA, Inc. (Toyota)	Georgetown, Kentucky (1988, 1993)
Mazda Motor Manufacturing, USA, Inc. (Mazda)	Flat Rock, Michigan (1987)
Diamond-Star Motors Corp. (Mitsubishi/Chrysler)	Normal, Illinois (1988)
Ford Motor Co. (Nissan/Ford)	Avon Lake, Ohio (1991)

- gain access to an expanding market at a time when the Japanese market was nearing saturation.
- provide a hedge against fluctuations in the yen-dollar exchange rate.

The rapid growth of Japanese investment in the U.S. auto industry led to concerns over the future of U.S.-owned auto-manufacturing and parts-supplier industries. Proponents of foreign direct investment maintained that it would foster improvement in the overall competitive position of the domestic auto-assembly and parts industries. They also argued that foreign investment generates jobs and provides consumers with a wider product choice at lower prices than would otherwise be available.

However, the United Auto Workers (UAW) union maintained that this foreign investment would result in job losses in the auto-assembly and parts-supplier industries. They and other critics argued that Japanese transplants would decrease the market share for U.S. automakers and parts suppliers and contribute to excess capacity at both automakers and parts-suppliers levels.

One factor that influences the number of workers hired is a company's *job classifications*, which stipulate the scope of work each employee performs. As the number of job classifications increases, the scope of work decreases, along with the flexibility of using available employees; this can lead to falling worker productivity and rising production costs.

Japanese-affiliated auto companies have traditionally used significantly fewer job classifications than traditional U.S. auto companies. Japanese transplants use work teams, and each team member is trained to do all the operations performed by the team. A typical Japanese-affiliated assembly plant has three to four job classifications: one team leader, one production technician, and one or two maintenance technicians. Often, jobs are rotated among team members. In contrast, traditional U.S. auto plants have enacted more than 90 different job classifications, and employees generally perform only those operations specifically permitted for their classifica-

tion. These trends have contributed to the superior labor productivity of Japanese transplants compared to the U.S. Big Three. Although powerful forces within the U.S. Big Three have resisted change, international competition has forced U.S. automakers to slowly dismantle U.S. management and production methods and remake them along Japanese lines.

For policy makers, the broader issue is whether the Japanese transplants have lived up to expectations. When the Japanese initiated investment in U.S. auto-manufacturing facilities in the 1980s, many Americans viewed them as models for a revitalized U.S. auto industry and new customers for U.S. auto-parts suppliers. Transplants were seen as a way of providing jobs for U.S. autoworkers whose jobs were dwindling as imports increased. When the transplant factories were announced, Americans anticipated that transplant production would be based primarily on American parts, material, and labor; transplant production would displace imports in the U.S. market while transferring new management techniques and technology to the United States.

Certainly, the transplant factories boosted the economies in the regions where they located. And there is no doubt that the transplants helped to transfer Japanese quality control, just-in-time delivery, and other production techniques to the United States. However, the original expectations of the transplants were only partially fulfilled. Skeptics contended that Japanese manufacturing operations were twice as likely to import parts for assembly in the United States as the average foreign company, and were four times as likely to import parts as the average U.S. company. Extensive use of imported parts by Japanese transplants would contribute to a U.S. automotive trade deficit with Japan and would result in fewer jobs for U.S. autoworkers.

How competitive are Japanese transplants relative to the U.S. Big Three auto manufacturers? Table 10.4 provides the estimated labor cost per vehicle for North American auto manufacturers in 1999. The table shows that Nissan's transplant factory was the most productive manufacturer in North America, with labor costs of $1,055 per vehicle for assembly, stamping, and powertrain.

FEARS AND FACTS ABOUT FOREIGN DIRECT INVESTMENT

In the 1980s, concerns arose in the United States that the rapid rise in inward foreign direct investment would have adverse effects on American workers. Some feared that foreign-controlled affiliates that displaced U.S. firms might change the composition of employment, moving "good" jobs to the home country and offering only "bad" jobs in the United States. In fact, foreign multinationals in the United States pay higher-than-average wages, suggesting that in fact they provide good jobs. When net foreign direct investment flows turned outward during the 1990s, the concern became that U.S. companies would begin outsourcing much of their production to other countries, again at the expense of jobs and wages at home. This seeming contradiction—that inward and outward foreign direct investment would have similar effects on U.S. workers—may reflect how little was actually known about the effects of foreign direct investment.

Unlike trade, which has been the subject of study for hundreds of years, foreign direct investment has been subjected to little rigorous study until recently. As more has been learned about foreign direct investment, many of these initial fears have subsided. The following are some fears that have been recently expressed about foreign direct investment, and the facts that we now know.

Fear: Won't U.S. industries leave for low-wage developing countries?

Fact: During the NAFTA debate, some voiced concern that lowering barriers to investment in Mexico would result in a large movement of U.S. industry there, as firms exploited low Mexican wages. But since the passage of NAFTA in 1993, Mexico's share of the U.S. outward foreign direct investment position has decreased. The reason there has been no mass exodus of U.S. industry to Mexico or to other low-wage countries is simple: There is no free lunch—for multinationals as for the rest of us. Real wages may vary significantly across countries, but studies show that these differences are linked to productivity differences, just as economic theory would predict. Low wages are not a sufficient reason to move production to a foreign country if low productivity there raises the labor cost per unit of output to a level close to that of the United States. The vast majority of U.S. foreign direct investment continues to be with other high-wage countries, so clearly other motivations than the

Table 10.4 Labor Cost per Vehicle for Selected North American Auto Manufacturers in 1999

	DaimlerChrysler	Ford	General Motors	Honda	Nissan	Toyota
Labor hours per vehicle (assembly, stamping powertrain)	43.58	36.24	43.03	29.34	29.30	30.96
Labor cost per vehicle*	$2,005	$1,667	$1,979	$1,056	$1,055	$1,115
Labor cost disadvantage relative to Nissan	$950	$612	$924	$1	——	$60
Annual production volume (million)	3.085	4.550	5.717	.686	.325	.688

*Labor cost of $46 per hour for DaimlerChrysler, Ford, and General Motors and $36 per hour for Honda, Nissan, and Toyota.

Source: J. D. Harbour and Associates, *The Harbour Report 2000*, Troy, MI, p. 172.

FEARS AND FACTS ABOUT FOREIGN DIRECT INVESTMENT *(continued)*

potential for low-wage outsourcing are behind the greater part of foreign direct investment.

Fear: Are U.S. firms that invest abroad exporting jobs?

Fact: It may seem reasonable to suppose that a U.S. firm that hires workers in an overseas affiliate is contributing to U.S. unemployment, because the firm could be hiring U.S. workers to do the same job here. Evidence shows, however, that generally this is not the case: Increases in employment in foreign affiliates of U.S. firms are often associated with increases in employment at the parent as well. What employment substitution there is seems to be occurring entirely offshore, between countries competing for U.S. FDI, not between U.S. parents and their foreign affiliates. Far from exporting jobs, it appears that creating jobs overseas creates jobs at home as well.

Fear: Doesn't U.S. foreign direct investment abroad represent domestic investment forgone?

Fact: With the surge in outward foreign direct investment in recent years, foreign direct investment outflows now amount to more than 10 percent of gross investment. However, when a U.S.

firm invests abroad, that does not necessarily mean it would have invested here instead if foreign direct investment had not been an option. It might then have chosen not to invest at all. Moreover, two-thirds of recorded outflows in 1996 were actually the reinvested earnings of foreign affiliates, not capital originating in the United States. Considering only actual capital outflows, a recent study estimated that outward foreign direct investment averaged only 0.9 percent of gross investment between 1970 and 1990—and the share has been deceasing. Capital outflows are also largely compensated by foreign investment inflows. Evidence suggests that a complementarity may exist between the United States and other industrial countries that increases total investment in all countries that participate.

In short, opponents of foreign direct investment have incorrectly framed it as a zero-sum venture, where for one country to gain, another must lose. Both the theoretical arguments of the benefits of FDI and the evidence now available suggest that foreign direct investment can provide net gains for all parties.

Source: *Economic Report of the President*, 1998, pp. 251–252.

The Honda plant was the second most productive, at $1,056 per vehicle. Ford was the most productive of the U.S. Big Three manufacturers with labor costs of $1,667 per vehicle. The labor cost disadvantages of DaimlerChrysler and General Motors, relative to Nissan, were larger than that of Ford.

INTERNATIONAL JOINT VENTURES

Another area of multinational enterprise involvement is **international joint ventures**. A joint venture is a business organization established by two or more companies that combines their skills and assets. It may have a limited objective (research or production) and be short-lived. It may also be multinational in character, involving cooperation among several domestic and foreign companies. Joint ventures differ from mergers in that they involve the creation of a *new* business firm, rather than the union of two existing companies. Table 10.5 provides examples of recent joint ventures between U.S. and foreign companies.

There are three types of international joint ventures. The first is a joint venture formed by two businesses that conduct business in a third country. For example, a U.S. oil firm and a British oil firm may form a joint venture for oil

Table 10.5 Joint Ventures Between U.S. and Foreign Companies

Joint Venture	U.S. Partner	Foreign Partner	Products
New United Motor Manufacturing	General Motors	Toyota (Japan)	Subcompact cars
National Steel	National Intergroup	Nippon Kokan	Steel
Siecor	Corning Glass Works	Siemens (Germany)	Optical cable
Himont	Hercules	Montedison (Italy)	Polypropylene resin
International Aero Engines	United Technologies	Rolls-Royce (Britain)	Aircraft engines
Tokyo Disneyland	Walt Disney Productions	Oriental Land Company	Entertainment

exploration in the Middle East. Next is the formation of a joint venture with local private interests. Honeywell Information Systems of Japan was formed by Honeywell, Inc., of the United States and Mitsubishi Office Machinery Company of Japan to sell information-systems equipment to the Japanese. The third type of joint venture includes participation by local government. Bechtel of the United States, Messerschmitt-Boelkow-Blom of West Germany, and National Iranian Oil (representing the government of Iran) formed Iran Oil Investment Company for oil extraction in Iran.

Several reasons have been advanced to justify the creation of joint ventures. Some functions, such as R&D, can involve costs too large for any one company to absorb by itself. Many of the world's largest copper deposits have been owned and mined jointly by the largest copper companies on the grounds that joint financing is required to raise enough capital. The exploitation of oil deposits is often done by a consortium of several oil companies. Exploratory drilling projects typically involve several companies united in a joint venture, and several refining companies traditionally own long-distance crude-oil pipelines. Oil refineries in foreign countries may be co-owned by several large U.S. and foreign oil companies.

Another factor that encourages the formation of international joint ventures is the restrictions some governments place on foreign ownership of local businesses. Governments in developing nations often close their borders to foreign companies unless they are willing to take on local partners. Mexico, India, and Peru require that their own national companies represent a major interest in any foreign company conducting business within their borders. The foreign investor is forced to either accept local equity participation or forgo operation in the country. Such government policies are defended on the grounds that joint ventures result in the transfer of managerial techniques and know-how to the developing nation. Joint ventures may also prevent the possibility of excessive political influence on the part of foreign investors. Finally, joint ventures help minimize dividend transfers abroad and thus strengthen the developing nation's balance of payments.

International joint ventures are also viewed as a means of forestalling protectionism against imports. Apparently motivated by fear that rising protectionism would restrict their access to U.S. markets, Japanese manufacturers (Toyota Motor Enterprise) increasingly formed joint ventures with U.S. enterprises in the 1980s. Such ventures typically resulted in U.S. workers' assembling Japanese components, with the finished goods sold to U.S. consumers. Not only did this process permit Japanese production to enter the U.S. market, but it also blurred the distinction between U.S. and Japanese production. Just who is us? And who is them? The rationale for protecting domestic output and jobs from foreign competition is thus lessened.

There are, however, disadvantages to forming an international joint venture. A joint venture is a cumbersome organization compared with a single organization. Control is divided, creating problems of "two masters." Success or failure depends on how well companies can work together despite having different objectives, corporate cultures, and ways of doing things. The action of corporate chemistry is difficult to predict, but it is critical, because joint-venture agreements usually provide both partners an ongoing role in management. When joint-venture ownership is divided equally, as often occurs, deadlocks in decision making can take place. If balance is to be preserved between different economic interests, negotiation must establish a hierarchical command. Even when negotiated balance is achieved, it can be upset by changing corporate goals or personnel.

WELFARE EFFECTS International joint ventures can yield both welfare-increasing effects and welfare-decreasing effects for the domestic economy. Joint ventures lead to *welfare gains* when (1) the newly established business adds to preexisting productive capacity and fosters additional competition, (2) the newly established business is able to enter new markets that neither parent could have entered individually, or (3) the business yields cost reductions that would have been unavailable if each parent performed the same function separately. However, the formation of a joint venture may also result in *welfare losses*. For instance, it may give rise to increased market power, suggesting greater ability to influence market output and price. This is especially likely to occur when the joint venture is formed in markets in which the parents conduct business. Under such circumstances, the parents, through their representatives in the joint venture, agree on prices and output in the very market that they themselves operate. Such coordination of activities limits competition, reinforces upward pressure on prices, and lowers the level of domestic welfare.

Let's consider an example that contrasts two situations: (1) Two competing companies sell autos in the domestic market. (2) The two competitors form a joint venture that operates as a single seller (a monopoly) in the domestic market. We would expect to see a higher price and smaller quantity when the joint venture behaves as a monopoly. This will always occur as long as the marginal cost curve for the joint venture is identical to the horizontal sum of the marginal cost curves of the individual competitors. The result of this *market-power effect* is a deadweight welfare loss for the domestic economy—a reduction in consumer surplus that is not offset by a corresponding gain to producers. If, however, the formation of the joint venture entails *productivity gains* that neither parent could realize prior to its formation, domestic welfare may increase. This is because a smaller amount of the domestic economy's resources is now required to produce any given output. Whether domestic welfare rises or falls because of the joint venture depends on the magnitudes of these two opposing forces.

Figure 10.3 illustrates the welfare effects of two parent companies' forming a joint venture in the market in which they operate.[1] Assume that Sony Auto Company of Japan and American Auto Company of the United States are the only two firms producing autos for sale in the U.S. market. Suppose each company realizes constant long-run costs, suggesting that average total cost equals marginal cost at each level of output. Let the cost schedules of each company prior to the formation of the joint venture be $MC_0 = ATC_0$, which equals \$10,000. $MC_0 = ATC_0$ thus becomes the long-run market supply schedule of autos.

Assume that Sony Auto Company and American Auto Company initially operate as competitors, charging a price equal to marginal cost. In Figure 10.3, market equilibrium exists at point *A*, where 100 autos are sold at a price of \$10,000 per unit. Consumer surplus totals area *a* + *b* + *c*. Producer surplus does not exist, given the horizontal supply schedule of autos (recall that producer surplus equals the sum of the differences between the market price and each of the minimum prices indicated on the supply schedule for quantities between zero and the market output).

[1] See Robert Carbaugh and Darwin Wassink, "International Joint Ventures and the U.S. Auto Industry," *The International Trade Journal*, Fall 1986.

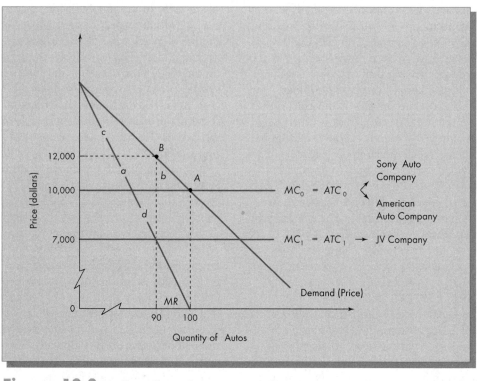

Figure 10.3 Welfare Effects of an International Joint Venture

An international joint venture can yield a welfare-decreasing market-power effect and a welfare-increasing cost-reduction effect. The source of the cost-reduction effect may be lower resource prices or improvements in technology and productivity. The joint venture leads to improvements in national welfare if its cost-reduction effect is due to improvements in technology and productivity and if it more than offsets the market-power effect.

Now suppose that the two competitors announce the formation of a joint venture known as JV Company, which manufactures autos for sale in the United States. The autos sold by JV replace the autos sold by the two parents in the United States.

Suppose the formation of JV Company entails new production efficiencies that result in cost reductions. Let JV's new cost schedule, $MC_1 = ATC_1$, be located at $7,000. As a monopoly, JV maximizes profit by equating marginal revenue with marginal cost. Market equilibrium exists at point B, where 90 autos are sold at a price of $12,000 per unit. The price increase leads to a reduction in consumer surplus equal to area $a + b$.

Of this amount, area a is transferred to JV as producer surplus. Area b represents the loss of consumer surplus that is not transferred to JV and that becomes a deadweight welfare loss for the U.S. economy (the consumption effect).

Against this deadweight welfare loss lies the efficiency effect of JV Company: a decrease in unit costs from $10,000 to $7,000 per auto. JV can produce its profit-maximizing output, 90 autos, at a cost reduction equal to area d as compared with the costs that would exist if the parent companies produced the same output. Area d thus represents additional producer surplus, which is a welfare gain for the U.S. economy. Our analysis concludes that, for the United States, the formation of JV Company is desirable if area *d* exceeds area *b*.

It has been assumed that JV Company achieves cost reductions that are unavailable to either parent as a stand-alone company. Whether the cost reductions benefit the overall U.S. economy depends on their source. If they result from *productivity* improvements (for example, new work rules leading to higher output per worker), a welfare gain exists for the economy, because fewer resources are required to produce a given number of autos and the excess can be shifted to other industries. However, the cost reductions stemming from JV Company's formation may be *monetary* in nature. Being a newly formed company, JV may be able to negotiate wage concessions from domestic workers that could not be achieved by American Auto Company. Such a cost reduction represents a transfer of dollars from domestic workers to JV profits and does not constitute an overall welfare gain for the economy.

MULTINATIONAL ENTERPRISES AS A SOURCE OF CONFLICT

The advocates of MNEs often point out the benefits these enterprises can provide for the nations they affect, including both the source country where the parent organization is located and the host country where subsidiary firms are established. Benefits allegedly exist in the forms of additional levels of investment and capital, creation of new jobs, and development of technologies and production processes. But critics contend that MNEs often create trade restraints, conflict with national economic and political objectives, and have adverse effects on a nation's balance of payments. These arguments perhaps explain why some nations frown on direct investment, while others welcome it. This section examines some of the more controversial issues involving multinationals. The frame of reference is the U.S. MNE, although the same issues apply no matter where the parent organization is based.

EMPLOYMENT One of the most hotly debated issues surrounding the MNE is its effects on employment in both the host and source countries. MNEs often contend that their foreign direct investment yields favorable benefits to the labor force of the recipient nation. Setting up a new multinational automobile manufacturing plant in Canada creates more jobs for Canadian workers. But the MNE's effect on jobs varies from business to business. One source of controversy arises when the direct investment spending of foreign-based MNEs is used to purchase already existing local businesses rather than to establish new ones. In this case, the investment spending may not result in additional production capacity and may not have noticeable effects on employment in the host country. Another problem arises when MNEs bring in foreign managers and other top executives to run the subsidiary in the host country. In the U.S. oil companies locating in Saudi Arabia, the Saudis are increasingly demanding that their own people be employed in higher-level positions.

As for the source country, the issues of runaway jobs and cheap foreign labor are of vital concern to home workers. Because labor unions are confined to individual countries, the multinational nature of these businesses permits them to escape much of the collective-bargaining influence of domestic unions. It is also pointed out that MNEs can seek out those countries where labor has minimal market power.

The ultimate impact that MNEs have on employment in the host and source countries seems to depend in part on the time scale. In the short run, the source country will likely experience an employment decline when production is shifted overseas. But other industries in the source country may find foreign sales rising over time. This is because foreign labor consumes as well as produces and tends to purchase more as employment and income increase as a result of increased investment. Perhaps the main source of controversy stems from the fact that the MNEs are involved in rapid changes in technology and in the transmission of productive enterprise to host countries. Although such efforts may promote global welfare in the long run, the potential short-run adjustment problems facing source-country labor cannot be ignored.

TECHNOLOGY TRANSFER Besides promoting runaway jobs, multinationals can foster the transfer of technology (knowledge and skills applied to how goods are produced) to other nations. Such a process is known as **technology transfer.**

Technology has been likened to a contagious disease: It spreads out farther and more quickly if there are more personal contacts. Foreign trade is viewed as a channel through which people in different nations make contacts and through which people in one nation get to know about the products of other nations. Foreign direct investment is an even more effective method of technology transfer. When foreign firms having technological advantages establish local production subsidiaries, the personal contacts between these subsidiaries and local firms are more frequent and closer than when firms are located abroad.

International trade and foreign direct investment also facilitate technology transfer via the so-called *demonstration effect*: As a firm shows how its products operate, this sends important information to other firms that such products exist and are usable. Technology diffusion is also aided by the *competition effect*: When a foreign firm manufacturers a superior product that is popular among consumers, other firms are threatened. To survive, they have to innovate and improve the quality of their products.

Although technology transfer may increase the productivity and competitiveness of recipient nations, donor nations may react against it because it is detrimental to their economic base. Donor nations contend that the establishment of production operations abroad by multinational enterprises decreases their export potential and leads to job losses for their workers. By sharing technical knowledge with foreign nations, a donor nation may eventually lose its international competitiveness, thus causing a decrease in its rate of economic growth.

Consider the case of U.S. technology transfer to China in the mid-1990s. After decades of mutual hostility, the United States hoped that by the 1990s China would open itself to the outside world and engage in free trade, so that foreign nations could trade with China according to the principle of comparative advantage. Instead, China used its leverage as a large buyer of foreign products to pressure multinational enterprises to localize production and transfer technology to China to help it become competitive. With multinational enterprises willing to outbid each other to woo Chinese bureaucrats, China was in a favorable position to reap the benefits of technology diffusion.

For example, Microsoft Corp., under threat of having its software banned, co-developed a Chinese version of Windows 95 with a local partner and agreed to aid efforts to develop a Chinese software industry. Another example was General Motors. To beat out Ford Motor for the right to become a partner in manufacturing sedans in Shanghai, General Motors agreed to bring in dozens of parts joint ventures and to design much of the car in China. It also agreed to establish five research institutes to teach Chinese engineers to turn technological theory in fields such as power trains and fuel-injection systems into commercial applications.

U.S. multinationals argued that transferring technology to China was largely risk-free because a competitive challenge from China was decades away. However, the acceleration of technology transfer in the mid-1990s became increasingly unpopular with U.S. labor unions, which feared that their members were losing jobs to lower-paid Chinese workers. U.S. government officials also feared that technology transfer was helping create a competitor of extreme proportions.

NATIONAL SOVEREIGNTY Another controversial issue involving the conduct of MNEs is their effect on the economic and political policies of the host and source governments. There is a suspicion in many nations that the presence of MNEs in a given country results in a loss of its national sovereignty. For example, MNEs may resist government attempts to redistribute national income through taxation. By using accounting techniques that shift

BOEING WORKERS CONTEST TECHNOLOGY TRANSFER TO CHINA

Sharing the manufacture of a product with foreign workers is a popular but controversial practice in today's global economy. Does it lead to job losses for domestic workers? Consider the case of commercial jet manufacturing.

In the mid-1990s, Boeing's domestic sales of jetliners weakened because of a post-Cold War decrease in U.S. defense spending and cost cutting by U.S. airlines in a mature travel market. Boeing increasingly looked to growing foreign markets, especially China, as a source of potential sales.

Being a major buyer in a sluggish market, China used its leverage to insist that if foreign producers wanted to sell jetliners to China, they would have to subcontract a portion of the planes' production to Chinese manufacturers. Such technological transfers would help China learn the art of jet-plane manufacturing and eventually result in China's becoming a builder of jetliners. China succeeded in pressuring Boeing, Airbus, and McDonnell Douglas to locate factories in China that produce airliner doors, tail fins, and a myriad of other parts.

The three Western airline producers bid to help China develop the hundred-seat jet, even though the winner would have only about a 20-percent stake in the venture. Each firm wanted to ensure that the design of the jet fit into its own line-up of larger jets, which cost $45 million to $185 million each.

The possibility of Boeing's helping China develop a jetliner threatened Boeing machinists, who saw the potential of their jobs being lost to the Chinese. The workers went on strike, demanding, among other things, that the firm cease or slow the granting of production contracts to China in exchange for orders of U.S. planes. The workers also pressed the Clinton Administration to halt U.S. exports of jetliner manufacturing and technology to China; they complained that the United States was moving toward becoming a seller of jetliner technology rather than a manufacturer of jets.

Boeing justified production sharing on the grounds that curtailment of subcontracting to China would cost its machinists more jobs than would be saved. Without any Boeing subcontracting, the contract would likely be awarded to Airbus, which indicated that it would subcontract production to China; more jobs would thus be lost by Boeing workers than would occur with Boeing's subcontracting some production to China. Boeing emphasized that its strategy was to share what it must, but only what it must, to maintain its 60-percent share of China's jetliner market.

After a lengthy strike, the machinists and Boeing agreed to a new contract. Boeing pledged to consult with the machinists' union on plans for subcontracting work. The firm also agreed to help its workers whose jobs were lost as a result of subcontracting, retraining them for other positions in the company as they became available.

As it happens, Boeing and McDonnell Douglas lost out to Airbus in the contest to become China's partner in building the hundred-seat jet. Some observers noted that Boeing and McDonnell Douglas may have been better off for having lost this contest, because China's Western partner stood to become embroiled in a long and costly development effort.

---

profits overseas, an MNE may be able to evade taxes of a host country. An MNE could accomplish this by raising prices on goods from its subsidiaries in nations with modest tax rates to reduce profits on its operations in a high-tax nation where most of its business actually takes place.

The political influence of MNEs is also questioned by many, as illustrated by the case of Chile. For years, U.S. businesses had pursued direct investments in Chile, largely in copper mining. When Salvador Allende was in the process of winning the presidency, he was opposed by U.S. businesses fearing that their Chilean operations would be expropriated by the host government. International Telephone and Telegraph tried to prevent the election of Allende and attempted to promote civil disturbances that would lead to his fall from power. Another case of MNEs' meddling in host-country affairs is that of United Brands (now Chiquita), the MNE engaged in food-product sales. In 1974, the company paid a $1.25 million bribe to the president of Honduras in return for an export-tax reduction applied to bananas. When the payoff was revealed, the president was removed from office.

There are other areas of controversy. Suppose a Canadian subsidiary of a U.S.-based MNE conducts trade with a country subject to U.S. trade embargoes. Should U.S. policy makers outlaw such activities? The Canadian subsidiary may be pressured by the parent organization to comply with U.S. foreign policy. During international crises, MNEs may move funds rapidly from one financial center to another to avoid losses (make profits) from changes in exchange rates. This conduct makes it difficult for national governments to stabilize their economies.

In a world where national economies are interdependent and factors of production are mobile, the possible loss of national sovereignty is often viewed as a necessary cost whenever direct investment results in foreign control of production facilities. Whether the welfare gains accruing from the international division of labor and specialization outweigh the potential diminution of national independence involves value judgments by policy makers and interested citizens.

BALANCE OF PAYMENTS The United States offers a good example of how an MNE can affect a nation's balance of payments. In brief, the *balance of payments* is an account of the value of goods and services, capital movements (including foreign direct investment), and other items that flow into or out of a country. Items that make a positive contribution to a nation's payments position include exports of goods and services and capital inflows (foreign investment entering the home country), whereas the oppo-

site flows would weaken the payments position. At first glance, we might conclude that when U.S. MNEs make foreign direct investments, these payments represent an outflow of capital from the United States and hence a negative factor on the U.S. payments position. Although this view may be true in the short run, it ignores the positive effects on trade flows and earnings that direct investment provides in the long run.

When a U.S. MNE sets up a subsidiary overseas, it generally purchases U.S. capital equipment and materials needed to run the subsidiary. Once in operation, the subsidiary tends to purchase additional capital equipment and other material inputs from the United States. Both of these factors stimulate U.S. exports, strengthening its payments position.

Another long-run impact that U.S. foreign direct investment has on its balance of payments is the return inflow of income generated by overseas operations. Such income includes earnings of overseas affiliates, interest and dividends, and fees and royalties. These items generate inflows of revenues for the economy and strengthen the balance-of-payments position.

TAXATION One of the most controversial issues involving MNEs for U.S. policy makers is the taxation of income stemming from foreign direct investment. Labor unions and other groups often contend that U.S. tax laws provide a disincentive to invest at home that results from tax concessions offered by the U.S. government on foreign direct investment. These concessions include *foreign tax credits* and *tax deferrals*.

According to U.S. tax law, an MNE headquartered in the United States is permitted credits against its U.S. income-tax liabilities in an amount equal to the income taxes it pays to foreign governments. Assuming that a Canadian subsidiary earns $100,000 taxable income and that Canada's income-tax rate is 25 percent, the company would pay the Canadian government $25,000. But if that income were applied to the parent organization in the United States, the tax owed to the U.S. government would be $48,000, given an income-tax rate of 48 percent. Under the tax credit system, the parent organization would pay the U.S. government only $23,000 ($48,000 − $25,000 = $23,000). The rationale of the foreign tax credit is that MNEs headquartered in the United States should not be subject to double taxation, whereby the same income would be subject to comparable taxes in two countries. The foreign tax credit is designed to prevent the combined tax rates of the foreign host and domestic source governments from exceeding the higher of the two national rates. In this example, should Canada's income tax rate be 48 percent, the parent organization would not pay any taxes in the United States on the income of its Canadian subsidiary.

U.S.-based MNEs also enjoy a tax-deferral advantage. Under U.S. tax laws, the parent organization has the option of deferring U.S. taxes paid on the income of its foreign subsidiary as long as that income is retained overseas rather than repatriated to the United States. This system amounts to an interest-free loan extended by the U.S. government to the parent for as long as the income is maintained abroad. Retained earnings of an overseas subsidiary can be reinvested abroad without being subject to U.S. taxes. No similar provisions apply to domestic investments. Such discriminatory tax treatment encourages foreign direct investment over domestic investment.

TRANSFER PRICING Another device that MNEs utilize in their effort to decrease their overall tax burden is **transfer pricing**. Using this technique, an MNE reports most of its profits in a low-tax country, even though the profits were earned in a high-tax country. For example, if corporate profit taxes are higher in the parent country than in the host country, and if the parent firm is exporting to its subsidiary in the host country, the MNE can lower its overall tax burden by *underpricing* its exports to its host-country subsidiary, thus shifting profits from the parent to the subsidiary, as illustrated in Figure 10.4. Profits are thus transferred from the branch in the high-tax country to the branch in the low-tax country. Conversely, if the host-country sub-

sidiary is exporting to the parent and the parent country has high tax levels, it would be in the interest of the subsidiary to *overprice* its exports, thus decreasing taxable profits in the parent country. The result is lower overall taxes for the MNE in question.

Both foreign governments and the U.S. government are interested in the part that transfer prices play in the realization of corporate profits. Abuses in pricing across national borders are illegal if they can be proved. According to U.S. Internal Revenue Service (IRS) regulations, enterprises dealing with their own subsidiaries are required to set prices "at arms length," just as they would for unrelated customers. However, proving that the prices that one subsidiary charges another are far from market prices is very difficult.

There's no question that transfer-pricing abuses can be enormous. It is estimated that foreign-based multinationals dodge more than $20 billion in U.S. taxes each year, while U.S. multinationals account for an additional $5 billion in lost U.S. taxes on profits dubiously allocated to foreign tax havens. In its biggest known tax-abuse victory, the IRS argued that Toyota of Japan had systematically overcharged its U.S. subsidiary for years on most of the automobiles, trucks, and parts sold in the United States. What would have been taxable profits from the United States were shifted back to Japan. Although Toyota denied improprieties, it agreed to a $1 billion settlement with the IRS, paid in part with tax rebates from the Japanese government.

U.S. PRODUCTION SHARING WITH MEXICO

The ships sail east from South Korea and Japan to the Mexican port of Guaymas. There, rolls of steel are transferred to trains and shipped to Ford Motor's assembly plant in Hermosillo, Sonora. Ford stamps and assembles the steel into Mercury auto bodies, puts in Japanese engines, and transports the autos to the United States.

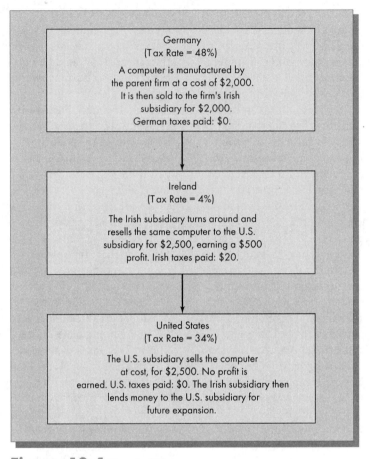

Figure 10.4 Transfer Pricing

This hypothetical example illustrates how MNEs can shift profits to countries with low corporate tax rates and thus get away with a smaller total tax bite. The MNE is headquartered in Germany (high-tax country) and has subsidiaries in Ireland (low-tax country) and in the United States. The bottom line is that the MNE pays no taxes either in Germany or in the United States!

Manufacturers such as Ford not only have changed the methods by which autos are produced but also have brought industry to Mexico's north, turning cow towns like Hermosillo into manufacturing centers.

Mexico's north, once a desert buffer between the capital, Mexico City, and the United States, has been the recipient of direct investment by foreign companies that have set up manufacturing facilities from the beaches south of San Diego to the Gulf Coast dunes beyond Brownsville, Texas. Mexico's **maquiladoras**, or industrial parks, typically host an assemblage of U.S.-owned companies that combine U.S. parts and supplies and Mexican assembly to manufacture goods that are exported to the United States. The mix of maquiladora products has traditionally been dominated by electronics (such as television sets) and automobiles. The largest concentration of maquiladora plants is in the border cities, including Ciudad Juárez, Tijuana, and Mexicali. Table 10.6 provides examples of companies that have located production facilities in Mexico.

Today, more than 1,300 maquiladoras operate in Mexico, employing more than half a million workers. The maquiladoras' managers point out that their workers are among the most highly skilled in Mexico and that they have trained large numbers of Mexican technicians, engineers, accountants, and middle managers.

The maquiladoras are engaged primarily in labor-intensive assembly operations that combine Mexican labor with U.S. capital and technology. Maquilas (firms) benefit from relatively low wages in Mexico and proximity to the United States. Proximity not only reduces transportation costs, compared with more distant low-wage countries (such as Taiwan), but also eases communication, facilitates supervision, and reduces lead times for delivery. Mexico's regional advantage is especially strong for such products as motor-vehicle parts that may require quick turnaround and benefit from good rail and highway connections between parts factories in the central United States, Mexican assembly plants in the Rio Grande Valley, and final auto-assembly plants in the central United States.

Mexico's attractiveness as an assembly location relative to that of other countries is reinforced by higher relative wage costs in such competing nations as Singapore, Taiwan, and South Korea.

The maquiladoras have drawn a considerable amount of capital to Mexico's northern border region, providing jobs and earning much-needed foreign exchange. But they have generated much controversy in both Mexico and the United States. Opposition in the United States has come mainly from labor unions that maintain that maquiladora investment by U.S. companies results in "runaway jobs." Proponents of the maquiladoras counter that northern Mexico is actually competing with other countries for labor-intensive factories and that jobs "lost" to the maquilas would eventually have been lost to other low-wage countries. Without the maquilas, many small and medium-sized U.S. companies would be driven out of business by foreign low-wage competitors in South Korea, Taiwan, and elsewhere. Having their unskilled jobs performed just across the border allows these companies to maintain the jobs of their skilled workers in the United States. They also contend that when U.S. jobs migrate to the border, a large amount of employment is generated in U.S. border communities and elsewhere in the United States because border production requires large quantities of U.S. inputs. Moreover, if it were not for the maquiladoras, additional Mexicans would likely be living in the United States as illegal immigrants.

In Mexico, critics of the maquiladoras contend that they make poor models for Mexican development. They assert that the maquilas exploit Mexican workers by paying them subsistence-level wages. Also, U.S. employers have relied on the most vulnerable and cheapest workers—young women and girls, who represent two-thirds of the maquiladora labor force. It is also maintained that a negligible fraction of the components used in the assembly of maquiladora output comes from Mexican suppliers. And the work itself is low-skilled, so workers receive minimal training. Because the maquiladoras do not transfer technology, there is little linkage between the maquiladoras and the rest of the Mexican economy, and few

Table 10.6 Companies with Production Facilities in Mexico: Selected Examples

Company	Product
Borg-Warner	Auto parts
Calmar Inc.	Plastics
Carrier	Metal
Emerson Electric	Electronics
General Instruments	Electronics
Honda	Auto parts
Lasating	Ceramics
Mattel	Toys
Motorola	Electronics
Unisys	Electronics

secondary benefits are generated. Maquiladoras tend to make Mexico more dependent on the rest of the world because important economic decisions are made outside of Mexico.

NAFTA, which went into force in 1994, has increased the competitiveness of production-sharing operations located in Mexico compared with those in East Asia and elsewhere. Producers within NAFTA have an incentive to purchase parts from fellow NAFTA beneficiaries to meet the NAFTA rules-of-origin requirements. Furthermore, U.S. and Canadian firms wishing to establish production-sharing facilities abroad are drawn to Mexico because products made in Mexico have preferential access to both NAFTA markets.

INTERNATIONAL LABOR MOBILITY: MIGRATION

Historically, the United States has been a favorite target for international **migration**. Because of its vast inflow of migrants, the United States has been described as the melting pot of the world. Table 10.7 indicates the volume of immigration to the United States from the 1820s to the 1990s. Western Europe was a major source of immigrants during this era, with Germany, Italy, and the United Kingdom among the largest contributors. In recent years, large numbers of Mexicans have migrated to the United States, as well as people from Asia. Migrants have been motivated by better economic opportunities and by noneconomic factors such as politics, war, and religion.

Although international labor movements can enhance the world economy's efficiency, they are often restricted by government controls. The United States, like most countries, limits immigration. Following waves of immigration at the turn of the century, the Immigration Act of 1924 was enacted. Besides restricting the overall flow of immigrants to the United States, the act implemented a quota that limited the number of immigrants from each foreign country. Because the quotas were based on the number of U.S. citizens who had previously emigrated from those coun-

Table 10.7 U.S. Immigration, 1820–1998

Period	Number (Thousands)
1820–1840	751
1841–1860	4,311
1861–1880	5,127
1881–1900	8,935
1901–1920	14,531
1921–1940	4,635
1941–1960	3,550
1961–1980	7,815
1981–1990	7,338
1991–1998	7,605

Source: U.S. Immigration and Naturalization Service, *Statistical Yearbook*, http://www.ins.usdoj.gov/graphics/index.htm. See also U.S. Department of Commerce, Bureau of the Census, *Statistical Abstracts of the United States*, Washington, DC, Government Printing Office.

tries, the allocation system favored emigrants from northern Europe relative to southern Europe. In the late 1960s, the quota formula was modified, which led to increasing numbers of Asian immigrants to the United States.

EFFECTS OF MIGRATION Figure 10.5 illustrates the economics of labor migration. Suppose the world consists of two countries, the United States and Mexico, that are initially in isolation. The horizontal axes denote the total quantity of labor in the United States and Mexico, and the vertical axes depict the wages paid to labor. For each country, the demand schedule for labor is designated by the value of the marginal product (VMP) of labor.[2] Also assume a fixed labor supply of 7 workers in the United States, denoted by $S_{U.S._0}$, and 7 workers in Mexico, denoted by S_{M_0}.

[2] The value of the marginal product of labor (VMP) refers to the amount of money producers receive from selling the quantity that was produced by the last worker hired; in other words, VMP = product price × the marginal product of labor. The VMP curve is the labor demand schedule. This follows from an application of the rule that a business hiring under competitive conditions finds it most profitable to hire labor up to the point at which the price of labor (wage rate) equals its VMP. The location of the VMP curve depends on the marginal productivity of labor and the price of the product that it produces. Under pure competition, price is constant. Therefore, it is because of diminishing marginal productivity that the labor demand schedule is downward sloping.

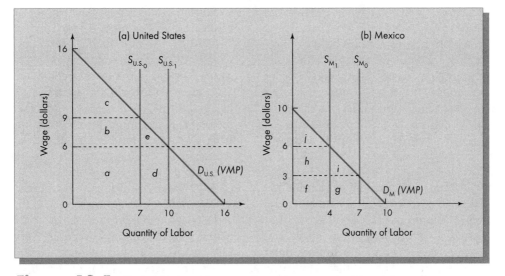

Figure 10.5 Effects of Labor Migration from Mexico to the United States

Prior to migration, the wage rate in the United States exceeds that of Mexico. Responding to the wage differential, Mexican workers migrate to the United States; this leads to a reduction in the Mexican labor supply and an increase in the U.S. labor supply. Wage rates continue to fall in Mexico and rise in the United States until they eventually are equalized. The labor migration hurts native U.S. workers but helps U.S. owners of capital; the opposite occurs in Mexico. Because migrant workers flow from uses of lower productivity to higher productivity, world output expands.

The equilibrium wage in each country is determined at the point of intersection of the supply and demand schedules for labor. In Figure 10.5(a), the U.S. equilibrium wage is $9, and total labor income is $63; this amount is represented by the area $a + b$. The remaining area under the labor demand schedule is area c, which equals $24.50; this represents the share of the nation's income accruing to owners of capital.[3] In Figure 10.5(b), the equilibrium wage for Mexico is $3; labor income totals $21, represented by area $f + g$; capital owners enjoy incomes equaling area $h + i + j$, or $24.50.

Suppose labor can move freely between Mexico and the United States and assume that migration is costless and occurs solely in response to wage differentials. Because U.S. wage rates are relatively high, there is an incentive for Mexican workers to migrate to the United States and compete in the U.S. labor market; this process will continue until the wage differential is eliminated. Suppose 3 workers migrate from Mexico to the United States. In the United States, the new labor supply schedule becomes $S_{U.S._1}$; the excess supply of labor at the $9 wage rate causes the wage rate to fall to $6. In Mexico, the labor emigration results in a new labor supply schedule at S_{M_1}; the excess demand for labor at wage rate $3 causes the wage rate to rise to $6. The effect of **labor**

---

[3] How do we know that area c represents the income accruing to U.S. owners of capital? Our analysis assumes two productive factors, labor and capital. The total income (value of output) that results from using a given quantity of labor with a fixed amount of capital equals the area under the *VMP* curve of labor for that particular quantity of labor. Labor's share of that area is calculated by multiplying the wage rate times the quantity of labor hired. The remaining area under the *VMP* curve is the income accruing to the owners of capital.

mobility is thus to equalize wage rates in the two countries.[4]

Our next job is to assess how labor migration in response to wage differentials affects the world economy's efficiency. Does world output expand or contract with open migration? For the United States, migration increases the labor supply from $S_{U.S._0}$ to $S_{U.S._1}$. This leads to an expansion of output; the value of the additional output is denoted by area $d + e$ ($22.50). For Mexico, the decrease in labor supply from S_{M_0} to S_{M_1} results in a contraction in output; the value of the lost output is represented by area $g + i$ ($13.50). The result is a net gain of $9 in world output as a result of labor migration. This is because the *VMP* of labor in the United States exceeds that of Mexico throughout the relevant range. Workers are attracted to the United States by the higher wages paid. These higher wages signal to Mexican labor the higher value of worker productivity, thus attracting workers to those areas where they will be most efficient. As workers are used more productively, world output expands.

Migration also affects the *distribution of income*. As we will see, the gains in world income resulting from labor mobility are not distributed equally among all nations and factors of production. The United States as a whole benefits from immigration; its overall income gain is the sum of the losses by native U.S. workers, gains by Mexican immigrants now living in the United States, and gains by U.S. owners of capital. Mexico experiences overall income losses as a result of its labor emigration; however, workers remaining in Mexico gain relative to Mexican owners of capital. As previously suggested, the Mexican immigrants gain from their relocation to the United States.

[4] Wage-rate equalization assumes unrestricted labor mobility in which workers are concerned only about their incomes. It also assumes that migration is costless for labor. In reality, there are economic and psychological costs of migrating to another country. Such costs may result in only a small number of persons' finding the wage gains in the immigrating country high enough to compensate them for their migration costs. Thus, complete wage equalization may not occur.

For the United States, the gain in income as a result of immigration is denoted by area $d + e$ ($22.50) in Figure 10.5(a). Of this amount, Mexican immigrants capture area d ($18), while area e ($4.50) is the extra income accruing to U.S. owners of capital thanks to the availability of additional labor to use with the capital. However, immigration forces wage rates down from $9 to $6. The earnings of the native U.S. workers fall by area b ($21); this amount is transferred to U.S. owners of capital.

As for Mexico, its labor emigration results in a decrease in income equal to $g + i$ ($13.50); this represents a transfer from Mexico to the United States. The remaining workers in Mexico gain area h ($12) as a result of higher wages. However, Mexican capital owners lose because less labor is available for use with their capital.

We can conclude that the effect of labor mobility is to increase overall world income and to redistribute income from labor to capital in the United States and from capital to labor in Mexico. Migration has an impact on the distribution of income similar to an increase in exports of labor-intensive goods from Mexico to the United States.

IMMIGRATION AS AN ISSUE The preceding example makes it clear why domestic labor groups in capital-abundant nations often prefer restrictions on immigration; open immigration tends to reduce their wages. When migrant workers are unskilled, as is typically the case, the negative effect on wages mainly affects unskilled domestic workers. Conversely, domestic manufacturers will tend to favor unrestricted immigration as a source of cheap labor.

Another controversy about immigrants is whether they are a drain on government resources. Nations that provide generous welfare payments to the economically disadvantaged may fear they will induce an influx of nonproductive people who will not produce as did the immigrants of Figure 10.5, but will enjoy welfare benefits at the expense of domestic residents and working immigrants. However, fiscal relief may not be far away. The children of immigrants will soon enter the labor force and begin paying taxes, thus supporting not only their kids' education, but also their parents' retirement. And, in a matter of two generations, most immigrant families tend to assimilate to the point that their fiscal burdens are indistinguishable from those of other natives. When it's all added up, most long-run calculations show that immigrants make a net positive contribution to public coffers.

Developing nations have sometimes feared open immigration policies because they can result in a **brain drain**—emigration of highly educated and skilled people from developing nations to industrial nations, thus limiting the growth potential of the developing nations. The brain drain has been encouraged by national immigration laws, as in the United States and other industrial nations, that permit the immigration of skilled persons while restricting that of unskilled workers. In the previous labor-migration example, we implicitly assumed that the Mexican workers' migration decision was more or less permanent. In practice, much labor migration is temporary, especially in the European Union. That is, a country such as France will allow the immigration of foreign workers on a temporary basis when needed; these workers are known as **guest workers**. During periods of business recession, France will refuse to issue work permits when foreign workers are no longer needed. Such a practice tends to insulate the French economy from labor shortages during business expansions and labor surpluses during business recessions. However, the labor-adjustment problem is shifted to the labor-emigrating countries.

There is also the problem of illegal migration. In the United States, this has become a political hot potato, with millions of illegal immigrants finding employment in the so-called underground economy, often at below-minimum wages. Some 3 to 15 million illegal immigrants are estimated to be in the United States, many of them from Mexico. For the United States, and especially the southwestern states, immigration of Mexican workers has provided a cheap supply

of agricultural and less skilled workers. For Mexico, it has been a major source of foreign exchange and a safety cushion against domestic unemployment. Illegal immigration also affects the distribution of income for U.S. natives because it tends to reduce the income of low-skilled U.S. workers.

On the other hand, immigrants not only diversify an economy, but they may also contribute to economic growth. It is because immigrants are often different from natives that the economy as a whole profits. In many instances, immigrants both cause prices to fall, which benefits all consumers, and enable the economy to domestically produce a wider variety of goods than natives could alone. If immigrants weren't different from natives, they would only augment the population and the scale of the economy, but not have an effect on the overall growth rate of per capita income. According to the National Research Council, the overall effect of immigration on the U.S. gross domestic product is between $1 billion and $10 billion a year.[5] While these amounts may seem negligible in an $8 trillion economy (about one-eighth of 1 percent at most), they are still a gain—and not the drain many believe immigration to be.

As we learned from Figure 10.5, immigrants increase the supply of labor in the economy. This results in a lower market wage for all workers *if all workers are the same*. But all workers are not the same. Some natives will compete with immigrants for positions because they possess similar skills; others will work alongside immigrants, complementing the immigrants' skills with their own. This skill distinction means that not all native workers will receive a lower wage. Those who compete with (are substitutes for) immigrants will receive a lower wage than they would without immigration, while those who complement immigrants will receive a higher wage. Most analyses of various countries have found

---

[5] See National Research Council Panel on the Demographic and Economic Impacts of Immigration, *The New Americans: Economic, Demographic, and Fiscal Effects of Immigration* (Washington D.C.: National Academy Press, 1997).

that a 10-percent increase in the immigrant share of the population reduces native wages by 1 percent at most. This finding suggests that most immigrants are not substituting for native labor—skilled or unskilled—but are, instead, complementing it.[6]

IMMIGRATION AND THE U.S. LABOR MARKET

By the 1970s and 1980s, immigration and trade had become increasingly significant for the U.S. labor market. The number of legal and illegal immigrants to the United States grew, modifying the size and composition of the work force and increasing the immigrant share of labor in so-called gateway cities, such as Los Angeles, New York, and Miami. The national origins of immigrants to the United States changed from primarily European to Mexican, Latin American, and Asian.

For native workers whose skills compete with those of new immigrants, immigration can adversely affect wages and employment, making their economic well-being a central issue in immigration policy. If certain segments of the native labor force, such as the low-wage workers for whom immigrants may be good substitutes, undergo sizable reductions in employment and earning opportunities, then the case for immigration controls to aid these workers is strengthened. Conversely, if the labor market can easily absorb additional immigrants without serious distributional impacts on native workers, allowing increasing numbers of immigrants seems more reasonable.

Critics of U.S. liberal trade and immigration policies maintain that they have depressed U.S. wages. In 1991, the National Bureau of Economic Research (NBER) analyzed this issue by considering the widening gap in earnings between lesser-educated and higher-educated U.S. workers during the 1980s.[7] This was a period in which college graduates' wages increased in inflationary-adjusted terms while inflationary-adjusted earnings of lesser-educated workers either failed to rise or actually decreased.

According to the NBER study, both trade and immigration augmented the effective U.S. supply of workers during the 1980s. The large U.S. trade deficits in manufacturers increased the "implicit" labor supply by some 6 percent annually during this period; the immigration flow increased the share of the U.S. workforce that was foreign born from 6.9 percent in 1980 to 9.3 percent in 1988. Moreover, trade and immigration augmented the supply of less-skilled workers more than they augmented the supply of more-skilled workers. This was because the largest portion of the U.S. trade deficit was concentrated in industries that intensively employed high-school dropouts, and the wave of new immigrants during the 1980s included many poorly educated workers. Many of these immigrants were non-English-speaking, sometimes barely literate in their own native languages, less able and less willing to adapt to American culture than earlier immigrants, and more of a burden on social services.

The NBER estimated that by 1988, the combination of the trade deficit and continued high immigration had increased the effective supply of high-school dropouts by approximately 30 percent. These two factors accounted for some 30 to 50 percent of the 10-percentage-point decline in dropout wages relative to those of high-school and college graduates during the period 1980 to 1988. In short, by increasing the effective supply of less-educated workers in the 1980s, imports and increased immigration depressed wages and thus widened the earnings gap between less-skilled and more-skilled Americans. By the 1990s, many Americans were expressing concerns that immigrants harmed the country by taking away jobs, driving down wages, and using too many government services.

Recent empirical work by labor economist George Borjas suggests that the increasing internationalization of the U.S. labor market, through both immigration and trade, has had an impor-

[6] Friedberg, R. M. and J. Hunt, "The Impact of Immigrants on Host Country Wages, Employment and Growth," *Journal of Economic Perspectives* (Spring 1995), pp. 23–44.

[7] Richard Freeman, ed., *Immigration, Trade, and the Labor Market* (Cambridge, MA: National Bureau of Economic Research, 1988).

tant impact on the wage structure. Immigration has tended to increase aggregate wage inequality because more recent immigrant waves tend to be less skilled than earlier waves. Also, it is likely that the large number of unskilled immigrants who entered the United States in the past two decades have had an adverse impact on the employment opportunities of less-skilled native workers. Trade in durable goods has increased wage inequality because durable-goods industries employ a disproportionately large number of less-skilled workers, and these workers previously received higher wages than comparable workers in more competitive sectors of the economy. The trade deficit in durable goods has decreased the returns going to domestic firms and workers and has had adverse spillover effects as displaced workers move from the trade-impacted industries into other sectors of the economy.[8]

The infusion of foreigners into the United States during the 1980s and 1990s, however, did not include only people with minimal skills and minimal education. Enjoying the benefits of a foreign brain drain, the United States reaped a bonanza of highly educated newcomers who enhanced the competitiveness of its companies. America's high-tech industries, from biotechnology to semiconductors, increasingly depended on immigrant scientists, engineers, and entrepreneurs to remain competitive; in Silicon Valley, the jewel of U.S. high-tech centers, much of the workforce is foreign born. With their bilingual skills, family ties, and knowledge of how things get done overseas, immigrants also contributed to the export of Made-in-USA goods and services. Moreover, they helped revitalize America by establishing new businesses and generating jobs, profits, and taxes to pay for social services. The infusion of new people into the United States thus helped improve the globally competitive top half of its economy. These benefits must be weighed against the economic disruptions caused

by the infusion of less educated and less capable people into the nation.

IS IMMIGRATION GOOD FOR CALIFORNIA?

The current national debate on immigration policy is especially intense in California, home to one-third of the country's immigrants. Economists at RAND, a private research institute, have analyzed the effects of immigration on California. Their conclusion: immigration is still a good thing, but its benefits are diminishing because of a growing mismatch between the needs of the economy and the quality of the new immigrants.[9]

According to RAND, California's employers, and its economy in general, have been the main beneficiaries of immigration. Immigrants are paid less than native workers at all skill levels but are equally productive employees. As a result, they have contributed to California's faster economic growth compared to the rest of the nation from 1960 to 1990. Even when California's growth advantage disappeared during the depths of the recession from 1990 to 1994, immigrants continued to arrive in the state in greater numbers and to hold down its labor costs.

However, these economic benefits have not come without certain costs. According to RAND, California's economy increasingly needs workers who have been educated beyond the high-school level. However, the latest immigrants appear to be less well educated than native-born Californians, and speak little or no English. Also, the educational level of immigrants has been decreasing relative to that of native Californians.

This results in several adverse consequences for California, according to RAND. First, the least-skilled native-born Californians have seen their wages hit and their job opportunities hurt by increased competition from immigrants. And the least-skilled immigrants have seen their earnings

---

[8] George Borjas, "The Internationalization of the U.S. Labor Market and the Wage Structure," *Economic Policy Review*, Federal Reserve Bank of New York, January 1995, pp. 3–8.

[9] Devin McCarthy and Georges Vernez, *Immigration in a Changing Economy: California's Experience* (RAND, Santa Monica, CA, 1997). See also "Immigration: Turn of the Tide?" *The Economist*, September 27, 1997, pp. 29–30.

decline both in relation to native-born workers and in relation to previous generations of immigrants. Second, the lower incomes and larger family sizes of recent immigrants have increased their demand for public services, particularly education, without increasing tax payments. The third effect is to erode California's claim to have America's most highly skilled labor force.

RAND does not hesitate to draw conclusions. For California, RAND argues that the state should develop policies for integrating immigrants both socially and economically. Because education is the most important determinant of the success of immigrants and their children, California must make special efforts to promote high-school graduation and college attendance for the children of immigrants, most of whom are born in the state. Moreover, the state should work with the federal government to sponsor programs that expedite English proficiency for adult immigrants already living and working in California. RAND also argues that the United States should decrease legal immigration, including refugees, and that it should expand the criteria for admission to include skills and education.

Critics of the RAND study maintain that its authors think that immigrants fill educationally graded slots in a predetermined economy. However, the entrepreneurs of Los Angeles's thriving toy and garment sector did not fill slots; they created businesses that would have not existed without the skills and capital they brought in from abroad. RAND places too much emphasis on education as compared with other resources, such as sheer willingness to work.

The second concern is RAND's emphasis on individuals rather than families, an emphasis that is especially misleading in its treatment of California's largest immigrant group, Hispanics. They try to make up for their low individual incomes by pooling family resources to purchase houses and small businesses.

Indeed, foreign-born Hispanics may have three advantages that help them make up for their lack of educational qualifications: the highest number of wage earners per family of any ethnic group, the highest participation in the labor force, and stable families. Thus, the households of American-born Hispanics—the descendants of immigrants—have almost the same average incomes as their white and Asian equivalents: 55 percent of them own their own homes, compared with 71 percent of white households and 44 percent of black ones.

S U M M A R Y

1. Today the world economy is characterized by the international movement of factor inputs. The multinational enterprise plays a central part in this process.

2. There is no single agreed-on definition of what constitutes an MNE. Some of the most identifiable characteristics of multinationals are the following: (a) Stock ownership and management are multinational in character; (b) Company headquarters may be far removed from the country where a particular activity occurs; and (c) Foreign sales represent a high proportion of total sales.

3. MNEs have diversified their operations along vertical, horizontal, and conglomerate lines.

4. Among the major factors that influence decisions to undertake foreign direct investment are (a) market demand, (b) trade restrictions, (c) investment regulations, and (d) labor productivity and costs.

5. In planning to set up overseas operations, a business must decide whether to construct (or purchase) plants abroad or extend licenses to foreign businesses to produce its goods.

6. The theory of multinational enterprise essentially agrees with the predictions of the comparative-advantage principle. However, conventional trade theory assumes that commodities are traded between independent, competitive businesses, whereas MNEs are

often vertically integrated businesses, with substantial intrafirm sales. Thus, MNEs may use transfer pricing to maximize overall company profits rather than the profits of any single subsidiary.

7. In recent years, companies have increasingly linked up with former rivals in a vast array of joint ventures. International joint ventures can yield welfare-increasing effects as well as market-power effects.

8. Some of the more controversial issues involving MNEs are (a) employment, (b) technology transfer, (c) national sovereignty, (d) balance of payments, and (e) taxation.

9. There are major differences between the theory of multinational enterprise and conventional trade theory. The conventional model assumes that commodities are traded between independent, competitive business-

es. However, MNEs are often vertically integrated businesses with substantial intrafirm sales. Also, MNEs may use transfer pricing to maximize overall company profits instead of the profits of any single subsidiary.

10. Mexico's maquiladoras are assemblages of foreign-owned companies that use foreign parts and Mexican assembly to produce goods that are exported to the United States. Maquiladora products have traditionally emphasized electronics and automobiles.

11. International labor migration occurs for economic and noneconomic reasons. Migration increases output and decreases wages in the country of immigration, as it decreases output and increasing wages in the country of emigration. For the world as a whole, migration leads to net increases in output.

STUDY QUESTIONS

1. Multinational enterprises may diversify their operations along vertical, horizontal, and conglomerate lines within the host and source countries. Distinguish among these diversification approaches.

2. What are the major foreign industries in which U.S. businesses have chosen to place direct investments? What are the major industries in the United States in which foreigners place direct investments?

3. Why is it that the rate of return on U.S. direct investments in the developing nations often exceeds the rate of return on its investments in industrial nations?

4. What are the most important motives behind an enterprise's decision to undertake foreign direct investment?

5. What is meant by the term *multinational enterprise*?

6. Under what conditions would a business wish to enter foreign markets by extending licenses or franchises to local businesses to produce its goods?

7. What are the major issues involving multinational enterprises as a source of conflict for source and host countries?

8. Is the theory of multinational enterprise essentially consistent or inconsistent with the traditional model of comparative advantage?

9. What are some examples of welfare gains and welfare losses that can result from the formation of international joint ventures among competing businesses?

10. What effects does labor migration have on the country of immigration? The country of emigration? The world as a whole?

11. Table 10.8 illustrates the revenue conditions facing ABC, Inc., and XYZ, Inc., which operate as competitors in the U.S. calculator market. Each firm realizes constant long-run costs ($MC = AC$) of $4 per unit. On graph paper, plot the enterprise demand, marginal revenue, and $MC = AC$ schedules. On the basis of this information, answer the following questions.

Table 10.8 Price and Marginal Revenue: Calculators

Quantity	Price ($)	Marginal Revenue ($)
0	9	—
1	8	8
2	7	6
3	6	4
4	5	2
5	4	0
6	3	-2
7	2	-4

a. With ABC and XYZ behaving as competitors, the equilibrium price is $ _____ and output is _____ . At the equilibrium price, U.S. households attain $ _____ of consumer surplus, while company profits total $ _____ .

b. Suppose the two organizations jointly form a new one, JV, Inc., whose calculators replace the output sold by the parent companies in the U.S. market. Assuming that JV operates as a monopoly and that its costs ($MC = AC$) equal $4 per unit, the company's output would be _____ at a price of $ _____ , and total profit would be $ _____ . Compared to the market equilibrium position achieved by ABC and XYZ as competitors, JV as a monopoly leads to a deadweight loss of consumer surplus equal to $ _____ .

c. Assume now that the formation of JV yields technological advances that result in a per-unit cost of only $2; sketch the new $MC = AC$ schedule in the figure. Realizing that JV results in a deadweight loss of consumer surplus, as described in *b*, the net effect of the formation of JV on U.S. welfare is a gain/loss of $ _____ . If JV's cost reduction was due to wage concessions of JV's U.S. employees, the net welfare gain/loss for the United States

would equal $ _____ . If JV's cost reductions resulted from changes in work rules leading to higher worker productivity, the net welfare gain/loss for the United States would equal $ _____ .

12. Table 10.9 illustrates the hypothetical demand and supply schedules of labor in the United States. Assume that labor and capital are the only two factors of production. On graph paper, plot these schedules.

a. Without immigration, suppose the labor force in the United States is denoted by schedule S_0. The equilibrium wage rate is $ _____ ; payments to native U.S. workers total $ _____ , while payments to U.S. capital owners equal $ _____ .

b. Suppose immigration from Hong Kong results in an overall increase in the U.S. labor force to S_1. Wages would rise/fall to $ _____ , payments to native U.S. workers would total $ _____ , and payments to Hong Kong immigrants would total $ _____ . U.S. owners of capital would receive payments of $ _____ .

c. Which U.S. factor of production would gain from expanded immigration? _____ Which U.S. factor of production would likely resist policies permitting Hong Kong workers to freely migrate to the United States? _____

Table 10.9 Demand and Supply of Labor

Wage ($)	Quantity Demanded	Quantity Supplied$_0$	Quantity Supplied$_1$
8	0	2	4
6	2	2	4
4	4	2	4
2	6	2	4
0	8	2	4

NetLink

10.1 Information about America's and the world's biggest companies, many of which are multinational, can be found by examining the Fortune 500 Giants and the Global 500. Set your browser to URL:

http://www.fortune.com/fortune

10.2 Comprehensive statistics on U.S. immigration can be found by visiting the Immigration and Naturalization Service (INS) home page. Set your browser to URL:

http://www.ins.usdoj.gov/graphics/aboutins/statistics/index.htm

To access NetLink Exercises and the Virtual Scavenger Hunt, visit the Carbaugh Web site at http://carbaugh.swcollege.com.

part two

INTERNATIONAL MONETARY RELATIONS

The Balance of Payments

When trade occurs between the United States and other nations, many types of financial transactions are recorded on a summary called the balance of payments. In this chapter, we examine the monetary aspects of international trade by considering the nature and significance of a nation's balance of payments.

The **balance of payments** is a record of the economic transactions between the residents of one country and the rest of the world. Nations keep record of their balance of payments over the course of a one-year period; the United States and some other nations also keep such a record on a quarterly basis.

An *international transaction* is an exchange of goods, services, or assets between residents of one country and those of another. But what is meant by the term *resident*? Residents include businesses, individuals, and government agencies that make the country in question their legal domicile. Although a corporation is considered to be a resident of the country in which it is incorporated, its overseas branch or subsidiary is not. Military personnel, government diplomats, tourists, and workers who emigrate temporarily are considered residents of the country in which they hold citizenship.

KEY CONCEPTS AND TERMS

- Balance of international indebtedness
- Balance of payments
- Capital account
- Credit transaction
- Current account
- Debit transaction
- Double-entry accounting
- Goods and services balance
- Merchandise trade balance
- Net creditor
- Net debtor
- Net foreign investment
- Official reserve assets
- Official settlements transactions
- Statistical discrepancy
- Trade balance
- Unilateral transfers

DOUBLE-ENTRY ACCOUNTING

The arrangement of international transactions into a balance-of-payments account requires that each transaction be entered as a credit or a debit. A **credit transaction** is one that results in a *receipt* of a payment from foreigners. A **debit transaction** is one that leads to a *payment* to foreigners.

This distinction is clarified when we assume that transactions take place between U.S. residents and foreigners and that all payments are financed in dollars.

From the U.S. perspective, the following transactions are credits (+), leading to the receipt of dollars from foreigners:

- Merchandise exports
- Transportation and travel receipts
- Income received from investments abroad
- Gifts received from foreign residents
- Aid received from foreign governments
- Investments in the United States by overseas residents

Conversely, the following transactions are debits (–) from the U.S. viewpoint because they involve payments to foreigners:

- Merchandise imports
- Transportation and travel expenditures
- Income paid on investments of foreigners
- Gifts to foreign residents
- Aid given by the U.S. government
- Overseas investment by U.S. residents

Although we speak in terms of credit transactions and debit transactions, every international transaction involves an exchange of assets and so has both a credit and a debit side. Each credit entry is balanced by a debit entry, and vice versa, so that the recording of any international transaction leads to two offsetting entries. In other words, the balance-of-payments accounts utilize a **double-entry accounting** system. The following two examples illustrate the double-entry technique.

EXAMPLE 1. IBM sells $25 million worth of computers to a German importer. Payment is made by a bill of exchange, which increases the balances of New York banks at their Bonn correspondents' bank. Because the export involves a transfer of U.S. assets abroad for which payment is to be received, it is entered in the U.S. balance of payments as a credit transaction. IBM's receipt of payment held in the German bank is classified as a short-term capital move-ment because the financial claims of the United States against the German bank have increased. The entries on the U.S. balance of payments would appear as follows:

	Credits (+)	Debits (−)
Merchandise exports	$25 million	
Short-term capital movement		$25 million

EXAMPLE 2. A U.S. resident who owns bonds issued by a Japanese company receives interest payments of $10,000. With payment, the balances owned by New York banks at their Tokyo affiliate are increased. The impact of this transaction on the U.S. balance of payments would be as follows:

	Credits (+)	Debits (−)
Service exports	$10,000	
Short-term capital movement		$10,000

These examples illustrate how every international transaction has two equal sides, a credit and a debit. If we add up all the credits as pluses and all the debits as minuses, the net result is zero; that is, the total credits must always equal the total debits. This means that the total balance-of-payments account must always be in balance. There is no such thing as an overall balance-of-payments surplus or deficit.

Even though the entire balance of payments must numerically balance by definition, it does not necessarily follow that any single subaccount or subaccounts of the statement must balance. For instance, total merchandise exports may or may not be in balance with total merchandise imports. When reference is made to a balance-of-payments surplus or deficit, it is particular subaccounts of the balance of payments that are referred to, not the overall value. A *surplus* occurs when the balance on a subaccount (subaccounts) is positive; a *deficit* occurs when the balance is negative.

INTERNATIONAL PAYMENTS PROCESS

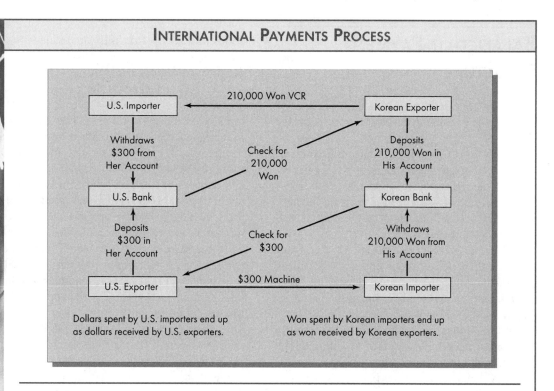

Dollars spent by U.S. importers end up as dollars received by U.S. exporters.

Won spent by Korean importers end up as won received by Korean exporters.

When residents in different countries contemplate selling or buying products, they must consider how payments will occur. Assume that you, as a resident of the United States, buy a VCR directly from a producer in South Korea. How, when, and where will the South Korean producer obtain his won so that he can spend the money in South Korea?

Initially, you would write a check for $300, which your U.S. bank would convert to 210,000 won (assuming an exchange rate of 700 won per dollar). When the South Korean producer receives your payment in won, he deposits the funds in his bank. The bank in South Korea thus holds a check from a U.S. bank that promises to pay a stipulated amount of won.

Assume that at the same time you paid for your VCR, a buyer in South Korea paid a U.S. producer $300 for machinery. The flowchart illustrates the path of both transactions.

When trade is in balance, money of different countries does not actually change hands across the oceans. In this example, the value of South Korea's exports to the United States equals the value of South Korea's imports from the United States; the won that South Korean importers use to purchase dollars to pay for U.S. goods are equal to the won that South Korean exporters receive in payment for the products they ship to the United States. The dollars that would flow, in effect, from U.S. importers to U.S. exporters exhibit a similar equality.

In theory, importers in a country pay the exporters in that same country in the national currency. In reality, however, importers and exporters in a given country do not deal directly with one another; to facilitate payments, banks carry out these transactions.

BALANCE-OF-PAYMENTS STRUCTURE

Let us now consider the structure of the balance of payments by examining its various subaccounts.

CURRENT ACCOUNT The **current account** of the balance of payments refers to the monetary value of international flows associated with transactions in goods and services, investment income, and unilateral transfers. Each of these flows will be described in turn.

Merchandise trade includes all of the goods the United States exports or imports: agricultural products, machinery, autos, petroleum, electronics, textiles, and the like. The dollar value of merchandise exports is recorded as a plus (credit), and the dollar value of merchandise imports is recorded as a minus (debit). Combining the exports and imports of goods gives the **merchandise trade balance**. When this balance is negative, the result is a merchandise trade deficit; a positive balance implies a merchandise trade surplus.

Exports and imports of *services* include a variety of items. When U.S. ships carry foreign products or foreign tourists spend money at U.S. restaurants and motels, valuable services are being provided by U.S. residents, who must be compensated. Such services are considered exports and are recorded as credit items on the goods and services account. Conversely, when foreign ships carry U.S. products or when U.S. tourists spend money at hotels and restaurants abroad, then foreign residents are providing services that require compensation. Because U.S. residents are, in effect, importing these services, the services are recorded as debit items. Insurance and banking services are explained in the same way. Services also include items such as transfers of goods under military programs, construction services, legal services, technical services, and the like.

To get a broader understanding of the international transactions of a country, we must add services to the merchandise trade account. This total gives the **goods and services balance**. When this balance is positive, the result is a surplus on goods and services transactions; a negative balance implies a deficit. Just what does a surplus or deficit balance appearing on the U.S. goods and services account mean? If the goods and services account shows a surplus, the United States has transferred more resources (goods and services) to foreigners than it has received from them over the period of one year. Besides measuring the value of the *net transfer of resources*, the goods and services balance also furnishes information about the status of a nation's gross domestic product (GDP). This is because the balance on the goods and services account is defined essentially the same way as the *net export of goods and services*, which is part of a nation's GDP.

Recall from your macroeconomics course that GDP is equal to the value of the goods and services produced in an economy over a period of time. In an economy with trade, GDP is equal to the sum of four different types of spending in the economy: consumption, gross investment, government spending, and net exports of goods and services. In effect, net exports represent the value of goods and services that are produced domestically but not included in domestic consumption.

For a nation's GDP, then, the balance on the goods and services account can be interpreted as follows. A positive balance on the account shows an excess of exports over imports, and this difference must be added to the GDP. When the account is in deficit, the excess of imports over exports must be subtracted from the GDP. If a nation's exports of goods and services equal its imports, the account will have a net imbalance of zero and will not affect the status of the GDP. Therefore, depending on the relative value of exports and imports, the balance on the goods and services account contributes to the level of a nation's national product.

Broadening our balance-of-payments summary further, we must include *income receipts and payments*. This item consists of the net earnings (dividends and interest) on U.S. investments abroad—that is, earnings on U.S. investments abroad less payments on foreign assets in the United States. It also includes compensation of employees.

Finally, our balance-of-payments summary is expanded to include **unilateral transfers.** These items include transfers of goods and services (gifts in kind) or financial assets (money gifts) between the United States and the rest of the world. *Private transfer payments* refer to gifts made by individuals and nongovernmental institutions to foreigners. These might include a remittance from an immigrant living in the United States to relatives back home, a birthday present sent to a friend overseas, or a contribution by a U.S. resident to a relief fund for underdeveloped nations.

Governmental transfers refer to gifts or grants made by one government to foreign residents or foreign governments. The U.S. government makes transfers in the form of money and capital goods to underdeveloped nations, military aid to foreign governments, and remittances such as retirement pensions to foreign workers who have moved back home. In some cases, U.S. governmental transfers represent payments associated with foreign assistance programs that can be used by foreign governments to finance trade with the United States. It should be noted that many U.S. transfer (foreign aid) programs are tied to the purchase of U.S. exports (such as military equipment or farm exports) and thus represent a subsidy to U.S. exporters. When investment income and unilateral transfers are combined with the balance on goods and services, we arrive at the current account balance. This is the broadest measure of a nation's balance of payments regularly quoted in the newspapers and in national television and radio news reports.

CAPITAL ACCOUNT Capital transactions in the balance of payments include all international purchases or sales of assets. The term *assets* is broadly defined to include items such as titles to real estate, corporation stocks and bonds, government securities, and ordinary commercial bank deposits. The **capital account** includes both private-sector and official (central bank) transactions. The following are examples of private-sector capital transactions:

DIRECT INVESTMENT. Direct investment occurs when residents of one country acquire a controlling interest (stock ownership of 10 percent or more) in a business enterprise in another country.

SECURITIES. Securities are private-sector purchases of short- and long-term debt securities, such as Treasury bills, Treasury notes, Treasury bonds, and securities of private enterprises.

BANK CLAIMS AND LIABILITIES. Bank claims consist of loans, overseas deposits, acceptances, foreign commercial paper, claims on affiliated banks abroad, and foreign government obligations. Bank liabilities include demand deposits and NOW (negotiable order of withdrawal) accounts, passbook savings deposits, certificates of deposit, and liabilities to affiliated banks abroad.

Capital transactions are recorded in the balance-of-payments statement by applying a plus sign (credit) to capital inflows and a minus sign (debit) to capital outflows. For the United States, a *capital inflow* might occur under the following circumstances: (1) U.S. liabilities to foreigners rise (for example, a French resident purchases securities of IBM); (2) U.S. claims on foreigners decrease (Citibank receives repayment for a loan it made to a Mexican enterprise); (3) foreign-held assets in the United States rise (Toyota builds an auto-assembly plant in the United States); (4) U.S. assets overseas decrease (Coca-Cola sells one of its Japanese bottling plants to a Japanese buyer). A *capital outflow* would imply the opposite.

The following rule may be helpful in appreciating the fundamental difference between credit and debit transactions that make up the capital account. Any transaction that leads to the home country's receiving payments from foreigners can be regarded as a credit item. A capital inflow can be likened to the *export* of goods and services. Conversely, any transaction that leads to foreigner's receiving payment from the home country is considered a debit item. A capital outflow is similar in effect to the *import* of goods and services.

Besides including private-sector transactions, the capital account includes **official settlements transactions** of the home country's central bank. Official settlements transactions refer to the movement of financial assets among official holders (for example, the U.S. Federal Reserve and the Bank of England). These financial assets fall into two categories: official reserve assets (U.S. government assets abroad) and liabilities to foreign official agencies (foreign official assets in the United States).

Table 11.1 summarizes the **official reserve assets** position of the United States as of 2000. One such asset is the stock of gold reserves held by the U.S. government. Next are convertible currencies, such as the Japanese yen, that are readily acceptable as payment for international transactions and can be easily exchanged for one another. Another reserve asset is the special drawing right (SDR), described in Chapter 18. Last is the reserve position that the United States maintains in the International Monetary Fund, also described in Chapter 18. Central banks often buy or sell international reserve assets in private-sector markets to affect their currencies' exchange rates, as will be discussed in Chapter 18.

Official settlements transactions also include liabilities to foreign official holders. These liabilities refer to foreign official holdings with U.S. commercial banks and official holdings of U.S. Treasury securities. Foreign governments often wish to hold such assets because of the interest earnings they provide. Table 11.2 illustrates the U.S. liabilities to foreign official holders as of 1999.

STATISTICAL DISCREPANCY: ERRORS AND OMISSIONS The data-collection process that underlies the published balance-of-payments figures is far from perfect. The cost of collecting balance-of-payments statistics is high, and a perfectly accurate collection system would be prohibitively costly. Government statisticians thus base their figures partly on information collected and partly on estimates. Probably the most reliable information consists of merchandise trade data, which are collected mainly from customs records. Capital account information is derived from reports by financial institutions indicating changes in their liabilities and claims to foreigners; these data are not matched with specific current account transactions. Because statisticians do not have a system whereby they can simultaneously record the credit side and debit side of each transaction, such information for any particular transaction tends to

Table 11.1 U.S. Reserve Assets, 2000*

Type	Amount (Billions of Dollars)
Gold stock**	$11.0
Special drawing rights	10.2
Reserve positions in the International Monetary Fund	17.7
Convertible foreign currencies	30.9
Total	69.8

*March

**Gold is valued at $42.22/fine troy ounce.

Source: *Federal Reserve Bulletin*, May 2000, p. A–51.

Table 11.2 Selected U.S. Liabilities to Foreign Official Institutions, 1999*

	Amount (Billions of Dollars)
BY TYPE	
Liabilities reported by U.S. banks**	124.2
U.S. Treasury bills and certificates	153.5
U.S. Treasury bonds and notes	423.2
Other U.S. securities	105.7
Total	806.6
BY AREA	
Europe	242.5
Canada	39.1
Latin America/Caribbean	72.3
Asia	441.0
Africa	7.1
Other	4.6
Total	806.6

*January

**Includes demand deposits, time deposits, bank acceptances, commercial paper, negotiable time certificates of deposit, and borrowings under repurchase agreements.

Source: *Federal Reserve Bulletin*, May, 2000, p. A–52.

come from different sources. Large numbers of transactions fail to get recorded.

When statisticians sum the credits and debits, it is not surprising when the two totals do not match. Because total debits must equal total credits in principle, statisticians insert a *residual* to make them equal. This correcting entry is known as **statistical discrepancy**, or errors and omissions. In the balance-of-payments statement, statistical discrepancy is treated as part of the capital account because short-term capital transactions are generally the most frequent source of error.

THE U.S. BALANCE OF PAYMENTS

For the United States, the method the U.S. Department of Commerce uses in presenting bal-

ance-of-payments statistics is shown in Table 11.3. This format groups specific transactions together along functional lines to provide analysts with information about the impact of international transactions on the domestic economy. The *partial balances* published on a regular basis include the merchandise trade balance, the balance on goods and services, the current account balance, and information about capital account transactions.

The *merchandise trade balance*, commonly referred to as the **trade balance** by the news media, is derived by computing the net exports (imports) in the merchandise accounts. Owing to its narrow focus on traded goods, the merchandise trade balance offers limited policy insight. The popularity of the merchandise trade balance is due largely to its availability on a monthly basis. Merchandise trade data can rapidly be gathered and reported, whereas measuring trade in services requires time-consuming questionnaires.

Table 11.3 U.S. Balance of Payments, 1999 (Billions of Dollars)*

Current Account		Capital Account	
Merchandise trade		Changes in U.S. assets abroad, net**	
Exports	683.0	U.S. official reserve assets	8.7
Imports	-1,030.1	Other U.S. government assets	-0.4
Balance	-347.1	U.S. private assets	-381.0
		All changes, net	-372.7
Services			
Travel and transportation receipts, net	5.3	Changes in foreign assets in the U.S.***	
Other services, net	74.3	Foreign official assets	44.6
Balance	79.6	Foreign private assets	706.2
		All changes, net	750.8
Balance on goods and services	-267.5		
		Allocation of SDRs	0
Income receipts and payments			
Investment income, net	-19.1	Statistical discrepancy	-39.2
Compensation of employees	-5.7		
Balance	-24.8	Balance on capital account	338.9
Unilateral transfers, net	-46.6		
Balance on current account	-338.9		

* Credits (+), debits (-).

**Increase/capital outflow (-).

***Increase/capital inflow (+).

Source: U.S. Department of Commerce, *Survey of Current Business*, March 2000, pp. 51–56. See also *Federal Reserve Bulletin*, May 2000.

As seen in Table 11.3, the United States had a merchandise trade deficit of $347.1 billion in 1999, resulting from the difference between U.S. merchandise exports ($683 billion) and U.S. merchandise imports ($1,030.1 billion). The United States was thus a net importer of merchandise. Table 11.4 shows that the United States has consistently faced merchandise trade deficits from the 1970s to the turn of the millennium. This situation contrasts with the 1950s and 1960s, when merchandise trade surpluses were common for the United States.

Trade deficits generally are not popular with domestic residents and policy makers because they tend to exert adverse consequences on the home nation's terms of trade and employment levels, as well as on the stability of the international money markets. For the United States, economists' concerns over persistent trade deficits have often focused on their possible effects on the terms at which the United States trades with other nations. With a trade deficit, the value of the dollar may fall in international currency markets as dollar outpayments exceed dollar inpayments. Foreign currencies would become more expensive in terms of dollars, so that imports would become more costly to U.S. residents. A trade deficit that induces a decrease in the dollar's international value imposes a real cost on U.S. residents in the form of higher import costs.

Another often-publicized consequence of a trade deficit is its adverse impact on employment levels in certain domestic industries, such as steel or autos. A worsening trade balance may injure domestic labor, not only by the number of jobs lost to foreign workers who produce our imports but also by the employment losses due to deteriorating export sales. It is no wonder that home-nation unions often raise the most vocal arguments about the evils of trade deficits for the domestic economy. Keep in mind, however, that a nation's trade deficit, which leads to decreased employment in some industries, is offset by capital account inflows that generate employment in other industries. Rather than determining total domestic employment, a trade

Table 11.4 U.S. Balance of Payments, 1970-1999 (in billions of dollars)

Year	Merchandise Trade Balance	Services Balance	Goods and Services Balance	Income Balance	Unilateral Transfers Balance	Current Account Balance
1970	$ 2.6	$-.3	$ 2.3	$ 6.2	$ -6.2	$ 2.3
1972	-6.4	1.0	-5.4	8.2	-8.5	-5.7
1974	-5.5	1.2	-4.3	15.5	-9.3	1.9
1976	-9.5	3.4	-6.1	16.1	-5.7	4.3
1978	-33.9	4.1	-29.8	20.4	-5.8	-15.2
1980	-25.5	6.1	-19.4	30.1	-8.3	2.4
1982	-36.5	12.3	-24.2	29.8	-17.1	-11.5
1984	-112.5	3.3	-109.2	30.0	-20.6	-99.8
1986	-145.1	6.3	-138.8	11.8	-24.2	-151.2
1988	-127.0	12.2	-114.8	11.6	-25.0	-128.2
1990	-109.0	30.2	-78.8	20.7	-33.7	-91.8
1992	-96.1	55.7	-40.4	4.5	-32.0	-67.9
1994	-166.1	59.9	-106.2	-9.2	-35.8	-151.2
1996	-191.3	87.0	-104.3	17.2	-42.1	-129.2
1998	-246.9	82.6	-164.3	-12.1	-44.1	-220.5
1999	-347.1	79.6	-267.5	-24.8	-46.6	-338.9

Source: U.S. Department of Commerce, *Survey of Current Business*, various issues.

deficit influences the distribution of employment among domestic industries.

Discussion of U.S. competitiveness in merchandise trade often gives the impression that the United States has consistently performed poorly relative to other industrial nations. However, the merchandise trade deficit is a narrow concept, because goods are only part of what the world trades. Another part of trade is services. A better indication of the nation's international payments position is the *goods and services balance*. Table 11.3 shows that in 1999, the United States generated a surplus of $79.6 billion on service transactions. Combining this surplus with the merchandise trade deficit of $347.1 billion yields a deficit on the goods and services balance of $267.5 billion. This means that the United States transferred fewer resources (goods and services) to other nations than it received from them during 1999.

In recent decades, the United States has generated a surplus in its services account, as seen in Table 11.4. The United States has been very competitive in the "other services" category, including transportation, construction, engineering, brokers' commissions, and certain health-care services. The United States also has traditionally registered large net receipts from transactions involving proprietary rights—fees, royalties, and other receipts derived mostly from long-established relationships between U.S.-based parent companies and their affiliates abroad.

Adjusting the balance on goods and services for income receipts and payments and net unilateral transfers gives the balance on current account. As Table 11.3 shows, the United States had a *current account* deficit of $338.9 billion in 1999. This means that an excess of imports over exports—of goods, services, investment income, and unilateral transfers—resulted in decreasing net foreign investment for the United States. However, we should not become unduly preoccupied with the current account balance, for it ignores capital account transactions. If foreigners purchase more U.S. assets in the United States (such as land, buildings, and bonds), then the United States can afford to import more goods and services from abroad. To look at one aspect

of a nation's international payment position without considering the others is misleading.

Taken as a whole, U.S. international transactions always balance. This means that any force leading to an increase or decrease in one balance-of-payments account sets in motion a process leading to exactly offsetting changes in the balances of other accounts. As seen in Table 11.3, the United States had a current account deficit in 1999 of $338.9 billion. Offsetting this deficit was a combined surplus of $338.9 billion in the remaining capital accounts, as follows: (1) U.S. assets abroad, deficit of $372.7 billion; (2) foreign assets in the United States, surplus of $750.8 billion; (3) SDR allocation, no change; (4) statistical discrepancy, $39.2 billion outflow.

WHAT DOES A CURRENT ACCOUNT DEFICIT (SURPLUS) MEAN?

Concerning the balance of payments, the current account and the capital account are not unrelated; they are essentially reflections of one another. Because the balance of payments is a double-entry accounting system, total debits will always equal total credits. It follows that if the current account registers a *deficit* (debits outweigh credits), the capital account must register a *surplus*, or net capital *inflow* (credits outweigh debits). Conversely, if the current account registers a *surplus*, the capital account must register a *deficit*, or net capital *outflow*.

To better understand this notion, assume that in a particular year your spending is greater than your income. How will you finance your "deficit"? The answer is by borrowing or by selling some of your assets. You might liquidate some real assets (for example, sell your personal computer) or perhaps some financial assets (sell a U.S. government security that you own). In like manner, when a nation experiences a current account deficit, its expenditures for foreign goods and services are greater than the income received from the international sales of its own goods and services, after making allowances for investment income flows and gifts to and from foreigners. The nation must somehow finance its current account deficit. But how? The answer lies in selling assets and borrowing. In other words, a nation's current account deficit (debits outweigh credits) is financed essentially by a net inflow of capital (credits outweigh debits) in its capital account.

NET FOREIGN INVESTMENT AND THE CURRENT ACCOUNT BALANCE
The current account balance is synonymous with **net foreign investment** in national income accounting. A *current account surplus* means an excess of exports over imports of goods, services, investment income, and unilateral transfers. This permits a net receipt of financial claims for home-nation residents. These funds can be used by the home nation to build up its financial assets or to reduce its liabilities to the rest of the world, improving its net foreign investment position (its net worth vis-à-vis the rest of the world). The home nation thus becomes a net supplier of funds (lender) to the rest of the world. Conversely, a *current account deficit* implies an excess of imports over exports of goods, services, investment income, and unilateral transfers. This leads to an increase in net foreign claims upon the home nation. The home nation becomes a net demander of funds from abroad, the demand being met through borrowing from other nations or liquidating foreign assets. The result is a worsening of the home nation's net foreign investment position.

The current account balance thus represents the bottom line on a nation's income statement. If it is positive, the nation is spending less than its total income and accumulating asset claims on the rest of the world. If it is negative, domestic expenditure exceeds income and the nation borrows from the rest of the world.

The net borrowing of an economy can be expressed as the sum of the net borrowing by each of its sectors: government and the private sector, including business and households. Net borrowing by government equals its budget

deficit: the excess of outlays (G) over taxes (T). Private-sector net borrowing equals the excess of private investment (I) over private saving (S). The net borrowing of the nation is given by the following identity:

$$(G - T) + (I - S) = \text{Current account deficit}$$

(G − T)	+	(I − S)	=	Current
Government deficit		Private investment	Private saving	account deficit

An important aspect of this identity is that the current account deficit is a macroeconomic phenomenon: It reflects imbalances between government outlays and taxes as well as imbalances between private investment and saving. Any effective policy to decrease the current account deficit must ultimately reduce these discrepancies. Reducing the current account deficit requires either decreases in the government's budget deficit or increases in private saving relative to investment, or both. However, these options are difficult to achieve. Decreasing budget deficits may require unpopular tax hikes or government program cutbacks. Efforts to reduce investment spending would be opposed because investment is a key determinant of the nation's productivity and standard of living. Finally, incentives to stimulate saving, such as tax breaks, may be opposed on the grounds that they favor the rich rather than the poor.

Decreasing a current account deficit is not entirely in the hands of the home nation. For the world as a whole, the sum of all nations' current account balances must equal zero. Thus, a reduction in one nation's current account deficit must go hand in hand with a decrease in the current account surplus of the rest of the world. Complementary policy in foreign nations, especially those with large current account surpluses, can help in successful transition.

THE IMPACT OF CAPITAL FLOWS ON THE CURRENT ACCOUNT
In the preceding section, we described a country's capital flows as responsive to developments in the current account—the United States imports a surfeit of foreign goods, and this causes an inflow of for-

eign capital. However, the process can, and often does, work the other way around, with capital flows initiating changes in the current account. For example, if foreigners want to purchase U.S. financial instruments exceeding the amount of foreign financial obligations that Americans want to hold, they must pay for the excess with shipments of foreign goods and services. Therefore, an inflow of foreign capital to the United States is associated with a U.S. current account deficit.

Let us elaborate on how a U.S. current account deficit can be caused by a net capital inflow. Suppose domestic saving falls short of desired domestic investment. Therefore, U.S. interest rates rise relative to interest rates abroad, which attracts an inflow of foreign saving to help support U.S. investment. The United States thus becomes a net importer of foreign saving, using the borrowed purchasing power to acquire foreign goods and services, and resulting in a like-sized net inflow of goods and services—a current account deficit. But how does a capital inflow cause a current account deficit for the United States? When foreigners start purchasing more of our assets than we are purchasing of theirs, the dollar becomes more costly in the foreign-exchange market (see Chapter 12). This causes U.S. goods become more expensive to foreigners, resulting in declining exports; also, foreign goods become cheaper to Americans, resulting in increasing imports. The result is a rise in the current account deficit, or a decline in the current account surplus.

Economists believe that, in the 1980s, a massive inflow of capital caused a current account deficit for the United States. The capital inflow was the result of an increase in the U.S. interest rate relative to interest rates abroad. The higher interest rate, in turn, was mainly due to the combined effects of the U.S. federal government's growing budget deficit and a decline in the private saving rate.

IS A CURRENT ACCOUNT DEFICIT A PROBLEM?

Contrary to commonly held views, a current account deficit has little to do with for-

eign trade practices or any inherent inability of a country to sell its goods on the world market. Instead, it is because of underlying macroeconomic conditions at home requiring more imports to meet current domestic demand for goods and services than can be paid for by export sales. In effect, the domestic economy spends more than it produces, and this excess of demand is met by a net inflow of foreign goods and services leading to the current account deficit. This tendency is minimized during periods of recession but expands significantly with the rising income associated with economic recovery and expansion.

When a nation realizes a current account deficit, it becomes a net borrower of funds from the rest of the world. Is this a problem? Not necessarily. The benefit of a current account deficit is the ability to push current spending beyond current production. However, the cost is the debt service that must be paid on the associated borrowing from the rest of the world.

Is it good or bad for a country to get into debt? The answer obviously depends on what the country does with the money. What matters for future incomes and living standards is whether the deficit is being used to finance more consumption or more investment. If used exclusively to finance an increase in domestic investment, the burden could be slight. We know that investment spending increases the nation's stock of capital and expands the economy's capacity to produce goods and services. The value of this extra output may be sufficient to both pay foreign creditors and also augment domestic spending. In this case, because future consumption need not fall below what it otherwise would have been, there would be no true economic burden. If, on the other hand, foreign borrowing is used to finance or increase domestic consumption (private or public), there is no boost given to future productive capacity. Therefore, to meet debt service expense, future consumption must be reduced below what it otherwise would have been. Such a reduction represents the burden of borrowing. This is not necessarily bad; it all depends on how one values current versus future consumption.

During the 1980s, when the United States realized current account deficits, the rate of domestic saving decreased relative to the rate of investment. In fact, the decline of the overall saving rate was mainly the result of a decrease of its public saving component, caused by large and persistent federal budget deficits in this period—budget deficits are in effect negative savings that subtract from the pool of savings. This indicated that the United States used foreign borrowing to increase current consumption, not productivity-enhancing public investment. The U.S. current account deficits of the 1980s were thus greeted by concern by many economists.

In the 1990s, however, U.S. current account deficits were driven by increases in domestic investment. This investment boom contributed to expanding employment and output. It could not, however, have been financed by national saving alone. Foreign lending provided the additional capital needed to finance the boom. In the absence of foreign lending, U.S. interest rates would have been higher, and investment would inevitably have been constrained by the supply of domestic saving. Therefore, the accumulation of capital and the growth of output and employment would all have been smaller had the United States not been able to run a current account deficit in the 1990s. Rather than choking off growth and employment, the large current account deficit allowed faster long-run growth in the U.S. economy, which improved economic welfare.

BUSINESS CYCLES, ECONOMIC GROWTH, AND THE CURRENT ACCOUNT

How is the current account related to a country's business cycle and long-run economic growth? Concerning the business cycle, *rapid* growth of production and employment is commonly associated with large or growing trade and current account *deficits*, whereas *slow* output and employment growth is associated with large or growing *surpluses*. For example, the U.S. current account improved during the recessions of 1973–1975, 1980, and 1990–1991, but declined during the cyclical upswings of 1970–1972, 1983–1990, and 1993–2000. This reflects both a decline in demand for imports during recessions and the usual cyclical movements of saving and investment.

During a recession, both saving and investment tend to fall. Saving falls as households try to maintain their consumption patterns in the face of a temporary fall in income; investment declines because capacity utilization declines and profits fall. However, because investment is highly sensitive to the need for extra capacity, it tends to drop more sharply than saving during recessions. The current account balance thus tends to rise. Consistent with this, but viewed from a different angle, the trade balance typically improves during a recession, because imports tend to fall with overall consumption and investment demand. The opposite occurs during periods of boom, when sharp increases in investment demand typically outweigh increases in saving, producing a decline of the current account. Of course, factors other than income influence saving and investment, so that the tendency of a country's current account deficit to decline in recessions is not ironclad.

The relationship just described between the current account and economic performance typically holds not only on a short-term or cyclical basis, but also on a long-term basis. Often, countries enjoying *rapid* economic growth possess long-run current account *deficits*, whereas those with *weaker* economic growth have long run current account *surpluses*. This relationship likely derives from the fact that rapid economic growth and strong investment often go hand in hand. Where the driving force is the discovery of new natural resources, technological progress, or the implementation of economic reform, periods of rapid economic growth are likely to be periods in which new investment is unusually profitable. However, investment must be financed with saving, and if a country's national saving is not sufficient to finance all new profitable investment projects, the country will rely on foreign saving to finance the difference. It thus experiences a net capital inflow and a corresponding current account deficit. As long as the new investments are profitable, they will generate the extra earnings needed to repay the claims contracted to undertake them. Thus, when current account deficits reflect strong, profitable investment programs, they work to raise the rate of output and employment growth, not to destroy jobs and production.

Historically, countries at relatively early stages of rapid economic development—such as the United States in the 1800s and Argentina, Australia, and Canada in the early 1900s—have enjoyed an excess of investment over saving, running large current account deficits for long periods. The same general pattern has held in more recent times: Faster-growing developing countries have generally run larger current account deficits than the slower-growing mature economies.

The link between trade, current account deficits, and economic growth is also confirmed by comparing the U.S. trade balance with those of other major industrial countries from 1992-1997. Figure 11.1 shows a negative correlation between output growth and the trade balance,

and between employment growth and the trade balance, respectively. During this period, the United States enjoyed the fastest output and employment growth—and the largest trade deficit—among the countries shown. Conversely, Japan had the largest trade surplus, but the second-slowest rate of growth. Trade surpluses were also the norm in Europe, where growth of output and employment was disappointing.

CAN THE UNITED STATES CONTINUE TO RUN CURRENT ACCOUNT DEFICITS YEAR AFTER YEAR? In the past two decades, the United States has run continuous deficits in its current account. Can the United States run deficits indefinitely? Because the current account deficit arises mainly because foreigners desire to purchase American assets, there is no economic reason why it cannot continue indefinitely. As long as the investment opportunities are large enough to provide foreign investors with competitive rates of return, they will be happy to continue supplying funds to the United States. Simply put, there is no reason why the process cannot continue indefinitely: There are no automatic

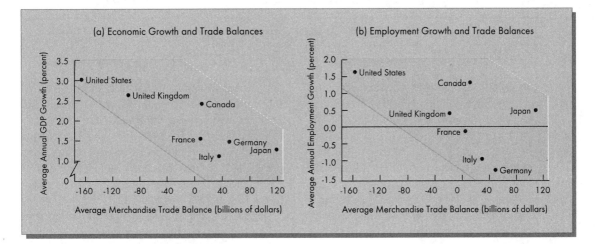

Figure 11.1 Economic Growth, Employment Growth, and Trade Balances of Major Industrial Countries, 1992–1997

Source: *Economic Report of the President*, Washington, DC, U.S. Government Printing Office, 1999, p. 260.

DO CURRENT ACCOUNT DEFICITS COST AMERICANS JOBS?

The sizable U.S. current account deficits that have occurred in recent years have prompted concerns that American jobs are in jeopardy. Increasing competition in the domestic market from low-cost Asian imports could put pressure on U.S. firms to lay off workers. Exporters such as Ford, whose sales decline as a strong dollar raises the price of its autos in foreign markets, could also move to restrict employment. Finally, jobs in export-oriented firms such as Boeing were hurt by the 1997-1998 recession in Asia, which weakened the demand for U.S. goods. Adding to concerns about the employment effects of current account deficit is the fear that increasing numbers of U.S. firms will shut down domestic operations and shift production to other countries, largely to take advantage of lower labor costs.

Nevertheless, although export and import trends raise concerns about U.S. job losses, employment statistics do not bear out the relationship between a rising current account deficit and lower employment. During the 1990s, the unemployment rate declined steadily, reaching a 25-year low in 1998, while the current account deficit mounted. Are the concerns over U.S. job losses from international trade misplaced?

According to economists at the Federal Reserve Bank of New York, the U.S. current account deficit is not a threat to employment for the economy as a whole. A high current account deficit may indeed hurt employment in particular firms and industries as workers are displaced by increased imports or by the relocation of production abroad. At the economy-wide level, however, the current account deficit is matched by an equal inflow of foreign capital, which finances employment-sustaining investment spending that would not otherwise occur. When viewed as the net inflow of foreign investment capital, the current account deficit produces jobs for the economy as a whole: both from the direct effects of higher employment in investment-oriented industries and from the indirect effects of higher investment spending on economy-wide employment. Viewing the current account deficit as a capital inflow thus helps to dispel misconceptions about the adverse consequences of economic globalization on the domestic job market.

Source: Matthew Higgins and Thomas Klitgaard, "Viewing the Current Account Deficit as a Capital Inflow," *Current Issues and Economics and Finance*, Federal Reserve Bank of New York, December 1999, pp. 1–6.

forces that will cause either a current account deficit or a current account surplus to reverse.

U.S. history illustrates this point. From 1820 to 1875, the United States ran current account deficits almost continuously. At this time, the United States was a relatively poor (by European standards) but rapidly growing country. Foreign investment helped foster that growth. This situation changed after World War I. The United States was richer, and investment opportunities were more limited. Thus, current account surpluses were present almost continuously between 1920 and 1970. During the last 25 years, the situation has again reversed. The current account deficits of the United States are underlaid by its system of secure property rights, a stable political and monetary environment, and a rapidly growing labor force (compared with Japan and Europe), which make the United States an attractive place to invest. Moreover, the U.S. saving rate is low compared to its major trading partners. The U.S. current account deficit reflects this combination of factors, and it is likely to continue as long as they are present.

However, the consequence of a current account deficit is a growing foreign ownership of the capital stock of the United States and a rising fraction of U.S. income that must be diverted overseas in the form of interest and dividends to foreigners. A possibly serious problem could emerge if foreigners lose confidence in the ability of the United States to generate the resources necessary to repay the funds borrowed from abroad. As a result, suppose that foreigners decide to reduce the fraction of their saving they send the United States in the form of a capital inflow, or they decide to repatriate part of their liquid capital. The initial effect could be both a sudden and large decline in the value of the dollar as the supply of dollars increases on the foreign-exchange market and a sudden and large increase in U.S. interest rates as an important source of saving was withdrawn from financial markets. Large increases in interest rates could cause problems for the U.S. economy as they reduce the market value of debt securities, cause prices on the stock market to decline, and raise questions about the solvency of various debtors. Simply put, whether the United States can sustain its current account deficit over the foreseeable future depends on whether foreigners are willing to increase their investments in U.S. assets. The current account deficit puts the economic fortunes of the United States partially in the hands of foreign investors.

Although the appropriate level of the U.S. current account deficit is difficult to assess, at least two principles are relevant should it prove necessary to reduce the deficit. First, the United States has an interest in policies that stimulate foreign growth, because it is better to reduce the current account deficit through faster growth abroad than through slower growth at home. A recession at home would obviously be a highly undesirable means of reducing the deficit.

Second, any reductions in the deficit are better achieved through increased national saving than through reduced domestic investment. If there are attractive investment opportunities in the United States, we are better off borrowing from abroad to finance these opportunities than forgoing them. On the other hand, incomes in this country would be even higher in the future if these investments were financed through higher national saving. Increases in national saving allow interest rates to remain lower than they would otherwise be. Lower interest rates would lead to higher domestic investment, which, in turn, would boost demand for equipment and

construction. For any given level of investment, increased saving would also result in higher net exports, which would again raise employment in these sectors.

BALANCE OF INTERNATIONAL INDEBTEDNESS

A main feature of the U.S. balance of payments is that it measures the economic transactions of the United States over a period of one year or one quarter. But at any particular moment, a nation will have a fixed stock of assets and liabilities against the rest of the world. The statement that summarizes this situation is known as the **balance of international indebtedness**. It is a record of the international position of the United States at a particular time (year-end data).

The U.S. balance of international indebtedness indicates the international investment position of the United States, reflecting the value of U.S. investments abroad as opposed to foreign investments in the United States. The United States is considered a **net creditor** to the rest of the world when U.S. claims on foreigners exceed foreign claims on the United States at a particular time. When the reverse occurs, the United States assumes a **net debtor** position.

The terms *net creditor* and *net debtor* in themselves are not particularly meaningful. We need additional information about the specific types of claims and liabilities involved. The balance of international indebtedness therefore looks at the short- and long-term investment positions of both the private and government sectors of the economy. Table 11.5 gives examples of the U.S. balance of international indebtedness.

Of what use is the balance of international indebtedness? Perhaps of greatest significance is that it breaks down international investment holdings into several categories so that policy implications can be drawn from each separate category about the *liquidity status* of the nation. For the short-term investment position, the strategic factor is the amount of short-term liabilities

Table 11.5 International Investment Position of the U.S. at Year-End (Billions of Dollars)

	1985	1990	1995	1998
Type of Investment*				
U.S. Assets Abroad				
U.S. government assets	205.7	256.7	257.2	228.4
U.S. private assets	1,067.1	1,893.3	3,148.6	4,702.5
Total	1,272.8	2,150.0	3,405.8	4,930.9
Foreign Assets in the United States				
Foreign official assets	202.5	373.3	671.7	836.1
Other foreign assets	1,012.9	2,017.2	3,234.2	5,334.0
Total	1,215.4	2,390.5	3,905.9	6,170.1
Net international investment position	57.4	−240.5	−500.1	−1,239.2

*At current cost.

Source: U.S. Department of Commerce, Bureau of Economic Analysis, *The International Investment Position of the United States at Year-End* 1998 at http://www.bea.doc.gov/. See also U.S. Department of Commerce, *Survey of Current Business*, various June and July issues.

(bank deposits and government securities) held by foreigners. This is because these holdings potentially can be withdrawn at very short notice, resulting in a disruption of domestic financial markets. The balance of official monetary holdings is also significant. Assume that this balance is negative from the U.S. viewpoint. Should foreign monetary authorities decide to liquidate their holdings of U.S. government securities and have them converted into official reserve assets, the financial strength of the dollar would be reduced. As for a nation's long-term investment position, it is of less importance for the U.S. liquidity position because long-term investments generally respond to basic economic trends and are not subject to erratic withdrawals.

THE UNITED STATES AS A DEBTOR NATION

In the early stages of its industrial development, the United States was a net international debtor. Relying heavily on foreign capital, the United States built up its industries by mortgaging part of its wealth to foreigners. After World War I, the United States became a net international creditor. The U.S. international investment position evolved steadily from a net-creditor position of $6 billion in 1919 to a position of $337 billion in 1983. By 1987, however, the United States had become a net international debtor, in the amount of $23 billion, for the first time since World War I; during the mid-1990s, the net-debtor position of the United States exceeded $500 billion, as seen in Table 11.5.

How did this turnabout occur so rapidly? The reason was that foreign investors placed more funds in the United States than U.S. residents invested abroad. The United States was considered attractive to investors from other countries because of its rapid economic recovery from the recession of the early 1980s, its political stability, and its relatively high interest rates. U.S. investments overseas fell because of a sluggish loan demand in Europe, a desire by commercial banks to reduce their overseas exposure as a reaction to the debt-repayment problems of Latin American countries, and decreases in credit demand by oil-importing developing nations as the result of declining oil prices. Of the foreign investment funds in the United States, less than one-fourth went to direct ownership of U.S. real estate and business. Most of the funds were in financial assets such as bank deposits, stocks, and bonds.

For the typical U.S. resident, the transition from net creditor to net debtor went unnoticed. However, the net-debtor status of the United States raised an issue of propriety. To many observers, it seemed inappropriate for the United States, one of the richest nations in the world, to be borrowing on a massive scale from the rest of the world.

S U M M A R Y

1. The balance of payments is a record of a nation's economic transactions with all other nations for a given year. A credit transaction is one that results in a receipt of payments from foreigners, whereas a debit transaction leads to a payment abroad. Owing to double-entry bookkeeping, a nation's balance of payments will always balance.

2. From a functional viewpoint, the balance of payments identifies economic transactions as (a) current account transactions and (b) capital account transactions.

3. The balance on goods and services is important to policy makers because it indicates the net transfer of real resources overseas. It also measures the extent to which a nation's exports and imports are part of its gross national product.

4. The capital account of the balance of payments shows the international movement of loans and investments. Capital inflows (outflows) are analogous to exports (imports) of goods and services because they result in the receipt (payment) of funds from (to) other nations.

5. Official reserves consist of a nation's financial assets: (a) monetary gold holdings, (b) convertible currencies, (c) special drawing rights, and (d) drawing positions on the International Monetary Fund.

6. The current method employed by the Department of Commerce in presenting the U.S. international payments position makes use of a functional format emphasizing the following *partial balances*: (a) merchandise trade balance, (b) balance on goods and services, and (c) current account balance.

7. Because the balance of payments is a double-entry accounting system, total debits will always equal total credits. It follows that if the current account registers a deficit (surplus), the capital account must register a surplus (deficit), or net capital inflow (outflow). If a country realizes a deficit (surplus) in its current account, it becomes a net demander (supplier) of funds from (to) the rest of the world.

8. Concerning the business cycle, rapid growth of production and employment is commonly associated with large or growing trade and current account deficits, whereas slow output and employment growth is associated with large or growing current account surpluses.

9. The international investment position of the United States at a particular time is measured by the balance of international indebtedness. Unlike the balance of payments, which is a flow concept (over a period of time), the balance of international indebtedness is a stock concept (at a single point in time).

S T U D Y   Q U E S T I O N S

1. What is meant by the balance of payments?
2. What economic transactions give rise to the receipt of dollars from foreigners? What transactions give rise to payments to foreigners?
3. Why does the balance-of-payments statement "balance"?
4. From a functional viewpoint, a nation's balance of payments can be grouped into several categories. What are these categories?

5. What financial assets are categorized as official reserve assets for the United States?
6. What is the meaning of a surplus (deficit) on the (a) merchandise trade balance, (b) goods and services balance, and (c) current account balance?
7. Why has the goods and services balance sometimes shown a surplus while the merchandise trade balance shows a deficit?
8. What does the balance of international indebtedness measure? How does this statement differ from the balance of payments?
9. Indicate whether each of the following items represents a debit or a credit on the U.S. balance of payments:
   a. A U.S. importer purchases a shipload of French wine.
   b. A Japanese automobile firm builds an assembly plant in Kentucky.
   c. A British manufacturer exports machinery to Taiwan on a U.S. vessel.
   d. A U.S. college student spends a year studying in Switzerland.
   e. U.S. charities donate food to people in drought-plagued Africa.
   f. Japanese investors collect interest income on their holdings of U.S. government securities.
   g. A German resident sends money to her relatives in the United States.
   h. Lloyds of London sells an insurance policy to a U.S. business firm.
   i. A Swiss resident receives dividends on her IBM stock.
10. Table 11.6 summarizes hypothetical transactions, in billions of U.S. dollars, that took place during a given year.
    a. Calculate the U.S. merchandise trade, services, goods and services, income, unilateral transfers, and current account balances.

Table 11.6 International Transactions of the United States (Billions of Dollars)

Travel and transportation receipts, net	$ 25
Merchandise imports	450
Unilateral transfers, net	−20
Allocation of SDRs	15
Receipts on U.S. investments abroad	20
Statistical discrepancy	40
Compensation of employees	-5
Changes in U.S. assets abroad, net	−150
Merchandise exports	375
Other services, net	35
Payments on foreign investments in the United States	−10

b. Which of these balances pertains to the net foreign investment position of the United States? How would you describe that position?

11. Given the hypothetical items shown in Table 11.7, determine the international investment position of the United States. Is the United States a net-creditor nation or a net-debtor nation?

Table 11.7 International Investment Position of the United State (Billions of Dollars)

Foreign official assets in the United States	$ 25
Other foreign assets in the United States	225
U.S. government assets abroad	150
U.S. private assets abroad	75

11.1 The Bureau of Economic Analysis compiles information on the U.S. balance of payments, U.S. exports and imports, and the international investment position of the United States. Go to International, then Data after setting your browser to URL:

http://www.bea.doc.gov/

You can go directly to the Survey of Current Business and Other BEA Publications page by setting your browser to URL:

http://www.bea.doc.gov/bea/pubs.htm

11.2 Summary statistics on international aspects of the economy can be found at the White House Briefing Room. Set your browser to URL:

http://www.whitehouse.gov/

To go directly to the Council of Economic Advisors Publications page that includes Economic Report of the President, log onto:

http://www.whitehouse.gov/WH/EOP/CEA/html/publications.html

To access NetLink Exercises and the Virtual Scavenger Hunt, visit the Carbaugh Web site at http://carbaugh.swcollege.com.

chapter 12

Foreign Exchange

Among the factors that make international economics a distinct subject is the existence of different national monetary units of account. In the United States, prices and money are measured in terms of the dollar. The peso represents Mexico's unit of account, whereas the franc and yen signify the units of account of Switzerland and Japan, respectively.

A typical international transaction requires two distinct purchases. First, the foreign currency is bought; second, the foreign currency is used to facilitate the international transaction. For example, before French importers can purchase commodities from, say, U.S. exporters, they must first purchase dollars to meet their international obligation. Some institutional arrangements are required that provide an efficient mechanism whereby monetary claims can be settled with a minimum of inconvenience to both parties. Such a mechanism exists in the form of the foreign-exchange market.[1]

FOREIGN-EXCHANGE MARKET

The **foreign-exchange market** refers to the organizational setting within which individuals, businesses, governments, and banks buy and sell foreign currencies and other debt instruments. Only a small fraction of daily transactions in foreign exchange actually involve trading of currency. Most foreign-exchange transactions involve the

[1] This chapter considers the foreign-exchange market in the absence of government restrictions. In practice, foreign-exchange markets for many currencies are controlled by governments; therefore, the range of foreign-exchange activities discussed in this chapter are not all possible.

KEY CONCEPTS AND TERMS

- Appreciation
- Arbitrage
- Bid rate
- Call option
- Covered interest arbitrage
- Cross exchange rate
- Currency swap
- Depreciation
- Destabilizing speculation
- Discount
- Effective exchange rate
- Exchange arbitrage
- Exchange rate
- Foreign-currency options
- Foreign-exchange market
- Forward market
- Forward rate
- Forward transaction
- Futures market
- Hedging
- Interbank market
- Interest arbitrage
- International Monetary Market (IMM)
- Long position
- Offer rate
- Option
- Option market
- Premium
- Put option
- Short position
- Speculation
- Spot market
- Spot transaction
- Spread
- Stabilizing speculation
- Strike price
- Three-point arbitrage
- Trade-weighted dollar
- Two-point arbitrage
- Uncovered interest arbitrage

transfer of bank deposits. Major U.S. banks, such as Citibank, maintain inventories of foreign exchange in the form of foreign-denominated deposits held in branch or correspondent banks in foreign cities. Americans can obtain this foreign exchange from hometown banks that, in turn, purchase it from Citibank.

The foreign-exchange market is by far the largest and most liquid market in the world. The estimated worldwide amount of foreign-exchange transactions is around $1.5 trillion a day. Individual trades of $200 million to $500 million are not uncommon. Quoted prices change as often as 20 times a minute. It has been estimated that the world's most active exchange rates can change up to 18,000 times during a single day.

Not all currencies are traded on foreign-exchange markets. Currencies that are not traded are avoided for reasons ranging from political instability to economic uncertainty. Sometimes a country's currency is not exchanged for the simple reason that the country produces very few products of interest to other countries.

Unlike stock or commodity exchanges, the foreign-exchange market is not an organized structure. It has no centralized meetingplace and no formal requirements for participation. Nor is the foreign-exchange market limited to any one country. For any currency, such as the U.S. dollar, the foreign-exchange market consists of all locations where dollars are exchanged for other national currencies. Three of the largest foreign-exchange markets in the world are located in London, New York, and Tokyo. A dozen or so other market centers also exist around the world, such as Paris and Zurich. Because foreign-exchange dealers are in constant telephone and computer contact, the market is very competitive; in effect, it functions no differently than if it were a centralized market.

The foreign-exchange market opens on Monday morning in Hong Kong, which is still Sunday evening in New York. As the day progresses, markets open in Tokyo, Frankfurt, London, New York, Chicago, San Francisco, and elsewhere. As the West Coast markets of the United States close, Hong Kong is only one hour away from opening for Tuesday business.

Indeed, the foreign-exchange market is a round-the-clock operation.

A typical foreign-exchange market functions at three levels: (1) in transactions between commercial banks and their commercial customers, who are the ultimate demanders and suppliers of foreign exchange; (2) in the domestic interbank market conducted through brokers; and (3) in active trading in foreign exchange with banks overseas.

Exporters, importers, investors, and tourists buy and sell foreign exchange from and to commercial banks rather than each other. As an example, consider the import of German autos by a U.S. dealer. The dealer is billed for each car it imports at the rate of 50,000 euros per car. The U.S. dealer cannot write a check for this amount because it does not have a checking account denominated in euros. Instead, the dealer goes to the foreign-exchange department of, say, Chase Manhattan Bank to arrange payment. If the exchange rate is 1.1 euros = $1, the auto dealer writes a check to Chase Manhattan Bank for $45,454.55 (50,000 / 1.1 = 45,454.55) per car. Chase Manhattan will then pay the German manufacturer 50,000 euros per car in Germany. Chase Manhattan is able to do this because it has a checking deposit in euros at its branch in Bonn.

The major banks who trade foreign exchange generally do not deal directly with one another but instead use the services of *foreign-exchange brokers*. The purpose of a broker is to permit the trading banks to maintain desired foreign-exchange balances. If at a particular moment a bank does not have the proper foreign-exchange balances, it can turn to a broker to buy additional foreign currency or sell the surplus. Brokers thus provide a wholesale, interbank market in which trading banks can buy and sell foreign exchange. Brokers are paid a commission for their services by the selling bank.

The third tier of the foreign-exchange market consists of the transactions between the trading banks and their overseas branches or foreign correspondents. Although several dozen U.S. banks trade in foreign exchange, it is the major New York banks that usually carry out transactions with foreign banks. The other, inland trading banks meet their foreign-exchange needs by maintaining correspondent relationships with the New York banks. Trading with foreign banks permits the matching of supply and demand of foreign exchange in the New York market. These international transactions are carried out primarily by telephone and computers.

TYPES OF FOREIGN-EXCHANGE TRANSACTIONS

When conducting purchases and sales of foreign currencies, banks promise to pay a stipulated amount of currency to another bank or customer on an agreed-upon date. Banks typically engage in three types of foreign-exchange transactions: spot, forward, and swap.

A **spot transaction** is an outright purchase and sale of foreign currency for cash settlement not more than two business days after the date the transaction is recorded as a spot deal. The two-day period is known as *immediate delivery*. By convention, the settlement date is the second business day after the date on which the transaction is agreed to by the two traders. The two-day period provides ample time for the two parties to confirm the agreement and arrange the clearing and necessary debiting and crediting of bank accounts in various international locations.

In many cases, a business or financial institution knows it will be receiving or paying an amount of foreign currency on a specific date in the future. For example, in August a U.S. importer may arrange for a special Christmas-season shipment of Japanese radios to arrive in October. The agreement with the Japanese manufacturer may call for payment in yen on October 20. To guard against the possibility of the yen's becoming more expensive in terms of the dollar, the importer might contract with a bank to buy yen at a stipulated price, but not actually receive them until October 20 when they are needed. When the contract matures, the U.S. importer pays for the yen with a known amount of dollars. This is known as a **forward transaction**.

Forward transactions differ from spot transactions in that their maturity date is more than two business days in the future. A forward-exchange contract's maturity date can be a few months or even years in the future. The exchange rate is fixed when the contract is initially made. No money necessarily changes hands until the transaction actually takes place, although dealers may require some customers to provide collateral in advance.

Trading foreign currencies among banks also involves swap transactions. A **currency swap** is the conversion of one currency to another currency at one point in time, with an agreement to reconvert it back to the original currency at a specified time in the future. The rates of both exchanges are agreed to in advance. Swaps provide an efficient mechanism through which banks can meet their foreign-exchange needs over a period of time. Banks are able to use a currency for a period in exchange for another currency that is not needed during that time.

For example, Chase Manhattan Bank may have excess balances of dollars but needs pounds to meet the requirements of its corporate clients. At the same time, Royal Bank of Scotland may have excess balances of pounds and insufficient amounts of dollars. The banks could negotiate a swap agreement in which Chase Manhattan Bank agrees to exchange dollars for pounds today and pounds for dollars in the future. The key aspect is that the two banks arrange the swap as a single transaction in which they agree to pay and receive stipulated amounts of currencies at specified rates.

INTERBANK TRADING

In the foreign-exchange market, currencies are actively traded around the clock and throughout the world. Banks are linked by telecommunications equipment that permits instantaneous communication. A relatively small number of money center banks carry out most of the foreign-exchange transactions in the United States. Virtually all the big New York banks have active currency-trading operations, as do their counterparts in London, Tokyo, Hong Kong, Frankfurt, and other financial centers. Large banks in cities such as Los Angeles, Chicago, San Francisco, and Detroit also have active currency-trading operations. For most U.S. banks, currency transactions are not a large part of their business; these banks have ties to correspondent banks in New York and elsewhere to conduct currency transactions.

All these banks are prepared to purchase or sell foreign currencies for their customers. Bank purchases from and sales to consumers are classified as *retail transactions* when the amount involved is less than 1 million currency units. *Wholesale transactions*, involving more than 1 million currency units, generally occur between banks or with large corporate customers. Bank transactions with each other constitute the **interbank market**. It is in this market that most foreign-exchange trading occurs.

Table 12.1 illustrates the distribution of foreign-exchange transactions by U.S. banking institutions in 1998, by transaction type and currency. The average daily amount of foreign-exchange transactions was estimated at $351 billion. The

U.S. dollar was by far the most important currency traded in foreign-exchange markets, being involved in more than 80 percent of all transactions. The next four most widely traded currencies were the German mark, Japanese yen, British pound, and Swiss franc. The average deal size for foreign-exchange transactions was $3.5 million per trade for spot transactions, $4 million per trade for forward transactions, and $31 million per trade for currency swaps.

Foreign-exchange departments of major commercial banks typically serve as profit centers. A bank's foreign-exchange dealers are in constant contact with other dealers to buy and sell currencies. In most large banks, dealers specialize in one or more foreign currencies. The chief dealer establishes the overall trading policy and direction of trading, trying to service the foreign-exchange needs of the bank's customers and make a profit for the bank. Currency trading is conducted on a 24-hour basis, and exchange rates may fluctuate at any moment. Bank dealers must be light sleepers, ready to react to a nighttime phone call that indicates exchange rates are moving sharply in foreign markets. Banks often allow senior dealers to conduct exchange trading at home in response to such developments.

With the latest electronic equipment, currency exchanges are negotiated on computer terminals; a push of a button confirms a trade. Dealers use electronic trading boards that permit them to instantly register transactions and verify their bank's positions. Besides trading currencies during daytime hours, major banks have established night-trading desks to capitalize on foreign-exchange fluctuations during the evening and to accommodate corporate requests for currency trades. In the interbank market, currencies are traded in amounts involving at least 1 million units of a specific foreign currency. Table 12.2 lists leading banks that trade in the foreign-exchange market.

How do banks such as Bank of America or Citibank earn profits in foreign-exchange transactions? Banks that regularly deal in the interbank market quote both a bid and an offer rate to other banks. The **bid rate** refers to the price

Table 12.1 Distribution of Foreign-Exchange Transactions by U.S. Banks, 1998

Transactions	Percentage		Percentage
BY TYPE		BY FOREIGN CURRENCY	
Swap	47%	German mark	25%
Spot	42	Japanese yen	22
Forward	11	British pound	8
	100%	Swiss franc	7
		French franc	4
		Canadian dollar	4
		Australian dollar	2
		Other	28
			100%

Source: Federal Reserve Bank of New York, Research Group/Capital Markets, *Survey of Foreign Exchange Market Activity in the United States*, April 1998. Updated every three years. See Internet address http://www.ny.frb.org.

Table 12.2 Top Ten Banks by Share of Foreign-Exchange Market*

Bank	Country	Share of Foreign-Exchange Market
Citibank/Salomon Smith Barney	United States	7.75
Deutsche Bank	Germany	7.12
Chase Manhatten Bank	United States	7.09
Warburg Dillon Read	United Kingdom	6.44
Goldman Sachs	United States	4.86
Bank of America	United States	4.39
JP Morgan	United States	4.00
HSBC	United Kingdom	3.75
ABN Amro	Netherlands	3.27
Merrill Lynch	United States	3.11

*Ranked by *Euromoney* survey of over 3,000 users of foreign exchange. This survey is updated annually.

Source: *Euromoney*, May 1999.

that the bank is willing to pay for a unit of foreign currency; the **offer rate** is the price at which the bank is willing to sell a unit of foreign currency. The difference between the bid and the offer rate is the **spread**. At any given time, a bank's bid quote for a foreign currency will be less than its offer quote. The spread is intended to cover the bank's costs of implementing the exchange of currencies. The large trading banks are prepared to "make a market" in a currency by providing bid and offer rates on request.

Foreign-exchange dealers who simultaneously purchase and sell foreign currency earn the spread as profit. For example, Citibank might quote bid and offer rates for the Swiss franc at $.5851/.5854. The bid rate is $.5851 per franc. At this price, Citibank would be prepared to buy 1 million francs for $585,100. The offer rate is $.5854 per franc. Citibank would be willing to sell 1 million francs for $585,400. If Citibank is able to simultaneously buy and sell 1 million francs, it will earn $300 on the transaction. This profit equals the spread ($.0003) multiplied by the amount of the transaction (1 million francs).

Table 12.3 illustrates the bid/offer spreads at the close of business on February 4, 2000, in London. When the London currency market closed, the Swedish krona price that a bank would pay for the dollar was 8.6320 krona per

dollar. Dollars would be sold for krona by the bank at 8.6420 francs per dollar. The spread thus equals (8.6420 − 8.6320) / 8.6420 = .0012. Tiny spreads, often less than one-tenth of 1 percent, are common in currency markets. For a particular currency, the spread varies according to the individual currency trader and the over-

Table 12.3 Closing Spreads on London Market, February 4, 2000

Country	Spread
Finland	6.0671–6.0702
Switzerland	1.6410–1.6420
United Kingdom*	1.5883–1.5888
Brazil	1.7730–1.7740
Canada	1.4435–1.4445
Australia	1.5819–1.5835
Japan	107.310–107.350
New Zealand	2.0255–2.0296
Saudi Arabia	3.7502–3.7505
South Korea	1,129.00–1,130.00

*Exchange-rate quote for the United Kingdom is in terms of U.S. dollars per British pound. All other exchange-rate quotes are in terms of domestic currency units per U.S. dollar.

Source: *Financial Times*, February 7, 2000, p. 26. The exchange rates printed in this table are also available on the Internet at http://www.FT.com.

all attitude of the trading bank concerning future market conditions. The spread that is quoted is generally larger for currencies that are traded in smaller quantities or when the trading bank views trading in a particular currency to be risky.

Besides earning profits from a currency's bid/offer spread, foreign-exchange dealers attempt to profit by anticipating correctly the future direction of currency movements. Suppose a Citibank dealer expects the Japanese yen to *appreciate* (strengthen) against the U.S. dollar. The dealer will likely raise both bid and offer rates, attempting to persuade other dealers to sell yen to Citibank and dissuade other dealers from purchasing yen from Citibank. The bank dealer thus purchases more yen than are sold. If the yen appreciates against the dollar as predicted, the Citibank dealer can sell the yen at a higher rate and earn a profit. Conversely, should the Citibank dealer anticipate that the yen is about to *depreciate* (weaken) against the dollar, the dealer will lower the bid and offer rates. Such action encourages sales and discourages purchases; the dealer thus sells more yen than are bought. If the yen depreciates as expected, the dealer can purchase yen back at a lower price to make a profit.

If exchange rates move in the desired direction, foreign-exchange traders earn profits. However, losses accrue if exchange rates move in the opposite, unexpected direction. To limit possible losses on exchange market transactions, banks impose financial restrictions on their dealers' trading volume. Dealers are subject to *position limits* that stipulate the amount of buying and selling that can be conducted in a given currency. Although banks maintain formal restrictions, they have sometimes absorbed substantial losses from unauthorized trading activity beyond position limits. Because foreign-exchange departments are considered by bank management to be profit centers, dealers feel pressure to generate an acceptable rate of return on the bank's funds invested in this operation.

TRADERS RUN CURRENCY MARKETS

Surrounded by flashing currency prices, ringing phones, and screaming traders, Fred Scala offers his view of people who use economic analysis to forecast currency rates.[2] "They might be right," he says, "but they don't know how to pull the trigger." And he knows. At age 27, he is Manufacturers Hanover Trust Co.'s top dealer in British pounds. Yesterday morning alone, he traded about $500 million in pounds, darting in and out of the market 100 times. As the dollar inched up, he bought. As it retreated, he sold. "We're mercenaries, soldiers of fortune," he says. "We have no alliances. We work for the bank."

Currency traders ride high. As politicians dicker about what to do about the dollar, young traders at the world's top 30 to 50 banks hold day-to-day control of the currency markets.

A look at Manufacturers Hanover's trading desk shows this trading mentality in firm command.

BRAVO FOR FRANC TRADER As traders arrived yesterday at 7 A.M., the Swiss franc trader, Scott Levy, gets a hero's welcome. He had bought $55 million of francs the night before, switched some into Austrian schilling, and benefited from a rising schilling in overnight Asian trading. "I did quite well," he tells colleagues, as he takes his seat. A Hong Kong trader woke him up at home with a 4 A.M. phone call—but helped Mr. Levy unwind his position at a profit of more than $165,000. Other traders greeted him with "high five"hand-slaps, like a football player who has just scored a touchdown.

The next 90 minutes are consumed by a blizzard of trades with European banks. Computerized trading systems let traders do business with London, Frankfurt, or Zurich by the

---

[2] Excerpts from "Young Traders Run Currency Markets," *The Wall Street Journal*, Nov. 5, 1987, p. A26; permission conveyed through the Copyright Clearance Center, Inc.

push of a button, without even a phone call. Typically, Manufacturers Hanover will buy "five dollars"—trader jargon for $5 million—then resell it at a razor-thin profit margin seconds later.

RUSSIAN INFLUENCE At 8:31 A.M., a British bank known for its Eastern European dealings calls. Mark Remigio, the No. 2 pound trader at Manufacturers Hanover, buys $10 billion from the bank, at a rate of .6073 British pounds. As soon as he finishes the call, he leaps up and shouts across the trading room: "The Russians are selling!"

"They tend to be big players, Mr. Seata observes. "If the Russians are selling, the chances are the market is going to go in that direction." A few minutes later, a currency broker calls for a bid. In the background, traders can hear the broker speaking in Russian on another call.

The Manufacturers Hanover traders start selling dollars, counting on more Soviet sales to drive the market down. The Soviets, however, unpredictably vanish from the market. But Manufacturers Hanover is able to reverse course without suffering for its quick reaction to the Soviet presence.

At 9:03 A.M., the day's first big new headlines hit the screen. "U.S. Commerce under Secretary Says Dollar Is Now Competitive," a news monitor reports. "That's good for the dollar," says Mr. Remigio. He and Mr. Scala buy $10 million at a rate of .6742 pounds. Moments later, a senior bank trader walks by and asks why the dollar is rising. Mr. Remigio starts to explain the new views expressed by the Commerce undersecretary. "What the hell does he know?" another trader snaps. The issue is settled. In a flurry of four transactions, Manufacturers Hanover dumps the $10 million it just bought, and sells another $8 million as well. It gets rates ranging from .6882 to .6998 pounds. The slight gain from its purchase price is infinitesimal to anyone but a currency trader. To Messengers, Scala, and Remigio, it is $450 quick profit for the bank.

DIFFICULT STRETCH About 10 A.M., the pound traders encounter their one difficult

stretch of the day. They have sold dollars, expecting further drops. But the dollar is inching up. Mr. Scala twirls his phone cord around his finger and taps his feet. Mr. Remigio slams his phone down, snarling: "It's up, it's up, it's going up."

Rather than fight the momentary trend, the traders begin by buying dollars. "The dollar is going uptown, " Mr. Remigio declares. He holds his new positive position on the dollar for only a brief spell, but profits from it as well.

All morning, calls from incoming banks and customers light up dealers' phone boards, which hold 120 direct phone lines. Only around 11 A.M. does the most important phone line—the one in the bottom left-hand corner—begin blinking at Manufacturers Hanover's pound desk. It is the Federal Reserve Bank of New York, agent for the U.S. government. And for a moment, Mr. Scala doesn't see the line light up.

"When that line comes in, you've got to pick it up quick," Mr. Remigio chides his partner. "They could be wanting to deal."

The New York Fed in fact deals with any of a dozen big New York banks when it enters the market to buy or sell currencies, and it often doesn't let one bank know about its dealings with another. This time the Fed just wants information about the dollar. "It goes up. It goes down. It goes all around," the Fed's trader says over the phone. "What's going on?"

READING FED SIGNALS Mr. Scala tries to offer a quick summary of market activity. Then he asks the Fed, "Is there any level you want me to call you back at?"

With his low-key question, Mr. Scala is trying to get at perhaps the most important piece of information in the foreign-exchange market. Traders' one big worry currently is that if the dollar fails too fast, the Fed and foreign central banks may barge in with big buy orders to prop up the dollar. If a trader knows what dollar rate worries the Fed, he can better prepare for any possible intervention.

"Yeah," says the Fed trader. "Call me if it gets to .6871." A little later, the dollar does slip to that level. Mr. Scala calls the Fed. But instead of placing a big buy order, the Fed trader just says, "Call me back if it goes much lower."

Around this time, Manufacturers Hanover's pound traders back off from some bearish market positions they have taken against the dollar. But that is straightforward profit-taking, the traders say, unrelated to the Fed's call.

The trading frenzy continues until about noon New York time, when the European trading day ends. Only then can Manufacturers' New York traders relax. For their efforts, the pound traders break even after making about 200 trades involving nearly $1 billion. The bank's entire currency-trading operation did better, however, bringing in a profit of about $300,000 for the day.

Although young traders are in the front lines, big banks like Manufacturers Hanover have top managers looking over their shoulders, setting position limits and trying to make sure the bank doesn't get stuck with unexpected losses. But the foreign-exchange market has grown so fast, and takes such a toll on traders, that there are few veterans.

Mr. Remigio, the 27-year-old No. 2 pound trader, received an MBA from Hofstra University before coming to Manufacturers Hanover a couple of years ago. His colleague, Mr. Scala, has only a high-school diploma. Mr. Scala has something more valuable to the bank, though: nearly a decade of experience. He started as a broker's clerk, then advanced to trading when he was all of 20 years old. Individual traders, many still in their 20s, earn more than $100,000 a year in salary and bonus.

THE ROLE OF LUCK But there are no illusions about succeeding on skill alone around the trading room. Within reach of nearly every trader is a good-luck charm. At the desk where Japanese yen are traded, dealers can rub the tummy of a cherubic statuette or slap a bobbling-head doll representing Japan's rising sun. It then cries out, in Japanese: "Try, you can do it!" The Japanese writing on a headband wrapped around a speakerphone reads: "We're definitely going to win!"

Traders joke that for them, 10 minutes is a long-term outlook. One of Manufacturers

Hanover's economists, Mark Goloven, says that he can sense the difference when he visits trading floors to get a feel for market trends. "When I sit down there, I can feel the tension rising," he says. "That's tough duty. I sympathize with them." His one quibble, he says, is that many traders "aren't attuned to looking at economic fundamentals as much as we think they should."

Down in the trading room, the traders generally agree. "I like to see what the economist thinks, but he's thinking long-term," say James Young, Manufacturers' top yen trader. "And there are 13 floors between here and long-term."

Bank officials doubt that the dollar's decline is over. "It isn't 'un-American' to sell dollars and profit from the currency's decline," Mr. Young says. "It's how the game is played."

The dollar's chronic slump is worrisome for the U.S. economy, adds Mr. Remigio. But there's no room at the trading desk for sentimentality. "I don't like seeing the dollar down here," he says. "My money doesn't buy as much when I travel overseas. But in trading, if the thing's going down. I'm going to sell it."

READING FOREIGN-EXCHANGE QUOTATIONS

Most daily newspapers publish foreign-exchange rates for major currencies. The **exchange rate** is the price of one currency in terms of another—for example, the number of dollars required to purchase 1 British pound (£). In shorthand notation, ER = $ / £, where ER is the exchange rate. For example, if ER = 2, then purchasing £1 will require $2 (2 / 1 = 2). It is also possible to define the exchange rate as the number of units of foreign currency required to purchase 1 unit of domestic currency, or ER′ = £ / $. In our example, ER′ = 0.5 (1 / 2 = 0.5) which implies that it requires £0.5 to buy $1. Of course, ER′ is the reciprocal of ER (ER′ = 1 / ER).

Table 12.4 shows the exchange rates listed for January 5, 2000, in *The Wall Street Journal*. In columns 2 and 3 (*U.S. dollar equivalent*) of the

Table 12.4 Foreign-Exchange Quotations

Wednesday, January 5, 2000

EXCHANGE RATES

The New York foreign exchange mid-range rates below apply to trading among banks in amounts of $1 million and more, as quoted at 4 p.m. Eastern time by Reuters and other sources. Retail transactions provide fewer units of foreign currency per dollar. Rates for the 11 Euro currency countries are derived from the latest dollar-euro rate using the exchange ratios set 1/1/99.

Country	U.S. $ equiv. Wed	U.S. $ equiv. Tue	Currency per U.S. $ Wed	Currency per U.S. $ Tue
Argentina (Peso)	1.0001	1.0001	.9999	.9999
Australia (Dollar)	.6585	.6551	1.5185	1.5266
Austria (Schilling)	.07497	.07491	13.338	13.349
Bahrain (Dinar)	2.6525	2.6525	.3770	.3770
Belgium (Franc)	.0256	.0256	39.1025	39.1325
Brazil (Real)	.5441	.5408	1.8380	1.8490
Britain (Pound)	1.6425	1.6370	.6088	.6109
1-month forward	1.6427	1.6372	.6088	.6108
3-months forward	1.6426	1.6371	.6088	.6108
6-months forward	1.6419	1.6365	.6091	.6111
Canada (Dollar)	.6900	.6887	1.4493	1.4521
1-month forward	.6905	.6892	1.4482	1.4510
3-months forward	.6914	.6902	1.4463	1.4489
6-months forward	.6926	.6915	1.4438	1.4462
Chile (Peso) (d)	.001889	.001890	529.25	529.05
China (Renminbi)	.1208	.1208	8.2798	8.2799
Colombia (Peso)	.0005236	.0005238	1910.00	1909.00
Czech. Rep. (Koruna)				
Commercial rate	.02848	.02839	35.116	35.226
Denmark (Krone)	.1387	.1385	7.2106	7.2186
Ecuador (Sucre)				
Floating rate	.00004237	.00004202	23600.00	23800.00
Finland (Markka)	.1735	.1734	5.7633	5.7678
France (Franc)	.1573	.1572	6.3584	6.3633
1-month forward	.1576	.1575	6.3440	6.3488
3-months forward	.1583	.1582	6.3157	6.3205
6-months forward	.1593	.1592	6.2755	6.2800
Germany (Mark)	.5275	.5273	1.8959	1.8966
1-month forward	.5287	.5285	1.8916	1.8922
3-months forward	.5310	.5308	1.8831	1.8838
6-months forward	.5344	.5343	1.8712	1.8717
Greece (Drachma)	.003120	.003120	320.48	320.52
Hong Kong (Dollar)	.1286	.1286	7.7778	7.7773
Hungary (Forint)	.004052	.004044	246.79	247.30
India (Rupee)	.02299	.02300	43.490	43.480
Indonesia (Rupiah)	.0001398	.0001396	7155.00	7165.00
Ireland (Punt)	1.3103	1.3094	.7632	.7637
Israel (Shekel)	.2405	.2413	4.1578	4.1436
Italy (Lira)	.0005328	.0005324	1876.87	1878.33
Japan (Yen)	.009588	.009681	104.30	103.29
1-month forward	.009639	.009730	103.75	102.77

Country	U.S. $ equiv. Wed	U.S. $ equiv. Tue	Currency per U.S. $ Wed	Currency per U.S. $ Tue
3-months forward	.009730	.009825	102.77	101.79
6-months forward	.009879	.009974	101.23	100.26
Jordan (Dinar)	1.4085	1.4085	.7100	.7100
Kuwait (Dinar)	3.2927	3.2927	.3037	.3037
Lebanon (Pound)	.0006634	.0006634	1507.50	1507.50
Malaysia (Ringgit)	.2632	.2632	3.8000	3.8001
Malta (Lira)	2.4722	2.4691	.4045	.4050
Mexico (Peso)				
Floating rate	.1050	.1045	9.5205	9.5700
Netherland (Guilder)	.4681	.4678	2.1361	2.1378
New Zealand (Dollar)	.5204	.5209	1.9216	1.9198
Norway (Krone)	.1260	.1260	7.9359	7.9388
Pakistan (Rupee)	.01929	.01929	51.850	51.850
Peru (new Sol)	.2849	.2841	3.5100	3.5200
Philippines (Peso)	.02494	.02509	40.100	39.850
Poland (Zloty)	.2421	.2427	4.1300	4.1195
Portugal (Escudo)	.005146	.005142	194.33	194.49
Russia (Ruble) (a)	.03670	.03632	27.250	27.530
Saudi Arabia (Riyal)	.2666	.2666	3.7506	3.7510
Singapore (Dollar)	.6035	.6039	1.6571	1.6560
Slovak Rep. (Koruna)	.02433	.02434	41.100	41.077
South Africa (Rand)	.1649	.1643	6.0650	6.0875
South Korea (Won)	.0008815	.0008909	1134.50	1122.50
Spain (Peseta)	.006200	.006196	161.28	161.41
Sweden (Krona)	.1195	.1195	8.3673	8.3671
Switzerland (Franc)	.6431	.6429	1.5550	1.5555
1-month forward	.6455	.6454	1.5491	1.5494
3-months forward	.6500	.6498	1.5384	1.5389
6-months forward	.6569	.6567	1.5224	1.5228
Taiwan (Dollar)	.03255	.03276	30.725	30.525
Thailand (Baht)	.02695	.02683	37.100	37.265
Turkey (Lira)	.00000186	.00000186	537285.00	536260.00
United Arab (Dirham)	.2723	.2722	3.6730	3.6731
Uruguay (New Peso)				
Financial	.08604	.08607	11.623	11.619
Venezuela (Bolivar)	.001540	.001538	649.51	650.00
SDR	1.3820	1.3820	.7236	.7236
Euro	1.0317	1.0313	.9693	.9696

Special Drawing Rights (SDR) are based on exchange rates for the U.S., German, British, French, and Japanese currencies. Source: International Monetary Fund.

a-Russian Central Bank rate. Trading band lowered on 8/17/98. b-Government rate. d-Floating rate; trading band suspended on 9/2/99.

The 3-month and 6-month forward rates for France, Germany, Japan and Switzerland appearing in the Foreign Exchange column were incorrectly calculated for the period beginning with August 13 and ending with October 7. Corrected data is available from Readers' Reference Service (413) 592-3600.

Key Currency Cross Rates — Late New York Trading Jan 5, 2000

	Dollar	Euro	Pound	SFranc	Guilder	Peso	Yen	Lira	D-Mark	FFranc	CdnDlr
Canada	1.4493	1.4952	2.3805	0.9320	.67848	.15223	.01390	.00077	.76444	.22793	
France	6.3584	6.5600	10.4437	4.0890	2.9766	.66786	.06096	.00339	3.3538		4.3872
Germany	1.8959	1.9560	3.1140	1.2192	.88755	.19914	.01818	.00101		.29817	1.3081
Italy	1876.9	1936.4	3082.8	1207.0	878.65	197.14	17.995		989.97	295.18	1295.0
Japan	104.30	107.61	171.31	67.074	48.827	10.955		.05557	55.013	16.403	71.966
Mexico	9.5205	9.8223	15.637	6.1225	4.4570		.09128	.00507	5.0216	1.4973	6.5690
Netherlands	2.1361	2.2038	3.5085	1.3737		.22437	.02048	.00114	1.1267	.33595	1.4739
Switzerland	1.555	1.6043	2.5541		.72796	.16333	.01491	.00083	.82019	.24456	1.0729
U.K.	.60880	.6281		.3915	.28502	.06395	.00584	.00032	.32113	.09575	.42008
Euro	.96930		1.5920	.62333	.45376	.10181	.00929	.00052	.51125	.15244	.66879
U.S.		1.0317	1.6425	.64309	.46814	.10504	.00959	.00053	.52745	.15727	.68999

Source: Reuters

upper portion of Table 12.4, the selling prices of foreign currencies are listed in dollars. The columns state how many dollars are required to purchase one unit of a given foreign currency. For example, the quote for the Austrian schilling for Wednesday was .07497. This means that $.07497 was required to purchase 1 schilling. Columns 4 and 5 (*Currency per U.S. dollar*) show the foreign-exchange rates from the opposite perspective, telling how many units of a foreign currency are required to buy a U.S. dollar. Again referring to Wednesday, it would take 13.338 Austrian schillings to purchase 1 U.S. dollar.

The term *selling rate* in the table's heading refers to the price at which a New York bank will sell foreign exchange, in amounts of $1 million and more, to another bank. The table heading also states at what time during the day the quotation was made because currency prices fluctuate throughout the day in response to changing supply and demand conditions. *The Wall Street Journal* customarily quotes the rates at the close of trading, 4 P.M. Eastern time. Next-day readers of the newspaper are thus offered the most recent currency prices. Retail foreign-exchange transactions, in amounts under $1 million, carry an additional service charge and are thus made at a different exchange rate.

An exchange rate determined by free-market forces can and does change frequently. When the dollar price of pounds increases, for example, from $2 = £1 to $2.10 = £1, the dollar has *depreciated* relative to the pound. Currency **depreciation** means that it takes more units of a nation's currency to purchase a unit of some foreign currency. Conversely, when the dollar price of pounds decreases, say, from $2 = £1 to $1.90 = £1, the value of the dollar has *appreciated* relative to the pound. Currency **appreciation** means that it takes fewer units of a nation's currency to purchase a unit of some foreign currency.

In the upper portion of Table 12.4, look at columns 2 and 3 (*U.S. dollar equivalent*). Going forward in time from Tuesday (January 4) to Wednesday (January 5), we see that the dollar cost of a British pound increased from $1.6370 to $1.6425; the dollar thus depreciated against

the pound. This means that the pound appreciated against the dollar. To verify this conclusion, refer to columns 4 and 5 of the table (*Currency per U.S. dollar*). Going forward in time from Tuesday to Wednesday, we see that the pound cost of the dollar decreased from .6109 pound = $1 to .6088 pound = $1. In similar fashion, we see that from Tuesday to Wednesday the dollar appreciated against the Japanese yen from $0.009681 = 1 yen to $0.009588 = 1 yen; the yen thus depreciated against the dollar, from 103.29 yen = $1 to 104.30 yen = $1.

Most tables of exchange-rate quotations express currency values relative to the U.S. dollar, regardless of the country where the quote is provided. Yet there are many instances in which the U.S. dollar is not part of a foreign-exchange transaction. In such cases, the people involved need to obtain an exchange quote between two nondollar currencies. As an example, if a British importer needs francs to purchase Swiss watches, the exchange rate of interest is the Swiss franc relative to the British pound. The exchange rate between any two currencies (such as the franc and the pound) can be derived from the rates of these two currencies in terms of a third currency (the dollar). The resulting rate is called the **cross exchange rate**.

Referring to the New York foreign-exchange market quotations in the upper portion of Table 12.4, we see that, as of Wednesday, the dollar value of the British pound is $1.6425 and the dollar value of the Swiss franc is $0.6431. We can then calculate the value of the British pound relative to the Swiss franc as follows:

$$\frac{\$ \text{ Value of British Pound}}{\$ \text{ Value of Swiss Franc}} = \frac{\$1.6425}{\$0.6431} = 2.55$$

Thus, each British pound buys about 2.55 Swiss francs; this is the cross exchange rate between the pound and the franc. In similar fashion, cross exchange rates can be calculated between any other two nondollar currencies in Table 12.4.

The lower portion of Table 12.4 gives the cross exchange rates for several leading currencies. Here, to find the value of the British pound relative to the Swiss franc, we simply locate the intersection of the pound column and the Switzerland row. The cross rate is given as 2.5541. In like manner, the cross exchange rates of other key currencies can be read directly from the table.

FORWARD AND
FUTURES MARKETS

Foreign exchange can be bought and sold for delivery immediately (the **spot market**) or for future delivery (the **forward market**). Forward contracts are normally made by those who will receive or make payment in foreign exchange in the weeks or months ahead. As seen in Table 12.4, the New York foreign-exchange market is a spot market for most currencies of the world. Regular forward markets, however, exist only for the more widely traded currencies. Exporters and importers, whose foreign-exchange receipts and payments are in the future, are the primary participants in the forward market. The forward quotations for currencies such as the British pound, Canadian dollar, Japanese yen, and Swiss franc are for delivery 1 month, 3 months, or 6 months from the date indicated in the table's caption (January 5, 2000).

Trading in foreign exchange can also be done in the **futures market**. In this market, contracting parties agree to future exchanges of currencies and set applicable exchange rates in advance. The futures market is distinguished from the forward market in that only a limited number of leading currencies are traded; moreover, trading takes place in standardized contract amounts and in a specific geographic location. Table 12.5 summarizes the major differences between the forward market and the futures market.

One such futures market is the **International Monetary Market (IMM)** of the Chicago Mercantile Exchange. Founded in 1972, the IMM is an extension of the commodity futures markets in which specific quantities of wheat, corn, and other commodities are bought and sold for future delivery at specific dates. The IMM provides trading facilities for the purchase and sale for future delivery of financial instruments (such as foreign currencies) and precious metals (such as gold). The IMM is especially popular with smaller banks and companies. Also, the IMM is one of the few places where individuals can speculate on changes in exchange rates.

Foreign-exchange trading on the IMM is limited to major currencies. Contracts are set for delivery on the third Wednesday of March, June,

Table 12.5 Forward Contract Versus Futures Contract

	Forward Contract	Futures Contract
Issuer	Commercial bank	International Monetary Market (IMM) of the Chicago Mercantile Exchange and other foreign exchanges such as the Tokyo International Financial Futures Exchange
Trading	"Over the counter" by telephone	On the IMM's market floor
Contract Size	Tailored to the needs of the exporter/importer/investor; no set size	Standardized in round lots
Date of Delivery	Negotiable	Only on particular dates
Contract Costs	Based on the bid/offer spread	Brokerage fees for sell and buy orders
Settlement	On expiration date only, at prearranged price	Profits or losses paid daily at close of trading

September, and December. Price quotations are in terms of U.S. dollars per unit of foreign currency, but futures contracts are for a fixed amount (for example, 62,500 British pounds).

Here is how to read the IMM's futures prices as listed in Table 12.6.[3] The size of each contract is shown on the same line as the currency's name and country. For example, a contract for yen covers the right to purchase 12.5 million yen. Moving to the right of the size of the contract, we see the expression *$ per yen (.00)*, which shows the number of cents required to purchase one yen. The first column of the table shows the **maturity months** of the contract; using March as an example, the remaining columns yield the following information:

Open refers to the price at which yen was first sold when the IMM opened on the morning of

January 5, 2000. Depending on overnight events in the world, the opening price may not be identical to the closing price from the previous trading day. Because prices are expressed in terms of cents per yen, the .9792 implies that yen opened for sale at .9792 cents per yen. Multiply this price by the size of a contract and you've calculated the full value of one contract at the open of trading for that day: .9792 cents × 12.5 million = $122,400.

The **high, low,** and **settle** columns indicate the contract's highest, lowest, and closing prices for the day. Viewed together, these figures provide an indication of how volatile the market for the yen was during the day. After opening at .9792 cents per yen, yen for March delivery never sold for more than .9832 cents per yen and never for less than .9682 cents per yen; trading finally settled, or ended, at .9683 cents per yen. Multiplying the size of the yen contract times the yen's settlement price gives the full value of a yen contract at the closing of the trading day: .9683 cents × 12.5 million = $121,037.50.

[3] This section is adapted from R. Wurman and others, *The Wall Street Journal: Guide to Understanding Money and Markets* (New York: Simon and Schuster, Inc., 1990).

Table 12.6 Foreign-Currency Futures, January 5, 2000: Selected Examples

	Open	High	Low	Settle	Change	Lifetime High	Low	Open Interest
JAPAN YEN (CME)—12.5 million yen; $ per yen (0.00)								
Mar	.9792	.9832	.9682	.9683	−.0108	1.0018	.8369	70,191
June	.9916	.9917	.9855	.9841	−.0108	1.0175	.8619	3,657
Sept	....	....	....	.9997	−.0108	1.0272	.9838	517
Est vol 17,360; vol Tue 34,487; open int 74,372, −2,444								
CANADIAN DOLLAR (CME)—100,000 dlrs.; $ per Can $								
Mar	.6898	.6917	.6880	.6916	+.0017	.6952	.6425	54,650
June	.6910	.6930	.6900	.6931	+.0017	.6964	.6547	5,386
Sept	.6925	.6940	.6925	.6943	+.0017	.6970	.6630	1,198
Dec	.6925	.6950	.6925	.6954	+.0017	.6980	.6640	444
Est vol 7,397; vol Tue 12,303; open int 61,690, +3780								
MEXICAN PESO (CME)—500,000 new Mex. peso; $ per MP								
Mar	.10200	.10275	.10150	.10260	+00425	.10450	.08135	12,573
June	.09820	.09930	.09800	.09905	+00500	.10075	.08350	2,208
Sept	....	....	....	.09600	+00500	.10295	.08500	137
Est vol 7,220; vol Tue 7,087; open int 15,009, +341								

Source: *The Wall Street Journal*, January 6, 2000, p. C20.

Change compares today's closing price with the closing price as listed in the previous day's paper. A plus (+) sign means prices ended higher; a minus (–) means prices ended lower. In the yen's case, the yen for March delivery settled .0108 cents lower than it did the previous trading day.

Lifetime high and **low** show the volatility that has occurred in the trading of this particular contract—an indication of risk and reward. We can see that the yen's March price of .9683 cents per yen is near the lifetime low for this particular contract.

Open interest refers to the total number of contracts outstanding; that is, those that have not been canceled by offsetting trades. It shows how much interest there is in trading a particular contract. The months closest to January 5 generally attract the most trading activity, as can be seen from the difference in March yen versus September yen.

The last line of Table 12.6 gives information concerning the estimated volume of trading on the current day, the actual volume on the previous trading day, the current number of contracts (open interest) across all maturity dates for this currency, and the change in the number of contracts since the previous trading day.

FOREIGN-CURRENCY OPTIONS

During the 1980s, a new feature of the foreign-exchange market was developed: the **option market**. An **option** is simply an agreement between a holder (buyer) and a writer (seller) that gives the holder the *right*, but not the obligation, to buy or sell financial instruments at any time through a specified date. Although the holder is not obligated to buy or sell currency, the writer is obligated to fulfill a transaction. Having a throw-away feature, options are a unique type of financial contract in that you only use the contract if you want to. By contrast, forward contracts *obligate* a person to carry out a transaction at a specified price, even if the market has changed and the person would rather not.

Foreign-currency options provide an options holder the right to buy or sell a fixed amount of foreign currency at a prearranged price, within a few days or a couple of years. The options holder can choose the exchange rate she wants to guarantee, as well as the length of the contract. Foreign-currency options have been used by companies seeking to hedge against exchange-rate risk as well as by speculators in foreign currencies.

There are two types of foreign-currency options. A **call option** gives the holder the right to *buy* foreign currency at a specified price, whereas a **put option** gives the holder the right to *sell* foreign currency at a specified price. The price at which the option can be exercised (that is, the price at which the foreign currency is bought or sold) is called the **strike price**. The holder of a foreign-currency option has the right to exercise the contract but may choose not to do so if it turns out to be unprofitable. The writer of the options contract (for example, Bank of America, Citibank, Merrill Lynch International Bank) must deliver the foreign currency if called on by a call-holder or must buy foreign currency if it is put to them by a put-holder. For this obligation, the writer of the options contract receives a *premium*, or fee (the option price). Financial institutions have been willing to write foreign-currency options because they generate substantial premium income (the fee income on a $5 million deal can run $100,000 or more). However, writing currency options is a risky business because the writer takes chances on tricky pricing.

Foreign-currency options are traded in a variety of currencies in Europe and the United States. The bank market for foreign-currency options consists of large U.S. banks that write options for their corporate customers. In addition, the Amsterdam, Montreal, and Philadelphia exchanges provide centralized trading floors devoted to foreign-currency-option trading.

In 1984, the IMM introduced a new option instrument to compete with the currency options issued by the major banks and exchanges: an *option on a foreign-currency futures contract*. This option provides the holder the right to buy or sell a futures contract for Swiss francs instead of the francs themselves. The options holder has the right to buy or sell a stipulated number of standardized futures contracts on a stipulated currency at a stipulated price up to a stipulated date. When the options holder exercises the right to buy or sell the foreign-currency futures, he buys or sells futures contracts that are actually executed at maturity.

A first impression might be that an option on a foreign-currency futures contract is an unnecessarily cumbersome instrument. But this instrument is especially attractive to small traders who desire to make large trades and who find it difficult to deal in the spot or forward market. In trading spot currencies with a bank, small traders typically must pay retail prices that are higher than the wholesale prices that are charged on large currency transactions. Moreover, banks often hesitate to make forward contracts that are large compared to the financial resources of small traders. In contrast, small traders can readily arrange with the IMM for a large futures contract to make delivery under an option.

ADVANTAGE OF FOREIGN-CURRENCY OPTIONS TO EXPORTERS

To see how exporters can use foreign-currency options to cope with exchange-rate risk, consider the hypothetical case of Boeing, which submits a bid for the sale of jet planes to an airline company in Japan. Boeing must deal not only with the uncertainty of winning the bid but also with exchange-rate risk. If Boeing wins the bid, it will receive yen in the future. But what if the yen depreciates in the interim, from, say, 115 yen = $1 to 120 yen = $1? Boeing's yen holdings would convert into fewer dollars, thus eroding the profitability of the jet sale.

Because Boeing wants to sell yen in exchange for dollars, it can offset this exchange-market risk by purchasing put options that give the company the right to sell yen for dollars at a specified price. Having obtained a put option, if Boeing wins the bid it has limited the exchange-rate risk. On the other hand, if the bid is lost, Boeing's losses are limited to the cost of the option. Foreign-currency options thus provide a worst-case rate of exchange for companies conducting international business. The maximum amount the company can lose by covering its exchange-rate risk is the amount of the option price.

UNDERSTANDING OPTION QUOTATIONS

The prices of futures options (Chicago Mercantile Exchange) and foreign-currency options (Philadelphia Exchange) are published daily in the financial press. Table 12.7 illustrates the prices for January 5, 2000, as listed in *The Wall Street Journal* on the following day.

Referring to the futures options of the Chicago Mercantile Exchange, let's look at the call options for the Swiss franc. These are the rights to buy franc futures at a specified price—the strike price. For example, consider the call option at the strike price 6400. This means that one can purchase an option to buy 125,000-franc February futures up to the January settlement date at 64 cents per franc. The price one pays to purchase the option (the premium of the option's writer) is 0.9 cents per franc, or $1,125 (125,000 × 0.9 cents), plus brokerage fees. The February option to buy February futures at 64 cents per franc will cost 1.43 cents per franc, or $1,787.50 (125,000 × 1.43 cents), plus brokerage fees.

Now refer to the Philadelphia Exchange quotations in Table 12.7. The Philadelphia Exchange deals with options for standardized bundles of currencies on the spot market. When a call option is exercised, foreign-currency is thus obtained immediately. The only difference in the presentation of the foreign-currency option prices, as compared with the futures options of the Chicago Mercantile Exchange, is that, the spot price is stated instead of the futures price. Referring to the Philadelphia Exchange, we see that call options on January 62,500 Swiss francs at the strike price of 65 cents per franc cost 0.38 cents per franc, or $237.50 (0.38 cents × 62,500), plus brokerage fees.

Table 12.7 Futures Options and Foreign-Currency Options, January 5, 2000: Swiss Franc

Futures Options:
Chicago Mercantile Exchange

Foreign-Currency Options:
Philadelphia Exchange

SWISS FRANC (CME)
125,000 francs; cents per franc

Strike	Calls-Settle			Puts-Settle		
Price	Jan	Feb	Mar	Jan	Feb	Mar
6400	0.90	1.43	1.77	0.08	0.61	0.96
6450	0.51	1.13	1.49	0.19	0.81	1.17
6500	0.24	0.88	1.22	0.42	1.06	1.40
6550	0.12	0.68	1.02	....	....	....
6600	0.07	0.53	0.83	....	....	2.00
6650	0.04	....	....	....	....	....

Est vol 647 Tu 452 calls 221 puts
Op int Tues 5,578 calls 2,711 puts

		Calls		Puts	
		Vol.	Last	Vol.	Last
62,500 Swiss francs—cents per unit					
63	Mar	.....	.....	2	0.56
64	Mar	.....	.....	5	0.87
65	Jan	7	0.38	.....	.....
67	Feb	.....	.....	4	2.36

Col Vol......1,670 Open Int.....13,149
Put Vol......507 Open Int.....9,474

Source: *The Wall Street Journal*, January 6, 2000, pp. C14 and C21.

EXCHANGE-RATE DETERMINATION

What determines the equilibrium exchange rate in a free market? Let us consider the exchange rate from the perspective of the United States—in dollars per unit of foreign currency. Like other prices, the exchange rate in a free market is determined by both supply and demand conditions.

DEMAND FOR FOREIGN EXCHANGE A nation's *demand for foreign exchange* is derived from, or corresponds to, the *debit* items on its balance of payments. For example, the U.S. demand for pounds may stem from its desire to import British goods and services, to make investments in Britain, or to make transfer payments to residents in Britain.

Like most demand schedules, the U.S. demand for pounds varies inversely with its price; that is, fewer pounds are demanded at higher prices than at lower prices. This relationship is depicted by

line D_0 in Figure 12.1. As the dollar depreciates against the pound (the dollar price of the pound rises), British goods and services become more expensive to U.S. importers. This is because more dollars are required to purchase each pound needed to finance the import purchases. The higher exchange rate reduces the number of imports bought, lowering the number of pounds demanded by U.S. residents. In like manner, an appreciation of the U.S. dollar relative to the pound would be expected to induce larger import purchases and more pounds demanded by U.S. residents.

SUPPLY OF FOREIGN EXCHANGE The *supply of foreign exchange* refers to the amount of foreign exchange that will be offered to the market at various exchange rates, all other factors held constant. The supply of pounds, for example, is generated by the desire of British residents and businesses to import U.S. goods and services, to lend funds and make investments in the United States, to repay debts owed to U.S. lenders, and to extend transfer payments to U.S. residents. In each of these cases, the British offer

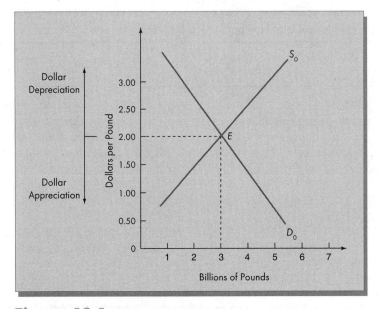

Figure 12.1 Exchange-Rate Determination

The equilibrium exchange rate is established at the point of intersection of the supply and demand schedules of foreign exchange. The demand for foreign exchange corresponds to the debit items on a nation's balance-of-payments statement; the supply of foreign exchange corresponds to the credit items.

pounds in the foreign-exchange market to obtain the dollars they need to make payments to U.S. residents. Note that the supply of pounds results from transactions that appear on the *credit* side of the U.S. balance of payments; thus, one can make a connection between the balance of payments and the foreign-exchange market.

The supply of pounds is denoted by schedule S_0 in Figure 12.1. The schedule represents the number of pounds offered by the British to obtain dollars with which to buy U.S. goods, services, and assets. It is depicted in the figure as a positive function of the U.S. exchange rate. As the dollar depreciates against the pound (dollar price of the pound rises), the British will be inclined to buy more U.S. goods. The reason, of course, is that at higher and higher dollar prices of pounds, the British can get more U.S. dollars and hence more U.S. goods per British pound. U.S. goods thus become cheaper to the British, who are induced to purchase addition-

al quantities. As a result, more pounds are offered in the foreign-exchange market to buy dollars with which to pay U.S. exporters.

EQUILIBRIUM RATE OF EXCHANGE As long as monetary authorities do not attempt to stabilize exchange rates or moderate their movements, the *equilibrium exchange rate* is determined by the market forces of supply and demand. In Figure 12.1, exchange-market equilibrium occurs at point E, where S_0 and D_0 intersect. Three billion pounds will be traded at a price of $2 per pound. The foreign-exchange market is precisely cleared, leaving neither an excess supply nor an excess demand for pounds.

Given the supply and demand schedules of Figure 12.1, there is no reason for the exchange rate to deviate from the equilibrium level. But in practice, it is unlikely that the equilibrium exchange rate will remain very long at the exist-

WEAK EURO IS BONANZA FOR AMERICAN TOURISTS

1999 was a bonanza for Americans vacationing in Europe. A sharp decrease in the exchange value of Europe's common currency, the euro, to near parity with the U.S. dollar made the continent a cheaper vacation destination for U.S. tourists. Travelers stayed in fancier hotels, dining in nicer restaurants and shopping with bargain-basement enthusiasm.

In 1999, the value of the euro fell from a high of $1.19 on January 4, its first day of trading, to about $1.01 in July. Because the currencies of the 11 European nations that adopted the euro were locked into fixed exchange rates, as the euro fell, so did French francs, Italian lire, German mark, and other key European currencies. In January 1999, one dollar bought about five French francs; by July it bought about six.

Adding to the bonanza for Americans, air fares to and from Europe declined. Therefore, airlines added jetliners to trans-Atlantic markets, even moving jumbo jets from Asia because of slumping economies there. In 1999, a record of 11.5 million Americans traveled to Europe, up about 5 percent from 1998.

U.S. travelers took advantage of the weak euro in several ways. For example, a round-trip business-class ticket between Chicago and Paris cost $7,428 on American Airlines. But purchasing two one-way tickets, one of which was priced in U.S. dollars ($3,700) and the other priced in French francs ($2,511) knocked the total cost down to $6,211—a savings of 16 percent for the same American flight.

Even better, a traveler could fly from Chicago to Paris via Toronto, where the U.S. dollar out-muscled its Canadian counterpart. That itinerary reduced the price of the business trip down to $4,357, including a first-class seat between Chicago and Toronto. Although the airlines didn't like the discounted fares, resulting from bargain exchange rates, they could not stop them.

U.S. travelers also booked their vacations through European Internet sites where tickets were denominated in local currencies. Credit-card companies converted the European currencies into U.S. dollars, giving the traveler the advantage of the favorable exchange rates. And if travelers thought the dollar would strengthen more against the European currencies, they could avoid prepaying as much as they could, and purchase their trip piecemeal rather than in a package. Once in Europe, they could pay for everything with a credit card. By the time the bill arrived, the exchange rate might be even more favorable.

Source: "Bon Voyage: Weak Euro Is Bonanza for U.S. Tourists," *The Wall Street Journal*, July 16, 1999, p. B1 and B4.

ing level. This is because the forces that underlie the location of the supply and demand schedules tend to change over time, causing shifts in the schedules. Should the *demand* for pounds shift *rightward* (an increase in demand), the dollar will *depreciate* against the pound; *leftward* shifts in the demand for pounds (a decrease in demand) cause the dollar to *appreciate*. Conversely, a *rightward* shift in the *supply* of pounds (increase in supply) causes the dollar to *appreciate* against the pound; a *leftward* shift in the supply of pounds (decrease in supply) results in a *depreciation* of the dollar. What causes shifts in these schedules? This topic will be considered in Chapter 13.

IS A STRONG DOLLAR ALWAYS GOOD AND A WEAK DOLLAR ALWAYS BAD?

Is a strong (appreciating) dollar always good and a weak (depreciating) dollar always bad? A strengthening or weakening dollar can affect many parties, among them consumers, tourists, investors, exporters, and importers. Table 12.8 summarizes these effects.

Consider also the effects of the fluctuating dollar on U.S. firms during the 1990s.[4] In 1995,

[4] "U.S. Importers Take on the Dollar's Fall," *The Wall Street Journal*, April 17, 1995, p. A2 and "Strong Dollar Creates Winners and Losers," *The Wall Street Journal*, February 6, 1997, p. A2.

Table 12.8 Advantages and Disadvantages of a Strengthening and Weakening Dollar

STRENGTHENING (APPRECIATING) DOLLAR	
Advantages	Disadvantages
1. U.S. consumers see lower prices on foreign goods	1. U.S. exporting firms find it harder to compete in foreign markets
2. Lower prices on foreign goods help keep U.S. inflation low	2. U.S. firms in import-competing markets find it harder to compete with lower-priced foreign goods
3. U.S. consumers benefit when they travel to foreign countries	3. Foreign tourists find it more expensive to visit the United States
4. U.S. investors can purchase foreign stocks and bonds at "lower" prices	4. It is more difficult for foreign investors to provide capital to the United States
WEAKENING (DEPRECIATING) DOLLAR	
Advantages	Disadvantages
1. U.S. exporting firms find it easier to sell goods in foreign markets	1. U.S. consumers face higher prices on foreign goods
2. Firms in the United States have less competitive pressure to keep prices low	2. Higher prices on foreign goods contribute to higher inflation in the United States
3. More foreign tourists can afford to visit the United States	3. U.S. consumers find traveling abroad more costly
4. U.S. capital markets become more attractive to foreign investors	4. It is more difficult for U.S. firms and investors to expand into foreign markets

the U.S. dollar's exchange value depreciated, especially against the Japanese yen. This meant that more dollars were needed to purchase the yen; as a result, goods imported by U.S. companies became more expensive. How did U.S. importers adjust to the dollar depreciation? Consider the following cases:

HIGH SIERRA SPORT CO., A LEATHER-GOODS MANUFACTURER IN ILLINOIS. As the dollar's exchange value plunged, faxes poured in from its Asian suppliers informing it of price hikes; one indicated nylon prices were going up, the next indicated zipper costs were increasing. When the firm decided to launch two new lines of handbags, Taiwanese and Korean suppliers warned it of pending increases in fabric prices. High Sierra's solution: raise the prices of leather goods rather than absorb the higher cost of imported inputs.

TREK BICYCLE INC., A BIKE MANUFACTURER IN WISCONSIN. This company manufac-

tured bikes and also imported bikes made to its design from Taiwanese manufacturers. In both cases, from 30 percent to 50 percent of the bike components came from Japanese suppliers. Trek paid its Taiwanese bike suppliers in dollars, but these firms had to purchase Japanese components with yen. As the dollar started depreciating, Trek was initially protected because the Taiwanese were absorbing the currency variance. As negotiations for the next year's models proceeded, however, the prices of Taiwanese bikes went up. To reduce the foreign content of its bikes, Trek announced plans to build a second Wisconsin factory.

From 1996 to 1999, the dollar rose on the foreign-exchange markets. This resulted in U.S. Treasury Secretary Robert Rubin declaring, "A strong dollar is in America's interest." The question is, which America was he talking about? As seen in the next two examples, not all Americans benefited from the rising dollar.

COMPUTER NETWORK TECHNOLOGY INC., A PRODUCER OF NETWORK SYSTEMS IN MINNESOTA. The dollar's climb in 1997 resulted in rising costs of its network systems to Japan. The systems produced by European firms thus became more competitive in the Japanese market. As a result, Computer Network Technology's sales fell and its earnings dropped by $100,000.

SONY COMPUTER ENTERTAINMENT, A U.S.-BASED UNIT OF SONY CORP. As the dollar steadily soared against the yen, many U.S.-based subsidiaries of Japanese companies questioned whether they should pack up and head home. For example, Sony Computer Entertainment Inc., seeking to capitalize on the appreciation of the dollar against the yen, announced that it would halt production of its PlayStation home-video game in the United States and shift it back to Japan.

EFFECTIVE EXCHANGE RATE: THE TRADE-WEIGHTED DOLLAR

Since 1973, the value of the U.S. dollar in terms of foreign currencies has changed daily. In this environment of market-determined exchange rates, measuring the international value of the dollar is a confusing task. Financial pages of newspapers may headline a *depreciation* in the value of the dollar relative to some currencies while at the same time reporting its *appreciation* relative to others. Such events may leave the general public confused as to the actual value of the dollar.

Suppose the U.S. dollar appreciates 10 percent relative to the yen and depreciates 5 percent against the pound. The change in the dollar's international value is some weighted average of the changes in these two bilateral exchange rates. Throughout the day, the value of the dollar may change relative to the values of any number of currencies under market-determined exchange rates. Direct comparison of the dollar's exchange rate over time thus requires a *weighted average*

of all the bilateral changes. This average is referred to as the dollar's **effective exchange rate** or the **trade-weighted dollar**.

The effective exchange rate is a weighted average of the exchange rates between the domestic currency and the nation's most important trading partners, with weights given by relative importance of the nation's trade with each of these trade partners. One popular index of effective exchange rates is constructed by the U.S. Federal Reserve Board of Governors. This index reflects the impact of changes in the dollar's exchange rate on U.S. exports and imports with ten industrial nations. The base period of the index is March 1973, when the major industrial nations adopted market-determined exchange rates.

Table 12.9 illustrates the trade-weighted value of the U.S. dollar. An *increase* in the dollar's nominal effective exchange rate (from year to year) indicates a dollar *appreciation* relative to

Table 12.9 Trade-Weighted Value of the U.S. Dollar (March 1973 = 100)

Year	Trade-Weighted Value of the Dollar*
1973 (March)	100.0
1980	87.4
1982	116.6
1984	138.3
1986	112.0
1988	92.7
1990	89.1
1992	86.6
1994	91.3
1996	87.4
1997	96.4
1998	95.8
1999	94.1
2000	96.3**

*The nations included in the construction of the index are Germany, Japan, Canada, France, United Kingdom, Italy, Netherlands, Belgium, Sweden, and Switzerland.

**April, 2000.

Source: *Federal Reserve Bulletin*, various issues.

the currencies of the ten other nations in the index and a *loss* of price competitiveness for the United States. Conversely, a *decrease* in the dollar's nominal effective exchange rate implies a dollar *depreciation* relative to the other currencies and an *improvement* in U.S. international price competitiveness.

ARBITRAGE

We have seen how the supply and demand for foreign exchange can set the market exchange rate. This analysis was from the perspective of the U.S. (New York) foreign-exchange market. But what about the relationship between the exchange rate in the U.S. market and that in other nations? When restrictions do not modify the ability of the foreign-exchange market to operate efficiently, normal market forces result in a consistent relationship among the market exchange rates of all currencies. That is to say, if £1 = $2 in New York, then $1 = £0.5 in London. The prices for the same currency in different world locations will be identical.

The factor underlying the consistency of the exchange rates is called **exchange arbitrage**. Exchange arbitrage refers to the *simultaneous* purchase and sale of a currency in different foreign-exchange markets in order to profit from exchange-rate differentials in the two locations. This process brings about an identical price for the same currency in different locations and thus results in one market.

Suppose that the dollar/pound exchange rate is £1 = $2 in New York but £1 = $2.01 in London. Foreign-exchange traders would find it profitable to purchase pounds in New York at $2 per pound and immediately resell them in London for $2.01. A profit of 1 cent would be made on each pound sold, less the cost of the bank transfer and the interest charge on the money tied up during the arbitrage process. This return may appear to be insignificant, but on a $1 million arbitrage transaction it would generate a profit of approximately $5,000—not bad for a few minutes' work! As the demand for pounds increases in New York,

the dollar price of a pound will rise above $2; as the supply of pounds increases in London, the dollar price of the pound will fall below $2.01. This arbitrage process will continue until the exchange rate between the dollar and the pound in New York is approximately the same as it is in London. Arbitrage between the two currencies thus unifies the foreign-exchange markets.

The preceding example illustrates **two-point arbitrage**, in which two currencies are traded between two financial centers. A more intricate form of arbitrage, involving three currencies and three financial centers, is known as **three-point arbitrage**, or triangular arbitrage. Three-point arbitrage involves switching funds among three currencies in order to profit from exchange-rate inconsistencies, as seen in the following example.

Consider three currencies—the U.S. dollar, the Swiss franc, and the British pound, all of which are traded in New York, Geneva, and London. Assume that the rates of exchange that prevail in all three financial centers are as follows: (1) £1 = $1.50; (2) £1 = 4 francs; (3) 1 franc = $0.50. Because the same exchange rates (prices) prevail in all three financial centers, two-point arbitrage is not profitable. However, these quoted exchange rates are mutually inconsistent. Thus, an arbitrager with $1.5 million could make a profit as follows:

1. Sell $1.5 million for £1 million.
2. Simultaneously, sell £1 million for 4 million francs.
3. At the same time, sell 4 million francs for $2 million.

The arbitrager has just made a risk-free profit of $500,000 ($2 million – $1.5 million) before transaction costs!

These transactions tend to cause shifts in all three exchange rates that bring them into proper alignment and eliminate the profitability of arbitrage. From a practical standpoint, opportunities for such profitable currency arbitrage have decreased in recent years, given the large number of currency traders—aided by sophisticated computer information systems—who monitor currency quotes in all financial markets. The result of this activity is that currency exchange rates tend to be consistent throughout the world, with only minimal deviations due to transaction costs.

THE FORWARD MARKET

Foreign-exchange markets, as we have seen, may be spot or forward. In the *spot market*, currencies are bought and sold for immediate delivery (generally two business days after the conclusion of the deal). In the *forward market*, currencies are bought and sold now for future delivery, typically 1 month, 3 months, or 6 months from the date of the transaction. The exchange rate is agreed on at the time of the contract, but payment is not made until the future delivery actually takes place. Only the most widely traded currencies are included in the regular forward market, but individual forward contracts can be negotiated for most national currencies.

THE FORWARD RATE The rate of exchange used in the settlement of forward transactions is called the **forward rate**. This rate is quoted in the same way as the spot rate: the price of one currency in terms of another currency. Table 12.10 provides examples of forward rates as of January 5, 2000. Thus, under the Tuesday quotations, the selling price of 1-month forward British pounds is $1.6427 per pound; the selling price of 3-month forward pounds is $1.6426 per pound, and for 6-month forward pounds it is $1.6419 per pound.

It is customary for a currency's forward rate to be stated in relation to its spot rate. When a foreign currency is worth more in the forward market than in the spot market, it is said to be at a **premium**; conversely, when the currency is worth less in the forward market than in the spot market, it is said to be at a **discount**. The per annum percentage premium (discount) in forward quotations is computed by the following formula:

$$\text{Premium (discount)} = \frac{\text{forward rate} - \text{spot rate}}{\text{spot rate}}$$

$$\times \frac{12}{\text{no. of months forward}}$$

If the result is a negative forward premium, it means that the currency is at a forward discount.

Table 12.10 Forward Exchange Rates: Selected Examples

EXCHANGE RATES
Wednesday, January 5, 2000

The New York foreign exchange mid-range rates below apply to trading among banks in amounts of $1 million and more, as quoted at 4 p.m. Eastern time by Reuters and other sources. Retail transactions provide fewer units of foreign currency per dollar.

Country	U.S. $ equiv.		Currency per U.S.$	
	Tue	Mon	Tue	Mon
Britain (Pound).......	1.6425	1.6370	.6088	.6109
1-month forward.....	1.6427	1.6372	.6088	.6108
3-months forward....	1.6426	1.6371	.6088	.6108
6- months forward...	1.6419	1.6365	.6091	.6111
Canada (Dollar).......	.6900	.6887	1.4493	1.4521
1-month forward......	.6905	.6892	1.4482	1.4510
3-months forward....	.6914	.6902	1.4463	1.4489
6-months forward....	.6926	.6915	1.4438	1.4462
Japan (Yen).............	.009588	.009681	104.30	103.29
1-month forward......	.009639	.009730	103.75	102.77
3-months forward....	.009730	.009825	102.77	101.79
6-months forward....	.009879	.009974	101.23	100.26
Switzerland (Franc)..	.6431	.6429	1.5550	1.5555
1-month forward......	.6455	.6454	1.5491	1.5494
3-months forward....	.6500	.6498	1.5384	1.5389
6-months forward....	.6569	.6567	1.5224	1.5228

Source: *The Wall Street Journal*, January 6, 2000, p. C14.

According to Table 12.10, on Tuesday the 1-month forward Swiss franc was selling at $0.6455, whereas the spot price of the franc was $0.6431. Because the forward price of the franc exceeded the spot price, the franc was at a 1-month forward premium of 0.24 cents, or at a 4.5 percent forward premium per annum against the dollar:

$$\text{Premium} = \frac{\$0.6455 - \$0.6431}{\$0.6431} \times \frac{12}{1} = .0448$$

Similarly, the franc was at a 3-month premium of 0.69 cents, or at a 4.3 percent forward premium per annum against the dollar:

$$\text{Premium} = \frac{\$0.6500 - \$0.6431}{\$0.6431} \times \frac{12}{3} = 0.0429$$

As for the British pound, the 6-month forward pound was at a discount of 0.07 percent per annum against the dollar:

$$\text{Discount} = \frac{\$1.6419 - \$1.6425}{\$1.6425} \times \frac{12}{6} = -0.0007$$

What determines the forward rate? Why might it be at a premium or discount compared to the spot rate? The forward rate is generally regarded as the exchange market's consensus forecast (average expectation) of what will happen to the spot rate over the period of the forward contract. If you desire to know the informed opinion of the market concerning what the pound will be worth in 1 month's time, you can look up the 1-month forward rate. For instance, if the spot rate of the pound is $1.60 and the 1-month forward rate is $1.56, the market's consensus is that the pound's spot rate will depreciate by 4 cents during the next month. To use a sports analogy, the forward rate is like the point spread on a baseball game, the number of runs by which the average gambler believes that the superior team will win.

FORWARD MARKET FUNCTIONS The forward market can be used to protect international traders and investors from the risks involved in fluctuations of the spot rate. The process of avoiding or covering a foreign-exchange risk is known as **hedging**. People who expect to make or receive payments in a foreign currency at a future date are concerned that if the spot rate changes, they will have to make a greater payment or will receive less in terms of the domestic currency than expected. This could wipe out anticipated profit levels.

In 1997, many Asian companies lost large sums when Asian currencies sharply depreciated against the U.S. dollar. For example, Siam Cement PCL, a chemicals giant in Thailand, was forced to absorb an extraordinary loss of $517 million in the third quarter of 1997. The company had $4.2 billion in foreign borrowing, and none of it was hedged. The foreign-exchange loss wiped out all of the profits that Siam Cement had chalked up between 1994 and 1996! Prior to 1997, few Asian economies bothered to hedge their foreign-exchange risks because most Asian currencies were tied to the dollar. The ties were broken, however, as a result of the Asian financial crises of 1997, and this caught many Asian

managers by surprise; they were unprepared for the adverse effects of volatile currencies.

How can firms and investors insulate themselves from volatile currency values? They can deal in the forward market, as shown in the following examples.

CASE 1:
U.S. importer hedges against a dollar depreciation.

Assume Sears Roebuck and Co. owes 1 million francs to a Swiss watch manufacturer in three month's time. During this period, Sears is in an exposed or uncovered position. Sears bears the risk that the dollar price of the franc might rise in three months (the dollar might depreciate against the franc), say, from $0.60 to $0.70 per franc; if so, purchasing 1 million francs would require an extra $100,000.

To cover itself against this risk, Sears could immediately buy 1 million francs in the spot market, but this would immobilize its funds for three months. Alternatively, Sears could contract to purchase 1 million francs in the forward market, at today's forward rate, for delivery in three months. In three months, Sears would purchase francs with dollars, at the contracted price, and use the francs to pay the Swiss exporter. Sears has thus hedged against the possibility that francs will be more expensive than anticipated in three months. Note that hedging in the forward market does not require Sears to tie up its own funds for three months.

CASE 2:
U.S. exporter hedges against a dollar appreciation.

Assume that Microsoft Corporation anticipates receiving 1 million francs in three months from its exports of computer software to a Swiss retailer. During this period, Microsoft is in an *uncovered* position. If the dollar price of the franc falls (the dollar appreciates against the franc), say, from $0.50 to $0.40 per franc, Microsoft's receipts will be worth $100,000 less when the 1 million francs are converted into dollars.

To avoid this foreign-exchange risk, Microsoft can contract to sell its expected franc receipts in the forward market at today's forward rate. By locking into a set forward-exchange rate, Microsoft is guaranteed that the value of its franc receipts will be maintained in terms of the dollar, even if the value of the franc should happen to fall.

The forward market thus eliminates the uncertainty of fluctuating spot rates from international transactions. Exporters can hedge against the possibility that the domestic currency will appreciate against the foreign currency, and importers can hedge against the possibility that the domestic currency will depreciate against the foreign currency. Hedging is not limited to exporters and importers. It applies to anyone who is obligated to make a foreign-currency payment or who will enjoy foreign-currency receipts at a future time. International investors, for example, also make use of the forward market for hedging purposes.

DOES FOREIGN-CURRENCY HEDGING ALWAYS PAY OFF?

As a firm that realizes more than half of its sales in profits in foreign currencies, Minnesota Mining & Manufacturing Co. is very sensitive to fluctuations in exchange rates. As the dollar appreciates against other currencies, 3M's profits decline; as the dollar depreciates, its profits increase. Indeed, when currency markets go wild, like they did during 1997–1998 when Asian currencies and the Russian ruble crashed relative to the dollar, deciding whether or not to hedge is a crucial business decision. Yet 3M didn't use hedges, such as the forward market or currency options market, to guard against currency fluctuations.[5]

In 1998, the producer of Scotch Tape and Post-its announced that the appreciating dollar had cost the firm $330 million in profits and $1.8 billion in revenue during the previous three years. Indeed, 3M's no-hedging policy had investors nervous. Was 3M unwise in not hedg-

ing its currency risk? Not according to many analysts and other big firms that chose to hedge very little, if at all. Firms ranging from Exxon to Deere to Kodak have maintained that currency fluctuations improve profits as often as they hurt them. In other words, although an appreciation of the dollar would detract from their profits, a dollar depreciation would add to them. As a result, hedging isn't necessary, as the ups and down of currencies even out over the long run.

The standard argument for hedging is increased stability of cash flows and earnings. Surveys of Corporate America's largest companies have found that one-third of them do some kind of foreign-currency hedging. For example, drug giant Merck and Co. hedges some of its foreign cash flows using the currency options market to sell the currencies for dollars at fixed rates. Merck maintains that it can protect against adverse currency moves by exercising its options, or enjoy favorable moves by not exercising them. Either way, the firm aims to guarantee that cash flow from foreign sales remains stable so that it can sustain research spending in years when a strong dollar trims foreign earnings. According to Merck's chief financial officer, the firm pays money for insurance to dampen volatility from unknown events.

Yet many well-established companies see no need to pay for protection against currency risk. Instead, they often choose to cover the risks out of their own deep pockets. According to 3M officials, if you consider the cost of hedging over the entire cycle, the drain on your earnings is very high for purchasing that insurance. Indeed, foreign-currency hedging eats into profits. A simple forward contract that locks in an exchange rate costs up to half a percentage point per year of the revenue being hedged. Other techniques such as currency options are more costly. What's more, fluctuations in a firm's business can detract from the effectiveness of foreign-currency hedging.

Indeed, many companies have decided heging is not worth the trouble. For example, in late 1993 Eastman Kodak concluded that the benefits

[5] "Perils of the Hedge Highwire," *Business Week*, October 26, 1998, pp. 74–76.

EXCHANGE-RATE RISK: THE HAZARD OF INVESTING ABROAD

Return on a 3-Month German Investment

	Deutsche Mark Return	Percentage Change in $/DM Exchange Rate	Dollar Return
May 27–August 26	2.4%	16.6%	19.0%
September 30–December 30	2.3	-12.5	-10.2

Exchange-rate fluctuations can substantially change the returns on assets denominated in a foreign currency. A real-world demonstration follows.

Throughout 1992, short-term interest rates in Germany were significantly higher than those in the United States; however, an American choosing between a dollar-denominated and Deutsche mark-denominated certificate of deposit (CD) with similar liquidities and default risks would not necessarily have earned a higher return on the German CD.

On May 27, 1992, an American saver with $10,000 to invest had the choice between a 3-month CD with an annual interest rate of 3.85 percent from an American bank and a 3-month CD with an annual interest rate of 9.65 percent (approximately 2.4 percent for 3 months) from a German bank. After 3 months, the U.S. CD was worth $10,096 and the German CD was worth $11,900 after exchanging the marks for dollars. As the table shows, the substantially larger value of the German CD was due primarily to a 16.6-percent appreciation of the mark against the dollar from May 27 to August 26.

Now consider the choice facing our investor on September 30, 1992: a 3-month U.S. CD offering an annual interest rate of 3.09 percent, and a comparable German investment offering an annual interest rate of 9.1 percent (approximately 2.3 percent for 3 months). After 3 months, the U.S. CD was worth $10,077. If the investor purchased the German CD, however, she would have had only $8,964 at the end of the 3 months—$1,036 less than the purchase price. This loss resulted from the 12.5-percent appreciation of the dollar against the mark between September and December 1992. With hindsight, the American saver would have preferred the U.S. CD to the German CD, even though the German interest rate was higher.

These examples provide a clear message. Even though interest rates play a key role in determining the relative attractiveness of assets denominated in domestic and foreign currencies, the effects of exchange-rate changes can swamp the effects of interest-rate differentials. Such large differences in returns illustrate why many investors choose to hedge against exchange-rate changes.

Source: Patricia S. Pollard, "Exchange-Rate Risk: The Hazard of Investing Abroad," *International Economic Conditions*, Federal Reserve Bank of St. Louis, February 1993, p. 1.

of extensive use of foreign-currency hedging did not justify the costs because the ups and downs of currencies would even out over the long run. As a result, the firm switched from hedging its overall receipts and payments to hedging only a few specific contracts. Moreover, IBM had reduced the impact of currency fluctuations without hedging by locating plants in many countries where it does business, so its costs are in the same currency as its revenues.

INTEREST ARBITRAGE

Investors make their financial decisions by comparing the rates of return of foreign investment with those of domestic investment. If rates of return from foreign investment are larger, they will desire to shift their funds abroad. **Interest arbitrage** refers to the process of moving funds into foreign currencies to take advantage of higher investment yields abroad. But investors assume a risk when they have foreign investments: When the investment's proceeds are converted back into the home currency, their value may fall because of a change in the exchange rate. Investors can eliminate this exchange risk by obtaining "cover" in the forward market.

UNCOVERED INTEREST ARBITRAGE Uncovered interest arbitrage occurs when an investor does not obtain exchange-market cover to protect investment proceeds from foreign-currency fluctuations. Although this practice is rarely used, it is a good pedagogical starting point.

Suppose the interest rate on 3-month Treasury bills is 6 percent (per annum) in New York and 10 percent (per annum) in London, and that the current spot rate is $2 per pound. A U.S. investor would seek to profit from this opportunity by exchanging dollars for pounds at the rate of $2 per pound and using these pounds to purchase 3-month British Treasury bills in London. The investor would earn 4 percent more per year, or 1 percent more for the 3 months, than if the same dollars had been used to buy 3-month Treasury bills in New York. These results are summarized in Table 12.11.

However, it is not necessarily true that our U.S. investor realizes an extra 1-percent rate of return (per 3 months) by moving funds to London. This amount will be realized only if the exchange value of the pound remains constant over the investment period. If the pound *depreciates* against the dollar, the investor makes *less*; if the pound *appreciates* against the dollar, the investor makes *more*!

Table 12.11 Uncovered Interest Arbitrage: An Example

	Rate per Year	Rate per 3 Months
U.K. 3-month Treasury bill interest rate	10%	2.5%
U.S. 3-month Treasury bill interest rate	6%	1.5%
Uncovered interest differential favoring the U.K.	4%	1.0%

Suppose our investor earns an extra 1 percent by purchasing 3-month British Treasury bills rather than U.S. Treasury bills. Over the same period, suppose the dollar price of the pound falls from $2.00 to $1.99 (the pound *depreciates* against the dollar). When the proceeds are converted back into dollars, the investor *loses* 0.5 percent—($2 − $1.99) / $2 = .005). The investor thus earns only 0.5 percent more (1 percent − 0.5 percent) than if the funds had been placed in U.S. Treasury bills. The reader can verify that if the dollar price of the pound fell from $2 to $1.98 over the investment period, the U.S. investor would earn nothing extra by investing in British Treasury bills.

Alternatively, suppose that over the 3-month period the pound rises from $2 to $2.02, a 1-percent *appreciation* against the dollar. This time, in addition to the extra 1-percent return on British Treasury bills, our investor realizes a return of 1 percent from the appreciation of the pound. The reason? When she bought pounds to finance her purchase of British Treasury bills, she paid $2 per pound; when she converted her investment proceeds back into dollars, she received $2.02 per pound—($2.02 − $2) / $2 = .01). Because the pound's appreciation adds to her investment's profitability, she earns two percent more than if she had purchased U.S. Treasury bills.

In summary, a U.S. investor's extra rate of return on an investment in the United Kingdom, as compared to the United States, equals the interest-rate differential adjusted for any change in the value of the pound, as follows:

Extra return = (U.K. interest rate – U.S. interest rate) – % depreciation of the pound

or

Extra return = (U.K. interest rate – U.S. interest rate) + % appreciation of the pound

COVERED INTEREST ARBITRAGE Investing funds in a foreign financial center involves an exchange-rate risk. Because investors typically desire to avoid this risk, interest arbitrage is usually *covered*.

Covered interest arbitrage involves two basic steps. First, an investor exchanges domestic currency for foreign currency, at the current spot rate, and uses the foreign currency to finance a foreign investment. At the same time, the investor contracts in the forward market to sell the amount of the foreign currency that will be received as the proceeds from the investment, with a delivery date to coincide with the maturity of the investment. It pays for the investor to make the foreign investment if the positive interest-rate differential in favor of the foreign investment more than offsets the cost of obtaining the forward cover.

Suppose the interest rate on 3-month Treasury bills is 12 percent (per annum) in London and 8 percent (per annum) in New York; the interest differential in favor of London is 4 percent per annum, or 1 percent for the 3 months. Suppose also that the current spot rate for the pound is $2, while the 3-month forward pound sells for $1.99. This means that the 3-month forward pound is at a 0.5 percent *discount*—($1.99 – $2) / $2 = –.005.

By purchasing 3-month Treasury bills in London, a U.S. investor could earn 1 percent more for the 3 months than if he bought 3-month Treasury bills in New York. To eliminate the uncertainty over how many dollars will be received when the pounds are reconverted into dollars, the investor sells enough pounds on the 3-month forward market to coincide with the anticipated proceeds of the investment. The cost of the forward cover equals the difference between the spot rate and the contracted 3-month forward rate; this difference is the discount on the forward pound, or 0.5 percent. Subtracting this 0.5 percent from the interest-rate differential of 1 percent, the investor is able to realize a net rate of return that is 0.5 percent higher than if he had bought U.S. Treasury bills. These results are summarized in Table 12.12.

This investment opportunity will not last long, because the net profit margin will soon disappear. As U.S. investors purchase spot pounds, the spot rate will rise. Concurrently, the sale of forward pounds will push the forward rate downward. The result is a widening of the discount on the forward pounds, which means that the cost of covering the exchange-rate risk increases. This arbitraging process will continue until the forward discount on the pound widens to 1 percent, at which point the extra profitability of the foreign investment vanishes. The discount on the pound now equals the interest-rate differential between New York and London:

Pound forward discount = U.K. interest rate – U.S. interest rate

Table 12.12 Covered Interest Arbitrage: An Example

	Rate per Year	Rate per 3 Months
U.K. 3-month Treasury bill interest rate	12%	3%
U.S. 3-month Treasury bill interest rate	8%	2%
Uncovered interest-rate differential favoring the U.K.	4%	1%
Forward discount on the 3-month pound		–0.5%
Covered interest-rate differential favoring the U.K.		0.5%

In short, the theory of foreign exchange suggests that the forward discount or premium on one currency against another reflects the difference in the short-term interest rates between the two nations. The currency of the higher-interest-rate-nation should be at a *forward* discount while the currency of the lower-interest-rate nation should be at a forward *premium*.

International differences in interest rates do exert a major influence on the relationship between the spot and forward rates. But on any particular day, one would hardly expect the spread on short-term interest rates between financial centers to precisely equal the discount or premium on foreign exchange, for several reasons. First, changes in interest-rate differentials do not always induce an immediate investor response necessary to eliminate the investment profits. Second, investors sometimes transfer funds on an uncovered basis; such transfers do not have an effect on the forward rate. Third, factors such as governmental exchange controls and speculation may weaken the connection between the interest-rate differential and the spot and forward rates.

FOREIGN-EXCHANGE MARKET SPECULATION

Besides being used for the financing of commercial transactions and investments, the foreign-exchange market is also used for exchange-rate speculation. **Speculation** is the attempt to profit by trading on expectations about prices in the future. Some speculators are traders acting for financial institutions or firms; others are individuals. In either case, speculators buy currencies that they expect to go up in value and sell currencies that they expect to go down in value.

Note the difference between arbitrage and speculation. With arbitrage, a currency trader *simultaneously* buys a currency at a low price and sells that currency at a high price, thus making a riskless profit. A speculator's goal is to buy a currency at one moment (such as today) and

sell that currency at a higher price in the future (such as tomorrow). Speculation thus implies the deliberate assumption of exchange risk: If the price of the currency falls between today and tomorrow, the speculator loses money.

SPECULATING IN THE SPOT MARKET
Imagine that you are a currency speculator in New York, willing to risk money on your opinion about future prices of a foreign currency—say, the Swiss franc. Consider the following scenarios.

CASE 1:
Speculating on a Swiss franc appreciation.

GIVEN: Today's spot price is $0.40 per franc.

ASSUMPTION: In 3 months, the spot price of the franc will rise to $0.50.

PROCEDURE
1. Purchase francs at today's spot price of $0.40 and deposit them in a bank to earn interest.
2. In 3 months, sell the francs at the prevailing spot price of $0.50 per franc.

OUTCOME: If assumption is right, profit = $0.10 per franc. If assumption is wrong and the spot price of the franc falls instead, you incur a loss, reselling francs at a price lower than the purchase price.

CASE 2:
Speculating on a Swiss franc depreciation.

GIVEN: Today's spot price is $0.40 per franc.

ASSUMPTION: In 3 months, the spot price of the franc will fall to $0.25.

PROCEDURE
1. Borrow francs today, exchange them for dollars at the prevailing spot price of $0.40 per franc, and deposit the dollars in a bank to earn interest.
2. In 3 months, buy francs at the prevailing spot price of $0.25 per franc and use them to pay back the loan.

OUTCOME: If assumption is right, profit = $0.15 per franc. (This return is reduced by the interest paid on borrowed money, but increased by the interest received on the bank savings account). If assumption is wrong and the spot price of the franc rises in 3 months instead, you incur a loss buying francs at a higher price than the initial selling price.

SPECULATING IN THE FORWARD MARKET

Although speculation on the spot market can lead to profits, it has a serious drawback: The speculator must have a large amount of idle cash or borrowing privileges, which require interest payments. Speculation in the forward market, however, does not require cash or credit facilities. All the speculator needs to do is sign a forward contract with a bank to either purchase or sell a specified amount of foreign currency at a specified date. The bank may impose a *margin requirement*, requiring the speculator to put up, say, 10 percent of the value of the foreign contract as security. In practice, most speculation is done in the forward market.

Forward market speculation occurs when a speculator believes that a currency's spot price at some future date will differ from today's forward price for that same date. For example, suppose the 30-day forward pound is selling at a 10-percent discount; this discount is the market's consensus (average expectation) that in 30 days the spot rate of the pound will be 10 percent lower than it is today. As a speculator, however, you feel you have better information than the market. You believe that in 30 days the pound's spot rate will be only 5 percent lower (or maybe 15 percent higher) than it is today. You are willing to bet your money that the market consensus is wrong. Your gains or losses will equal the difference between the current forward rate and the spot rate 30 days from now. Consider the following scenarios.

CASE 1:

Speculating that the spot rate of the Swiss franc in 3 months will be higher *than its current 3-month forward rate.*

GIVEN: The current price of the 3-month forward franc is $0.40.

ASSUMPTION: In 3 months, the prevailing spot price of the franc will be $0.50.

PROCEDURE

1. Contract to purchase a specified amount of francs in the forward market, at $0.40 per

franc, for 3-month delivery.
2. After receiving delivery of the francs in 3 months, resell them in the spot market at the prevailing price of $0.50 per franc.

OUTCOME: If assumption is right, profit = $0.10 per franc. If assumption is wrong and the prevailing spot price in 3 months is lower than $0.40 per franc, you incur a loss.

CASE 2:

Speculating that the spot rate of the Swiss franc in 3 months will be lower *than its current 3-month forward rate.*

GIVEN: The current price of the 3-month forward franc is $0.40.

ASSUMPTION: In 3 months, the prevailing spot price of the franc will be $0.30.

PROCEDURE

1. Contract to sell a specified amount of francs (which you do not currently have) for delivery in 3 months at the forward price of $0.40 per franc.
2. In 3 months, purchase an identical amount of francs in the spot market at $0.30 per franc and deliver them to fulfill the forward contract.

OUTCOME: If assumption is right, profit = $0.10 per franc. If assumption is wrong and the prevailing spot price in 3 months is higher than $0.40 per franc, you incur a loss.

When speculators purchase foreign currency on the spot or forward market with the anticipation of selling it at a higher future spot price, they are said to take a **long position** in the currency. But when speculators borrow or sell forward a foreign currency with the anticipation of purchasing it at a future lower price to repay the foreign-exchange loan or fulfill the forward sale contract, they are said to take a **short position** (that is, they are selling what they do not presently have).

OTHER FORMS OF SPECULATION Besides speculation in the spot and forward markets, there are other ways of capitalizing on expectations of currency movements. One way is to *purchase securities* denominated in a foreign currency. A U.S. speculator who anticipates that the

Japanese yen's spot rate will significantly appreciate in the near future might purchase bonds issued by Japanese corporations and expressed in yen. The bonds are paid for in yen, which are purchased by converting dollars into yen at the prevailing spot rate. If the yen goes up, the speculator gets not only the accrued interest from the bond but also its appreciated value in dollars. The catch is that, in all likelihood, others have the same expectations. The overall demand for the bonds may be sufficient to force up the bond price, resulting in a lower interest rate. For the speculator to win, the yen's appreciation must exceed the loss of interest income. In many cases, the exchange-rate changes are not large enough to make such investments worthwhile.

Rather than investing in foreign securities, some speculators choose to *purchase stocks* of foreign corporations, denominated in foreign currencies. The speculator in this case is trying to predict the trend of not only the foreign currency but also its stock market. The speculator must be highly knowledgeable about both financial and economic affairs in the foreign country.

For investors who expect that the spot rate of a foreign currency will soon rise, the answer lies in a *savings account* denominated in a foreign currency. For example, a U.S. investor may contact a major New York bank or a U.S. branch of a foreign bank and take out an interest-bearing certificate of deposit expressed in a foreign currency. An advantage of such a savings account is that the investor is guaranteed a fixed interest rate. An investor who has guessed correctly also enjoys the gains stemming from the foreign currency's appreciation. However, the investor must be aware of the possibility that governments might tax or shut off such deposits or interfere with the investor's freedom to hold another nation's currency.

SPECULATION AND EXCHANGE-MARKET STABILITY

An exchange-market speculator deliberately assumes foreign-exchange risk on the expectation of profiting from future changes in the spot exchange rate. Such activity can exert either a stabilizing or a destabilizing influence on the foreign-exchange market.

STABILIZING SPECULATION Stabilizing speculation goes against market forces by *moderating* or *reversing* a rise or fall in a currency's exchange rate. It occurs when a speculator buys foreign currency with domestic currency when the domestic price of the foreign currency falls, or depreciates. The hope is that the domestic price of the foreign currency will soon increase, leading to a profit. Such purchases increase the demand for the foreign currency, which moderates its depreciation. Stabilizing speculation also occurs when a speculator sells foreign currency when the domestic price of the foreign currency rises, or appreciates, in the hope that the price will soon fall. Such sales moderate the appreciation of the foreign currency. Stabilizing speculation performs a useful function for bankers and businesspeople, who desire stable exchange rates.

DESTABILIZING SPECULATION Destabilizing speculation goes with market forces by *reinforcing* fluctuations in a currency's exchange rate. It occurs when a speculator sells a foreign currency when it depreciates, on the expectation that it will depreciate further in the future. Such sales depress the foreign currency's value. It also occurs when speculators buy a foreign currency when its exchange rate appreciates, on the expectation that it will appreciate even further in the future. Such purchases increase the foreign currency's value. Destabilizing speculation reinforces exchange-rate fluctuations and can disrupt international trade and investment.

Should destabilizing speculation against a currency be sufficiently large, it may induce sizable forward discounts on the currency. If speculators view a currency as particularly weak, they may anticipate a significant decline in its value. Immediately they would begin selling the currency forward for future delivery, in the hope of fulfilling their futures contracts at lower spot rates. These sales tend to further weaken the forward rate, causing the forward discount to become larger. When there is a sizable forward discount on a currency, the ability of interest-rate differentials to promote order in the exchange market may be limited.

Destabilizing speculation can disrupt international transactions in several ways. Because of the uncertainty of financing exports and imports, the cost of hedging may become so high that international trade is impeded. What is more, unstable exchange rates may disrupt international investment activity. This is because the cost of obtaining forward cover for international capital transactions may rise significantly as foreign-exchange risk intensifies.

A slight variation of the concept of foreign market speculation is that of *capital flight*. This is motivated not by the expectation of profit but rather by the fear of exchange-market loss. Capital flight may be induced by fear of currency devaluation, political instability, or government restrictions on foreign-exchange movements. Such short-run monetary flows, sometimes referred to as *hot money*, created marked disruptions in the international monetary system during the late 1960s and early 1970s. Major capital flights out of the overvalued U.S. dollar in 1971 and 1973 touched off the termination of the dollar's gold convertibility.

SHOULD SPECULATORS BE SHOT? Currency speculators have never had a good press. In the late 1960s, British politicians found it convenient to blame speculators for a big depreciation of the pound. Nowadays, London itself has become the world's biggest foreign-exchange market, and the complaints have moved elsewhere. During the East Asian currency crisis of 1997, the currencies of Malaysia, Thailand, South Korea, Indonesia, and the Philippines plummeted against the dollar. According to Prime Minister Mahathir of Malaysia, entire regions can be bankrupted by just a few speculators whose only objective is to enrich themselves and their wealthy clients. He added that currency trading, beyond the level necessary to finance trade, is unnecessary, unpro-

ductive, and immoral, and that speculators should be shot!

There is no doubt that the volume of currency trading has mushroomed relative to trade. At the turn of the millennium, the value of currency trading was only six times greater than the value of world trade in goods and services. By 1995, currency trading was about 50 times the value of world trade. Put simply, much currency trading occurs for reasons other than to provide liquidity for world trade.

The case against currency speculators assumes that their decisions are underlain by their desire for profit, and thus that they pay negligible attention to the underlying health of economies. However, speculators do not select their targets at random. True, their goal is to make money, but the best way to do this over the long run is to identify currencies that are out of line with economic fundamentals (see Chapter 13) and whose prices are thus likely to change. The depreciations of the East Asian currencies in 1997 all reflected imbalances. Therefore, the changes in the prices of these currencies were necessary. The speculators, arguably, just called the change first.

Analysts estimate that speculators can mobilize between $600 billion and $1 trillion to bet against currencies—for example, selling a currency forward in the hope that they can buy it back later at a cheaper rate. If such sales are conducted in massive amounts, speculators may be able to force a currency's value downward. However, speculators devote much time to studying economic and political fundamentals, identifying those economic imbalances that offer profitable opportunities. Generally, speculators do not attack currencies that are underlain by credible economic policies.

This does not imply that currency markets are perfect. They are vulnerable to "bubbles" and excess waves of optimism followed by excessive pessimism. In a bubble, it may be profitable to buy a currency even when its price is high, as long as it is expected to increase further—until the bubble bursts. A speculator will lose money if she does not jump on the bandwagon.

SHOULD FOREIGN-EXCHANGE TRANSACTIONS BE TAXED?

The 1997 financial crises in East Asia, in which several nations were forced to abandon their fixed-exchange-rate regimes, produced demands for more stability and government regulation in the foreign-exchange markets. Indeed, market volatility was blamed for much of the trouble sweeping the region.

Economists generally argue that the free market is the best device for determining how money should be invested. Global capital markets provide sneedy countries with funds to grow, while permitting foreign investors to diversify their portfolios. If capital is allowed to flow freely, they contend, markets will reward countries that pursue sound economic policies and will pressure the rest to do the same. Indeed, most countries welcome and even encourage capital inflows such as foreign direct investment in factories and businesses, which represent long-lasting commitments. But some have become skeptical of financial instruments such as stocks and bonds, bank deposits, and short-term debt securities, which can be pulled out of a country with a stroke of a computer key. That's what occurred in East Asia in 1997, in Mexico in 1994 and 1995, and in the United Kingdom and Italy in 1992 and 1993.

To prevent international financial crises, several notable economists have called for sand to be thrown in the wheels of international finance by imposing a tax on foreign-exchange transactions. The idea is that a tax would increase the cost of these transactions, which would discourage massive responses to minor changes in information about the economic situation, and thus dampen volatility in exchange rates. Proponents argue that such a tax would give traders an incentive to look at long-term economic trends, not short-term hunches, when buying and selling foreign exchange and securities. Traders must pay a small tax, say, 0.1 percent for every transaction, so they won't buy or sell unless expected returns justify the additional expense. Fewer transactions suggest less volatility and more stable exchange rates.

Proponents of a tax may well contend that they are not trying to interfere with free markets, but only to prevent excess volatility. However, we do not know how much volatility is excessive or irrational. It's true that economists cannot explain all exchange-rate volatility in terms of changes in the economic fundamentals of nations, but it does not follow from this that we should seek to regulate such fluctuations. Indeed, some of the volatility may be produced by uncertainty about government policies.

There are other drawbacks to the idea of taxing foreign-exchange transactions. Such a tax could impose a burden on countries that are quite rationally borrowing overseas. By raising the cost of capital for these countries, it would discourage investment and hinder their development. Also, a tax on foreign-exchange transactions would be difficult to implement. Foreign-exchange trading can be conducted almost anywhere in the world, and a universal agreement to impose such a tax seems extremely unlikely. Those countries that refused to implement the tax would become centers for foreign-exchange trading.

If foreign-currency markets are to be regulated by government, will such intervention be superior to the outcome that occurs in a free market? Will government be able to identify better than markets what the "correct" exchange rate is? Many analysts contend that government would make even bigger mistakes. Moreover, markets are better than government in admitting their mistakes and reversing out of them. That is because, unlike governments, markets have no pride.

S U M M A R Y

1. The foreign-exchange market provides the institutional framework within which individuals, businesses, and financial institutions purchase and sell foreign exchange. Two of the world's largest foreign-exchange markets are located in New York and London.

2. The exchange rate is the price of one unit of foreign currency in terms of the domestic currency. From a U.S. viewpoint, the exchange rate might refer to the number of dollars necessary to buy a Swiss franc. A dollar depreciation (appreciation) is an increase (decrease) in the number of dollars required to buy a unit of foreign exchange.

3. In the foreign-exchange market, currencies are traded around the clock and throughout the world. Most foreign-exchange trading is in the interbank market. Banks typically engage in three types of foreign-exchange transactions: spot, forward, and swap.

4. *The Wall Street Journal's* foreign-exchange quotations include those of the New York foreign-exchange market and the International Monetary Market located in Chicago. Both spot quotations and forward quotations are provided.

5. The equilibrium rate of exchange in a free market is determined by the intersection of the supply and demand schedules of foreign exchange. These schedules are derived from the credit and debit items in a nation's balance of payments.

6. Exchange arbitrage permits the rates of exchange in different parts of the world to be kept the same. This is achieved by selling a currency when its price is high and purchasing when the price is low.

7. Foreign traders and investors often deal in the forward market for protection from possible exchange-rate fluctuations. However, speculators also buy and sell currencies in the futures markets in anticipation of sizable profits. In general, interest arbitrage determines the relationship between the spot rate and the forward rate.

8. Speculation in the foreign-exchange markets may be either stabilizing or destabilizing in nature.

S T U D Y   Q U E S T I O N S

1. What is meant by the foreign-exchange market? Where is it located?

2. What is meant by the forward market? How does this differ from the spot market?

3. The supply and demand for foreign exchange are considered to be derived schedules. Explain.

4. Explain why exchange-rate quotations stated in different financial centers tend to be consistent with one another.

5. Who are the participants in the forward exchange market? What advantages does this market afford these participants?

6. What explains the relationship between the spot rate and the forward rate?

7. What is the strategy of speculating in the forward market? In what other ways can one speculate on exchange-rate changes?

8. Distinguish between stabilizing speculation and destabilizing speculation.

9. If the exchange rate changes from $1.70 = £1 to $1.68 = £1, what does this mean for the dollar? For the pound? What if the exchange rate changes from $1.70 = £1 to $1.72 = £1?

10. Suppose $1.69 = £1 in New York and $1.71 = £1 in London. How can foreign-exchange arbitragers profit from these exchange rates? Explain how foreign-exchange arbitrage results in the same dollar/pound exchange rate in New York and London.

11. Table 12.13 shows supply and demand schedules for the British pound. Assume that exchange rates are flexible.

   a. The equilibrium exchange rate equals _____ . At this exchange rate, how many pounds will be purchased, and at what cost in terms of dollars?

   b. Suppose the exchange rate is $2 per pound. At this exchange rate, there is an excess (supply/demand) of pounds. This imbalance causes (an increase/a decrease) in the dollar price of the pound, which leads to (a/an) _____ in the quantity of pounds supplied and (a/an) _____ in the quantity of pounds demanded.

   c. Suppose the exchange rate is $1 per pound. At this exchange rate, there is an excess (supply/demand) for pounds. This imbalance causes (an increase/ a decrease) in the price of the pound, which leads to (a/an) _____ in the quantity of pounds supplied and (a/an) _____ in the quantity of pounds demanded.

12. Suppose the spot rate of the pound today is $1.70 and the 3-month forward rate is $1.75.

   a. How can a U.S. importer who has to pay 20,000 pounds in 3 months hedge her foreign-exchange risk?

   b. What occurs if the U.S. importer does not hedge and the spot rate of the pound in 3 months is $1.80?

13. Suppose the interest rate (on an annual basis) on 3-month Treasury bills is 10 percent in

Table 12.13 Supply and Demand of British Pounds

Quantity of Pounds Supplied	Dollars per Pound	Quantity of Pounds Demanded
50	$2.50	10
40	2.00	20
30	1.50	30
20	1.00	40
10	.50	50

London and 6 percent in New York, and the spot rate of the pound is $2.

   a. How can a U.S. investor profit from uncovered interest arbitrage?

   b. If the price of the 3-month forward pound is $1.99, will a U.S. investor benefit from covered interest arbitrage? If so, by how much?

14. Table 12.14 gives hypothetical dollar/franc exchange values for Wednesday, May 5, 1999.

   a. Fill in the last two columns of the table with the reciprocal price of the dollar in terms of the franc.

   b. On Wednesday, the spot price of the two currencies was _____ dollars per franc, or _____ francs per dollar.

   c. From Tuesday to Wednesday, in the spot market the dollar (appreciated/depreciated) against the franc; the franc (appreciated/depreciated) against the dollar.

Table 12.14 Dollar/Franc Exchange Values

	U.S. Dollar Equivalent		Currency per U.S. Dollar	
	Wed.	Tues.	Wed.	Tues.
Switzerland (franc)	.5851	.5846		
30-Day Forward	.5853	.5848		
90-Day Forward	.5854	.5849		
180-Day Forward	.5851	.5847		

d. In Wednesday's spot market, the cost of buying 100 francs was _____ dollars; the cost of buying 100 dollars was _____ francs.

e. On Wednesday, the 30-day forward franc was at a (premium/discount) of _____ dollars, which equaled _____ percent on an annual basis? What about the 90-day forward franc?

15. Assume a speculator anticipates that the spot rate of the franc in 3 months will be lower than today's 3-month forward rate of the franc, $0.50 = 1 franc.

a. How can this speculator use $1 million to speculate in the forward market?

b. What occurs if the franc's spot rate in 3 months is $0.40? $0.60? $0.50?

16. You are given the following spot exchange rates: $1 = 3 francs, $1 = 4 schillings, and 1 franc = 2 schillings. Ignoring transaction costs, how much profit could a person make via 3-point arbitrage?

12.1 The Web site of the Wells Fargo Bank provides an overview of exchange rates and international trade in its International Services section. Set your browser to URL:

http://www.wellsfargo.com/

12.2 L.P. Bloomberg, a well-known financial-services firm, provides currency information at its Web site, including its currency calculator, key cross-country rate, and currency by region. Go to Markets after setting your browser to URL:

http://www.bloomberg.com/

12.3 Olsen and Associates is a leading developer of online forecasting technology for business and finance. OANDA, its Internet subsidiary, offers a currency converter that will tell you current and historical exchange rates for 192 currencies. Set your browser to URL:

http://www.oanda.com/

12.4 J.P. Morgan, a global financial-services firm, publishes a daily trade-weighted currency index that measures nominal exchange-rate strength of individual OECD currencies relative to a basket of 18 other OECD currencies. It can be reached at URL:

http://www.jpmorgan.com/MarketDataInd/Forex/currIndex.html

To access NetLink Exercises and the Virtual Scavenger Hunt, visit the Carbaugh Web site at http://carbaugh.swcollege.com.

chapter 13

Exchange-Rate Determination

S ince the introduction of market-determined exchange rates by the major industrial nations in the 1970s, wide shifts in exchange rates have been observed. This chapter seeks to explain the forces that underlie currency appreciation and depreciation under a system of market-determined (floating) exchange rates.

EXCHANGE-RATE DETERMINATION IN A FREE MARKET

We have learned that foreign-exchange markets are highly competitive by nature. Large numbers of sellers and buyers meet in these markets, which are located in the major cities of the world and are connected electronically to form one worldwide market. Participants in the foreign-exchange market have excellent, up-to-the-minute information about the exchange rates between any two currencies. As a result, currency values are determined by the unregulated forces of supply and demand as long as central banks do not attempt to stabilize them. The supplies and demands for a currency are those of private individuals, corporations, banks, and government agencies other than central banks. In a free market, the equilibrium exchange rate occurs at the point at which the quantity demanded of a foreign currency equals the quantity of that currency supplied.

To say that supply and demand determine exchange rates in a free market is at once to say everything and to say nothing. If we are to

KEY CONCEPTS AND TERMS

- Asset-markets approach
- Forecasting exchange rates
- Fundamental analysis
- International capital movements
- Judgmental forecasts
- Law of one price
- Market expectations
- Market fundamentals
- Monetary approach
- Nominal interest rate
- Overshooting
- Purchasing-power-parity approach
- Real interest rate
- Relative purchasing power parity
- Speculative bubble
- Technical analysis

understand why some currencies depreciate and others appreciate, we must investigate the factors that cause the supply and demand schedules of currencies to change. These factors include **market fundamentals** (economic variables) and **market expectations:**[1]

MARKET FUNDAMENTALS
Current account balances
Real income
Real interest rates
Inflation rates
Consumer preferences for domestic or foreign products
Productivity changes affecting production costs
Profitability and riskiness of investments
Product availability
Monetary policy and fiscal policy
Government trade policy

MARKET EXPECTATIONS
News about future market fundamentals
Speculative opinion about future exchange rates

Because economists believe that the determinants of exchange-rate fluctuations are rather different in the short run (a few weeks or even days), medium run (several months), and long run (1, 2, or even 5 years), we will consider these time frames when analyzing exchange rates. In the *short run*, foreign-exchange transactions are dominated by transfers of financial assets (bank deposits) that respond to differences in real interest rates and to shifting expectations of future exchange rates; such transactions have the major influence on short-run exchange rates. Over the *medium run*, exchange rates are governed by cyclical factors such as cyclical fluctuations in economic activity. Over the *long run*, foreign-

exchange transactions are dominated by flows of goods, services, and investment capital, which respond to forces such as inflation rates, investment profitability, consumer tastes, real income, productivity, and government trade policy; such transactions have the dominant impact on long-run exchange rates.

Note that day-to-day influences on foreign exchange rates can cause the rate to move in the opposite direction from that indicated by longer-term fundamentals. Although today's exchange rate may be out of line with long-term fundamentals, this should not be construed as implying that it is necessarily inconsistent with short-term determinants—for example, interest-rate differentials, which are among the relevant fundamentals at the short end of the time dimension.

Figure 13.1 highlights the framework in which exchange rates are determined.[2] The figure views exchange rates as simultaneously determined by long-run structural, medium-run cyclical, and short-run speculative forces. The figure illustrates the idea that there exists some equilibrium level or path to which a currency will eventually gravitate. A currency's long-run equilibrium path is likely to rest on market fundamentals, such as differences in national inflation rates or balance-of-payments considerations. This equilibrium path serves as a long-run magnet or anchor; it ensures that exchange rates will not fluctuate aimlessly without limit but rather will tend to gravitate over time toward the long-run equilibrium path.

Medium-run cyclical forces can induce fluctuations of a currency above and below its long-run equilibrium path. However, fundamental forces serve to push a currency toward its long-run equilibrium path. Note that medium-run cyclical fluctuations from a currency's long-run equilibrium path can be large at times, if economic disturbances induce significant changes in either trade flows or capital movements.

Longer-run structural forces and medium-run cyclical forces interact to establish a currency's fun-

---

[1] This approach to exchange-rate determination is known as the balance-of-payments approach. It emphasizes the flow of goods, services, and investment funds and their impact on foreign-exchange transactions and exchange rates. The approach predicts that exchange-rate depreciation (appreciation) tends to occur for a nation that spends more (less) abroad in combined purchases and investments than it acquires from abroad over a sustained period of time.

[2] This figure and its analysis are adapted from Michael Rosenberg, *Currency Forecasting* (Homewood, IL: Richard D. Irwin, 1996), pp. 3–5.

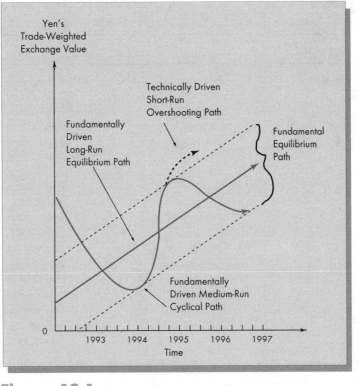

Figure 13.1 The Path of the Yen's Exchange Rate

The figure views the exchange value of a nation's currency as being determined by long-run structural, medium-run cyclical, and short-run speculative forces.

damental equilibrium path. Exchange rates may sometimes move away from this fundamental equilibrium path, if short-run forces (for example, changing market expectations) induce fluctuations in exchange rates beyond those based on fundamental factors. Although such overshooting behavior can persist for significant periods, fundamental forces generally push the currency back into its fundamental equilibrium path.

Unfortunately, exchange-rate determination (forecasting) is a difficult job. That is because economic forces affect exchange rates through a variety of channels—some of which may induce negative impacts on a currency's value, others of which may exert positive impacts on a currency's value. Some of those channels may be more

important in determining short- or medium-run tendencies, whereas other channels may be more important in explaining the long-run trend that a currency follows.

Let us first analyze the impact of market fundamentals on exchange rates, as summarized in Table 13.1. We will then consider the effects of changing market expectations on exchange rates.

REAL INCOME AND EXCHANGE RATES

Consider how changes in *real income differentials* affect the exchange rate between two currencies,

Table 13.1 Market Fundamentals and the Dollar's Exchange Value

Factor	Change	Effect on the Dollar's Exchange Value
Foreign demand for U.S. exports	Decrease	Depreciation
	Increase	Appreciation
Foreign demand for U.S. assets	Decrease	Depreciation
(stocks, bonds, bank deposits)	Increase	Appreciation
U.S. demand for foreign exports	Decrease	Appreciation
	Increase	Depreciation
U.S. demand for foreign assets	Decrease	Appreciation
	Increase	Depreciation
U.S. price level*	Decrease	Appreciation
	Increase	Depreciation
U.S. interest rates*	Decrease	Depreciation
	Increase	Appreciation
U.S. real income*	Decrease	Appreciation
	Increase	Depreciation
U.S. productivity*	Decrease	Depreciation
	Increase	Appreciation
U.S. trade restrictions*	Increase	Appreciation
	Decrease	Depreciation

*Relative to foreign nations.

say, the U.S. dollar and the British pound. Figure 13.2 illustrates the foreign-exchange market in which the demand and supply schedules of pounds are denoted by D_0 and S_0, respectively, and the equilibrium exchange rate is $1.50 per pound. Suppose there occurs an increase in the growth rate of the U.S. economy that results in higher real incomes for U.S. households, while the economy of the United Kingdom remains stagnant. Rising real income causes U.S. consumers to purchase more domestically produced goods and also more goods from the United Kingdom. The demand for pounds thus increases from D_0 to D_1 in the figure. Given supply-of-pounds schedule S_0, the dollar depreciates to $1.60 per pound. Conversely, a decrease in U.S. real income, holding U.K. income constant, would cause the exchange value of the dollar to appreciate against the pound.

Suppose that increased government spending leads the economies of the United States and the United Kingdom to expand at the same time. Which nation's currency will depreciate? As real income rises in the United States, Americans will import more goods from the United Kingdom. The demand for pounds will increase, causing a depreciation in the dollar's exchange value against the pound. At the same time, however, rising real income in the United Kingdom causes the British to import more goods from the United States. The supply of pounds thus increases, which causes the exchange value of the dollar to appreciate against the pound. On balance, the dollar may or may not depreciate. The outcome depends on whether U.S. exports to the United Kingdom are growing faster than U.S. imports from the United Kingdom.

The general rule relating real income to exchange rates is as follows: Holding other determinants of exchange rates constant, a country experiencing *faster* economic growth than the rest of the world tends to find its currency's

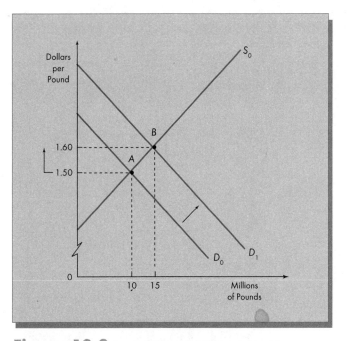

Figure 13.2 Income Growth Differentials and Exchange-Rate Fluctuations

An increase in real income in the United States has the effect of increasing U.S. spending on imports from the United Kingdom, which leads to an increase in the demand for pounds and a depreciation in the dollar's exchange value. Should U.S. real income fall, the effects will be to reduce the demand for pounds and to appreciate the dollar's exchange value. In general, a country experiencing faster economic growth than its trading partners tends to find its currency's exchange value depreciating, and vice versa.

exchange value *depreciating*. This is because its imports rise faster than its exports, and thus its demand for foreign currency rises more rapidly than its supply of foreign currency. Thus, in our example, if the income-growth differential favors the United States, the dollar will depreciate against the pound; if the differential favors the United Kingdom, the pound will depreciate against the dollar.

One should not conclude that a strong currency is an indicator of a strong economy. A country that realizes a more rapid growth rate than its trading partners may find that the exchange value of its currency is depreciating! As an example, during 1993 and 1994, the U.S. economy was expanding, while Europe's economies were weak and Japan was mired in a prolonged slump; during this period the dollar depreciated against these currencies.

A caution must be added to this reasoning, however. Income is not an independent force that can simply fluctuate by itself. What leads to its fluctuation has a major impact on the exchange rate. In our example, we assumed that real income was increased by the effects of increased government spending; this caused aggregate demand to

INTEREST RATES AND THE DOLLAR'S EXCHANGE VALUE

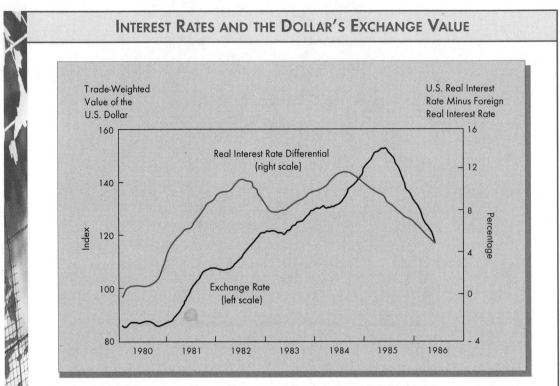

Source: Craig Hakkio, "Interest Rates and Exchange Rates: What Is the Relationship?" Federal Reserve Bank of Kansas City, *Economic Review*, November 1986.

The theory of flexible exchange rates helps explain the behavior of the dollar in the 1980s. When real interest rates in the United States are increasing relative to real interest rates overseas, the U.S. dollar should appreciate as investors seek to locate their funds in the United States.

The figure shows the real-interest-rate differential between the United States and other industrial nations in the 1980s. Over the period 1980–1984, the real interest rate rose in the United States relative to the other nations. This attracted investment funds into the United States and promoted a steady appreciation in the dollar's value until early 1985. Subsequently, the dollar's exchange value decreased sharply as the real-interest-rate differential moved lower.

rise, which led to an increase in imports and a weakening of the domestic currency. Now assume that the rise in real income is due to a supply-side factor—an improvement in the nation's productivity. If productivity gains are passed forward to foreign buyers in the form of lower prices, the nation's exports will increase, as will its real income. In this case, the nation's currency will appreciate because of the additional exports made possible by the rising productivity.

REAL INTEREST RATES AND EXCHANGE RATES

Although the cyclical position of a country's economy is an important determinant of exchange rates over the longer run, other factors affect exchange rates in the short run. One such factor is *short-term interest-rate differentials* between nations, which influence **international capital movements**. These are the movements of investment funds—held by corporations, banks, and individuals—that travel around the world in search of the highest interest rates.

Holding constant other exchange-rate determinants, *easy credit* and relatively *low short-term interest rates* lead to exchange-rate *depreciation* for a nation, whereas *tight credit* and relatively *high short-term interest rates* cause a nation's currency to *appreciate*. These conclusions are based on the assumption that short-term interest-rate differentials between any two nations are a key determinant of international capital movements, as seen in the following example.

Referring to Figure 13.3, suppose the equilibrium exchange rate for the U.S. dollar and the Japanese yen is \$.0075 per yen, determined at the point of intersection of schedules S_0 and D_0. Assume that an expansionary monetary policy of the U.S. Federal Reserve results in a fall in U.S. short-term interest rates to 8 percent, while interest rates in Japan are at 10 percent. U.S. investors will be attracted by the relatively high interest rates in Japan and will demand more yen to buy Japanese securities. The demand for yen thus rises to D_1 in the figure. Concurrently, the Japanese will find investing in the United States less attractive than before, so fewer yen will be offered to buy dollars for purchases of U.S. securities. The supply of yen thus shifts to S_1 in the

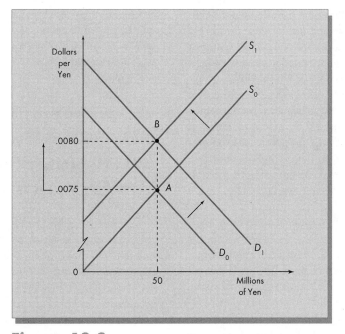

Figure 13.3 Interest-Rate Differentials and Exchange-Rate Fluctuations

As U.S. interest rates fall relative to Japanese interest rates, Japanese citizens make fewer investments in the United States, and the supply of yen decreases. But U.S. citizens will make more investments in Japan in order to take advantage of relatively high interest rates; the demand for yen thus increases. The result is a depreciation in the dollar's exchange value against the yen.

figure. The combined effect of these two shifts is to move the market equilibrium from point *A* to point *B*, and the dollar depreciates to $.0080 per yen. Alternatively, if interest rates were lower in Japan than in the United States, the dollar would appreciate against the yen as Americans made fewer investments in Japan and the Japanese made more investments in the United States.

Most experts in international finance agree that interest-rate differentials are a major determinant of exchange rates in the short run. Observers point to the U.S. dollar during 1983 and 1984 as an example of currency appreciation caused by high interest rates. During this period, the U.S. economy enjoyed rapid recovery from recession, while sluggish economic growth plagued its trading partners. The result was a decrease in the value of U.S. exports relative to the value of U.S. imports. This situation by itself would have caused the dollar to depreciate. However, during this period U.S. interest rates rose well above comparable interest rates abroad; this differential led to net investment inflows for the United States. That the dollar appreciated suggested that the downward pressure of a worsening trade deficit was being more than offset by the upward pressure of an increasing demand for dollars by international investors. In 1985 and 1986, when U.S. interest rates fell relative to those in foreign nations, the exchange value of the dollar depreciated against such key currencies as the mark and the yen.

Things may not always be so simple, though, concerning the relationship between interest rates and exchange rates. It is important to distinguish between the **nominal** (money) **interest rate** and the **real interest rate** (the nominal interest rate minus the inflation rate). For international investors, it is relative changes in the real interest rate that matter.

If a rise in the nominal interest rate in the United States is accompanied by an equal rise in the U.S. inflation rate, the real interest rate remains constant. In this case, higher nominal interest rates do not make dollar-denominated securities more attractive to British investors. This is because rising U.S. inflation will encourage U.S. buyers to seek out low-priced British goods, which will increase the demand for pounds and cause the dollar to depreciate. British investors will expect the exchange rate of the dollar, in terms of the pound, to depreciate along with the declining purchasing power of the dollar. The higher nominal return on U.S. securities will thus be offset by the expectation of a lower future exchange rate, leaving the motivation for increased British investment in the United States unaffected. Only if higher nominal interest rates in the United States signal an increase in the real interest rate will the dollar appreciate; if they signal rising inflationary expectations and a falling real interest rate, the dollar will depreciate. Table 13.2 provides examples of short-term real interest rates for various nations.

In summary, we expect to see appreciating currencies in countries whose real interest rates are higher than abroad because these countries will attract investment funds from all over the world. Countries that experience relatively low real interest rates tend to find their currencies depreciating.

INFLATION RATES, PURCHASING POWER PARITY, AND EXCHANGE RATES

Determining the long-run equilibrium value of an exchange rate (the value toward which the actual rate tends to move, given current economic conditions and policies) is important for successful exchange-rate management. For example, if a nation's exchange rate rises above the level warranted by economic conditions, so that its currency becomes *overvalued*, the nation's costs will no longer be competitive and a trade *deficit* will likely occur. An *undervalued* currency tends to lead to a trade *surplus*. National authorities have tried to forecast the long-run equilibrium rate and initiate exchange-rate adjustments to keep the actual rate in line with the forecasted rate. The **purchasing-power-parity approach** can be used to make predictions about exchange rates.

Table 13.2 Short-Term Nominal and Real Interest Rates, 1998

Country	Nominal Interest Rate*	Inflation Rate**	Real Interest Rate
Canada	4.7	2.1	2.6
France	3.5	0.1	3.4
Germany	3.0	0.1	2.9
India	13.5	13.2	0.3
Italy	4.6	2.0	2.6
Japan	0.4	0.1	0.3
South Korea	15.8	7.5	8.3
Mexico	24.8	15.9	8.9
United States	5.3	2.5	2.8
United Kingdom	6.8	3.4	3.4

*Rates are for 3-month Treasury bills.

**Measured by the consumer price index.

Source: *International Financial Statistics*, February 2000.

LAW OF ONE PRICE The simplest concept of purchasing power parity is the **law of one price**. It asserts that identical goods should cost the same in all nations, assuming that it is costless to ship goods between nations and there are no barriers to trade (such as tariffs).

Before the costs of goods in different nations can be compared, prices must first be converted into a common currency. Once converted at the going market-exchange rate, the prices of identical goods from any two nations should be identical. After converting francs into dollars, for example, machine tools purchased in Switzerland should cost the same as identical machine tools bought in the United States.

In theory, the pursuit of profits tends to equalize the price of identical products in different nations. Assume that machine tools bought in Switzerland are cheaper than the same machine tools bought in the United States, after converting francs into dollars. Swiss exporters could realize a profit by purchasing machine tools in Switzerland at a low price and selling them in the United States at a high price. Such transactions would force prices up in Switzerland and force prices down in the United States until the price of the machine tools would eventually become equal in both nations, whether prices are expressed in francs or dollars. As a result, the law of one price would prevail.

In practice, however, the law of one price does not always prevail. International trade is more complicated than suggested by simple theories. For example, tariffs and other trade barriers tend to drive a wedge between prices of identical products in different nations. Moreover, the cost of transporting goods from one nation to another restricts the potential profit from buying and selling identical products with different prices.

RELATIVE PURCHASING POWER PARITY Rather than focusing on a particular good when applying the purchasing-power-parity concept, most analysts look at market baskets consisting of many goods. They consider a nation's overall inflation (deflation) rate as measured by, say, the producer price index or consumer price index.

According to the theory of **relative purchasing power parity**, changes in relative national price levels determine changes in exchange rates over the long run. The theory predicts that the foreign-exchange value of a currency tends to

THE "BIG MAC" INDEX AND THE LAW OF ONE PRICE

The Price of a Big Mac, April 25, 2000

Country	Prices in Local Currency	U.S. Equivalent (in Dollars)	Local Currency Overvaluation (+), Undervaluation (−)
United States	$2.51	$2.51	—
Israel	14.5 shekel	3.58	+43%
Switzerland	5.9 francs	3.48	+39
Denmark	24.75 krone	3.08	+23
Britain	1.90 pounds	3.00	+20
Japan	294 yen	2.78	+11
Argentina	2.50 pesos	2.50	0
Chile	1,260 pesos	2.45	−2
Euro area	2.56 euros	2.37	−5
Canada	$2.85 Canadian	1.94	−23
South Africa	9.0 rands	1.34	−47

Source: " Big MacCurrencies," *The Economist*, April 29, 2000, p. 75.

The "Big Mac" hamburger sandwich sold by McDonalds has been viewed as an international monetary standard. Although economists generally prefer vast indexes based on thousands of commodities and prices to measure purchasing power, playful ones have opted for hamburger sandwiches. After all, the amount you pay for a Big Mac is a reflection of everything from sesame-seed prices to labor costs.

The so-called Big Mac Index is a popular stand-in for a much more serious concept, the law of one price. Based solely on the price of a Big Mac, the index is used to roughly assess which currencies are *overvalued* and which are *undervalued* relative to the U.S. dollar. *The Economist* magazine publishes Big Mac updates each year.

Consistent with the law of one price, the Big Mac Index suggests that the exchange rate between the dollar and the yen is in equilibrium when it equates the prices of hamburger sandwiches in the United States and Japan. Big Macs should thus cost the same in each country when the prices are converted to the dollar. When Big Macs do not cost the same, the yen is said to be overvalued or undervalued compared to the dollar.

The table shows what a Big Mac cost in different countries as of April 25, 2000. The U.S. equivalent prices denote which currencies are overvalued and which are undervalued relative to the dollar. In the United States (New York), a Big Mac cost $2.51. In Switzerland, the dollar-equivalent price of a Big Mac was $3.48. Compared to the dollar, the franc was *overvalued* by 39 percent (3.48 / 2.51 = 1.39). The Big Mac was a bargain in Canada, however, where the U.S. dollar equivalent price was $1.94; the Canadian dollar was *undervalued* by 23 percent (1.94 / 2.51 = 0.77).

To be sure, the Big Mac Index is primitive and has many flaws. However, it is widely understood by noneconomists and serves as an approximation of which currencies are too weak or strong, and by how much.

appreciate or depreciate at a rate equal to the difference between foreign and domestic inflation. As an example, if U.S. inflation exceeds Switzerland's inflation by 4 percentage points per year, the purchasing power of the dollar falls 4 points relative to the franc. The foreign-exchange value of the dollar should therefore depreciate 4 percent per year. Conversely, the U.S. dollar should appreciate against the franc if U.S. inflation is less than Switzerland's inflation.

The purchasing-power-parity theory can be used to predict long-run exchange rates. We'll consider an example using the price indexes (P) of the United States and Switzerland. Letting 0 be the base period and 1 represent period 1, the purchasing-power-parity theory is given in symbols as[3]

$$S_1 = S_0 \frac{P_{US_1} / P_{US_0}}{P_{S_1} / P_{S_0}}$$

where S_0 equals the equilibrium exchange rate existing in the base period and S_1 equals the estimated target at which the actual rate should be in the future.

For example, let the price indexes of the United States and Switzerland and the equilibrium exchange rate be as follows:

$$P_{US_0} = 100 \qquad P_{S_0} = 100 \qquad S_0 = \$0.50$$
$$P_{US_1} = 200 \qquad P_{S_1} = 100$$

[3] This chapter presents the so-called *relative version* of the purchasing-power-parity theory, which addresses changes in prices and exchange rates over a period of time. Another variant is the *absolute version*, which states that the equilibrium exchange rate will equal the ratio of domestic to foreign prices of an appropriate market basket of goods and services at a given point in time.

Putting these figures into the previous equation, we can determine the new equilibrium exchange rate for period 1:

$$S_1 = \$0.50 \left(\frac{200 / 100}{100 / 100} \right) = \$0.50(2) = \$1.00$$

Between one period and the next, the U.S. inflation rate rose 100 percent, whereas Switzerland's inflation rate remained unchanged. Maintaining purchasing power parity between the dollar and the franc requires the dollar to depreciate against the franc by an amount equal to the difference in the percentage rates of inflation in the United States and Switzerland. The dollar must depreciate by 100 percent, from $0.50 per franc to $1 per franc, to maintain its purchasing power parity. If the example assumed instead that Switzerland's inflation rate doubled while the U.S. inflation rate remained unchanged, the dollar would appreciate to a level of $0.25 per franc, according to the purchasing-power-parity theory.

An application of the purchasing-power-parity concept is provided in Table 13.3, which gives the dollar/peso exchange rate over the period 1985–1989, during which time Mexico experienced high inflation. From 1985 to 1989, U.S. prices rose by about 15 percent, whereas Mexico's prices skyrocketed more than 1,100 percent. Applying the purchasing-power-parity formula to these figures, we would forecast the dollar to appreciate against the peso, from $0.0039 per peso to $0.0004 per peso, owing to the relative decline in the peso's domestic purchasing power. In fact, the dollar did appreciate to $0.0004 per peso.

Table 13.3 Purchasing Power Parity in Action, 1985–1989

Year	U.S. Consumer Price Index	Mexican Consumer Price Index	Actual Exchange Rate: Dollars/Peso	Forecast Exchange Rate: Dollars/Peso
1985	100.0	100.0	0.0039	——
1987	105.7	431.7	0.0007	0.0010
1989	115.2	1,109.6	0.0004	0.0004

Source: International Monetary Fund, *IMF Financial Statistics*, Washington, DC, May 1990.

Purchasing power parity can be illustrated in terms of the supply and demand for foreign exchange. In Figure 13.4, D_0 and S_0 represent the demand and supply schedules of pounds, and the equilibrium exchange rate is $1.50 per pound. Suppose the domestic price level increases rapidly in the United States and remains constant in the United Kingdom. U.S. consumers will desire relatively low-priced British goods. The demand for pounds thus increases to D_1 in the figure. Conversely, the British will be less interested in purchasing relatively high-priced U.S. goods, thus reducing the supply of pounds to S_1. The increase in the demand for pounds and the decrease in the supply of pounds result in a depreciation of the dollar to $1.70 per pound.

Although the purchasing-power-parity theory can be helpful in forecasting appropriate levels to which currency values should be adjusted, it is not an infallible guide to exchange-rate determination. For instance, the theory overlooks the fact that exchange-rate movements may be influenced by capital flows. The theory also faces the problems of choosing the appropriate price index to be used in price calculations (for example, consumer prices or producer prices) and of determining the equilibrium period to use as a base. Moreover, government policy may interfere with

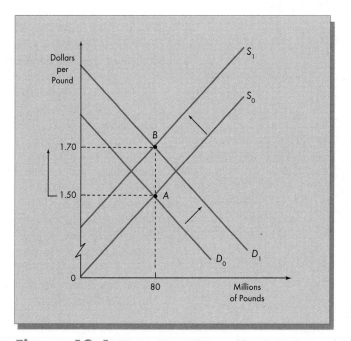

Figure 13.4 Inflation-Rate Differentials and Exchange-Rate Fluctuations

If the U.S. price level rises relative to the U.K. price level, imports become relatively less expensive in the United States. U.S. consumers tend to increase their spending on imports from the United Kingdom, which leads to an increase in the demand for pounds. At the same time, U.K. consumers see U.S. goods becoming more expensive. As they reduce their demand for exports from the United States, the supply of pounds decreases. The result is a depreciation in the dollar's exchange value against the pound.

INFLATION DIFFERENTIALS AND THE EXCHANGE RATE

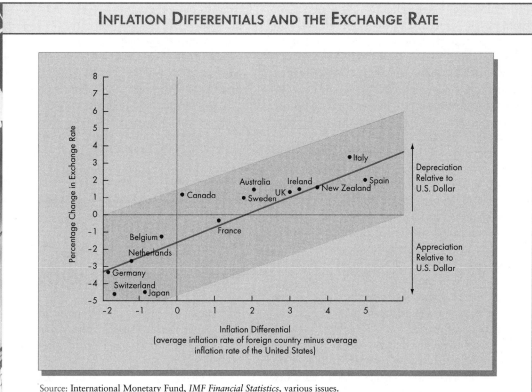

Source: International Monetary Fund, *IMF Financial Statistics*, various issues.

The purchasing-power-parity theory helps explain the behavior of a currency's exchange value. According to this theory, changes in relative national price levels determine changes in exchange rates over the long run. A currency would be expected to depreciate by an amount equal to the excess of domestic inflation over foreign inflation; it would appreciate by an amount equal to the excess of foreign inflation over domestic inflation.

The figure shows the relationship between inflation and the exchange rate for selected countries. The horizontal axis shows the country's average inflation minus the U.S. average inflation during the 1960–1997 period. The vertical axis shows the average percentage change in a country's exchange rate (foreign currency per dollar) over that period. Consistent with the predictions of the purchasing-power-parity theory, the figure shows that countries with relatively low inflation rates tend to have appreciating currencies, and countries with relatively high inflation tend to have depreciating currencies.

the operation of the theory (for example, trade restrictions that disrupt the flow of exports and imports among nations).

Evidence concerning the validity of the purchasing-power-parity theory is mixed. The theory appears roughly valid as a guide to exchange-rate determination when inflation is extreme.

Over the period from 1982 to 1985, Israel's annual inflation rate was in the triple-digit range. The Israeli shekel depreciated against the U.S. dollar in an amount that approximated the excess of Israeli inflation over U.S. inflation. The currencies of Latin American countries, such as Argentina and Mexico, also tend to follow this rule. However, where inflation differentials are small, factors other than price comparisons can become more important in the determination of exchange rates. The purchasing-power-parity theory also does not appear to hold as well when tests are conducted over relatively short (such as year-to-year) time periods, because of lags in the balance-of-payments adjustment process, government interference, and so on.

For many years, the purchasing-power-parity theory appeared to operate reasonably well. Although precise exchange-rate predictions based on purchasing-power-parity calculations were not always accurate, nations having higher inflation rates did at least experience depreciating currencies. In the early 1980s, however, even this broke down. For example, between 1980 and 1983 the U.S. inflation rate was much *higher* than Japan's and modestly higher than Germany's. Nevertheless, the dollar *appreciated* against both the yen and the mark during this period.

Observers maintain that exchange-rate movements are often caused by news that, by its very nature, is unpredictable. Foreign-exchange rates have been viewed to behave similarly to asset markets (such as stock markets), which incorporate new information quickly and adjust their prices continuously. However, purchasing-power-parity calculations are based on commodity prices (such as the consumer price index), which respond sluggishly to changing economic circumstances. To the extent that exchange rates respond quickly to new information and commodity prices respond slowly, departures from the purchasing-power-parity theory will occur. Most economists maintain that other factors are much more important than relative price levels for exchange-rate determination in the short run.

Although the purchasing-power-parity theory is of limited value in the short run, over a sufficiently long period it is possible that economic forces work to maintain purchasing-power-parity levels. One study used annual data over the period 1869–1984 to estimate the degree to which the dollar/pound exchange rate returns to purchasing power-parity equilibrium. Over the course of this period, the estimated speed of adjustment to purchasing power parity was 14 percent per year. This means that 50 percent of the adjustment toward purchasing power parity occurs after 4.5 years, and 90 percent of the adjustment occurs by the end of 15 years. These results suggest that the purchasing-power-parity theory provides a rough approximation of the long-run exchange rate if the adjustment process is analyzed over many years. A time horizon of such length, however, is of little relevance to decision makers.[4]

OTHER MARKET FUNDAMENTALS AND THEIR EFFECTS ON EXCHANGE RATES

In addition to real income, interest rates, and inflation, other market fundamentals that can affect exchange-rate movements include the following:

BILATERAL TRADE RELATIONSHIPS. A chronic U.S. trade deficit with Japan would create an ongoing supply of dollars to the Japanese marketplace. If Japanese investors are not willing to absorb these dollars, it weakens the dollar's exchange value against the yen.

CONSUMER TASTES. Should consumer tastes in the United States change in favor of goods produced abroad, the demand for foreign exchange would increase, causing a depreciation of the dollar. Conversely, if U.S. consumers followed a "Buy American" policy over a sustained period of time, an increased preference for domestic products over foreign products would lead to a reduced demand for foreign exchange and an appreciation in the dollar's exchange value.

INVESTMENT PROFITABILITY. If the profitability of Japanese assets (such as corporations, real estate) rises relative to the profitability of assets in

---

[4] J. Frenkel, "International Capital Mobility and Crowding Out in the U.S. Economy," in R. Hafer, ed., *How Open Is the U.S. Economy?* (Springfield, MA: Lexington Books/Heath, 1986).

foreign countries, foreign investors demand additional yen to make investments in Japan, which causes the yen's exchange value to appreciate.

PRODUCT AVAILABILITY. If Canada experiences a disastrous wheat-crop failure, it will have to import more wheat. This adds to the Canadian demand for foreign exchange, which causes the dollar's exchange value to depreciate.

PRODUCTIVITY CHANGES. If France realizes technological improvements in the production of computers, which lowers its costs relative to those of foreign producers, French computer exports will rise. This increases the demand for the franc and leads to an appreciation in its exchange value.

TRADE POLICY. Should the Mexican government implement policies that restrict imports (encourage exports), Mexico's demand for foreign exchange falls (supply of foreign exchange rises), which causes the peso's exchange value to appreciate.

MARKET EXPECTATIONS AND EXCHANGE RATES

We have seen that exchange-rate volatility stems in part from volatility in market fundamentals, such as real-income differentials and price differentials. Fluctuations in exchange rates, however, are sometimes too large and too sudden to be explained solely by such factors. For example, exchange rates can change by 2 percentage points or more in a single day. But variations in market fundamentals usually do not occur frequently or significantly enough to fully account for such exchange-rate irascibility. When exchange rates respond immediately to market forces, they are subject to *expectations*; that is, rather than reflecting existing market fundamentals, rates can move in anticipation of future changes.

A parallel exists between the foreign-exchange markets and the stock markets. In each, the exchange rate (or price) responds quickly as new information reaches the market. Elections, wars, or even personnel changes at the Federal Reserve may signal changes in future monetary policy. These or similar events—or simply rumors about them—can affect exchange rates in the same manner as they affect daily stock prices.

Suppose it is widely expected that the U.S. economy will (1) grow faster than the Japanese economy, (2) have lower future interest rates than Japan, (3) experience more rapid inflation than Japan, and (4) have a greater growth in its money supply than Japan. All these expectations suggest that the dollar in the future will depreciate against the yen. To avoid the exchange-market loss resulting from this projected dollar depreciation, holders of dollars will try to convert them into yen, thus increasing the demand for the yen. This conversion leads to an appreciation in the yen and a depreciation in the dollar. Table 13.4 summarizes the effects of changing market expectations on a currency's exchange value.

Figure 13.5 can be used to illustrate how expectations of future inflation can affect the dollar/franc exchange rate. Exchange-market equilibrium initially exists at point A, where $S_0 = D_0$, and the equilibrium

Table 13.4 Market Expectations and the Dollar's Exchange Value

Factor	Change	Effect on the Dollar's Exchange Value
Expected U.S. price level*	Increase	Depreciation
	Decrease	Appreciation
Expected U.S. interest rate*	Increase	Appreciation
	Decrease	Depreciation
Expected U.S. trade barriers*	Increase	Appreciation
	Decrease	Depreciation
Expected U.S. import demand	Increase	Depreciation
	Decrease	Appreciation
Expected demand for U.S. exports	Increase	Appreciation
	Decrease	Depreciation
Expected U.S. productivity*	Increase	Appreciation
	Decrease	Depreciation

*Relative to foreign nations.

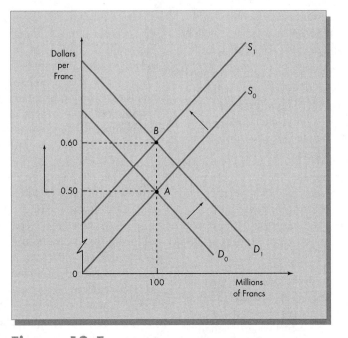

Figure 13.5 Market Expectations and Exchange-Rate Fluctuations

Given future expectations of a depreciation in the dollar's exchange value against the franc, U.S. importers of Swiss goods have the incentive to purchase additional francs before they become more expensive; the demand for francs thus increases. But Swiss importers of U.S. goods will be less willing to sell francs for dollars that are expected to soon become less expensive; the supply of francs thus decreases. The result is a depreciation in the dollar's exchange value against the franc.

exchange rate is $.50 per franc. Suppose that an unanticipated rise in the growth rate of the U.S. money supply is interpreted as a signal that the U.S. inflation rate will rise, which in turn signals a possible depreciation in the dollar's exchange rate. With these expectations, U.S. buyers who intend to make purchases in Switzerland are motivated to obtain francs prior to the anticipated depreciation of the dollar (when the franc would become more expensive in dollars). Accordingly, the demand for francs rises in the foreign-exchange market, say, to D_1.

Concurrently, the Swiss, who hold the same set of expectations, will be less willing to give up

francs in exchange for dollars that will soon decrease in value. The supply of francs offered in the foreign-exchange market thus shifts to the left, say, to S_1. The shifts in these schedules result in a depreciation of the dollar to $.60 per franc at equilibrium point *B*. In this way, future expectations of a dollar depreciation can be *self-fulfilling*.

Sometimes investors change their expectations about future exchange rates even without new information about market fundamentals. These changed expectations can also affect the exchange rate. An example is when the exchange rate is affected by a **speculative bubble**. To illustrate, suppose a significant number of speculators antic- ipate an appreciation in the Swiss franc. This expectation need not be based on any knowledge of Swiss market fundamentals; perhaps the spec- ulators charting the day-to-day movements of the exchange rate simply conclude that the franc is ripe for a takeoff. They will buy the currency, leading to a rise in its value; thus, the speculators' expectations become self-fulfilling. As specula- tors' confidence in the franc becomes stronger, they purchase additional francs. Thus, the franc can appreciate on a steady or even a spectacular climb with no change in market fundamentals underlying the upward movement. At any time, of course, a speculative bubble is likely to burst. Investors may suddenly realize that market fun- damentals do not justify a rise in the value of the franc and will attempt to sell it, driving the franc's value sharply downward. In short, actions by speculators can increase the volatility of exchange rates. Bubbles can drive a currency upward for no fundamental reason; then, when the bubble bursts, the currency can suddenly fall back down.

INTERACTION OF EXCHANGE- RATE DETERMINANTS

We have learned that in a free market, exchange rates fluctuate according to changes in market fundamentals and market expectations. Most of the time, these factors don't all point in the same direction; over a particular period, some factors may be causing a currency's exchange value to depreciate while others may be causing it to appre- ciate. What is the net effect on the exchange rate of these conflicting determinants?

For example, assume that the United States simultaneously experiences the following scenar- ios: (1) a sudden rise in real interest rates; (b) a sudden rise in national income; and (3) a sudden rise in inflation. Assume also that the Japanese economy remains unchanged. The first scenario would cause the dollar's exchange value to appre- ciate against the yen, while the second two sce- narios would cause a depreciation of the dollar.

Whether the dollar will rise or fall against the yen depends on the nature of the international trans- actions between the United States and Japan. If the two countries engage in a large amount of international investment but only a small amount of international trade, rising U.S. real interest rates will likely be more influential and the dol- lar's exchange value will appreciate. Conversely, if the two countries engage in a large amount of international trade but only a small amount of international investment, the increases in U.S. national income and inflation will likely be more influential, and the dollar's exchange value will depreciate.

As an application of this concept, assume that IBM of the United States desires to forecast the direction of the dollar's exchange value against the yen and the peso, because the firm obtains computer components from Japan and Mexico. Suppose IBM analysts develop one-year projec- tions like those in Table 13.5. Also assume that trade in goods between the United States and Japan is large, but investment flows between the countries are small, and that trade in goods between the United States and Mexico is small, but that investment flows between the two coun- tries are large. What will IBM predict concerning the exchange value of the dollar against these two currencies?

Because of Japan's large trade volume with the United States, the dollar/yen rate would be affected most by trade-related factors. The fore- casted income and inflationary changes lead to the expectation that the dollar will depreciate

Table 13.5 IBM's One-Year Forecast

Exchange-Rate Determinant	United States	Japan	Mexico
Percentage change in:			
National income	+3%	−2%	0%
Inflation	+2%	−3%	−2%
Interest rates	+1%	−1%	−3%

against the yen. The forecasted changes in interest rates would not be expected to have a significant direct affect on the dollar/yen rate because of the small volume of investment flows between Japan and the United States.

The dollar/peso rate, on the other hand, would be most influenced by interest rates, because of Mexico's large investment transactions with the United States. The forecasted interest-rate changes lead to the expectation that the dollar will appreciate against the peso. The forecasted changes in income and inflation would not be expected to have much of a direct effect on the dollar/peso rate, because of the modest amount of trade between the two nations.

In practice, forecasting exchange rates is tricky. Even if analysts understand the determinants of exchange rates, this does not mean that they can predict how those determinants will change. More will be said about forecasting later in this chapter.

The Federal Reserve and the Monetary Approach to Exchange-Rate Determination

Some economists find fault with the exchange-rate analysis considered so far in this chapter. They view its reliance on the relative supply and demand of goods, services, and investment flows as indirect at best—and theoretically misleading at worst—as an explanation of exchange rates. Unlike our previous analysis, which discusses exchange-rate determination in terms of the *flow* of funds in the foreign-exchange market over a period of time, the **monetary approach** sees exchange rates as determined by the free-market responses to changes in the *stock* (or total) demands and supplies of national currencies.

The monetary approach emphasizes the fact that the foreign-exchange market is a monetary phenomenon, where monies are traded for monies.

The money supply and money demand at home and abroad are thus used to explain a nation's exchange-rate trend. Because money supplies can be controlled by central banks, the monetary approach emphasizes a nation's demand for money and its determinants.

According to the monetary approach, the aggregate demand for money in a nation depends on the level of *real income*, *prices*, and *interest rates*. As the economy grows and real income rises, the public's demand for money increases in order to finance rising transactions. If prices rise, the public will demand more money to cover their economic transactions. The interest rate represents the opportunity cost of holding money. Lower interest rates induce the public to hold more money because the opportunity cost of holding cash balances is decreased. In other words, during eras of low interest rates, the public has less incentive to shift away from money balances, which pay no interest, to interest-bearing financial assets. Conversely, as these determinants change in the opposite direction, the demand for money decreases.

The following example illustrates how an *increase* in the domestic money *supply* causes the home currency's exchange rate to *depreciate*, according to the monetary approach. Given an initial equilibrium in the domestic money market and foreign-exchange market, suppose the Federal Reserve increases the U.S. money supply. The monetary expansion makes it easier for individuals and companies to borrow money. A rise in domestic spending and income thus occurs, leading to increased imports and a rise in the demand for foreign currency. The monetary expansion also results in lower interest rates, assuming the absence of inflationary expectations. Lower domestic interest rates motivate U.S. investment overseas, again increasing the demand for foreign currency.

With the demand for foreign currency now exceeding the supply, the dollar depreciates in value under market-determined exchange rates. The dollar depreciation induces higher prices for imports and a greater demand for exports, leading to higher domestic prices. Higher-priced transactions result in an increase in the demand for money. The adjustment process continues until the excess supply of money is eliminated. According to the monetary approach, the depreciation of the U.S. dollar and the appreciation of the German mark during the 1970s were attributable to excessive monetary growth in the United States and to a much smaller rate of monetary growth in Germany than in the rest of the world.

Similar reasoning can be used to determine how an *increase* in the *demand* for money leads to an *appreciation* in the nation's exchange rate. Given initial equilibrium in the domestic money market and foreign-exchange market, suppose Egypt's real income increases after new oil reserves are discovered. Because additional oil sales lead to a larger money value of goods exchanged in the economy, a larger amount of money will be needed to negotiate these transactions. The demand for Egypt's pound as a currency thus increases. But this demand cannot be fulfilled by the existing money supply (recall the initial assumption that money supply equals money demand in the domestic market). Efforts to get additional pounds, say, by exporting Egyptian goods, result in foreign nations' needing pounds to pay Egyptian exporters. The demand for the pound thus rises, which leads to an increase in its value.

The monetary approach emphasizes that under a system of market-determined exchange rates, movements in currency values play a primary role in restoring equilibrium between money demand and money supply. Table 13.6 summarizes the impact of changes in the money supply and money demand on domestic currency values according to the monetary approach. (The monetary approach to the balance of payments under a system of *fixed* exchange rates will be considered in the following chapter.)

The monetary approach to exchange-rate determination has made a significant contribution to economic theory by stressing monetary assets. However, empirical tests of the monetary approach have failed to provide an adequate explanation of exchange-rate movements during the floating rate period. Simply put, the

Table 13.6 Changes in Money Supply and Money Demand Under Market-Determined Exchange Rates: Impact on the Exchange Rate According to the Monetary Approach

Change*	Impact
Increase in money supply	Depreciation
Decrease in money supply	Appreciation
Increase in money demand	Appreciation
Decrease in money demand	Depreciation

*Starting from the point of equilibrium between money supply and money demand.

approach offers only a partial view of the forces influencing exchange rates—it assumes away the role of nonmonetary assets such as government bonds and stocks, and it takes no explicit account of supply and demand conditions in goods and services markets. Despite its limitations, the monetary approach offers very useful insights. It highlights the importance of monetary policy in influencing exchange rates, and correctly warns that excessive monetary expansion leads to currency depreciation.

FINANCIAL ASSETS AS DETERMINANTS OF EXCHANGE RATES

Traditional models of exchange-rate forecasting, such as the purchasing-power-parity theory, focus mainly on the prices of traded goods and services. That was fine when tight controls restricted the movement of capital around the world. But now that those controls have been largely eliminated, capital flows have become more important than trade in determining exchange rates. Today, only 1 to 2 percent of all foreign-exchange transactions are related to the financing of exports and imports.

Therefore, over short periods of time such as six or nine months, decisions to hold foreign or domestic financial assets play a much greater role in the determination of exchange rates than the demand for imports and exports does.

Despite America's huge and growing current account deficit at the turn of the millennium, the dollar was strong because foreign investors were happy to finance the deficit. According to this view, the relative prices of financial assets in different countries matter more than the prices of goods and services. Until recently, the financial assets involved were largely government bonds. International money tended to move in response to differences on bond yields. Recently, however, some economists reckon that equity (stock) markets are in the driving seat. Let us consider two explanations of how holdings of these financial assets influence exchange rates.

GOVERNMENT BONDS The **asset-markets** (or portfolio balance) **approach** takes a short-term view of exchange rates and broadens the focus from the demand and supply conditions for money to take account of the demand and supply conditions for other financial assets as well. Unlike the monetary approach, the assets-markets approach assumes that domestic and foreign bonds are not perfect substitutes. Firms and individuals balance their portfolios among domestic money, domestic bonds, and foreign-currency bonds, and they modify their portfolios as conditions change. It is the process of equilibrating the total demand for, and supply of, financial assets in each country that determines the exchange rate.

Each individual and firm chooses a portfolio to suit its needs, based on a variety of considerations: the holder's wealth and tastes, the level of domestic and foreign interest rates, expectations of future inflation, and so on. Any significant change in the underlying factors will cause the holder to adjust her portfolio and seek a new equilibrium. These actions to balance portfolios will influence exchange rates.

Accordingly, a nation with a sudden increase in money supply would immediately purchase both domestic and foreign bonds, resulting in a decline in both countries' interest rates and, to the extent of the shift to foreign bonds, a depreciation in the nation's home currency. Over time, the depreciation in the home currency would lead to growth in the nation's exports and a decline in its imports, and thus, to an improved trade balance and reversal of part of the original depreciation.

As yet, there is no unified theory of exchange-rate determination based on the asset-markets approach that has proved reliable in forecasting. These results reflect both conceptual problems and the lack of adequate data on the size and currency composition of private-sector portfolios. A more detailed discussion of the asset-markets approach can be found in Appendix I at the end of this chapter.

STOCKS AND MERGERS It's not every day that you can see the foreign-exchange market in action. However, February 3, 2000, was one such day. When the European Central Bank increased interest rates by $1/4$ of one percent at 11:30 A.M., the euro broke tradition and depreciated against the dollar. Later in the day, news emerged that Germany's Mannesmann was about to merge with Britain's Vodafone AirTouch PLC. Contrary to what would be expected, the euro appreciated against the dollar by almost 2.5 cents, to 99.5 cents.

The appreciation of the euro was a striking indication that foreign-exchange traders were not simply monitoring changes in interest rates in deciding whether to buy or sell a currency. Traditional rules suggest that a central bank's decision to raise or lower interest rates underlays a currency's exchange value and directly affects foreign investors' demand for debt instruments. Smart investors typically play these interest-rate differentials via securities.

Therefore, during the 1980s, record-high interest rates attracted billions in foreign capital to U.S. Treasury securities, and the dollar skyrocketed. To be sure, long-term trends in the U.S. economic health and investment history eventually asserted their influence on the dollar's exchange value. Over the short run, however, interest rates mattered most to foreign-exchange dealers.

But at the turn of the millennium, dealers seemed to respond to other factors in their daily game of buying and selling currencies. Equity flows from stock investments in foreign countries and cross-border merger deals became increasingly important.

Equity markets have become more important for two reasons. The first is that they have grown rapidly compared with government-bond markets. The second reason is that cross-border equity investment has increased even more dramatically. When they ventured abroad, investors used to purchase government bonds almost exclusively. Today, they are increasingly purchasing equities.

Therefore, foreign-exchange dealers now appear to analyze business acquisition news with much enthusiasm. The rationale: If foreign companies are ready to initiate major takeovers in a market, they will force up demand for the currency—a foreign-exchange market "purchase" signal if there ever was one. And traders can play the deal-driven surge in currencies by taking long positions in the currency they anticipate is about to depreciate.

According to analysts, the impact of deals and stock prices on currencies was apparent by 1999. The Bank of Japan kept interest rates close to zero for months, hoping to stimulate the economy. Those low rates would suggest a weak yen. However, the yen appreciated from May 1999 to February 2000, from 124 to the dollar to about 109 to the dollar. That's because traders ignored Japan's low interest rates and focused instead on stocks and deal news that showed a surge of foreign investment coming into Japan and a restructuring of the Japanese economy to make it more competitive.

The opposite effect occurred in the euro's case. When the euro was launched in 1999, investors and even the Continent's own executives were still down on the region's economy and far more attracted to deals and portfolio investments in the United States and Japan. So while the eurozone ran a $60 billion surplus in its current account, its companies spent some $120 billion on mergers and other direct investments abroad, forcing down the demand for euros and causing the euro to depreciate. Indeed, currency traders appeared to be getting a little help from merger and acquisition artists.[5]

EXCHANGE-RATE OVERSHOOTING

Changes in expected future values of market fundamentals contribute to exchange-rate volatility in the short run. For example, announcements by the Federal Reserve of changes in monetary-growth targets or by the President and Congress of changes in tax or spending programs cause changes in expectations of future exchange rates that can lead to immediate changes in equilibrium exchange rates. In this manner, frequent changes in policy contribute to volatile exchange rates in a system of market-determined exchange rates.

The volatility of exchange rates is further intensified by the phenomenon of **overshooting**. An exchange rate is said to overshoot when its short-run response (depreciation or appreciation) to a change in market fundamentals is *greater* than its long-run response. Changes in market fundamentals thus exert a disproportionately large *short-run* impact on exchange rates. Exchange-rate overshooting is an important phenomenon because it helps explain why exchange rates depreciate or appreciate so sharply from day to day.

Exchange-rate overshooting can be explained by the tendency of elasticities to be smaller in the short run than in the long run. Referring to Figure 13.6, the short-run supply schedule and demand schedule of the British pound are denoted by S_0 and D_0, respectively, and the equilibrium exchange rate is $2 per pound. If the demand for pounds increases to D_1, the dollar depreciates to $2.20 per pound in the short run. Because of the dollar depreciation, however, there occurs a decrease in the British price of U.S. exports, an increase in the quantity of U.S. exports demanded, and thus an

---

[5] "The Currency Game Has Brand-New Rules," *Business Week*, February 21, 2000, p. 136, and "Test-Driving a New Model," *The Economist*, March 18, 2000, pp. 75–76.

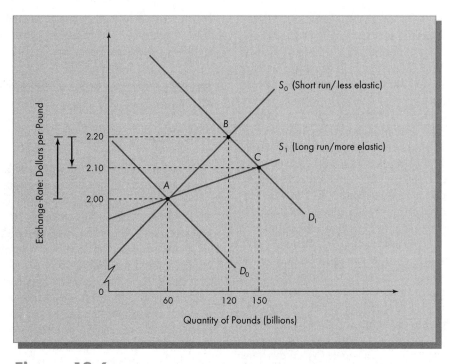

Figure 13.6 Short-Run/Long-Run Equilibrium Exchange Rates: Overshooting

Given the short-run supply of pounds (S_0), if the demand for pounds increases from D_0 to D_1, the dollar depreciates from $2 per pound to a short-run equilibrium of $2.20 per pound. In the long run, the supply of pounds is more elastic (S_1), and the equilibrium exchange rate is lower, at $2.10 per pound. Because of the difference in these elasticities, the short-run depreciation of the dollar overshoots its long-run depreciation.

increase in the quantity of pounds supplied. The longer the time period, the greater the rise in the quantity of exports is likely to be, and the greater the rise in the quantity of pounds supplied will be. The long-run supply schedule of pounds is thus more elastic than the short-run supply schedule, as shown by S_1 in the figure. Following the increase in the demand for pounds to D_1, the long-run equilibrium exchange rate is $2.10 per pound, as compared to the short-run equilibrium exchange rate of $2.20 per pound. Because of differences in these elasticities, the dollar's depreciation in the short run overshoots its long-run depreciation.

Overshooting can also be explained by the fact that exchange rates tend to be more flexible than

many other prices. Many prices are written into long-term contracts (for example, workers' wages) and do not respond immediately to changes in market fundamentals. Exchange rates, however, tend to be highly sensitive to current demand and supply conditions. Exchange rates often depreciate or appreciate more in the short run than in the long run so as to compensate for other prices that are slower to adjust to their long-run equilibrium levels. As the general price level slowly gravitates to its new equilibrium level, the amount of exchange-rate overshooting dissipates, and the exchange rate moves toward its long-run equilibrium level.

FORECASTING FOREIGN-EXCHANGE RATES

Previous sections of this chapter have examined various factors that determine exchange-rate movements. But even a clear understanding of how factors influence exchange rates does not guarantee that we can forecast how exchange rates will change. Not only do exchange-rate determinants often point in the opposite direction, but predicting how these determinants will change is difficult. Forecasting exchange rates is tricky.

A major issue, as far as business is concerned, however, is whether **forecasting exchange rates** is feasible and, if so, how to do it. Because the future is unclear, participants in international financial markets are unsure what the spot rate will be in the months ahead. Exchange-rate forecasts are required by exporters, importers, investors, bankers, and foreign-exchange dealers.

Multinational enterprises need short-term currency-price forecasts for a variety of reasons. For example, corporations often have for brief periods large amounts of cash, used to make bank deposits in various currencies. Choosing a currency in which to make deposits requires some idea of what the currency's exchange rate will be in the future. Long-term corporate planning, especially concerning decisions about foreign investment, necessitates an awareness of where exchange rates will move over an extended time period—hence the need for long-term forecasts. For multinational enterprises, short-term forecasting tends to be more widespread than long-term forecasting. Most corporations revise their currency forecasts at least every quarter.

Table 13.7 illustrates three exchange-rate forecasts made by the Morgan Guaranty Trust Company for December 31, 1999, based on the following factors:

- Real interest rates
- Current account balance as a percentage of GDP
- Deviation of the real foreign-exchange rate from its long-run average rate

Table 13.7 How Accurate Were the Exchange-Rate Forecasts of Morgan Guaranty Trust Company?

Currency	Actual Exchange Rate 12-31-99*	Exchange-Rate Forecast 2½ Months Prior to 12-31-99*	Exchange-Rate Forecast 6 Months Prior to 12-31-99*	Exchange-Rate Forecast 1½ Years Prior to 12-31-99*
Canadian dollar	1.47	1.44	1.40	1.35
Brazilian real	1.84	1.90	1.90	1.44
Mexican peso	9.40	10.00	10.00	10.25
Japanese yen	103.00	108.00	130.00	130.00
Australian dollar	0.64	0.67	0.70	0.70
Chinese yuan	8.28	8.28	8.28	9.25
Hong Kong dollar	7.77	7.77	7.76	7.75
New Zealand dollar	1.96	1.85	1.69	1.81
South African rand	6.15	6.10	6.40	6.25
Venezuelan bolivar	644.00	655.00	655.00	720.00
South Korean won	1,137.00	1,200.00	1,100.00	1,500.00

*Currency units per U.S. dollar.

Source: Morgan Guaranty Trust Company, *World Financial Markets*, various issues and *Federal Reserve Bulletin*, March 2000, p. A62.

• Change in official foreign-exchange reserves over the past year

Overall, according to Morgan Guaranty Trust, a nation with high real interest rates, a large current account deficit, a real exchange-rate level well above its long-run average, and falling reserves over the past year is a strong a priori candidate for a currency crisis, in the absence of corrective policy measures to narrow its current account deficit. As the table suggests, forecasting exchange rates is difficult, especially the longer the time horizon involved.

The need of multinational enterprises and investors for forecasted currency values has resulted in the emergence of *consulting firms*, including Predex, Goldman Sachs, and Wharton Econometric Forecasting Associates. In addition, large banks such as Chase Manhattan Bank, Chemical Bank, and Citibank have provided free currency forecasts to corporate clients. Customers of consulting firms often pay fees ranging up to $25,000 per year or more for expert opinions. Consulting firms provide forecast services ranging from video screens to "listening-post" interviews with forecast service employees who provide their predictions of exchange-rate movements and respond to specific questions from the client. It has become customary for corporate managers to use home or hotel telephones to connect portable terminals to advisory services that make available foreign-exchange forecasts.

Most exchange-rate forecasting methods use accepted economic (fundamental) relationships to formulate a model that is then refined through statistical analysis of past data. The forecasts generated by the models are usually tempered by the additional insights or intuition of the forecaster before being offered to the final user.

In the current system of market-determined exchange rates, currency values fluctuate almost instantaneously in response to new information regarding changes in interest rates, inflation rates, money supplies, trade balances, and the like. To successfully forecast exchange-rate movements, it is necessary to estimate the future values of these economic variables and determine the relationship between them and future exchange rates. Even the most sophisticated analysis, however, can be rendered worthless by unexpected changes in government policy, market psychology, and so forth. Indeed, people who deal in the currency markets on a daily basis have come to feel that market psychology is a dominant influence on future exchange rates. Despite these problems, exchange-rate forecasters are in current demand. Their forecasting approaches are classified as judgmental, technical, or fundamental (econometric). Table 13.8 provides examples of exchange-rate forecasting organizations and their methodologies.

Table 13.8 Exchange-Rate Forecasters

Forecasting Organization	Methodology	Horizon
Chase Econometrics	Econometric	8 quarters
Chase Manhattan Bank	Judgmental	Under 12 months
Data Resources	Econometric	6 quarters
Exchange Rate Outlook	Judgmental	12 months ahead
Goldman Sachs	Technical	Under 12 months
	Econometric	Over 12 months
Phillips & Drew	Judgmental, econometric	6, 12 months ahead
Predex Forecast	Econometric	7 quarters
Predex Short-Term forecast	Technical	1–3 months ahead
Wharton Econometric Forecasting Associates	Econometric	24 months ahead

Source: *Euromoney*, various issues.

JUDGMENTAL FORECASTS Judgmental forecasts are sometimes known as subjective or commonsense models. They require the gathering of a wide array of political and economic data and the interpretation of these data in terms of the timing, direction, and magnitude of exchange-rate changes. Judgmental forecasters formulate projections based on a thorough examination of individual nations. They consider economic indicators, such as inflation rates and trade data; political factors, such as a future national election; technical factors, such as potential intervention by a central bank in the foreign-exchange market; and psychological factors that relate to one's "feel for the market."

TECHNICAL FORECASTS Technical analysis involves the use of historical exchange-rate data to estimate future values. The approach is technical in that it extrapolates from past exchange-rate trends and ignores economic and political determinants of exchange-rate movements. Technical analysts look for specific exchange-rate patterns. Once the beginning of a particular pattern has been determined, it automatically implies what the short-run behavior of the exchange rate will be.

Technical analysis encompasses a variety of charting techniques involving a currency's price, cycles, or volatility. A common starting point for technical analysis is a chart that plots a trading period's opening, high, low, and closing prices. These charts most often plot one trading day's range of prices, but also are created on a weekly, monthly, and yearly basis. Traders watch for new highs and lows, broken trendlines, and patterns that are thought to predict price targets and movement.

To illustrate technical analysis, assume you have formed an opinion about the yen's exchange value against the dollar based on your analysis of economic fundamentals. Now you want to look at what the markets can tell you; you're looking for price trends, and you can use charts to do it. As shown in Figure 13.7, you might want to look at the relative highs and lows of the yen for the past several months; the trendlines in the figure connect the higher highs and the lower lows for the yen. If the yen's exchange rate moves substantially above or below the trendlines, it might signal that a trend is changing. Changes in trends help you decide when to purchase or sell yen in the foreign-exchange market.

Technicians do not necessarily deny the value of fundamental information such as national inflation-rate differentials. Many technical analysts believe that exchange rates eventually close in on the fundamental values. Technicians believe, nevertheless, that shifts in market fundamentals can be discerned before the impact of those shifts is fully reflected in exchange rates. As the market adjusts to a new equilibrium, astute traders can exploit these exchange-rate trends. Technicians also believe that market fundamentals can be perturbed by irrational factors. More or less random fluctuations in exchange rates will accompany any underlying trend. If these fluctuations dissipate slowly, they can be exploited for abnormal profits.

Technical analysts use computer-based statistical programs to find recurring exchange-rate patterns and then issue sell or buy instructions if exchange rates deviate from their past pattern. For example, time-series models are used to analyze moving averages of exchange rates. They permit a forecaster to formulate some rule, such as "The franc tends to rise in value after a fall in the franc's average over four consecutive periods." Generally, consultants who adopt such an approach will not disclose their particular rules for forecasting. If they did, their potential customers might use the rules themselves instead of purchasing the consultants' forecasts.

Because technical analysis follows the market closely, it is used to forecast exchange-rate movements in the *very near future*. Determining an exchange-rate pattern is useful only as long as the market continues to consistently follow that pattern. No pattern, however, can be relied on to continue more than a few days, perhaps weeks. A client must therefore respond quickly to a technical recommendation to buy or sell a currency. And clients require immediate communication of technical recommendations, so as to make timely financial decisions.

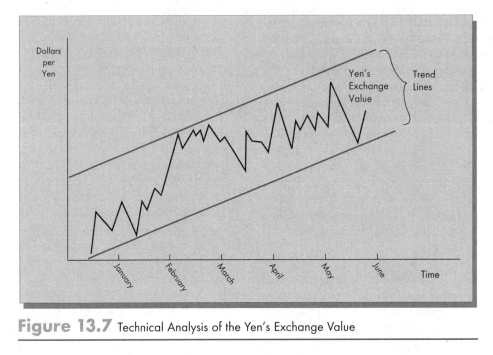

Figure 13.7 Technical Analysis of the Yen's Exchange Value

When forecasting exchange rates, technical analysts watch for new highs and lows, broken trendlines, and patterns that are thought to predict price targets and movement.

Although fundamental-based models have not been successful in forecasting exchange-rate movements over short- and medium-run periods, many technical-based models have been useful in explaining exchange-rate movements over short-run periods. It is not surprising that most foreign-exchange dealers use some technical model input to help them formulate their forecast for exchange rates, especially for intraday and one-week horizons. However, complete reliance on technical analysis for currency forecasting leaves one vulnerable to whipsaw losses caused by false technical signals when markets are not moving in discernible trends. Forecasters may also feel reluctant to make a prediction on the basis of technical analysis if there are no fundamental data supporting the prediction. Moreover, a major shortcoming of technical analysis is that although it may be useful for forecasting short-term exchange rates, it is of negligible value in forecasting medium- and long-run trends.

FUNDAMENTAL ANALYSIS Fundamental analysis is the opposite of technical analysis. It involves consideration of macroeconomic variables and policies that are likely to affect a currency's value. Fundamental analysis uses computer-based econometric models, which are statistical estimations of economic theories. To generate forecasts, econometricians develop models for individual nations that attempt to incorporate the fundamental variables that underlie exchange-rate movements: trade and investment flows, industrial activity, inflation rates, income levels, and the like (see Appendix II at the end of this chapter).

Econometricians assume that changes in key economic variables will induce changes in future exchange rates in approximately the same patterns as in the past. The formulation of an econometric model requires specifying *independent variables* (for example, previous quarterly percentage changes in interest rates or inflation rates) that influence the *dependent variable* (for example, quarterly percentage change in a currency's value). The econometrician must also identify the nature of the relationship (for example, linear, exponential) that best explains the dependent variable. The econometric model determines the direction and degree to which a currency's exchange rate is affected by each independent variable.

Econometric models used to forecast exchange rates, however, face limitations. They often rely on predictions of key independent variables, such as inflation rates or interest rates, and obtaining reliable information can be difficult. Moreover, there are always factors affecting exchange rates that cannot easily be quantified (such as intervention by a country's central bank in currency markets). Also, the precise timing of a factor's effect on a currency's exchange rate may be unclear. For example, inflation-rate changes may not have their full impact on a currency's value until three or six months in the future. Because econometric models may not always generate accurate forecasts, econometricians must exercise judgment when the results of their equations appear to be questionable. By the same token, users of econometric forecasts must allow for a margin of error and must recognize the potential for error when applying forecasts to financial decision making.

Econometric models are best suited for forecasting *long-term* exchange-rate trends. This is because exchange rates in the short run are influenced by many factors that change on a day-to-day basis (for example, the release of information concerning the nation's inflation rate), resulting in considerable short-term volatility.

Econometric models are generally used to forecast an exchange rate over a period of time rather than a specific exchange rate at a particular time. If one asks an econometric forecaster for a currency forecast for, say, March 1 of next year, she will likely respond by giving a range. The critic might conclude that she is improving her odds of getting the forecast right. Although there may be some truth in this, the critic should also recognize that because she is forecasting an average, over time, there is no way she can accurately forecast an exchange rate for a particular moment. Despite a wide range, the actual

exchange rate may lie outside it, even if the average forecast is still accurate.

FOREIGN-EXCHANGE FORECASTING IN PRACTICE

Most of the approaches to exchange-rate determination tell only part of the story—like the several blindfolded men touching different parts of the elephant's body—and other, more comprehensive explanations cannot, in practice, be used for precise forecasting. We do no yet have a way of bringing together all of the factors that help determine the exchange rate in a single comprehensive approach that will provide reliable short- to medium-term predictions.

The exchange rate is a pervasive and complex mechanism, influencing and being influenced by many different forces, with the effects and the relative importance of the different influences continuously changing as conditions change. To the extent that the trade flows are a force in the market, competitiveness is obviously important to the exchange rate, and the many factors affecting competitiveness must be considered. To the extent that the money market is a factor, the focus should be on the short-term interest rates, and on monetary policy and other factors influencing those short-term interest rates. To the extent that portfolio capital flows matter, the focus should be broadened to include bond market conditions and long-term interest rates. Particularly at times of great international tension, all other factors affecting the dollar exchange rate may be overwhelmed by considerations of "safe haven." Indeed, countless forces influence the exchange rate, and they are subject to continuous and unpredictable changes over time, by a market that is broad and heterogenous in terms of the participants, their interests, and their time frames.

With conditions always changing, the impact of particular events and the response to particular policy actions can vary greatly with the circumstances at the time. Higher interest rates might strengthen a currency or weaken it, by a small amount or by a lot—much depends on why the interest rates went up, whether a move was anticipated, what subsequent moves are expected, and the implications for other financial markets, decisions, or government policy moves. Similarly, the results of exchange-rate changes are not always predictable: Importers might expect to pay more if their domestic currency depreciates, but not if foreign producers are "pricing to market" in order to establish a beachhead or maintain a market share, or if the importers or exporters had anticipated the rate move and had acted in advance to protect themselves from it.

Nonetheless, those participating in the market must make their forecasts, implicitly and explicitly, day after day, all of the time. Every piece of information that becomes available can be the basis for an adjustment of each participant's viewpoint or expectations—in other words, a forecast, informal or otherwise. When the screen flashes with an unexpected announcement that, say, Germany has reduced interest rates by a quarter of one percent, that is not just news: It is the basis for countless assessments of the significance of that event and countless forecasts of its impact in number of basis points.

As we have learned, those who forecast foreign-exchange rates often are divided into those who use technical analysis and those who rely on analysis of fundamentals such as productivity, inflation, balance-of-payments position, and the like. Nearly all traders acknowledge their use of technical analysis and charts. According to surveys, a majority say they employ technical analysis to a greater extent than fundamental analysis, and that they regard it as more useful than fundamental analysis—a contrast to 20 years ago when most said they relied more heavily on fundamental analysis. Perhaps traders use technical analysis in part because, at least superficially, it seems simpler, or because the data are more current and timely. Perhaps they use it because traders often have a very short-term time frame and are interested in very short-term moves. They might agree that fundamentals determine the course of prices in the long run, but they may not regard that as relevant to their immediate task, particularly since many fundamental data become available only with long lags and are often subject to major revisions. Perhaps traders think technical analysis will be effective in part because they know many other market participants are relying on it.

Still, spotting trends is of real importance to traders—"a trend is a friend" is a comment often-heard, and technical analysis can add some discipline and sophistication to the process of discovering and following a trend. Technical analysis may add more objectivity to making the difficult decision on when to give up on a position—enabling one to see that a trend has changed or run its course, and it is now time for reconsideration.

Most market participants probably use a combination of fundamental, technical, and judgmental analysis, with the emphasis on each shifting as conditions change. They form a general view about whether a particular currency is overvalued or undervalued in a structural or longer-term sense, and within that longer-term framework, assess all current economic forecasts, news events, political developments, statistical releases, rumors, and changes in sentiment, while also carefully studying the charts and technical analysis.[6]

FORECAST PERFORMANCE OF ADVISORY SERVICES To be successful, a forecasting model should provide better information about future exchange rates than is available to the market in general. Successful forecasters are those who can consistently profit from their forecasting activities by predicting *more accurately* than the rest of the market.

In evaluating the performance of forecasters, it is important to determine what a naive forecast would be in the absence of any specific model or information. Assuming efficient foreign-exchange markets in which prices reflect all available information, what exchange-rate prediction is implicit in market quotations? As discussed in Chapter 12, the *forward-exchange rate* (the spot rate plus the interest-rate differential) is the rational approximation of the market's expectation of the spot rate that will exist at the end of the forward period. This means that the forward *premium* or *discount* on a currency serves as a rough benchmark of the expected rate of appreciation or depreciation of a currency. The forward rate is widely considered to

---

[6] This section is drawn from Sam Cross, *The Foreign-Exchange Market in the United States*, Federal Reserve Bank of New York, 1998, pp. 113–115.

be useful as a forecasting device for a period of one to three months. A successful forecaster should thus be able to predict spot rates better than what is implied by the forward rate.

When evaluating a consulting firm, one might compare its currency forecasts to the forward rates, which are quoted in newspapers and magazines. Although forward rates provide simple and easy-to-use currency forecasts, several studies have shown that forward rates are not reliable predictors of future spot rates. It appears that unanticipated news and the market's expectations of future policies can have a frequent and noticeable impact on spot rates, making them inherently volatile and unpredictable in the short run. Caution must be exercised when attempting to interpret forward-exchange rates.

Consulting firms are not always successful in forecasting currency values. One study compared the forward rate to the forecasts of several consulting firms concerning nine different currencies. Of all the consulting firms and all the currencies forecasted, only 5 percent of the forecasts for 1 month ahead were more accurate than the forward rate; and only 14 percent of forecasts for 3 months ahead were more accurate.[7] These results can be discouraging to clients who pay thousands of dollars for advisory services, when the forward rate is readily available in the newspaper, virtually cost-free.

---

[7] R. Levich, "Currency Forecasters Lose Their Way," *Euromoney*, August 1983, pp. 140–147.

S U M M A R Y

1. In a free market, exchange rates are determined by market fundamentals and market expectations. The former include real income, real interest rates, consumer preferences for domestic or foreign products, productivity, investment profitability, product availability, monetary policy and fiscal policy, and government trade policy. Economists generally agree that the major determinants of exchange-rate fluctuations are different in the long run than in the short run.

2. With market-determined exchange rates, a nation that experiences faster (slower) economic growth than the rest of the world tends to find its currency's exchange value depreciating (appreciating).

3. Short-term interest-rate differentials between any two nations are an important determinant of international investment flows and short-term exchange rates. More important, international investors are concerned about relative changes in the real interest rate, which is the nominal rate adjusted for inflation. With market-determined exchange rates, a nation that has relatively high (low) real interest rates finds its currency's exchange value appreciating (depreciating).

4. According to the purchasing-power-parity theory, changes in relative national price levels determine changes in exchange rates over the long run. A currency maintains its purchasing power parity if it depreciates (appreciates) by an amount equal to the excess of domestic (foreign) inflation over foreign (domestic) inflation.

5. In the short run, market expectations influence exchange-rate movements. Future expectations of rapid domestic economic growth, falling domestic interest rates, and high domestic inflation rates tend to cause the domestic currency to depreciate.

6. The monetary approach suggests that an increase in the domestic money supply causes the home currency's exchange rate to depreciate, and vice versa. It also maintains that an increase in the domestic demand for money leads to an appreciation in the home country's exchange rate. The monetary approach appears to be most valid as a predictor of exchange-rate movements over the long run.

7. The asset-markets approach contends that stock adjustments among financial assets are a key determinant of short-run movements in exchange rates. The demand for domestic

assets is primarily determined by the interest rate payable in domestic currency on domestic securities, the interest rate payable in foreign currency on foreign securities, and expected changes in the domestic currency's exchange rate.

8. Exchange-rate volatility is intensified by the phenomenon of overshooting. An exchange rate is said to overshoot when its short-run response to a change in market fundamentals is greater than its long-run response.

9. Currency forecasters use several methods to predict future exchange-rate movements: (a) judgmental forecasts, (b) technical analysis, and (c) fundamental analysis.

S T U D Y   Q U E S T I O N S

1. In a free market, what factors underlie currency exchange values? Which factors best apply to long-run exchange rates and to short-run exchange rates?

2. Why are international investors especially concerned about the real interest rate as opposed to the nominal rate?

3. What predictions does the purchasing-power-parity theory make concerning the impact of domestic inflation on the home country's exchange rate? What are some limitations of the purchasing-power-parity theory?

4. If a currency becomes overvalued in the foreign-exchange market, what will be the likely impact on the home country's trade balance? What if the home currency becomes undervalued?

5. What is meant by the monetary approach to exchange-rate determination? What are its major predictions concerning exchange-rate movements?

6. How does the asset-markets approach attempt to improve on the monetary approach in the determination of exchange rates?

7. Explain how the following factors affect the dollar's exchange rate under a system of market-determined exchange rates: (a) a rise in the U.S. price level, with the foreign price level held constant; (b) tariffs and quotas placed on U.S. imports; (c) increased demand for U.S. exports and decreased U.S. demand for imports; (d) rising productivity in the United States relative to other countries; (e) rising real interest rates overseas, relative to U.S. rates; (f) an increase in U.S. money growth; (g) an increase in U.S. money demand.

8. What is meant by exchange-rate overshooting? Why does it occur?

9. What methods do currency forecasters use to predict future changes in exchange rates?

10. Assuming market-determined exchange rates, use supply and demand schedules for pounds to analyze the effect on the exchange rate (dollars per pound) between the U.S. dollar and the British pound under each of the following circumstances:

   a. Voter polls suggest that Britain's conservative government will be replaced by radicals who pledge to nationalize all foreign-owned assets.

   b. Both the British economy and U.S. economy slide into recession, but the British recession is less severe than the U.S. recession.

   c. The Federal Reserve adopts a tight monetary policy that dramatically increases U.S. interest rates.

   d. Britain's oil production in the North Sea decreases, and exports to the United States fall.

   e. The United States unilaterally reduces tariffs on British products.

   f. Britain encounters severe inflation, while price stability exists in the United States.

   g. Fears of terrorism reduce U.S. tourism in Britain.

   h. The British government invites U.S. firms to invest in British oil fields.

   i. The rate of productivity growth in Britain decreases sharply.

j. An economic boom occurs in Britain, which induces the British to purchase more U.S.-made autos, trucks, and computers.

k. Ten-percent inflation occurs in both Britain and the United States.

11. Explain why you agree or disagree with each of the following statements:

a. "A nation's currency will depreciate if its inflation rate is less than that of its trading partners."

b. "A nation whose interest rate falls more rapidly than that of other nations can expect the exchange value of its currency to depreciate."

c. "A nation whose economy grows more slowly than its major trading partners can expect the exchange value of its currency to appreciate."

d. "A nation's currency will depreciate if its interest rate falls relative to that of its trading partners and its income level rises relative to that of its trading partners."

12. The appreciation in the dollar's exchange value from 1980 to 1985 made U.S. products (less/ more) expensive and foreign products (less/more) expensive, (decreased, increased) U.S. imports, and (decreased, increased) U.S. exports.

13. Suppose the dollar/franc exchange rate equals $0.50 per franc. According to the purchasing-power-parity theory, what will happen to the dollar's exchange value under each of the following circumstances?

a. The U.S. price level increases by 10 percent and the price level in Switzerland stays constant.

b. The U.S. price level increases by 10 percent and the price level in Switzerland increases by 20 percent.

c. The U.S. price level decreases by 10 percent and the price level in Switzerland increases by 5 percent.

d. The U.S. price level decreases by 10 percent and the price level in Switzerland decreases by 15 percent.

14. Suppose that the nominal interest rate on 3-month Treasury bills is 8 percent in the United States and 6 percent in the United Kingdom, and the rate of inflation is 10 percent in the United States and 4 percent in the United Kingdom.

a. What is the real interest rate in each nation?

b. In which direction would international investment flow in response to these real interest rates?

c. What impact would these investment flows have on the dollar's exchange value?

NETLINK

13.1 The Web page of J.P. Morgan, a global financial-services firm, contains its Event Risk Indicator (ERI), which reports an index of likelihood of a currency crash from 0 to 100. Set your browser to URL:

http://www.jpmorgan.com/

13.2 Historical information on exchange rates can be found at the home page of the Federal Reserve Bank of St. Louis. Go to Economic Research, FRED, and then Exchange Rate and

Balance of Payments Data. Set your browser to URL:

http: //www.stls.frb.org/

13.3 The Pacific Rate Exchange Service provides information on current and past daily exchange rates, as well as exchange-rate forecasts for the Canadian dollar relative to five other major currencies. Set your browser to URL:

http://pacific.commerce.ubc.ca/xr/

To access NetLink Exercises and the Virtual Scavenger Hunt, visit the Carbaugh Web site at http://carbaugh.swcollege.com.

A P P E N D I X   I

THE ASSET-MARKETS APPROACH TO EXCHANGE-RATE DETERMINATION

As discussed earlier in this chapter, the asset-markets approach considers domestic currency as only one among a spectrum of financial assets that residents of a nation may desire to hold. That is, an individual may choose to hold financial wealth in some combination of domestic currency, domestic securities, foreign securities denominated in a foreign currency, or even foreign currency.

The asset-markets approach recognizes that short-term capital movements among nations can have both a continuing-flow component and a stock-adjustment component. The *continuing-flow* component entails investors' shifting a growing supply of funds among assets in different nations as their wealth expands. The *stock-adjustment* component involves the reallocation of an existing stock of wealth among assets in various nations. It is the stock-adjustment component of international capital movements that the asset-markets approach emphasizes.

According to the asset-markets approach, stock adjustments among financial assets are a key determinant of *short-run* movements in exchange rates. These stock adjustments are guided by the profit motive—the expected return on one financial asset compared with the expected return on another asset. The asset-markets approach maintains that it is mainly through the medium of market expectations of future returns that exchange rates are affected in the short run; other variables, such as the current account balance or the growth rate in the money supply, affect the exchange rate primarily by influencing market expectations.

Concerning the demand for financial assets, an individual's desire to hold domestic or foreign securities is based on the income they are expected to generate. In addition, foreign securities may be desired because they enable domestic investors to spread their risks. Such investments, however, carry the risk of possible default and variations in their market values over time. For foreign securities denominated in a foreign currency, there is the additional risk that the foreign currency may depreciate. Investors also desire to maintain a portion of their financial wealth in currency in order to make business payments. Although holding domestic currency is riskless, it provides no interest income. The opportunity cost of holding domestic currency is the interest income sacrificed by not holding securities.

Suppose the United States is the home country and U.S. assets are denominated in dollars; the United Kingdom represents the foreign country. The asset-markets approach contends that the most important factor influencing the *demand* for dollar-denominated assets is the anticipated return on these assets relative to the anticipated return on British assets. If the anticipated return on dollar-denominated assets is high compared with that of British assets, there is a larger demand for dollar-denominated assets, and vice versa. This expected return depends on (1) the interest rate payable in dollars on U.S. securities, (2) the interest rate payable in pounds on British securities, and (3) the expected changes in the dollar's exchange rate against the pound.

Consider a U.S. or British resident's decision to hold dollar-denominated assets versus pound-denominated assets. If the annual interest rate on dollar-denominated assets is 10 percent and the dollar is anticipated to *appreciate* by 5 percent per year against the pound, the expected return on the dollar-denominated assets is 15 percent in terms of the pound. Conversely, if the annual interest rate on the dollar-denominated assets is 10 percent and the dollar is anticipated to *depreciate* by 5 percent per year against the pound, the anticipated return on dollar-denominated assets would be only 5 percent (the 10 percent interest less the 5 percent anticipated depreciation). In general, we can conclude that a U.S. or British resident would demand more dollar-denominated assets if the interest rate on these assets increases relative to the interest rate on British-denominated assets, assuming exchange-rate expectations are constant. More dollar-denominated assets would also be demanded if the expected rate of appreciation in the dollar increases, assuming the interest rate is constant.

Figure 13.8 illustrates the foreign-exchange market according to the asset-markets approach. In panel (a), demand schedule D_0 denotes the quantity of dollar-denominated financial assets demanded at various current pound/dollar exchange rates by all potential holders, both domestic and foreign. The demand for dollar-denominated financial assets (dollars) is *inversely* related to the value of the U.S. dollar; that is, as the current exchange rate (pounds/dollar) rises, fewer exchange-market participants are willing to trade an increasing quantity of pounds for dollars, assuming that no change in the exchange rate is

anticipated.[8] The supply schedule of dollar-denominated assets in the international exchange market is ultimately fixed by the total quantity of assets in the U.S. economy (S_0). Exchange-market equilibrium exists at point *A*, where the quantity of dollar-denominated assets equals the quantity supplied.

We know that the demand for dollar-denominated assets is directly related to the anticipated return on dollar assets relative to the anticipated return on British assets. This return depends on the interest rate payable in dollars on U.S. securities, the interest rate payable in pounds on British securities, and the expected change in the dollar's exchange rate against the pound. As we have seen, *movements* along the demand schedule for dollar-denominated assets are caused by changes in the current pound/dollar exchange rate. *Shifts* in the demand schedule are caused by changes in interest rates and in future exchange-rate expectations. Let's see how the asset-markets approach explains short-run fluctuations in exchange rates.

Refer now to panel (b) which illustrates shifts in the demand schedule of dollar-denominated assets. Assume that exchange-market equilibrium exists at point *A*, where $S_0 = D_0$, and the equilibrium

---

[8] Stated more technically, demand schedule D_0 is downward sloping because a lower current exchange rate suggests a higher expected appreciation of the dollar, a higher expected return on dollar assets compared with foreign assets, and thus a higher quantity of dollar assets demanded. See F. S. Mishkin, *The Economics of Money, Banking, and Financial Markets* (Boston: Little, Brown, 1986), pp. 636–638.

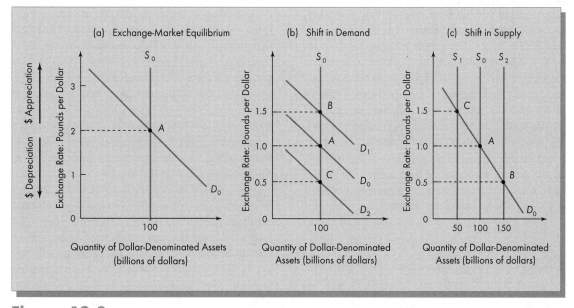

Figure 13.8 Exchange Market Equilibrium According to the Asset-Markets Approach

exchange rate is 1 pound per dollar. Suppose now that U.S. real interest rates rise, all else being equal. Residents will want to take advantage of the higher expected return on U.S. financial assets. This leads to a shift in the demand schedule for dollar assets to D_1 and an appreciation in the dollar's value to 1.5 pounds per dollar at equilibrium point B. Conversely, if U.S. real interest rates fall, the demand for dollar assets decreases, and the dollar depreciates in value.

Now suppose that British real interest rates rise. In this case, the expected return on British assets increases relative to dollar-denominated assets. As a result, the quantity of dollar assets demanded falls, and the dollar depreciates against the pound. Conversely, a fall in British real interest rates leads to an increased demand for dollar-denominated assets and a rise in the dollar's value. This analysis applies to *expected*, as well as actual, interest-rate changes. The reader is left to determine how factors that influence the expected future pound/dollar exchange rate (such as anticipating higher U.S. tariffs) would affect the demand for dollar assets and the pound/dollar exchange rate.

Refer now to panel (c), which illustrates shifts in the supply schedule of dollar-denominated assets. Suppose the U.S. Federal Reserve purchases $5 billion of its currency in the foreign-exchange market, using its international currency reserves to do so. This action causes the overall supply of dollar assets to fall. The supply schedule of dollar assets thus shifts from S_0 to S_1, and the dollar appreciates against the pound. Conversely, if the Federal Reserve sells $5 billion of its currency in the foreign-exchange market, increasing its international reserves, this means a rise in the overall supply of dollar assets. The supply schedule shifts to S_2, which results in a depreciation in the dollar's value. Obviously, central banks can have a major impact on exchange rates by intervening in the foreign-exchange market.[9]

The asset-markets approach can be used to explain volatile exchange rates, such as occurred in the 1980s. Although variables such as the current account balance or the rate of monetary growth affect exchange rates over the long run, changes in short-run exchange rates are more likely to reflect adjustments in financial assets and expectations. Whenever changes occur in expectations of variables (such as monetary policy), there tends to be an immediate impact on exchange rates. The asset-markets model thus views exchange-rate determination as similar to the stock market, in which future expectations are important and prices are volatile.

As we have seen, the asset-markets approach emphasizes the influence on exchange rates of expected returns on investments. Such was the case with the appreciation of the U.S. dollar from 1980 to February 1985, as discussed earlier in this chapter. According to the asset-markets approach, most of the dollar appreciation probably stemmed from portfolio shifts into U.S. dollar assets because of the increased expected returns relative to assets denominated in other currencies. In 1980, real (inflation-adjusted) interest rates paid on long-term U.S. government securities were approximately 2 percentage points below those paid on a weighted average of similar securities among U.S. trading partners. By 1985, the real interest rate on U.S. securities was some 3 percentage points above that on securities of U.S. trading partners. According to the asset-markets approach, this 5 percentage points of swing in real interest rates in favor of the United States motivated investors to channel funds into dollar-denominated assets, thus adding to the demand for the dollar and reinforcing its appreciation in the foreign-exchange market.

In general, tests of the asset-markets approach have produced mixed or inconclusive results concerning its empirical validity. What's more, such tests are hampered because data on currencies in private holdings of foreign assets are usually not available. It is clear, however, that asset managers working for commercial banks, investment banks, pension funds, and insurance companies

[9] In practice, virtually all exchange-market intervention is carried out by central banks of other nations and not by the Federal Reserve; hence, this example is somewhat unrealistic. However, the Federal Reserve occasionally conducts foreign-exchange market operations, and we continue to use the United States as the home country to maintain consistency with the rest of this section.

do use portfolio theory in determining where and how to invest their funds. A reasonable guess is that short-term exchange-rate movements that occur in practice between major currencies tend to approximate those implied by portfolio theory. But because market expectations are not readily known, it is difficult to test the asset-markets approach.

A P P E N D I X   1 1

FUNDAMENTAL FORECASTING— REGRESSION ANALYSIS

Recall that fundamental forecasting involves estimating an exchange rate's response to changes in economic factors. By determining how these factors have influenced exchange-rate fluctuations in the past, one can get insight about the future course of the exchange rate. Regression analysis is often used to make such an assessment. Forecasting organizations, such as Chase Econometrics, construct regression models based on 20 or more economic determinants of exchange rates.

Suppose we wish to forecast the percentage change in the Swiss franc's exchange value against the dollar in the next quarter. For simplicity, assume that our forecast for the franc is dependent on only two factors that influence the franc's exchange value: (1) the inflation-rate differential between the United States and Switzerland; and (2) the income-growth differential, measured as a percentage change, between the United States and Switzerland. Assume also that these factors have a lagged effect on the franc's exchange rate. A regression model can be constructed as follows:

$$Y_t = b_0 + b_1 X1_{t-n} + b_2 X2_{t-n} + u_t$$

wherein the dependent variable, the quarterly percentage change in the franc's exchange value (Y), is related to quarterly percentage changes in the two independent variables, the U.S./Swiss inflation differential (X1) and the U.S./Swiss income-growth differential (X2). In the model, b_0 is a constant, b_1 indicates the sensitivity of the franc's exchange value to changes in the inflation differential between the United States and Switzerland, b_2 indicates the sensitivity of the franc's exchange value to changes in the income-growth differential between the United States and Switzerland, t stands for the time period, n indicates the number of quarters lagged, and u_t is an error term with all assumed statistical properties.

Once the regression model is constructed, a set of historical data must be compiled for quarterly changes in the franc's exchange rate, the U.S./Swiss inflation differential, and the U.S./Swiss income-growth differential. A large time-series database is desirable, generally consisting of thirty or more quarters of information. Using these data, suppose our model estimates the following regression coefficients:

$$b_1 = 0.6$$
$$b_2 = 0.4$$

The regression coefficient $b_1 = 0.6$ implies that for every one-unit percentage change in the U.S.\Swiss inflation differential, the predicted percentage change in the franc's exchange value is 0.6 percent, the income-growth differential remaining constant. Underlying this positive relationship is the tendency for relatively high inflation in the United States to cause a rise (appreciation) in the franc's value against the dollar, and vice versa. The regression coefficient $b_2 = 0.4$ suggests that for each one-unit percentage change in the U.S./Swiss income-growth differential, the predicted percentage change in the franc's exchange value is 0.4 percent, the inflation-rate differential remaining constant. The positive relationship suggests that relatively high income growth in the United States leads to an appreciation in the franc against the dollar, and vice versa. Once the regression coefficients have been estimated, and any potential statistical problems have been corrected, the coefficients can be tested to determine if they are statistically significant. If so, there exists a predictable relationship between a given exchange-rate determinant and the franc's exchange rate.

Our regression model can now be used for exchange-rate forecasting. Suppose that in the most recent year the U.S. inflation rate exceeded the Swiss inflation rate by 3 percentage points and that the U.S. income-growth rate exceeded the Swiss income-growth rate by 1 percentage point. Combining these data with the estimated regression coefficients, the forecast for the franc's exchange value is:

$$
\begin{aligned}
Y_t &= b_0 + b_1 X1_{t-n} + b_2 X2_{t-n} + u_t \\
&= .01 + .6(3\%) + .4(1\%) \\
&= 1\% + 1.8\% + .4\% \\
&= 3.2\%
\end{aligned}
$$

Our forecast is that the franc will appreciate by about 3.2 percent against the dollar in the next quarter.

In practice, using regression analysis to forecast exchange rates is more difficult than our simplified model suggests. Recall that our model was based on the impact of inflation differentials and income-growth differentials on trade flows and their effects on foreign-exchange market trading. In reality, much foreign-exchange market trading is related to investment flows and speculation, which requires that other variables be included in our model, such as relative interest rates and future expectations. Finally, other exchange-rate determinants, such as labor strikes, are difficult to measure and cannot be included in our model. As a result of these limitations, even the most sophisticated regression models cannot produce consistently accurate exchange-rate forecasts. Forecasters typically modify the results of regression models with their own commonsense judgments.

chapter 14

Balance-of-Payments Adjustments Under Fixed Exchange Rates

Chapter 11 examined the meaning of a balance-of-payments deficit and surplus. Recall that, owing to double-entry bookkeeping, total inpayments (credits) always equal total outpayments (debits) when all balance-of-payments accounts are considered. A deficit refers to an excess of outpayments over inpayments for selected accounts grouped along functional lines. For example, a current account deficit suggests an excess of imports over exports of goods, services, and unilateral transfers. A current account surplus implies the opposite.

A nation finances or covers a current account deficit out of its international reserves or by attracting investment (such as purchases of factories or securities) from its trading partners. The capacity of a *deficit nation* to cover the excess of outpayments over inpayments is limited by its stocks of international reserves and the willingness of its trading partners to invest in the deficit nation. For a surplus nation, once it believes that its stocks of international reserves or overseas investments are adequate—although history shows that this belief may be a long time in coming—it will be reluctant to run prolonged surpluses. In general, the incentive for reducing a payments surplus is not so direct and immediate as that for reducing a payments deficit.

The **adjustment mechanism** works for the return to equilibrium after the initial equilibrium has been disrupted. The process of payments

KEY CONCEPTS AND TERMS

- *Adjustment mechanism*
- *Automatic adjustment*
- *Foreign repercussion effect*
- *Foreign-trade multiplier*
- *Gold standard*
- *Income determination*
- *Multiplier process*
- *Quantity theory of money*
- *Rules of the game*

adjustment takes two different forms. First, under certain conditions, there are adjustment factors that automatically promote equilibrium. Second, should the automatic adjustments be unable to restore equilibrium, discretionary government policies may be adopted to achieve this objective.

This chapter emphasizes the **automatic adjustment** of the balance-of-payments process that occurs under a fixed exchange-rate system.[1] The adjustment variables that we will examine include prices, interest rates, and income. The impact of money on the balance of payments is also considered. Subsequent chapters discuss the adjustment mechanism under flexible exchange rates and the role of government policy in promoting payments adjustment.

Although the various automatic adjustment approaches have their contemporary advocates, each was formulated during a particular period and reflects a different philosophical climate. That the balance of payments could be adjusted by prices and interest rates stemmed from the *classical* economic thinking of the 1800s and early 1900s. The *classical approach* was geared toward the existing gold standard associated with fixed exchange rates. That income changes could promote balance-of-payments adjustments reflected the *Keynesian theory* of income determination, which grew out of the Great Depression of the 1930s. That money plays a crucial role in the long run as a disturbance and adjustment in the nation's balance of payments is an extension of domestic monetarism. This approach originated during the late 1960s and is associated with the *Chicago school* of economic thought.

PRICE ADJUSTMENTS

The original theory of balance-of-payments adjustment is credited to David Hume (1711–1776), the English philosopher and economist.[2] Hume's theory arose from his concern with the prevailing mercantilist view that advocated government controls to ensure a continuous favorable balance of payments. According to Hume, this strategy was self-defeating over the long run because a nation's balance of payments tends to move toward equilibrium automatically. Hume's theory stresses the role that adjustments in national *price levels* play in promoting balance-of-payments equilibrium.

GOLD STANDARD The classical **gold standard** that existed from the late 1800s to the early 1900s was characterized by three conditions. (1) Each member nation's money supply consisted of gold or paper money backed by gold. (2) Each member nation defined the official price of gold in terms of its national currency and was prepared to buy and sell gold at that price. (3) Free import and export of gold was permitted by member nations. Under these conditions, a nation's money supply was directly tied to its balance of payments. A nation with a balance-of-payments surplus would acquire gold, directly expanding its money supply. Conversely, the money supply of a deficit nation would decline as the result of a gold outflow.

The balance of payments can also be tied directly to a nation's money supply under a modified gold standard, requiring that the nation's stock of money be fractionally backed by gold at a constant ratio. It would also apply to a fixed exchange-rate system in which payments disequilibria are financed by some acceptable international reserve asset, assuming that a constant ratio between the nation's international reserves and its money supply is maintained.

---

[1] Under a fixed exchange-rate system, the supply of and demand for foreign exchange reflect credit and debit transactions in the balance of payments. These forces of supply and demand, however, are not permitted to determine the exchange rate. Instead, government officials peg, or fix, the exchange rate at a stipulated level by intervening in the foreign-exchange markets to purchase and sell currencies. This topic is examined further in the next chapter.

[2] David Hume, "Of the Balance of Trade." Reprinted in Richard N. Cooper, ed., *International Finance: Selected Readings* (Harmondsworth, England: Penguin Books, 1969), Chapter 1.

QUANTITY THEORY OF MONEY The essence of the classical price-adjustment mechanism is embodied in the **quantity theory of money**. Consider the *equation of exchange*:

$$MV = PQ$$

M refers to a nation's money supply. *V* refers to the velocity of money—that is, the number of times per year the average currency unit is spent on final goods. The expression *MV* corresponds to the aggregate demand, or total monetary expenditures on final goods. Alternatively, the monetary expenditures on any year's output can be interpreted as the physical volume of all final goods produced (*Q*) multiplied by the average price at which each of the final goods is sold (*P*). As a result, $MV = PQ$.

This equation is an identity. It says that total monetary expenditures on final goods equals the monetary value of the final goods sold; the amount spent on final goods equals the amount received from selling them.

The classical economists made two additional assumptions. First, they took the volume of final output (*Q*) to be fixed at the full employment level in the long run. Second, they assumed that the velocity of money (*V*) was constant, depending on institutional, structural, and physical factors that rarely changed. With *V* and *Q* relatively stable, a change in *M* must induce a *direct and proportionate change* in *P*. The model linking changes in *M* to changes in *P* became known as the *quantity theory of money*.

BALANCE-OF-PAYMENTS ADJUSTMENT

The preceding analysis showed how, under the classical gold standard, the balance of payments is linked to a nation's money supply, which is linked to its domestic price level. Let us consider how the price level is linked to the balance of payments.

Suppose that, under the classical gold standard, a nation realized a balance-of-payments deficit. The deficit nation would experience a gold outflow, which would reduce its money supply and thus its price level. The nation's international competitiveness would be enhanced, so that its exports would rise and imports fall. This process would continue until its price level had fallen to the point where balance-of-payments equilibrium was restored. Conversely, a nation with a balance-of-payments surplus would realize gold inflows and an increase in its money supply. This process would continue until its price level had risen to the point where balance-of-payments equilibrium was restored. Thus, the opposite price-adjustment process would occur at the same time in each trading partner.

The price-adjustment mechanism as devised by Hume illustrated the impossibility of the mercantilist notion of maintaining a continuous favorable balance of payments. The linkages (balance of payments—money supply—price level—balance of payments) demonstrated to Hume that, over time, balance-of-payments equilibrium tends to be achieved automatically.

With the advent of Hume's price-adjustment mechanism, classical economists had a very powerful and influential theory. It was not until the Keynesian revolution in economic thinking during the 1930s that this theory was effectively challenged. Even today, the price-adjustment mechanism is a hotly debated issue. A brief discussion of some of the major criticisms against the price-adjustment mechanism is in order.

The classical linkage between changes in a nation's gold supply and changes in its money supply no longer holds. Central bankers can easily offset a gold outflow (or inflow) by adopting an expansionary (or contractionary) monetary policy. The experience of the gold standard of the late 1800s and early 1900s indicates that these offsetting monetary policies often occurred. The classical view that full employment always exists has also been challenged. When an economy is far below its full employment level, there is a smaller chance that prices in general will rise in response to an increase in the money supply than if the economy is at full employment. It has also been pointed out that, in a modern industrial world, prices and wages are inflexible in a downward direction. If prices are inflexible downward, then changes in *M* will affect not *P* but rather *Q*. A deficit nation's falling money supply will bring about a fall in output and employment. Furthermore, the stability and predictability of V have been questioned. Should a gold inflow that results in an increase in M be offset by a decline in V, total spending (MV) and PQ would remain unchanged.

These issues are part of the current debate over the price-adjustment mechanism's relevance. They have caused sufficient doubts among economists to warrant a search for additional balance-of-payments adjustment explanations. The most notable include the effect of interest-rate changes on capital movements and the effect of changing incomes on trade flows.

INTEREST-RATE ADJUSTMENTS

Under the classical gold standard, the price-adjustment mechanism was not the only vehicle that served to restore equilibrium in the balance of payments. Another monetary effect of a payments surplus or deficit lay in its impact on *short-term interest rates* and hence on short-term private capital flows.

Consider a world of two countries: nation A, enjoying a surplus, and nation B, facing a deficit. The inflow of gold from the deficit to the surplus nation automatically results in an increase in nation A's money supply and a decline in the money supply of nation B. Given a constant demand for money, the increase in nation A's money supply would lower domestic interest rates. At the same time, nation B's gold outflow and declining money supply would bid up interest rates. In response to falling domestic interest rates and rising foreign interest rates, the investors of nation A would find it attractive to send additional investment funds abroad. Conversely, nation-B investors would not only be discouraged from sending money overseas, but might find it beneficial to liquidate foreign investment holdings and put the funds into domestic assets.

This process facilitates the automatic restoration of payments equilibrium in both nations. Because of the induced changes in interest rates,

stabilizing capital movements automatically flow from the surplus to the deficit nation, thereby reducing the payment imbalances of both nations. Although this induced short-term capital movement is temporary rather than continuous, it nevertheless facilitates the automatic balance-of-payments adjustment process.

During the actual operation of the gold standard, however, central bankers were not totally passive in response to these automatic adjustments. They instead agreed to reinforce and speed up the interest-rate adjustment mechanism by adhering to the so-called **rules of the game**. This required central bankers in a *surplus nation* to *expand credit*, leading to lower interest rates; central bankers in *deficit nations* would *tighten credit*, bidding interest rates upward. Private short-term capital presumably would flow from the surplus nation to the deficit nation. Not only would the deficit nation's ability to finance its payments imbalance be strengthened, but also the surplus nation's gold inflows would be checked.

CAPITAL FLOWS AND THE BALANCE OF PAYMENTS

The classical economists were aware of the impact of changes in interest rates on international capital movements, even though this factor was not the central focus of their balance-of-payments adjustment theory. With national financial systems closely integrated today, it is recognized that interest-rate fluctuations can induce significant changes in a nation's capital account and balance-of-payments position.

Recall that the capital account of the balance of payments records net changes in a nation's international financial assets and liabilities, excluding changes in official reserves, over a one-year period. Its size depends on all the factors that cause financial assets to move across national borders. The most important of these factors is interest rates in domestic and foreign markets. However, other factors are important too, such as investment profitability, national tax policies, and political stability.

Figure 14.1 shows the hypothetical capital account schedules for the United States. Capital account *surpluses* (net capital inflows) and *deficits* (net capital outflows) are measured on the vertical axis. Capital flows between the United States and the rest of the world are assumed to respond to *interest-rate differentials* between the two areas (U.S. interest rate minus foreign interest rate) for a particular set of economic conditions in the United States and abroad.

Referring to capital account schedule CA_0, the U.S. capital account is in *balance* (zero net capital flow) at point A, where the U.S. interest rate is equal to that abroad. Should the United States reduce its monetary growth, the scarcity of money would tend to raise interest rates in the United States compared with the rest of the world. Suppose U.S. interest rates rise 1 percent above those overseas. Investors, seeing higher U.S. interest rates, will tend to sell foreign securities to purchase U.S. securities that offer a higher yield. The 1-percent interest-rate differential leads to *net capital inflows* of $5 billion for the United States, which thus moves to point B on schedule CA_0. Conversely, should foreign interest rates rise above those in the United States, the United States will face *net capital outflows* as investors sell U.S. securities to purchase foreign securities offering a higher yield.

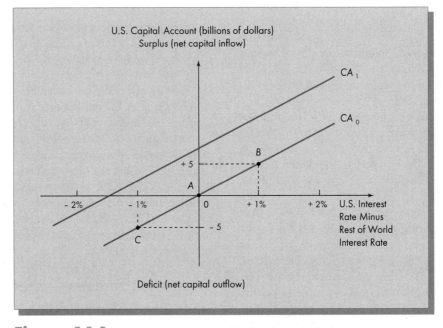

Figure 14.1 Capital Account Schedule for the United States

Interest-rate differentials between the United States and the rest of the world induce movements along the U.S. capital account schedule. Relatively high (low) U.S. interest rates trigger net capital inflows (outflows) and an upward (downward) movement along the capital account schedule. The capital account schedule shifts upward/downward in response to changes in non-interest-rate determinants such as investment profitability, tax policies, and political stability.

Figure 14.1 assumes that interest-rate differentials are the basic determinant of capital flows for the United States. Movements along a given capital account schedule are caused by changes in the interest rate in the United States relative to that in the rest of the world. However, there are certain determinants other than interest-rate differentials that might cause the United States to import (or export) more or less capital at each possible interest-rate differential and thereby change the location of the capital account schedule.

To illustrate, assume the United States is located along capital account schedule CA_0 at point A. Suppose that rising U.S. income leads to higher sales and increased profits. Direct investment (in an auto-assembly plant, for example) becomes more profitable in the United States. Nations such as Japan will invest more in their U.S. subsidiaries, whereas General Motors will invest less overseas. The higher profitability of direct investment leads to a greater flow of capital into the United States at each possible interest-rate differential and an upward shift in the capital account schedule (illustrated by schedule CA_1).

Suppose the U.S. government levies an *interest equalization tax*, as it did from 1964 to 1974. This tax was intended to help reverse the large capital outflows that the United States faced when European interest rates exceeded those in the United States. By taxing U.S. investors on dividend and interest income from foreign securities, the tax reduced the net profitability (that is, the after-tax yield) of foreign securities. At the same time, the U.S. government enacted a foreign-credit-restraint program, which placed direct restrictions on foreign lending by U.S. banks and financial institutions and later on foreign lending of nonfinancial corporations. By discouraging capital outflows from the United States to Europe, these policies resulted in an upward shift in the U.S. capital account schedule in terms of Figure 14.1, suggesting that less capital would flow out of the United States in response to higher interest rates overseas.

INCOME ADJUSTMENTS

The classical balance-of-payments adjustment theory relied primarily on the price-adjustment mechanism, while delegating a secondary role to the effects of interest rates on private short-term capital movements. A main criticism of the classical theory was that it almost completely neglected the effect of *income adjustments*. The classical economists were aware that the income, or purchasing power, of a surplus nation rose relative to that of the deficit nation. This would have an impact on the level of imports in each nation. But the income effect was viewed as an accompaniment of price changes. Largely because the gold movements of the nineteenth century exerted only minor impacts on price and interest-rate levels, economic theorists began to look for alternate balance-of-payments adjustment explanations under a fixed exchange-rate system. The theory of **income determination** developed by John Maynard Keynes in the 1930s, provided such an explanation.[3]

Keynes asserted that under a system of fixed exchange rates, the influence of income changes in surplus and deficit nations will help restore payments equilibrium automatically. Given a persistent payments imbalance, a surplus nation will experience rising income, and its imports will increase. Conversely, a deficit nation will experience a fall in income, resulting in a decline in imports. These effects of income changes on import levels will reverse the disequilibrium in the balance of payments.

INCOME DETERMINATION IN A CLOSED ECONOMY

To illustrate the Keynesian theory of income determination, let us first assume a *closed econ-*

---

[3] John Maynard Keynes, *The General Theory of Employment, Interest, and Money* (London: Macmillan, 1936).

omy with no foreign trade, with price and interest-rate levels constant. In this simple Keynesian model, national income (Y) is the sum of consumption expenditures (C) plus savings (S):

$$Y = C + S$$

Total expenditures on national product are C plus business investment (I). This relationship is given by

$$Y = C + I$$

Figure 14.2 represents the familiar income-determination model found in introductory economics textbooks. Referring to Figure 14.2(a), consumption is assumed to be functionally dependent on income, whereas investment spending is autonomous—that is, independent of the level of income. The economy is in equilibrium when the level of planned expenditures equals income. This occurs at Y_E, where the 45° line intersects the (C

$+ I$) schedule. At any level of income lower (or higher) than Y_E, planned expenditure would exceed (or fall below) income and income would rise (or fall).

Combining these relationships yields the following:

$$Y = C + S = C + I$$

The basic equilibrium condition can thus be stated as

$$S = I$$

or

$$S - I = 0$$

This equivalent condition for equilibrium income is illustrated in Figure 14.2(b). Like consumption, saving is assumed to be functionally related to income. Given a constant level of investment, the ($S - I$) schedule is upward sloping. Savings

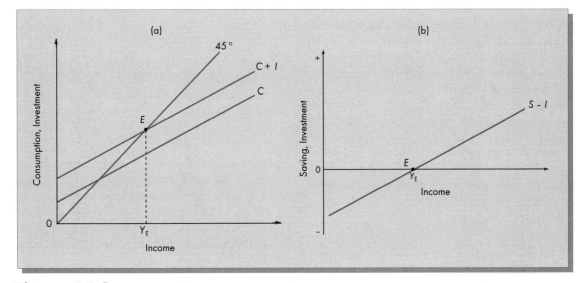

Figure 14.2 Income Determination in a Closed Economy

In an economy not exposed to international trade, equilibrium income occurs where the level of planned expenditures (consumption plus investment) equals income: $Y = C + I$. An equivalent condition for equilibrium income is planned saving equals planned investment: $S = I$, or $S - I = 0$.

can be regarded as a leakage from the income stream, whereas investment is an injection into the income stream. At income levels below Y_E, I exceeds S, and the level of income rises. The opposite holds equally true. The economy is thus in equilibrium where $S = I$ (or $S - I = 0$). Figure 14.2(b) will be used later to illustrate income determination in an open economy.

Suppose an economy that is initially in equilibrium experiences some disturbance, say, an increase in investment spending. This would bid up the level of equilibrium income. This result comes about through a **multiplier process**; that is, the initial investment sets off a chain reaction that results in greater levels of spending, so that income increases by some multiple of the initial investment. Given an autonomous injection of investment spending into the economy, the induced increase in income is given by

$$\Delta Y = k \Delta I$$

where k represents some multiplier.

Let's see how the multiplier is derived for a closed economy. First, remember that in equilibrium, an economy will find planned saving equal to planned investment. It follows that any I must be matched by an equivalent S if the economy is to remain in balance. Because it has been assumed that saving is functionally dependent on income, changes in saving will be related to changes in income. If we use s to represent the marginal propensity to save out of additional income levels, then $S = sY$. Given an autonomous increase in investment, the equilibrium condition suggests that

$$\Delta I = \Delta S = s \Delta Y$$

From the preceding expression, the multiplier can be derived as

$$\Delta Y = \frac{1}{s} \Delta I$$

Suppose, for example, a nation finds that its marginal propensity to save (s) is 0.25, and there occurs an autonomous increase in investment of $100. According to the multiplier principle, the induced change in income stemming from the initial increase in investment spending equals the increase in investment spending times the multiplier (k). Because the s is assumed to equal 0.25, $k = 1/s = 1/0.25 = 4$. The $100 increase in investment expenditure ultimately results in a $400 increase in the level of income.

INCOME DETERMINATION IN AN OPEN ECONOMY

Now assume an *open economy* subject to international trade. The condition for equilibrium income, as well as the formulation of the spending multiplier, must both be modified. In an open economy, imports (M), like savings, constitute a leakage out of the income stream, whereas exports (X), like investment, represent an injection into the stream of national income. The condition for equilibrium income, which relates leakages to injections in an open economy's income stream, becomes

$$S + M = I + X$$

Rearranging terms, this becomes

$$S - I = X - M$$

Assume that exports are unrelated to the level of domestic income. Also assume that imports are functionally dependent on domestic income—that is,

$$\Delta M = m \Delta Y$$

where m represents the marginal propensity to import. We are now in a position to derive what is known as the **foreign-trade multiplier**.

First, let the injections into and leakages from the income stream rise by the same amount, so that the induced change in income will be of equilibrium magnitude. This yields

$$\Delta S + \Delta M = \Delta I + \Delta X$$

Given that

$$\Delta S = s \Delta Y$$

and

$$\Delta M = m \Delta Y$$

the induced change in income stemming from the changes in injections and leakages can be shown as follows:

$$(s + m) \, \Delta Y = \Delta I + \Delta X$$

Holding exports constant, $(\Delta X = 0)$ the induced change in income is equal to the change in investment times the foreign trade multiplier, or

$$\Delta Y = \left(\frac{1}{s + m} \right) \times \Delta I$$

The preceding expression states that *the foreign-trade multiplier equals the reciprocal of the sum of the marginal propensities to save and to import.* In this formulation, an autonomous change in exports, investment remaining fixed, would have an impact on domestic income identical to that of an equivalent change in investment.

IMPLICATIONS OF THE FOREIGN-TRADE MULTIPLIER

To show the adjustment implications of the foreign-trade multiplier, we construct a diagram based on the framework of Figure 14.2. Remember that the $(S - I)$ schedule is positively sloped. This is because changes in savings are assumed to be directly related to changes in income, investment being unaffected. Subtracting investment from saving yields an upward-sloping $(S - I)$ schedule, as shown in Figure 14.3. Similarly, it has been assumed that changes in imports are directly related to changes in income, exports remaining constant. When imports are subtracted from exports, the result is a downward-sloping $(X - M)$ schedule. As before, the equilibrium condition of an open economy with no government is $(X - M) = (S - I)$.

Starting at equilibrium income level $1,000 in Figure 14.3, suppose a disturbance results in an autonomous increase in exports by, say, $200. This is shown by shifting the $(X - M)$ schedule upward by $200, resulting in the new schedule $(X' - M)$. The level of income rises, generating increases in imports and savings. Domestic equilibrium is established at income level $1,400, where $(S - I) = (X' - M)$. The trade account is no longer in balance; there is a trade surplus of

$100. This trade surplus is less than the initial $200 rise in exports because part of the surplus is offset by increases in imports induced by the rise in income from $1,000 to $1,400.

In this example, we can use the concept of a foreign-trade multiplier to determine the effect of the increase in exports on the home economy. Inspection of the $(S - I)$ schedule in Figure 14.3 reveals that the slope of the schedule, which represents the marginal propensity to save, equals 0.25. The slope of the $(X - M)$ schedule indicates that the marginal propensity to import also equals 0.25. The foreign-trade multiplier is the reciprocal of the sum of the marginal propensities to save and to import—that is, 1 / 0.50, or 2. An autonomous increase in exports of $200 thus generates a twofold increase in domestic income, and equilibrium income rises from $1,000 to $1,400.

As for the trade-account effect, the $400 rise in domestic income induces a $100 increase in imports, given a marginal propensity to import of 0.25. Part of the initial export-led surplus is neutralized, lowering it from $200 to $100. Over time, the increase in imports generated by increased domestic expenditures will tend to reduce the trade surplus, but not enough to restore balance-of-payments equilibrium.

Consider another case that illustrates the national-income and balance-of-payments effects of a change in expenditures. Assume that, owing to improved profit expectations, domestic investment rises autonomously by $200. Starting at equilibrium level $1,000 in Figure 14.3, the increase in investment will displace the $(S - I)$ schedule downward by $200 because the negative term is increased. This gives us the new schedule $(S - I')$. Domestic income rises from $1,000 to $1,400, which stimulates a rise in imports, producing a trade deficit of $100. Unlike the previous case of export-led expansion, an autonomous increase in domestic investment spending (or government expenditures) increases domestic income but at the expense of a balance-of-payments deficit. This should serve as a reminder to economic policy makers that under a system of fixed exchange rates, the impact of domestic policies on the balance of payments cannot be overlooked.

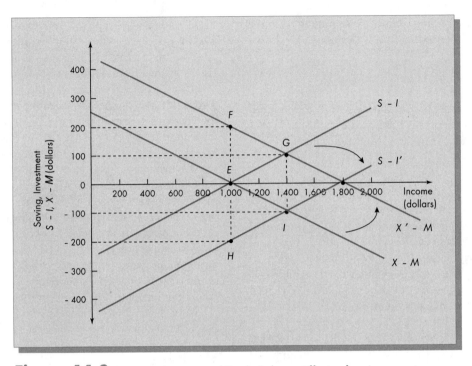

Figure 14.3 Domestic Income and Trade-Balance Effects of an Increase in Exports and an Increase in Investment

Starting at equilibrium income, an autonomous increase in domestic exports leads to a rise in domestic income, which promotes an increase in imports and savings. Because of the multiplier effect, the induced increase in income tends to be larger than the initial increase in exports. The trade account moves into surplus because the induced increase in imports tends to be less than the initial increase in exports. Again starting at equilibrium income, an autonomous increase in domestic investment generates an increase in income, which promotes additional savings and imports. Because of the multiplier effect, the increase in investment generates a magnified increase in income. As the increase in income induces a rise in imports, a trade deficit appears.

FOREIGN REPERCUSSIONS The preceding income-adjustment analysis needs to be modified to include the impact that changes in domestic expenditures and income levels have on foreign economies. This process is referred to as the **foreign repercussion effect.**

Assume a two-country world, the United States and Canada, in which there initially exists balance-of-payments equilibrium. Owing to changing consumer preferences, suppose the United States faces an autonomous increase in imports from Canada. This results in an increase in Canada's exports. According to the multiplier principle, U.S. income will fall, and Canada's income will rise. The fall in U.S. income induces a fall in the level of U.S. imports (and a fall in Canada's exports). At the same time, the rise in Canada's income induces a rise in Canada's imports (and a rise in U.S. exports). This feedback process is repeated again and again.

The consequence of this process is that both the rise in income of the surplus nation (Canada)

and the fall in income of the deficit nation (United States) are dampened. This is because the autonomous increase in U.S. imports (and Canada's exports) will cause the U.S. income to decrease as imports are substituted for home-produced goods. Given the marginal propensity to import, the decline in U.S. income will generate a reduction in its imports. Because U.S. imports are Canada's exports, the result will be to moderate the rise in Canada's income. From the perspective of the United States, the decline in its income will be cushioned by an increase in exports to Canada stemming from a rise in Canada's income.

The importance of the foreign repercussion effect depends in part on the economic size of a country as far as international trade is concerned. A small nation that increases its imports from a large nation will have little impact on the large nation's income level. But for major trading nations, the foreign repercussion effect is likely to be significant and must be taken into account when the income-adjustment mechanism is being considered.

Table 14.1 gives estimated spending multipliers with foreign repercussions for five industrial nations. Inspecting the table's top row, we see that U.S. national income would increase 1.3 percent if aggregate spending increased by 1 percent in the United States alone, or by 0.1 percent if spending rose in Japan alone, 0.1 percent if spending increased by 1 percent in Germany, and so on. Inspecting the numbers down the Japan column, we see that a 1-percent increase in Japanese spending would increase U.S. national income by 0.1 percent, Japanese national income by 2.1 percent, German national income by 0.2 percent, and so on. The implication of the table is that the larger the nation, the greater the impact of its spending on other nations. For example, Germany is more affected by changes of spending in the United States (0.9 percent) than it is by those in the United Kingdom (0.3 percent) or Canada (0.1 percent).

DISADVANTAGES OF AUTOMATIC ADJUSTMENT MECHANISMS The preceding sections have considered automatic balance-of-payments adjustment mechanisms under a system of fixed exchange rates. According to the classical school of thought, adjustments occur as prices and interest rates respond to international gold movements. Keynesian theory emphasized another adjustment process, the effect of changes in national income on a nation's balance of payments.

Although elements of price, interest rate, and income adjustments may operate in the real

Table 14.1 Spending Multipliers* Subject to Foreign-Income Repercussions for Five Industrial Nations

On Real National Income in	The Impact of a 1-Percent Increase in Spending in				
	United States	Japan	Germany	United Kingdom	Canada
United States	1.3%	0.1%	0.1%	0.05%**	0.1%
Japan	1.0	2.1	0.1	0.1	0.1
Germany	0.9	0.2	1.7	0.3	0.1
United Kingdom	0.5	0.1	0.2	1.1	0.05**
Canada	0.8	0.1	0.05**	0.05**	1.0

*These multipliers are the results for the third year following the initial increase in spending.

**Less than.

Source: Richardson, P. "The Structure and Simulation Properties of OECD's Interlink Model," *OECD Economic Studies*, Spring 1988, pp. 57–121, Annex Table 2.

world, these adjustment mechanisms have a major shortcoming. The problem is that an efficient adjustment mechanism requires central bankers to forgo their use of monetary policy to promote the goal of full employment without inflation; each nation must be willing to accept inflation or recession when balance-of-payments adjustment requires it. Take the case of a nation that faces a deficit caused by an autonomous increase in imports or decrease in exports. For income adjustments to reverse the deficit, monetary authorities must permit domestic income to decrease and not undertake policies to offset its decline. The opposite applies equally to a nation with a balance-of-payments surplus.

To the classical economists, abandoning an independent monetary policy would not be considered a disadvantage. This is because classical thought envisioned a system that would automatically move toward full employment over time and placed a high priority on balance-of-payments adjustment. In today's world, *unemployment* is often the norm, and its elimination is generally given priority over balance-of-payments equilibrium. Modern nations are thus reluctant to make significant internal sacrifices for the sake of external equilibrium. The result is that reliance on an automatic payments-adjustment process is politically unacceptable.

MONETARY ADJUSTMENTS

The previous sections have examined how changes in national price, interest rate, and income levels automatically lead to balance-of-payments adjustment. During the 1960s and 1970s, a new theory emerged, called the *monetary approach* to the balance of payments.[4] The monetary approach views disequilibrium in the

balance of payments primarily as a monetary phenomenon. Money acts as both a *disturbance* and an *adjustment* to the balance of payments. As in the classical and Keynesian approaches, adjustment in the balance of payments is viewed as an automatic process.

PAYMENTS IMBALANCES UNDER FIXED EXCHANGE RATES The monetary approach emphasizes that disequilibrium in the balance of payments reflects an imbalance between the demand and the supply of money. A first assumption is that, over the long run, the nation's demand for money is a stable function of real income, prices, and the interest rate.

The quantity of nominal money balances demanded is *directly* related to income and prices. Increases in income or prices trigger increases in the value of transactions and an increased need for money to finance the transactions, and vice versa. The quantity of money demanded is *inversely* related to the interest rate. Whenever money is held rather than used to make an investment, the money holder sacrifices interest that could have been earned. If interest rates are high, people will try to keep as little money on hand as possible, putting the rest into interest-earning investments. Conversely, a decline in interest rates increases the quantity of money demanded.

The nation's *money supply* is a multiple of the monetary base that includes two components. The *domestic component* refers to credit created by the nation's monetary authorities (such as Federal Reserve liabilities for the United States). The *international component* refers to the foreign-exchange reserves of a nation, which can be increased or decreased as the result of balance-of-payments disequilibrium.

The monetary approach maintains that all payments *deficits* are the result of an *excess supply of money* in the home country. Under a fixed exchange-rate system, the excess supply of money results in a flow overseas of foreign-exchange reserves, and thus a reduction in the domestic money supply. Conversely, an *excess demand for money* in the home country leads to a payments surplus, resulting in the inflow of for-

---

[4] The monetary approach to the balance of payments had its intellectual background at the University of Chicago. It originated with Robert Mundell, *International Economics* (New York: Macmillan, 1968) and Harry Johnson, "The Monetary Approach to Balance-of-Payments Theory," *Journal of Financial and Quantitative Analysis*, March 1972.

eign-exchange reserves from overseas and an increase in the domestic money supply. Balance in the nation's payments position is restored when the excess supply of money, or the excess demand for money, has fallen enough to restore the equilibrium condition: *money supply equals money demand*. Table 14.2 summarizes the conclusions of the monetary approach, given a system of fixed exchange rates.

Assume that to finance a budget deficit, the Canadian government creates additional money. Considering this money to be in excess of desired levels (excess money supply), Canadian residents choose to increase their spending on goods and services instead of holding extra cash balances. Given a fixed exchange-rate system, the rise in home spending will push up the prices of Canadian goods and services relative to those abroad. Canadian buyers will be induced to decrease purchases of Canadian-produced goods and services, as will foreign buyers. Conversely, Canadian sellers will offer more goods at home and fewer abroad, whereas foreign sellers will try to increase sales to Canada. By encouraging a rise in imports and a fall in exports, these forces tend to worsen the Canadian payments position. As Canada finances its deficit by transferring international reserves to foreign nations, the Canadian money supply will fall back toward

desired levels. This, in turn, will reduce Canadian spending and demand for imports, restoring payments balance.

The monetary approach views balance-of-payments adjustment as an automatic process. Any payments imbalance reflects a disparity between actual and desired money balances that tends to be eliminated by inflows or outflows of foreign-exchange reserves, which lead to increases or decreases in the domestic money supply. This self-correcting process requires time. Except for implying that the adjustment process takes place over the long run, the monetary approach does not consider the time period needed to achieve equilibrium. The monetary approach thus emphasizes the economy's final, long-run equilibrium position.

The monetary approach assumes that flows in foreign-exchange reserves associated with payments imbalances do exert an influence on the domestic money supply. This is true as long as central banks do not use monetary policies to neutralize the impact of flows in foreign-exchange reserves on the domestic money supply. If they do neutralize such flows, payments imbalances will continue, according to the monetary approach.

POLICY IMPLICATIONS What implications does the monetary approach have for domestic economic policies? The approach suggests that economic policy affects the balance of payments through its impact on the domestic demand for and supply of money. Policies that *increase the supply of money* relative to the demand for money will lead to a payments *deficit*, an outflow of foreign-exchange reserves, and a reduction in the domestic money supply. Policies that *increase the demand for money* relative to the supply of money will trigger a payments *surplus*, an inflow of foreign-exchange reserves, and an increase in the domestic money supply.

The monetary approach also suggests that nonmonetary policies that attempt to influence a nation's balance of payments (such as tariffs, quotas, or currency devaluation) are unnecessary because payments disequilibria are self-correcting

Table 14.2 Changes in the Supply of Money and Demand for Money Under Fixed Exchange Rates: Impact on the Balance of Payments According to the Monetary Approach	
Change*	Impact
Increase in money supply	Deficit
Decrease in money supply	Surplus
Increase in money demand	Surplus
Decrease in money demand	Deficit

*Starting from a position at which the nation's money demand equals the money supply and its balance of payments is in equilibrium.

over time. However, in the short run, such policies may speed up the adjustment process by reducing excesses in the supply of money or the demand for money.

For example, given an initial equilibrium, suppose the Canadian government creates money in excess of that demanded by the economy, leading to a payments deficit. The monetary approach maintains that, in the long run, foreign-exchange reserves will flow out of Canada and the Canadian money supply will decrease. This automatic adjustment process will continue until the money supply decreases enough to restore the equilibrium condition: money supply equals money demand. Suppose Canada, to speed the return to equilibrium, imposes a tariff on imports. The tariff increases the price of imports as well as the prices of nontraded goods (goods produced exclusively for the domestic market, which face no competition from imports), owing to interproduct substitution. Higher Canadian prices trigger an increase in the quantity of money demanded, because Canadians now require additional funds to finance higher-priced purchases. The increase in the quantity of money demanded absorbs part of the excess money supply. The tariff therefore results in a speedier elimination of the excess money supply and payments deficit than would occur under an automatic adjustment mechanism.[5]

The monetary approach also has policy implications for the growth of the economy. Starting from the point of equilibrium, as the nation's output and real income expand, so do the number of transactions and the quantity of money demanded. If the government does not increase the domestic component of the money supply commensurate with the increase in the quantity of money demanded, the excess demand will induce an inflow of funds from abroad and a payments surplus. This explanation is often advanced for the German payments surpluses that occurred during the late 1960s and early 1970s, a period when the growth in German national output and money demand surpassed the growth in the domestic component of the German money supply.

[5] An import quota would also promote payments equilibrium by restricting the supply of Canadian imports and increasing their price. The quantity of money demanded by Canadians would rise, reducing the excess money supply and the payments deficit. As discussed in the next chapter, a currency devaluation also leads to higher-priced imports. This generates a higher demand for money and a shrinking payments deficit, according to the monetary approach.

S U M M A R Y

1. Because persistent balance-of-payments disequilibrium—whether surplus or deficit—tends to have adverse economic consequences, there exists a need for adjustment.

2. Balance-of-payments adjustment can be classified as automatic or discretionary. Under a system of fixed exchange rates, automatic adjustments can occur through variations in prices, interest rates, and incomes. The demand for and supply of money can also influence the adjustment process.

3. David Hume's theory provided an explanation of the automatic adjustment process that occurred under the gold standard. Starting from a condition of payments balance, any surplus or deficit would automatically be eliminated by changes in domestic price levels. Hume's theory relied heavily on the quantity theory of money.

4. Another important consequence of international gold movements under the classical theory was their impact on short-term interest rates. A deficit nation suffering gold losses would face a shrinking money supply, which would force up interest rates, promoting capital inflows and payments equilibrium. The opposite held true for a surplus nation. Rather than relying on automatic

adjustments in interest rates to restore payments balance, central bankers often resorted to monetary policies designed to reinforce the adjustment mechanism during the gold-standard era.

5. With the advent of Keynesian economics during the 1930s, greater emphasis was put on the income effects of trade in explaining adjustment.

6. The foreign repercussion effect refers to a situation in which a change in one nation's macroeconomic variables relative to another nation will induce a chain reaction in both nations' economies.

7. An automatic balance-of-payments adjustment mechanism has several disadvantages.

Nations must be willing to accept adverse changes in the domestic economy when required for balance-of-payments adjustment. Policy makers must forgo using discretionary economic policy to promote domestic equilibrium.

8. The monetary approach to the balance of payments is presented as an alternative, rather than a supplement, to traditional adjustment theories. It maintains that, over the long run, payments disequilibria are rooted in the relationship between the demand for and the supply of money. Adjustment in the balance of payments is viewed as an automatic process.

STUDY QUESTIONS

1. What is meant by the term *balance-of-payments adjustment*? Why does a deficit nation have an incentive to undergo adjustment? What about a surplus nation?

2. Under a fixed exchange-rate system, what automatic adjustments promote payments equilibrium?

3. What is meant by the quantity theory of money? How did it relate to the classical price-adjustment mechanism?

4. How can adjustments in domestic interest rates help promote payments balance?

5. In the gold-standard era, there existed the so-called rules of the game. What were these rules? Were they followed in practice?

6. Keynesian theory suggests that under a system of fixed exchange rates, the influence of income changes in surplus and deficit nations helps promote balance-of-payments equilibrium. Explain.

7. When analyzing the income-adjustment mechanism, one must account for the foreign repercussion effect. Explain.

8. What are some major disadvantages of the automatic adjustment mechanism under a system of fixed exchange rates?

9. According to the monetary approach, balance in a nation's payments position is restored when the excess supply of money or the excess demand for money has fallen to restore the equilibrium condition: money supply equals money demand. Explain.

10. What implications does the monetary approach have for domestic economic policies?

14.1 To get the foreign-exchange rates releases, summary indexes, currency weights, historical bilateral rates, and daily update, log on to The Federal Reserve Board Statistics: Releases and Historical Data page at:
http://www.bog.frb.fed.us/releases/

14.2 The Asian Development Bank, based in the Philippines, promotes the economic and social progress of its developing member countries. It has extensive reports and statistics on a number of Asian countries. Find it by setting your browser to URL:
http://www.adb.org/

To access NetLink Exercises and the Virtual Scavenger Hunt, visit the Carbaugh Web site at http://carbaugh.swcollege.com.

chapter 15

Exchange-Rate Adjustments and the Balance of Payments

The previous chapter demonstrated that balance-of-payments disequilibriums tend to be reversed by automatic adjustments in prices, interest rates, and incomes. If these adjustments are allowed to operate, however, reversing balance-of-payments disequilibriums may come at the expense of domestic recession or price inflation. The cure may be perceived as worse than the disease.

Instead of relying on adjustments in prices, interest rates, and incomes to counteract payments imbalances, governments permit alterations in exchange rates. By adopting a floating exchange-rate system, a nation permits its currency to depreciate or appreciate in a free market in response to shifts in either the demand for or supply of the currency. Under a fixed exchange-rate system, rates are set by government in the short run. However, if the official exchange rate becomes overvalued over a period of time, a government may initiate policies to *devalue* its currency.

Currency devaluation causes a depreciation of a currency's exchange value; it is initiated by government policy rather than by the free-market forces of supply and demand. When a nation's currency is undervalued, it may be *revalued* by the government; this policy causes the currency's exchange value to appreciate. Currency devaluation and revaluation will be discussed further in the next chapter.

In this chapter, we examine the impact of exchange-rate adjustments on the balance of payments. We will learn under what conditions currency depreciation (devaluation) and appreciation

KEY CONCEPTS AND TERMS

- *Absorption approach*
- *Currency pass-through*
- *Elasticity approach*
- *J-curve effect*
- *Marshall–Lerner condition*
- *Monetary approach*

(revaluation) will improve/worsen a nation's payments position.

EFFECTS OF EXCHANGE-RATE CHANGES ON COSTS AND PRICES

Industries that compete with foreign producers, or that rely on imported inputs in production, can be noticeably affected by exchange-rate fluctuations. Changing exchange rates influence the international competitiveness of a nation's industries through their influence on relative costs. How do exchange-rate fluctuations affect relative costs? The answer depends on the extent to which a firm's costs are denominated in terms of the home currency or foreign currency.

CASE 1

No foreign sourcing—all costs are denominated in dollars.

Table 15.1 illustrates the hypothetical production costs of Bethlehem Steel, a U.S. manufacturer. Assume that in its production of steel, Bethlehem utilizes U.S. labor, coal, iron, and other inputs whose costs are denominated in dollars. In period 1, the exchange value of the dollar is assumed to be 50 cents per Swiss franc (2 francs per dollar). Assume that the firm's cost of producing a

ton of steel is $500, which is equivalent to 1,000 francs at this exchange rate.

Suppose that in period 2, because of changing market conditions, the dollar's exchange value *appreciates* from 50 cents per franc to 25 cents per franc, a 100-percent appreciation (the franc depreciates from 2 to 4 francs per dollar). With the dollar appreciation, Bethlehem's labor, iron, coal, and other input costs remain constant in dollar terms. In terms of the franc, however, these costs rise from 1,000 francs to 2,000 francs per ton, a 100-percent increase. The 100-percent dollar appreciation induces a 100-percent increase in Bethlehem's franc-denominated production cost. The international competitiveness of Bethlehem is thus reduced.

This example assumes that all of a firm's inputs are acquired domestically and that their costs are denominated in the domestic currency. In many industries, however, some of a firm's inputs are purchased in foreign markets (foreign sourcing), and these input costs are denominated in a foreign currency. What impact does a change in the home-currency's exchange value have on a firm's costs in this situation?

CASE 2

Foreign sourcing—some costs denominated in dollars and some costs denominated in francs.

Table 15.2 again illustrates the hypothetical production costs of Bethlehem Steel, whose costs of labor, iron, coal, and certain other inputs are assumed to

Table 15.1 Effects of a Dollar Appreciation on a U.S. Steel Firm's Production Costs When All Costs Are Dollar-Denominated

	Cost of Producing a Ton of Steel			
	Period 1 $.50 per franc (2 francs = $1)		Period 2 $.25 per franc (4 francs = $1)	
	Dollar Cost	Franc Equivalent	Dollar Cost	Franc Equivalent
Labor	$160	320 francs	$160	640 francs
Materials (iron/coal)	300	600	300	1,200
Other costs (energy)	40	80	40	160
Total	$500	1,000 francs	$500	2,000 francs
Percentage change	—	—	—	100 %

Table 15.2 Effects of a Dollar Appreciation on a U.S. Steel Firm's Production Costs When Some Costs Are Dollar-Denominated and Other Costs Are Franc-Denominated

| | Cost of Producing a Ton of Steel | | | |
| | Period 1 $.50 per franc (2 francs = $1) | | Period 2 $.25 per franc (4 francs = $1) | |
	Dollar Cost	Franc Equivalent	Dollar Cost	Franc Equivalent
Labor	$160	320 francs	$160	640 francs
Materials				
Dollar-denominated (iron/coal)	120	240	120	480
Franc-denominated (scrap iron)	180	360	90	360
Total	300	600	210	840
Other costs (energy)	40	80	40	160
Total cost	$500	1,000 francs	$410	1,640 francs
Percentage change	—	—	-18%	+64%

be denominated in dollars. However, suppose Bethlehem acquires scrap iron from Swiss suppliers (foreign sourcing), and these costs are denominated in francs. Once again, assume the dollar's exchange value appreciates from 50 cents per franc to 25 cents per franc. As before, the cost in francs of Bethlehem's labor, iron, coal, and certain other inputs rise by 100 percent following the dollar appreciation; however, the franc cost of scrap iron remains constant. As can be seen in the table, Bethlehem's franc cost per ton of steel rises from 1,000 francs to 1,640 francs—an increase of only 64 percent. Thus, the dollar appreciation worsens Bethlehem's international competitiveness, but not as much as in the previous example.

In addition to influencing Bethlehem's franc-denominated cost of steel, a dollar appreciation affects a firm's dollar cost when franc-denominated inputs are involved. Because scrap-iron costs are denominated in francs, they remain at 360 francs after the dollar appreciation; however, the dollar-equivalent scrap-iron cost falls from $180 to $90. Since the costs of Bethlehem's other inputs are denominated in dollars and do not change following the dollar appreciation, the firm's total dollar cost falls from $500 to $410 per ton—a

decrease of 18 percent. This cost reduction offsets some of the cost disadvantage that Bethlehem incurs relative to Swiss exporters as a result of the dollar appreciation (franc depreciation).

The preceding examples suggest the following generalization: As franc-denominated costs become a larger portion of Bethlehem's total costs, a dollar appreciation (depreciation) leads to a smaller increase (decrease) in the franc cost of Bethlehem steel and a larger decrease (increase) in the dollar cost of Bethlehem steel compared to the cost changes that occur when all input costs are dollar-denominated. As franc-denominated costs become a smaller portion of total costs, the opposite conclusions apply. These conclusions have been especially significant for the world trading system during the 1980s to 2000s as industries—e.g., autos and computers—have become increasingly internationalized and utilize increasing amounts of imported inputs in the production process.

Changes in relative costs because of exchange-rate fluctuations also influence relative prices and the volume of goods traded among nations. By increasing relative U.S. production costs, a dollar *appreciation* tends to *raise* U.S. export prices in foreign-currency terms, which induces a decrease in the quantity of U.S. goods sold abroad; similarly, the dollar appreciation leads to an increase in U.S. imports. By decreasing relative U.S. production costs, a dollar *depreciation* tends to *lower* U.S. export prices in foreign-currency terms, which induces an increase in the quantity of U.S. goods sold abroad; similarly, the dollar depreciation leads to a decrease in U.S. imports.

Several factors govern the extent by which exchange-rate movements lead to relative price changes among nations. Some U.S. exporters may be able to offset the price-increasing effects of an appreciation in the dollar's exchange value by reducing profit margins to maintain competitiveness. Perceptions concerning long-term trends in exchange rates also promote price rigidity: U.S. exporters may be less willing to raise prices if the dollar's appreciation is viewed as temporary. The extent to which industries implement pricing strategies depends significantly on the substitutability of their product: The greater the degree of product differentiation (as in quality or service), the greater control producers can exercise over prices; the pricing policies of such producers are somewhat insulated from exchange-rate movements.

The U.S. International Trade Commission (USITC) has estimated the effect of exchange-rate changes on prices of U.S. imports and exports of selected steel products over the period from 1981 to 1989. Table 15.3 summarizes their findings for two products, hot-rolled sheet steel and cold-rolled sheet steel. According to the USITC's estimates, a 1-percent appreciation in the dollar's exchange value induces a much smaller percentage change in steel import and export prices. Moreover, most of the induced price changes do not occur until 9 to 12 months later. These results are not surprising given the lead time required to order, produce, and ship steel and the fact that steel export pricing tends to be especially sensitive to foreign levels of steel consumption and domestic costs.

Is there any way in which companies can offset the impact of currency swings on their competitiveness? Suppose the exchange value of the Japanese yen appreciates against other curren-

Table 15.3 Estimated Effects of a 1-Percent Dollar Appreciation on Prices of U.S. Steel Imports and Exports

	Price Change (%)
Import Price	
Hot-rolled sheet	−0.78%
Cold-rolled sheet	−0.36
Export Price	
Hot-rolled sheet	0.22
Cold-rolled sheet	0.52

Source: U.S. International Trade Commission, *Steel Industry Annual Report*, Washington, DC, September 1991, Appendix G.

cies, which causes Japanese goods to become less competitive in world markets. To insulate themselves from the squeeze on profits caused by the rising yen, Japanese companies could move production to affiliates located in countries whose currencies have depreciated against the yen. This would be most likely to occur if the yen's appreciation is sizable and is regarded as being permanent. Even if the yen's appreciation is not permanent, shifting production offshore can help reduce the uncertainties associated with currency swings. Indeed, Japanese companies have resorted to offshore production to protect themselves from an appreciating yen.

COST-CUTTING STRATEGIES OF JAPANESE MANUFACTURERS IN RESPONSE TO YEN APPRECIATION

From 1990 to 1996, the value of the Japanese yen relative to the U.S. dollar increased by almost 40 percent. In other words, if the yen and dollar prices in the two nations had remained unchanged, Japanese products in 1996 would have been roughly 40 percent more expensive, compared with U.S. products, than they were in 1990. How then did Japanese manufacturers respond to a development that could have had disastrous consequences for their competitiveness in world markets?

Japanese firms remained competitive by using the yen's strength to cheaply establish integrated manufacturing bases in the United States and in dollar-linked Asia. This allowed Japanese firms to play both sides of fluctuations in the yen/dollar exchange rate: using cheaper dollar-denominated parts and materials to offset higher yen-related costs. While they maintained their U.S. markets, many Japanese companies also used the strong yen to purchase cheaper components from around the world and ship them home for assembly. That provided a competitive edge in Japan for these firms.

Consider the Japanese electronics manufacturer Hitachi, whose TV sets were a global production effort in the mid-1990s, as shown in Figure

15.1. The small tubes that projected information onto Hitachi TV screens came from a subsidiary in South Carolina, while the TV chassis and circuitry were manufactured by an affiliate in Malaysia. From Japan came only computer chips and lenses, which amounted to 30 percent of the value of the parts used. By sourcing TV production in countries whose currencies had fallen against the yen, Hitachi was able hold down the dollar price of its TV sets in spite of the rising yen.

To limit their vulnerability to a rising yen, Japanese exporters also shifted production from commodity-type goods to high-value products. The demand for commodities—for example, metals and textiles—is quite sensitive to price changes because these goods are largely indistinguishable, except by price. Customers, therefore, could easily switch to non-Japanese suppliers if an increase in the yen shoved the dollar price of Japanese exports higher. In contrast, more sophisticated, high-value

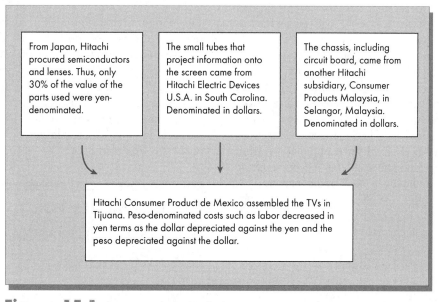

Figure 15.1 Coping with the Yen's Appreciation: Hitachi's Geographic Diversification as a Manufacturer of Television Sets

In 1995, Hitachi's global diversification permitted it to sell TVs in the United States without raising prices as the yen appreciated against the dollar.

Source: "What the Strong Yen Is Breeding: Japanese Multinationals," *Business Week*, April 10, 1995, p. 119.

products—for example, transportation equipment and electrical machinery—are less sensitive to price increases. For these goods, factors such as embedded advanced technology and high-quality standards work to neutralize the effect on demand if prices are driven up by an appreciating yen. Shifting production from commodity-type products to high-value products from 1990 to 1996 enhanced the competitiveness of Japanese firms.

Another example is the Japanese auto industry. To offset the rising yen, Japanese automakers cut the yen prices of their autos and thus realized falling unit-profit margins. They also reduced manufacturing costs by increasing worker productivity, importing materials and parts whose prices were denominated in currencies that had depreciated against the yen, and by outsourcing larger amounts of a vehicle's production to transplant factories in countries whose currencies had depreciated against the yen.

In 1994, Toyota Motor Corporation announced that its competitiveness had been eroded by as much as 20 percent as a result of the yen's recent appreciation. Toyota therefore convinced its subcontractors to cut part prices by 15 percent over three years. By using common parts in various vehicles and shortening the time needed to design, test, and commercialize automobiles, Toyota was also able to cut costs. Moreover, Toyota pressured Japanese steelmakers to produce less costly galvanized sheet steel for use in its vehicles. Finally, Toyota reintroduced less expensive models with fewer options in an effort to reduce costs and prices and thus recapture sales in the midsize-family-car segment of the market.

Foreign-made parts, once rejected by Japanese automakers as inferior to domestically produced parts, became much less alien to them in the 1990s. Foreign parts steadily made their way into Japanese autos, helped by both the strong yen and Japanese automakers' urgency to slash costs. Moreover, Japanese auto-parts makers set up manufacturing operations in Southeast Asia and South America to cut costs; these parts were then exported to Japan for assembly into autos. In 1995, for example, parts-manufacturing costs in the Philippines were estimated to be from 15 to 20 percent lower than in Japan, due to the strong yen and lower Philippine wage rates. By 1995,

Japanese automakers were importing some of their steel from low-cost South Korean steel companies rather than buying it from Japanese companies.

The yen's appreciation made it less costly for Japanese firms to build cars and trucks in the United States than in Japan. In 1995, Japanese firms made several production changes in response to these conditions:

- Toyota stopped exporting compact pickup trucks to the United States and expanded truck production at the NUMMI assembly plant that it shared with General Motors in the United States.
- Honda's Acura luxury division introduced a model to be designed and manufactured entirely by the company's U.S. operations. The company also announced plans for double-digit production increases at its U.S. and Canadian factories and expected to boost exports from Canada and the United States to more than 150,000 vehicles in 1999 from 75,000 in 1994.

Throughout 1996 and 1997, market forces reversed themselves, and the yen depreciated against the dollar. Japanese carmakers responded by reversing their previous policy of building autos in the United States; instead, they exported hundreds of thousands of them to America. Even Honda sharply curtailed its own imports of Made-in-America Hondas into Japan because of the strong dollar.

REQUIREMENTS FOR A SUCCESSFUL DEPRECIATION (DEVALUATION)

We have seen that currency depreciation tends to improve a nation's competitiveness by reducing its costs and prices, while currency appreciation implies the opposite. Under what circumstances will currency depreciation (devaluation) succeed in reducing a payments deficit?

Several approaches to currency depreciation (devaluation) must be considered, and each of them will be dealt with in a separate section. The **elasticity approach** emphasizes the relative *price effects* of depreciation and suggests that depreciation works best when demand elasticities are high. The **absorption approach** deals with the *income effects* of depreciation; the implication is that a decrease in domestic expenditure relative to income must occur for depreciation to promote payments equilibrium. The **monetary approach** stresses the effects depreciation has on the *purchasing power of money* and the resulting impact on domestic expenditure levels.

THE ELASTICITY APPROACH TO EXCHANGE-RATE ADJUSTMENT

Currency devaluation (depreciation) affects a country's balance of trade through changes in the relative prices of goods and services internationally. A trade-deficit nation may be able to reverse its imbalance by lowering its relative prices, so that exports increase and imports decrease. The nation can lower its relative prices by permitting its exchange rate to depreciate in a free market or by formally devaluing its currency under a system of fixed exchange rates. The ultimate outcome of currency depreciation (devaluation) depends on the price elasticity of demand for a nation's imports and the price elasticity of demand for its exports.

Recall that *elasticity of demand* refers to the responsiveness of buyers to changes in price. It indicates the percentage change in the quantity demanded stemming from a 1-percent change in price. Mathematically, elasticity is the ratio of the percentage change in the quantity demanded to the percentage change in price. This can be symbolized as

$$Elasticity = \frac{\Delta Q}{Q} \div \frac{\Delta P}{P}$$

The elasticity coefficient is stated numerically, without regard to the algebraic sign. If the preceding ratio exceeds 1, a given percentage change in price results in a larger percentage change in quantity

demanded; this is referred to as relatively *elastic demand*. If the ratio is less than 1, demand is said to be relatively *inelastic*, because the percentage change in quantity demanded is less than the percentage change in price. A ratio precisely equal to 1 denotes *unitary elastic demand*, meaning that the percentage change in quantity demanded just matches the percentage change in price.

Next we investigate the effects of a currency depreciation (devaluation) on a nation's balance of trade—that is, the value of its exports minus imports. Suppose the British monetary authorities decide to devalue the pound by 10 percent to correct a trade deficit with the United States. Whether the British trade balance will be improved depends on what happens to the dollar inpayments for Britain's exports as opposed to the dollar outpayments for its imports. This, in turn, depends on whether the U.S. demand for British exports is elastic or inelastic and whether the British demand for imports is elastic or inelastic.

Depending on the size of the demand elasticities for British exports and imports, Britain's trade balance may improve, worsen, or remain unchanged in response to the pound devaluation. The general rule that determines the actual outcome is the so-called **Marshall–Lerner condition**. The Marshall–Lerner condition states: (1) Devaluation (depreciation) will *improve* the trade balance if the devaluing nation's demand elasticity for imports plus the foreign demand elasticity for the nation's exports exceeds 1. (2) If the sum of the demand elasticities is less than 1, devaluation (depreciation) will *worsen* the trade balance. (3) The trade balance will be *neither helped nor hurt* if the sum of the demand elasticities equals 1. The Marshall–Lerner condition may be stated in terms of the currency of either the nation undergoing a devaluation (depreciation) or its trading partner. Our discussion is confined to the currency of the devaluing (depreciating) country, Great Britain.

CASE 1
Improved trade balance.

Referring to Table 15.4, assume that the British demand elasticity for imports equals 2.5 and the U.S. demand elasticity for British exports equals

CHEAP IMPORTS? NOT SO FAST

When East Asia's currencies crashed in 1997, many analysts predicted that a flood of cheap, East Asian exports would pour into the United States. As things turned out, however, East Asia's export boom met resistance.

The crash of East Asia's currencies provided an opportunity for Vigor International President Wang Yu-len. Like many Asian middlemen who exported handicrafts and garments to big retailers in the United States, Taipei-based Vigor relied heavily on low-cost factories in China. With the Thai baht, Malaysian ringgit, Indonesian rupiah, and Philippine peso all suddenly trading at less than half their old values against the dollar—while China's renminbi remained stable—Wang anticipated that bargains would be abundant in East Asia. But after a swing through East Asia in 1998, Wang returned empty-handed. Why? Most East Asian manufacturers sought foreign orders. However, they so lacked cash that they could not purchase the imported materials needed to run their factories. That made it much more difficult to generate the exports.

To the depressed economies of East Asia, the situation was frustrating. They had anticipated that their cheaper currencies would translate into a big increase in export competitiveness in everything from computer chips to toys, thus permitting their countries to quickly recover from the economic decline. However, this expectation did not materialize for many exporters. East Asian exporters could sell at a discount, but not so much that they could steal much market share from U.S. rivals.

East Asian exporters met resistance when nervous local suppliers, fearful of more currency depreciations, demanded dollars up front. Other key suppliers went bankrupt. Moreover, the region's financial systems were so squeezed that many manufacturers could not get financing to fill exports. For

many normally sound manufacturers, getting export financing from shell-shocked Asian banks was nearly impossible. A manager at a trading branch of an elite Korean conglomerate said his firm faced difficulty in all export areas, including machinery, electronics, automobiles, and textiles. Also, furniture makers noted that they were not able to purchase imported raw materials. To fill export orders, they had to draw down inventories. Financing costs also soared in East Asia after the currency crash. Interest rates in some countries tripled to around 30 percent, as panicked central banks attempted to stabilize currencies. The increases in financial costs added to the costs of goods sold abroad.

True, the depreciation in Southeast Asian currencies made the labor costs of East Asian manufacturers more competitive. However, this advantage was offset by higher import costs caused by depreciating currencies. Most East Asian producers purchased most of their raw materials and components from abroad and thus were sensitive to exchange-rate fluctuations. For example, Nike noted that 65 percent of the materials of its shoes made in Indonesia were imported. Inflation of raw-material costs thus negated most of the price cuts that would normally be expected to occur following a large depreciation in currency values.

In the United States, retailers initially expected discounts of 35 percent to 75 percent on items purchased from East Asia as a result of the currency realignment. However, East Asian manufacturers found that they could not afford to cut prices much more than 10 percent. This dampened the tidal wave of cheap exports going to the United States. Moreover, the Asian crisis amplified the commitment of U.S. producers to reduce costs and prices in an effort to protect their share of the market.

1.5; the sum of the elasticities is 4.0. To improve its payments position, Britain officially devalues the pound by 10 percent, which leads to a depreciation of the pound against the dollar by the same

amount. An assessment of the overall impact of the devaluation on Britain's payments position requires identification of the devaluation's impact on import expenditures and export receipts.

Table 15.4 British Devaluation: Improved Trade Balance

| Sector | Trade-Balance Effect | | |
	Change in Pound Price (%)	Change in Quantity Demanded (%)	Net Effect (in Pounds)
Import	+10	-25	-15% outpayments
Export	0	+15	+15% inpayments

Assumptions:
British demand elasticity for imports = 2.5 } Sum = 4.0
Demand elasticity for British exports = 1.5 }
Pound devaluation = 10%

If prices of imports remain constant in terms of foreign currency, then a devaluation increases the home-currency price of goods imported. Because of the devaluation, the pound price of British imports rises 10 percent. British consumers would thus be expected to reduce their purchases from abroad. Given an import demand elasticity of 2.5, the devaluation triggers a 25-percent decline in the quantity of imports demanded. The 10-percent price increase in conjunction with a 25-percent quantity reduction results in approximately a 15-percent decrease in British outpayments in pounds. This cutback in import purchases actually reduces import expenditures, which reduces the British deficit.

How about British export receipts? The pound price of the exports remains constant, but after devaluation of the pound, consumers in the United States find British exports costing 10 percent less in terms of dollars. Given a U.S. demand elasticity of 1.5 for British exports, the 10-percent British devaluation will stimulate foreign sales by 15 percent, so that export receipts in pounds will increase by approximately 15 percent. This strengthens the British payments position. The 15-percent reduction in import expenditures coupled with a 15-percent rise in export receipts means that the pound devaluation will reduce the British payments deficit. *With the sum of the elasticities exceeding 1, the devaluation strengthens Britain's trade position.*

CASE 2
Worsened trade balance.

In Table 15.5, the British demand elasticity for imports is 0.2 and the U.S. demand elasticity for British exports is 0.1; the sum of the elasticities is 0.3. The 10-percent British devaluation raises the pound price of imports by 10 percent, inducing a 2-percent reduction in the quantity of imports demanded. In contrast to the previous case, under relatively inelastic conditions the devaluation contributes to an *increase*, rather than a decrease, in import expenditures of some 8 percent. As before, the pound price of British exports is unaffected by the devaluation, whereas the dollar price of exports falls 10 percent. U.S. purchases from abroad increase by 1 percent, resulting in an increase in pound receipts of about 1 percent. With expenditures on imports rising 8 percent while export receipts increase only 1 percent, the British deficit will tend to *worsen*. As stated in the Marshall–Lerner condition, *if the sum of the elasticities is less than 1, devaluation will cause a deterioration in a nation's trade position.* The reader is left to verify that a nation's trade balance remains unaffected by devaluation if the sum of the demand elasticities equals 1.

Although the Marshall–Lerner condition provides a general rule as to when a currency devaluation (depreciation) will be successful in restoring payments equilibrium, it depends on some simplifying assumptions. For one, it is assumed

Table 15.5 British Devaluation: Worsened Trade Balance

Sector	Change in Pound Price (%)	Change in Quantity Demanded (%)	Net Effect (in Pounds)
		Trade-Balance Effect	
Import	+10	−2	+8% outpayments
Export	0	+1	+1% inpayments

Assumptions:
British demand elasticity for imports = 0.2 ⎱ Sum = 0.3
U.S. demand elasticity for British exports = 0.1 ⎰
Pound devaluation = 10%

that a nation's trade balance is in equilibrium when the devaluation occurs. If there is initially a very large trade deficit, with imports exceeding exports, then a devaluation might cause import expenditures to change more than export receipts, even though the sum of the demand elasticities exceeds 1. The analysis also assumes no change in the sellers' prices in their own currency. But this may not always be true. To protect their competitive position, foreign sellers may lower their prices in response to a home-country devaluation; domestic sellers may raise home-currency prices so that the devaluation's effects are not fully transmitted into lower foreign-exchange prices for their goods. However, neither of these assumptions invalidates the Marshall–Lerner condition's spirit, which suggests that devaluations work best when demand elasticities are high.

EMPIRICAL MEASUREMENT: IMPORT/EXPORT DEMAND ELASTICITIES

The Marshall–Lerner condition illustrates the price effects of a nation's depreciation (devaluation) on its trade balance. The extent to which price changes affect the volume of goods traded depends on the elasticity of demand for imports and exports. If the elasticities were known in advance, it would be possible to determine the proper exchange-rate policy to restore payments equilibrium. Without such knowledge, nations often have been reluctant to change the par values of their currencies.

During the 1940s and 1950s, there was considerable debate among economists concerning the empirical measurement of demand elasticities. Several early studies suggested low demand elasticities. Those findings led to the formation of the *elasticity pessimist* school of thought, which contended that currency devaluations and revaluations would be largely ineffectual in promoting changes in a nation's trade balance. By the 1960s, most economists considered themselves *elasticity optimists*, estimating the demand elasticities for most nations to be rather high. Table 15.6 shows estimated price elasticities of demand for total imports and exports by country.

TIME PATH OF DEPRECIATION (DEVALUATION)

Empirical estimates of price elasticities in international trade suggest that, according to the Marshall–Lerner condition, devaluation (depreciation) is likely to improve a nation's trade balance. A basic problem in measuring world price elasticities, however, is that there tends to be a *time lag* between changes in exchange rates and their ultimate effect on real trade. One popular description of the time path of trade flows is the so-called **J-curve effect**. This view suggests that in the very short run, a currency devaluation will lead to a worsening of a nation's trade balance. But as time passes, the trade balance will likely improve. This is because it takes time for new information about the price effects of devaluation to be disseminated throughout the economy and for economic units to adjust their behavior accordingly.

Table 15.6 Price Elasticities of Demand for Total Imports and Exports of Selected Countries

Country	Import Price Elasticity	Export Price Elasticity	Sum of Import and Export Elasticities
United States	0.92	0.99	1.91
United Kingdom	0.47	0.44	0.91
Germany	0.60	0.66	1.26
Japan	0.93	0.93	1.86
Canada	1.02	0.83	1.85
Other developed countries	0.49	0.83	1.32
Less developed countries	0.81	0.63	1.44
OPEC	1.14	0.57	1.71

Source: Jaime Marques, "Bilateral Trade Elasticities," *Review of Economics and Statistics*, 72, No. 1, February 1990, pp. 75–76.

J-CURVE EFFECT. A currency devaluation (depreciation) affects a nation's trade balance through its net impact on export receipts and import expenditures. Export receipts and import expenditures are calculated by multiplying the commodity's per-unit price times the quantity being demanded. Figure 15.2 illustrates the process by which devaluation influences export receipts and import expenditures.

The immediate effect of devaluation is a change in relative prices. If a nation devalues its currency 10 percent, it means that import prices initially increase 10 percent in terms of the home currency. The quantity of imports demanded will then fall according to home demand elasticities. At the same time, exporters will initially receive 10 percent more in home currency for each unit of foreign currency they earn. This means they can become more competitive and lower their export prices measured in terms of foreign currencies. Export sales will then rise in accordance with foreign demand elasticities. The problem with this process is that for devaluation to take effect, time is required for the pricing mechanism to induce changes in the volume of exports and imports.

The time path of the response of trade flows to a devaluation can be described in terms of the J-curve effect, so called because the trade balance continues to get worse for a while after devaluation (sliding down the hook of the J) and then gets better (moving up the stem of the J). This effect

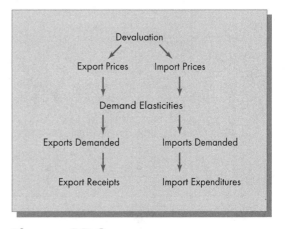

Figure 15.2 Devaluation Flowchart

occurs because the initial effect of devaluation is an increase in import expenditures: The home-currency price of imports has risen, but the volume is unchanged owing to prior commitments. As time passes, the quantity adjustment effect becomes relevant: import volume is depressed, whereas exports become more attractive to foreign buyers.

Advocates of the J-curve effect use the devaluation of the British pound as an example. In 1967, the British balance of trade showed a $1.3 billion deficit. To improve its trade position, Britain devalued the pound by 14.3 percent in November 1967. The initial impact of the devaluation was negative: In 1968, the British balance of trade showed a $3 billion deficit. After a lag, however, the British balance of trade improved, with a reduction in the growth of imports and a rise in the growth of exports. By 1969, the British balance of trade showed a $1 billion surplus; by 1971, the surplus was $6.5 billion.

Another example of the J-curve effect is the experience of the U.S. balance of trade during the 1980s and 1990s. As seen in Figure 15.3, between 1980 and 1987 the U.S. trade deficit expanded at a very rapid rate. The deficit decreased substantially between 1988 and 1991. The rapid increase in the trade deficit that took place during the early 1980s occurred mainly because of the appreciation of the dollar at the time, which resulted in a steady increase in imports and a drop in U.S.

exports. The depreciation of the dollar that began in 1985 led to a boom in exports in 1988 and a drop in the trade deficit through 1991.

What factors might explain the time lags in a devaluation's adjustment process? The types of lags that may occur between changes in relative prices and the quantities of goods traded include the following:

- *Recognition lags* of changing competitive conditions
- *Decision lags* in forming new business connections and placing new orders
- *Delivery lags* between the time new orders are placed and their impact on trade and payment flows is felt

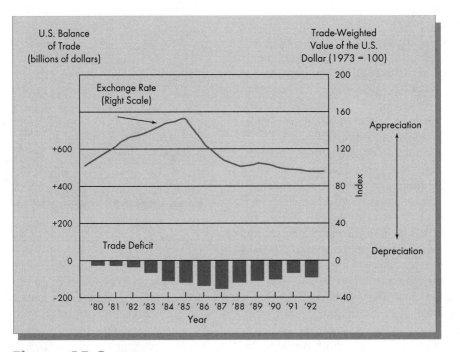

Figure 15.3 Time Path of U.S. Balance of Trade, in Billions of Dollars, in Response to Dollar Appreciation and Depreciation

Between 1980 and 1987, the U.S. merchandise trade deficit expanded at a rapid rate. The trade deficit decreased substantially between 1988 and 1991. The rapid increase in the trade deficit that took place during the early 1980s occurred mainly because of the appreciation of the dollar at the time, which resulted in a steady increase in imports and a drop in U.S. exports. The depreciation of the dollar that began in 1985 led to a boom in exports in 1988 and a drop in the trade deficit through 1991.

- *Replacement lags* in using up inventories and wearing out existing machinery before placing new orders
- *Production lags* involved in increasing the output of commodities for which demand has increased

Empirical evidence suggests that the trade-balance effects of devaluation do not materialize until years afterward. Adjustment lags may be four years or more, although the major portion of adjustment takes place in about two years. One study made the following estimates of the lags in the devaluation adjustment process for trade in manufactured goods: (1) The response of trade flows to relative price changes stretches out over a period of some four to five years. (2) Following a price change, almost 50 percent of the full trade-flow response occurs within the first three years, and about 90 percent takes place during the first five years.[1]

The experience of the United States during the 1980s is consistent with the idea of time lags in the market adjustment to changes in the exchange rate. The dollar appreciated by almost 60 percent, against the currencies of the major industrial nations, from the second quarter of 1980 to the first quarter of 1985; however, the U.S. current account did not begin to deteriorate until the first quarter of 1983. Moreover, the dollar continued to depreciate from the first quarter of 1985 through the end of 1990; however, the U.S. current account balance did not start to improve until the third quarter of 1987. Consistent with the J-curve concept, the U.S. current account balance during the 1980s appeared to respond to exchange-rate movements only after a lengthy time lag.

CURRENCY PASS-THROUGH. The J-curve analysis assumes that a given change in the exchange rate brings about a proportionate change in import prices. In practice, this relationship may be less than proportionate, thus weakening the influence of a change in the exchange rate on the volume of trade.

The extent to which changing currency values lead to changes in import and export prices is known as the **currency pass-through** relationship. Pass-through is important because buyers have incentives to alter their purchases of foreign goods only to the extent that the prices of these goods change in terms of their domestic currency following a change in the exchange rate. This depends on the willingness of exporters to permit the change in the exchange rate to affect the prices they charge for their goods, measured in terms of the buyer's currency.

Assume that Toyota of Japan exports autos to the United States and that the prices of Toyota are fixed in terms of the yen. Suppose the dollar's value depreciates 10 percent relative to the yen. Assuming no offsetting actions by Toyota, U.S. import prices will rise 10 percent. This is because 10 percent more dollars are needed to purchase the yen that are used to pay for the import purchases. *Complete pass-through* thus exists: Import prices in dollars rise by the full proportion of the dollar depreciation.

To illustrate the calculation of complete currency pass-through, assume that Caterpillar charges $50,000 for a tractor exported to Japan. If the exchange rate is 150 yen per U.S. dollar, the price paid by the Japanese buyer will be 7,500,000 yen. Assuming the dollar price of the tractor remains constant, a 10-percent appreciation in the dollar's exchange value will increase the tractor's yen price 10 percent, to 8,250,000 yen (165 × 50,000 = 8,250,000). Conversely, if the dollar depreciates by 10 percent, the yen price of the tractor will fall by 10 percent, to 6,750,000. So long as Caterpillar keeps the dollar price of its tractor constant, changes in the dollar's exchange rate will be fully reflected in changes in the foreign-currency price of exports. The ratio of changes in the foreign-currency price to changes in the exchange rate will be 100 percent, implying complete currency pass-through.

Empirical evidence suggests, however, that the more typical real-world situation is *partial pass-through*, with significant time lags. Concerning the United States, it is estimated that for every 10-percent change in the value of the dollar, both

[1] Helen Junz and Rudolf R. Rhomberg, "Price Competitiveness in Export Trade among Industrial Countries," *American Economic Review*, May 1973, pp. 412–419.

import prices and export prices change about 6 percent. Moreover, exchange-rate changes tend to be absorbed by profit margins for as long as two years or more before affecting product prices. These lags depend on the length of time before dollar-denominated contracts expire as well as on the extent to which businesses view exchange-rate changes as permanent rather than temporary.

The dollar depreciation of the mid-1980s provides an example of partial currency pass-through. Following a five-year rise in value, the dollar began to depreciate in 1985. By 1986, the value of the dollar had fallen more than 25 percent against the currencies of the major U.S. trading partners on a trade-weighted basis and more than 47 percent against the Japanese yen. Other things being equal, the dollar depreciation should have led to higher U.S. exports and lower U.S. imports. But other things were not equal. Foreign manufacturers, particularly the Japanese, were not willing to sacrifice their share of the U.S. market without a struggle.

Rather than permit increases in the prices of their goods sold in the United States, Japanese firms absorbed the dollar depreciation in reduced profits—and even losses—which triggered accusations of dumping by their U.S. competitors. But Japanese companies could not cut profits or absorb losses indefinitely. Therefore, many concerns attempted to reduce manufacturing costs, either by leaving Japan for lower-cost sites such as South Korea or by overhauling products and factories in Japan. The result was only a partial pass-through of the dollar depreciation into retail price increases in the United States.

Prior to the dollar depreciation, Japanese automakers enjoyed an estimated 12-percent profit margin on their exports to the United States—nearly double that of U.S. companies. As a way of compensating for the depreciating dollar, throughout 1986 Japanese automakers pared profits by some $518 per vehicle. Yet foreign businesses could not persistently operate on razor-thin profit margins because they would lack money for product development and sales promotion. Eventually the businesses would have to reduce their emphasis on market share, and the

U.S. trade deficit would shrink. However, it was estimated that if foreigners kept profit margins thin, they could preserve their market share for two years or longer.

U.S. imports also remained strong because of pricing policies of U.S. companies. As foreign prices inched upward as a result of the dollar depreciation, many U.S. businesses followed the price increases, although at a slower rate. In April 1986, General Motors surprised the auto industry with price increases, which were matched by Ford in July. It was argued that with such price hikes, U.S. companies would fritter away a chance to increase market share and close the U.S. trade deficit.

Currency pass-through also had implications for U.S. exporters. A factor that contributed to sluggish U.S. exports was that U.S. prices in foreign markets did not fall proportionate to the dollar depreciation, implying partial pass-through. Throughout 1986, many U.S. exporters sought to restore profit margins, which had deteriorated when the dollar was so strong in the early 1980s, by maintaining or even increasing export prices.

Other U.S. exporters passed through the dollar depreciation as price reductions, only to have these reductions offset by foreign intermediaries along the distribution network who pocketed the price cuts instead of passing them through to customers. A survey of Japan's Ministry of International Trade and Industry found that only 10 to 15 percent of the savings from the dollar's depreciation were passed through to Japanese customers via price cuts in 1986. Moreover, some U.S. companies that cut export prices in 1986 were hampered by the aggressive price cuts of foreign competitors intent on maintaining market share.

THE PASS-THROUGH EFFECT AND PROFIT MARGINS. In this chapter, we learned how changing currency values result in changes in import and export prices, a process known as the currency pass-through relationship. What explains the magnitude of the pass-through effect?

Data concerning U.S. trade show that changing profit margins are a significant factor in explaining the size of the pass-through effect. Researchers at the Federal Reserve analyzed prices and profit margins for the 1977–1980 period of dollar depreciation (15.5 percent) and the 1980–1985 period of dollar appreciation (74.9 percent). Table 15.7 shows the evidence for U.S. imports and exports.

Concerning the evidence regarding U.S. *imports*, notice that during the period of dollar depreciation, foreign firms usually reduced profit margins. This meant that the dollar price of foreign goods sold in the United States did not increase by the full amount of the dollar depreciation. When the dollar appreciated during the period 1980–1985, foreign firms increased their profit margins on goods shipped to the United States. Therefore, the dollar price of such foreign goods did not decrease by the full amount of the dollar appreciation. The experience of the U.S. import sector thus shows that there was

only a modest pass-through of changing currency values to changes in import prices during these periods.

The lower portion of the table considers U.S. *exports*. During the 1977–1980 period of dollar depreciation and the 1980–1985 period of dollar appreciation, the profit margins of U.S. exporters changed by small amounts compared to the changes in the dollar's exchange rate. This may have been caused by the large size of the home market in the United States: Pricing decisions by U.S. companies may have been more closely tied to domestic market conditions than to global conditions. As a result, there was significant pass-through of changing currency values to changes in export prices during these periods. Conclusion: The foreign-currency prices of U.S. exports are more likely to have a significant pass-through of exchange-rate changes than the dollar prices of U.S. imports are.

Table 15.7 Percentage Change in Profit Margins for Selected U.S. Industries

Industry	1977–1980	1980–1985
Exchange Value of the Dollar	–15.5%	74.9%
Imports		
Leather footwear	–4.2	87.3
Textiles	–9.1	28.0
Construction machinery	–9.2	11.6
Paper products	–2.3	17.6
Apparel	–4.9	4.1
Canned fruits and vegetables	–14.1	6.8
Steel	14.6	4.1
Exports		
Semiconductors	–5.9	–9.6
Power-driven hand tools	–5.0	–6.9
Pulp-mill products	4.6	–17.1
Internal combustion engines	–4.5	4.2
Valves and pipe fittings	–2.7	8.7
Oil-field and gas-field equipment	–2.0	1.0
Printing trades machinery	–3.9	5.3
Farm machinery	–2.9	4.5
Meat packing	–3.6	17.7

Source: Catherine Mann, "Prices, Profit Margins, and Exchange Rates," *Federal Reserve Bulletin*, June 1986. See also Joseph Gagnon and Michael Knetter, "Markup Adjustment and Exchange Rate Fluctuations: Evidence from Panel Data on Automobiles," *Journal of International Money and Finance*, April 1995.

INFLATION WORKS AGAINST THE GAINS OF DEPRECIATION

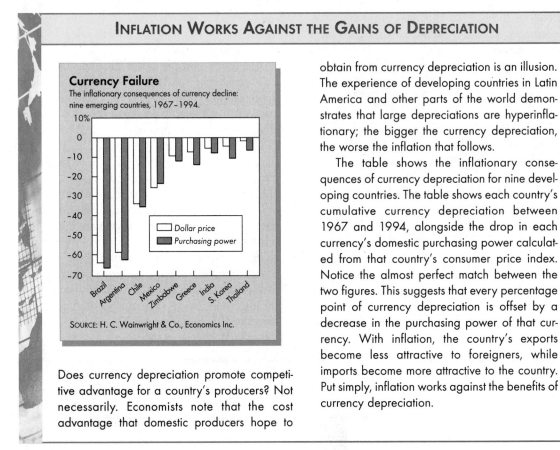

Currency Failure
The inflationary consequences of currency decline: nine emerging countries, 1967–1994.

SOURCE: H. C. Wainwright & Co., Economics Inc.

Does currency depreciation promote competitive advantage for a country's producers? Not necessarily. Economists note that the cost advantage that domestic producers hope to obtain from currency depreciation is an illusion. The experience of developing countries in Latin America and other parts of the world demonstrates that large depreciations are hyperinflationary; the bigger the currency depreciation, the worse the inflation that follows.

The table shows the inflationary consequences of currency depreciation for nine developing countries. The table shows each country's cumulative currency depreciation between 1967 and 1994, alongside the drop in each currency's domestic purchasing power calculated from that country's consumer price index. Notice the almost perfect match between the two figures. This suggests that every percentage point of currency depreciation is offset by a decrease in the purchasing power of that currency. With inflation, the country's exports become less attractive to foreigners, while imports become more attractive to the country. Put simply, inflation works against the benefits of currency depreciation.

Source: David Ranson, "Inflation Steals the Benefits of Devaluation," *The Wall Street Journal*, April 28, 1998, p. A18.

THE DOLLAR AND U.S. MANUFACTURING

As we have learned, a dollar appreciation can affect the revenues and costs of U.S. manufacturers. Concerning revenues, a stronger dollar pushes up the prices of U.S. goods in export markets, making those goods less attractive to foreign buyers and ultimately resulting in reduced export sales for U.S. producers. Also a stronger dollar can jeopardize the domestic sales of U.S. manufacturers by giving the foreign producers that have penetrated U.S. markets a competitive edge in pricing. For example, if the dollar appreciates against the yen, then Japanese producers selling to U.S. markets will find that their dollar revenues translate into more yen than in the past. This increase in their "local currency profit" enables the Japanese producers to reduce the prices they charge in U.S. markets and thus to draw customers away from rival U.S. producers.

A stronger dollar also affects the costs of U.S. manufacturers. In recent years, U.S. firms have increasingly relied on foreign equipment and components in producing their goods. When the dollar rises, the cost of such imported inputs falls. The resulting savings can at least partially offset the revenue losses associated with a dollar appreciation and thereby help to stabilize industries' profits. Indeed, for some industries, the cost benefits of the appreciation may outweigh the adverse revenue effects.

Economists at the Federal Reserve Bank of New York have captured both the revenue and cost sides of an industry's exposure to dollar movements by constructing a measure called "net external orientation." This measure is computed as the share of an industry's total revenues that is derived from exports less the share of its total spending that is attributable to imported inputs. An industry has a positive (negative) net external orientation when its export revenues are greater (less) than its imported input costs.

To assess the vulnerability of U.S. manufacturers to a rise in the dollar's exchange value, refer to Table 15.8. In many industries, exports represent a large fraction of total revenues: Chemicals, industrial machinery, electronic equipment, transportation, equipment, and instruments generate more than 15 percent of their revenues through exports. This shared focus on exports would seem to suggest that the profitability of all these industries would suffer significantly under a dollar appreciation. But once we take into account the offsetting effects of imported input use, we find that these industries would not, in fact, all fare alike with a rise in the dollar.

In the electronic equipment industry, exports account for 24.2 percent of revenues, while imported inputs account for a much smaller share of costs—11.6 percent. Subtracting the imported input share from the export share yields a relatively high net external orientation of 12.6 percent. By contrast, in the transportation equipment industry, the share of total revenues attributable to exports is a sizable 17.8 percent, but spending on imports—15.7 percent of total spending—largely offsets the high export share, producing a net external orientation of only 2.1 percent. The contrasting net figures for the two industries indicate that a strong dollar is likely to have significant adverse effects on the profitability of U.S. electronic equipment manufacturers, while the profitability of the transportation equipment industry should be more insulated from exchange rate effects. As Table 15.8 shows, the industries most likely to be hurt by a stronger dollar are those with high net external orientation—tobacco, industrial machinery, electronic equipment, and instruments. For some industries, such as petroleum refining and leather

Table 15.8 Trade Orientation of U.S. Manufacturing Industries in 1995

Industry	Export Revenues as a Percent of Total Revenues	Imported Input Spending as a Percent of Total Spending	Net External Orientation	
Instruments	21.3	6.3	15.0	Profits More Vulnerable
Industrial machinery	25.8	11.0	14.8	to a Dollar Appreciation
Electronic equipment	24.2	11.6	12.6	
Tobacco products	14.0	2.1	11.9	↑
Chemicals	15.8	6.3	9.5	
Apparel	7.4	3.2	4.2	
Rubber and plastics	9.2	5.3	3.9	
Lumber	7.6	4.3	3.3	
Transportation equipment	17.8	15.7	2.1	
Food products	5.9	4.2	1.7	
Stone and concrete products	5.6	4.7	0.9	↓
Petroleum refining	3.9	5.3	-1.4	Profits Less Vulnerable
Leather products	14.4	20.5	-6.1	to a Dollar Appreciation

Source: Linda Goldberg and Keith Crockett, "The Dollar and U.S. Manufacturing," *Current Issues in Economics and Finance*, Federal Reserve Bank of New York, November 1998, p. 3.

WILL THE STRONGER POUND DRIVE JAPANESE CAR MAKERS OUT OF THE UNITED KINGDOM?

At the turn of the millennium, the appreciation of the pound against the euro tested the patience of the big Japanese auto makers that emerged as the backbone of Britain's auto industry now that others have sold out, packed up, or withered away. The question being asked in the U.K. by Toyota, Nissan, and Honda was whether they would stay or would exit, too.

From 1999 to 2000, the pound appreciated 16 percent against the euro. The strong pound made British-manufactured products more expensive to consumers on the Continent (Western Europe). Toyota, Nissan, and Honda booked most of their parts and costs in pounds. With the majority of their sales going to the Continent, that hurt. About half of what went into Toyota cars was purchased in the U.K., and half on the Continent. But 80 percent of sales were to the 11 Continental nations that used the euro.

Determined to increase their European market share, the Japanese were reluctant to pass the exchange-rate costs on to Continental customers in the form of higher prices. Toyota, Nissan, and Honda together had only 7.6 percent of Western Europe's car market in 2000. However, it was difficult to remain competitive in the face of climbing costs. Industry sources noted that Nissan was losing money on its Micra model, even though it was manufactured at the most efficient auto plant in Europe, the Sunderland facility in northeast England.

Nissan and Toyota wouldn't rule out moving production to the Continent. But analysts questioned whether they really would go. These companies make their location decisions based on the fundamentals—which in Britain's favor included the English language and lower labor costs. The weak euro was not considered to be a fundamental.

In reaction to the appreciating pound, each Japanese company tried to cut costs to protect profits. Nissan aimed at a 30-percent reduction at its Sunderland factory and pressed U.K. suppliers to reduce prices. Honda asked its suppliers to cut costs 10 percent to 20 percent.

And it wasn't easy simply to switch sourcing to eurozone suppliers: The Japanese have long-standing relationships with U.K. suppliers, with which they often work closely to develop components. While the Japanese complained, other auto makers did more than talk. In 2000, Germany's Bayerische Motoren Werke AG sold Britain's Rover Group to a British consortium; it blamed the strong pound for its difficulties. Moreover, Ford Motor Co. announced plans to stop manufacturing cars at its London plant and to move production of its Fiesta model to Germany.

In the short term, the Japanese didn't have much flexibility. Unlike their European and American competitors, they had little manufacturing capacity in Europe outside of the U.K.; of the three, only Nissan operated a plant on the Continent. However, Nissan stated that it would make a decision by 2001 whether to manufacture the next-generation Micra at the Sunderland plant in the U.K. or in France with its partner, Renault. Moreover, Toyota announced that it would open a new factory in 2001 in France, where it would manufacture its popular Yaris; a company spokesman wouldn't rule out the possibility of shifting production from the U.K. to that factory.

Source: "Will Japan's Car Makers Leave the U.K.?" *The Wall Street Journal*, September 5, 2000, p. A–28.

products, the cost benefits of a dollar appreciation outweigh and adverse revenue effects.

U.S. manufacturing industries are becoming increasingly sensitive to changes in the international value of the dollar. This increased sensitivity is largely attributable to the growing reliance of this sector on international trade. Firms now export a greater share of their products than in the past and make more extensive use of foreign parts and materials in the production of their goods.

THE ABSORPTION APPROACH TO EXCHANGE-RATE ADJUSTMENT

According to the elasticities approach, currency devaluation offers a price incentive to reduce imports and increase exports. But even if elasticity conditions are favorable, whether the home country's trade balance will actually improve may depend on how the economy reacts to the devaluation. The *absorption approach*[2] provides insights into this question by considering the impact of devaluation on the spending behavior of the domestic economy and the influence of domestic spending on the trade balance.

The absorption approach starts with the idea that the value of total domestic output (Y) equals the level of total spending. Total spending consists of consumption (C), investment (I), government expenditures (G), and net exports ($X - M$). This can be written as

$$Y = C + I + G + (X - M)$$

The absorption approach then consolidates $C + I + G$ into a single term A, which is referred to as absorption, and designates net exports ($X - M$) as B. Total domestic output thus equals the sum of absorption plus net exports, or

$$Y = A + B$$

This can be rewritten as

$$B = Y - A$$

This expression suggests that the balance of trade (B) equals the difference between total domestic output (Y) and the level of absorption (A). If national output exceeds domestic absorption, the economy's trade balance will be positive. Conversely, a negative trade balance suggests that an economy is spending beyond its ability to produce.

The absorption approach predicts that a currency devaluation will improve an economy's trade balance only if national output rises relative to absorption. This means that a country must increase its total output, reduce its absorption, or do some combination of the two. The following examples illustrate these possibilities.

Assume that an economy faces *unemployment* as well as a *trade deficit*. With the economy operating below maximum capacity, the price incentives of devaluation would tend to direct idle resources into the production of goods for export, in addition to diverting spending away from imports to domestically produced substitutes. The impact of the devaluation is thus to expand domestic output as well as to improve the trade balance. It is no wonder that policy makers tend to view currency devaluation as an effective tool when an economy faces unemployment with a trade deficit.

In the case of an economy operating at *full employment*, however, there are no unutilized resources available for additional production. National output is at a fixed level. The only way in which devaluation can improve the trade balance is for the economy to somehow cut domestic absorption, freeing resources needed to produce additional export goods and import substitutes. For example, domestic policy makers could decrease absorption by adopting restrictive fiscal and monetary policies in the face of higher prices resulting from the devaluation. But this would result in sacrifice on the part of those who bear the burden of such measures. Devaluation may thus be considered inappropriate when an economy is operating at maximum capacity.

The absorption approach goes beyond the elasticity approach, which views the economy's trade balance as distinct from the rest of the economy. Instead, devaluation is viewed in relation to the economy's utilization of its resources and level of production. The two approaches are therefore complementary.

2 Sidney S. Alexander, "Effects of a Devaluation on a Trade Balance," *IMF Staff Papers*, April 1952, pp. 263–278.

THE MONETARY APPROACH TO EXCHANGE-RATE ADJUSTMENT

A survey of the traditional approaches to devaluation reveals a major shortcoming. According to the elasticities and absorption approaches, monetary consequences are not associated with balance-of-payments adjustment; or, to the extent that such consequences exist, they can be neutralized by domestic monetary authorities. The elasticities and absorption approaches apply only to the trade account of the balance of payments, neglecting the implications of capital movements. The *monetary approach* to devaluation addresses this shortcoming.[3]

According to the monetary approach, currency devaluation may induce a *temporary* improvement in a nation's balance-of-payments position. For example, assume that equilibrium initially exists in the home country's money market. A devaluation of the home currency would increase the price level—that is, the domestic-currency prices of potential imports and exports. This increase would increase the demand for money, because larger amounts of money are needed for transactions. If that increased demand is not fulfilled from domestic sources, an inflow of money from overseas occurs. This inflow results in a balance-of-payments surplus and a rise in international reserves. But the surplus does not last forever. By adding to the international component of the home-country money supply, the devaluation leads to an increase in spending (absorption), which reduces the surplus. The surplus eventually disappears when equilibrium is restored in the home country's money market. The effects of devaluation on real economic variables are thus temporary. *Over the long run, currency devaluation merely raises the domestic price level.*

[3] See Donald S. Kemp, "A Monetary View of the Balance of Payments," *Review*, Federal Reserve Bank of St. Louis, April 1975, pp. 14–22; and Thomas M. Humphrey, "The Monetary Approach to Exchange Rates: Its Historical Evolution and Role in Policy Debates," *Economic Review*, Federal Reserve Bank of Richmond, July–August 1978, pp. 2–9.

SUMMARY

1. Currency depreciation or devaluation may affect a nation's trade position through its impact on relative prices, incomes, and purchasing power of money balances.
2. When all of a firm's inputs are acquired domestically and their costs are denominated in the domestic currency, an appreciation in the domestic currency's exchange value tends to increase the firm's costs by the same proportion, in terms of the foreign currency. Conversely, a depreciation of the domestic currency's exchange value tends to reduce the firm's costs by the same proportion in terms of the foreign currency.
3. Manufacturers often obtain inputs from abroad (foreign sourcing) whose costs are denominated in terms of a foreign currency. As foreign-currency-denominated costs become a larger portion of a producer's total costs, an appreciation of the domestic currency's exchange value leads to a smaller increase in the foreign-currency cost of the firm's output and a larger decrease in the domestic cost of the firm's output—compared to the cost changes that occur when all input costs are denominated in the domestic currency. The opposite applies for currency depreciation.
4. By increasing (decreasing) relative U.S. production costs, a dollar appreciation (depreciation) tends to raise (lower) U.S. export prices in terms of a foreign currency, which induces a decrease (increase) in the quantity of U.S. goods sold abroad; similarly, a dollar

appreciation (depreciation) tends to raise (lower) the amount of U.S. imports.

5. According to the elasticities approach, currency depreciation or devaluation leads to the greatest improvement in a country's trade position when demand elasticities are high. Recent empirical studies indicate that the estimated demand elasticities for most nations are quite high.

6. The time path of currency depreciation or devaluation can be explained in terms of the J-curve effect. According to this concept, the response of trade flows to changes in relative prices increases with the passage of time. Currency depreciation tends to worsen a country's trade balance in the short run, only to be followed by an improvement in the long run (assuming favorable elasticities).

7. The extent to which exchange-rate changes lead to changes in import prices and export prices is known as the pass-through relationship. Complete (partial) pass-through occurs when a change in the exchange rate brings

about a proportionate (less than proportionate) change in export prices and import prices. Empirical evidence suggests that pass-through tends to be partial rather than complete.

8. The absorption approach emphasizes the income effects of currency devaluation. According to this view, a devaluation may initially stimulate a nation's exports and production of import-competing goods. But this will promote excess domestic spending unless real output can be expanded or domestic absorption reduced. The result would be a return to a payments deficit.

9. The monetary approach to devaluation emphasizes the effect that devaluation has on the purchasing power of money balances and the resulting impacts on domestic expenditures and import levels. According to the monetary approach, the influence of currency devaluation on real output is temporary; over the long run, devaluation merely raises the domestic price level.

STUDY QUESTIONS

1. How does a currency depreciation or devaluation affect a nation's balance of trade?

2. Three major approaches to analyzing the economic impact of currency depreciation or devaluation are (a) the elasticities approach, (b) the absorption approach, and (c) the monetary approach. Distinguish among the three.

3. What is meant by the Marshall–Lerner condition? Do recent empirical studies suggest that world elasticity conditions are sufficiently high to permit successful depreciations or devaluations?

4. How does the J-curve effect relate to the time path of currency depreciation or devaluation?

5. What implications does currency pass-through have for a nation whose currency depreciates or is devalued?

6. According to the absorption approach, does it make any difference whether a nation devalues

its currency when the economy is operating at less than full capacity versus at full capacity?

7. How can devaluation-induced changes in household money balances promote payments equilibrium?

8. Suppose ABC Inc., a U.S. auto manufacturer, obtains all of its auto components in the United States and that its costs are denominated in dollars. Assume the dollar's exchange value appreciates by 50 percent against the Mexican peso. What impact does the dollar appreciation have on the firm's international competitiveness? What about a dollar depreciation?

9. Suppose ABC Inc., a U.S. auto manufacturer, obtains some of its auto components in Mexico and that the costs of these components are denominated in pesos; the costs of the remaining components are denominated in dollars. Assume the dollar's exchange value

appreciates by 50 percent against the peso. Compared to your answer in study question 8, what impact will the dollar appreciation have on the firm's international competitiveness? What about a dollar depreciation?

10. Assume the United States exports 1,000 computers at a price of $3,000 each and imports 150 British autos at a price of £10,000 each. Assume that the dollar/pound exchange rate is 2 dollars per pound.

   a. Calculate, in dollar terms, the U.S. export receipts, import payments, and trade balance prior to a depreciation of the dollar's exchange value.

   b. Suppose the dollar's exchange value depreciates by 10 percent. Assuming that the price elasticity of demand for U.S. exports equals 3.0 and the price elasticity of demand for U.S. imports equals 2.0, calculate the U.S. export receipts, import payments, and trade balance. Does the dollar depreciation improve or worsen the U.S. trade balance? Why?

   c. Now assume that the price elasticity of demand for U.S. exports equals 0.3 and the price elasticity of demand for U.S. imports equals 0.2. Does this change the outcome? Why?

NetLink

15.1 Changes in the exchange rate can have a significant impact on various sectors of the economy. For a detailed look at the various countries' exports and imports of agricultural products to the U.S., visit the home page of the U.S. Department of Agriculture/Foreign Agricultural Service. Set your browser to URL:

http://www.fas.usda.gov/

15.2 The Council on Foreign Relations is a national organization that is committed to the study and debate of America's global role. Visit its Web site to view some of their recent studies on international finance and trade. Set your browser to URL:

http://www.cfr.org/p/

To access NetLink Exercises and the Virtual Scavenger Hunt, visit the Carbaugh Web site at http://carbaugh.swcollege.com.

Exchange-Rate Systems

Previous chapters have discussed the determination of exchange rates and their effects on the balance of payments. This chapter surveys the exchange-rate practices that have been used during the post–World War II era. The discussion focuses on the nature and operation of actual exchange-rate systems and identifies economic factors that influence the choice of alternative exchange-rate systems.

EXCHANGE-RATE PRACTICES

In choosing an exchange-rate system, a nation must decide whether to allow its currency to be determined by free-market forces (floating rate) or to be fixed (pegged) against some standard of value. If a nation adopts floating rates, it must decide whether to float independently, to float in unison with a group of other currencies, or to crawl according to a predetermined formula such as relative inflation rates. The decision to peg a currency includes the options of pegging to a single currency, to a basket of currencies, or to gold. Since 1971, however, the technique of expressing official exchange rates in terms of gold has not been used; gold has been phased out of the international monetary system.

Members of the International Monetary Fund (IMF) have been free to follow any exchange-rate policy that conforms to three principles: (1) Exchange rates should not be manipulated to prevent effective balance-of-payments adjustments or to gain unfair competitive advantage over other members. (2) Members should act to counter short-term disorderly conditions in exchange markets. (3) When members intervene in exchange markets, they should take into account

KEY CONCEPTS AND TERMS

- *Adjustable pegged exchange rates*
- *Bretton Woods system*
- *Clean float*
- *Crawling peg*
- *Currency board*
- *Devaluation*
- *Dirty float*
- *Dollarization*
- *Dual exchange rates*
- *Exchange controls*
- *Exchange-stabilization fund*
- *Fixed exchange rates*
- *Floating exchange rates*
- *Fundamental disequilibrium*
- *Key currency*
- *Leaning against the wind*
- *Managed floating system*
- *Multiple exchange rates*
- *Official exchange rate*
- *Par value*
- *Revaluation*
- *Seigniorage*
- *Special drawing right (SDR)*
- *Target exchange rates*

the interests of other members. Table 16.1 summarizes the exchange-rate practices of IMF member countries as of 1999; Table 16.2 highlights some of the factors that affect the choice of an exchange-rate system.

Fixed (pegged) **exchange rates** are used primarily by small, developing nations that maintain pegs to a **key currency,** such as the U.S. dollar or the French franc. A key currency is widely traded on world money markets, has demonstrated relatively stable values over time, and has been widely accepted as a means of international settlement. Table 16.3 identifies the major key currencies of the world.

One reason why developing nations choose to tie their currencies to a key currency is that it is used as a means of international settlement. Consider a Norwegian importer who wants to purchase Argentinean beef over the next year. If the Argentine exporter is unsure of what the Norwegian krone will purchase in one year, he might reject the krone

Table 16.1 Exchange-Rate Arrangements of IMF Members, 1999

Exchange Arrangement	Number of Countries
Exchange arrangements with no separate legal tender*	37
Currency board arrangements	8
Conventional pegged (fixed) exchange rates	44
Pegged exchange rates within horizontal bands	8
Crawling pegged exchange rates	6
Exchange rates within crawling bands	9
Managed floating exchange rates	25
Independently floating exchange rates	48
	185

*The currency of another country circulates as the sole legal tender, or the member belongs to a monetary or currency union in which the same legal tender is shared by the members of the union.

Source: *International Financial Statistics*, June 2000, p. 2

Table 16.2 Choosing an Exchange-Rate System

Characteristics of Economy	Implication for the Desired Degree of Exchange-Rate Flexibility
Size and openness of the economy	If trade is a large share of national output, then the costs of currency fluctuations can be high. This suggests that small, open economies may best be served by fixed exchange rates.
Inflation rate	If a country has much higher inflation than its trading partners, its exchange rate needs to be flexible to prevent its goods from becoming uncompetitive in world markets. If inflation differentials are more modest, a fixed rate is less troublesome.
Labor-market flexibility	The more rigid wages are, the greater the need for a flexible exchange rate to help the economy respond to an external shock.
Degree of financial development	In developing countries with immature financial markets, a freely floating exchange rate may not be sensible because a small number of foreign-exchange trades can cause big swings in currencies.
Credibility of policy makers	The weaker the reputation of the central bank, the stronger the case for pegging the exchange rate to build confidence that inflation will be controlled.
Capital mobility	The more open an economy to international capital, the harder it is to sustain a fixed rate.

Source: International Monetary Fund, *World Economic Outlook*, October 1997, p. 83.

Table 16.3 Key Currencies: Share of National Currencies in Total Identified Official Holdings of Foreign Exchange, 1998

Key Currency	All Countries	Industrial Countries	Developing Countries
U.S dollar	60.3	64.3	57.1
British pound	3.9	3.1	4.6
German mark	12.1	14.7	10.1
French franc	1.3	1.4	1.2
Swiss franc	0.7	0.2	1.0
Netherlands guilder	0.4	0.3	0.4
Japanese yen	5.1	7.0	3.7
European currency unit	0.8	1.8	—
Other	15.4	7.2	21.9
	100.0	100.0	100.0

Source: International Monetary Fund, *Annual Report*, 1999, p.133.

in settlement. Similarly, the Norwegian importer might doubt the value of Argentina's peso. One solution is for the contract to be written in terms of a key currency such as the U.S. dollar. Generally speaking, smaller nations with relatively undiversified economies and large foreign-trade sectors have been inclined to peg their currencies to one of the key currencies.

Maintaining pegs to a key currency provides several benefits for developing nations. First, the prices of the traded products of many developing nations are determined primarily in the markets of industrialized nations such as the United States; by pegging, say, to the dollar, these nations can stabilize the domestic-currency prices of their imports and exports. Second, many nations with high inflation have pegged to the dollar (the United States has relatively low inflation) in order to exert restraint on domestic policies and reduce inflation. By making the commitment to stabilize their exchange rates against the dollar, governments hope to convince their citizens that they are willing to adopt the responsible monetary policies necessary to achieve low inflation. Pegging the exchange rate may thus lessen inflationary expectations, leading to lower interest rates, a lessening of the loss of output due to disinflation, and a moderation of price pressures.

In maintaining fixed exchange rates, nations must decide whether to peg their currencies to another currency or to a currency basket. Pegging to a *single currency* is generally done by developing nations whose trade and financial relationships are mainly with a single industrial-country partner. For example, Ivory Coast, which trades primarily with France, pegs its currency to the French franc.

Developing nations with more than one major trading partner often peg their currencies to a group or *basket of currencies*. The basket is composed of prescribed quantities of foreign currencies in proportion to the amount of trade done with the nation pegging its currency. Once the basket has been selected, the currency value of the nation is computed using the exchange rates of the foreign currencies in the basket. Pegging the domestic-currency value of the basket enables a nation to average out fluctuations in export or import prices caused by exchange-rate movements. The effects of exchange-rate changes on the domestic economy are thus reduced.

Rather than constructing their own currency basket, many nations peg the value of their currencies to the **special drawing right (SDR)**, a basket of five currencies established by the IMF. The IMF requires that the valuation of the SDR basket be reviewed every five years; the basket is to include, in proportional amounts, the currencies of the members having the largest exports of goods and services during the previous five years. The currencies comprising the basket as of 1999, along with their amounts and percentage weights, are listed in Table 16.4.

The idea behind the SDR basket valuation is to make the SDR's value more stable than the foreign-currency value of any single national currency. The SDR is valued according to an index based on the moving average of those currencies in the basket. Should the values of the basket currencies either depreciate or appreciate against one another, the SDR's value would remain in the center. The SDR would depreciate against those currencies that are rising in value and appreciate against currencies whose values are falling. Nations desiring exchange-rate stability are attracted to the SDR as a currency basket against which to peg their currency values.

FIXED EXCHANGE-RATE SYSTEM

Few nations have allowed their currencies' exchange values to be determined solely by the forces of supply and demand in a free market. Until the industrialized nations adopted managed floating exchange rates in the 1970s, the practice generally was to maintain a pattern of relatively fixed (pegged) exchange rates among national currencies. Changes in national

Table 16.4 Special Drawing Right Basket of Currencies

Currency	Amount
U.S. dollar	0.5821
Euro (Germany)	0.2280
Japanese yen	27.2000
Euro (France)	0.1239
Pound sterling	0.1050

Source: International Monetary Fund, *Annual Report*, 1999, p. 109.

exchange rates presumably were to be initiated by domestic monetary authorities when long-term market forces warranted it.

PAR VALUE AND OFFICIAL EXCHANGE RATE Under a fixed exchange-rate system, governments assign their currencies a **par value** in terms of gold or other key currencies. By comparing the par values of two currencies, we can determine their **official exchange rate**. For example, the official exchange rate between the U.S. dollar and the British pound was $2.80 = £1 as long as the United States bought and sold gold at a fixed price of $35 per ounce and Britain bought and sold gold at £12.50 per ounce (35.00 / 12.50 = 2.80). The major industrial nations set their currencies' par values in terms of gold until gold was phased out of the international monetary system in the early 1970s.

Today, many developing nations choose to define their par values in terms of certain key currencies, such as the U.S. dollar. Under this arrangement, the monetary authority first defines its official exchange rate in terms of the key currency. It then defends the fixed parity by purchasing and selling its currency for the key currency at that rate. Assume, for example, that Bolivian central bankers fix their peso at 20 pesos = US$1, whereas Ecuador's sucre is set at 10 sucres = US$1. The official exchange rate between the peso and sucre becomes 1 peso = 0.5 sucre.

EXCHANGE-RATE STABILIZATION A first requirement for a nation participating in a fixed exchange-rate system is to determine an official exchange rate for its currency. The next step is to set up an **exchange-stabilization fund** to defend the official rate. Through purchases and sales of foreign currencies, the exchange-stabilization fund attempts to ensure that the market exchange rate does not move above or below the official exchange rate.

In Figure 16.1, assume that the market exchange rate equals $2.80 per pound, seen at the intersection of the demand and supply schedules of British pounds, D_0 and S_0. Also assume that the official exchange rate is defined as $2.80

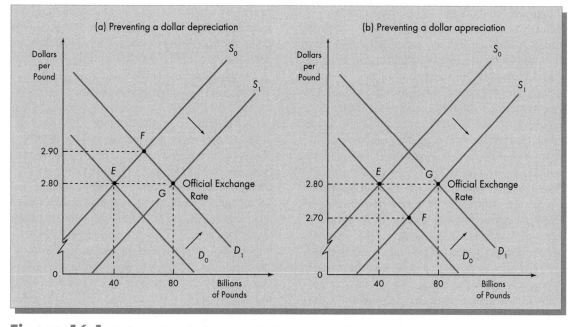

Figure 16.1 Exchange-Rate Stabilization Under a Fixed Exchange-Rate System

To defend the official exchange rate of $2.80 per pound, the central bank must supply all of the nation's currency that is demanded at the official rate and demand all of the nation's currency that is supplied to it at the official rate. To prevent a dollar depreciation, the central bank must purchase the excess supply of dollars with an equivalent amount of pounds. To prevent a dollar appreciation, the central bank must purchase the excess supply of pounds with an equivalent amount of dollars.

per pound. Now suppose that rising interest rates in Britain cause U.S. investors to demand additional pounds to finance the purchase of British securities; let the demand for pounds rise from D_0 to D_1 in Figure 16.1(a). Under free-market conditions, the dollar would depreciate from $2.80 per pound to $2.90 per pound. But under a fixed exchange-rate system, the monetary authority will attempt to defend the official rate of $2.80 per pound. At this rate, there exists an excess demand for pounds equal to £40 billion; this means that the British face an excess supply of dollars in the same amount. To keep the market exchange rate from depreciating beyond $2.80 per pound, the U.S. exchange-stabilization fund would purchase the excess supply of dollars with pounds. The supply of pounds thus rises from S_0 to S_1, resulting in a stabilization of the market exchange rate at $2.80 per pound.

Conversely, suppose that increased prosperity in the United Kingdom leads to rising imports from the United States; the supply of pounds thus increases from, say, S_0 to S_1 in Figure 16.1(b). At the official exchange rate of $2.80 per pound, there exists an excess supply of pounds equal to £40 billion. To keep the dollar from appreciating against the pound, the U.S. stabilization fund would purchase the excess supply of pounds with dollars. The demand for pounds thus increases from D_0 to D_1, resulting in a stabilization of the market exchange rate at $2.80 per pound.

This example illustrates how an exchange-stabilization fund undertakes its pegging operations to offset short-term fluctuations in the market exchange rate. Over the long run, however, the official exchange rate and the market exchange rate may move apart, reflecting changes in fundamental economic conditions—income levels, tastes and preferences, and technological factors. In the case of a **fundamental disequilibrium**, the cost of defending the existing official rate may become prohibitive.

Consider the case of a deficit nation that finds its currency depreciating in the exchange market. Maintaining the official rate may require the exchange-stabilization fund to purchase sizable quantities of its currency with foreign currencies or other reserve assets. This may impose a severe drain on the deficit nation's stock of international reserves. Although the deficit nation may be able to borrow reserves from other nations or from the International Monetary Fund to continue the defense of its exchange rate, such borrowing privileges are generally of limited magnitude. At the same time, the deficit nation will be undergoing internal adjustments to curb the disequilibrium. These measures will likely be aimed at controlling inflationary pressures and raising interest rates to promote capital inflows and discourage imports. If the imbalance is persistent, the deficit nation may view such internal adjustments as too costly in terms of falling income and employment levels. Rather than continually resorting to such measures, the deficit nation may decide that the reversal of the disequilibrium calls for an adjustment in the exchange rate itself. Under a system of pegged exchange rates, a chronic imbalance may be counteracted by a currency devaluation or revaluation.

DEVALUATION AND REVALUATION Under a fixed exchange-rate system, a nation's monetary authority may decide to pursue balance-of-payments equilibrium by devaluing or revaluing its currency. The purpose of **devaluation** is to cause the home currency's exchange value to *depreciate*, thus counteracting a payments *deficit*. The purpose of currency **revaluation** is to cause the home currency's exchange value to *appreciate*, thus counteracting a payments *surplus*.

The terms *devaluation* and *revaluation* refer to a legal redefinition of a currency's par value under a system of fixed exchange rates. The terms *depreciation* and *appreciation* refer to the actual impact on the market exchange rate caused by a redefinition of a par value or to changes in an exchange rate stemming from changes in the supply of or demand for foreign exchange.

Devaluation and revaluation policies are considered to be *expenditure-switching* instruments because they work on relative prices to divert domestic and foreign expenditures between domestic and foreign goods. By raising the home price of the foreign currency, a devaluation makes the home country's exports cheaper to foreigners in terms of the foreign currency, while making the home country's imports more expensive in terms of the home currency. Expenditures are diverted from foreign to home goods as home exports rise and imports fall. In like manner, a revaluation discourages the home country's exports and encourages its imports, diverting expenditures from home goods to foreign goods.

Before implementing a devaluation or revaluation, the monetary authority must decide (1) if an adjustment in the official exchange rate is necessary to correct a payments disequilibrium, (2) when the adjustment will occur, and (3) how large the adjustment should be. Exchange-rate decisions of government officials may be incorrect—that is, ill timed and of improper magnitude.

In making the decision to undergo a devaluation or revaluation, monetary authorities generally attempt to hide behind a veil of secrecy. Just hours before the decision is to become effective, public denials of any such policies by official government representatives are common. This is to discourage currency speculators, who try to profit by shifting funds from a currency falling in value to one rising in value. Given the destabilizing impact that massive speculation can exert on financial markets, it is hard to criticize monetary authorities for being secretive in their actions. However, the need for devaluation tends to be obvious to outsiders as well as to government officials and in the past has nearly always resulted in heavy speculative pressures.

LEGAL VERSUS ECONOMIC IMPLICATIONS Currency devaluations and revaluations are used in conjunction with a *fixed* exchange-rate system. The monetary authority changes a currency's exchange rate by decree, usually by a sizable amount at one time. How is such a policy implemented?

Recall that under a fixed exchange-rate system, the home currency is assigned a par value by the nation's monetary authorities. The par value is the amount of a nation's currency that is required to purchase a fixed amount of gold, a key currency, or the special drawing right. These assets represent the legal *numeraire*, or the unit of contractual obligations. By comparing various national currency prices of the numeraire, monetary authorities determine the official rate of exchange for the currencies.

In the *legal* sense, a devaluation or revaluation occurs when the home country redefines its currency price of the official numeraire, changing the par value. The *economic* effect of the par value's redefinition is the impact on the market rate of exchange. Assuming that other trading nations retain their existing par values, one would expect (1) a devaluation to result in a depreciation in the currency's exchange value; (2) a revaluation to result in an appreciation in the currency's exchange value.

Figure 16.2 illustrates the legal and economic implications of devaluation/revaluation policies. Assume that the SDR serves as the numeraire by which the value of individual currencies can be defined relative to each other—Burundi's franc and Uganda's shilling. The diagram's vertical axis denotes the shilling price of an SDR, and the horizontal axis depicts the franc price of an SDR. Three price ratios are illustrated by each point in the figure: (1) the shilling price of the SDR, (2) the

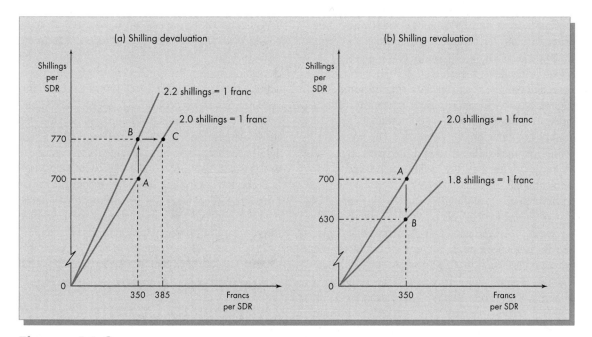

Figure 16.2 Devaluation/Revaluation: Legal Versus Economic Implications

Starting at the official exchange rate of 2 Uganda shillings per Burundi franc, a 10-percent devaluation of the shilling results in the shilling's depreciating 10 percent against the franc, to 2.2 shillings per franc; if Burundi retaliates and devalues its franc by 10 percent, the exchange rate will revert back to 2 shillings per franc. A 10-percent revaluation of the Uganda shilling, unaccompanied by an offsetting currency revaluation by Burundi, leads to a 10-percent appreciation of the shilling against the franc.

franc price of the SDR, and (3) the shilling price of the franc, indicated by the slope of a ray connecting the origin with any point in the figure.

Referring to Figure 16.2(a), suppose Uganda sets its par value at 700 shillings per SDR, whereas Burundi's par value equals 350 francs per SDR. Connecting these two prices yields point *A* in the diagram. Relative to each other, the official exchange rate between the shilling and the franc is 2 shillings = 1 franc, denoted by the slope of the ray *0A* (700 / 350 = 2.0).

Assume that Uganda wishes to devalue the shilling by, say, 10 percent to correct a payments deficit. Starting at point *A*, Uganda would raise the shilling price of the SDR from 700 to 770 shillings per SDR, a 10-percent increase. This results in a movement from point *A* to point *B* in the figure. Corresponding to the slope of ray *0B*, the new exchange rate is 2.2 shillings = 1 franc (770 / 350 = 2.2). Uganda's devaluation results in a depreciation in the shilling's exchange value from 2 shillings = 1 franc to 2.2 shillings = 1 franc, a 10-percent change. Conversely, suppose that Uganda revalues the shilling by 10 percent to reverse a payments surplus. Starting at point *A* in Figure 16.2(b), Uganda would lower the official price of the SDR from 700 shillings to 630 shillings, a 10-percent decrease. The exchange value of the shilling would increase from 2 shillings = 1 franc to 1.8 shillings = 1 franc, a 10-percent change.

To change the shilling/franc exchange rate, it is not sufficient for Uganda to redefine the shilling's par value. It is also necessary that the par value of the Burundi franc remain constant or be altered by a smaller fraction. In Figure 16.2(a), a change in the shilling/franc exchange rate requires a change in the *slope* of ray *OA*. Acting by itself, Uganda can establish only the vertical position in the diagram. Because Burundi determines the horizontal position, any redefinition of Uganda's par value can be neutralized by an equivalent change in Burundi's par value. In other words, Burundi can offset any change in the slope of the ray that Uganda may wish to undertake.

Let us start again at point *A* in Figure 16.2(a), where the exchange rate is set at 2 shillings = 1 franc. Facing a payments deficit, suppose Uganda devalues the shilling 10 percent by increasing the official price of the SDR from 700 to 770 shillings. This would cause a movement from point *A* to point *B*, where the exchange rate is 2.2 shillings = 1 franc. But what if Burundi determines that the shilling's devaluation gives Uganda an unfair competitive advantage? Suppose Burundi retaliates by devaluing the franc 10 percent, thus increasing the official price of the SDR from 350 to 385 francs. A movement from point *B* to point *C* in the diagram would result. Although both currencies have been officially devalued by 10 percent, the exchange rate between them remains constant at 2 shillings = 1 franc. The conclusion is that a devaluation in the legal sense does not necessarily ensure a devaluation in the economic sense—that is, a depreciation in the exchange rate. This occurs only if other nations do not retaliate by initiating offsetting devaluations of their own.

Currency devaluations do have foreign repercussions similar to those of domestic economic policies. The larger and more significant the devaluing nation, the greater the economic effects transmitted abroad. A nation that devalues to initiate an export-led economic recovery may be the cause of recession in its trading partners. This was often the case during the Great Depression of the 1930s, when competitive devaluations were widespread. It is no wonder that when currency realignments involving devaluations and revaluations are called for, they usually require intense negotiations and the harmonization of economic interests among participating nations.

STABILIZING CURRENCIES OF DEVELOPING COUNTRIES: CURRENCY BOARDS VERSUS DOLLARIZATION

In recent years, stabilization of the beleaguered currencies of the developing countries has been a hotly debated topic. Rather than relying on a central bank's exchange-stabilization fund,

ARE FIXED EXCHANGE RATES GOOD FOR DEVELOPING COUNTRIES?

After more than a decade of maintaining the Thai baht's peg to the U.S. dollar, Thai authorities abandoned the peg in July 1997. By October, market forces had led the baht to depreciate by 60 percent against the dollar! The depreciation triggered a wave of speculation against other Southeast Asian currencies. Over the same period, the Indonesian rupiah, Malaysia ringgit, Philippine peso, and South Korean won abandoned links to the dollar and depreciated 47, 35, 34, and 16 percent, respectively. This episode reopened one of the oldest debates in economics: whether a currency should have a fixed or floating exchange rate. Consider the case of Thailand.

Although Thailand was widely regarded as one of Southeast Asia's outstanding performers throughout the 1980s and 1990s, it relied heavily on inflows of short-term foreign capital, attracted both by the stable baht and by Thai interest rates, which were much higher than comparable interest rates elsewhere. The capital inflow supported a broad-based economic boom that was especially visible in the real estate market.

By 1996, however, Thailand's economic boom fizzled. As a result, both local and foreign investors got nervous and began withdrawing funds from Thailand's financial system, which put downward pressure on the baht. However, the Thai government resisted the depreciation pressure by purchasing baht with dollars in the foreign-exchange market and also raising interest rates, which increased the attractiveness of the baht. But the purchases of the baht greatly depleted Thailand's reserves of hard currency. Moreover, raising interest rates adversely affected an already weak financial sector by dampening economic activity. These factors ultimately contributed to the abandonment of the baht's link to the dollar.

Although Thailand and other Southeast Asian countries abandoned fixed exchange rates in 1997, some economists questioned whether such a policy would be in their best interest in the long run. Their reasoning was that these economies were relatively small and wide open to international trade and investment flows. Moreover, inflation rates were modest by the standards of a developing country, and labor markets were relatively flexible. In other words, freely floating exchange rates were probably not the best long-run option. Indeed, these economists maintained that unless the Southeast Asian governments anchored their currencies to something, currencies might drift into a vicious cycle of depreciation and higher inflation. There was certainly a concern that central banks in the region lacked the credibility to enforce tough monetary policies without the external constraint of a fixed exchange rate.

Simply put, neither fixed exchange rates nor floating exchange rates offer a magical solution. What really makes a difference to a country's prospects is the quality of the overall economic policies that are pursued.

Source: Ramon Moreno, "Lessons from Thailand," *Economic Letter*, Federal Reserve Bank of San Francisco, November 7, 1997.

developing countries have increasingly resorted to currency boards and dollarization as stabilization devices. Let us examine these techniques.

CURRENCY BOARD A **currency board** is a monetary authority that issues notes and coins convertible into a foreign anchor currency at a *fixed exchange rate*. The anchor currency is a currency chosen for its expected stability and international acceptability. For most currency boards, the U.S. dollar or British pound has been the anchor currency. Also, a few currency boards have used gold as the anchor. Usually, the fixed exchange rate is set by law, making changes to the exchange rate very costly for governments. Put simply, currency boards offer the strongest form of a fixed exchange rate that is possible short of full currency union.

The commitment to exchange domestic currency for foreign currency at a fixed exchange rate requires that the currency board have sufficient foreign exchange to honor this commitment. This means that its holdings of foreign exchange must at least equal 100 percent of its notes and coins in circulation, as set by law. A currency board can operate in place of a central bank or as a parallel issuer alongside an existing central bank. Usually, a currency board takes over the role of a central bank in strengthening the currency of a developing country.

By design, a currency board has no discretionary powers. Its operations are completely passive and automatic. The sole function of a currency board is to exchange its notes and coins for the anchor at a fixed rate. Unlike a central bank, a currency board does not lend to the domestic government, to domestic companies, or to domestic banks. In a currency-board system, the government can finance its spending only by taxing or borrowing, not by printing money and thereby creating inflation. This results from the stipulation that the backing of the domestic currency must be at least 100 percent.

A country that adopts a currency board thus puts its monetary policy on autopilot. It is as if the chairman of the Board of Governors of the Federal Reserve System were replaced by a personal computer. When the anchor currency flows in, the board issues more domestic currency and interest rates fall; when the anchor currency flows out, interest rates rise. The government sits back and watches, even if interest rates skyrocket and a recession ensues.

Many economists maintain that, especially in the developing world, central banks are incapable of retaining nonpolitical independence and thus instill less confidence than is necessary for the smooth functioning of a monetary system. They are answerable to the prerogatives of populism or dictatorship and are at the beck and call of political changes. The bottom line is that central banks should not be given the onerous responsibility of maintaining the value of currencies. This job should be left to an independent body whose sole mandate is to issue currency

against a strict and inalterable set of guidelines that require a fixed amount of foreign exchange or gold to be deposited for each unit of domestic currency issued.

Currency boards can confer considerable credibility on fixed exchange-rate regimes. The most vital contribution a currency board can make to exchange-rate stability is by imposing discipline on the process of money creation. This results in greater stability of domestic prices, which, in turn, stabilizes the value of the domestic currency. In short, the major benefits of the currency-board system are:

- making a nation's currency and exchange-rate regimes more rule-bound and predictable
- placing an upper bound on the nation's base money supply
- arresting any tendencies in an economy toward inflation
- forcing the government to restrict its borrowing to what foreign and domestic lenders are willing to lend it at market interest rates
- engendering confidence in the soundness of the nation's money, thus assuring citizens and foreign investors that the domestic currency can always be exchanged for some other strong currency
- creating confidence and promoting trade, investment, and economic growth

Proponents cite Hong Kong as a country that has benefited from a currency board. In the early 1980s, Hong Kong had a floating exchange rate. The immediate cause of Hong Kong's economic problems was uncertainty about its political future. In 1982, the United Kingdom and China began talks about the fate of Hong Kong after the United Kingdom's lease on the territory expired in 1997. Fear that China would abandon Hong Kong's capitalist system sent Hong Kong's stock market down by 50 percent. Hong Kong's real estate market weakened also, and small banks with heavy exposure in real estate suffered runs. The result was a 16-percent depreciation in the Hong Kong dollar against the U.S. dollar. With this loss of confidence, many merchants refused to accept Hong Kong dollars and quoted prices in U.S. dollars instead. Panic buying of vegetable oil, rice, and other staples emptied merchants' shelves.

In 1983, the government of Hong Kong ended its economic crises by announcing that Hong Kong would adopt a currency-board system. It pegged its exchange rate at HK$7.8 = US$1. The currency reform immediately reversed the loss of confidence about Hong Kong's economy despite continuing troubles in the U.K.–China discussions. A stable currency provided the basis for Hong Kong to continue its rapid economic growth.

By maintaining a legal commitment to exchange domestic currency for a foreign currency at a fixed exchange rate, and a commitment to issue currency only if it is backed by foreign reserves, a currency board can be a good way of restoring confidence in a country gripped by economic chaos. Although a currency board cannot solve all of a country's economic problems, it may achieve more financial credibility than a domestic central bank can.

Although currency boards help discipline government spending, therefore reducing a major source of inflation in developing countries, there are concerns about currency boards. Perhaps the most common objection is that a currency board prevents a country from pursuing a discretionary monetary policy and thus reduces its economic independence. Also, it is sometimes said that a currency-board system is susceptible to financial panics because it lacks a lender of last resort. Another objection is that a currency-board system creates a colonial relationship with the anchor currency. Critics cite the experiences of British colonies, which operated under currency-board systems in the early 1900s.

It is possible for a nation's monetary system to be orderly and disciplined under either a currency board or a central banking system. But neither system by itself guarantees either order or discipline. The effectiveness of both systems depends on other factors, such as fiscal discipline and a sound banking system. In other words, it is a whole network of responsible and mutually supporting policies and institutions that make for sound money and stable exchange rates. No monetary regime, however well conceived, can bear the entire burden alone.

DOLLARIZATION Instead of using a currency board to promote a stable currency, why not "dollarize" an economy? This is what several Latin American countries, such as Argentina and Mexico, were considering at the turn of the millennium.

Dollarization occurs when residents of, say, Argentina, use the U.S. dollar alongside or instead of the peso. *Unofficial dollarization* (partial dollarization) occurs when Argentines hold dollar-denominated bank deposits or Federal Reserve notes to protect against high inflation in the peso. Unofficial dollarization has existed for years in many Latin American and Caribbean countries, where the United States is a major trading partner and a major source of foreign investment.

Official dollarization (full dollarization) means the elimination of the Argentine peso, and its complete replacement with the U.S. dollar. The monetary base of Argentina, which initially consists entirely of peso-denominated currency, would be converted into U.S. Federal Reserve notes. To replace its currency, Argentina would sell foreign reserves (mostly U.S. Treasury securities) to buy dollars and exchange all outstanding peso notes for dollar notes. The U.S. dollar would be the sole legal tender and sole unit of account in Argentina. As of 2000, there were 13 officially dollarized countries in Latin America and the Caribbean.

WHY DOLLARIZE? Why would countries such as Argentina or Mexico want to fully dollarize their economies? Let us consider Argentina. The monetary history of Argentina over much of the post–World War II era is one of a very high and unstable rate of inflation with numerous episodes of exchange controls placed on external transactions, especially those related to capital outflows. The shocks that have unsettled the Argentina economy have generally stemmed from large budget deficits that were financed heavily by printing money. Although Argentina used a currency board to maintain a rigid link of its peso to the dollar, financial experts noted that domestic interest rates were unusually high, given the inflation rate, because Argentine lenders did not have confidence in the ability to maintain the rigid link of the peso to the dollar. Lenders felt that the Argentine government might abandon its resolve to maintain fixed ties to the dollar during periods of economic crisis. Because of this, lenders insisted that a substantial risk premium be added to loans, which translated into high real domestic interest rates. These high rates discouraged capital formation and growth across the economy. Advocates of dollarization argue that by adopting the dollar as the official currency in place of a peso rigidly linked to the dollar, the risk premium would fall, resulting in lower real interest rates and a higher rate of capital formation and economic growth. Simply put, dollarization is seen as a way to permanently protect Argentina's growth and prosperity from devastating, periodic bouts in inflation and peso depreciation.

EFFECTS OF DOLLARIZATION. A convenient way to think about Argentina in this context, or any country that plans to adopt the dollar as its official currency, is to treat it as one would treat any of the 50 states in the United States. Thus, in discussions about monetary policy in the United States, it is assumed that the Federal Reserve conducts monetary policy with reference to national economic conditions rather than the economic conditions in an individual state or region, even though economic conditions are not uniform throughout the country. The reason for this is that monetary policy works through interest rates on credit markets that are national in scope. Thus, monetary policy cannot be tailored to deal with business conditions in an individual state or region that are different from the national economy. Therefore, when Argentina dollarizes its economy, it essentially accepts the monetary policy of the Federal Reserve.

With dollarization in Argentina, U.S. monetary policy would presumably be carried out as it is now. If Argentine business cycles do not coincide with those in the United States, Argentina could not count on the Federal Reserve to come to its rescue, just as any state in the United States cannot count on the Federal Reserve to come to its rescue if its business conditions are out of sync with the national pattern. This may be a major downside for the Argentineans. Despite this, Argentina might still be better off without the supposed safety valve of an independent monetary policy. In Argentina and other Latin American countries, currency depreciations have led to higher interest rates, higher inflation, and falling output. Rather than counteracting economic shocks, independent monetary policies have actually exacerbated the ups and downs of the business cycle.

Another limitation facing the Argentineans is that the Federal Reserve would not be their lender of last resort as it is for Americans. That is, if the U.S. financial system should come under stress, the Federal Reserve could use its various monetary powers to aid these institutions and contain possible failures. Without the consent of the U.S. Congress, the Federal Reserve could not perform this function for Argentina or for any other country that decided to adopt the dollar officially as its currency.

A third shortcoming arising from the adoption of the dollar as the official currency is that Argentina could no longer get any **seigniorage** from its monetary system. This cost for Argentina stems from the loss of the foreign reserves (mainly U.S. Treasury securities) that Argentina would have to sell in exchange for dollars. These reserves bear interest and, therefore, are a source of income for Argentina. This income is called seigniorage. But once Argentina's reserves are replaced by dollar bills, this source of income disappears.

With dollarization, Argentina would enjoy the same freedom as the 50 states in the United States enjoy as to how to spend its tax dollars. Argentine state expenditures for education, police protection, social insurance, and the like would not be affected by its use of the U.S. dollar. Also, Argentina could establish its own tariffs, subsidies, and other trade policies. Therefore, Argentina's sovereignty would not be compromised in these areas. There would, however, be an overall constraint on Argentine fiscal policy: Argentina would not have recourse to printing more pesos to finance budget deficits and would thus have to exercise caution in its spending policies.

Official dollarization of Argentina's economy also has implications for the United States. First, when Argentines acquire dollars they surrender goods and services to Americans. Thus, for each dollar sent abroad, Americans enjoy a one-time increase in the amount of goods and services they are able to consume. Second, by opting to hold dollars rather than the interest-bearing debt of the United States, the United States, in effect, gets an interest-free loan from Argentina. The interest that does not have to be paid is a measure of seigniorage that accrues on an annual basis to the United States. On the other hand, use of U.S. currency abroad might hinder the formulation and execution of monetary policy by the Federal Reserve. Also, by making Argentina more dependent on U.S. monetary policy, dollarization could result in more pressure on the Federal Reserve to conduct policy according to the interests of Argentina rather than those of the United States.

FLOATING EXCHANGE RATES

Instead of utilizing fixed exchange rates, some nations allow their currencies to float in the foreign-exchange market. By **floating** (or flexible) **exchange rates**, we mean currency prices that are established daily in the foreign-exchange market, without restrictions imposed by government policy on the extent to which the prices can move. With floating rates, there is an equilibrium exchange rate that equates the demand for and supply of the home currency. Changes in the exchange rate will ideally correct a payments imbalance by bringing about shifts in imports and exports of goods, services, and short-term capital movements. The exchange rate depends on relative money supplies, income levels, interest rates, prices, and other factors discussed in Chapter 13.

Unlike fixed exchange rates, floating exchange rates are not characterized by par values and official exchange rates; they are determined by market supply and demand conditions rather than central bankers. Although floating rates do not have an exchange-stabilization fund to maintain existing rates, it does not necessarily follow that floating rates must fluctuate erratically. They will do so if the underlying market forces become unstable. Because there is no exchange-stabilization fund under floating rates, any holdings of international reserves serve as working balances rather than to maintain a given exchange rate for any currency.

ACHIEVING MARKET EQUILIBRIUM How do floating exchange rates promote payments equilibrium for a nation? Consider Figure 16.3, which illustrates the foreign-exchange market in Swiss francs in the United States. The intersection of supply schedule S_0 and demand schedule D_0 determines the equilibrium exchange rate of $0.50 per franc.

Referring to Figure 16.3(a), suppose a rise in real income causes U.S. residents to demand more Swiss cheese and watches, and therefore more francs; let the demand for francs rise from D_0 to D_1. Initially the market is in disequilibrium, because the quantity of francs demanded (60 francs) exceeds the quantity supplied (40 francs) at the exchange rate of $0.50 per franc. The excess demand for francs leads to an increase in the exchange rate from $0.50 to $0.55 per franc; the dollar thus falls in value, or depreciates, against the franc, while the franc rises in value, or appreciates, against the dollar. The higher value of the franc prompts Swiss residents to increase the quantity of francs supplied on the foreign-exchange market to purchase more U.S. goods, which are now cheaper in terms of the franc; at the same time, it dampens U.S. demand for more expensive Swiss goods. Market equilibrium is restored at the exchange rate of $0.55 per franc, at which the quantities of francs supplied and demanded are equal.

Suppose instead that real income in the United States falls, which causes U.S. residents to demand less Swiss cheese and watches, and

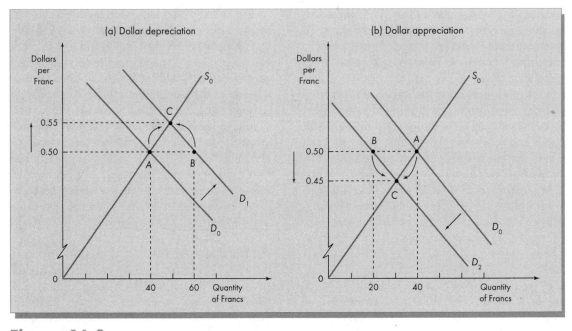

Figure 16.3 Market Adjustment Under Floating Exchange Rates

Under a floating exchange-rate system, continuous changes in currency values restore payments equilibrium at which the quantity supplied and quantity demanded of a currency are equal. Starting at equilibrium point A, an increase in the demand for francs leads to a depreciation of the dollar against the franc; conversely, a decrease in the demand for francs leads to an appreciation of the dollar against the franc.

therefore fewer francs. In Figure 16.3(b), let the demand for francs fall from D_0 to D_2. The market is initially in disequilibrium because the quantity of francs supplied (40 francs) exceeds the quantity demanded (20 francs) at the exchange rate of $0.50 per franc. The excess supply of francs causes the exchange rate to fall from $0.50 to $0.45 per franc; the dollar thus appreciates against the franc, while the franc depreciates against the dollar. Market equilibrium is restored at the exchange rate of $0.45 per franc, at which the quantities of francs supplied and demanded are equal.

This example illustrates one argument in favor of floating rates: When the exchange rate is permitted to adjust freely in response to market forces, market equilibrium will be established at a point where the quantities of foreign exchange supplied and demanded are equal. If the

exchange rate promotes market equilibrium, monetary authorities will not need international reserves for the purpose of intervening in the market to maintain exchange rates at their par value. Presumably, these resources can be used more productively elsewhere in the economy.

TRADE RESTRICTIONS, JOBS, AND FLOATING EXCHANGE RATES During the economic downturns of the 1980s and 1990s, U.S. labor unions increasingly lobbied for import restrictions in order to save jobs for American workers. Do import restrictions lead to rising total employment in the United States?

As long as the United States maintains a floating exchange rate, the implementation of import restrictions to help one industry will gradually shift jobs from other industries in the economy to the protected industry, with no significant impact on aggregate employment. Short-run employment gains in the protected industry will be offset by long-run employment losses in other industries.

Suppose the United States increases tariffs on autos imported from Japan. This policy would reduce auto imports, causing a decrease in the U.S. demand for yen to pay for imported vehicles. With floating exchange rates, the yen would depreciate against the dollar (the dollar would appreciate against the yen) until balance in international transactions was attained. The change in the exchange rate would encourage Americans to purchase more goods from Japan and the Japanese to purchase fewer goods from the United States. Sales and jobs would therefore be lost in other U.S. industries. Trade restrictions thus result in a zero-sum game within the United States. Job increases in Detroit are offset by job decreases in Los Angeles and Portland, with exchange-rate changes imposing costs on unprotected workers in the U.S. economy.

In 1982, the U.S. government considered implementing domestic-content legislation that would force U.S. and foreign auto firms that sell autos in the U.S. market to use greater amounts of U.S. production (labor and parts) in each vehicle. Because this policy would reduce the U.S. demand for Japanese-made autos and the demand for yen to pay for these autos, the yen would depreciate and the dollar would appreciate. The U.S. Department of Labor estimated that the protectionist policy would generate some 300,000 jobs in the automotive sector, but that the same number of jobs would be lost in other U.S. sectors, including apparel, aircraft, electronic components, and computers, as a result of exchange-rate changes.[1]

ARGUMENTS FOR AND AGAINST FLOATING RATES

One advantage claimed for floating rates is their simplicity. Floating rates allegedly respond quickly to changing supply and demand conditions, clearing the market of shortages or surpluses of a given currency. Instead of

[1] Robert Dunn, "Save an Auto Worker's Job, Put Another American Out of Work," *The Washington Post*, October 29, 1982, p. A23.

having formal rules of conduct among central bankers governing exchange-rate movements, floating rates are market determined. They operate under simplified institutional arrangements that are relatively easy to enact.

Because floating rates fluctuate throughout the day, they permit continuous adjustment in the balance of payments. The adverse effects of prolonged disequilibriums that tend to occur under fixed exchange rates are minimized under floating rates. It is also argued that floating rates partially insulate the home economy from external forces. This means that governments will not have to restore payments equilibrium through painful inflationary or deflationary adjustment policies. Switching to floating rates frees a nation from having to adopt policies that perpetuate domestic disequilibrium as the price of maintaining a satisfactory balance-of-payments position. Nations thus have greater freedom to pursue policies that promote domestic balance than they do under fixed exchange rates.

Although there are strong arguments in favor of floating exchange rates, this system is often considered to be of limited usefulness for bankers and businesspeople. Critics of floating rates maintain that an unregulated market may lead to wide fluctuations in currency values, discouraging foreign trade and investment. Although traders and investors may be able to hedge exchange-rate risk by dealing in the forward market, the cost of hedging may become prohibitively high.

Floating rates in theory are supposed to allow governments to set independent monetary and fiscal policies. But this flexibility may cause a problem of another sort: *inflationary bias*. Under a system of floating rates, monetary authorities may lack the financial discipline required by a fixed exchange-rate system. Suppose a nation faces relatively high rates of inflation compared with the rest of the world. This domestic inflation will have no negative impact on the nation's trade balance under floating rates because its currency will automatically depreciate in the exchange market. However, a protracted depreciation of the currency would result in persistently increasing import prices and a rising price level, making inflation self-perpetuating and the depreciation continuous. Because there is greater freedom for domestic financial management under floating rates, there may be less resistance to overspending and to its subsequent pressure on wages and prices.

ADJUSTABLE PEGGED RATES

Rather than maintaining completely fixed exchange rates or allowing the exchange rate to be determined by the free-market forces of supply and demand, nations have often pursued limited exchange-rate flexibility. Such is the case of the adjustable pegged-rate system.

In 1944, delegates from 44 member nations of the United Nations met at Bretton Woods, New Hampshire, to create a new international monetary system. They were aware of the unsatisfactory monetary experience of the 1930s, during which the international gold standard collapsed as the result of the economic and financial crises of the Great Depression and nations experimented unsuccessfully with floating exchange rates and exchange controls. The delegates wanted to establish international monetary order and avoid the instability and nationalistic practices that had been in effect until 1944.

The international monetary system that was created became known as the **Bretton Woods system.** The founders felt that neither completely fixed exchange rates nor floating rates were optimal; instead, they adopted a kind of managed exchange-rate system known as **adjustable pegged exchange rates.** The Bretton Woods system lasted from 1946 until 1973.

The main feature of the adjustable peg system is that currencies are tied to each other to provide stable exchange rates for commercial and financial transactions. When the balance of payments moves away from its long-run equilibrium position, however, a nation can repeg its exchange rate via devaluation or revaluation policies. Member nations agreed in principle to defend existing par values as long as possible in times of balance-of-payments

disequilibrium. They were expected to use fiscal and monetary policies first to correct payments imbalances. But if reversing a persistent payments imbalance would mean severe disruption to the domestic economy in terms of inflation or unemployment, member nations could correct this *fundamental disequilibrium* by repegging their currencies up to 10 percent without permission from the International Monetary Fund and by greater than 10 percent with the Fund's permission.

Under the Bretton Woods system, each member nation set the par value of its currency in terms of gold or, alternatively, the gold content of the U.S. dollar in 1944. Market exchange rates were almost but not completely fixed, being kept within a band of 1 percent on either side of parity for a total spread of 2 percent, as shown in Figure 16.4. National exchange-stabilization funds were used to maintain the band limits. In 1971, the exchange-support margins were widened to 2.25 percent on either side of parity to eliminate payments imbalances by setting in motion corrective trade and capital movements. As seen in Figure 16.4, devaluations or revaluations could be used to adjust the par value of a currency when it became overvalued or undervalued.

Although adjustable pegged rates are intended to promote a viable balance-of-payments adjustment mechanism, they have been plagued with operational problems. In the Bretton Woods system, adjustments in prices and incomes often conflicted with domestic-stabilization objectives. Also, currency devaluation was considered undesirable because it seemed to indicate a failure of domestic policies and a loss of international prestige. Conversely, revaluations were unacceptable to exporters, whose livelihoods were vulnerable to such policies. Repegging exchange rates only as a last resort often meant that when adjustments did occur, they were sizable. Moreover, adjustable pegged rates posed difficulties in estimating the equilibrium rate to which a currency should be repegged. Finally, once the market exchange rate reached the margin of the permissible band around parity, it in effect became a rigid fixed rate that presented speculators with a one-way bet. Given persistent weakening pressure, for example, at the

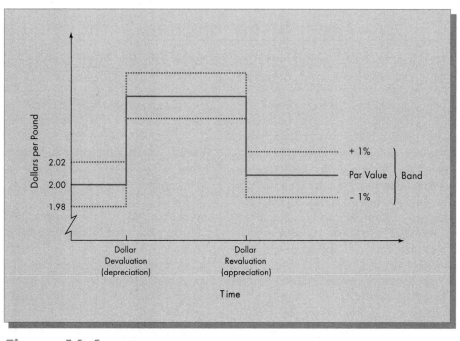

Figure 16.4 Adjustable Pegged Exchange Rates

Market exchange rates are almost completely fixed, being maintained within a narrow band around the currency's official exchange rate. When a nation experiences a fundamental disequilibrium, it can devalue (revalue) its currency to restore payments balance.

band's outer limit, speculators had the incentive to move out of a weakening currency that was expected to depreciate further in value as the result of official devaluation.

These problems reached a climax in the early 1970s. Faced with continuing and growing balance-of-payments deficits, the United States suspended the dollar's convertibility into gold in August 1971. This suspension terminated the U.S. commitment to exchange gold for dollars at $35 per ounce—a commitment that had existed for 37 years. This policy abolished the tie between gold and the international value of the dollar, thus floating the dollar and permitting its exchange rate to be set by market forces. The floating of the dollar terminated U.S. support of the Bretton Woods system of adjustable pegged rates and led to the demise of that system.

MANAGED FLOATING RATES

The adoption of managed floating exchange rates by the United States and other industrial nations in 1973 followed the breakdown of the international monetary system based on adjustable pegged rates. Before the 1970s, only a handful of economists gave serious consideration to a general system of floating rates. Because of defects in the decision-making process caused by procedural difficulties and political biases, however, adjustments of par values under the Bretton Woods system were often delayed and discontinuous. It was recognized that exchange rates should be adjusted more promptly and in small but continuous amounts in response to evolving market forces. In 1973, a **managed floating system** was adopted,

SPECULATIVE ATTACKS ON THE KRONA

By mounting an attack on a currency, speculators may be able to force a change in its value. Consider the case of the Swedish krona, which was attacked by speculators in the early 1990s.

In May 1991, Sweden applied to enter the Exchange Rate Mechanism (ERM) of the European Union in a bid to stabilize its currency. To stabilize the krona–mark exchange rate, interest rates in Sweden and Germany had to be the same. Thus, the Swedish and German central banks couldn't independently use monetary policy—that is, change short-term interest rates—if they wanted to keep the exchange rate stable. If Sweden wanted to act independently, it had to use fiscal policy (tax and government spending policies) to stimulate the country's growth rate.

However, a weak Swedish economy provoked speculators, who mounted an attack on the krona in September 1992. Speculators knew that the weak economy would tempt Sweden to abandon its fixed exchange rate and use monetary policy to cut short-term interest rates, especially since the new Swedish government was adopting restrictive fiscal policy. Speculators believed that if the Swedish central bank cut the short-term interest rate, the krona wouldn't be as attractive to investors. Thus, the speculators thought that after interest rates were cut, the currency would depreciate with respect to other ERM currencies. But since speculators expected the depreciation to happen, they decided to sell the krona immediately and thus mount a speculative attack on the currency.

This attack put the Swedish central bank in an uncomfortable position. To combat the currency's depreciation, the central bank raised short-term interest rates temporarily to repel the speculative attack—exactly the policy it didn't want in the face of sluggish economic growth. In fact, the Swedish central bank raised the short-term interest rate to an astonishing 500 percent and held it there for four days. The speculators were deterred, but not for long.

The speculators understood that the Swedish central bank had to raise short-term interest rates temporarily to support the currency. But they were betting that the central bank wouldn't fight off the attack for long, especially in the face of disquiet in the country resulting from weak economic growth and the higher interest rates needed to fight the speculative attack. The high short-term interest rates had made the economic situation in Sweden even more precarious, so, in November the speculators attacked again, selling the krona in favor of other ERM currencies. This time the Swedish central bank did not aggressively raise interest rates and the krona depreciated.

Profit opportunities such as this one can sometimes be exploited by speculators who recognize that a country's exchange-rate policy is inconsistent with the monetary policy needed, given a country's domestic situation. By paying careful attention to a country's economic and political developments, a speculator can sometimes forecast the direction of a currency's move when it breaks out of a stabilized exchange-rate system.

Source: Gregory Hopper, "What Determines the Exchange Rate: Economic Factors or Market Sentiment?" *Business Review*, Federal Reserve Bank of Philadelphia, September/October 1997, p. 23.

under which informal guidelines were established by the IMF for coordination of national exchange-rate policies.

The motivation for the formulation of guidelines for floating arose from two concerns. The first was that nations might intervene in the exchange markets to avoid exchange-rate alterations that would weaken their competitive position. When the United States suspended its gold-convertibility pledge and allowed its overvalued dollar to float in the exchange markets, it hoped that a free-market adjustment would result in a depreciation of the dollar against other, undervalued currencies. Rather than permitting a **clean float** (a free-market solution) to occur, foreign central banks refused to permit the dollar depreciation by intervening in the exchange market. The United States considered this a **dirty float**, because the free-market forces of supply and demand were not allowed to achieve their equilibrating role. A second motivation for floating guidelines was the concern that free floats over time might lead to disorderly markets with erratic fluctuations in exchange rates. Such destabilizing activity could create an uncertain business climate and reduce the level of world trade.

Under managed floating, a nation can alter the degree to which it intervenes on the foreign-exchange market. Heavier intervention moves the nation nearer the fixed exchange-rate case, whereas less intervention moves the nation nearer the floating exchange-rate case. Concerning day-to-day and week-to-week exchange-rate movements, a main objective of the floating guidelines has been to prevent the emergence of erratic fluctuations. Member nations should intervene on the foreign-exchange market as necessary to prevent sharp and disruptive exchange-rate fluctuations from day to day and week to week. Such a policy is known as **leaning against the wind**— intervening to reduce short-term fluctuations in exchange rates without attempting to adhere to any particular rate over the long run. Members should also not act aggressively with respect to their currency exchange rates; that is, they should not enhance the value when it is appreciating or depress the value when it is depreciating.

Under the managed float, some nations choose target exchange rates and intervene to support them. Target exchange rates are intended to reflect long-term economic forces that underlie exchange-rate movements. One way for managed floaters to estimate a target exchange rate is to follow statistical indicators that respond to the same economic forces as the exchange-rate trend. Then, when the values of indicators change, the exchange-rate target can be adjusted accordingly. Among these indicators are rates of inflation in different nations, levels of official foreign reserves, and persistent imbalances in international payments accounts. In practice, defining a target exchange rate can be difficult in a market based on volatile economic conditions.

MANAGED FLOATING RATES IN THE SHORT RUN AND LONG RUN

Managed floating exchange rates attempt to combine market-determined exchange rates with foreign-exchange market intervention in order to take advantage of the best features of floating exchange rates and fixed exchange rates. Under a managed float, market intervention is used to stabilize exchange rates in the short run; in the long run, a managed float allows market forces to determine exchange rates.

Figure 16.5 illustrates the theory of a managed float in a two-country framework, Switzerland and the United States. The supply and demand schedules for francs are denoted by S_0 and D_0; the equilibrium exchange rate, at which the quantity of francs supplied equals the quantity demanded, is $0.50 per franc.

Suppose there occurs a permanent increase in U.S. real income, as a result of which U.S. residents demand additional francs to purchase more Swiss chocolate. Let the demand for francs rise from D_0 to D_1, as shown in Figure 16.5(a). Because this increase in demand is the result of long-run market forces, a managed float permits supply and demand conditions to determine the exchange rate. With the increase in the demand for francs, the quantity of francs demanded (180 francs) exceeds the quantity supplied (100 francs) at the exchange rate of $0.50 per franc. The excess demand results in a rise in the exchange rate to $0.60 per franc, at which the quantity of francs supplied and the quantity demanded are equal. In this manner, long-run movements in exchange rates are determined by the supply and demand for various currencies.

Figure 16.5(b) illustrates the case of a short-term increase in the demand for francs. Suppose U.S. investors demand additional francs to finance purchases of Swiss securities, which pay relatively high interest rates; again, let the demand for francs rise from D_0 to D_1. In a few

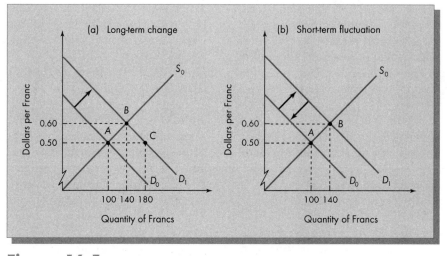

Figure 16.5 Managed Floating Exchange Rates

Under this system, central bank intervention is used to stabilize exchange rates in the short run; in the long run, market forces are permitted to determine exchange rates.

weeks, suppose Swiss interest rates fall, causing the U.S. demand for francs to revert to its original level, D_0. Under floating rates, the dollar price of the franc would rise from $0.50 per franc to $0.60 per franc and then fall back to $0.50 per franc. This type of exchange-rate irascibility is widely considered to be a disadvantage of floating rates because it leads to uncertainty regarding the profitability of international trade and financial transactions; as a result, the pattern of trade and finance may be disrupted.

Under managed floating rates, the response to this temporary disturbance is exchange-rate intervention by the Federal Reserve to keep the exchange rate at its long-term equilibrium level of $0.50 per franc. During the time period in which demand is at D_1, the central bank will sell francs to meet the excess demand. As soon as the disturbance is over, and demand reverts back to D_0, exchange-market intervention will no longer be needed. In short, central bank intervention is used to offset temporary fluctuations in exchange rates that contribute to uncertainty in carrying out transactions in international trade and finance.

Since the advent of managed floating rates in 1973, the frequency and size of U.S. foreign-exchange interventions have varied. Intervention was substantial from 1977 to 1979, when the dollar's exchange value was considered to be unacceptably low. U.S. stabilization operations were minimal during the Reagan Administration's first term, consistent with its goal of limiting government interference in markets; they were directed at offsetting short-run market disruptions. Intervention was again substantial in 1985, when the dollar's exchange value was deemed unacceptably high, hurting the competitiveness of U.S. producers. The most extensive U.S. intervention operations took place after the Louvre Accord of 1987, when the major industrial nations reached informal understandings about the limits of tolerance for exchange-rate fluctuations.

EXCHANGE-RATE STABILIZATION AND MONETARY POLICY We have seen how central banks can buy and sell foreign currencies to stabilize their values under a system of managed floating exchange rates. Another stabilization technique involves a nation's *monetary policy*. As we shall see, stabilizing a currency's exchange value requires the central bank to adopt (1) an *expansionary* monetary policy to offset currency *appreciation*, and (2) a *contractionary* monetary policy to offset currency *depreciation*.

Figure 16.6 illustrates the foreign-exchange market for the United States. Assume the supply schedule of British pounds is denoted by S_0 and the demand schedule of pounds is denoted by D_0. The equilibrium exchange rate, at which the quantity of pounds supplied and the quantity demanded are equalized, is $2 per pound.

Suppose that as a result of production shutdowns in Britain, caused by labor strikes, U.S. residents purchase fewer British products and therefore demand fewer pounds. Let the demand for pounds decrease from D_0 to D_1 in Figure 16.6(a). In the absence of central-bank intervention, the dollar price of the pound falls from $2 to $1.80; the dollar thus appreciates against the pound.

To offset the appreciation of the dollar, the Federal Reserve can increase the supply of money in the United States, which will decrease domestic interest rates in the short run. The reduced interest rates will cause the foreign demand for U.S. securities to decline. Fewer pounds will thus be supplied to the foreign-exchange market to buy dollars with which to purchase U.S. securities. As the supply of pounds shifts leftward to S_1, the dollar's exchange value reverts to $2 per pound. In this manner, the expansionary monetary policy has offset the dollar's appreciation.

Referring now to Figure 16.6(b), suppose a temporary surge in British interest rates causes U.S. investors to demand additional pounds with which to purchase additional British securities. Let the demand for pounds rise from D_0 to D_1. In the absence of central bank intervention, the dollar's exchange value would rise from $2 to $2.20 per pound; the dollar has depreciated against the pound.

To offset this dollar depreciation, the Federal Reserve can decrease the supply of money in the

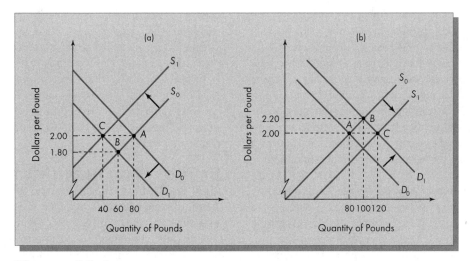

Figure 16.6 Exchange-Rate Stabilization and Monetary Policy

In the absence of international policy coordination, stabilizing a currency's exchange value requires a central bank to initiate (a) an expansionary monetary policy to offset an appreciation of its currency, and (b) a contractionary monetary policy to offset a depreciation of its currency.

United States, which will increase domestic interest rates and attract British investment. More pounds will thus be supplied to the foreign-exchange market to purchase dollars with which to buy U.S. securities. As the supply of pounds increases from S_0 to S_1, the dollar's exchange value reverts to $2 per pound. The contractionary monetary policy thus helps offset the dollar depreciation.

These examples illustrate how domestic monetary policies can be used to stabilize currency values. Such policies are not without costs, however, as seen in the following example.

Suppose the U.S. government increases federal spending without a corresponding increase in taxes. To finance the resulting budget deficit, assume the government borrows funds from the money market, which raises domestic interest rates. High U.S. interest rates enhance the attractiveness of dollar-denominated securities, leading to increased foreign purchases of these assets, an increased demand for dollars, and an appreciation in the dollar's exchange value. The appreciating dollar makes U.S. goods more expensive overseas and foreign goods less expensive in the United States, thus causing the U.S. trade account to fall into deficit.

Now suppose the Federal Reserve intervenes and adopts an expansionary monetary policy. The resulting increase in the supply of money dampens the rise in U.S. interest rates and the dollar's appreciation. By restraining the increase in the dollar's exchange value, the expansionary monetary policy enhances the competitiveness of U.S. businesses and keeps the U.S. trade account in balance.

However, the favorable effects of the expansionary monetary policy on the domestic economy are temporary. When pursued indefinitely (over the long run), a policy of increasing the domestic money supply leads to a *weakening* in the U.S. trade position, because the monetary expansion required to offset the dollar's appreciation eventually promotes higher prices in the United States. The higher prices of domestic goods offset the benefits to U.S. competitiveness that initially occur under the monetary expansion. U.S. spending eventually shifts back to foreign products and away from domestically produced goods, causing the U.S. trade account to fall into deficit!

This example shows how monetary policy can be used to stabilize the dollar's exchange value in the short run. But when monetary expansion occurs on a sustained, long-run basis, it brings with it eventual price increases that nullify the initial gains in domestic competitiveness. The long-run effectiveness of using monetary policy to stabilize the dollar's exchange value is limited, because the increase in the money supply to offset the dollar's appreciation does not permanently correct the underlying cause of the trade deficit—the increase in domestic spending.

Attempting to stabilize both the domestic economy and the dollar's exchange value can be difficult for the Federal Reserve. In early 1995, for example, the dollar was taking a nosedive against the yen and the mark, and the U.S. economy showed signs of slowing. To boost the dollar's exchange value would have required the Federal Reserve to adopt a restrictive monetary policy which would have led to higher interest rates and net investment inflows. However, further increases in domestic interest rates would heighten the danger that the U.S. economy would be pushed into a recession by the next year. The Federal Reserve thus had to choose between supporting domestic economic expansion or the dollar's exchange value. In this case, the Federal Reserve adopted a policy of lower interest rates, thus appearing to respond to U.S. domestic needs.

BANK OF JAPAN INTERVENES TO SLOW YEN'S RISE Another example of managed floating exchange rates involves Japan. In June and July of 1999, the Bank of Japan conducted several direct interventions in the currency market as expectations that Japan could be emerging from its decade-long recession rippled through the market. Currency traders reported that they took orders from the Bank of Japan to buy dollars with yen to force the value of the yen down against the dollar. In June alone, the Bank of Japan flooded the market with $23 billion in yen.

Officials at the Bank of Japan feared that a strong yen would undermine Japan's fragile economy. Should the exchange value of the yen increase against the dollar, stemming from an inflow of foreign money into Japan, Japanese exports would become more expensive and less competitive overseas. Therefore, the central bank was committed to forcing down the value of the yen to protect its exporters of cars, steel, CD players, VCRs, and the like.

The initial intervention by the Bank of Japan was successful in bringing the dollar from 119 per yen to 120 per yen. Currency traders said, however, that the central bank had to spend double what it normally spends to influence the value of the currency, just to keep the yen stable. As one currency trader put it, "There was not much bang for the buck." As time passed, market forces continued to push the value of the yen upward against the dollar, which resulted in additional interventions by the central bank. As seen in Figure 16.7, the Bank of Japan intervened in the currency market six times during June and July of 1999 to hold the value of the yen down against the dollar.

Although officials at the Bank of Japan welcomed economic growth and a stronger stock market, they maintained that higher bond yields and a stronger currency weren't what Japan's fragile economy needed at the moment. And they used every opportunity to let the markets know they were ready to take action if financial markets turned against economic recovery.

Despite record U.S. trade deficits with Japan, President Bill Clinton was willing to tolerate the currency interventions of the Bank of Japan as a means of supporting its exporters. He stated that unless Japan pulls out of its prolonged economic slump, emerging Asia's rebound from its recession could be snuffed out, therefore undermining the stability of the global economy. However, Clinton indicated that sound economic policies—not market intervention—were essential to an appropriate yen-dollar exchange rate. The foreign-exchange market is too big and deep to successfully fight it for long, according to Clinton.

THE CRAWLING PEG

Since 1968, the Brazilian government has announced a change in the par value of the cruzeiro several times a year. The frequent adjustments in Brazil's exchange rate occur in response to the following indicators: (1) the movement in prices in Brazil relative to those of its main trading partners, (2) the level of foreign-exchange reserves, (3) export performance, and (4) the position of the current account of the balance of payments. These exchange-rate adjustments are an application of a mechanism dubbed the **crawling peg**. Not only has Brazil adopted this system, but it also has been used by Argentina, Chile, Israel, and Peru.

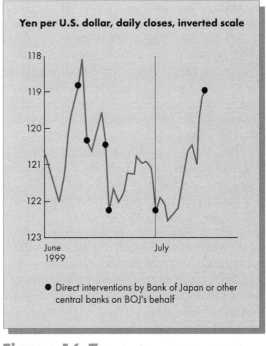

Figure 16.7 Bank of Japan Tries to Hold the Yen Down

Source: "Japan Continues Solo Intervention to Hold down Yen," *The Wall Street Journal*, July 21, 1999, p. A15 and "Bank of Japan Intervenes to Slow Yen's Rise," *The Wall Street Journal*, June 15, 1999, p. A12.

The crawling-peg system, a compromise between fixed and floating rates, means that a nation makes small, frequent changes in the par value of its currency to correct balance-of-payments disequilibriums. Deficit and surplus nations both keep adjusting until the desired exchange-rate level is attained. The term *crawling peg* implies that par-value changes are implemented in a large number of small steps, making the process of exchange-rate adjustment continuous for all practical purposes. The peg thus crawls from one par value to another.

The crawling-peg mechanism has been used primarily by nations with high inflation rates. Some developing nations, mostly South American, have recognized that a pegging system can operate in an inflationary environment only if there is provision for frequent changes in the par values. Associating national inflation rates with international competitiveness, these nations have generally used price indicators as a basis for adjusting crawling pegged rates. In these nations, the primary concern is the criterion that governs exchange-rate movements, rather than the currency or basket of currencies against which the peg is defined.

The crawling peg differs from the system of adjustable pegged rates. Under the adjustable peg, currencies are tied to a par value that changes infrequently (perhaps once every several years) but suddenly, usually in large jumps. The idea behind the crawling peg is that a nation can make small, frequent changes in par values, perhaps several times a year, so that they creep along slowly in response to evolving market conditions.

Supporters of the crawling peg argue that the system combines the flexibility of floating rates with the stability usually associated with fixed rates. They contend that a system providing continuous, steady adjustments is more responsive to changing competitive conditions and avoids a main problem of adjustable pegged rates—that changes in par values are frequently wide of the mark. Moreover, small, frequent changes in par values made at random intervals frustrate speculators with their irregularity.

In recent years, the crawling-peg formula has been used by developing nations facing rapid and persistent inflation. But the IMF has generally contended that such a system would not be in the best interests of nations such as the United States or Germany, which bear the responsibility for international currency levels. The IMF has felt that it would be hard to apply such a system to the industrialized nations, whose currencies serve as a source of international liquidity. Although even the most ardent proponents of the crawling peg admit that the time for its widespread adoption has not yet come, the debate over its potential merits is bound to continue.

EXCHANGE CONTROLS

The exchange-rate mechanisms discussed so far all have one important characteristic in common: All are based on the principle of a free exchange market and automatic market forces. It is true that monetary authorities may modify the exchange-rate outcome by purchasing and selling national currencies, but the foreign-exchange transactions conducted among private exporters and importers are free from government regulation. A private foreign-exchange market thus exists.

A government that does not wish to permit a free foreign-exchange market can set up a system of exchange measures to keep its balance of payments under control when the exchange rate moves away from its equilibrium level. Among the devices that have been used to achieve this objective are direct control over balance-of-payments transactions and multiple exchange rates.

Exchange controls achieved prominence during the economic crises of the late 1930s and immediately after World War II. It was not until the late 1950s that the industrialized nations of Western Europe considered themselves financially stable enough so that most controls could be dismantled and a high degree of freedom provided for many international transactions. Exchange controls are still widespread today in the less developed nations of Africa, South America, and the Far East.

At one extreme, a government may seek to gain control over its payments position by directly circumventing market forces through the imposition of direct controls on international transactions. For example, a government that has a virtual monopoly over foreign-exchange dealings may require that all foreign-exchange earnings be turned over to authorized dealers. The government then allocates foreign exchange among domestic traders and investors at government-set prices.

The advantage of such a system is that the government can influence its payments position by regulating the amount of foreign exchange allocated to imports or capital outflows, limiting the extent of these transactions. Exchange controls also permit the government to encourage or discourage certain transactions by offering different rates for foreign currency for different purposes. Furthermore, exchange controls can give domestic monetary and fiscal policies greater freedom in their stabilization roles. By controlling the balance of payments through exchange controls, a government can pursue its domestic economic policies without fear of balance-of-payments repercussions.

A related method of gaining control of the balance of payments is the practice of **multiple exchange rates**. Used primarily by the developing nations, multiple exchange rates attempt to ensure that necessary goods are imported and less essential goods are discouraged. Essential imports, such as raw materials or capital goods, are subsidized when the government sets a low exchange rate for these commodities, resulting in lower prices to domestic buyers. For less desirable imports, such as luxury products, a higher price will be set when the government makes foreign exchange available only at a high rate. Multiple exchange rates can thus be used to subsidize or tax import purchases so that a nation's scarce supply of foreign exchange will be rationed among only the most essential commodities. Obviously, the implementation of such a mechanism requires an elaborate classification system, as well as strict penalties against smuggling. Table 16.5 illustrates the multiple exchange rates used by Chile during the early 1970s.

Table 16.5 Chile's Multiple Exchange Rate System, 1972

Foreign-Exchange Usage	Exchange Rate: Chilean Escudos per U.S. dollar
Residential travel	130
Luxury imports	80
Tourism (to Chile)	46
Machinery imports	40
Student expenses	36
Specified exports	30
Raw material imports	25
General trade	25
Special trade	20

Source: *Pick's Currency Yearbook 1977–1979*, New York: Pick Publishing Co., 1979, p. 150.

Nations have also used **dual** (*two-tier*) **exchange rates** to cope with destabilizing international capital flows. Short-term capital tends to move across national borders in response to anticipated changes in exchange rates and interest-rate differentials. Such movements may prevent monetary authorities from pursuing policies insulated from balance-of-payments considerations or even from defending official exchange rates.

Dual exchange rates attempt to insulate a nation from the balance-of-payments effects of capital flows while providing a stable business climate for commercial (current account) transactions involving merchandise trade and services. This is accomplished by having separate exchange rates for commercial and capital transactions. *Commercial* transactions must be conducted in a market where exchange rates are officially *pegged* by national monetary authorities, whereas *capital* transactions occur in a financial market in which exchange rates are *floating*. Although history gives no example of a dual exchange-rate system in which complete segregation of commercial and capital transactions has been achieved, the experiences of Belgium, France, and Italy have approximated such a mechanism.

S U M M A R Y

1. Most nations maintain neither completely fixed nor floating exchange rates. Contemporary exchange-rate systems generally embody some features of each of these standards.

2. Small, developing nations often peg their currencies to a single currency or a currency basket. Pegging to a single currency is generally used by small nations whose trade and financial relationships are mainly with a single trading partner. Small nations with more than one major trading partner often peg their currencies to a basket of currencies.

3. The special drawing right (SDR) is a currency basket composed of five currencies of International Monetary Fund members. The basket-valuation technique attempts to make the SDR's value more stable than the foreign-currency value of any single currency in the basket. Developing nations often choose to peg their exchange rates to the SDR.

4. Under a fixed exchange-rate system, a government defines the official exchange rate for its currency. It then establishes an exchange-stabilization fund, which buys and sells foreign currencies to prevent the market exchange rate from moving above or below the official rate.

5. Under a fixed exchange-rate system, nations may officially devalue/revalue their currencies to restore trade equilibrium. The purpose of devaluation is to promote a depreciation in the home currency's exchange value, which helps reduce a trade deficit. The purpose of revaluation is to promote an appreciation in the home currency's exchange value, which helps reduce a trade surplus.

6. Currency boards are a method of stabilizing exchange rates of developing countries. A currency board is a monetary authority that issues notes and coins convertible into a foreign currency at a fixed exchange rate. Usually, the fixed exchange rate is set by law, making changes to the exchange rate very costly for governments. The most vital contribution a currency board can make to exchange-rate stability is to impose discipline on the process of money creation. This results in greater stability on domestic prices which, in turn, stabilizes the value of the domestic currency.

7. Rather than using a currency board to stabilize currency values, countries may dollarize their monetary systems. Dollarization occurs when residents of a country use the U.S. dollar alongside or instead of their own currency. Dollarization is seen as a way to protect a country's growth and prosperity from bouts of inflation and currency depreciation.

8. Under floating exchange rates, market forces of supply and demand determine currency values. Among the major arguments for floating rates are (a) simplicity, (b) continuous adjustment, (c) independent domestic policies, and (d) reduced need for international reserves. Arguments against floating rates stress (a) disorderly exchange markets, (b) reckless financial policies on the part of governments, and (c) conduciveness to price inflation.

9. The adjustable pegged exchange-rate system resulted from the Bretton Woods Agreement of 1944. The idea was to provide participating nations with stable but flexible exchange rates. In the short run, nations would use exchange-stabilization funds to maintain fixed exchange rates; in the long run, currency devaluations and revaluations would be used to help reverse persistent payment imbalances.

10. With the breakdown of the Bretton Woods system, the major industrial nations adopted a system of managed floating exchange rates. Under this system, central-bank intervention in the foreign-exchange market is intended to prevent disorderly market conditions in the short run. In the long run, exchange rates are permitted to float in accordance with changing supply and demand.

11. To offset a depreciation in the home currency's exchange value, a central bank can (1) use its international reserves to purchase quantities of that currency on the foreign-exchange market; (2) initiate a contractionary monetary policy, which leads to higher domestic interest rates, increased investment inflows, and increased demand for the home currency. To offset an appreciation in the home currency's exchange value, a central bank can sell additional quantities of its currency on the foreign-exchange market or initiate an expansionary monetary policy.

12. Under a crawling-peg exchange-rate system, a nation makes frequent devaluations (or revaluations) of its currency to restore payments balance. Developing nations suffering from high inflation rates have been major users of this mechanism.

13. Exchange controls are sometimes used by governments in an attempt to gain control of the balance of payments. To limit imports, the government may ration foreign exchange to domestic traders and investors. Multiple exchange rates are sometimes used in an attempt to ensure that only necessary goods will be imported.

14. Nations such as Belgium have resorted to dual exchange rates to insulate the balance of payments from short-term capital movements while providing exchange-rate stability for commercial transactions.

STUDY QUESTIONS

1. What factors underlie a nation's decision to adopt floating exchange rates or fixed exchange rates?

2. How do managed floating exchange rates operate? Why were they adopted by the industrialized nations in 1973?

3. Why do some developing countries adopt currency boards? Why do others dollarize their monetary systems?

4. Discuss the philosophy and operation of the Bretton Woods system of adjustable pegged exchange rates.

5. Why have nations such as Brazil adopted a crawling-peg exchange-rate system?

6. What is the purpose of exchange controls? Are they still being used today?

7. How do dual exchange rates attempt to provide a steady environment for commercial transactions while insulating the balance of payments from destabilizing capital movements?

8. Why do small nations adopt currency baskets against which to peg their exchange rates?

9. What advantage does the SDR offer to small nations seeking to peg their exchange rates?

10. Present the case for and the case against a system of floating exchange rates.

11. What techniques can a central bank use to stabilize the exchange value of its currency?

12. What is the purpose of a currency devaluation? What about a currency revaluation?

NETLINK

16.1 The Federal Reserve Bank of New York regularly reports on its intervention in foreign-exchange markets. Go to News Items and Foreign Exchange after setting your browser to URL:

http://www.ny.frb.org/

16.2 Throughout the world, central banks intervene in the foreign market. For a quick link to numerous central banks, go to the Bank for International Settlements Web page at:

http://www.bis.org/cbanks.htm

16.3 The International Monetary Fund (IMF) provides loans, technical assistance, and policy guidance to developing members in order to reduce poverty, improve living standards, and safeguard the stability of the international monetary system. Learn about exchange-rate practices by setting your browser to URL:

http://www.imf.org/

To access NetLink Exercises and the Virtual Scavenger Hunt, visit the Carbaugh Web site at http://carbaugh.swcollege.com.

chapter 17

Macroeconomic Policy in an Open Economy

A nation with a closed economy can select its economic policies in view of its own goals. In an open world economy, however, consequences of a nation's activities are felt by its trading partners. The result has been efforts among nations to coordinate their economic policies. This chapter examines government policies designed to achieve full employment with price stability and equilibrium in the balance of payments. The importance of international economic-policy cooperation is emphasized throughout the discussion.

ECONOMIC POLICY IN AN OPEN ECONOMY

International economic policy refers to activities of national governments that affect the movement of trade and factor inputs among nations. Included are not only the obvious measures such as import tariffs and quotas, but also domestic measures such as monetary policy and fiscal policy. Policies that are undertaken to improve the conditions of one sector in a nation tend to have repercussions that spill over into other sectors. Since an economy's *internal* (domestic) sector is tied to its *external* (foreign) sector, one cannot designate economic policies as purely domestic or purely foreign. Rather, the effects of economic policy should be viewed as being located on a continuum between two poles—an internal-effects pole and an external-effects pole. Although the primary impact of an import

KEY CONCEPTS AND TERMS

- *Bank for International Settlements (BIS)*
- *Demand-pull inflation*
- *Direct controls*
- *Expenditure-changing policies*
- *Expenditure-switching policies*
- *External balance*
- *Fiscal policy*
- *Group of Five (G-5)*
- *Group of Seven (G-7)*
- *Institutional constraints*
- *Internal balance*
- *International economic policy*
- *International economic-policy coordination*
- *Leaning with the wind*
- *Louvre Accord*
- *Monetary policy*
- *Operation Twist*
- *Overall balance*
- *Policy agreement*
- *Policy conflict*
- *Wage and price controls*

restriction is on a nation's trade balance, for example, there are secondary effects on national output, employment, and income. Most economic policies are located between the external and internal poles rather than falling directly on either one.

ECONOMIC OBJECTIVES OF NATIONS

What are the basic objectives of economic policies? Since the Great Depression of the 1930s, governments have actively pursued the goal of economic stability at full employment. Known as **internal balance**, this objective has two dimensions: (1) a fully employed economy, and (2) no inflation—or, more realistically, a reasonable amount of inflation. Nations traditionally have considered internal balance to be of primary importance and have formulated economic policies to attain this goal.

Policy makers are also aware of a nation's balance-of-payments (BOP) position. A nation is said to be in **external balance** when it realizes neither BOP deficits nor BOP surpluses.[1] In practice, policy makers usually express external balance in terms of a BOP subaccount, such as the current account. In this context, external balance occurs when the current account is neither so deeply in deficit that the home nation is incapable of repaying its foreign debts in the future nor so strongly in surplus that foreign nations cannot

repay their debts to it. Although nations usually consider internal balance to be the highest priority, they are sometimes forced to modify priorities when confronted with large and persistent external imbalances.

Nations have economic targets other than internal balance and external balance, such as long-run economic development and a reasonably equitable distribution of national income. Although these and other commitments may influence international economic policies, the discussion in this chapter is confined to the pursuit of internal balance and external balance.

POLICY INSTRUMENTS

To attain the objectives of external balance and internal balance, policy makers enact expenditure-changing policies, expenditure-switching policies, and direct controls. **Expenditure-changing policies** alter the level of aggregate demand for goods and services, including those produced domestically and those imported. They include **fiscal policy**, which refers to changes in government spending and taxes, and **monetary policy**, which refers to changes in the money supply by a nation's central bank (such as the Federal Reserve). Depending on the direction of change, expenditure-changing policies are either expenditure increasing or expenditure reducing.

If *inflation* is a problem, it is likely to be because the level of aggregate demand (total spending) is too high for the level of output that can be sustained by the nation's resources at constant prices. The standard recommendation in this case is for policy makers to reduce aggregate demand by implementing *expenditure-decreasing policies* such as reductions in government expenditures, tax increases, or decreases in the money supply; these policies offset the upward pressure on prices resulting from excess aggregate demand. If *unemployment* is excessive, the standard recommendation is for policy makers to increase aggregate demand for goods and services by initiating *expenditure-increasing policies*.

---

[1] Recall from Chapter 11 that BOP transactions are grouped into two categories: the current account and the capital account. Private-sector transactions and official (central bank) transactions are included in the capital account. With double-entry accounting, total debits equal total credits in the BOP statement. This implies that a current account deficit (surplus) will equal a capital account surplus (deficit).

In this chapter, we assume that BOP equilibrium occurs when the current account deficit (surplus) is equal to the surplus (deficit) on private-sector capital transactions; the balance on official capital transactions thus equals zero. This measure is known as the official reserve transaction balance; it emphasizes the role of all private-sector transactions in a nation's international payments position. It follows that a BOP deficit (surplus) occurs if the deficit (surplus) on current account transactions exceeds the surplus (deficit) on private-sector capital transactions.

Expenditure-switching policies modify the direction of demand, shifting it between domestic output and imports. Under a system of fixed exchange rates, a trade-deficit nation could devalue its currency to increase the international competitiveness of its industries, thus diverting spending from foreign goods to domestic goods. To increase its competitiveness under a managed floating exchange-rate system, the nation could purchase other currencies with its currency, thereby causing the exchange value of its currency to depreciate. The success of these policies in promoting trade balance largely depends on switching demand in the proper direction and amount, as well as on the capacity of the home economy to meet the additional demand by supplying more goods. Exchange-rate adjustments are general switching policies that influence the balance of payments indirectly, through their effects on the price mechanism and national income.

Direct controls consist of government restrictions on the market economy. They are selective expenditure-switching policies whose objective is to control particular items in the balance of payments. Direct controls, such as automobile tariffs and dairy quotas, are levied on imports in an attempt to switch domestic spending away from foreign goods to domestic goods. Similarly, the object of an export subsidy is to enhance exports by switching foreign spending to domestic output. When a government wishes to limit the volume of its overseas sales, it may impose an export quota (such as Japan's automobile export quotas of the 1980s). Direct controls may also be levied on capital flows so as to either restrain excessive capital outflows or stimulate capital inflows.

Economic policy formation is subject to **institutional constraints** that involve considerations of fairness and equity.[2] Policy makers are aware of the needs of groups they represent, such as labor and business, especially when pursuing conflicting economic objectives. For example, to what extent are policy makers willing to permit reductions in

national income, output, and employment at the cost of restoring BOP equilibrium? The outcry of adversely affected groups within the nation may be more than sufficient to convince policy makers not to pursue external balance as a goal. During election years, government officials tend to be especially sensitive to domestic economic problems. Reflecting perceptions of fairness and equity, policy formation tends to be characterized by negotiation and compromise.

Figure 17.1 illustrates the two basic policy dimensions of internal balance and external balance. The vertical axis of the diagram depicts the size of a nation's BOP deficit or surplus. External balance is reached at the diagram's origin, with neither BOP surplus nor BOP deficit. The horizontal axis indicates the extent of domestic recession or inflation. Full employment (zero recession) without inflation, or internal balance, is also achieved at the diagram's origin. An economy reaches overall balance when it attains internal balance and external balance.

EXCHANGE-RATE POLICIES AND OVERALL BALANCE

As noted previously, expenditure-switching policies can help a nation attain overall balance. Although these measures are designed primarily to influence the nation's external sector, they have secondary impacts on its internal sector. Let us examine one expenditure-switching instrument, the exchange rate, and its impact on a nation's external sector and internal sector.

Referring to Figure 17.1, suppose a nation is located in the disequilibrium zone of *BOP deficit with recession*, indicated by point C in the figure. A depreciation (devaluation) of the nation's currency increases the international competitiveness of its goods; this leads to rising exports and a reduction in the BOP deficit. Additional export sales provide an injection of spending into the economy, which encourages additional production and thus reduces the level of unemployment. In terms of the figure, the currency depreciation

[2] See A. C. Day, "Institutional Constraints and the International Monetary System," in R. Mundell and A. Swoboda, eds., *Monetary Problems of the International Economy* (Chicago: University of Chicago Press, 1969), pp. 333–342.

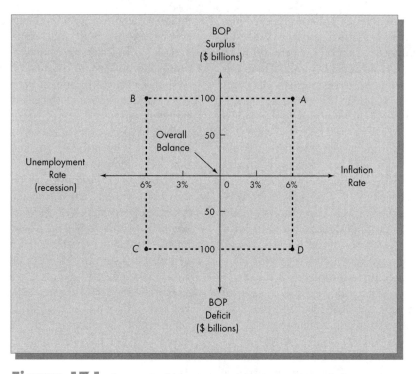

Figure 17.1 Economic Objectives and Macroeconomic Policy

A nation attains overall balance when it simultaneously achieves internal balance and external balance. When overall balance is not realized, nations can implement expenditure-changing policies (such as monetary/fiscal policy) or expenditure-switching policies (such as currency devaluation/revaluation) to help eliminate internal disequilibrium and/or external disequilibrium, thus pushing the economy toward overall balance.

induces movement in a northeasterly direction, promoting both internal balance and external balance.

Conversely, suppose that a nation experiences *BOP surplus with inflation*, indicated by point *A* in Figure 17.1. If this nation permits an appreciation (revaluation) of its currency, the international competitiveness of its goods will decline, causing exports to fall. Falling export sales decrease the level of spending in the economy, thus reducing its inflation rate. By promoting internal balance and external balance, the currency's appreciation induces a southwesterly movement in the figure.

As these examples suggest, the ability to implement exchange-rate policies is subject to

international policy cooperation for several reasons. A *depreciation* of one nation's currency implies an *appreciation* for its trading partners. If the dollar depreciates by 30 percent, this can be equivalent to a 30-percent subsidy on U.S. exports and a 30-percent tax on U.S. imports. Furthermore, changes in the exchange rate influence the external sectors and internal sectors of both the home country and its trading partners. In a global system, one nation cannot achieve overall balance single-handedly by means of its own policy tools. Other nations can implement retaliatory policies—such as tariffs and currency devaluations—that offset the nation's pursuit of overall balance, as occurred during the Great Depression of the 1930s.

MONETARY POLICY AND FISCAL POLICY: EFFECTS ON INTERNAL BALANCE

The previous section suggested that exchange-rate policies primarily affect the economy's external sector, while having secondary effects on its internal sector. Let us now consider monetary policy and fiscal policy as stabilization tools. These tools are generally used to stabilize the economy's internal sector, while having secondary effects on its external sector. How successful are monetary policy and fiscal policy in achieving full employment and price stability?

Let us assume that the mobility of international capital is high. This suggests that a small change in the relative interest rate across nations induces a large international flow of capital (investment funds). This assumption is consistent with capital movements among many industrial nations, such as the United States and Germany, and the conclusions of many analysts that capital mobility is increasing as national financial markets have become internationalized.

Two conclusions will emerge from our discussion: (1) Under a fixed exchange-rate system, fiscal policy is successful in promoting internal balance, whereas monetary policy is unsuccessful. (2) Under a floating rate system, monetary policy is successful in promoting internal balance, whereas fiscal policy is unsuccessful. These conclusions are summarized in Table 17.1.

In practice, most industrial nations maintain neither rigidly fixed exchange rates nor freely float-ing exchange rates. Rather, they maintain managed floating exchange rates in which central banks buy and sell currencies in an attempt to prevent exchange-rate movements from becoming disorderly. Heavier exchange-rate intervention moves a nation closer to our fixed exchange-rate conclusions for monetary and fiscal policy; less intervention moves a nation closer to our floating exchange-rate conclusions.

FISCAL POLICY WITH FIXED EXCHANGE RATES AND FLOATING EXCHANGE RATES

Assume that a nation operates under a fixed exchange-rate system and encounters high unemployment. Let us follow the case of an expansionary fiscal policy—say, an increase in government purchases of goods and services. The rise in government spending increases aggregate demand, which leads to higher output, employment, and income, as seen in the upper portion of Figure 17.2(a).

Now refer to the lower portion of Figure 17.2(a). As total spending rises, so does the demand for money. Given the supply of money, interest rates increase; this encourages foreigners to invest more in the home nation and discourages its residents from investing abroad. The resulting net capital inflows push the nation's capital account into surplus. Concurrently, the increase in spending results in higher imports and a trade deficit. If investment flows are highly mobile, it is likely that the capital account surplus will exceed the trade-account deficit; the overall BOP thus moves into surplus. Because the nation is committed to fixed exchange rates, its central bank buys foreign currency, thus preventing an appreciation of the home currency. This

Table 17.1 The Effectiveness of Fiscal Policy and Monetary Policy in Promoting Internal Balance*

Exchange-Rate Regime	Monetary Policy	Fiscal Policy
Floating exchange rates	Effective	Ineffective
Fixed exchange rates	Ineffective	Effective

*Assuming a high degree of capital mobility.

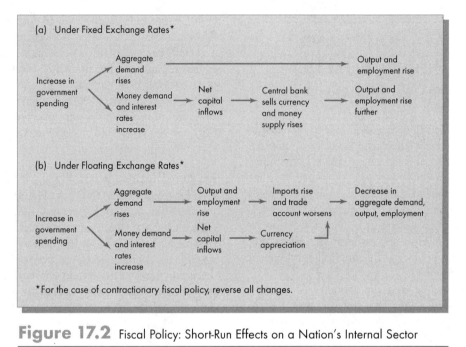

(a) Under Fixed Exchange Rates*

(b) Under Floating Exchange Rates*

*For the case of contractionary fiscal policy, reverse all changes.

Figure 17.2 Fiscal Policy: Short-Run Effects on a Nation's Internal Sector

(a) Under fixed exchange rates, an expansionary (contractionary) fiscal policy helps correct the problem of recession (inflation). (b) Under floating exchange rates, an expansionary (contractionary) fiscal policy is unsuccessful in correcting the problem of recession (inflation).

increases the money supply, which leads to additional spending, output, and employment. In this manner, the expansionary fiscal policy promotes internal balance.

If capital mobility is low, however, the trade-account deficit may more than offset the capital account surplus, pulling the overall BOP into deficit. To prevent the home currency from depreciating, central bankers would purchase it on the foreign-exchange market. This would cause a decrease in the money supply, an increase in interest rates, a decline in investment spending, and a decrease in output. The attempt to use expansionary fiscal policy to jumpstart the economy could backfire.

The result is different if the country has floating exchange rates. As before, fiscal expansion leads to higher output and income as well as higher interest rates. Higher income induces rising

imports, which push the trade account into deficit. Higher interest rates lead to net investment inflows and a surplus in the capital account. With highly mobile capital, it is likely that the surplus in the capital account will exceed the deficit in the trade account, so that the overall BOP moves into surplus. This leads to an appreciation in the home currency's exchange value. With a floating exchange-rate system, however, the central bank does nothing to offset this appreciation. By making the nation less competitive, the appreciation leads to falling exports and rising imports; the ensuing decrease in aggregate demand, output, and employment offsets the initial gains of the fiscal expansion. The expansionary fiscal policy is thus unable to mitigate the economy's recession. Adjustment following an increase in government spending under floating exchange rates is summarized in Figure 17.2(b).

MONETARY POLICY WITH FIXED EXCHANGE RATES AND FLOATING EXCHANGE RATES

Suppose that a nation experiences domestic recession and that it allows its currency to float in the foreign-exchange market. To stimulate domestic output, assume that the central bank adopts an expansionary monetary policy. By increasing the supply of money relative to the money demand, the monetary policy leads to lower interest rates, which stimulate aggregate demand and output. Lower interest rates also discourage foreigners from investing in the home country and encourage its residents to invest abroad. The resulting net capital outflows induce a depreciation of the nation's currency and an improvement in its international competitiveness. The subsequent rise in exports and fall in imports lead to further increases in output and employment; the expansionary monetary policy thus promotes internal balance. Adjustment following an expansionary monetary policy under floating exchange rates is summarized in Figure 17.3(a).

Contrast this outcome with the effects of monetary policy under a system of fixed exchange rates. The monetary expansion reduces interest rates, leading to rising aggregate demand, output, and employment. Lower interest rates result in net capital outflows and a depreciation in the currency's exchange value. To maintain a fixed exchange rate, however, the central bank intervenes on the foreign-exchange market and purchases the home currency with foreign currency. This decreases the money supply and offsets the initial increase in the money supply. The initial output and employment expansion resulting from the expansionary monetary policy is thus blunted, and internal balance is

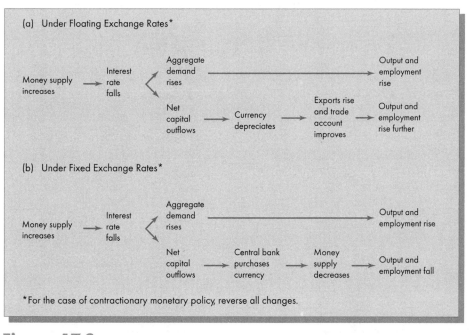

(a) Under Floating Exchange Rates*

(b) Under Fixed Exchange Rates*

*For the case of contractionary monetary policy, reverse all changes.

Figure 17.3 Monetary Policy: Short-Run Effects on a Nation's Internal Sector

(a) Under floating exchange rates, an expansionary (contractionary) monetary policy is successful in correcting the problem of recession (inflation). (b) Under fixed exchange rates, an expansionary (contractionary) monetary policy is unsuccessful in correcting the problem of recession (inflation).

not attained. Adjustment following an expansionary monetary policy under fixed exchange rates is summarized in Figure 17.3(b)

MONETARY AND FISCAL POLICIES: EFFECTS ON EXTERNAL BALANCE

What are the effects of monetary policy and fiscal policy on a nation's external balance? We assume that the exchange rate is fixed, because BOP surpluses and BOP deficits are issues only when the exchange rate is fixed; recall that floating exchange rates automatically adjust to promote BOP equilibrium.

The short-run effects of monetary policy on the BOP are definite: An expansion in the money supply worsens the BOP, whereas a contraction in the money supply improves the BOP. These effects are illustrated in Figure 17.4.

To illustrate, assume the central bank increases the money supply, relative to the money demand, which pushes interest rates downward. Falling interest rates encourage additional investment spending, which leads to an increase in aggregate demand, output, and income. The rise in income, in turn, increases imports and worsens the trade balance. At the same time, falling interest rates (relative to those abroad) induce net investment outflows and a deterioration in the capital account. By worsening the trade balance and the capital account balance, the monetary expansion worsens overall BOP. In the long run, the overseas

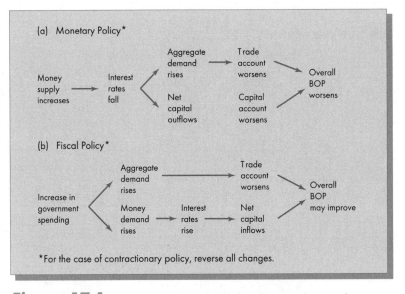

Figure 17.4 Monetary Policy and Fiscal Policy Under Fixed Exchange Rates: Short-Run Effects on a Nation's External Sector

(a) An expansionary (contractionary) monetary policy leads to a worsening (improving) trade account and capital account, thus worsening (improving) the overall balance of payments. (b) An expansionary (contractionary) fiscal policy leads to a worsening (improving) trade account and an improving (worsening) capital account. The overall balance of payments improves (worsens) depending on the relative strength of these two opposing forces.

investments will be repaid with interest, resulting in a positive feedback into the BOP; but the negative effect on the trade balance will persist.

The short-run effects on the BOP of expansionary fiscal policy are not as clear as those of monetary policy. Assume the government increases its purchases of goods and services, leading to increases in aggregate demand, output, and income. Rising income, in turn, induces rising imports and a worsening trade balance. Meanwhile, increased government spending leads to increased money demand and rising interest rates. The higher interest rates, in turn, induce net investment inflows and an improvement in the capital account. If capital mobility is sufficiently high, the improvement in the capital account more than offsets the trade-account deterioration, and the overall BOP improves. Eventually, however, foreign investors must be repaid with interest, and this more than offsets the investment inflows caused by higher interest rates. As a result, the fiscal expansion probably worsens the overall BOP in the long run, albeit improving it in the short run if enough investment inflows occur in response to higher interest rates.

MONETARY POLICY AND FISCAL POLICY: POLICY AGREEMENT AND POLICY CONFLICT

With fixed exchange rates, let us consider monetary policy and fiscal policy and see what effects they have on a nation's internal balance and external balance.

Consider monetary policy first. Referring to Figure 17.1, suppose that a nation experiences *unemployment with BOP surplus*, shown by point *B*. The previous section suggested that if the central bank increases the money supply, which leads to rising aggregate demand, unemployment will fall and the BOP surplus will decrease. In this case, the expansionary monetary policy clearly promotes overall balance. Alternatively, suppose that a country experiences *inflation with BOP deficit*, shown

by point *D* in Figure 17.1. A reduction in the money supply, which reduces aggregate demand, decreases the inflation rate as well as the BOP deficit, thus promoting overall balance. These two disequilibrium zones illustrate **policy agreement** for monetary policy. Changes in the money supply move the economy toward both internal balance and external balance.

Not all disequilibrium zones, however, are as favorable for monetary policy. Suppose now that a nation experiences *unemployment with BOP deficit*, shown by point *C* in Figure 17.1. The previous section suggested that an expansionary monetary policy, which raises aggregate demand, will reduce unemployment—but at the cost of a larger BOP deficit (southeast from point *C*). If a country experiences *inflation with BOP surplus*, shown by point *A* in Figure 17.1, a contractionary monetary policy leads to less inflation but increased BOP surplus (northwest from point *A*). These disequilibrium zones imply **policy conflict** for monetary policy. Although changes in the money supply improve one economic objective, they detract from another objective. A dilemma thus exists for monetary authorities concerning which objective to pursue.

Instead of utilizing monetary policy in policy-conflict zones, suppose a nation resorts to fiscal policy. Assume, for example, that a country experiences *unemployment and BOP deficit*, as shown by point *C* in Figure 17.1. Recall that an expansionary fiscal policy, which raises aggregate demand, promotes full employment; however, it reduces a nation's BOP deficit only if the ensuing improvement in the capital account more than offsets the deterioration in the trade account. If a country experiences *inflation and BOP surplus*, shown by point *A* in Figure 17.1, a contractionary fiscal policy lessens inflation; whether the BOP surplus rises or falls depends on whether the worsening of its capital account more than offsets the improvement of its trade account. It is thus not clear whether fiscal policy is able to promote overall balance for a nation situated in one of these policy-conflict zones.

When a nation finds itself in a policy-conflict zone, fiscal policy or monetary policy alone will not necessarily restore both internal and external balance. A combination of policies is generally needed. Suppose, for example, that a nation experiences *unemployment with BOP deficit*, shown by point C in Figure 17.1. An expansionary monetary policy to combat unemployment might be accompanied by tariffs or quotas, or possibly currency devaluation, to reduce imports and improve the BOP. Each economic objective is matched with an appropriate policy instrument so that both objectives can be attained at the same time.

In U.S. history, the Federal Reserve has attempted to line up policy instruments with targets during conflict situations. During the early 1960s, the conflict was *domestic recession with BOP deficit*. The Federal Reserve attempted to match instruments with targets by manipulating the structure of domestic interest rates in a program called **Operation Twist**. Under this program, the U.S. interest-rate structure was modified so that short-term rates were used primarily to promote external balance whereas long-term rates were used primarily for internal balance. By keeping short-term interest rates high, the United States could expect to experience net investment inflows, thereby improving its BOP position. Low long-term rates would presumably stimulate domestic investment, output, and employment, thus correcting the recession. At best, Operation Twist was only partially successful in promoting overall balance. The policy was initially successful in keeping short-term rates above long-term rates. As time passed, however, the differential between them disappeared as inflation pushed both short-term and long-term rates upward, thus moderating the program's success.

INFLATION WITH UNEMPLOYMENT

The analysis so far has looked at internal balance under special circumstances. It has been assumed that as the economy advances to full employment, domestic prices remain unchanged until full employment is reached. Once the nation's capac-ity to produce has been achieved, further increases in aggregate demand pull prices upward. This type of inflation is known as **demand-pull inflation**. Under these conditions, internal balance (full employment with stable prices) can be viewed as a single target that requires but one policy instrument: reductions in aggregate demand via monetary policy or fiscal policy.

A more troublesome problem is the appropriate policy to implement when a nation experiences *inflation with unemployment*. Here the problem is that internal balance cannot be achieved just by manipulating aggregate demand. To decrease inflation, a reduction in aggregate demand is required; to decrease unemployment, an expansion in aggregate demand is required. Thus, the objectives of full employment and stable prices cannot be considered as one and the same target; rather, they are two independent targets, requiring two distinct policy instruments.

Achieving overall balance thus involves three separate targets: (1) BOP equilibrium, (2) full employment, and (3) price stability. To ensure that all three objectives can be achieved simultaneously, monetary/fiscal policies and exchange-rate adjustments may not be enough; direct controls may also be needed.

Inflation with unemployment has been a problem for the United States. In 1971, for example, the U.S. economy experienced *inflation with recession and BOP deficit*. Increasing aggregate demand to achieve full employment would presumably intensify inflationary pressures. The President therefore implemented a comprehensive system of **wage and price controls** to remove the inflationary constraint. Later the same year, the United States entered into exchange-rate realignments that resulted in a depreciation of the dollar's exchange value by 12 percent against the trade-weighted value of other major currencies. The dollar depreciation was intended to help the United States reverse its BOP deficit. In short, it was the President's view that the internal and external problems of the United States could not be eliminated through expenditure-changing policies alone.

INTERNATIONAL ECONOMIC-POLICY COORDINATION

Policy makers have long been aware that the welfare of their economies is linked to that of the world economy. Because of the international mobility of goods, services, capital, and labor, economic policies of one nation have spillover effects on others. This spillover is especially true for the larger industrial economies, but even here, the linkages are stronger among some nations, such as those within Western Europe, than for others. Recognizing these spillover effects, governments have often made attempts to coordinate their economic policies.

Economic relations among nations can be visualized along a spectrum, illustrated in Figure 17.5, ranging from *open conflict* to *integration*, where nations implement policies jointly in a supranational forum to which they have ceded a large degree of authority, such as the European Union. At the spectrum's midpoint lies policy *independence*: Nations take the actions of other nations as a given; they do not attempt to influence those actions or be influenced by them. Between independence and integration lie various forms of policy coordination and cooperation.

Cooperative policy making can take many forms, but in general it occurs whenever officials from different nations meet to evaluate world economic conditions. During these meetings, policy makers may present briefings on their individual economies and discuss current policies. Such meetings represent a simple form of cooperation. A more involved format might consist of economists' studies on a particular subject, combined with an in-depth discussion of possible solutions. True policy coordination, however, goes beyond these two forms of cooperation; policy coordination is a formal agreement among nations to initiate particular policies.

International economic-policy coordination is the attempt to significantly modify national policies—monetary policy, fiscal policy, exchange-rate policy—in recognition of international economic interdependence. Policy coordination does not necessarily imply that nations give precedence to international over domestic concerns. It does recognize, however, that the policies of one nation can spill over to influence the objectives of others; nations should therefore communicate with one another and attempt to coordinate their policies so as to take these linkages into account. Presumably, they will be better off than if they had acted independently.

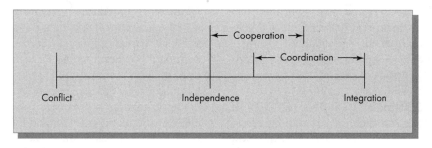

Figure 17.5 Relations Among National Governments

Relations among national governments can be visualized along a spectrum ranging from policy conflict to policy integration. Between these extremes are a variety of forms of cooperation and coordination.

Source: Dobson, *Economic Policy Coordination: Requiem or Prologue?* Washington, DC, Institute for International Economics, 1991, p. 3.

There are many examples of international economic-policy coordination. The Smithsonian Agreement of 1971 was a coordinated attempt by the major industrial nations to realign the exchange values of their currencies using currency devaluations and revaluations. The 1978 Bonn Summit resulted in the enactment by Germany and Japan of expansionary fiscal and monetary policies to stimulate their demand for U.S. goods and reduce the U.S. trade deficit; in return, the United States raised its price of oil to the world level. In the Plaza Accord of 1985, Germany and Japan agreed to adopt stimulative fiscal policies to promote imports from the United States and to intervene in foreign currency markets to further a depreciation in the dollar's exchange value.

To facilitate policy coordination, economic officials of the major governments talk with one another frequently in the context of the International Monetary Fund (IMF) and the Organization for Economic Cooperation and Development (OECD). Also, central bank senior officials meet monthly at the Basel meetings of the **Bank for International Settlements (BIS)**. Since 1975, government officials of the seven largest industrial economies (United States, Canada, Japan, United Kingdom, Germany, France, and Italy), known as the **Group of Seven (G-7)**, have met in annual economic summits to discuss economic issues of common concern. Not only do the G-7 nations initiate dialogues concerning economic objectives and policy, but they also devise economic indicators that provide a framework for multilateral surveillance of their economies and help monitor the international consequences of domestic policies.

POLICY COORDINATION IN THEORY

If economic policies in each of two nations affect the other, then the case for policy coordination would appear to be obvious. Policy coordination is considered important in the modern world because economic disruptions are transmitted rapidly from one nation to another. Without policy coordination, national economic policies can destabilize other economies. The logic of policy coordination is illustrated in the following basketball-spectator problem.[3]

Suppose you are attending a basketball game between the Seattle Supersonics and the Chicago Bulls. If everyone is sitting, someone who stands has a superior view. Spectators usually can see well if everyone sits or if everyone stands. Sitting in seats is more comfortable than standing. When there is no cooperation, everyone stands; each spectator does what is best for herself/himself given the actions of other spectators. If all spectators sit, someone, taking what the others will do as a given, will stand. If all spectators are standing, then it is best to remain standing. With spectator cooperation, the solution is for everyone to sit. The problem is that each spectator may be tempted to get a better view by standing. The cooperative solution will not be attained, therefore, without an outright agreement on coordination—in this situation, everyone remains seated.

Consider the following economic example. Suppose the world consists of just two nations, Germany and Japan. Although these nations freely trade goods with each other, they desire to pursue their own domestic economic priorities. Germany wants to avoid trade deficits with Japan, while achieving full employment for its economy; Japan desires full employment for its economy, while avoiding trade deficits with Germany. Assume that both nations achieve balanced trade with each other, but each nation's economy operates below full employment. Germany and Japan contemplate enacting expansionary government spending policies that would stimulate demand, output, and employment. But each nation rejects the idea, recognizing the policy's adverse impact on the trade balance. Germany and Japan realize that bolstering domestic income to increase jobs has the side effect of stimulating the demand for imports, thus pushing the trade account into deficit.

The preceding situation is *favorable* for successful policy coordination. If Germany and Japan agree to simultaneously expand their government spending, then output, employment,

[3] See S. Fischer, "International Macroeconomic Policy Coordination," in M. Feldstein, *International Economic Cooperation* (Chicago: University of Chicago Press, 1988), p. 19.

and incomes will rise concurrently. While higher German income promotes increased imports from Japan, higher Japanese income promotes increased imports from Germany. An appropriate increase in government spending results in each nation's increased demand for imports being offset by an increased demand for exports, which leads to balanced trade between Germany and Japan. In our example of mutual implementation of expansionary fiscal policies, policy coordination permits each nation to achieve full employment and balanced trade.

This is an optimistic portrayal of international economic-policy coordination. The synchronization of policies appears simple because there are only two economies and two objectives. In the real world, however, policy coordination generally involves many countries and many diverse objectives, such as low inflation, high employment, economic growth, and trade balance.

If the benefits of international economic-policy coordination are really so obvious, it may seem odd that agreements do not occur more often than they do. Several obstacles hinder successful policy coordination. Even if national economic objectives are harmonious, there is no guarantee that governments can design and implement coordinated policies. Policy makers in the real world do not always have sufficient information to understand the nature of the economic problem or how their policies will affect economies. Implementing appropriate policies when governments disagree about economic fundamentals is difficult.

Policy coordination is also complicated by different national starting points:[4]

Different economic objectives. Some nations give higher priority to price stability, for instance, or to full employment, than others.

Different national institutions. Some nations have a stronger legislature, or weaker trade unions, than others.

Different national political climates. The party pendulums in different nations, for example, shift with elections occurring in different years.

Different phases in the business cycle. One nation may experience economic recession while another nation experiences rapid inflation.

Although the theoretical advantages of international economic-policy coordination are fairly clearly established, attempts to quantify their gains are rare. Skeptics point out that, in practice, the gains from policy coordination are smaller than what is often suggested. Let us consider some examples of international economic-policy coordination.

PLAZA AGREEMENT OF 1985 AND LOUVRE ACCORD OF 1987

By early 1984, the U.S. economy was recovering from the recession of 1981–1983; domestic output was rising and unemployment was falling. While an expansionary fiscal policy contributed to economic recovery, growing U.S. government budget deficits were causing concern about the stability of the world financial system. Equally problematic was the appreciation in the dollar's exchange value, which encouraged U.S. consumers to purchase cheaper imports, and resulted in large U.S. trade deficits. By 1985, it was estimated that the dollar was overvalued by about 30 to 35 percent. As the U.S. recovery slowed, protectionist pressures skyrocketed in the U.S. Congress.

U.S. trading partners were also exasperated by the hands-off approach of the Reagan Administration. During the early 1980s, they had pleaded for a reduction in the U.S. budget deficits and a depreciation in the dollar's exchange value, but to no avail. The exchange values of the industrial nations' currencies oscillated, straining the world trading system. Trade wars, both between the United States and Western Europe and between the United States and Japan, seemed a possibility. This was the environment that led to the *Plaza Agreement* of 1985.

Fearing a disaster in the world trading system,

[4] See R. Putnam and C. R. Henning, "The Bonn Summit of 1978: A Case Study in Coordination," in R. Cooper et al., *Can Nations Agree?* (Washington, D.C.: The Brookings Institution, 1989), p. 17.

government officials of the **Group of Five (G-5)** nations—the United States, Japan, Germany, Great Britain, and France—met at New York's Plaza Hotel in September 1985. There was widespread agreement that the dollar was overvalued and that the twin U.S. deficits (trade and federal budget) were too large. The Plaza strategy was threefold: (1) to combat protectionism in the U.S. Congress, a short-term strategy; (2) to promote world economic expansion by stimulating demand in Germany and Japan, a medium-term strategy; and (3) to ease the burden of U.S. debt service, a long-term strategy.

The Plaza strategy was presented as a comprehensive package that included monetary, fiscal, and exchange-rate policies. To stimulate demand, German and Japanese officials agreed to more expansionary fiscal policies—accelerating planned tax cuts and expanding spending programs, respectively. For its part, the United States agreed to attempt to bring down its budget deficit. Moreover, all participants agreed to intervene in the currency markets, when necessary, to further the dollar's orderly decline. The Plaza Agreement represented an abrupt change in policy for the Reagan Administration, a reversal of its opposition to foreign-exchange intervention.

Prior to the 1985 Plaza meeting, some participants were skeptical that concerted intervention could push the U.S. dollar down sufficiently to dampen protectionist sentiments in the U.S. Congress. Nevertheless, concerted intervention was decided upon, and the operation succeeded beyond expectations. The objective of intervention was to **lean with the wind**, accelerating the downward pace of the already depreciating U.S. dollar. Large-scale intervention occurred in the month after the Plaza agreement; the dollar's trade-weighted exchange value fell sharply after the agreement and continued to fall through the spring of 1986. At that time, central bankers began to indicate reservations about the dollar's continued depreciation, and central bankers in the industrial countries other than the United States intervened heavily to support the dollar's value.

The Plaza Agreement complicated the Federal Reserve's mission of pursuing both domestic and international objectives. To lower the dollar's

exchange value, the Federal Reserve would have to adopt an expansionary monetary policy that would force down domestic interest rates; this would induce investment outflows, a lower demand for the dollar, and a depreciation in the dollar's value. The Federal Reserve's concern, however, was that such a policy would intensify U.S. inflation. It would then have to decide whether to give higher priority to fighting inflation, which would call for a restrictive monetary policy, or to promoting a dollar depreciation, which would call for an expansionary monetary policy. It turned out that 1985 was a year of modest inflation, and the Federal Reserve was able to give higher priority to international objectives.

The Plaza Agreement was generally viewed as a success, though not an unqualified one. In 1987, citing increased inflationary pressures, German officials were cautious in approaching implementation of the coordinated fiscal policy expansion agreed to in the Plaza Agreement. This development did not sit well with the United States, which disagreed over the extent to which accelerating inflation was a problem in West Germany. The slow progress on reducing the federal budget deficit in the United States, especially during the second half of 1987, also strained the pact. Other nations were understandably reluctant to enact stimulative policies without evidence of fiscal restraint in the United States. The agreement, however, survived numerous attacks, with the participating nations repeatedly expressing their support for it.

By early 1987, the dollar's exchange value had become a topic of disagreement among the G-5 nations. The United States continued to pressure foreign governments for further dollar depreciation to help restore current account balance. Officials of other G-5 nations, however, maintained that appreciation of their currencies against the dollar had gone far enough. In February 1987, the G-5 nations plus Canada met at the Louvre in Paris. In the **Louvre Accord**, these six nations agreed to stabilize exchange rates around levels then prevailing, which officials considered to be generally harmonious with underlying economic fundamentals.

S U M M A R Y

1. International economic policy refers to various government activities that influence trade patterns among nations, including (a) monetary and fiscal policies, (b) exchange-rate adjustments, (c) tariff and nontariff trade barriers, (d) foreign-exchange controls and investment controls, and (e) export-promotion measures.

2. Since the 1930s, nations have actively pursued internal balance (full employment without inflation) as a primary economic objective. Nations also consider external balance (balance-of-payments equilibrium) as an economic objective. A nation realizes overall balance when it attains internal balance and external balance.

3. To achieve overall balance, nations implement expenditure-changing policies (monetary and fiscal policies), expenditure-switching policies (exchange-rate adjustments), and direct controls (price and wage controls).

4. Although exchange-rate adjustments primarily influence a nation's BOP position, they have secondary impacts on the domestic economy. A nation with a BOP deficit and high unemployment could devalue its currency to resolve these problems; a nation with a BOP surplus and inflation could revalue its currency. Such policies are dependent upon the willingness of other nations to refrain from implementing offsetting exchange-rate adjustments. International economic-policy cooperation is thus essential when nations are economically interdependent.

5. Under a fixed exchange-rate system, fiscal policy is successful in promoting internal balance, whereas monetary policy is unsuccessful. Under a floating exchange-rate system, monetary policy is successful in promoting internal balance, whereas fiscal policy is unsuccessful.

6. Given a fixed exchange-rate system, in the short run, an expansionary monetary policy worsens the BOP position, and a contractionary monetary policy improves the BOP position. An expansionary fiscal policy leads to a worsening of the trade account and an improvement in the capital account; the impact on the overall BOP depends on the relative strength of these opposing forces.

7. Policy agreement occurs when an economic policy helps eliminate internal disequilibrium and external disequilibrium, thus promoting overall balance for the nation. Policy conflict occurs when an economic policy helps eliminate one economic problem (such as internal disequilibrium), but aggravates another economic problem (such as external disequilibrium).

8. Given a fixed exchange-rate system, for monetary policy the disequilibrium zones of unemployment-with-BOP-surplus and inflation-with-BOP-deficit are zones of policy agreement. The disequilibrium zones of unemployment-with-BOP-deficit and inflation-with-BOP-surplus are zones of policy conflict; a dilemma exists for monetary authorities concerning which objective to pursue. A combination of policies may be needed to resolve these economic problems.

9. When a nation experiences inflation with unemployment, achieving overall balance involves three separate targets: BOP equilibrium, full employment, and price stability. Three policy instruments may be needed to achieve these targets.

10. International economic-policy coordination is the attempt to significantly modify national policies in recognition of international economic interdependence. Nations regularly consult with each other in the context of the IMF, OECD, Bank for International Settlements, and Group of Seven. The Smithsonian Agreement, Plaza Agreement, and Louvre Accord are examples of international economic-policy coordination.

11. Several problems confront international economic-policy coordination: (a) different national economic objectives, (b) different national institutions, (c) different national political climates, (d) different phases in the business cycle. Moreover, there is no guarantee that governments can design and implement policies that are capable of achieving the intended results.

STUDY QUESTIONS

1. Distinguish among external balance, internal balance, and overall balance.
2. What are the most important instruments of international economic policy?
3. What is meant by the terms *expenditure-changing policy* and *expenditure-switching policy*? Give some examples of each.
4. What institutional constraints bear on the formation of economic policies?
5. Assume that a nation faces a BOP deficit with high unemployment. What exchange-rate adjustment can be made to resolve these problems? What if the nation experiences a BOP surplus with inflation?
6. Under a system of fixed exchange rates, is monetary policy or fiscal policy better suited for promoting internal balance? Why?
7. Under a system of floating exchange rates, is monetary policy or fiscal policy better suited for promoting internal balance? Why?

8. With fixed exchange rates, what impact does an expansionary monetary policy have on the nation's BOP? What about a contractionary monetary policy?
9. With fixed exchange rates, when does an expansionary fiscal policy improve the nation's BOP? When does it worsen the BOP?
10. What is meant by the terms *policy agreement* and *policy conflict*?
11. Given a system of fixed exchange rates, for monetary policy, is unemployment-with-BOP-surplus a zone of policy agreement or policy conflict? What about inflation-with-BOP-deficit, unemployment-with-BOP-deficit, or inflation-with-BOP-surplus?
12. What are some obstacles to successful international economic-policy coordination?

International Banking: Reserves, Debt, and Risk

The world's banking system plays a vital role in facilitating international transactions and maintaining economic prosperity. Commercial banks, such as Citicorp, help finance trade and investment and provide loans to international borrowers. Central banks, such as the Federal Reserve, serve as a lender of last resort to commercial banks and sometimes intervene in foreign-currency markets to stabilize currency values. Finally, the International Monetary Fund serves as a lender to nations having long-term deficits in their balance of payments. This chapter concentrates on the role that banks play in world financial markets, the risks associated with international banking, and strategies employed to deal with these risks.

We'll begin with an investigation of the nature of international reserves and their importance for the world financial system. This is followed by a discussion of banks as international lenders and the problems associated with international debt.

NATURE OF INTERNATIONAL RESERVES

The need of a central bank, such as the Bank of England, for international reserves is similar to an individual's desire to hold cash balances (currency and checkable deposits). At both levels, monetary reserves are intended to bridge the gap between monetary receipts and monetary payments.

KEY CONCEPTS AND TERMS

- *Basket valuation*
- *Buffer-stock facility*
- *Compensatory financing facility*
- *Conditionality*
- *Country risk*
- *Credit risk*
- *Currency risk*
- *Debt/equity swap*
- *Debt forgiveness*
- *Debt reduction*
- *Debt service/export ratio*
- *Debt-to-export ratio*
- *Demand for international reserves*
- *Demonetization of gold*
- *Eurocurrency market*
- *General Arrangements to Borrow*
- *Gold exchange standard*
- *Gold standard*
- *IMF drawings*
- *International Monetary Fund*
- *International reserves*
- *Liquidity problem*
- *Oil facility*
- *Special drawing rights*
- *Supply of international reserves*
- *Swap arrangements*

Suppose that an individual receives income in equal installments every minute of the day and that expenditures for goods and services are likewise evenly spaced over time. The individual will require only a minimum cash reserve to finance purchases, because no significant imbalances between cash receipts and cash disbursements will arise. In reality, however, individuals purchase goods and services on a fairly regular basis from day to day, but receive paychecks only at weekly or longer intervals. A certain amount of cash is therefore required to finance the discrepancy that arises between monetary receipts and payments.

When an individual initially receives a paycheck, cash balances are high. But as time progresses, these holdings of cash may fall to virtually zero just before the next paycheck is received. Individuals are thus concerned with the amount of cash balances that, on average, are necessary to keep them going until the next paycheck arrives.

Although individuals desire cash balances primarily to fill the gap between monetary receipts and payments, this desire is influenced by a number of other factors. The need for cash balances may become more acute if the absolute dollar volume of transactions increases, because larger imbalances may result between receipts and payments. Conversely, to the extent that individuals can finance their transactions on credit, they require less cash in hand.

Just as an individual desires to hold cash balances, national governments have a need for **international reserves**. The chief purpose of international reserves is to enable nations to finance disequilibriums in their balance-of-payments positions. When a nation finds its monetary receipts falling short of its monetary payments, the deficit is settled with international reserves. Eventually, the deficit must be eliminated, because central banks tend to have limited stocks of reserves.

From a policy perspective, the advantage of international reserves is that they enable nations to sustain temporary balance-of-payments deficits until acceptable adjustment measures can operate to correct the disequilibrium. Holdings of international reserves facilitate effective policy formation because corrective adjustment measures need not be implemented prematurely. Should a deficit nation possess abundant stocks of reserve balances, however, it may be able to resist unpopular adjustment measures, making eventual adjustments even more troublesome.

DEMAND FOR INTERNATIONAL RESERVES

When a nation's international monetary payments exceed its international monetary receipts, some means of settlement is required to finance its payments deficit. Settlement ultimately consists of transfers of international reserves among nations. Both the magnitude and the longevity of a balance-of-payments deficit that can be sustained in the absence of equilibrating adjustments are limited by a nation's stock of international reserves.

On a global basis, the **demand for international reserves** depends on two related factors: (1) the monetary value of international transactions and (2) the disequilibrium that can arise in balance-of-payments positions. The demand for international reserves is also contingent on such things as the speed and strength of the balance-of-payments adjustment mechanism and the overall institutional framework of the world economy.

EXCHANGE-RATE FLEXIBILITY One determinant of the demand for international reserves is the *degree of exchange-rate flexibility* of the international monetary system. This is because exchange-rate flexibility in part underlies the efficiency of the balance-of-payments adjustment process.

Figure 18.1 represents the exchange-market position of the United States in trade with Great Britain. Starting at equilibrium point E, suppose that an increase in imports increases the U.S. demand for pounds from D_0 to D_1. The prevailing exchange-rate system will determine the quantity of international reserves needed to bridge the gap between the number of pounds demanded and the number supplied.

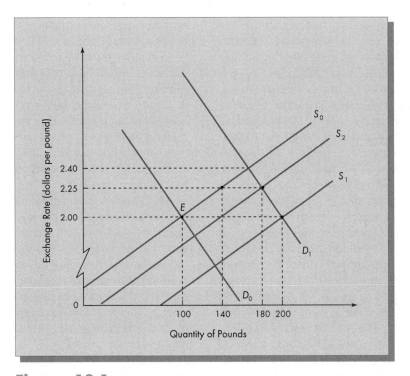

Figure 18.1 The Demand for International Reserves and Exchange-Rate Flexibility

When exchange rates are fixed (pegged) by monetary authorities, international reserves are necessary for the financing of payments imbalances and the stabilization of exchange rates. With floating exchange rates, payments imbalances tend to be corrected by market-induced fluctuations in the exchange rate; the need for exchange-rate stabilization and international reserves disappears.

If exchange rates are fixed or pegged by the monetary authorities, international reserves play a crucial role in the exchange-rate stabilization process. In Figure 18.1, suppose the exchange rate is pegged at $2 per pound. Given a rise in the demand for pounds from D_0 to D_1, the United States would face an excess demand for pounds equal to £100 at the pegged rate. If the U.S. dollar is not to depreciate beyond the pegged rate, the monetary authorities—that is, the Federal Reserve—must enter the market to supply pounds, in exchange for dollars, in the amount necessary to eliminate the disequilibrium. In the figure, the pegged rate of $2 per pound can be maintained if the monetary authorities supply £100 on the market. Coupled with the existing supply schedule S_0, the added supply will result in a new supply schedule at S_1. Market equilibrium is restored at the pegged rate.

Rather than operating under a rigidly pegged system, suppose a nation makes an agreement to foster some automatic adjustments by allowing market rates to float within a narrow band around the official exchange rate. This limited exchange-rate flexibility would be aimed at correcting minor payments imbalances, whereas large and persistent disequilibriums would require other adjustment measures.

Referring to Figure 18.1, assume that the U.S. official exchange rate is $2 per pound, but with a band of permissible exchange-rate fluctuations whose upper limit is set at $2.25 per pound. Given a rise in the U.S. demand for pounds, the value of the dollar will begin to decline. Once the exchange rate depreciates to $2.25 per pound, domestic monetary authorities will need to supply £40 on the market to defend the band's outer limit. This will have the effect of shifting the market supply schedule from S_0 to S_2. Under a system of limited exchange-rate flexibility, then, movements in the exchange rate serve to reduce the payments disequilibrium. Smaller amounts of international reserves are required for exchange-rate stabilization purposes under this system than if exchange rates are rigidly fixed.

A fundamental purpose of international reserves is to facilitate government intervention in exchange markets to stabilize currency values. The more active a government's stabilization activities, the greater is the need for reserves. Most exchange-rate standards today involve some stabilization operations and require international reserves. However, if exchange rates were allowed to float freely without government interference, theoretically there would be no need for reserves. This is because a floating rate would serve to eliminate an incipient payments imbalance, negating the need for stabilization operations. Referring again to Figure 18.1, suppose the exchange market is initially in equilibrium at a rate of $2 per pound. Given an increase in the demand for foreign exchange from D_0 to D_1, the home currency would begin to depreciate. It would continue to weaken until it reached an exchange value of $2.50 per pound, at which point market equilibrium would be restored. The need for international reserves would thus be nonexistent under freely floating rates.

OTHER DETERMINANTS The lesson of the previous section is that changes in the degree of exchange-rate flexibility are inversely related to changes in the quantity of international reserves demanded. In other words, a monetary system characterized by more rapid and flexible exchange-rate adjustments requires smaller reserves, and vice versa.

In addition to the degree of exchange-rate flexibility, several other factors underlie the demand for international reserves, including (1) automatic adjustment mechanisms that respond to payments disequilibriums, (2) economic policies used to bring about payments equilibrium, and (3) the international coordination of economic policies.

Our earlier analysis has shown that adjustment mechanisms involving prices, interest rates, incomes, and monetary flows automatically tend to correct balance-of-payments disequilibriums. A payments deficit or surplus initiates changes in each of these variables. The more efficient each of these adjustment mechanisms is, the smaller and more short-lived market imbalances will be and the fewer reserves will be needed. The demand for international reserves therefore tends to be smaller with speedier and more complete automatic adjustment mechanisms.

The demand for international reserves is also influenced by the choice and effectiveness of government policies adopted to correct payments imbalances. Unlike automatic adjustment mechanisms, which rely on the free market to identify industries and labor groups that must bear the adjustment burden, the use of government policies involves political decisions. All else being equal, the greater a nation's propensity to apply commercial policies (including tariffs, quotas, and subsidies) to key sectors, the less will be its need for international reserves. This assumes, of course, that the policies are effective in reducing payments disequilibriums. Because of uncertainties about the nature and timing of payments disturbances, however, nations are often slow to initiate such trade policies and find themselves requiring international reserves to weather periods of payments disequilibriums.

The international coordination of economic policies is another determinant of the demand for international reserves. A primary goal of economic cooperation among finance ministers is to reduce the frequency and extent of payments imbalances and hence the demand for international reserves. Since the end of World War II, nations have moved toward the harmonization of national economic objectives by establishing programs through such organizations as the International Monetary Fund and the Organization of Economic Cooperation and Development. Another example of international economic organization has been the European Union, whose goal is to achieve a common macroeconomic policy and full monetary union. By reducing the intensity of disturbances to payments balance, such policy coordination reduces the need for international reserves.

Other factors influence the demand for international reserves. The quantity demanded is positively related to the level of world prices and income. One would expect rising price levels to inflate the market value of international transactions and, therefore, to increase the potential demand for reserves. The need for reserves would also tend to rise with the level of global income and trade activity.

In summary, central banks need international reserves to cover possible or expected excess payments to other nations at some future time. The quantity of international reserves demanded is directly related to the size and duration of these payment gaps. If a nation with a payments deficit is willing and able to initiate quick actions to increase receipts or decrease payments, the amount of reserves needed will be relatively small. Conversely, the demand for reserves will be relatively large if nations initiate no actions to correct payments imbalances or adopt policies that prolong such disequilibriums.

SUPPLY OF INTERNATIONAL RESERVES

The analysis so far has emphasized the demand for international reserves. But what about the **supply of international reserves?**

The total supply of international reserves consists of two distinct categories: *owned reserves* and *borrowed reserves*. Reserve assets such as gold, acceptable foreign currencies, and SDRs

are generally considered to be directly owned by the holding nations. But if nations with payments deficits find their stocks of owned reserves falling to unacceptably low levels, they may be able to borrow international reserves as a cushioning device. Lenders may be foreign nations with excess reserves, foreign financial institutions, or international agencies such as the IMF.

FOREIGN CURRENCIES

International reserves are a means of payment used in financing foreign transactions. One such asset is holdings of *national currencies* (foreign exchange). As seen in Table 18.1, the largest share of international reserves today consists of holdings of national currencies.

Over the course of the 1800s–1900s, two national currencies in particular have gained prominence as means of financing international transactions. These currencies, the U.S. dollar and the British pound, have been considered *reserve currencies* (or *key currencies*), because trading nations have traditionally been willing to hold them as international reserve assets. Since World War II, the U.S. dollar has been the dominant reserve currency. Other reserve currencies are the French franc, Japanese yen, and a few

Table 18.1 International Reserves, 1999, All Countries (in Billions of SDRs*)

Item	Amount	Percentage
Foreign exchange	1,197.9	91.7
IMF reserve positions	57.2	4.3
Gold**	29.6	2.3
SDRs	21.5	1.7
Total	1,306.2	100.0

*For 1999, 1 SDR = $1.34.

**At 35 SDRs per ounce.

Source: International Monetary Fund, *International Financial Statistics*, April 1999.

other currencies that are acceptable in payment for international transactions.

The role of the pound as a reserve currency is largely due to circumstances of the late 1800s and early 1900s. Not only did Britain at that time play a dominant role in world trade, but the efficiency of London as an international money market was widely recognized. This was the golden age of the gold standard, and the pound was freely convertible into gold. Traders and investors felt confident financing their transactions with pounds. With the demise of the gold standard and the onset of the Great Depression during the 1930s, Britain's commercial and financial status began to deteriorate, and the pound lost some of its international luster. Today, the pound still serves as an important international-reserve asset, but it is no longer the most prestigious reserve currency.

The emergence of the U.S. dollar as a reserve currency stems from a different set of circumstances. Emerging from World War II, the U.S. economy was not only unharmed but actually stronger. Because of the vast inflows of gold into the United States during the 1930s and 1940s, the dollar was in a better position than the pound to assume the role of a reserve currency.

The mechanism that supplied the world with dollar balances was the balance-of-payments deficits of the United States. These deficits stemmed largely from U.S. foreign aid granted to Europe immediately after World War II, as well as from the flow of private investment funds abroad from U.S. residents. The early 1950s were characterized as a *dollar-shortage era*, when the massive development programs of the European nations resulted in an excess demand for the dollars used to finance such efforts. As the United States began to run modest payments deficits during the early 1950s, the dollar outflow was appreciated by the recipient nations.

By the late 1950s, the U.S. payments deficits had become larger. As foreign nations began to accumulate larger dollar balances than they were accustomed to, the dollar-shortage era gave way to a *dollar glut*. Throughout the 1960s, the United States continued to provide reserves to the world through its payments deficits. However, the persistently weak position of the U.S. balance of payments increasingly led foreigners to question the soundness of the dollar as a reserve currency. By 1970, the amount of dollar liabilities in the hands of foreigners was several times as large as U.S. reserve assets. Lack of confidence in the soundness of the dollar inspired several European nations to exercise their rights to demand that the U.S. Treasury convert their dollar holdings into gold, which in turn led the United States to suspend its gold convertibility pledge to the rest of the world in 1971.

Using the dollar as a reserve currency meant that the supply of international reserves varied with the payments position of the United States. During the 1960s, this situation gave rise to the so-called **liquidity problem**. To preserve confidence in the dollar as a reserve currency, the United States had to strengthen its payments position by eliminating its deficits. But correction of the U.S. deficits would mean elimination of additional dollars as a source of reserves for the international monetary system. The creation in 1970 of SDRs as reserve assets and their subsequent allocations have been intended as a solution for this problem.

Gold

The historical importance of gold as an international reserve asset should not be underemphasized. At one time, gold served as the key monetary asset of the international payments mechanism; it also constituted the basis of the money supplies of many nations.

As an international money, gold fulfilled several important functions. Under the historic **gold standard**, gold served directly as an international means of payments. It also provided a unit of account against which commodity prices as well as the parities of national currencies were quoted. Although gold holdings do not yield interest income, gold has generally served as a viable store of value despite inflation, wars, and revolutions. Perhaps the greatest advantage of gold as a monetary asset is its overall acceptability, especially when compared with other forms of international monies.

Today, the role of gold as an international reserve asset has declined. Over the past 30 years, gold has fallen from nearly 70 percent to less than 3 percent of world reserves. Private individuals rarely use gold as a medium of payment and virtually never as a unit of account. Nor do central banks currently use gold as an official unit of account for stating the parities of national currencies. The monetary role of gold is currently recognized by only a few nations, mostly in the Middle East. In most nations outside the United States, private residents have long been able to buy and sell gold as they would any other commodity. On December 31, 1974, the U.S. government revoked a 41-year ban on U.S. citizens' ownership of gold. The monetary role of gold today is only that of a glittering ghost haunting efforts to reform the international monetary system.

INTERNATIONAL GOLD STANDARD Under the international gold standard, whose golden age was about 1880 to 1914, the values of most national currencies were anchored in gold. Gold coins circulated within these countries as well as across national boundaries as generally accepted means of payment. Monetary authorities were concerned about maintaining the public's confidence in the paper currencies that supplemented gold's role as money. To maintain the integrity of paper currencies, governments agreed to convert them into gold at a fixed rate. This requirement was supposed to prevent monetary authorities from producing excessive amounts of paper money. The so-called *discipline* of the gold standard was achieved by having the money supply bear a fixed relation to the monetary stock of gold. Given the cost of producing gold relative to the cost of other commodities, a monetary price of gold could be established to produce growth in monetary gold—and thus in the money supply—at a rate that corresponded to the growth in real national output.

Over the course of the gold standard's era, the importance of gold began to decline, whereas both paper money and demand deposits showed marked increases. From 1815 to 1913, gold as a share of the aggregate money supply of the United States, France, and Britain fell from about 33 percent to 10 percent. At the same time, the proportion of bank deposits skyrocketed from a modest 6 percent to about 68 percent. By 1913, paper monies plus demand deposits accounted for approximately 90 percent of the U.S. money supply.

After World War I, popular sentiment favored a return to the discipline of the gold standard, in part because of the inflation that gripped many economies during the war years. The United States was the first to return to the gold standard, followed by several European nations. Efforts to restore the prewar gold standard, however, ended in complete collapse during the 1930s. In response to the economic strains of the Great Depression, nations one by one announced that they could no longer maintain the gold standard.

In the United States, the Great Depression brought an important modification of the gold standard. In 1934, the Gold Reserve Act gave the U.S. government title to all monetary gold and required citizens to turn in their private holdings to the U.S. Treasury. This was done to end the pressure on U.S. commercial banks to convert their liabilities into gold. The U.S. dollar was also devalued in 1934, when the official price of gold was raised from $20.67 to $35 per ounce. The dollar devaluation was not specifically aimed at defending the U.S. trade balance. The rationale was that a rise in the domestic price of gold would encourage gold production, adding to the money supply and the level of economic activity. The Great Depression would be solved! In retrospect, the devaluation may have had some minor economic effects, but there is no indication that it did anything to lift the economy out of its depressed condition.

GOLD EXCHANGE STANDARD Emerging from the discussions among the world powers during World War II was a new international monetary organization, the **International Monetary Fund**. A main objective of the fund was to

THE INTERNATIONAL MONETARY FUND

The International Monetary Fund (IMF) was one of two international institutions established near the end of World War II to ease the transition from a wartime to a peacetime environment and to help prevent a recurrence of the turbulent economic conditions of the Great Depression era. The IMF and the World Bank (the International Bank for Reconstruction and Development) were established at the United Nations Monetary and Financial Conference held at Bretton Woods, New Hampshire, in July 1944. The World Bank's main purpose is to make loans for long-term development and reconstruction, whereas the IMF provides short-term loans for balance-of-payments adjustment.

Today the IMF includes more than 180 nations. The goals of the IMF are (1) to promote international cooperation by providing the means for members to consult on international monetary issues; (2) to facilitate the growth of international trade and foster a multilateral system of international payments; (3) to promote stability of exchange rates and seek the elimination of exchange restrictions that disrupt international trade; and (4) to make short-term financial resources available to member nations on a temporary basis so as to allow them to correct payments disequilibriums without resorting to measures that would destroy national prosperity.

The IMF can be thought of as a bank for the central banks of member nations. Over a given time period, some nations will face balance-of-payments surpluses, and others will face deficits. A nation experiencing payments deficits initially draws on its stock of international reserves, such as the dollar, that are accepted in payment by other nations. However, the deficit nation will sometimes have insufficient amounts of international reserves. That is when other nations, via the IMF, can provide assistance. By making available international reserves to the IMF, the surplus nations channel funds to nations with temporary payments deficits. Over the long run, payments deficits must be corrected, and the IMF attempts to ensure that this adjustment will be as prompt and orderly as possible.

The IMF's loanable resources come from two major sources: quotas and loans. Quotas (or subscriptions), which are pooled funds of member nations, generate most of the IMF's loanable funds. The size of a member's quota depends on its economic and financial importance in the world; nations with larger economic importance have larger quotas. The quotas are increased periodically as a means of boosting the IMF's resources. The IMF also obtains loanable resources through loans from member nations. The

reestablish a system of fixed exchange rates, with gold serving as the primary reserve asset. Gold became an international unit of account when member nations officially agreed to state the par values of their currencies in terms of gold or, alternatively, the gold content of the U.S. dollar.

The post–World War II international monetary system as formulated by the fund nations was nominally a **gold exchange standard**. The idea was to economize on monetary gold stocks as international reserves, because they could not expand as fast as international trade was growing. This required the United States, which emerged from the war with a dominant economy in terms of productive capacity and national wealth, to assume the role of world banker. The dollar was to become the chief reserve currency of the international monetary system. The coexistence of both dollars and gold as international reserve assets led to this system's being dubbed the *dollar-gold system*.

As a world banker, the United States assumed responsibility for buying and selling gold at a fixed price to foreign official holders of dollars. The dollar was the only currency that was made

THE INTERNATIONAL MONETARY FUND *(continued)*

IMF has lines of credit with major industrial nations as well as with Saudi Arabia. Interest and other terms on IMF borrowing arrangements vary considerably. Frequently, interest is charged according to a floating rate, and loans are repaid within five to seven years.

Member nations can draw against the IMF's pooled and borrowed funds to finance temporary balance-of-payments deficits. Deficit nations borrow from the IMF by purchasing the currencies of other member nations (typically, dollars or other major currencies) or SDRs with their own currencies. The IMF's resources are available for limited periods, and members that purchase foreign currencies from the IMF must subsequently repurchase their own currencies, thus repaying the loan.

All IMF loans are subject to some degree of *conditionality*. This means that to obtain a loan, a deficit nation must agree to implement economic and financial policies as stipulated by the IMF. These policies are intended to correct the member's balance-of-payments deficit and promote noninflationary economic growth. However, the conditionality attachment to IMF lending has often met strong resistance among deficit nations. The IMF has sometimes demanded that deficit nations undergo austerity programs including severe reductions in public spending, private consump-tion, and imports in order to live within their means.

Critics of the IMF note that its bailouts often contribute to the so-called *moral-hazard* problem, whereby economic actors realize the benefits of their decisions when things go well but are protected when things go poorly. If investors and borrowers do not suffer the costs of bad decisions, won't they be encouraged to make other bad decisions in the future? A second area of concern is the deflationary effect of the IMF's restrictive monetary and fiscal policy conditions. Won't such conditions cause business and bank failures, induce a deeper recession, and limit government spending to help the poor? Many analysts feel the answer is yes. However, is there a viable alternative? Imagine how foreign investors would react to the IMF's advising a financially weak country to increase deficit spending and relax monetary policy.

The IMF makes its assistance available through a number of different programs, which vary with international economic conditions (for example, buffer-stock facility or oil facility). The IMF generally finances only part of a member's payments deficit. In addition, IMF assistance is sometimes made in loose connection with World Bank lending, a portion of which can be used for balance-of-payments adjustment loans.

---

convertible into gold; other national currencies were pegged to the dollar. The dollar was therefore regarded as a reserve currency that was as good as gold because it was thought that the dollar would retain its value relative to other currencies and remain convertible into gold.

As long as the monetary gold stocks of the United States were large relative to outstanding dollar liabilities abroad, confidence in the dollar as a viable reserve currency remained intact. Immediately following World War II, the U.S. monetary gold stocks peaked at $24 billion, about two-thirds of the world total. But as time passed, the amount of foreign dollar holdings rose significantly because of the U.S. payments deficits, whereas the U.S. monetary gold stock dwindled as some of the dollars were turned back to the U.S. Treasury for gold. By 1965, the total supply of foreign-held dollars exceeded the U.S. stock of monetary gold. With the United States unable to redeem all outstanding dollars for gold at $35 per ounce, its ability as a world banker to deliver on demand was questioned.

These circumstances led to speculation that the United States might attempt to solve its gold-shortage problem by devaluing the dollar. By increasing the official price of gold, a dollar devaluation would lead to a rise in the value of U.S. monetary gold stocks. To prevent speculative profits from any rise in the official price of gold, the United States along with several other nations in 1968 established a *two-tier gold system*. This consisted of an *official tier*, in which central banks could buy and sell gold for monetary purposes at the official price of $35 per ounce, and a *private market*, where gold as a commodity could be traded at the free-market price. By separating the official gold market from the private gold market, the two-tier system was a step toward the complete demonetization of gold.

DEMONETIZATION OF GOLD

The formation of the two-tier gold system was a remedy that could only delay the inevitable collapse of the gold exchange standard. By 1971, the U.S. stock of monetary gold had declined to $11 billion, only a fraction of U.S. dollar liabilities to foreign central banks. The U.S. balance-of-payments position was also deteriorating. In August 1971, U.S. President Richard Nixon announced that the United States was suspending its commitment to buy and sell gold at $35 per ounce. The closing of the gold window to foreign official holders brought an end to the gold exchange standard, and the last functional link between the dollar and monetary gold was severed.

It took several years for the world's monetary authorities to formalize the **demonetization of gold** as an international reserve asset. On January 1, 1975, the official price of gold was abolished as the unit of account for the international monetary system. National monetary authorities could enter into gold transactions at market-determined prices, and the use of gold was terminated by the IMF. It was agreed that one-sixth of the fund's gold would be auctioned at prevailing prices and the profits distributed to the less developed nations.

As for the United States, the 41-year ban on gold ownership for U.S. residents was ended on January 1, 1975. Within a few weeks, the U.S. Treasury was auctioning a portion of its gold on the commodity markets. These actions were a signal by the United States that it would treat gold in the same way it treats any other commodity.

SPECIAL DRAWING RIGHTS

The liquidity and confidence problems of the gold exchange standard that resulted from reliance on the dollar and gold as international monies led in 1970 to the creation by the IMF of a new reserve asset, termed **special drawing rights** (**SDRs**). The objective was to introduce into the payments mechanism a new reserve asset, in addition to the dollar and gold, that could be transferred among participating nations in settlement of payments deficits. With the IMF managing the stock of SDRs, world reserves would presumably grow in line with world commerce.

SDRs are unconditional rights to draw currencies of other nations. When the fund creates a certain number of SDRs, they are allocated to the member nations in proportion to the relative size of their fund quotas. Nations can then draw on their SDR balances in financing their payments deficits. The key point is that certain surplus nations are designated by the fund to trade their currencies for an equivalent amount in SDRs to deficit nations in need of foreign-exchange reserves. Nations whose currencies are acquired as foreign exchange are not required to accept more than three times their initial SDR allotments.

SDRs pay interest to surplus nations on their net holdings (the amount by which a nation's SDR balance exceeds its allocation as determined by its fund quota). Interest payments come from deficit nations that draw their SDR balances below their original allotments. The SDR interest rate is adjusted periodically in line with the short-term interest rates in world money markets. It is reviewed quarterly and adjusted on the basis of a formula that takes into account the short-term interest rates of the United States, the United Kingdom, Germany, France, and Japan.

When the SDR was initially adopted, it was agreed that its value should be maintained at a fixed tie to the U.S. dollar's par value, which was then expressed in terms of gold. The value of the

SDR was originally set at US $1. After several monetary developments, this linkage became unacceptable. With the suspension of U.S. gold convertibility in 1971, it was doubted whether the gold value of the dollar should serve as the official unit of account for international transactions. The United States was making it known that it wished to phase out gold as an international monetary instrument. Furthermore, the dollar's exchange rate against gold fell twice as the result of U.S. devaluations in 1971 and 1973. Finally, under the system of managed floating exchange rates, adopted by the industrialized nations in 1973, it became possible for the SDR's value to fluctuate against other currencies while still bearing a fixed tie to the dollar's value. In view of these problems, in 1974, a new method of SDR valuation was initiated—the **basket valuation**.

Basket valuation is intended to provide stability for the SDR's value under a system of fluctuating exchange rates, making the SDR more attractive as an international reserve asset. The SDR is called a basket currency because it is based on the value of five currencies: the U.S. dollar, German mark, Japanese yen, French franc, and British pound. An appreciation, or increase in value, of any one currency in the basket in terms of all other currencies will raise the value of the SDR in terms of each of the other currencies. Conversely, a depreciation, or decline in value, of any one currency will lower the value of the SDR in terms of each other currency. Because the movements of some currencies can be offset or moderated by the movements of other currencies, the value of the SDR in terms of a group of currencies is likely to be relatively stable.

Besides helping nations finance balance-of-payments deficits, SDRs have a number of other uses. Some of the fund's member nations peg their currency values to the SDR. The SDR is the unit of account for IMF transactions and is used as a unit of account for individuals (such as exporters, importers, or investors) who desire protection against the risk of fluctuating exchange rates.

For example, several major banks in London offer certificates of deposit (CDs) denominated in SDRs. The major attraction of SDR-denominated CDs is that they offer investors a financial instrument that is less susceptible to exchange-rate fluctuations than financial assets denominated in any single currency. Although the SDR-denominated CDs are sold for and repaid in dollars, their dollar value at, or any time before, maturity depends on the dollar/SDR exchange rate. Because the dollar/SDR rate is a weighted average of the dollar exchange rates relative to other currencies in the SDR basket, the exchange-rate gains or losses over the term of the deposit will be less than those for any one of the currencies making up the SDR. Therefore, by purchasing SDR-indexed CDs, investors can reduce their overall exchange-rate risk, because losses on one currency may be offset by gains on another in the SDR basket.

FACILITIES FOR BORROWING RESERVES

The discussion so far has considered the different types of *owned reserves*—national currencies, gold, and SDRs. Various facilities for *borrowing reserves* have also been implemented for nations with weak balance-of-payments positions. Borrowed reserves do not eliminate the need for owned reserves, but they do add to the flexibility of the international monetary system by increasing the time available for nations to correct payments disequilibriums. Let's examine the major forms of international credit.

IMF DRAWINGS One of the original purposes of the IMF was to help member nations finance balance-of-payments deficits. The fund has furnished a pool of revolving credit for nations in need of reserves. Temporary loans of foreign currency are made to deficit nations, which are expected to repay them within a stipulated time. The transactions by which the fund makes foreign-currency loans available are called **IMF drawings**.

Deficit nations do not borrow from the fund. Instead they purchase with their own currency the foreign currency required to help finance deficits. When the nation's balance-of-payments position improves, it is expected to reverse the transaction and make repayment by repurchasing its currency from the fund. The fund currently allows members to purchase other currencies at their own option up to the first 50 percent of their fund quotas, which are based on the nation's economic size. Special permission must be granted by the fund if a nation is to purchase foreign currencies in excess of this figure. The fund extends such permission once it is convinced that the deficit nation has enacted reasonable measures to restore payments equilibrium.

Since the early 1950s, the fund has also fostered liberal exchange-rate policies by entering into *standby arrangements* with interested member nations. These agreements guarantee that a member nation may draw specified amounts of foreign currencies from the fund over given time periods. The advantage is that participating nations can count on credit from the fund should it be needed. It also saves the drawing nation from administrative time delays when the loans are actually made.

GENERAL ARRANGEMENTS TO BORROW

During the early 1960s, the question was raised whether the IMF had sufficient amounts of foreign currencies to meet the exchange-stabilization needs of its deficit member nations. Owing to the possibility that large drawings by major nations might exhaust the fund's stocks of foreign currencies, the **General Arrangements to Borrow** were initiated in 1962. Ten leading industrial nations, called the Group of Ten, originally agreed to lend the fund up to a maximum of $6 billion. In 1964, the Group of Ten expanded when Switzerland joined the group. By serving as an intermediary and guarantor, the fund could use these reserves to offer compensatory financial assistance to one or more of the participating nations. Such credit arrangements were expected to be used only when the deficit nation's borrowing needs exceeded the amount of assistance that could be provided under the fund's own drawing facilities.

The General Arrangements to Borrow do not provide a permanent increase in the supply of

world reserves once the loans are repaid and world reserves revert back to their original levels. However, these arrangements have made world reserves more flexible and adaptable to the needs of deficit nations.

SWAP ARRANGEMENTS

During the early 1960s, there occurred a wave of speculative attacks against the U.S. dollar, based on expectations that it would be devalued in terms of other currencies. To help offset the flow of short-term capital out of the dollar into stronger foreign currencies, the U.S. Federal Reserve agreed with several central banks in 1962 to initiate reciprocal currency arrangements, commonly referred to as **swap arrangements**. Today, the swap network on which the United States depends to finance its interventions in the foreign-exchange market includes the central banks of Canada and Mexico.[1]

Swap arrangements are bilateral agreements between central banks. Each government provides for an exchange, or swap, of currencies to help finance temporary payments disequilibriums. If Mexico, for example, is short of dollars, it can ask the Federal Reserve to supply them in exchange for pesos. A drawing on the swap network is usually initiated by telephone, followed by an exchange of wire messages specifying terms and conditions. The actual swap is in the form of a foreign-exchange contract calling for the sale of dollars by the Federal Reserve for the currency of a foreign central bank. The nation requesting the swap is expected to use the funds to help ease its payments deficits and discourage speculative capital outflows. Swaps are to be repaid (reversed) within a stipulated period of time, normally within 3 to 12 months.

COMPENSATORY FINANCING FOR EXPORTS

In 1963, the IMF approved a special credit facili-

---

[1] Because of the formation of the European Central Bank and in light of 15 years of disuse, the bilateral swap arrangements of the Federal Reserve with many European central banks, such as Austria, Germany, and Belgium, were jointly deemed no longer necessary in view of the well-established, present-day arrangements for international monetary cooperation. Accordingly, the respective parties to the arrangements mutually agreed to allow them to lapse in 1998.

ty to aid the less developed nations. The idea was to extend the fund's balance-of-payments assistance to member nations suffering from fluctuations in receipts from exports of primary products owing to circumstances beyond their control. Borrowings from the so-called **compensatory financing facility** are separate from and in addition to a nation's regular borrowing privileges from the fund. A nation facing temporary declines in its commodity export earnings can, under this facility, borrow an amount up to 50 percent of its fund quota.

OIL FACILITY In 1974, the IMF established a special facility to help member nations cushion the impact on their balance of payments of the skyrocketing costs of oil imports generated by the OPEC price increases of 1973 and 1974. Under the **oil facility**, fund resources are made available to members as a supplement to other fund-drawing arrangements. Although the oil facility has been used primarily by the less developed nations, industrialized nations including Italy and the United Kingdom have borrowed reserves under these arrangements.

BUFFER-STOCK FINANCING FACILITY A major concern of the less developed nations has been erratic fluctuations in their commodity-export prices. To correct such disturbances, commodity producers have often banded together and formulated price-stabilization schemes based on buffer stocks, as discussed in Chapter 8.

Consistent with the IMF's support of commodity-price stabilization for the less developed nations, in 1969 the fund established a facility to aid members in financing their contributions to buffer stocks. Under this scheme, a member nation with a balance-of-payments need can obtain financial assistance from the fund in amounts up to the value of the nation's buffer stocks calculated at the floor price of the agreement or at the average market price of these stocks should the market price fall below the floor price. Borrowing under the **buffer-stock facility** cannot exceed 50 percent of a member's fund quota. Like the fund's compensatory financing facility,

buffer-stock arrangements are separate from and additional to normal fund facilities for dealing with balance-of-payments difficulties. The borrowings are generally expected to be repaid within a period of three to five years after the date of the loan.

The preceding sections have analyzed the nature of international reserves and the role of central banks in the international monetary system. Let us now consider *commercial banks* as international lenders and the problems associated with international debt.

INTERNATIONAL LENDING RISK

In many respects, the principles that apply to international lending are similar to those of domestic lending: The lender needs to determine the credit risk that the borrower will default. When making international loans, however, bankers face two additional risks: country risk and currency risk.

Credit risk is financial and refers to the probability that part or all of the interest or principal of a loan will not be repaid. The larger the potential for default on a loan, the higher the interest rate that the bank must charge the borrower.

Assessing credit risk on international loans tends to be more difficult than on domestic loans. U.S. banks are often less familiar with foreign business practices and economic conditions than those in the United States. Obtaining reliable information to evaluate foreign credit risk can be time-consuming and costly. Many U.S. banks, therefore, confine their international lending to major multinational corporations and financial institutions. To attract lending by U.S. banks, a foreign government may provide assurances against default by a local private borrower, thus reducing the credit risk of the loan.

Country risk is political and is closely related to political developments in a country, especially the government's views concerning international investments and loans. Some governments encourage the inflow of foreign funds to foster domestic economic development. Fearing loss of national sovereignty, other governments may discourage such inflows by enacting additional taxes, profit restrictions, and wage/price controls that can hinder the ability of local borrowers to repay loans. In the extreme, foreign governments can expropriate the assets of foreign investors or make foreign loan repayments illegal.

Currency risk is economic and is associated with currency depreciations and appreciations as well as exchange controls. Some loans of U.S. banks are denominated in foreign currency instead of dollars. If the currency in which the loan is made depreciates against the dollar during the period of the loan, the repayment will be worth fewer dollars. If the foreign currency has a well-developed forward market, the loan may be hedged. But many foreign currencies, especially of the developing nations, do not have such markets, and loans denominated in these currencies cannot always be hedged to decrease this type of currency risk. Another type of currency risk arises from exchange controls, which are common in developing nations. Exchange controls restrict the movement of funds across national borders or limit a currency's convertibility into dollars for repayment, thus adding to the risk of international lenders.

When lending overseas, bankers must evaluate credit risk, country risk, and currency risk. Evaluating risks in foreign lending often results in detailed analyses, compiled by a bank's research department, that are based on a nation's financial, economic, and political conditions. When international lenders consider detailed analyses too expensive, they often use reports and statistical indicators to help them determine the risk of lending.

Analyses of international lending risk have been conducted by several organizations, one of which is Political Risk Services. Each month this organization publishes the *International Country Risk Guide*. The guide provides individual ratings on more than 120 nations for political, financial, and economic risk, plus a composite rating for a nation's overall risk. The ratings are based on a number of risk factors, weighted to reflect current conditions. Table 18.2 shows the

Table 18.2 International Lending Risk: Selected Country Ratings, 1999

	Composite Risk Rating (100 Points Possible)
Switzerland	87.3
Japan	83.3
United States	82.8
Canada	82.8
Germany	82.8
United Kingdom	81.3
Poland	80.5
India	63.0
Romania	57.8
Russia	49.8
Indonesia	48.5
Sierra Leone	29.5

Source: Political Risk Services (East Syracuse, NY), *International Country Risk Guide*, February 1999, pp. 153–155. See also the World Bank, *World Development Report 1999–2000*, p. 262 and various issues of *Euromoney*.

International Country Risk Guide ratings for selected nations. In assessing a nation's composite risk, a higher score (100-point maximum) indicates a lower overall risk; a lower score indicates a higher overall risk. The composite risk rating of a particular nation can be assessed using the following fairly broad categories: (1) low risk, 85–100 points; (2) moderate risk, 60—84 points; (3) high risk, 0–59 points.

THE PROBLEM OF INTERNATIONAL DEBT

Much concern has been voiced over the volume of international lending in recent years. At times, the concern has been that international lending was insufficient. Such was the case after the oil shocks in 1974–1975 and 1979–1980, when it was feared that some oil-importing developing nations might not be able to obtain loans to finance trade deficits resulting from the huge increases in the price of oil. It so happened that many oil-importing nations were able to borrow dollars from commercial banks. They paid the dollars to OPEC nations, who redeposited the money in commercial banks, which then re-lent the money to oil importers, and so on. In the 1970s, the banks were part of the solution; if they had not lent large sums to the developing nations, the oil shocks would have done far more damage to the world economy.

By the 1980s, however, commercial banks were viewed as part of an international debt problem because they had lent so much to developing nations. Flush with OPEC money after the oil price increases of the 1970s, the banks actively sought borrowers and had no trouble finding them among the developing nations. Some nations borrowed to prop up consumption because their living standards were already low and hit hard by oil-price hikes. Most nations borrowed to avoid cuts in development programs and to invest in energy projects. It was generally recognized that banks were successful in recycling their OPEC deposits to developing nations following the first round of oil-price hikes in 1974 and 1975. But the international lending mechanism encountered increasing difficulties beginning with the global recession of the early 1980s. In particular, some developing nations were unable to pay their external debts on schedule.

Table 18.3 summarizes the magnitude of the international debt problem of the developing nations. As of 1996, the external debt of the non-oil developing nations stood at $1,934 billion; this was a sharp increase from the $328 billion level of the late 1970s. Much of this debt was incurred by Latin American nations, including Mexico and Brazil. As a percentage of the gross domestic product of developing nations, external debt stood at 30 percent in 1996.

Most of the external debt of the developing nations is denominated in U.S. dollars. Repayment of this debt thus requires developing nations to earn foreign exchange through exports of goods and services to industrial nations. One measure of a nation's debt burden is its external debt relative to its current export earnings. Changes in this **debt-to-export ratio** indicate whether a nation's debt burden is rising or falling in relation to its ability to pay. From the late 1970s to 1987, the ratio of developing-nation external debt to export revenues rose from 133 percent to 171 percent. This suggests that the external debt exceeded and grew more rapidly than export revenues over this period. By 1998, the debt-to-export ratio had moderated to 143 percent.

Another indicator of debt burden is the **debt service/export ratio**, which refers to scheduled interest and principal payments as a percentage of export earnings. The debt service/export ratio

Table 18.3 Developing Nations' External Debt

	1987	1993	1999*
Outstanding debt (billions)	$1,156.5	$1,461.0	$1,942.3
Outstanding debt by area (billions)			
Africa	$203.0	$259.0	$288.1
Asia	317.6	455.3	663.2
Middle East/Europe	209.3	208.1	256.6
Western Hemisphere	426.7	538.6	734.4
Ratio of external debt to gross domestic product	40.6%	37.3%	35.1%
Ratio of external debt to exports of goods and services	171.1%	192.8%	158.1%
Debt service/export ratio	9.1%	9.3%	9.1%

*Estimated.

Source: International Monetary Fund, *World Economic Outlook*, May 1999, pp. 198-205.

permits one to focus on two key indicators of whether a reduction in the debt burden is possible in the short run: (1) the interest rate that the nation pays on its external debt and (2) the growth in its exports of goods and services. All else being constant, a rise in the interest rate increases the debt service/export ratio, while a rise in exports decreases the ratio. It is a well-known rule of international finance that a nation's debt burden rises if the interest rate on the debt exceeds the rate of growth of exports. As of 1998, the developing nations' debt service/export ratio was 9 percent.

A nation may experience debt-servicing problems for a number of reasons: (1) It may have pursued improper macroeconomic policies that contribute to large balance-of-payments deficits, (2) It may have borrowed excessively or on unfavorable terms, or (3) It may have been affected by adverse economic events that it could not control.

A nation facing debt-servicing difficulties has several options. First, it can cease repayments on its debt. Such an action, however, undermines confidence in the nation, making it difficult (if not impossible) for it to borrow in the future. Furthermore, the nation might be declared in default, in which case its assets (such as ships and aircraft) might be confiscated and sold to discharge the debt. As a group, however, developing nations in debt may have considerable leverage in winning concessions from their lenders.

A second option is for the nation to try to service its debt at all costs. To do so may require the restriction of other foreign-exchange expenditures, a step that may be viewed as socially unacceptable.

Finally, a nation may seek debt rescheduling, which generally involves stretching out the original payment schedule of the debt. There is a cost because the debtor nation must pay interest on the amount outstanding until the debt has been repaid.

When a nation faces debt-servicing problems, its creditors seek to reduce their exposure by collecting all interest and principal payments as they come due, while granting no new credit. But there is an old adage that goes as follows: When a man owes a bank $1,000, the bank owns him; but when a man owes the bank $1 million, he owns the bank. Banks with large amounts of international loans find it in their best interest to help the debtor recover financially. To deal with debt-servicing problems, therefore, debtor nations and their creditors generally attempt to negotiate rescheduling agreements. That is, creditors agree to lengthen the time period for repayment of the principal and sometimes part of the interest on existing loans. Banks have little option but to accommodate demands for debt rescheduling because they do not want the debtor to officially default on the loan. With default, the bank's assets become nonperforming and subject to markdowns by government regulators. This could lead to possible withdrawals of deposits and bank insolvency.

Besides rescheduling debt with commercial banks, developing nations may obtain emergency loans from the IMF. The IMF provides loans to nations experiencing balance-of-payments difficulties provided that the borrowers initiate programs to correct these difficulties.

By insisting on **conditionality**, the IMF asks borrowers to adopt austerity programs to shore up their economies and put their muddled finances in order. Such measures have resulted in the slashing of public expenditures, private consumption, and, in some cases, capital investment. Borrowers must also cut imports and expand exports. The IMF views austerity programs as a necessity because with a sovereign debtor, there is no other way to make it pay back its loans. The IMF faces a difficult situation in deciding how tough to get with borrowers. If it goes soft and offers money on easier terms, it sets a precedent for other debtor nations. But if it miscalculates and requires excessive austerity measures, it risks triggering political turmoil and possibly a declaration of default.

The IMF has been criticized, notably by developing nations, for demanding austerity policies that excessively emphasize short-term improvements in the balance of payments rather than fostering long-run economic growth. Developing nations also contend that the IMF austerity programs promote downward pressure on economic activity in nations that are already exposed to recessionary forces. The crucial issue faced by the IMF is how to resolve the economic problems of the debtor nations in a manner most advantageous to them, to their creditors, and to the world as a whole. The mutually advantageous solution is one that enables these nations to achieve sustainable, noninflationary economic growth, thus assuring creditors of repayment and benefiting the world economy through expansion of trade and economic activity.

At the 1985 annual meetings of the IMF and World Bank, the Reagan administration proposed that the international debt problem could best be solved through economic growth in the debtor nations. It was argued that the World Bank should make large loans, co-financed by commercial banks, that permit debtor nations to resume investment and capital formation. The Reagan proposal called for a larger role for the World Bank and a smaller role for the austerity measures of the IMF. These measures were incorporated into a 1986 loan accord reached by Mexico and its creditors.

REDUCING BANK EXPOSURE TO DEVELOPING-NATION DEBT

When developing nations cannot meet their debt obligations to foreign banks, the stability of the international financial system is threatened. Banks may react to this threat by increasing their capital base, setting aside reserves to cover losses, and reducing new loans to debtor nations.

Banks have additional means to improve their financial position. One method is to liquidate developing-nation debt by engaging in outright *loan sales* to other banks in the secondary market. But if there occurs an unexpected increase in the default risk of such loans, their market value

will be less than their face value. The selling bank thus absorbs costs because its loans must be sold at a discount. Following the sale, the bank must adjust its balance sheet to take account of any previously unrecorded difference between the face value of the loans and their market value. Many small and medium-sized U.S. banks, eager to dump their bad loans in the 1980s, were willing to sell them in the secondary market at discounts as high as 70 percent, or 30 cents on the dollar. But many banks could not afford such huge discounts. Even worse, if the banks all rushed to sell bad loans at once, prices would fall further. Sales of loans in the secondary market were often viewed as a last-resort measure.

Another debt-reduction technique is the *debt buyback*, in which the government of the debtor nation buys the loans from the commercial bank at a discount. Banks have also engaged in *debt-for-debt swaps*, in which a bank exchanges its loans for securities issued by the debtor nation's government at a lower interest rate or discount.

Cutting losses on developing-nation loans has sometimes involved banks in **debt/equity swaps**. Under this approach, a commercial bank sells its loans at a discount to the developing-nation government for local currency, which it then uses to finance an equity investment in the debtor nation. In the late 1980s, Citicorp converted some of its Chilean loans into pesos, which were used to purchase ownership shares in Chilean gold mines and pulp mills. Citicorp maintained that it could get better value by selling and swapping the loans without using the secondary market. In Chile, Citicorp typically converted debt at about 87 cents worth of local currency for each $1 of debt. Although debt/equity swaps enhance a bank's chances of selling developing-nation debt, they do not necessarily decrease its risk. Some equity investments in developing nations may be just as risky as the loans that were swapped for local factories or land. Moreover, banks that acquire an equity interest in developing-nation assets may not have the knowledge to manage those assets. Debtor nations also worry that debt/equity swaps will allow major companies to fall into foreign hands.

HOW A DEBT/EQUITY SWAP WORKS

Brazil owes Manufacturers Hanover Trust (of New York) $1 billion. Manufacturers Hanover decides to swap some of the debt for ownership shares in Companhia Suzano del Papel e Celulose, a pulp and paper company. Here is what occurs:

- Manufacturers Hanover takes $115 million in Brazilian government-guaranteed loans to a Brazilian broker. The broker takes the loans to the Brazilian central bank's monthly debt auction, where they are valued at an average of 87 cents on the dollar.

- Through the broker, Manufacturers Hanover exchanges the loans at the central bank for $100 million worth of Brazilian cruzados. The broker is paid a commission, and the central bank retires the loans.

- With its cruzados, Manufacturers Hanover purchases 12 percent of Suzano's stock, and Suzano uses the bank's funds to increase capacity and exports.

DEBT REDUCTION AND DEBT FORGIVENESS

Another method of coping with developing-nation debt involves programs enacted for debt reduction and debt forgiveness. **Debt reduction** refers to any voluntary scheme that lessens the burden on the debtor nation to service its external debt. Debt reduction is accomplished through two main approaches. The first is the use of negotiated modifications in the terms and conditions of the contracted debt, such as debt reschedulings, retiming of interest payments, and improved borrowing terms. Debt reduction may also be achieved through measures such as debt/equity swaps and debt buybacks. The purpose of debt reduction is to foster comprehensive policies for economic growth by easing the ability of the debtor nation to service its debt, thus freeing resources that will be used for investment.

An example of a debt-reduction proposal is the Brady Initiative of 1989, named after U.S. Treasury Secretary Nicholas Brady. During the late 1980s, the persistence of serious problems in the debtor economies and concern over the economic hardships sustained by their populations resulted in the Brady Initiative. This proposal called for the mobilization of private-sector financing to generate growth in debtor nations. The major innovation of the initiative is that it emphasized debt reduction by commercial banks. It also called for the IMF and the World Bank to provide financial support for debt reduction to those nations that enact effective economic-reform policies.

Some proponents of debt relief maintain that the lending nations should permit **debt forgiveness**. Debt forgiveness refers to any arrangement that reduces the value of contractual obligations of the debtor nation; it includes schemes such as markdowns or write-offs of developing-nation debt or the abrogation of existing obligations to pay interest.

Debt-forgiveness advocates maintain that the most heavily indebted developing nations are unable to service their external debt and maintain an acceptable rate of per capita income growth because their debt burden is overwhelming. They contend that if some of this debt were forgiven, a debtor nation could use the freed-up foreign-exchange resources to increase its imports and invest domestically, thus increasing domestic economic growth rates. The release of the limitation on foreign exchange would provide the debtor nation additional incentive to invest because it would not have to share as much of the benefits of its increased growth and investment with its creditors in the form of interest payments. Moreover, debt forgiveness would allow the debtor nation to service its debt more easily; this would reduce the debt-load burden of a debtor nation and could potentially lead to greater inflows of foreign investment.

Debt-forgiveness critics question whether the amount of debt is a major limitation on developing-nation growth and whether that growth would in fact resume if a large portion of that debt were forgiven. They contend that nations such as Indonesia and South Korea have experienced large amounts of external debt relative to national output but have not faced debt-servicing problems. Also, debt forgiveness does not guarantee that the freed-up foreign-exchange resources will be used productively—that is, invested in sectors that will ultimately generate additional foreign exchange.

FINANCIAL CRISES AND THE INTERNATIONAL MONETARY FUND

The financial experiences of Mexico and Southeast Asia provide examples of the costs that can be inflicted on an economy when it neglects its balance of payments and borrows heavily from other nations.

MEXICAN CRISES IN 1994 AND 1995

From the late 1980s to 1993, Mexico followed a strategy of economic adjustment and reform intended to reduce inflation, decrease the role of the government in the economy, and lay the foundation for growth led by the private sector. The key elements of the strategy were the maintenance of tight financial policies, a major restructuring of external debt, and reforms based in privatization and trade liberalization. Mexico also established a target range for the dollar value of the peso.

In addition to the privatization of large public enterprises and commercial banks, Mexico embarked on an ambitious trade reform comprising further unilateral cuts in import tariffs and negotiation of free-trade agreements with several Western Hemisphere nations, including the NAFTA with the United States and Canada. Restrictions on foreign investment and foreign ownership were eased, and a number of key sectors—including agriculture, mining, telecommunications, and transportation— were deregulated. Overall, these reforms signaled a strong commitment by the Mexican government to deepen Mexico's transformation into a market-based economy.

By late 1993, the peso had appreciated significantly, making foreign goods cheaper for Mexican consumers. This led to trade and current account deficits for Mexico, which were financed by borrowing from foreign investors, a large portion of which took the form of short-term government securities. As the Mexican presidential election approached in 1994, an uprising in the state of Chiapas and the subsequent assassination of the ruling party's candidate contributed to investor uncertainty.

As investors lost confidence and the inflow of foreign investment funds disappeared, the government found it increasingly difficult to maintain its target exchange rate against the dollar. In December 1994, Mexico disbanded its target exchange rate and allowed the market to determine the peso's value. What appeared to be a minor correction in the peso quickly developed into a broader financial crunch felt in and outside Mexico. By March 1995, the peso had fallen more than 50 percent against the dollar, and Mexico's inflation was growing at an annual rate in excess of 60 percent.

At the request of Mexico, the United States orchestrated a $53 billion multilateral effort to assist in Mexico's stabilization and made available $20 billion in U.S. credit. Other support came from the International Monetary Fund, the Bank for International Settlements, and several nations including Canada, Argentina, and Brazil. These efforts helped alleviate the impact of the financial crisis on other nations' markets. At the same time, the Mexican government took the

MEXICO: ELECTIONS AND CURRENCY CRISES

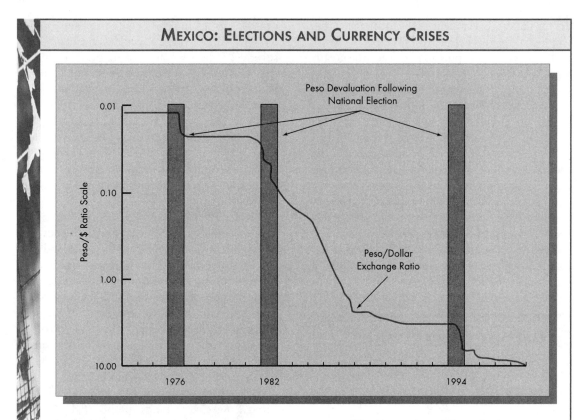

In developing countries, elections are often accompanied by currency crises. In Mexico, for example, major devaluations of the peso and economic crises followed three of the four national elections during 1976–1994, as shown in the figure—the elections of 1976, 1982, and 1994. Why do crises often occur in election years?

Election years have led to several forces that make the economy vulnerable to crisis. Incumbent governments in Mexico, like those in many other countries, have the incentive to keep the economy growing in an election year to attract as many votes as possible. Going into an election year, the government tries to sustain or increase fiscal spending. Monetary policy is kept loose, and the pace of lending to the public and private sectors is maintained.

This causes inflationary pressures to build up and, given a highly managed nominal exchange rate, leads to appreciation and overvaluation of the real (inflationary adjusted) exchange rate. An overvalued real exchange rate reflects a drop in international competitiveness and results in reduced exports and increased imports. This, in turn, generates a widening current account deficit and increased speculation of an impending devaluation, which lowers international reserves as capital flees the country. Eventually, under mounting pressures, a balance-of-payments crisis erupts, and the currency is devalued.

Source: David Gould, *Mexico: Election Economics*, Federal Reserve Bank of Dallas, 1999.

difficult steps essential to restoring stability and growth in Mexico. Government spending was slashed, and a tight monetary policy was implemented. These actions led to a stabilization in the peso's exchange value, although at the cost of a severe recession in Mexico.

Three years after Mexico's economic collapse, its economy was expanding at a 9-percent clip, its exports soared, and its foreign-exchange reserves were piling up. But Mexico achieved this turnaround by committing itself to free trade, balancing the budget, boosting the productivity of its industries, and allowing a wave of restructuring in banks and other sectors.

THE EAST ASIAN FINANCIAL CRISIS OF 1997 AND 1998

During the 1980s and 1990s, the economies of East Asia were growing at rates of 5 to 10 percent per year. East Asia was also opening its economies to foreign direct investments, foreign goods and services, and capital flows and was relying heavily on dollar markets, especially the United States, to absorb its exports. In 1997, however, the currencies of several economies in East Asia came under severe downward pressure. The strongest pressures emerged initially in Thailand, where concerns about the sustainability of the existing exchange-rate peg to the U.S. dollar prompted a run on the currency. The crisis soon spread to Indonesia, Malaysia, the Philippines, and South Korea, which saw their currencies rapidly depreciate against the U.S. dollar. What caused the financial crisis?

Prior to the financial crisis, the financial-services sector in most of the East Asian economies had been developing rapidly and without sufficient regulation, oversight, and government controls. As capital markets became liberalized, banks in these countries could borrow abroad at relatively low rates of interest and re-lend the funds domestically. Whereas in the 1970s the governments might have borrowed from the World Bank for infrastructure development, in the 1990s a local bank might borrow directly from a large New York money center bank. The financial crisis in East Asia began in currency markets, but this exchange-rate instability was underlain by problems in the banking sectors of the countries in question.

Most analysts felt that the financial difficulties in East Asia were triggered by the misallocation of investment due to easy access to cheap foreign capital. Translation? In Thailand, Malaysia, Indonesia, and South Korea, politicians and bureaucrats used government-controlled banks to funnel money to friends, family, or chosen entrepreneurs, who then returned the favor by kicking back campaign contributions or personal gratuities. Markets thus played a small role in allocating investments. Politicians used taxpayers' money to build huge public-works monuments to themselves. Businesspeople speculated in property and constructed enormous overcapacity in chips, steel, cars, textiles, and electronics. Cheap capital from the United States and elsewhere eventually overheated Asia's economic growth. Asia's inexpensive labor, high savings rates, and strong exports would have supported adequate growth rates. But throwing billions of extra dollars into an economic system that was immune to market discipline resulted in a financial crisis.

Another factor that initially enabled the crisis to occur was that the exchange rates of most East Asian currencies had been aligned with the dollar or a basket of currencies dominated by the dollar. The advantage of this system to the countries involved was that it kept the countries' exchange rates relatively constant with respect to the dollar and allowed their traders to import from and export to dollar areas, especially the United States, with little exchange-rate risk. It also provided a stable financial environment that encouraged foreign sources of capital for loans and investments.

The linking of official exchange rates to the dollar, however, had one major shortcoming. As the value of the dollar changed, so did the value of these currencies relative to others, such as the German mark and Japanese yen, that were not tied to the U.S. dollar. Problems began to arise in 1996 and 1997 as the dollar appreciated and the official values of these currencies deviated from their underlying market values. While the dollar was pulling up the value of these currencies, some of the countries in question encountered increasing difficulty in balancing their international accounts. Their exports grew more costly to buyers not using dollars, and their imports from nondollar areas became cheaper. The weak yen, in particular, was reducing the competitiveness of their products relative to those of Japan. The consequent rising deficits in their trade accounts placed downward pressure on their exchange rates, which required more and more government intervention to maintain. Eventually, the East Asian governments had to concede failure and allow their currencies to depreciate.

In order to ensure that the financial crisis would not spread throughout the world, the IMF agreed to help bail out the troubled Asian countries, as shown in Table 18.4. In exchange for receiving IMF loans, the Asian countries committed themselves to big policy changes to cure the problems that produced the crisis. Let us consider the case of South Korea.

South Korea asked for IMF loans in 1997 after its currency, the won, began depreciating rapidly, straining the country's hard-currency reserves. As shown in Table 18.5, the IMF-led rescue consist-

ed of a package of loans and loan pledges totaling $57 billion. The loans were designed to replenish Korea's currency reserves and to bolster the confidence of investors, so that they would reschedule billions of dollars in short-term loans.

It was widely recognized that East Asia did not have the traditional financial problems of excessive government spending that once typified Mexico and other Latin American countries, and certainly not their huge trade deficits. So traditional IMF remedies, aimed at reducing domestic spending and putting people out of work, wouldn't cure this Asian economic flu. Instead, East Asia needed deep structural change that would promote markets and break up elite power.

Therefore, the IMF insisted on radical reforms in the Korean economic system before agreeing to extend Korea any credit. Among the changes: foreign banks would be able to buy Korean ones; Korean firms would be able to borrow more freely abroad; banks in Korea would make loans according to commercial considerations, not government fiat; insolvent Korean merchant banks would be closed; insolvent commercial banks would be merged with wealthy ones or closed; and tariffs would be lowered, according to commitments Korea had made at the World Trade Organization. In short, the Korean government agreed to broadly dismantle the country's interlocked financial and industrial system as a price for winning a $57 billion bailout by the IMF.

Table 18.4 IMF to the Rescue: International Bailout Packages

Country (Year)	Total Package	IMF Share
Mexico (1995)	$53 billion	$18 billion
Thailand (1997)	17	4
Indonesia (1997)	40	10
South Korea (1997)	57	21

Source: International Monetary Fund.

Table 18.5 The Rescue of South Korea in 1997: Terms and Conditions

Loans to South Korea		And Their Conditions
Source	Amount	
IMF	$21 billion	Strengthen fiscal and monetary policies
World Bank	10	Implement far-reaching financial reform
Asia Development Bank	4	Liberalize trade and capital-flow laws
Back-up funds from U.S., Japan, U.K., Germany, France, and Italy	22	Change structure of Korean corporations
	$57 billion	

Source: International Monetary Fund.

THE EUROCURRENCY MARKET

One of the most widely misunderstood topics in international finance is the nature and operation of the **Eurocurrency market**. This market operates as a financial intermediary, bringing together lenders and borrowers. It serves as one of the most important tools for moving short-term funds across national borders. When the Eurocurrency market first came into existence in the 1950s, its volume was estimated to be approximately $1 billion. The size of the Eurocurrency market in the mid-1990s was estimated to be more than $5 trillion.

Eurocurrencies are deposits, denominated and payable in dollars and other foreign currencies—such as the Swiss franc—in banks outside the United States, primarily in London, the market's center. The term *Eurocurrency market* is something of a misnomer because much Eurocurrency trading occurs in non-European centers, such as Hong Kong and Singapore. Dollar deposits located in banks outside the United States are known as *Eurodollars*, and banks that conduct trading in the markets for Eurocurrencies (including the dollar) are designated *Eurobanks*.

Eurocurrency depositors may be foreign exporters who have sold products in the United States and have received dollars in payment. They may also be U.S. residents who have withdrawn funds from their accounts in the United States and put them in a bank overseas. Foreign-currency deposits in overseas banks are generally for a specified time period and bear a stated yield, because most Eurocurrency deposits are held for investment rather than as transaction balances.

Borrowers go to Eurocurrency banks for a variety of purposes. When the market was first developed, borrowers were primarily corporations that required financing for international trade. But other lending opportunities have evolved with the market's development. Borrowers currently include the British government and U.S. banks.

DEVELOPMENT OF THE EUROCURRENCY MARKET Although several hundred banks currently issue Eurocurrency deposits on investor demand, it was not until the late 1950s and early 1960s that the market began to gain prominence as a major source of short-term capital. Several factors contributed to the Eurocurrency market's growth.

One factor was fear that deposits held in the United States would be frozen by the government in the event of an international conflict. The Eastern European countries, notably Russia, were among the first depositors of dollars in European banks, because during World War II the United States had impounded Russian dollar holdings located in U.S. banks. Russia was thus motivated to maintain dollar holdings free from U.S. regulation.

Ceilings on interest rates that U.S. banks could pay on savings deposits provided another reason for the Eurocurrency market's growth. These ceilings limited the U.S. banks in competing with foreign banks for deposits. During the 1930s, the Federal Reserve system under Regulation Q established ceiling rates to prevent banks from paying excessive interest rates on savings accounts and thus being forced to make risky loans to generate high earnings. By the late 1950s, when London was paying interest rates on dollar deposits that exceeded the levels set by Regulation Q, it was profitable for U.S. residents and foreigners to transfer their dollar balances to London. Large U.S. banks directed their foreign branches to bid for dollars by offering higher interest rates than those allowed in the United States. The parent offices then borrowed the money from their overseas branches. To limit such activity, the Federal Reserve in 1969 established high reserve requirements on head-office borrowings from abroad. In 1973, the Federal Reserve system made large-denomination certificates of deposit exempt from Regulation Q ceilings, further reducing the incentive to borrow funds from overseas branches.

Throughout the 1970s, 1980s, and 1990s, the Eurocurrency market has continued to grow. A major factor behind the sustained high growth of the market has been the risk-adjusted interest-rate advantage of Eurocurrency deposits relative to domestic deposits, reflecting increases in the level of dollar interest rates and reductions in the perceived riskiness of Euromarket deposits.

FINANCIAL IMPLICATIONS Eurocurrencies have significant implications for international finance. By increasing the financial interdependence of nations involved in the market, Eurocurrencies facilitate the financing of international trade and investment. They may also reduce the need for official reserve financing, because a given quantity of dollars can support a large volume of international transactions. On the other hand, it is argued that Eurocurrencies may under-mine a nation's efforts to implement its monetary policy. Volatile movements of these balances into and out of a nation's banking system complicate a central bank's attempt to hit a monetary target.

Another concern is that the Eurocurrency market does not face the same financial regulations as do the domestic banking systems of most industrialized nations. Should the Eurocurrency banks not maintain sound reserve requirements or enact responsible policies, the pyramid of Eurocurrency credit might collapse. Such fears became widespread in 1974 with the failure of the Franklin National Bank in the United States and the Bankus Herstatt of Germany, both of which lost huge sums speculating in the foreign-exchange market.

S U M M A R Y

1. The purpose of international reserves is to permit nations to bridge the gap between monetary receipts and payments. Deficit nations can use international reserves to buy time in order to postpone adjustment measures.

2. The demand for international reserves depends on two major factors: (a) the monetary value of international transactions and (b) the size and duration of balance-of-payments disequilibriums.

3. The need for international reserves tends to become less acute under a system of floating exchange rates than under a system of fixed rates. The more efficient the international adjustment mechanism and the greater the extent of international policy coordination, the smaller the need for international reserves.

4. The supply of international reserves consists of owned and borrowed reserves. Among the major sources of reserves are (a) foreign currencies, (b) monetary gold stocks, (c) special drawing rights, (d) IMF drawing positions, (e) the General Arrangements to Borrow, and (f) swap arrangements.

5. When making international loans, bankers face credit risk, country risk, and currency risk.

6. Among the indicators used to analyze a nation's external debt position are its debt-to-export ratio and debt service/export ratio.

7. A nation experiencing debt-servicing difficulties has several options: (a) cease repayment on its debt, (b) service its debt at all costs, or (c) reschedule its debt. Debt rescheduling has been widely used by borrowing nations in recent years.

8. A bank can reduce its exposure to developing-nation debt through outright loan sales in the secondary market, debt buybacks, debt-for-debt swaps, and debt/equity swaps.

9. Eurocurrencies are deposits, denominated and payable in dollars and other foreign currencies, in banks outside the United States. Dollar deposits located in banks outside the United States are called Eurodollars, and banks that conduct trading in markets for Eurocurrencies are known as Eurobanks.

S T U D Y   Q U E S T I O N S

1. A nation's need for international reserves is similar to an individual's desire to hold cash balances. Explain.
2. What are the major factors that determine a nation's demand for international reserves?
3. The total supply of international reserves consists of two categories: (a) owned reserves and (b) borrowed reserves. What do these categories include?
4. In terms of volume, which component of world reserves is currently most important? Which is currently least important?
5. What is meant by a reserve currency? Historically, which currencies have assumed this role?
6. What is the current role of gold in the international monetary system?
7. What advantages does a gold exchange standard have over a pure gold standard?
8. What are special drawing rights? Why were they created? How is their value determined?
9. What facilities exist for trading nations that wish to borrow international reserves?
10. What caused the international debt problem of the developing nations in the 1980s? Why did this debt problem threaten the stability of the international banking system?
11. What is a Eurocurrency? How did the Eurocurrency market develop?
12. What risks do bankers assume when making loans to foreign borrowers?
13. Distinguish between debt-to-export ratio and debt service/export ratio.
14. What options are available to a nation experiencing debt-servicing difficulties? What limitations apply to each option?
15. What methods do banks use to reduce their exposure to developing-nation debt?
16. How can debt/equity swaps help banks reduce losses on developing-nation loans?

18.1 The World Bank provides various forms of assistance to developing countries in order to promote economic growth and investment in people. Learn more about the World Bank by setting your browser to URL:

http://www.worldbank.org/

18.2 The European Central Bank was formed in June 1998 with 11 member states. Information on Eurocurrency, including pictures of its design and discussion of the changeover process, can be found at this home page. Set your browser to URL:

http://www.ecb.int/

18.3 The Stern School of Business at New York University maintains a Web site that provides extensive information and articles relating to instability in Asian financial markets. Visit this site by setting your browser to URL:

http://stern.nyu.edu/globalmacro/

18.4 The NYU Salomon Center for Research in Financial Institutions and Markets, a center within New York University's Stern School of Business, supports academic research for the study of problems and issues related to the U.S. and global financial structure. Log onto their Web page at:

http://www.stern.nyu.edu/Academic/Centers/

To access NetLink Exercises and the Virtual Scavenger Hunt, visit the Carbaugh Web site at http://carbaugh.swcollege.com.

INDEX